5.4 Perform preventative maintenance of networks including securing and protecting network cabling	
DOMAIN 6 SECURITY	
6.1 Identify the fundamental principles of security	4, 10
6.2 Install, configure, upgrade and optimize security	2, 4, 8, 9, 10
6.3 Identify tools, diagnostic procedures and troubleshooting techniques for security	4, 8, 9, 10
6.4 Perform preventative maintenance for security	10
DOMAIN 7 SAFETY & ENVIRONMENTAL ISSUES	
7.1 Identify potential hazards and proper safety procedures including power supply, display devices and environment (e.g, trip, liquid, situational, atmospheric hazards and high-voltage and moving equipment)	
DOMAIN 8 PROFESSIONALISM AND COMMUNICATION	
8.1 Use good communication skills including listening and tact/discretion, when communicating with customers and colleagues	12
8.2 Use job-related professional behavior including notation of privacy, confidentiality and respect for the customer and customers' property	12

CompTIA A+ 220-603

Objectives	Chapters
DOMAIN 1 PERSONAL COMPUTER COMPONENTS	
1.1 Install, configure, optimize, and upgrade personal computer components	8
1.2 Identify tools, diagnostic procedures, and troubleshooting techniques for personal computer components	8, 11
1.3 Perform preventative maintenance on personal computer components	3, 4, 11
DOMAIN 2 OPERATING SYSTEMS—UNLESS OTHERWISE NOTED, OPERATING SYSTEMS REFERRED TO WITHIN INCLUDE MICROSOFT WINDOWS 2000, XP PROFESSIONAL, XP HOME AND MEDIA CENTER.	
2.1 Identify the fundamental principles of using operating systems	1, 2, 3, 4, 5, 8, 9, 10
2.2 Install, configure, optimize and upgrade operating systems	2, 3, 4, 5, 9
2.3 Identify tools, diagnostic procedures and troubleshooting techniques for operating	1, 3, 4, 5, 9, 10, 11
2.4 Perform preventative maintenance for operating systems	2, 3, 4, 10
DOMAIN 3 PRINTERS AND SCANNERS	
3.1 Identify the fundamental principles of using printers and scanners	11
3.2 Install, configure, optimize and upgrade printers and scanners.	11
3.3 Identify tools, diagnostic procedures and troubleshooting techniques for printers and scanners	11
DOMAIN 4 NETWORKS	
4.1 Identify the fundamental principles of networks	8, 9
4.2 Install, configure, optimize and upgrade networks	4, 8, 9, 10
4.3 Identify tools, diagnostic procedures and troubleshooting techniques for networks	4, 8, 9, 10
DOMAIN 5 SECURITY	
5.1 Identify the fundamental principles of security	4, 10
5.2 Install, configure, optimize and upgrade security	4, 8, 9, 10
5.3 Identify tools, diagnostic procedures and troubleshooting techniques for security issues	4, 8, 9, 10
5.4 Perform preventative maintenance for security.	10
DOMAIN 6 PROFESSIONALISM AND COMMUNICATION	
6.1 Use good communication skills, including listening and tact/discretion, when communicating with customers and colleagues	12
6.2 Use job-related professional behavior including notation of privacy, confidentiality and respect for the customer and customers' property	12

CompTIA A+ 220-604

Objectives	Chapters
DOMAIN 1 PERSONAL COMPUTER COMPONENTS	
1.1 Install, configure, optimize and upgrade personal computer components	3, 8
1.2 Identify tools, diagnostic procedures and troubleshooting techniques for personal computer components	8, 11
1.3 Perform preventative maintenance of personal computer components	8, 11
DOMAIN 2 LAPTOPS AND PORTABLE DEVICES	
2.1 Identify the fundamental principles of using laptops and portable devices	8
2.2 Install, configure, optimize and upgrade laptops and portable devices	
2.3 Identify tools, diagnostic procedures and troubleshooting techniques for laptops and portable devices	8
DOMAIN 3 PRINTERS AND SCANNERS	
3.1 Identify the fundamental principles of using printers and scanners	11
3.2 Install, configure, optimize and upgrade printers and scanners	11
3.3 Identify tools, diagnostic methods and troubleshooting procedures for printers and scanners	11
3.4 Perform preventative maintenance of printer and scanner problems	11
DOMAIN 4 SECURITY	
4.1 Identify the names, purposes and characteristics of physical security devices and processes	4, 10
4.2 Install hardware security	9, 10
DOMAIN 5 SAFETY AND ENVIRONMENTAL ISSUES	
5.1 Identify potential hazards and proper safety procedures including power supply, display devices and environment (e.g., trip, liquid, situational, atmospheric hazards, high-voltage and moving equipment)	10

A+ Guide to Software: Managing, Maintaining and Troubleshooting

FOURTH EDITION

Jean Andrews, Ph.D.

COURSE TECHNOLOGY
CENGAGE Learning™

Australia • Canada • Mexico • Singapore • Spain • United Kingdom • United States

COURSE TECHNOLOGY
CENGAGE Learning™

A+ Guide to Software: Managing, Maintaining and Troubleshooting, FOURTH EDITION

Jean Andrews

Executive Editor: Steve Helba

Managing Editor: Larry Main

Acquisitions Editor: Nick Lombardi

Senior Product Manager: Michelle Ruelos Cannistraci

Developmental Editor: Jill Batistick

Marketing Manager: Guy Baskaran

Editorial Assistant: Jessica Reed

Copy Editor: Karen Annett

Proofreaders: Christine Clark Kim Kosmatka

Manufacturing Coordinator: Susan Carroll

Senior Content Project Manager: Catherine G. DiMassa

Quality Assurance: Christian Kunciw

Cover Design: Betsy Young

Interior Design: Betsy Young

Compositor: Integra, Inc.—Pondicherry

For product information and technology assistance, contact us at
Cengage Learning Customer & Sales Support, 1-800-354-9706

For permission to use material from this text or product, submit all requests online at **cengage.com/permissions**.
Further permissions questions can be emailed to
permissionrequest@cengage.com

ISBN-10 0-619-21760-x
ISBN-13 978-0-619-21760-0

Instructor Edition ISBN-10 0-619-21770-7
Instructor Edition ISBN-13 978-0-619-21770-9

Course Technology
25 Thomson Place,
Boston, Massachusetts, 02210.

Disclaimer

Cengage Course Technology reserves the right to revise this publication and make changes from time to time in its content without notice.

Printed in United States of America
4 5 6 7 8 9   11 10 09

Table of Contents

CHAPTER 1

Introducing Operating Systems 1

CHAPTER 2

Installing Windows 2000/XP 55

CHAPTER 3

Maintaining Windows 2000/XP 107

CompTIA A+ Essentials
2006 Examination Objectives

DOMAIN 1 PERSONAL COMPUTER COMPONENTS

1.1   Identify the fundamental principles of using personal computers

OBJECTIVES	CHAPTERS	PAGE NUMBERS
Identify the names, purposes, and characteristics of storage devices		
◢ FDD		See *A+ Guide to Hardware*
◢ HDD		See *A+ Guide to Hardware*
◢ CD/DVD/RW (e.g., drive speeds, media types)		See *A+ Guide to Hardware*
◢ Removable storage (e.g., tape drive, solid state such as thumb drives, flash and SD cards, USB, external CD-RW and hard drive)		See *A+ Guide to Hardware*
Identify the names, purposes, and characteristics of motherboards		
◢ Form Factor (e.g., ATX/BTX, microATX/NLX)		See *A+ Guide to Hardware*
◢ Components		See *A+ Guide to Hardware*
• Integrated I/Os (e.g., sound, video, USB, serial, IEEE 1394/firewire, parallel, NIC, modem)		
• Memory slots (e.g. RIMM, DIMM)		
• Processor sockets		
• External cache memory		
• Bus architecture		
• Bus slots (e.g., PCI, AGP, PCIE, AMR, CNR)		
• EIDE/PATA		
• SATA		
• SCSI Technology		
◢ Chipsets		See *A+ Guide to Hardware*
◢ BIOS/CMOS/Firmware	1, 2, 10	26/77–78/545–547 More content in *A+ Guide to Hardware*
◢ Riser card/daughter board		See *A+ Guide to Hardware*
Identify the names, purposes and characteristics of power supplies, for example: AC adapter, ATX, proprietary, voltage		See *A+ Guide to Hardware*
Identify the names, purposes, and characteristics of processor/CPUs		
◢ CPU chips (e.g., AMD, Intel)		See *A+ Guide to Hardware*
◢ CPU technologies		
• Hyperthreading		
• Dual core		
• Throttling	3	164–166
• Micro code (MMX)		More content in *A+ Guide to Hardware*
• Overclocking		
• Cache		
• VRM		
• Speed (real vs. actual)		
• 32 vs. 64 bit		
Identify the names, purposes, and characteristics of memory		
◢ Types of memory (e.g., DRAM, SRAM, SDRAM, DDR/DDR2, RAMBUS)		See *A+ Guide to Hardware*

◢ Operational characteristics • Memory chips (8, 16, 32) • Parity versus non-parity • ECC vs. non-ECC • Single-sided vs. double-sided		See *A+ Guide to Hardware*
Identify the names, purposes, and characteristics of display devices, for example: projectors, CRT and LCD		
◢ Connector types (e.g., VGA, DVI/HDMi, S-Video, Component / RGB)		See *A+ Guide to Hardware*
◢ Settings (e.g., V-hold, refresh rate, resolution)		See *A+ Guide to Hardware*
Identify the names, purposes, and characteristics of input devices, for example: mouse, keyboard, bar code reader, multimedia (e.g., web and digital cameras, MIDI, microphones), biometric devices, touch screen	10	581–583 More content in *A+ Guide to Hardware*
Identify the names, purposes, and characteristics of adapter cards		
◢ Video including PCI/PCI-E and AGP		See *A+ Guide to Hardware*
◢ Multimedia		See *A+ Guide to Hardware*
◢ I/O (SCSI, serial, USB, Parallel)		See *A+ Guide to Hardware*
◢ Communications including network and modem	8	402–403, 423–429 More content in *A+ Guide to Hardware*
Identify the names, purposes and characteristics of ports and cables, for example: USB 1.1 and 2.0, parallel, serial, IEEE1394/firewire, RJ45 and RJ11, PS2/MINI-DIN, centronics (e.g., mini, 36), multimedia (e.g., 1/8 connector, MIDI, COAX, SPDIF)		See *A+ Guide to Hardware*
Identify the names, purposes, and characteristics of cooling systems, for example: heat sinks, CPU and case fans, liquid cooling systems, thermal compound		See *A+ Guide to Hardware*

1.2 Install, configure, optimize and upgrade personal computer components

OBJECTIVES	CHAPTERS	PAGE NUMBERS
Add, remove, and configure internal and external storage devices		
◢ Drive preparation of internal storage devices including format/file systems and imaging technology	3	114–119 More content in *A+ Guide to Hardware*
Install display devices	1	29–30 More content in *A+ Guide to Hardware*
Add, remove and configure basic input and multimedia devices		See *A+ Guide to Hardware*

1.3 Identify tools, diagnostic procedures and troubleshooting techniques for personal computer components

OBJECTIVES	CHAPTERS	PAGE NUMBERS
Recognize the basic aspects of troubleshooting theory, for example:		
◢ Perform backups before making changes	3, 4, 5, 12	140–148/233–237/ 261–263/ 645–647 More content in *A+ Guide to Hardware*
◢ Assess a problem systematically and divide large problems into smaller components to be analyzed individually	4, 5, 11, 12	233–237/261–263/627–632/645–647 More content in *A+ Guide to Hardware*
◢ Verify even the obvious, determine whether the problem is something simple and make no assumptions	5, 11, 12	261–263/627–632/645–647 More content in *A+ Guide to Hardware*

◢ Research ideas and establish priorities	5, 11, 12	261–263/627–632/ 645–647 More content in *A+ Guide to Hardware*
◢ Document findings, actions and outcomes	4, 11, 12	233–237/627– 632/645–647 More content in *A+ Guide to Hardware*
Identify and apply basic diagnostic procedures and troubleshooting techniques, for example: ◢ Identify the problem including questioning user and identifying user changes to computer	4, 5, 11, 12	233–237/261–263/627– 632/645–647 More content in *A+ Guide to Hardware*
◢ Analyze the problem including potential causes and make an initial determination of software and/or hardware problem	4, 5, 11, 12	233–237/261–263/627– 632/645–647 More content in *A+ Guide to Hardware*
◢ Test related components including inspection, connections, hardware/software configurations, device manager and consult vendor documentation	3, 4, 5, 11, 12	119–124/233–237/ 261–263/627–632/642 More content in *A+ Guide to Hardware*
◢ Evaluate results and take additional steps if needed such as consultation, use of alternate resources, manuals	4, 5, 11, 12	233–237/261–263/627– 632/642, 645–647 More content in *A+ Guide to Hardware*
◢ Document activities and outcomes	4, 11, 12	233–237/627–632/ 642, 645–647 More content in *A+ Guide to Hardware*
Recognize and isolate issues with display, power, basic input devices, storage, memory, thermal, POST errors (e.g., BIOS, hardware)	11	627–632 More content in *A+ Guide to Hardware*
Apply basic troubleshooting techniques to check for problems (e.g., thermal issues, error codes, power, connections including cables and/or pins, compatibility, functionality, software/drivers) with components, for example:		
◢ Motherboards		See *A+ Guide to Hardware*
◢ Power supply		See *A+ Guide to Hardware*
◢ Processor/CPUs		See *A+ Guide to Hardware*
◢ Memory		See *A+ Guide to Hardware*
◢ Display devices		See *A+ Guide to Hardware*
◢ Input devices		See *A+ Guide to Hardware*
◢ Adapter cards	8	457–460 More content in *A+ Guide to Hardware*
Recognize the names, purposes, characteristics, and appropriate application of tools, for example: BIOS, self-test, hard drive self-test and software diagnostic test	11	627–634 More content in *A+ Guide to Hardware*

1.4   Perform preventative maintenance on personal computer components

OBJECTIVES	CHAPTERS	PAGE NUMBERS
Identify and apply basic aspects of preventative maintenance theory, for example: ◢ Visual/audio inspection	11	619–634 More content in *A+ Guide to Hardware*
◢ Driver/firmware updates	10, 11	579–580/619–634 More content in *A+ Guide to Hardware*

◢ Scheduling preventative maintenance	10, 11	578/619–634 More content in *A+ Guide to Hardware*
◢ Use of appropriate repair tools and cleaning materials	11	619–634 More content in *A+ Guide to Hardware*
◢ Ensuring proper environment	11	619–634 More content in *A+ Guide to Hardware*
Identify and apply common preventative maintenance techniques for devices such as input devices and batteries	11	619–634 More content in *A+ Guide to Hardware*

DOMAIN 2 LAPTOPS AND PORTABLE DEVICES

2.1   Identify the fundamental principles of using laptops and portable devices

OBJECTIVES	CHAPTERS	PAGE NUMBERS
Identify names, purposes, and characteristics of laptop-specific:		
◢ Form factors such as memory and hard drives		See *A+ Guide to Hardware*
◢ Peripherals (e.g., docking station, port replicator and media/accessory bay)		See *A+ Guide to Hardware*
◢ Expansion slots (e.g., PCMCIA I, II and III, card and express bus)		See *A+ Guide to Hardware*
◢ Ports (e.g., mini PCI slot)		See *A+ Guide to Hardware*
◢ Communication connections (e.g., Bluetooth, infrared, cellular WAN, Ethernet)	8	404–409 More content in *A+ Guide to Hardware*
◢ Power and electrical input devices (e.g., auto-switching and fixed-input power supplies, batteries)		See *A+ Guide to Hardware*
◢ LCD technologies (e.g., active and passive matrix, resolution such as XGA, SXGA+ , UXGA, WUXGA, contrast radio, native resolution)		See *A+ Guide to Hardware*
◢ Input devices (e.g., stylus/digitizer, function (Fn) keys and pointing devices such as touch pad, point stick/track point)		See *A+ Guide to Hardware*
Identify and distinguish between mobile and desktop motherboards and processors including throttling, power management and WiFi	8	432–443 More content in *A+ Guide to Hardware*

2.2   Install, configure, optimize and upgrade laptops and portable devices

OBJECTIVES	CHAPTERS	PAGE NUMBERS
Configure power management		
◢ Identify the features of BIOS-ACPI		See *A+ Guide to Hardware*
◢ Identify the difference between suspend, hibernate and standby		See *A+ Guide to Hardware*
Demonstrate safe removal of laptop-specific hardware such as peripherals, hot-swappable devices and non-hot-swappable devices		See *A+ Guide to Hardware*

2.3   Identify tools, basic diagnostic procedures and troubleshooting techniques for laptops and portable devices

OBJECTIVES	CHAPTERS	PAGE NUMBERS
Use procedures and techniques to diagnose power conditions, video, keyboard, pointer and wireless card issues, for example:		See *A+ Guide to Hardware*
◢ Verify AC power (e.g., LEDs, swap AC adapter)		See *A+ Guide to Hardware*
◢ Verify DC power		See *A+ Guide to Hardware*
◢ Remove unneeded peripherals		See *A+ Guide to Hardware*
◢ Plug in external monitor		See *A+ Guide to Hardware*

3.2 **Install, configure, optimize and upgrade operating systems—references to upgrading from Windows 95 and NT may be made**

OBJECTIVES	CHAPTERS	PAGE NUMBERS
Identify procedures for installing operating systems including:		
◢ Verification of hardware compatibility and minimum requirements	2	75–100 More content in *A+ Guide to Hardware*
◢ Installation methods (e.g., boot media such as CD, floppy or USB, network installation, drive imaging)	2	75–100 More content in *A+ Guide to Hardware*
◢ Operating system installation options (e.g., attended/ unattended, file system type, network configuration)	2	75–100
◢ Disk preparation order (e.g., start installation, partition and format drive)	2, 3	75–100/114–119
◢ Device driver configuration (e.g., install and upload device drivers)	2, 3	75–100/108–114, 119–124 More content in *A+ Guide to Hardware*
◢ Verification of installation	2, 3	91–100/108–114, 119–124 More content in *A+ Guide to Hardware*
Identify procedures for upgrading operating systems including:		
◢ Upgrade considerations (e.g., hardware, application and/ or network compatibility)	2	75–100
◢ Implementation (e.g., backup data, install additional Windows components)	2	75–100
Install/add a device including loading, adding device drivers and required software including:	3	108–114, 119–124
◢ Determine whether permissions are adequate for performing the task	3, 4	108–114, 119–124/ 186–199 More content in *A+ Guide to Hardware*
◢ Device driver installation (e.g., automated and/or manual search and installation of device drivers)	3, 11	108–114, 119–124/ 608–619, 620–624 More content in *A+ Guide to Hardware*
◢ Using unsigned drivers (e.g., driver signing)	3, 8	108–114, 119–124/ 432–443 More content in *A+ Guide to Hardware*
◢ Verify installation of the driver (e.g., device manager and functionality)	3, 11	108–114, 119–124/ 608–619, 620–624 More content in *A+ Guide to Hardware*
Identify procedures and utilities used to optimize operating systems, for example, virtual memory, hard drives, temporary files, service, startup and applications	3, 4, 5	124–140, 160–179/ 219–233 282–287

3.3 **Identify tools, diagnostic procedures and troubleshooting techniques for operating systems**

OBJECTIVES	CHAPTERS	PAGE NUMBERS
Identify basic boot sequences, methods and utilities for recovering operating systems		
◢ Boot methods (e.g., safe mode, recovery console, boot to restore point)	5, 10	246–295/589–593 More content in *A+ Guide to Hardware*
◢ Automated System Recovery (ASR) (e.g., Emergency Repair Disk (ERD))	3, 5	148–152/290–295

Identify and apply diagnostic procedures and troubleshooting techniques, for example:		
▲ Identify the problem by questioning user and identifying user changes to computer	3, 4, 5, 12	119–124/233–237/261–263/645–647
▲ Analyze problem including potential causes and initial determination of software and/or hardware problem	3, 4, 5, 10	119–124/233–237/275–295/583–589
▲ Test related components including connections, hardware/software configurations, device manager and consulting vendor documentation	3, 4, 5, 12	119–124/233–237/246–295/645–647
▲ Evaluate results and take additional steps if needed such as consultation, alternate resources and manuals	3, 4, 5, 10, 12	119–124/233–237/246–295/589–599/642
▲ Document activities and outcomes	3, 4, 5, 10, 12	119–124/233–237/261–263/589/645–647
Recognize and resolve common operational issues such as bluescreen, system lock-up, input/output device, application install, start or load and Windows-specific printing problems(e.g., print spool stalled, incorrect/incompatible driver for print)	4, 5, 10, 11	233–237/275–295/589–599/619–634
Explain common error messages and codes, for example:		
▲ Boot (e.g., invalid boot disk, inaccessible boot drive, missing NTLDR)	5	275–295 More content in *A+ Guide to Hardware*
▲ Startup (e.g., device/service failed to start, device/program in registry not found)	4, 5	233–237/275–295/589–599
▲ Event Viewer	3, 4, 10	132–138/222/572–577
▲ Registry	3, 10	134–138/589–599
▲ Windows reporting	3	128–130
Identify the names, locations, purposes, and characteristics of operating system utilities, for example:		
▲ Disk management tools (e.g., DEFRAG, NTBACKUP, CHKDSK, Format)	3, 4, 5, 8	114–119/219–233/252–258/448–450
▲ System management tools (e.g., device and task manager, MSCONFIG.EXE)	3, 5	108–114, 161–170/275–295
▲ File management tools (e.g., Windows Explorer, ATTRIB.EXE)	1, 4, 10	34–39/204–205, 219–233/595–596

3.4 Perform preventative maintenance on operating systems

OBJECTIVES	CHAPTERS	PAGE NUMBERS
Describe common utilities for performing preventative maintenance on operating systems, for example: software and Windows updates (e.g., service packs), scheduled backups/restore, restore points	2, 3, 4, 10	94–97, 100/140–152/207–209, 219–233/578

DOMAIN 4 PRINTERS AND SCANNERS

4.1 Identify the fundamental principles of using printers and scanners

OBJECTIVES	CHAPTERS	PAGE NUMBERS
Identify differences between types of printer and scanner technologies (e.g., laser, inkjet, thermal, solid ink, impact)		See *A+ Guide to Hardware*
Identify names, purposes, and characteristics of printer and scanner components (e.g., memory, driver, firmware) and consumables (e.g., toner, ink cartridge, paper)		See *A+ Guide to Hardware*
Identify the names, purposes and characteristics of interfaces used by printers and scanners including port and cable types, for example:		
▲ Parallel	11	607 More content in *A+ Guide to Hardware*

6.2   Install, configure, upgrade and optimize security

8.2 Use job-related professional behavior including privacy, confidentiality and respect for the customer and customers' property (e.g., telephone, computer)

OBJECTIVES	CHAPTERS	PAGE NUMBERS
Behavior		
◢ Maintain a positive attitude and tone of voice	12	642–650
◢ Avoid arguing with customers and/or becoming defensive	12	642–650
◢ Do not minimize costumers' problems	12	642–650
◢ Avoid being judgmental and/or insulting or calling the customer names	12	642–650
◢ Avoid distractions and/or interruptions when talking with customers	12	642–650
Property		
◢ Telephone, laptop, desktop computer, printer, monitor, etc.	12	642–650

CompTIA A+ 220-602
2006 Examination Objectives

DOMAIN 1 PERSONAL COMPUTER COMPONENTS

1.1 Install, configure, optimize and upgrade personal computer components

OBJECTIVES	CHAPTERS	PAGE NUMBERS
Add, remove and configure personal computer components including selection and installation of appropriate components, for example:		
◢ Storage devices		See A+ Guide to Hardware
◢ Motherboards		See A+ Guide to Hardware
◢ Power supplies		See A+ Guide to Hardware
◢ Processors/CPUs		See A+ Guide to Hardware
◢ Memory		See A+ Guide to Hardware
◢ Display devices		See A+ Guide to Hardware
◢ Input devices (e.g., basic, specialty and multimedia)		See A+ Guide to Hardware
◢ Adapter cards	8	457–460 More content in A+ Guide to Hardware
◢ Cooling systems		See A+ Guide to Hardware

1.2 Identify tools, diagnostic procedures and troubleshooting techniques for personal computer components

OBJECTIVES	CHAPTERS	PAGE NUMBERS
Identify and apply basic diagnostic procedures and troubleshooting techniques	8, 11	457–460/619–634 More content in A+ Guide to Hardware
◢ Isolate and identify the problem using visual and audible inspection of components and minimum configuration	11	619–634 More content in A+ Guide to Hardware
Recognize and isolate issues with peripherals, multimedia, specialty input devices, internal and external storage and CPUs	11	619–634 More content in A+ Guide to Hardware
Identify the steps used to troubleshoot components (e.g., check proper seating, installation, appropriate component, settings and current driver), for example:		
◢ Power supply		See A+ Guide to Hardware
◢ Processor/CPUs and motherboards		See A+ Guide to Hardware
◢ Memory		See A+ Guide to Hardware

DOMAIN 3 OPERATING SYSTEMS—UNLESS OTHERWISE NOTED, OPERATING SYSTEMS REFERRED TO WITHIN INCLUDE MICROSOFT WINDOWS 2000, XP PROFESSIONAL, XP HOME AND MEDIA CENTER.

3.1   Identify the fundamental principles of operating systems

3.2 Install, configure, optimize and upgrade operating systems—references to upgrading from Windows 95 and NT may be made

OBJECTIVES	CHAPTERS	PAGE NUMBERS
Identify procedures and utilities used to optimize operating systems, for example:		
◢ Virtual memory	3	175–179
◢ Hard drives (e.g., disk defragmentation)	2, 4	75–100/219–233
◢ Temporary files	4, 9	219–233/516–520
◢ Services	3, 5	161–170/282–287
◢ Startup	2, 5	75–100/282–287
◢ Application	3, 5	119–130, 161–175/ 282–287

3.3 Identify tools, diagnostic procedures and troubleshooting techniques for operating systems

OBJECTIVES	CHAPTERS	PAGE NUMBERS
Demonstrate the ability to recover operating systems (e.g., boot methods, recovery console, ASR, ERD)	3, 4, 5	148–152/233–237/ 246–295
Recognize and resolve common operational problems, for example:		
◢ Windows-specific printing problems (e.g., print spool stalled, incorrect/incompatible driver form print)	11	619–634
◢ Auto-restart errors	5	258–263
◢ Bluescreen error	5, 10	275–295/589–599
◢ System lock-up	5, 10	275–295/589–599
◢ Device drivers failure (input/output devices)	3, 5, 11	119–124/275–295/ 619–634 More content in A+ Guide to Hardware
◢ Application install, start or load failure	3, 5, 10	124–130, 170–175/275– 295/589–599
Recognize and resolve common error messages and codes, for example:		
◢ Boot (e.g., invalid boot disk, inaccessible boot drive, missing NTLDR)	5	275–295 More content in A+ Guide to Hardware
◢ Startup (e.g., device/service has failed to start, device/program in registry not found)	3, 4, 5, 10	170–175/233–237/ 275–295/589–599
◢ Event viewer	3, 5, 10	134–138/275–295/ 572–577
◢ Registry	3, 5, 10	152–160, 170–175/263– 295/589–599
◢ Windows reporting	3	128–130
Use diagnostic utilities and tools to resolve operational problems, for example:		
◢ Bootable media	5	275–295 More content in A+ Guide to Hardware
◢ Startup modes (e.g., safe mode, safe mode with command prompt or networking, step-by-step/single step mode)	5, 10	246–295/589–599
◢ Documentation resources (e.g., user/installation manuals, internet/web based, training materials)	4, 5, 10	233–237/246–295/ 589–599 More content in A+ Guide to Hardware
◢ Task and Device Manager	1, 3, 5, 10	41–44/119–124/275–295/ 589–599 More content in A+ Guide to Hardware

DOMAIN 5 NETWORKS

5.1 **Identify the fundamental principles of networks**

OBJECTIVES	CHAPTERS	PAGE NUMBERS
Identify names, purposes, and characteristics of basic network protocols and terminologies, for example:		
◢ ISP	9	477–478
◢ TCP/IP (e.g., gateway, subnet mask, DNS, WINS, static and automatic address assignment)	8, 9	409–422/468–474
◢ IPX/SPX (NWLink)	8	409–422
◢ NETBEUI/NETBIOS	8	409–422
◢ SMTP	9	468–474, 522–524
◢ IMAP	9	468–474, 522–524
◢ HTML	9	511–516
◢ HTTP	9	468–474, 511–516
◢ HTTPS	9	468–474, 520–522
◢ SSL	9	468–474, 520–522
◢ Telnet	9	468–474
◢ FTP	9	468–474, 524–527
◢ DNS	8	409–422
Identify names, purposes, and characteristics of technologies for establishing connectivity, for example:		
◢ Dial-up networking	9	477–490, 493–494 More content in *A+ Guide to Hardware*
◢ Broadband (e.g., DSL, cable, satellite)	8, 9	402–409/477–485
◢ ISDN Networking	8, 9	402–409/477–485
◢ Wireless (all 802.11)	8, 9	402–409/477–485
◢ LAN/WAN	8, 9	402–409/477–485
◢ Infrared	8	402–409 More content in *A+ Guide to Hardware*
◢ Bluetooth	8	402–409
◢ Cellular	8	402–409
◢ VoIP	8, 9	402–409/527–530

5.2 **Install, configure, optimize and upgrade networks**

OBJECTIVES	CHAPTERS	PAGE NUMBERS
Install and configure browsers		
◢ Enable/disable script support	9, 10	511–520/558
◢ Configure proxy and security settings	9, 10	511–520/558
Establish network connectivity		
◢ Install and configure network cards	8	423–429, 432–443
◢ Obtain a connection	8	423–429, 432–443 More content in *A+ Guide to Hardware*
◢ Configure client options (e.g., Microsoft, Novell) and network options (e.g., domain, workgroup, tree)	8	443–446
◢ Configure network options	8	450–451
Demonstrate the ability to share network resources		
◢ Models	2, 8	62–64/443–446, 450–451
◢ Configure permissions	4, 8, 10	186–199, 209–212/443–446, 450–451/549–552
◢ Capacities/limitations for sharing for each operating system	4, 8, 9, 10	223–227/443–446, 450–451/ 495–498/549–552

◢ Encryption and encryption technology issues	8, 9, 10	405–408, 432–443, 451–457/508–510/560–566 More content in *A+ Guide to Hardware*

6.4 Perform preventative maintenance for security

OBJECTIVES	CHAPTERS	PAGE NUMBERS
Recognize social engineering and address social engineering situations	10	567–569

DOMAIN 7 SAFETY & ENVIRONMENTAL ISSUES

7.1 Identify potential hazards and proper safety procedures including power supply, display devices and environment (e.g., trip, liquid, situational, atmospheric hazards and high-voltage and moving equipment)		See *A+ Guide to Hardware*

DOMAIN 8 PROFESSIONALISM AND COMMUNICATION

8.1 Use good communication skills including listening and tact/discretion, when communicating with customers and colleagues

OBJECTIVES	CHAPTERS	PAGE NUMBERS
Use clear, concise and direct statements	12	642–650
Allow the customer to complete statements—avoid interrupting	12	642–650
Clarify customer statements—ask pertinent questions	12	642–650
Avoid using jargon, abbreviations and acronyms	12	642–650
Listen to customers	12	642–650

8.2 Use job-related professional behavior including notation of privacy, confidentiality and respect for the customer and customers' property

OBJECTIVES	CHAPTERS	PAGE NUMBERS
Behavior		
◢ Maintain a positive attitude and tone of voice	12	642–650
◢ Avoid arguing with customers and/or becoming defensive	12	642–650
◢ Do not minimize customers' problems	12	642–650
◢ Avoid being judgmental and/or insulting or calling the customer names	12	642–650
◢ Avoid distractions and/or interruptions when talking with customers	12	642–650
Property		
◢ Telephone, laptop, desktop computer, printer, monitor, etc.	12	642–650

CompTIA A+ 220-603
2006 Examination Objectives

DOMAIN 1 PERSONAL COMPUTER COMPONENTS

1.1 Install, configure, optimize, and upgrade personal computer components

OBJECTIVES	CHAPTERS	PAGE NUMBERS
Add, remove, and configure display devices and adapter cards including basic input and multimedia devices	8	451–457 More content in *A+ Guide to Hardware*

1.2   Identify tools, diagnostic procedures, and troubleshooting techniques for personal computer components

OBJECTIVES	CHAPTERS	PAGE NUMBERS
Identify and apply basic diagnostic procedures and troubleshooting techniques, for example:	11	619–634 More content in *A+ Guide to Hardware*
◢ Identify and analyze the problem/potential problem	8, 11	451–457/ 619–634 More content in *A+ Guide to Hardware*
◢ Test related components and evaluate results	8, 11	451–457/619–634 More content in *A+ Guide to Hardware*
◢ Identify additional steps to be taken if/when necessary	8	451–457 More content in *A+ Guide to Hardware*
◢ Document activities and outcomes	3, 4, 5, 10, 12	119–124/233–237/261–263/589/645–647
Recognize and isolate issues with display, peripheral, multimedia, specialty input device and storage	8, 11	451–457/619–634 More content in *A+ Guide to Hardware*
Apply steps in troubleshooting techniques to identify problems (e.g., physical environment, functionality and software/driver settings) with components including display, input devices and adapter cards	8, 11	451–457/619–634 More content in *A+ Guide to Hardware*

1.3   Perform preventative maintenance on personal computer components

OBJECTIVES	CHAPTERS	PAGE NUMBERS
Identify and apply common preventative maintenance techniques for storage devices, for example:		See *A+ Guide to Hardware*
◢ Software tools (e.g., Defrag, CHKDSK)	3, 4	114–119/219–233
◢ Cleaning (e.g., optics, tape heads)		See *A+ Guide to Hardware*

DOMAIN 2 OPERATING SYSTEMS—UNLESS OTHERWISE NOTED, OPERATING SYSTEMS REFERRED TO WITHIN INCLUDE MICROSOFT WINDOWS 2000, XP PROFESSIONAL, XP HOME AND MEDIA CENTER.

2.1   Identify the fundamental principles of using operating systems

OBJECTIVES	CHAPTERS	PAGE NUMBERS
Use command-line functions and utilities to manage Windows 2000, XP Professional and XP Home, including proper syntax and switches, for example:		
◢ CMD	1, 4	12/199–207
◢ HELP	4, 5	199–207/263–274
◢ DIR	4, 5	199–207/263–274
◢ ATTRIB	4, 5, 10	199–207/263–274/ 595–596
◢ EDIT	4	199–207
◢ COPY	4, 5	199–207/263–274
◢ XCOPY	4	199–207
◢ FORMAT	4, 5	199–207/263–274
◢ IPCONFIG	8 9	451–457/474–477
◢ PING	8, 9	451–457/474–477
◢ MD/CD/RD	4, 5, 10	199–207/263–274/ 595–596
Identify concepts and procedures for creating, viewing, managing disks, directories and files in Windows 2000, XP Professional and XP Home, for example:		
◢ Disks (e.g., active, primary extended and logical partitions)	1, 2, 3, 10	12–19/65–74, 81/ 114–119/560–566

2.2 Install, configure, optimize and upgrade operating systems

2.3 Identify tools, diagnostic procedures and troubleshooting techniques for operating systems

◢ Install and configure print drivers (e.g., PCL™, Postscript™, and GDI)	11	607–619, 624–625
◢ Validate compatibility with OS and applications	11	607–619, 624–625
◢ Educate user about basic functionality	11	607–619, 624–625
Optimize scanner performance, for example: resolution, file format and default settings	11	607–619, 624–625

3.3 Identify tools, diagnostic procedures and troubleshooting techniques for printers and scanners

OBJECTIVES	CHAPTERS	PAGE NUMBERS
Gather information required to troubleshoot printer/ scanner problems	11	619–634
Troubleshoot a print failure (e.g., lack of paper, clear queue, restart print spooler, recycle power on printer, inspect for jams, check for visual indicators)	11	619–634

DOMAIN 4 NETWORKS

4.1 Identify the fundamental principles of networks

OBJECTIVES	CHAPTERS	PAGE NUMBERS
Identify names, purposes, and characteristics of the basic network protocols and terminologies, for example:		
◢ ISP	9	477–478
◢ TCP/IP (e.g., Gateway, Subnet mask, DNS, WINS, Static and automatic address assignment)	8, 9	409–422/468–474
◢ IPX/SPX (NWLink)	8	409–422
◢ NETBEUI/NETBIOS	8	409–422
◢ SMTP	9	468–474, 522–524
◢ IMAP	9	468–474, 522–524
◢ HTML	9	511–516
◢ HTTP	9	468–474, 511–516
◢ HTTPS	9	468–474, 520–522
◢ SSL	9	468–474, 520–522
◢ Telnet	9	468–474
◢ FTP	9	468–474, 524–527
◢ DNS	8	409–422
Identify names, purposes, and characteristics of technologies for establishing connectivity, for example:		
◢ Dial-up networking	9	477–490, 493–494 More content in *A+ Guide to Hardware*
◢ Broadband (e.g., DSL, cable, satellite)	8, 9	402–409/477–485
◢ ISDN Networking	8, 9	402–409/477–485
◢ Wireless	8, 9	402–409/477–485
◢ LAN/WAN	8, 9	402–409/477–485

4.2 Install, configure, optimize and upgrade networks

OBJECTIVES	CHAPTERS	PAGE NUMBERS
Establish network connectivity and share network resources	4, 8, 9, 10	186–199, 209–212, 223–227/423–429, 432–446, 450–451/495–498/ 549–552 More content in *A+ Guide to Hardware*

4.3 Identify tools, diagnostic procedures and troubleshooting techniques for networks

OBJECTIVES	CHAPTERS	PAGE NUMBERS
Identify the names, purposes, and characteristics of command line tools, for example:		
◢ IPCONFIG.EXE	8, 9	451–457/474–477
◢ PING.EXE	8, 9	451–457/474–477
◢ TRACERT.EXE	8, 9	451–457/474–477
◢ NSLOOKUP.EXE	8, 9	451–457/474–477
Diagnose and troubleshoot basic network issues, for example:		
◢ Driver/network interface	8	451–457
◢ Protocol configuration	8, 9	451–457/477–485
• TCP/IP (e.g., Gateway, Subnet mask, DNS, WINS, static and automatic address assignment)	8, 9	451–457/477–485
• IPX/SPX (NWLink)	8	423–429
◢ Permissions	4, 10	186–199, 209–212/ 549–552
◢ Firewall configuration	9	497–507
◢ Electrical interference	8, 9	451–457/527–530

DOMAIN 5 SECURITY

5.1 Identify the fundamental principles of security

OBJECTIVES	CHAPTERS	PAGE NUMBERS
Identify the names, purposes, and characteristics of access control and permissions		
◢ Accounts including user, admin and guest	4, 10	186–199, 223–227, 209–212/544–553, 559–560
◢ Groups	4, 10	186–199, 223–227, 209–212/544–553, 559–560
◢ Permission levels, types (e.g., file systems and shared) and actions (e.g., read, write, change and execute)	4, 10	186–199, 223–227, 209–212/544–553, 559–560

5.2 Install, configure, optimizing and upgrade security

OBJECTIVES	CHAPTERS	PAGE NUMBERS
Install and configure hardware, software, wireless and data security, for example:		
◢ Smart card readers	10	579–583
◢ Key fobs	10	581–583
◢ Biometric devices	10	581–583 More content in *A+ Guide to Hardware*
◢ Authentication technologies	9, 10	508–510/581–583 More content in *A+ Guide to Hardware*
◢ Software firewalls	9, 10	497–499/554 More content in *A+ Guide to Hardware*
◢ Auditing and event logging (enable/disable only)	10	572–577
◢ Wireless client configuration	8, 10	405–408, 432–443, 451–457/579–580
◢ Unused wireless connections	8	405–408, 432–443/ 451–457
◢ Data access (e.g., permissions, security policies)	4, 10	186–199, 209–212/ 544–553, 559–560

◢ Encryption and encryption technologies	8, 9, 10	405–408, 432–443, 451–457/508–510/ 560–566

5.3 Identify tools, diagnostic procedures and troubleshooting techniques for security issues

OBJECTIVES	CHAPTERS	PAGE NUMBERS
Diagnose and troubleshoot software and data security issues, for example:		
◢ Software firewall issues	9, 10	497–499/554
◢ Wireless client configuration issues	8	405–408, 432–443, 451–457
◢ Data access issues (e.g., permissions, security policies)	4, 10	186–199, 209–212/ 544–553, 559–560
◢ Encryption and encryption technologies issues	8, 9, 10	405–408, 432–443, 451–457/508–510/ 560–566 More content in *A+ Guide to Hardware*

5.4 Perform preventative maintenance for security.

OBJECTIVES	CHAPTERS	PAGE NUMBERS
Recognize social engineering and address social engineering situations	10	567–569

DOMAIN 6 PROFESSIONALISM AND COMMUNICATION

6.1 Use good communication skills, including listening and tact/discretion, when communicating with customers and colleagues

OBJECTIVES	CHAPTERS	PAGE NUMBERS
Use clear, concise and direct statements	12	642–650
Allow the customer to complete statements— avoid interrupting	12	642–650
Clarify customer statements—ask pertinent questions	12	642–650
Avoid using jargon, abbreviations and acronyms	12	642–650
Listen to customers	12	642–650

6.2 Use job-related professional behavior including notation of privacy, confidentiality and respect for the customer and customers' property

OBJECTIVES	CHAPTERS	PAGE NUMBERS
	12	642–650

CompTIA A+ 220-604
2006 Examination Objectives

DOMAIN 1 PERSONAL COMPUTER COMPONENTS

1.1 Install, configure, optimize and upgrade personal computer components

OBJECTIVES	CHAPTERS	PAGE NUMBERS
Add, remove and configure internal storage devices, motherboards, power supplies, processor/CPUs, memory and adapter cards, including:		
◢ Drive preparation	3	114–119 More content in *A+ Guide to Hardware*
◢ Jumper configuration		See *A+ Guide to Hardware*
◢ Storage device power and cabling		See *A+ Guide to Hardware*
◢ Selection and installation of appropriate motherboard		See *A+ Guide to Hardware*

◢ BIOS set-up and configuration		See *A+ Guide to Hardware*
◢ Selection and installation of appropriate CPU		See *A+ Guide to Hardware*
◢ Selection and installation of appropriate memory		See *A+ Guide to Hardware*
◢ Installation of adapter cards including hardware and software/drivers	8	451–457 More content in *A+ Guide to Hardware*
◢ Configuration and optimization of adapter cards including adjusting hardware settings and obtaining network card connection	8	451–457 More content in *A+ Guide to Hardware*
Add, remove and configure cooling systems		See *A+ Guide to Hardware*

1.2 Identify tools, diagnostic procedures and troubleshooting techniques for personal computer components

OBJECTIVES	CHAPTERS	PAGE NUMBERS
Identify and apply diagnostic procedures and troubleshooting techniques, for example:	11	619–634 More content in *A+ Guide to Hardware*
◢ Identify and isolate the problem using visual and audible inspection of components and minimum configuration	11	619–634 More content in *A+ Guide to Hardware*
Identify the steps used to troubleshoot components (e.g., check proper seating, installation, appropriate component, settings, current driver), for example:		
◢ Power supply		See *A+ Guide to Hardware*
◢ Processor/CPUs and motherboards		See *A+ Guide to Hardware*
◢ Memory		See *A+ Guide to Hardware*
◢ Adapter cards	8	451–457 More content in *A+ Guide to Hardware*
Recognize names, purposes, characteristics and appropriate application of tools, for example:		
◢ Multi-meter		See *A+ Guide to Hardware*
◢ Anti-static pad and wrist strap		See *A+ Guide to Hardware*
◢ Specialty hardware/tools		See *A+ Guide to Hardware*
◢ Loop back plugs		See *A+ Guide to Hardware*
◢ Cleaning products (e.g., vacuum, cleaning pads)		See *A+ Guide to Hardware*

1.3 Perform preventative maintenance of personal computer components

OBJECTIVES	CHAPTERS	PAGE NUMBERS
Identify and apply common preventive maintenance techniques, for example:		
◢ Thermally sensitive devices (e.g., motherboards CPUs, adapter cards, memory)		See *A+ Guide to Hardware*
• Cleaning		See *A+ Guide to Hardware*
• Air flow (e.g., slot covers, cable routing)		See *A+ Guide to Hardware*
◢ Adapter cards (e.g., driver/firmware updates)	8	451–457 More content in *A+ Guide to Hardware*

DOMAIN 2 LAPTOPS AND PORTABLE DEVICES

2.1 Identify the fundamental principles of using laptops and portable devices

OBJECTIVES	CHAPTERS	PAGE NUMBERS
Identify appropriate applications for laptop-specific communication connections, for example:		
◢ Bluetooth	8	404–409 More content in *A+ Guide to Hardware*

◢ Infrared devices	8	404–409 More content in *A+ Guide to Hardware*
◢ Cellular WAN	8	404–409 More content in *A+ Guide to Hardware*
◢ Ethernet	8	404–409 More content in *A+ Guide to Hardware*
Identify appropriate laptop-specific power and electrical input devices, for example: ◢ Output performance requirements for amperage and voltage		See *A+ Guide to Hardware*
Identify the major components of the LCD (e.g., inverter, screen, video card)		See *A+ Guide to Hardware*

2.2   Install, configure, optimize and upgrade laptops and portable devices

OBJECTIVES	CHAPTERS	PAGE NUMBERS
Demonstrate the safe removal of laptop-specific hardware including peripherals, hot-swappable and non hot-swappable devices		See *A+ Guide to Hardware*
Identify the effect of video sharing on memory upgrades		See *A+ Guide to Hardware*

2.3   Identify tools, diagnostic procedures and troubleshooting techniques for laptops and portable devices

OBJECTIVES	CHAPTERS	PAGE NUMBERS
Use procedures and techniques to diagnose power conditions, video issues, keyboard and pointer issues and wireless card issues, for example:		
◢ Verify AC power (e.g., LEDs, swap AC adapter)		See *A+ Guide to Hardware*
◢ Verify DC power		See *A+ Guide to Hardware*
◢ Remove unneeded peripherals		See *A+ Guide to Hardware*
◢ Plug in external monitor		See *A+ Guide to Hardware*
◢ Toggle Fn keys		See *A+ Guide to Hardware*
◢ Check LCD cutoff switch		See *A+ Guide to Hardware*
◢ Verify backlight functionality and pixilation		See *A+ Guide to Hardware*
◢ Stylus issues (e.g., digitizer problems)		See *A+ Guide to Hardware*
◢ Unique laptop keypad issues		See *A+ Guide to Hardware*
◢ Antenna wires	8	432–443 More content in *A+ Guide to Hardware*

DOMAIN 3 PRINTERS AND SCANNERS

3.1   Identify the fundamental principles of using printers and scanners

OBJECTIVES	CHAPTERS	PAGE NUMBERS
Describe the processes used by printers and scanners including laser, inkjet, thermal, solid ink and impact printers		See *A+ Guide to Hardware*

3.2   Install, configure, optimize and upgrade printers and scanners

OBJECTIVES	CHAPTERS	PAGE NUMBERS
Identify the steps used in the installation and configuration processes for printers and scanners, for example:		
◢ Power and connect the device using network or local port	11	607–619
◢ Install and update the device driver	11	607–619
◢ Calibrate the device	11	607–619
◢ Configure options and default settings	11	607–619
◢ Print test page	11	607–619
Install and configure printer/scanner upgrades including memory and firmware	11	607–619

3.3 Identify tools, diagnostic methods and troubleshooting procedures for printers and scanners

OBJECTIVES	CHAPTERS	PAGE NUMBERS
Gather data about printer/scanner problem	11	619–634
Review and analyze data collected about printer/scanner problems	11	619–634
Implement solutions to solve identified printer/scanner problems	11	619–634
Identify appropriate tools used for troubleshooting and repairing printer/scanner problems		
◢ Multi-meter		See *A+ Guide to Hardware*
◢ Screw drivers		See *A+ Guide to Hardware*
◢ Cleaning solutions		See *A+ Guide to Hardware*
◢ Extension magnet		See *A+ Guide to Hardware*
◢ Test patterns		See *A+ Guide to Hardware*

3.4 Perform preventative maintenance of printer and scanner problems

OBJECTIVES	CHAPTERS	PAGE NUMBERS
Perform scheduled maintenance according to vendor guidelines (e.g., install maintenance kits, reset page counts)		See *A+ Guide to Hardware*
Ensure a suitable environment		See *A+ Guide to Hardware*
Use recommended supplies		See *A+ Guide to Hardware*

DOMAIN 4 SECURITY

4.1 Identify the names, purposes, and characteristics of physical security devices and processes

OBJECTIVES	CHAPTERS	PAGE NUMBERS
Control access to PCs, servers, laptops and restricted spaces		
◢ Hardware	10	544–553, 559–560
◢ Operating systems	4, 10	186–199, 223–227, 209–212/544–553, 559–560

4.2 Install hardware security

OBJECTIVES	CHAPTERS	PAGE NUMBERS
Smart card readers	10	579–583
Key fobs	10	579–583
Biometric devices	9, 10	508–510/581–583 More content in *A+ Guide to Hardware*

DOMAIN 5 SAFETY AND ENVIRONMENTAL ISSUES

5.1 Identify potential hazards and proper safety procedures including power supply, display devices and environment (e.g., trip, liquid, situational, atmospheric hazards, high-voltage and moving equipment)

OBJECTIVES	CHAPTERS	PAGE NUMBERS
	10	544, 572 More content in *A+ Guide to Hardware*

Introduction

A+ Guide to Software, Fourth Edition, was written to be the very best tool on the market today to prepare you to support operating systems used on personal computers. Updated to include the most current technologies, with a new chapter on securing your PC and small network, and new content on supporting Windows 2000/XP, this book takes you from the just-a-user level to the I-can-fix-this level for PC operating system matters. This book achieves its goals with an unusually effective combination of tools that powerfully reinforce both concepts and hands-on, real-world experiences. In combination with its companion book, *A+ Guide to Hardware,* these two books provide thorough preparation for the new 2006 CompTIA A+ Certification exams and the older (but still alive) CompTIA 2003 A+ Certification exams. Competency in using a computer is a pre-requisite to using this book. An appropriate pre-requisite course for this book would be a general course in microcomputer applications.

This book includes:

- **Comprehensive review and practice end-of-chapter material**, including a chapter summary, key terms, review questions, critical thinking questions, hands-on projects, and real-world problems to solve.
- **Step-by-step instructions** on installation, maintenance, optimization of system performance, and troubleshooting.
- **Video clips** featuring Jean Andrews illustrating key points from the text to aid your understanding of the material.
- **A wide array of photos, drawings, and screen shots** support the text, displaying in detail exactly how to best understand, purchase, install, and maintain software.
- **Several in-depth, hands-on projects** at the end of each chapter designed to make certain that you not only understand the material, but also execute procedures and make decisions on your own.

In addition, the carefully structured, clearly written text is accompanied by graphics that provide the visual input essential to learning. For instructors using the book in a classroom, a special CD-ROM is available that includes an Instructor's Manual, an Online Testing system, and a PowerPoint presentation.

Coverage is balanced— while focusing on Windows 2000/XP and application support, the text also covers what you need to support Windows 9x/Me and DOS. Because Windows XP is currently the preferred Windows OS, four full chapters are devoted to supporting it and Windows 2000. In addition, two chapters are dedicated to DOS and Windows 9x, because these operating systems are still present in the workplace. The four Windows 2000/XP chapters precede the two DOS and Windows 9x chapters, although the six chapters are written so that you can choose to cover the two DOS and Windows 9x chapters before you study the four Windows 2000/XP chapters. Because occasionally a PC technician sees a Linux installation on the desktop, an appendix covers this OS. You'll also find an appendix on the Mac OS.

This book together with its companion book, *A+ Guide to Hardware,* provide thorough preparation for CompTIA's A+ 2006 and 2003 Certification examinations, and the two books in tandem map completely to these new and older exam objectives. This certification credential's popularity among employers is growing exponentially, and obtaining certification increases your ability to gain employment and improve your salary. To get more information on A+ certification and its sponsoring organization, the Computing Technology Industry Association, see their Web site at *www.comptia.org.*

FEATURES

To ensure a successful learning experience, this book includes the following pedagogical features:

⊿ **Learning Objectives:** Every chapter opens with a list of learning objectives that sets the stage for you to absorb the lessons of the text.

⊿ **Comprehensive Step-by-Step Troubleshooting Guidance:** Troubleshooting guidelines are included in almost every chapter.

⊿ **Step-by-Step Procedures:** The book is chock full of step-by-step procedures covering subjects from operating system installation and maintenance to optimizing system performance.

⊿ **Art Program:** Numerous detailed photographs, three-dimensional art, and screenshots support the text, displaying software features exactly as you will see them in your work.

⊿ **CompTIA A+ Table of Contents:** This table of contents indicates every page that relates to each certification objective. You'll find mapping grids for both the 2006 and 2003 objectives. This is a valuable tool for quick reference. (CompTIA has announced that the 2003 exams will stay live until June 2007, and the 2006 exams are expected to go live by the time this book is in print.) The mapping grids for all of the CompTIA A+ 2006 objectives (CompTIA A+ Essentials, CompTIA A+ 220-602, CompTIA A+ 220-603, and CompTIA A+ 220-604) are placed here in the front of the book. The mapping grids for the CompTIA A+ 2003 objectives are placed on the accompanying CD.

⊿ **Applying Concepts:** These sections offer practical applications for the material being discussed. Whether outlining a task, developing a scenario, or providing pointers, the Applying Concepts sections give you a chance to apply what you've learned to a typical PC problem.

 **Notes:** Note icons highlight additional helpful information related to the subject being discussed.

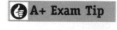 **A+ Icons:** All of the content that relates to CompTIA's A+ 2006 Essentials and 220-602 Certification exams, whether it's a page or a sentence, is highlighted with an A+ icon. The icon notes the exam name and the objective number. This unique feature highlights the relevant content at a glance, so you can pay extra attention to the material.

 **A+ Exam Tip Boxes:** These boxes highlight additional insights and tips to remember if you are planning to take the CompTIA A+ Exams.

 **Caution Icons:** These icons highlight critical safety information. Follow these instructions carefully to protect the PC and its data and to ensure your own safety.

 **Video Clips:** Short video passages reinforce concepts and techniques discussed in the text, and offer insight into the life of a PC repair technician.

 End-of-Chapter Material: Each chapter closes with the following features, which reinforce the material covered in the chapter and provide real-world, hands-on testing:

 Chapter Summary: This bulleted list of concise statements summarizes all major points of the chapter.

Key Terms: The content of each chapter is further reinforced by an end-of-chapter key-term list. The definitions of all terms are included at the end of the book in a full-length glossary.

Review Questions: You can test your understanding of each chapter with a comprehensive set of review questions. The "Reviewing the Basics" questions check your understanding of fundamental concepts, while the "Thinking Critically" questions help you synthesize and apply what you've learned.

Hands-On Projects: You get to test your real-world understanding with hands-on projects involving a full range of software and hardware problems. Each hands-on activity in this book is preceded by the Hands-On icon and a description of the exercise that follows.

Real World, Real Problems: Each comprehensive problem allows you to find out if you can apply what you've learned in the chapter to a real-life situation.

CD Resource Pak: The CD placed in the book includes video clips which feature Jean Andrews illustrating key concepts in the text and providing advice on the real world of PC repair. Other helpful tools on the CD include mapping grids to the CompTIA A+ 2003 exams, Frequently Asked Questions, Sample Reports, Troubleshooting Flowcharts, and an electronic Glossary.

Web Site: For additional content and updates to this book and information about our complete line of CompTIA A+ and PC Repair topics, please visit our Web site at *www.course.com/pcrepair*.

INSTRUCTOR RESOURCES

The following supplemental materials are available when this book is used in a classroom setting. All of the supplements available with this book are provided to the instructor on a single CD-ROM.

Electronic Instructor's Manual: The Instructor's Manual that accompanies this textbook includes additional instructional material to assist in class preparation, including suggestions for classroom activities, discussion topics, and additional projects.

Solutions: Answers to the end-of-chapter material are provided. These include the answers to the Review Questions and to the Hands-On Projects (when applicable).

ExamView®: This textbook is accompanied by ExamView, a powerful testing software package that allows instructors to create and administer printed, computer (LAN-based), and Internet exams. ExamView includes hundreds of questions that correspond to the topics covered in this text, enabling students to generate detailed study guides that include page references for further review. The computer-based and Internet testing components allow students to take exams at their computers, and also save the instructor time by grading each exam automatically.

PowerPoint Presentations: This book comes with Microsoft PowerPoint slides for each chapter. These are included as a teaching aid for classroom presentation, to make available to students on the network for chapter review, or to be printed for classroom distribution. Instructors, please feel at liberty to add your own slides for additional topics you introduce to the class.

Figure Files: All of the figures in the book are reproduced on the Instructor Resource CD, in bit-mapped format. Similar to the PowerPoint presentations, these are included as a teaching aid for classroom presentation, to make available to students for review, or to be printed for classroom distribution.

Daily Lesson Planner: This free teaching tool enables instructors to use our CompTIA A+ products with even greater ease. It includes detailed lecture notes and teaching instructions that incorporate all of the components of the CompTIA A+ Total Solutions. A user name and password are required for download. The Daily Lesson Planner is available on the Instructor's CD and online at *www.course.com/pcrepair*.

ACKNOWLEDGMENTS

Thank you to the wonderful people at Thomson Course Technology who continue to provide support, warm encouragement, patience, and guidance: Nick Lombardi, Michelle Ruelos Cannistraci, and Catherine DiMassa. You've truly helped make this fourth edition fun! Thank you, Jill Batistick, Developmental Editor, for your careful attention to detail and your genuine friendship, and to Karen Annett, our excellent copy editor. Thank you, Susan Whalen and Serge Palladino, for your careful attention to the technical accuracy of the book. Thank you, Abigail Reip, for your research efforts.

Thank you to all the people who took the time to voluntarily send encouragement and suggestions for improvements to the previous editions. Your input and help is very much appreciated. The reviewers all provided invaluable insights and showed a genuine interest in the book's success. Thank you to:

Paul J. Bartoszewicz, Hudson Valley Community College, Troy, NY
Steve Belville, Bryant & Stratton, Milwaukee, WI
Keith Conn, Cleveland Institute of Electronics, Cleveland, OH
Kevin Crawford, Community College of Rhode Island
Chuck Lund, Central Lakes College, Brainerd, MN
Erik Schmid, The Chubb Institute, Cherry Hill, NJ

Thank you to Joy Dark who was here with me making this book happen. I'm very grateful. This book is dedicated to the covenant of God with man on earth.

Jean Andrews, Ph.D.

PHOTO CREDITS

Figure 4-46	Courtesy of Kaguru Solutions
Figure 8-58	Courtesy of D-Link Corporation
Figure 10-5	Courtesy of wesecure.com
Figure 10-42	Courtesy of RSA Security
Figure 10-43	Courtesy of IDenticard Systems
Figure 10-44	Courtesy of Athena Smartcard Solutions Ltd.
Figure 10-45	Courtesy of Aladdin
Figure 11-1	Courtesy of Hewlett-Packard Company

Most of the other photos are courtesy of Joy Dark and Jennifer Dark.

READ THIS BEFORE YOU BEGIN

The following hardware, software, and other equipment are needed to do the Hands-on Projects in each chapter:

▲ You need a working PC on which you can install an operating system.
▲ Chapter 1 relies solely on Windows XP, although you can substitute Windows 2000 Professional or Windows 98/Me. Microsoft Windows XP Professional and Windows 2000

Professional are needed for Chapters 2-5. (Except for a few instances, you can substitute Windows XP Home Edition for Windows XP Professional in these four chapters.) Windows 98/Me is needed for Chapters 6 and 7.

COMPTIA AUTHORIZED CURRICULUM PROGRAM

The logo of the CompTIA Authorized Curriculum Program and the status of this or other training material as "Authorized" under the CompTIA Authorized Curriculum Program signifies that, in CompTIA's opinion, such training material covers the content of the CompTIA's related certification exam. CompTIA has not reviewed or approved the accuracy of the contents of this training material and specifically disclaims any warranties of merchantability or fitness for a particular purpose. CompTIA makes no guarantee concerning the success of persons using any such "Authorized" or other training material in order to prepare for any CompTIA certification exam.

The contents of this training material were created for the CompTIA A+ 2006 certification exams.

STATE OF THE INFORMATION TECHNOLOGY (IT) FIELD

Most organizations today depend on computers and information technology to improve business processes, productivity, and efficiency. Opportunities to become global organizations and reach customers, businesses, and suppliers are a direct result of the widespread use of the Internet. Changing technology further changes how companies do business. This fundamental change in business practices has increased the need for skilled and certified IT workers across industries. This transformation has moved many IT workers out of traditional IT businesses and into various IT-dependent industries such as banking, government, insurance, and healthcare.

In the year 2004, the U.S. Department of Labor, Bureau of Labor Statistics, reported that there were 1.1 million computer and data processing services jobs within organizations and an additional 132,000 self-employed workers.

In any industry, the workforce is important to continuously drive business. Having correctly skilled workers in IT is a struggle with the ever-changing technologies. It has been estimated that technologies change approximately every 2 years. With such a quick product life cycle, IT workers must strive to keep up with these changes to continue to bring value to their employer.

CERTIFICATIONS

Different levels of education are required for the many jobs in the IT industry. Additionally, the level of education and type of training required varies from employer to employer, but the need for qualified technicians remains constant. As technology changes and advances in the industry continue to rapidly evolve, many employers consistently look for employees who possess the skills necessary to implement these new technologies. Traditional degrees and diplomas do not identify the skills that a job applicant has. With the growth of the IT industry, companies increasingly rely on technical certifications to identify the skills a particular job applicant possesses. Technical certifications are a way for employers to ensure the quality and skill qualifications of their computer professionals, and they can offer job seekers a competitive edge. According to Thomas Regional Industrial Market Trends, one of the 15 trends that will transform the workplace over the next decade is a severe labor and skill shortage, specifically in technical fields, which are struggling to locate skilled and educated workers.

There are two types of certifications: vendor neutral and vendor specific. Vendor neutral certifications are those that test for the skills and knowledge required in specific industry job roles and do not subscribe to a specific vendor's technology solution. Vendor neutral certifications include all of the Computing Technology Industry Association's (CompTIA) certifications, Project Management Institute's certifications, and Security Certified Program certifications. Vendor specific certifications validate the skills and knowledge necessary to be successful by utilizing a specific vendor's technology solution. Some examples of vendor specific certifications include those offered by Microsoft, IBM, Novell, and Cisco.

As employers struggle to fill open IT positions with qualified candidates, certifications are a means of validating the skill sets necessary to be successful within an organization. In most careers, salary and compensation are determined by experience and education, but in IT, the number and type of certifications an employee earns also factors into salary and wage increases. The Department of Labor, Bureau of Labor Statistics, reported that the computer and data processing industry is expected to grow about 40% by the year 2014, compared to a 14% increase in the entire economy.

Certifications provide job applicants with more than just a competitive edge over their non-certified counterparts who apply for the same IT positions. Some institutions of higher education grant college credit to students who successfully pass certification exams, moving them further along in their degree programs. Certifications also give individuals who are interested in careers in the military the ability to move into higher positions more quickly. And many advanced certification programs accept, and sometimes require, entry-level certifications as part of their exams. For example, Cisco and Microsoft accept some CompTIA certifications as prerequisites for their certification programs.

CAREER PLANNING

Finding a career that fits a person's personality, skill set, and lifestyle is challenging and fulfilling, but can often be difficult. What are the steps individuals should take to find that dream career? Is IT interesting to you? Chances are that if you are reading this book, this question has been answered. What about IT do you like? The world of work in the IT industry is vast. Some questions to ask include the following: Are you a person who likes to work alone, or do you like to work in a group? Do you like speaking directly with customers or do you prefer to stay behind the scenes? Is your lifestyle conducive to a lot of travel, or do you need to stay in one location? All of these factors influence your decision when faced with choosing the right job. Inventory assessments are a good first step to learning more about your interests, work values, and abilities. There are a variety of Web sites that offer assistance with career planning and assessments.

The Computing Technology Industry Association (CompTIA) hosts an informational Web site called the TechCareer Compass™ (TCC) that defines careers in the IT industry. The TCC is located at *tcc.comptia.org*. This Web site was created by the industry and outlines over 100 industry jobs. Each defined job includes a job description, alternate job titles, critical work functions, activities and performance indicators, and skills and knowledge required by the job. In other words, it shows exactly what the job entails so that you can find one that best fits your interests and abilities. Additionally, the TCC maps over 750 technical certifications to the skills required by each specific job, allowing you to research and plan your certification training. The Web site also includes a resource section, which is updated regularly with articles and links to other career Web sites. The TechCareer Compass is the one-stop location for IT career information.

In addition to CompTIA's TechCareer Compass, there are many other Web sites that cover components of IT careers and career planning. Many of these sites can also be found in the TCC Resources section. Some of these other career planning sites include *YourITFuture.com*, *ITCompass.net*, and *About.com*.

CITATION

Bureau of Labor Statistics, U.S. Department of Labor. *Career Guide to Industries, 2006-7 Edition, Computer and Data Processing Services.* On the Internet at http://www.bls.gov/oco/cg/cgs033.htm (visited September 6, 2006).

Bureau of Labor Statistics, U.S. Department of Labor, *Occupational Outlook Handbook, 2006-7 Edition, Computer Support Specialists and System Administrators.* On the Internet at http://www.bls.gov/oco/home.htm (visited September 3, 2006).

Thomas Regional Industrial Market Trends. July 8, 2003 Newsletter: *15 Trends that Will Transform the Workforce.* On the Internet at http://www.thomasregional.com/newsarchive2.html?us=3f61ed4162269&to=5&from=0&id=1057266649 (visited September 3, 2006).

WHAT'S NEW WITH COMPTIA A+ CERTIFICATION

In June 2006, CompTIA *(www.comptia.org)* published the objectives for the 2006 CompTIA A+ Certification exams. These exams go live in September 2006. However, you can still become CompTIA A+ certified by passing the older 2003 exams that are to remain live until the end of 2006 and, in some educational environments, until June 2007. The 2003 exams consist of two exams: the CompTIA A+ Core Hardware Service Technician exam and the CompTIA A+ Operating System Technologies exam. You must past both exams to become CompTIA A+ certified. Content on hardware and operating systems on these two hardware and OS exams does not overlap, except for a few instances. Most students have found it convenient to study for one exam and pass it before preparing for the other exam.

The format of the 2006 exams is new. Here are the key facts regarding these exams:

- Currently, there are four 2006 exams. Everyone must pass the CompTIA A+ Essentials exam. You must also pass one of three advanced exams, which are named the CompTIA A+ 220-602 exam, the CompTIA A+ 220-603 exam, and the CompTIA A+ 220-604 exam.
- All four exams cover the same content, which includes both hardware and software. The advanced exams cover the content in a greater depth than does the CompTIA A+ Essentials exam.
- The CompTIA A+ 220-602 exam is the most comprehensive of the three advanced exams. Basically, the CompTIA A+ 220-603 and CompTIA A+ 220-604 exams are subsets of the CompTIA A+ 220-602 exam.
- The type of CompTIA A+ Certification you receive depends on which of the three advanced exams you pass, as diagrammed in Figure 1.
- By passing the CompTIA A+ 220-602 and CompTIA A+ Essentials exams, you are awarded the CompTIA A+ Certification for IT Technician. This certification targets those who intend to work in a "mobile or corporate technical environment with a high level of face-to-face client interaction." Job roles include IT administrator, enterprise technician, field service technician, and PC support technician.
- By passing the CompTIA A+ 220-603 and CompTIA A+ Essentials exams, you are awarded the CompTIA A+ Certification for Remote Support Technician. This certification targets those who intend to work "in a remote-based work environment where client interaction, client training, operating system and connectivity issues are emphasized." Job roles include help desk technician, remote support technician, and call center technician.
- By passing the CompTIA A+ 220-604 and CompTIA A+ Essentials exams, you are awarded the CompTIA A+ Certification for Depot Technician. This certification targets those who intend to work in settings where hardware is emphasized. Job roles include bench technician and depot technician.

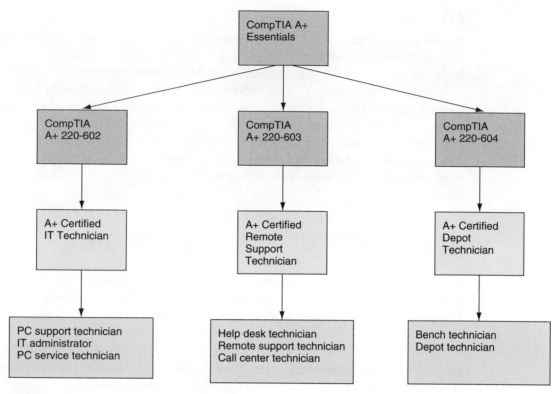

Figure 1 Paths to CompTIA A+ Certification and job roles

All of the four 2006 A+ exams contain content on both hardware and software. Basically, the software content for all four exams is contained in this book and the hardware content for all four exams is contained in the companion book, *A+ Guide to Hardware*. Here is a breakdown of the domains covered on each of the four exams:

Domain	CompTIA A+ Essentials	CompTIA A+ 220-602	CompTIA A+ 220-603	CompTIA A+ 220-604
1.0 Personal Computer Components	21%	18%	15%	45%
2.0 Laptop and Portable Devices	11%	9%	0	20%
3.0 Operating Systems	21%	20%	29%	0
4.0 Printers and Scanners	9%	14%	10%	20%
5.0 Networks	12%	11%	11%	0
6.0 Security	11%	8%	15%	5%
7.0 Safety and Environmental Issues	10%	5%	0	10%
8.0 Communication and Professionalism	5%	15%	20%	0

HOW TO BECOME COMPTIA CERTIFIED

This training material can help you prepare for and pass a related CompTIA certification exam or exams. In order to achieve CompTIA certification, you must register for and pass a CompTIA certification exam or exams. In order to become CompTIA certified, you must:

1. Select a certification exam provider. For more information, please visit the following Web site: *www.comptia.org/certification/general_information/test_locations.asp*.

2. Register for and schedule a time to take the CompTIA certification exam(s) at a convenient location.

3. Read and sign the Candidate Agreement, which will be presented at the time of the exam(s). The text of the Candidate Agreement can be found at the following Web site: *www.comptia.org/certification/general_information/candidate_agreement.asp*.

4. Take and pass the CompTIA certification exam(s).

For more information about CompTIA's certifications, such as their industry acceptance, benefits, or program news, please visit *www.comptia.org/certification/default.asp*.

CompTIA is a non-profit information technology (IT) trade association. CompTIA's certifications are designed by subject matter experts from across the IT industry. Each CompTIA certification is vendor-neutral, covers multiple technologies, and requires demonstration of skills and knowledge widely sought after by the IT industry.

To contact CompTIA with any questions or comments, call + 1 630 678 8300 or send an email to *questions@comptia.org*.

Introducing Operating Systems

Personal computers have changed the way we work, play, and do business. Everyone, no matter how young or old they are or how they make their living, encounters a personal computer in some way almost daily. No matter how experienced a computer user you are, this book can take you from the just-a-user stage to understanding what happens behind the scenes when you click a Web site or install a new screen saver. Not only will you understand what happened, but you'll also be able to customize your operating system (OS) and applications, troubleshoot and solve problems with the OS, and optimize your system for best performance.

The goals of this book are to help you understand, troubleshoot, customize, and optimize a Windows operating system and to make wise buying decisions about operating systems. The only assumption made here is that you are a computer user—that is, you can turn on your machine, load a software package, and use that software to accomplish a task. In addition, this book, together with its companion book, *A+ Guide to Managing and Troubleshooting Hardware* (Thomson Learning, ISBN 0-619-21672-6), prepares you to pass the A+ Essentials exam and any one of the advanced exams, which are the A+ 220-602, A+ 220-603, and A+ 220-604 exams, required by CompTIA (*www.comptia.org*) for A+ Certification. At the time this book went to print, the older 2003 A+ exams were still live; therefore, the book also includes the content on the 2003 A+ Operating System Technologies exam.

In this chapter, you'll learn about the different operating systems, what they do, and how they work to control several of the more significant hardware devices. You'll also see how an OS provides the interface that users and applications need to command and use hardware devices. Finally, you'll learn to use several Windows tools and utilities that are useful to examine a system, change desktop settings, and view and manage some hardware devices.

OPERATING SYSTEMS PAST AND PRESENT

An **operating system** (OS) is software that controls a computer. It manages hardware, runs applications, provides an interface for users, and stores, retrieves, and manipulates files. In general, you can think of an operating system as the middleman between applications and hardware, between the user and hardware, and between the user and applications (see Figure 1-1).

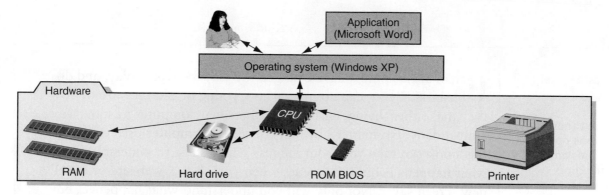

Figure 1-1 Users and applications depend on the OS to relate to all applications and hardware components

Several applications might be installed on a computer to meet various user needs, but a computer really needs only one operating system. You need to be aware of the older and current operating systems described in the following sections of the chapter and how operating systems have evolved to support new hardware technologies and expanding user needs.

DOS (DISK OPERATING SYSTEM)

DOS was the first OS among IBM computers and IBM-compatible computers. Figure 1-2 shows a computer screen using the DOS operating system. DOS is outdated as a viable option for a desktop computer operating system today. However, you need to know about it because it is sometimes still used in specialized systems that still use older applications

```
C:\>DIR \GAME

 Volume in drive C has no label
 Volume Serial Number is 0F52-09FC
 Directory of C:\GAME

 .            <DIR>      02-18-93    4:50a
 ..           <DIR>      02-18-93    4:50a
 CHESS        <DIR>      02-18-93    4:50a
 NUKE         <DIR>      02-18-93    4:51a
 PENTE        <DIR>      02-18-93    4:52a
 NETRIS       <DIR>      02-18-93    4:54a
 BEYOND       <DIR>      02-18-93    4:54a
        7 file(s)            0 bytes
                     9273344 bytes free

C:\>
```

Figure 1-2 DOS provides a command-line prompt to receive user commands

and hardware that were created for DOS. For example, a microcomputer dedicated to controlling an in-house phone system might run DOS. Sometimes DOS is used on a floppy disk or CD that contains utilities to upgrade and diagnose problems with a hard drive or motherboard. That's because DOS can be used to boot and troubleshoot a computer when a more sophisticated OS is too cumbersome and has too much overhead.

DOS was the OS used by early versions of Windows, including Windows 3.1 and Windows 3.11 (collectively referred to as Windows 3.x). Windows 3.x had to use DOS because Windows 3.x didn't perform OS functions, but simply served as a user-friendly intermediate program between DOS, applications, and the user (see Figure 1-3). Windows 3.x is totally outdated and not covered in this book.

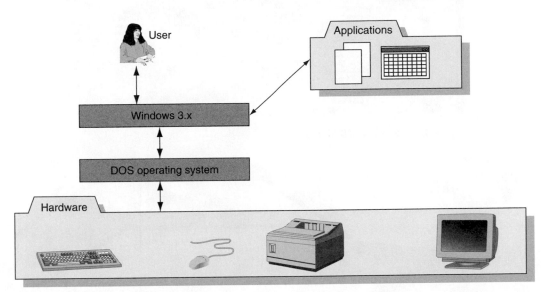

Figure 1-3 Windows 3.x was layered between DOS and the user and applications to provide a graphics interface for the user and a multitasking environment for applications

Windows 9x/Me uses some DOS programs as part of the underlying OS (called a DOS core), and therefore has some DOS characteristics. When the Windows 9x/Me desktop fails, DOS can be used to troubleshoot the OS. DOS is covered as a troubleshooting OS in Chapter 6. Also, Windows 2000/XP offers a Recovery Console and a Command Prompt window where you use DOS-like commands. You'll learn about the Command Prompt window in Chapter 4 and the Recovery Console in Chapter 5.

WINDOWS 9X/ME

Early OSs that used a DOS core are Windows 95, Windows 98, and Windows Me, collectively called Windows 9x/Me. These are true operating systems built on a DOS core that provide a user-friendly interface shown in Figure 1-4. Windows XP has largely replaced Windows 9x/Me, but you still occasionally see Windows 98 on a notebook or desktop computer for home use. (Many people chose not to upgrade from Windows 98 to Windows Me because they did not consider it a significant-enough upgrade to warrant the cost and hassle involved.)

Windows 9x/Me is a blend of low-end and high-end technologies. These operating systems fulfill the Microsoft commitment to be **backward-compatible** with older software and hardware while still taking advantage of newer technology. Windows 9x/Me is an OS that bridges two worlds (see Figure 1-5).

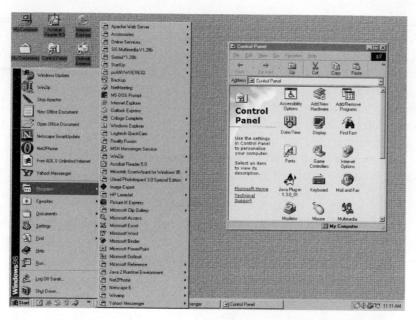

Figure 1-4   Windows 98 SE desktop

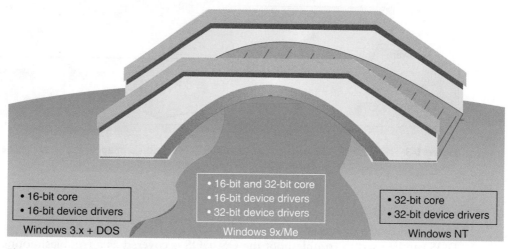

- 16-bit core
- 16-bit device drivers

Windows 3.x + DOS

- 16-bit and 32-bit core
- 16-bit device drivers
- 32-bit device drivers

Windows 9x/Me

- 32-bit core
- 32-bit device drivers

Windows NT

Figure 1-5   Windows 9x/Me is the bridge from DOS to Windows NT

Table 1-1 lists the hardware requirements of Windows 9x/Me. Note that Table 1-1 gives the *recommended* minimum to run each version of Windows 9x/Me. You may find different values in other documentation, because these OSs might need more or less memory depending on whether you are installing on a new system or upgrading an older system, as well as which applications and OS features you choose to install. Also, sometimes Microsoft lists the minimum requirements to *install* an OS, which might be different from the requirements to *run* an OS. (Requirements in Table 1-1 are for running the OS.)

Description	Windows 95	Windows 98	Windows Me
Processor	486 or higher	Pentium	Pentium 150 MHz
RAM	8 MB	24 MB	32 MB
Free hard drive space	50 MB	195 MB	320 MB

Table 1-1   Recommended minimum hardware requirements for Windows 9x/Me

Keep these differences in mind when reviewing the lists of minimum hardware requirements for OSs throughout this chapter. Windows 9x/Me is covered in Chapter 7.

You cannot buy a new license for Windows 9x/Me, so the OS is considered a legacy OS. Microsoft no longer supports Windows 9x/Me. As a support technician, the only reason you would install an existing copy of Windows 9x/Me on a computer is in a situation where you are repairing a corrupted installation or replacing a hard drive.

> **Notes**
>
> Some instructors prefer to cover DOS and Windows 9x/Me before they cover Windows 2000/XP, and others prefer to start with Windows 2000/XP. To satisfy both approaches, know that Chapters 6 and 7 on DOS and Windows 9x/Me are written so that they can be covered first before you study the four Windows 2000/XP Chapters 2, 3, 4, and 5. On the other hand, Chapters 2 through 7 function well when covered sequentially.

WINDOWS NT

Windows NT (New Technology) came in two versions: Windows NT Workstation for workstations, and Windows NT Server to control a network. Windows NT corrected many problems with Windows 9x/Me because it completely rewrote the OS core, totally eliminating the DOS core, and introduced many new problems of its own that were later solved by Windows 2000 and Windows XP.

The minimum hardware requirements for Windows NT on an IBM-compatible PC are listed below for informational purposes only. Because it's such a problem-riddled OS, don't install it unless you absolutely have no other option. For more information about Windows NT, see Appendix D, "Windows NT Workstation."

- Pentium-compatible processor or higher
- 16 MB of RAM (32 MB is recommended)
- 125 MB of hard disk space

A+ ESS
3.1

WINDOWS 2000

Windows 2000 is an upgrade of Windows NT, and also came in several versions, some designed for the desktop and others designed for high-end servers. Windows 2000 Professional was popular as an OS for the corporate desktop. Windows 2000 Server, Advanced Server, and Datacenter Server are network server OSs. Windows 2000 offered several improvements over Windows NT, including a more stable environment, support for Plug and Play, Device Manager, Recovery Console, Active Directory, better network support, and features specifically targeting notebook computers. The Windows 2000 Professional desktop is shown in Figure 1-6.

Hardware and software must qualify for all the Windows 2000 operating systems. To see if your hardware and applications qualify, check the Windows Marketplace Tested Products List at *testedproducts.windowsmarketplace.com* (see Figure 1-7). Alternately, for hardware, you can check the HCL at *www.microsoft.com/whdc/hcl/search.mspx*.

The recommended system requirements for Windows 2000 Professional are:

- 133 MHz Pentium-compatible processor
- 2 GB hard drive with at least 650 MB free space
- 64 MB RAM

Windows 2000 is considered a dying OS. You cannot buy a new license for it, and, except for providing security patches, Microsoft no longer supports the OS. Windows 2000 Professional and Windows XP are covered together in Chapters 2, 3, 4, and 5. Server OSs are not covered in this book.

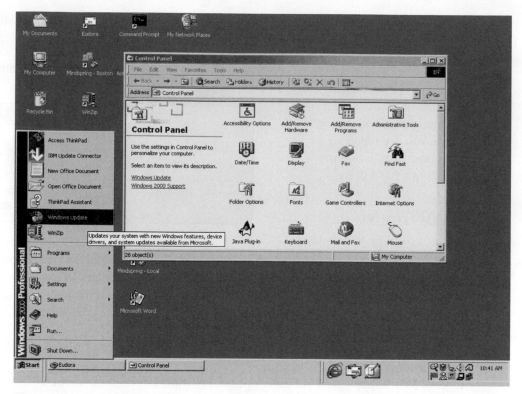

Figure 1-6 The Windows 2000 Professional desktop

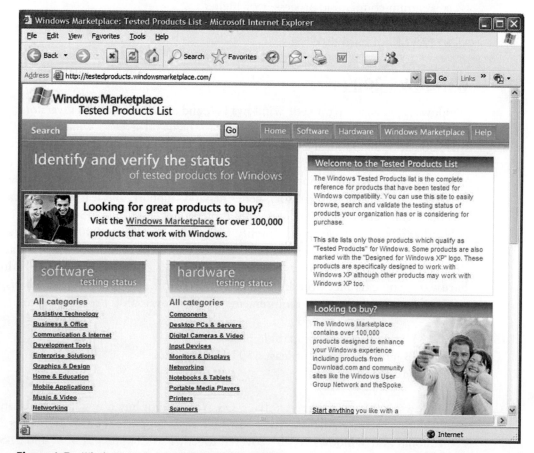

Figure 1-7 Windows Marketplace Tested Products List

A+ ESS
3.1

WINDOWS XP

Windows XP is an upgrade of Windows 2000 and attempts to integrate Windows 9x/Me and 2000, while providing added support for multimedia and networking technologies. The two main versions are Windows XP Home Edition and Windows XP Professional, though other less significant editions include Windows XP Media Center Edition, Windows XP Tablet PC Edition, and Windows XP Professional x64 Edition. This book focuses on Windows XP Professional and Windows XP Home Edition.

The Windows XP desktop (see Figure 1-8) has a different look from the desktops for earlier Windows. Windows XP has the ability for two users to log on simultaneously, both with their own applications open. Windows Messenger and Windows Media Player are inherent parts of Windows XP. And XP includes several advanced security features, including Windows Firewall.

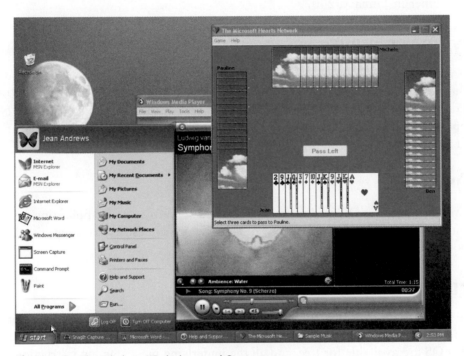

Figure 1-8 The Windows XP desktop and Start menu

The minimum requirements for Windows XP Professional are:

- A minimum of 64 MB of RAM, with 128 MB recommended
- At least 1.5 GB of free hard drive space, with 2 GB recommended
- A CPU that runs at least 233 MHz, with a 300-MHz CPU recommended. Windows XP can support two processors.

Windows XP is replacing all previous versions of Windows in the home market and for the corporate desktop.

Notes

To know the Windows XP version, the CPU speed, and the amount of RAM installed on your computer, click the **Start** button on the Windows XP desktop and right-click **My Computer**. Select **Properties** on the shortcut menu and select the **General** tab.

A+ Tip

The A+ Essentials exam expects you to know the system requirements for Windows 2000 Professional and Windows XP.

At the time this book went to print, when you buy a new Windows computer, Windows XP is installed. When deciding to upgrade to Windows XP, the only reasons you would not upgrade are to avoid the time and expense of the upgrade or when you have compatibility issues with older hardware and software. Windows XP is covered in Chapters 2, 3, 4, and 5 along with Windows 2000 Professional.

WINDOWS VISTA

Windows Vista, code-named Longhorn, is the next generation of Windows operating systems by Microsoft. Windows Vista has a new graphical interface, a revamped engine, and a new interface between it and applications. At the time this book went to print, Microsoft had announced that it intended to release desktop and server versions of Windows Vista for multiple-license business users in November, 2006, and for the consumer in January, 2007.

WINDOWS SERVER 2003

Windows Server 2003 is a suite of Microsoft operating systems including Windows Small Business Server 2003, Storage Server 2003, Server 2003 Web Edition, Server 2003 Standard Edition, Server 2003 Enterprise Edition, and Server 2003 Datacenter Edition. None of these operating systems are intended to be used for a personal computer, and they are not covered in this book.

UNIX

Unix is a popular OS used to control networks and to support applications used on the Internet. There are several versions of Unix, which are called flavors or distributions. Unix is not covered in this book.

LINUX

A variation of Unix that has recently gained popularity is Linux, an OS created by Linus Torvalds when he was a student at the University of Helsinki in Finland. Basic versions of this OS are available for free, and all the underlying programming instructions (called source code) are also freely distributed. Like Unix, Linux is distributed by several different companies, whose versions of Linux are sometimes called **distributions**. Popular distributions of Linux include SuSE (*www.novell.com/linux/suse*), RedHat (*redhat.com*), and TurboLinux (*www.turbolinux.com*). Linux can be used both as a server platform and a desktop platform, but its greatest popularity has come in the server market.

A+ Tip

The A+ Essentials exam expects you to know when it is appropriate to use the Linux and Mac OS.

Network services such as a Web server or e-mail server often are provided by a computer running the Linux operating system. Linux is well-suited to support various types of server applications. Because Linux is very reliable and does not require a lot of computing power, it is sometimes used as a desktop OS, although it is not as popular for this purpose because it is not easy to install or use and few Linux applications are available. Linux is an excellent training tool for learning Unix.

Here are tips about the requirements to use the Linux OS:

▲ You don't have to install Linux on a hard drive in order to run it. You can download Linux from the Internet and burn it to a CD or DVD and boot from the disc to run Linux. You can also buy books on Linux that include the Linux OS on CD.

A+ ESS
3.1

▲ You can download some distributions of Linux for free, but in most cases, you must pay for technical support.

▲ The minimum and recommended system requirements for Linux vary from one distribution to another. Expect to need at least a Pentium III or AMD Athlon processor with 256 MB of RAM. If you install the OS on your hard drive, you'll need at least 4 GB of free space.

Because many users prefer a Windows-style desktop, several applications have been written to provide a GUI shell for Unix and Linux. These shells are called X Windows. A typical X Windows screen is shown in Figure 1-9.

You can find out more about Linux by reading Appendix B, "Introducing Linux".

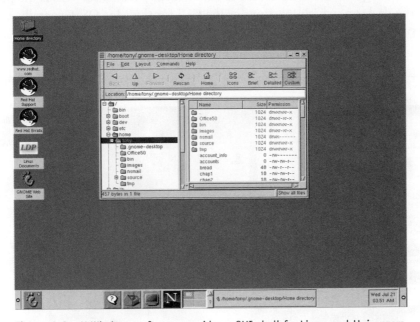

Figure 1-9 X Windows software provides a GUI shell for Linux and Unix users

OS/2

OS/2, developed by IBM and Microsoft, is less common for home desktop PCs, but is used in certain types of networks. Microsoft developed Windows NT using some of the core components of OS/2 and intended it to replace OS/2. OS/2 is not covered in this book.

A+ ESS
3.1

MAC OS

Currently, the Mac OS, which has its roots in the Unix OS, is available only on Macintosh computers by Apple Corporation (*www.apple.com*). The Mac and the Mac OS were first introduced in 1984. Several versions of the Macintosh OS have been written since 1984, the latest being Mac OS X (ten), which offers easy access to the Internet and allows any Macintosh computer to become a Web server for a small network.

Until recently, all Macintosh computers were built using PowerPC processors by IBM. Now, some Macs use processors by Intel, which means that it is now possible for Mac OS X to work on other Intel-based computers. It remains to be seen

> **Notes**
>
> Recently, Apple released Boot Camp software, which makes it possible to install Windows on a Mac computer as a dual boot with Mac OS X. A dual boot makes it possible to boot a computer into one of two installed OSs.

if Apple will make versions of the Mac OS X available for purchase and use on computers other than the Macintosh. Speculation says that if Apple chooses this route, Mac OS X will compete with Windows for the desktop OS market for IBM-compatible computers.

Because it is easy to use, the Mac OS has been popular in educational environments, from elementary school through the university level. It also provides excellent support for graphics and multimedia applications and is popular in the professional desktop publishing and graphics markets. Because IBM-compatible PCs have a larger share of the computer market, applications compatible with the Mac OS are not as readily available. Mac OS X requires at least 128 MB of RAM and 1.5 GB of hard drive space.

The Mac OS X interface is significantly different from that of the Mac OS 9, including two new features called the dock and the toolbar, as shown in Figure 1-10. When a Mac is turned on, a program called the Finder is automatically launched. This is the program that provides the desktop, which functions as the GUI for the Mac OS. Generally, under normal Mac OS operation, you cannot quit the Finder program.

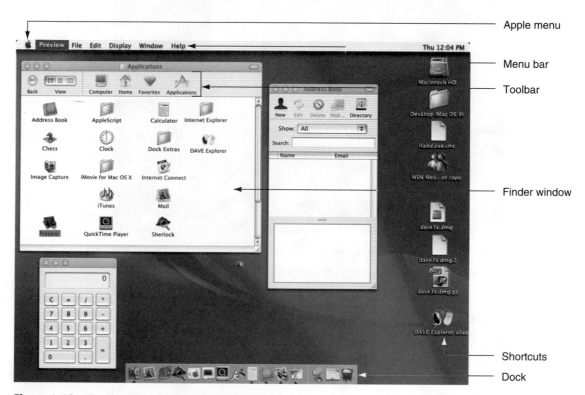

Figure 1-10 The Mac OS X desktop is intuitive and easy to use

The Mac OS X tries to make installing hardware as smooth as possible without much user interaction by providing superior Plug and Play capabilities, so that new hardware devices can be added easily and are automatically recognized by the OS. Another important difference between Mac OS X and earlier versions is that Mac OS X provides better support for multitasking and is thus less likely to freeze when several applications are running simultaneously.

You can learn more about the Mac OS by reading Appendix C, "Introducing the Mac OS".

> **Notes**
>
> Although the initial cost of setting up a Macintosh system is generally higher than for a comparable IBM-compatible system, the cost of support and maintenance is generally lower for the Mac.

1

WHAT AN OPERATING SYSTEM DOES

A+ ESS 3.1

Although there are important differences among them, OSs share the following four main functions:

 Notes

All Windows operating systems are produced by Microsoft (*www.microsoft.com*). Different flavors of Unix and Linux are produced by various manufacturers. You can learn more about Unix and Linux at *www.unix.org* and *www.linux.org*. For more information about the Mac OS, see *www.apple.com*, and for information about OS/2, see *www.ibm.com*.

- ◢ Providing a user interface
  - Performing housekeeping procedures requested by the user, often concerning secondary storage devices, such as formatting new disks, deleting files, copying files, and changing the system date
  - Providing a way for the user to manage the desktop, hardware, applications, and data
- ◢ Managing files
  - Managing files on hard drives, DVD drives, CD drives, floppy drives, and other drives
  - Creating, storing, retrieving, deleting, and moving files
- ◢ Managing applications
  - Installing and uninstalling applications
  - Running applications and managing the interface to the hardware on behalf of an application
- ◢ Managing hardware
  - Managing the BIOS (programs permanently stored on hardware devices)
  - Managing memory, which is a temporary place to store data and instructions as they are being processed
  - Diagnosing problems with software and hardware
  - Interfacing between hardware and software (that is, interpreting application software needs to the hardware and interpreting hardware needs to application software)
- ◢ Before we look more closely at each of these four main functions, let's turn our attention to the core components common to every operating system.

OPERATING SYSTEM COMPONENTS

Every operating system has two main internal components: the shell and the kernel (see Figure 1-11). A **shell** is the portion of the OS that relates to the user and to applications. The shell provides a way for the user to do such things as select music to burn to a CD, install an application, or change the wallpaper on the Windows desktop. The shell does this using various interface tools such as Windows Explorer, the Control Panel, or My Computer, which can have command, menu, or icon-driven interfaces for the user. For applications, the shell provides commands and procedures that applications can call on to do such things as print a spreadsheet, read from a database, or display a photograph onscreen.

The core, or **kernel**, of the OS is responsible for interacting with hardware. It has more power to communicate with hardware devices than the shell has. Therefore, applications operating under the OS cannot get to hardware devices without the shell passing those requests to the kernel. This module approach that says, "You do your job and I'll do mine,

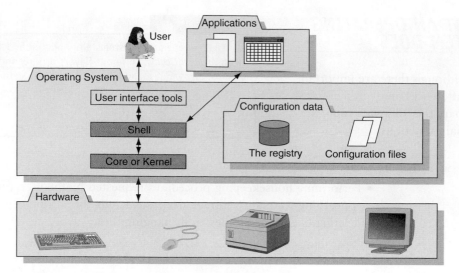

Figure 1-11 Inside an operating system, different components perform various functions

and we won't mess with each other's work" provides for a more stable system. If you think of an OS as a restaurant, the shell is like the hosts and waiters that serve customers, and the kernel is like the chefs and kitchen staff. Hosts and waiters are responsible for customer interaction but aren't allowed in the kitchen where the food is prepared.

An operating system needs a place to keep hardware and software configuration information, user preferences, and application settings that are used when the OS is first loaded and are accessed as needed by hardware, applications, and users. This information can be kept in databases or text files. Windows uses a database called the **registry** for most of this information. In addition, Windows keeps some data in text files called **initialization files**, which often have an .ini or .inf file extension. For example, an application might store in a text file or in the registry the settings preferred by the last user, such as background color, fonts, and text size. When the application is launched, the first thing it does is read the registry or text file and then loads the user's preferred settings.

Now let's look at a more detailed explanation of each of the four functions of an OS.

AN OS PROVIDES A USER INTERFACE

When you first turn on a PC, the operating system is loaded. After the OS is in control, it provides an interface on the computer screen (called the desktop) and waits for the user to do something (point, click, double-click, or type). The user is clicking a menu, typing a command, or double-clicking an icon using an interface that is command-driven, menu-driven, or icon-driven.

COMMAND-DRIVEN INTERFACES

With a command-driven interface, you type commands to tell the OS to perform operations. Computer technicians who are good typists and are very familiar with DOS-like commands often prefer this kind of OS interface. For example, to type a command using Windows XP, click the **Start** button on the Windows taskbar and then click **Run**. The Run dialog box appears where you can type a command such as DEFRAG C:, which is the command to arrange data on your hard drive for better performance. You can also enter the command **Cmd** in the Run dialog box to get a Command Prompt window such as the one in Figure 1-12. From this window, you can enter commands such as Defrag C:. You will learn more about this and other commands in Chapters 4 and 5.

1

A+ ESS
3.1

A+
220-602
3.1

```
C:\WINDOWS\system32\cmd.exe - defrag C:                          _ □ ×

Microsoft Windows XP [Version 5.1.2600]
(C) Copyright 1985-2001 Microsoft Corp.

C:\Documents and Settings\Jean Andrews>dir
 Volume in drive C has no label.
 Volume Serial Number is DCB8-611B

 Directory of C:\Documents and Settings\Jean Andrews

03/15/2006  07:43 PM    <DIR>          .
03/15/2006  07:43 PM    <DIR>          ..
03/31/2006  02:01 PM    <DIR>          Desktop
03/23/2006  02:40 PM    <DIR>          Favorites
12/05/2005  12:07 PM    <DIR>          My Documents
04/11/2006  02:38 PM         4,980,736 ntuser.dat
09/30/2004  04:04 PM    <DIR>          Start Menu
07/30/2005  02:05 PM    <DIR>          WINDOWS
               1 File(s)      4,980,736 bytes
               7 Dir(s)  46,515,404,800 bytes free

C:\Documents and Settings\Jean Andrews>defrag C:
Windows Disk Defragmenter
Copyright (c) 2001 Microsoft Corp. and Executive Software International, Inc.
```

Figure 1-12   Enter command lines in a Command Prompt window

ICON-DRIVEN AND MENU-DRIVEN INTERFACES

Most Windows interface tools use a combination of menus and icons. An example is Windows Explorer in Windows XP. From the drop-down menus, you can format disks, rename files, copy and delete files, and perform many other operations to manage files and storage devices (see Figure 1-13). You can also see in the figure many yellow file folder icons representing Windows folders.

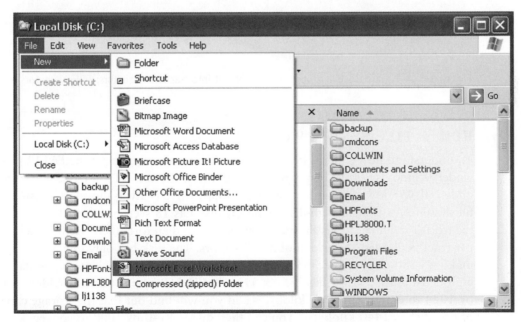

Figure 1-13   A menu-driven interface: Windows Explorer in Windows XP

With an icon-driven interface, sometimes called a **graphical user interface (GUI)**, you perform operations by clicking icons (or pictures) on the screen. When an OS is first executed, the initial screen that appears, together with its menus, commands, and icons, is called the **desktop**.

AN OS MANAGES FILES AND FOLDERS

An operating system is responsible for storing files and folders on a secondary storage device, such as a DVD, CD, flash drive, or hard drive, using an organizational method called the **file system**.

For hard drives, Windows uses either the FAT or the NTFS file system. The FAT file system is named after the **file allocation table (FAT)**, a table on a hard drive or floppy disk that tracks how space on a disk is used to store files. The latest version of FAT, FAT32, is a more efficient method of organization for large hard drives than FAT16 (the earlier version). The **New Technology file system (NTFS)** is supported by Windows NT/2000/XP and is designed to provide greater security and to support more storage capacity than the FAT file system.

> **A+ Tip**
>
> The A+ Essentials exam expects you to know all the key terms in this section.

A hard drive or floppy disk is composed of **tracks**, which are concentric circles (one circle inside the next) on the disk surface, shown in Figure 1-14. Each track is divided into several segments, each called a **sector**. Each sector can hold 512 bytes of data. A **cluster**, the smallest unit of space on a disk for storing a file, is made up of one or more sectors. A file system, either FAT or NTFS, tracks how these clusters are used for each file stored on the disk.

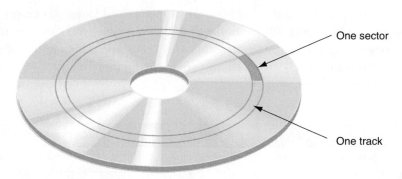

One sector

One track

Figure 1-14 A hard drive or floppy disk is divided into tracks and sectors; several sectors make one cluster

HOW A FILE SYSTEM WORKS

To understand how a file system works, we'll use as our example the FAT12 file system. Under Windows 2000/XP, a hard drive can use either the NTFS or FAT file system, but under all Windows operating systems, a floppy drive is always formatted using the FAT12 file system. A $3\frac{1}{2}$-inch, high-density floppy disk has 18 sectors per track, as shown in Figure 1-15. The disk has 80 tracks on each side; therefore, there are 80 tracks x 18 sectors per track x 2 sides, for a total of 2,880 sectors. The disk has only one sector per cluster, making 2880 clusters. Because each cluster holds 512 bytes (one sector) of data, a $3\frac{1}{2}$-inch, high-density floppy disk has 2880 x 512 = 1,474,560 bytes of data. Divide this number by 1024 to convert bytes to kilobytes and you will find out that the storage capacity of this disk is 1440 kilobytes. You can then divide 1440 by 1000 to convert kilobytes to megabytes, and the storage is 1.44 MB.

> **Notes**
>
> There is a discrepancy in the way the computer industry defines a megabyte. Sometimes 1 megabyte = 1,000 kilobytes; at other times, we use the relationship 1 megabyte = 1,024 kilobytes.

Most floppy disks come already formatted, but occasionally you will need to format one. To do that, you

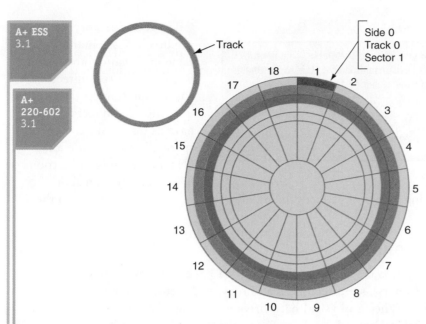

Figure 1-15 3 $\frac{1}{2}$-inch , high-density floppy disk showing tracks and sectors

can use the Format command or Windows Explorer. Either way, when you format a disk, a file system is written to the disk, and the following are created:

- ▲ *Tracks and sectors.* The tracks and sectors are created by writing tracks as a series of F6s in hex and, as necessary, writing the sector address mark to identify the beginning sector on a track

- ▲ *The boot record.* The first sector on the disk, called the **boot sector** or **boot record,** contains the information about the disk including the total number of sectors, the number of sectors per cluster, the number of bits in each FAT entry, and the version of DOS or Windows used to format the disk. The boot record also includes the name of the program it searches for to load an OS, either Io.sys or Ntldr. If one of these files is on the disk, this program searches for and loads the rest of the OS files needed on the disk to boot; then the disk is said to be bootable. The boot sector is always located at the beginning of the disk at track 0, sector 1 (bottom of the disk, outermost track). This uniform layout and content allows any version of DOS or Windows to read any floppy disk.

- ▲ *Two copies of the file allocation table (FAT).* Because the width of each entry in the FAT is 12 bits, the FAT on a floppy disk is called a 12-bit FAT, or **FAT12.** The FAT lists how each cluster (or file allocation unit) on the disk is currently used. A file is stored in one or more clusters that do not have to be contiguous on the disk. In the FAT, some clusters might be marked as bad (the 12 bits to mark a bad cluster are FF7h). An extra copy of the FAT immediately follows the first. If the first is damaged, sometimes you can recover your data and files by using the copy.

- ▲ *The root directory.* The root directory contains a fixed number of rows to accommodate a predetermined number of files and subdirectories. A 3 $\frac{1}{2}$-inch, high-density floppy disk has 224 entries in the root directory. Some important items in a directory are a list of filenames and their extensions, the time and date of creation or last update of each file, and the file attributes. These are on/off switches indicating the archive, system file, hidden file, and read-only file status of the file or directory.

A+ ESS
3.1

A+
220-602
3.1

Notes

For tech-hungry readers, you can use the Debug command to view the contents of the boot record or FAT. How to do that is covered in the online content, "Behind the Scenes with DEBUG." Also, to see a group of tables showing the contents of the floppy disk boot record, the root directory, and the meaning of each bit in the attribute byte, see the online content, "FAT Details."

The root directory and all subdirectories contain the same information about each file. Only the root directory has a limitation on the number of entries. Subdirectories can have as many entries as disk space allows. Because long filenames require more room in a directory than short filenames, assigning long filenames reduces the number of files that can be stored in the root directory.

FILES AND DIRECTORIES

Regardless of the file system used, every OS manages a hard drive by using directories (Windows calls these folders), subdirectories, and files. A **directory table** is a list of subdirectories and files. When a physical hard drive is first installed, it can be divided into one or more logical drives such as drive C and drive D. These logical drives are sometimes called volumes. When each logical drive is formatted, a single directory table is placed on the drive called the **root directory**. For a logical drive, such as drive C, the root directory is written as C:\. (Logical drives are discussed in more detail in the next section of the chapter.)

As shown in Figure 1-16, this root directory can hold files or other directories, which can have names such as C:\Tools. These directories, called **subdirectories, child directories**, or **folders**, can, in turn, have other directories listed in them. Any directory can have files and other subdirectories listed in it; for example, Figure 1-16 shows C:\wp\data\myfile.txt. In this path to the file, Myfile.txt, the C: identifies the logical drive. If a directory is on a floppy disk, then either A: or B: identifies it. If a directory is on a logical drive on a hard drive or on a CD, flash drive, or DVD, a letter such as C:, D:, or F: identifies it.

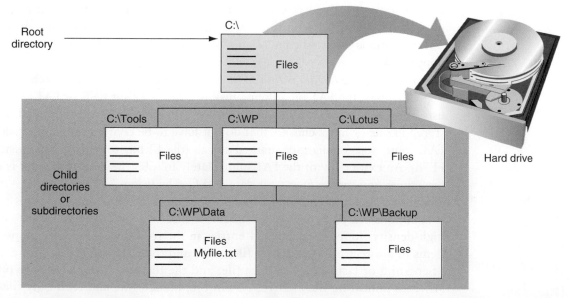

Figure 1-16 A hard drive is organized into directories and subdirectories that contain files

1

A+ ESS
3.1

A+
220-602
3.1

When you refer to a drive and directories that are pointing to the location of a file, as in C:\wp\data\myfile.txt, the drive and directories are called the **path** to the file (see Figure 1-17). When naming a file, the first part of the name before the period is called the **filename** (myfile), and the part after the period is called the **file extension** (txt), which, for Windows and DOS, always has three characters or fewer. The file extension identifies the file type, such as .doc for Microsoft Word document files or .xls for Microsoft Excel spreadsheet files.

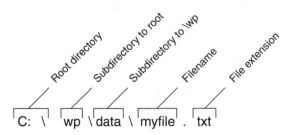

Figure 1-17 The complete path to a file includes the logical drive letter, directories, filename, and file extension; the colon, backslashes, and period are required to separate items in the path

PARTITIONS AND LOGICAL DRIVES ON A HARD DRIVE

A hard drive is organized into one or more **partitions**. A partition can be a primary partition or an extended partition (see Figure 1-18). A primary partition can have only one logical drive, and an extended partition can have one or more logical drives. For example, a hard drive can have one primary partition with one logical drive in it called drive C, and one extended partition with two logical drives most likely called drive D and drive E.

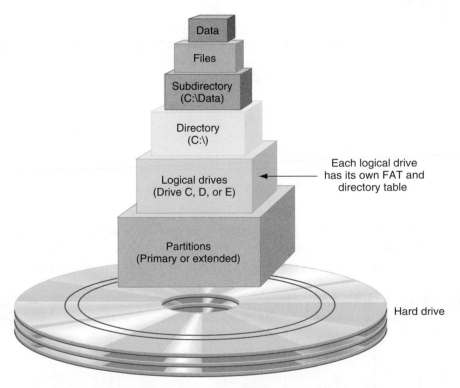

Figure 1-18 A hard drive is divided and organized at several levels

Each **logical drive**, sometimes called a **volume**, is formatted using its own file system. For example, if a hard drive is divided into two logical drives, drive C might be formatted using the FAT32 file system and drive D might use the NTFS file system. Each logical drive has its own root directory and subdirectories.

Partitions can be created on a hard drive when the drive is first installed, when an OS is first installed, or after an existing partition becomes corrupted. When an OS is first installed, the installation process partitions and formats the drive if necessary. After Windows 2000/XP is installed, you can use the Disk Management tool to view partitions, create new ones, and format logical drives. To open the Disk Management utility, use one of these methods:

◢ For Windows XP, click **Start, Control Panel**. (For Windows 2000, click **Start, Settings, Control Panel**.) Open the **Administrative Tools** applet. The Computer Management window opens. Click **Disk Management**. The Disk Management window opens.

◢ Click **Start, Run** and enter **Diskmgmt.msc** in the Run dialog box. Press **Enter**.

The Disk Management window in Figure 1-19 shows one hard drive that contains three primary partitions, which are formatted as drives C, E, and F. Drive C is using the NTFS file system and drives E and F are using the FAT32 file system. This drive has no extended partitions. You will learn more about how to manage partitions and logical drives using Disk Management in Chapter 2.

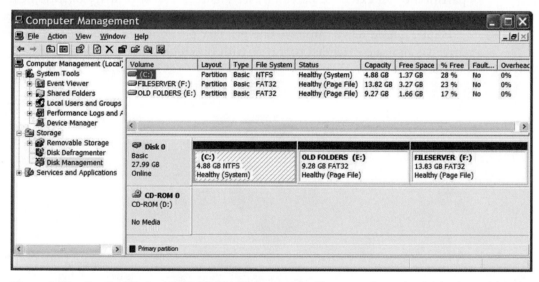

Figure 1-19 Use the Windows 2000/XP Disk Management utility to see how a hard drive is partitioned

For Windows 9x/Me, the Fdisk command is used to create partitions, and the Format command is used to format logical drives. Chapter 6 covers how to use the Fdisk and Format commands. Table 1-2 lists the three file systems for Windows and DOS operating systems.

	DOS	Windows 95	Windows 98	Windows NT	Windows 2000	Windows XP
FAT16	X	X	X	X	X	X
FAT32		X (for OSR2)	X		X	X
NTFS				X	X	X

Table 1-2 Operating system support for file systems

A+ ESS
3.1

A+
220-602
3.1

APPLYING|CONCEPTS

When using Windows Explorer or My Computer, Windows does not distinguish between logical drives stored on the same hard drive or on different hard drives. For example, Figure 1-20 shows three drives, C, E, and F, that are logical drives on one physical hard drive shown earlier in Figure 1-19. If you right-click one drive, such as drive E in the figure, and select Properties on the shortcut menu, you can see the amount of space allotted to this logical drive and how much of it is currently used. Also note in the figure that drive E is formatted using the FAT32 file system.

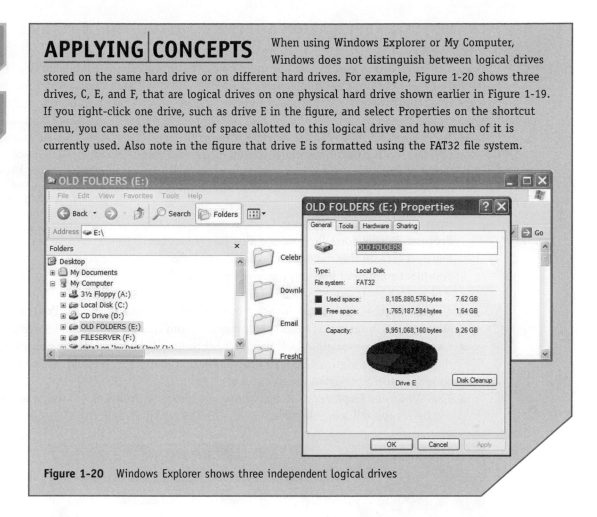

Figure 1-20   Windows Explorer shows three independent logical drives

AN OS MANAGES APPLICATIONS

An operating system installs and runs all the other software on a PC. Software designed to perform a task for the user is called an application. An application, such as Microsoft Word, depends on an OS to provide access to hardware resources, to manage its data in memory and in secondary storage, and to perform many other background tasks.

A+
220-602
3.1

An application built to work with one OS, such as Windows 95, does not necessarily work with another, such as Windows XP, because of the different ways each OS manages an application. Windows 9x/Me was written to work with DOS or Windows 3.x applications, which was an early selling point for Windows 9x/Me, but Windows 2000/XP does not claim to support many legacy applications. So, when it's important that your application work correctly, make sure you use applications written specifically for your OS.

INSTALLING APPLICATION SOFTWARE

The operating system is responsible for installing software using the installation program provided by the application. Application software is downloaded from the Internet or comes written on CDs, DVDs, or floppy disks. Usually it must be installed on a hard drive in order to run. During the installation, the install program creates folders on the hard drive and copies files to them. For Windows, it also makes entries in the Windows registry, and it can place icons on the desktop and add entries to the Start menu. Because the install program does all the work for you, installing a software package usually is very easy. Installing software is covered in later chapters.

A+ ESS
3.1

LAUNCHING APPLICATION SOFTWARE USING THE WINDOWS DESKTOP

Before an application can be used, it must be started up, which is called running, loading, launching, or executing the application. Windows 2000/XP and Windows 9x/Me offer four ways to run software:

▲ *Use a shortcut icon.* Place a shortcut icon directly on the desktop for the applications you use often and want to get to quickly. A shortcut contains the command line that executes the application. To view this command line, right-click an application icon on the desktop to open a shortcut menu. On the shortcut menu, select **Properties**. The icon's Properties dialog box opens (see Figure 1-21). In this dialog box, you can view the complete command line that the icon represents. You will learn how to create shortcuts later in the chapter.

▲ *Use the Start menu.* Click the **Start** button, select **Programs** (or **All Programs** in Windows XP), and then select the program from the list of installed software.

▲ *Use the Run command.* Click the **Start** button, and then click **Run** to display the Run dialog box (see Figure 1-22). In this dialog box, enter a command line or click **Browse** to search for a program file to execute.

▲ *Use Windows Explorer or My Computer.* Execute a program or launch an application file by double-clicking the filename in Windows Explorer or My Computer.

A+ Tip

The A+ Essentials exam often expects you to know more than one way to do something. Knowing the four ways to load an application is a good example.

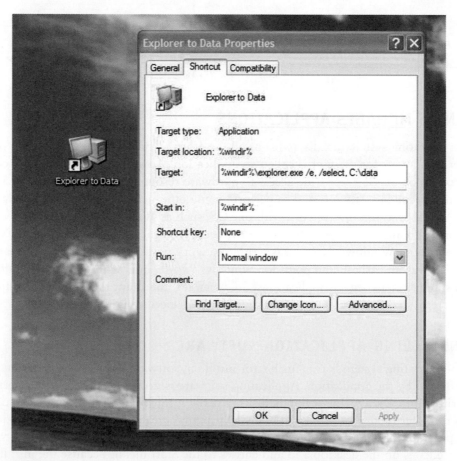

Figure 1-21 The target for this shortcut is the C:\data folder, which will be displayed by Windows Explorer

A+ ESS
3.1

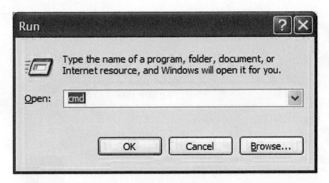

Figure 1-22 The Windows Run dialog box allows you to enter DOS-like commands

APPLYING|CONCEPTS

Practice the last three ways listed to load an application. Use Microsoft Paint as your sample application. The program file is Mspaint.exe. Execute the application by using the Start menu, using the Run dialog box, and using Windows Explorer.

REAL (16-BIT), PROTECTED (32-BIT), AND LONG (64-BIT) OPERATING MODES

CPUs operate in three modes: 16-bit, 32-bit, or 64-bit modes, which are also called real mode, protected mode, and long mode, respectively. There are several differences between these three modes, but fundamentally, in 16-bit mode, or **real mode**, the CPU processes 16 bits of data at one time, in 32-bit mode, or **protected mode**, it processes 32 bits at a time, and in 64-bit mode, or **long mode**, it processes 64 bits at a time.

Early computers all used real mode, but no OS today uses this mode. In real mode, an application has complete access to all hardware resources. This sounds good on the surface, but this open-door policy can create problems when applications make conflicting or erroneous commands to hardware. On the other hand, in protected mode and long mode, the OS controls how an application can access hardware. This helps when more than one program is working at the same time, which is a type of **multitasking**, so that each program is protected from other programs making conflicting demands on hardware. In protected mode and long mode, the OS provides to each program a limited and controlled access to hardware resources. If a system has only a single CPU, then two programs cannot literally multitask. This is because a CPU can only do one thing at a time. The two programs only appear to multitask because, in protected mode or long mode, the OS allots CPU time to an application for a specified period. Then it preempts the processing to give the CPU to another application in a process called preemptive multitasking (see Figure 1-23). The end result is that the computer appears to be multitasking when it really is not. Windows 95 was the first version of Windows to provide preemptive multitasking.

Some computers have more than one CPU either embedded in the same processor housing or installed as two separate processors on the same motherboard. For these systems, if the operating system is capable of it, it can feed tasks to each CPU working independently of each other in what is called true multiprocessing. Windows NT was the first Windows OS to support multiprocessing.

DOS uses 16-bit mode; Windows 9x/Me and Windows NT/2000/XP all use 32-bit mode, although each OS is backward compatible with earlier modes. In other words, Windows 9x/Me and Windows NT/2000/XP can support an application that uses 16-bit mode.

Figure 1-23 Using preemptive multitasking, more than one application appears to be using CPU resources

---

> ✎ **Notes**
>
> Real mode means that the software has "real" access to the hardware; protected mode means that more than one program can be running, and each one is "protected" from other programs accessing its hardware resources. Long mode processes twice as many bits at a time than protected mode.

Windows XP Professional x64 Edition uses 64-bit mode, and is backward compatible with many applications that use 32-bit or 16-bit mode. Processors today are built to run in either 32-bit mode or 64-bit mode, but are backward compatible with 16-bit mode so that any PC can be booted up using DOS—a useful troubleshooting OS when more complex OSs fail.

All Pentium processors operate in 32-bit mode. Three high-end processors that operate in 64-bit mode are the Intel Itanium, the AMD Opteron, and the AMD Athlon 64. For these three processors, in order to use 64-bit mode, you need to install Windows XP Professional x64 Edition.

16-BIT, 32-BIT, AND 64-BIT SOFTWARE

Software written for Windows 3.x is called 16-bit Windows software. Data access is 16 bits at a time, and each program is written so that it should not infringe on the resources of other programs that might be running. Software programs written for Windows NT/2000/XP and Windows 9x/Me are called 32-bit programs, and software programs written for Windows XP Professional x64 Edition are called 64-bit programs.

Nearly all software written today is 32-bit or 64-bit (for the Itaniums, Opterons, and Athlon 64 processors), although 16-bit applications software still exists and might still work under any version of Windows. However, a 16-bit device driver won't work under Windows 2000/XP or Windows Me. The next section explains what a device driver is.

AN OS MANAGES HARDWARE

An operating system is responsible for communicating with hardware, but the OS does not relate directly to the hardware. Rather, the OS uses device drivers or the BIOS to do the job. Figure 1-24 shows these relationships. Therefore, most software falls into three categories:

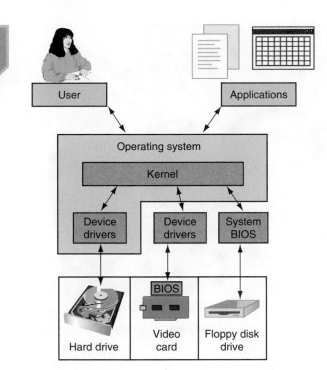

Figure 1-24 An OS relates to hardware by way of BIOS and device drivers

- Device drivers or the BIOS
- Operating system
- Application software

HOW AN OS USES DEVICE DRIVERS TO MANAGE DEVICES

Device drivers are small programs stored on the hard drive that tell the computer how to communicate with a specific hardware device such as a printer, network card, or modem. These drivers are installed on the hard drive when the OS is first installed or when new hardware is added to the system.

The OS provides some device drivers, and the manufacturer of the specific hardware device with which they are designed to interface provides others. In either case, device drivers are usually written for a particular OS and most likely need to be rewritten for use with another.

When you purchase a printer, DVD drive, Zip drive, digital camera, scanner, or other hardware device, bundled with the device might be a CD or set of floppy disks that contains the device drivers (see Figure 1-25). Sometimes, the device also comes bundled with a user manual and applications software that uses the device. You use the operating system to install the device drivers so it will have the necessary software to control the device. In most cases, you install the device and then install the device drivers. There are a few exceptions, such as a digital camera using a USB port to download pictures. Most often in this case, you install the software to drive the digital camera before you plug in the camera.

There are three kinds of device drivers: 16-bit real-mode drivers, 32-bit protected-mode drivers, and 64-bit long-mode drivers. Windows 95 and Windows 98 support 16-bit and 32-bit drivers. Windows Me,

> **Notes**
>
> Device drivers come from a number of sources. Some come with and are part of the operating system, some come with hardware devices when they are purchased, and some are provided for downloading over the Internet from a device manufacturer's Web site.

Figure 1-25 A device such as this video card comes packaged with its device drivers stored on a CD; alternately, you can use device drivers built into the OS

> **Notes**
>
> This book focuses on using 32-bit drivers because 16-bit drivers are not supported by Windows 2000/XP, and Windows XP Professional x64 Edition is not currently popular as a desktop OS.

Windows NT/2000, Windows XP Home Edition, and Windows XP Professional use only 32-bit drivers. Windows XP Professional x64 Edition only uses 64-bit drivers. Windows 9x/Me and Windows 2000/XP provide hundreds of 32-bit drivers for many different kinds of devices, and device manufacturers also provide their own 16-bit, 32-bit, and 64-bit drivers, which come bundled with the device or can be downloaded from the device manufacturer's Web site.

Device Drivers Under Windows 2000/XP

> **Video**
>
> Device with Bundled Software

Before installing a new hardware device on a Windows 2000/XP system, check the Microsoft Windows Marketplace Web site to verify that the hardware has been tested by Microsoft, which assures you that the device driver provided by the manufacturer should not give you problems under Windows. To search the site, go to *http://testedproducts.windowsmarketplace.com*. (Hey, don't forget that the period at the end of the preceding sentence is *not* part of the URL.)

When 32-bit device drivers are installed, Windows 2000/XP and Windows 9x/Me record information about the drivers in the Windows registry. Each time Windows starts up, it reads these entries in the registry to know how to load the drivers needed at startup.

Sometimes, to address bugs, make improvements, or add features, manufacturers release device drivers that are more recent than those included with Windows or bundled with the device. Whenever possible, it is best to use the latest driver available for a device provided by the device manufacturer. You can usually download these updated drivers from the manufacturer's Web site. You will learn how to install, update, and troubleshoot drivers in later chapters.

> **A+ Tip**
>
> The A+ Essentials exam expects you to know how to find and download a device driver.

A+ ESS
3.1

APPLYING CONCEPTS

Suppose you have just borrowed an HP Photosmart 7760 Deskjet printer from a friend, but you forgot to borrow the CD with the printer drivers on it. Instead of going back to your friend's apartment, you can go to the Hewlett-Packard Web site (*www.hp.com*), download the drivers to a folder on your PC, and install the driver under Windows. Figure 1-26 shows a Web page from the site listing downloadable drivers for ink-jet printers.

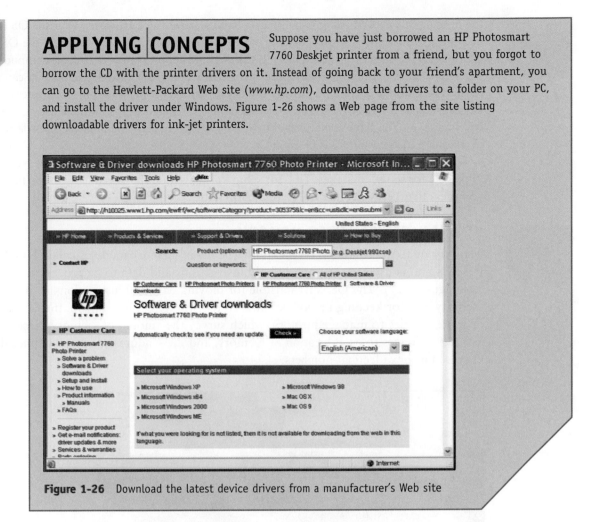

Figure 1-26   Download the latest device drivers from a manufacturer's Web site

Device Drivers Under Windows 9x/Me

Windows 9x/Me comes with 32-bit drivers for hundreds of hardware devices. However, Windows does not provide drivers for all older devices, so a system might sometimes need to use an older 16-bit real-mode device driver. These 16-bit drivers are loaded by entries in the **Config.sys, Autoexec.bat,** and **System.ini** files, text files used to configure DOS and Windows 3.x that Windows 95 and Windows 98 support for backward compatibility. Windows Me does not support 16-bit drivers. In Chapter 7, you will learn how to install 32-bit drivers under Windows 9x/Me and 16-bit drivers under Windows 95/98.

A+ ESS
1.1

HOW AN OS USES SYSTEM BIOS TO MANAGE DEVICES

The system BIOS (basic input/output system) on the motherboard is a group of programs hard-coded or permanently coded into a computer chip called the firmware or ROM BIOS chip. The OS can communicate with simple devices, such as floppy drives or keyboards, through this system BIOS. In addition, system BIOS can be used to access the hard drive. An OS has a choice of using system BIOS or device drivers to access a device. Because device drivers are faster, the trend today is to use device drivers rather than the BIOS to manage devices.

When you think about it, you know that Windows does not load on a computer until after the monitor screen displays information, the keyboard can be used, and the computer has searched a floppy disk inserted into its drive, a CD, or the hard drive to find the OS to load. This means that the CPU knows how to communicate with these devices without the help of an OS. The CPU got the instructions needed for communication from system BIOS. However, after the OS is loaded, it might provide its own instructions to use for communication with a device or the OS can continue to use system BIOS for this job. As a rule of thumb, know that if the computer can use a device such as a monitor or keyboard before the OS is loaded, then system BIOS can control the device even though the OS might later use device drivers for the job. If the computer can't use a device, such as a mouse or a printer, until after an OS is loaded, then it must use device drivers to communicate. You have some control over how system BIOS recognizes and uses devices—changes are made using CMOS setup.

To access CMOS setup, you press a key early in the boot process. For example, you might see "Press F2 for setup" or "Press DEL for setup" displayed on the screen early in the boot. When you press that key, you enter the CMOS setup utility.

HOW AN OS MANAGES MEMORY

Memory or RAM is housed on the motherboard in memory modules called DIMMs or RIMMs and is used to temporarily hold instructions and data to be processed by the CPU (see Figure 1-27). The OS is responsible for moving data and instructions in and out of memory and for keeping up with what is stored where. During startup, the OS launches one or more utilities to manage memory, which survey the amount of memory present. The OS assigns addresses to each location of memory, and these addresses are sometimes displayed onscreen as hexadecimal numbers.

Figure 1-27 This DIMM module installed on a motherboard holds 512 MB of RAM

After memory addresses have been assigned to memory, they can be used for communication with all software layers. Device drivers, the OS, and application software are all working when a computer is running. During output operations, application software must pass information to the OS, which, in turn, passes that information to a device driver. The device drivers managing input devices must pass information to the OS, which passes it to the application software. These layers of software all identify the data they want to share by referring to the memory address of the data (see Figure 1-28).

 Tip

The A+ Essentials exam expects you to know the purpose and characteristics of virtual memory.

Figure 1-28 Applications, the OS, and drivers pass data among them by communicating the address of memory holding the data

In a 16-bit real mode environment, DOS allowed applications to have direct access to memory, and Windows 9x/Me offered a hybrid environment whereby applications could run in real mode (having direct access to memory) or in protected mode (the OS controls access to memory). Windows NT/2000/XP forces all programs to run in protected mode, and it controls how that software accesses memory. For example, in Figure 1-29, you can see that the 16-bit program running in real mode has direct access to RAM. But in protected mode, more than one program can run, and the programs must depend on the OS to access RAM. This arrangement also allows the OS some latitude in how it uses RAM. If the OS is low on RAM, it can store

> **Notes**
>
> For more information on how an OS manages hardware resources, especially as this information applies to Windows 9x/Me, see Appendix A, "How an OS Uses System Resources."

Real mode: One program has direct access to hardware

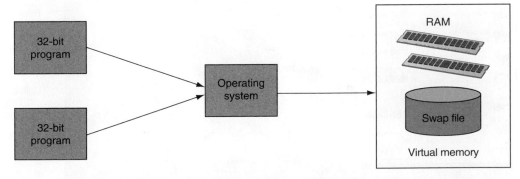

Protected mode: Multiple programs depend on the OS to access hardware

Figure 1-29 Protected mode allows more than one program to run, each protected from the other by the operating system

some data on the hard drive. This method of using the hard drive as though it were RAM is called **virtual memory**, and data stored in virtual memory is stored in a file on the hard drive called a **swap file** or **page file**. The Windows 2000/XP swap file is Pagefile.sys, and the Windows 9x/Me swap file is Win386.swp. The OS manages the entire process, and the applications know nothing about this substitution of hardware resources for RAM. How to manage the Windows swap files is covered in later chapters.

OS TOOLS TO EXAMINE A SYSTEM

You have learned about many operating systems and OS components and functions in this chapter. When maintaining and troubleshooting a system, it is important for you to know how to use OS tools to examine and change the system. In this section, you'll learn how to use several of these tools, and others will be covered in future chapters.

🔵 A+ Tip

The A+ Essentials exam expects you to be familiar with and know how to use the Windows 2000/XP desktop, My Computer, Windows Explorer, System Properties, Control Panel, Device Manager, and System Information. All these tools are discussed in this section. If the utility can be accessed by more than one method, you are expected to know all of the methods.

THE WINDOWS DESKTOP

The Windows desktop is the primary tool provided by the Windows shell. The Windows 2000/XP desktop can be customized and maintained to provide a user-friendly place to manage applications and often-used files. Figure 1-30 shows the Windows XP desktop after the user has clicked the Start button. Notice in the figure for Windows XP that the username for the person currently logged on is shown at the top of the Start menu.

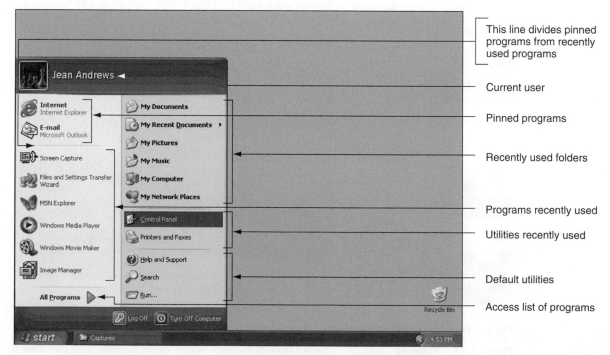

Figure 1-30   The Windows XP desktop and Start menu

1

A+ ESS
3.1

> ✎ **Notes**
>
> If you know how to move around in the Windows XP Start menu, you pretty much know how to move around in the Windows 2000 and Windows 9x/Me Start menus as well.

Applications at the top of the Start menu are said to be "pinned" to the menu—in other words, permanently listed there until you change them in a Start menu setting. Applications that are used often are listed below the pinned applications and can change from time to time. The programs in the white column on the left side of the Start menu are user-oriented applications, and the programs in the dark column on the right side of the menu are OS-oriented, and are most likely to be used by an administrator or technician responsible for the system.

When you point to **All Programs** in Figure 1-30, the list of currently installed software appears. Figure 1-31 shows the default entries that appear when you point to **Accessories** and then **System Tools**. You can use these tools to back up data, clean up a hard drive, schedule tasks, restore Windows settings, and do various other things when solving problems with Windows.

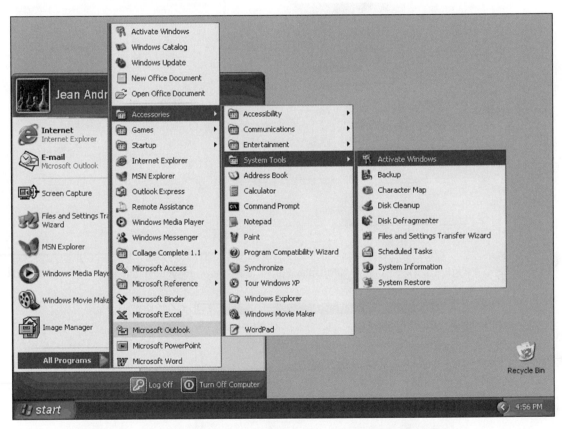

Figure 1-31 Click Start, All Programs to view the list of currently installed software

You can do several things to customize the Windows desktop. For example, you can make applications automatically load at startup, change the background on the desktop (called the wallpaper), create shortcuts to files and applications, control what goes in the taskbar, and make the environment more user-friendly. Let's now look at several tools to make the desktop look and work the way you want it to.

> 🔿 **A+ Tip**
>
> The A+ Essentials exam expects you to know how to configure Windows display settings.

DISPLAY PROPERTIES WINDOW

One tool useful for changing the way the desktop looks is the Display Properties window. To access this window, right-click anywhere on the desktop and select Properties from the shortcut menu, or you can open the Display applet in Control Panel.

The left side of Figure 1-32 shows the Desktop tab of the Display Properties window for Windows XP; Figure 1-33 shows the Display Properties window for Windows 98. The Windows 98 window is similar to that of Windows 2000. Some things you can do from the Display Properties window are:

◢ Select a desktop wallpaper photo or a pattern, and pick a color scheme for the desktop.
◢ Select a screen saver and change its settings.

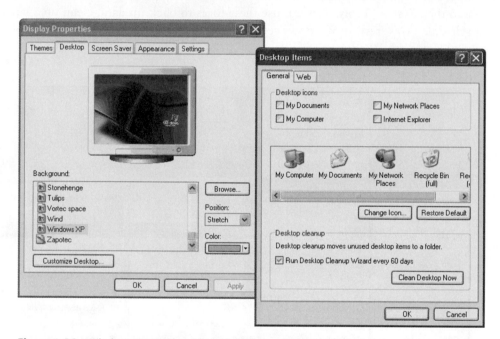

Figure 1-32   Windows XP Display Properties window lets you change settings for your desktop

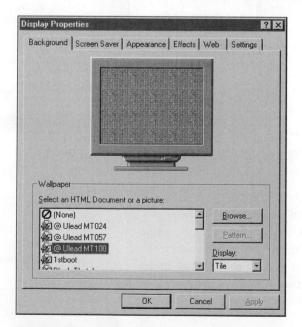

Figure 1-33   The Display Properties window for Windows 98

1

A+ ESS
1.2
1.3

▲ Change power settings for the monitor.

▲ Change icon and shortcut settings.

▲ Change the color range, screen resolution, and screen refresh rate.

▲ Change drivers for the video card and monitor.

▲ Enable or display multiple monitors installed on the system.

APPLYING CONCEPTS

Changing the wallpaper (desktop background) is easy in Windows XP. All you have to do is click the **Desktop** tab, select the wallpaper, and click **Apply**. Any photographs you have stored in your Windows XP default folder for photographs (most likely, My Pictures) appear in the list for you to use as wallpaper. You can also use photographs you have stored in other folders as your wallpaper, but you will have to click the **Browse** button to go off and look for them. Another method to change your wallpaper is to use Windows Explorer. In Explorer, right-click the photograph's filename and select **Set as Desktop Background** from the shortcut menu.

When you first install Windows XP, only the Recycle Bin shows on the desktop by default. You can add other shortcuts by using the Display Properties window. In the window, click **Customize Desktop** to display the Desktop Items window, which is shown in Figure 1-32. You can check My Documents, My Computer, My Network Places, and Internet Explorer to add these icons to the desktop. Also notice on this window the option to have Windows clean up your desktop by moving any shortcuts that you have not used in the last 60 days to a separate folder.

A+ ESS
3.1

THE TASKBAR AND SYSTEM TRAY

The **taskbar** is normally located at the bottom of the Windows desktop, displaying information about open programs and providing quick access to others (see Figure 1-34). The system tray is usually on the right side of the taskbar and displays open services. A **service** is a program that runs in the background to support or serve Windows or an application.

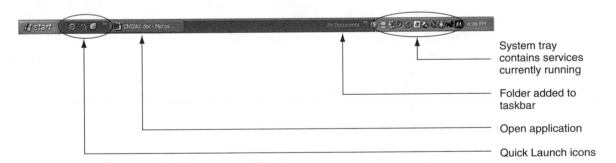

System tray contains services currently running

Folder added to taskbar

Open application

Quick Launch icons

Figure 1-34 The Windows XP taskbar

You can control the taskbar, system tray, and Start menu from the Taskbar and Start Menu Properties window. To access this window, do the following:

▲ In Windows XP, right-click **Start** and select **Properties** from the shortcut menu. Another method is to right-click the taskbar and select Properties from the shortcut menu. A third method is to use Control Panel. From Control Panel, open the Taskbar Start Menu applet.

▲ In Windows 2000 or Windows 9x/Me, click **Start, Settings, Taskbar & Start Menu** or right-click the **taskbar** and select **Properties** from the shortcut menu.

For Windows XP, the window in Figure 1-35 opens. From it you can add items to and remove items from the Start menu, control how the taskbar manages items in the system tray, and specify how the taskbar is displayed.

Figure 1-35 Use the Taskbar and Start Menu Properties window to control what appears in the Start menu and taskbar

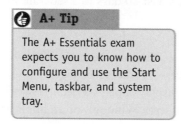

A+ Tip

The A+ Essentials exam expects you to know how to configure and use the Start Menu, taskbar, and system tray.

Items displayed in the taskbar can be applications and services launched or not launched. An open application displays its title in the taskbar (see Figure 1-34). Quick Launch icons on the left are displayed in the taskbar so you can quickly find and launch them. To turn the Quick Launch display on or off, right-click the **taskbar**, select **Toolbars**, and then click **Quick Launch**. To add a new toolbar folder to the taskbar, right-click the **taskbar**, select **Toolbars**, and click **New Toolbar**. Then select the folder you want displayed in the taskbar, such as the My Documents folder in Figure 1-34.

The **system tray** is on the right side of the taskbar and displays icons for running services; these services include the volume control and network connectivity. Windows XP automatically hides these icons. To display them, click the left arrow on the right side of the taskbar. If you have a sluggish Windows system, one thing you can do is look at all the running services in the system tray and try to disable the services that are taking up system resources. How to do that is covered in later chapters.

For Windows 2000, the Taskbar and Start Menu Properties window is organized slightly differently than for Windows XP, but works about the same way. For Windows 9x/Me, the window is called the Taskbar Properties window, and is shown in Figure 1-36.

SHORTCUTS

A **shortcut** on the desktop is an icon that points to a program you can execute, or to a file or folder. The user double-clicks the icon to load the software. Using Windows 2000/XP or Windows 9x/Me, you can create a shortcut in several ways:

▲ Select the file, folder, or program in Windows Explorer or in a My Computer window. From the **File** menu, select **Create Shortcut**.

▲ From the File menu in Explorer, click **New** and then click **Create Shortcut**.

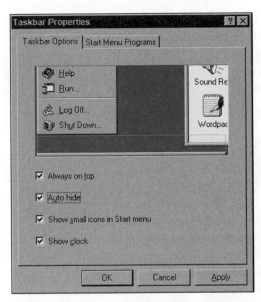

Figure 1-36 Use the Windows 98 Taskbar Properties window to change taskbar and Start menu settings

- ◢ Right-click the file, folder, or program to which you want to create a shortcut, and select **Create Shortcut** from the menu.
- ◢ Drag the file, folder, or program to the desktop.
- ◢ Right-click the file, folder, or program and hold down the mouse button while dragging the item to the desktop. When you release it, a dialog box opens. Choose **Create Shortcut(s) Here**.
- ◢ Right-click the file, folder, or program and select **Create Shortcut** from the shortcut menu (see Figure 1-37).
- ◢ To edit a shortcut, right-click it and select **Properties** from the menu. To delete a shortcut, select **Delete** from this same menu.

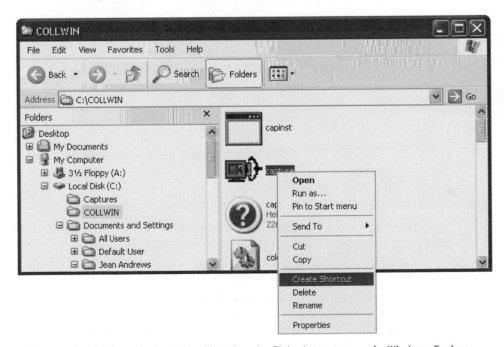

Figure 1-37 Create a shortcut to a file using the file's shortcut menu in Windows Explorer

For Windows 9x/Me, another way to create a shortcut is to use the Taskbar Properties window (refer back to Figure 1-36). Click the **Start Menu Programs** tab. Then click the

Add button. The Create Shortcut Wizard appears, as shown in Figure 1-38. Enter the name of the program to which you want to create a shortcut, or browse for the file on your computer. In this example, we are creating a desktop shortcut to the Notepad application. Click **Next**. On the next window, you must select where to place the shortcut. Select **Desktop** at the top of the folder list to create a desktop shortcut, and then click **Next**. Follow the directions in the wizard to complete the process.

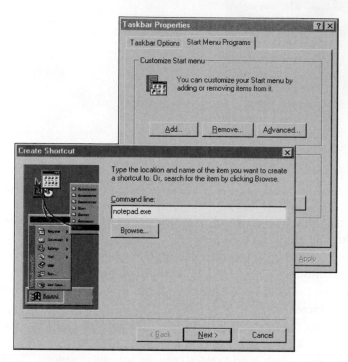

Figure 1-38 Select the item to which you want the shortcut to point

A+ ESS
3.1

A+
220-602
3.1

MY COMPUTER AND WINDOWS EXPLORER

The two most useful tools to explore files and folders on your computer are My Computer and Windows Explorer. Under Windows 2000 and Windows 9x/Me, the tools work pretty much the same way. With Windows XP, they are really the same tools with different names.

To access My Computer, use one of these methods:

◢ For Windows XP, click **Start** and click **My Computer**.
◢ For Windows XP, open Windows Explorer and click **My Computer** in the left pane of the Explorer window.
◢ For Windows 2000 or Windows 9x/Me, double-click **My Computer** on the desktop.

Figure 1-39 shows the Windows XP My Computer window, and Figure 1-40 shows the My Computer folder as seen when using Windows 98 Explorer.

Windows Explorer can be opened in different ways, as follows:

◢ Right-click **My Computer** and select **Explore** from the menu.
◢ Right-click **Start** and select **Explore** from the menu.
◢ Open **My Computer** and then click the **View** menu, **Explorer Bar**, and **Folders**.
◢ For Windows 2000/XP, right-click either **My Network Places** or the **Recycle Bin** and select **Explore** from the menu.
◢ For Windows 9x/Me, click **Start**, **Programs**, and **Windows Explorer**.

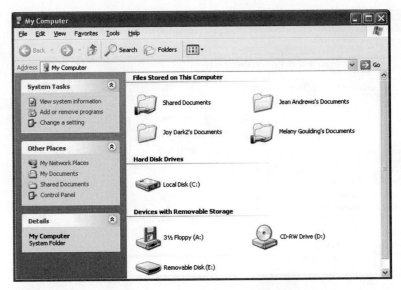

Figure 1-39 Use Windows XP My Computer to manage system resources

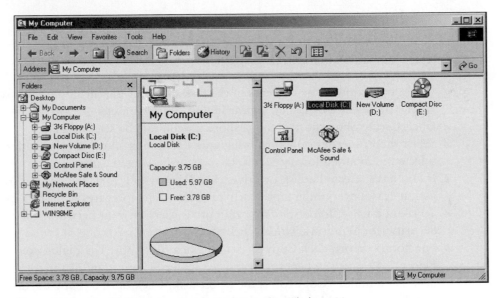

Figure 1-40 The My Computer view in Explorer using Windows 98

▲ For Windows 9x/Me, right-click either the **Network Neighborhood** icon or the **Recycle Bin** icon and select **Explore** from the menu.

Let's now turn our attention to how to use My Computer or Explorer to manage files and folders and other system resources.

USING SHORTCUT MENUS

The easiest way to manage drives, disks, folders, and files in Explorer or My Computer is to use the shortcut menus. To access a shortcut menu, right-click the icon representing the item you want to work with. Figure 1-41 shows the shortcut menu for the floppy drive as an example. Here are some tasks you can perform from a shortcut menu:

▲ Click **Explore** or **Open** to view the contents of the disk or folder. For Windows XP, contents of the disk or folder appear in a separate window. For Windows 9x/Me, if

A+ ESS
3.1

A+
220-602
3.1

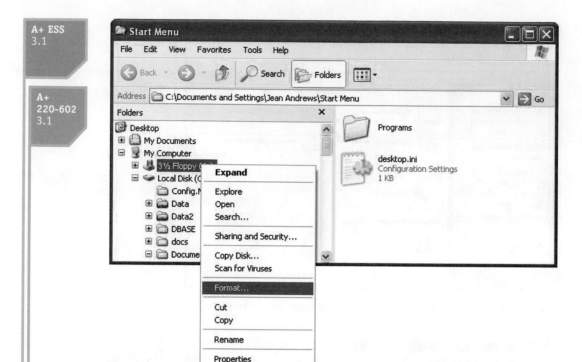

Figure 1-41   Use the shortcut menu to manage items in Explorer

you select **Explore,** the contents of the disk or folder appear in the same window, but when you select **Open,** they appear in a separate window.

▲ Click **Create Shortcut** to create a shortcut icon for the selected item.

▲ Select the **Properties** option to bring up a dialog box showing information about the selected item and allowing you to change settings for the item.

▲ If you have selected a disk or drive, click **Format** to format the disk or drive. This action erases everything on the disk or drive and/or prepares it for first use.

▲ To share a drive, folders, or files with other users on your network, click **Sharing and Security** (for Windows 9x/Me, click **Sharing**).

▲ For floppy drives, click **Copy Disk** to make a disk copy. The dialog box shown in Figure 1-42 opens, where the disk listed under "Copy from" is the source disk and the disk listed under "Copy to" is the target disk. Click **Start** to copy the disk.

▲ For Windows 9x/Me, click **Backup** to make a backup of a disk.

▲ When a file is selected, use additional options on the shortcut menu for files to do such things as editing, printing, and e-mailing the file and scanning the file for viruses.

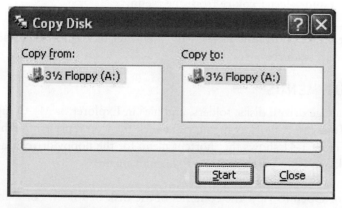

Figure 1-42   Copying a disk using Windows

1

A+ ESS
3.1

A+
220-602
3.1

◢ To create a file, for Windows 2000/XP, right-click in the unused white area in the right window of Explorer and select **New** from the shortcut menu. The menu lists applications you can use to create the file in the current folder (see Figure 1-43). For Windows 9x/Me, right-click a folder name and select **New** from the shortcut menu.

Figure 1-43   Create a new file using Windows Explorer

As you can see, some options on shortcut menus are the same for files, folders, drives, and disks; others are specific to particular items. The additional shortcut menu options may differ, depending on what programs you have installed to work with a particular item.

Now let's look in more detail at ways to use Windows Explorer to work with files and folders on your floppy disk or hard drive.

CREATING A FOLDER

To create a folder, first select the folder you want to be the parent folder. (Remember that a parent folder is the folder that contains the child folder.) You select a folder by clicking the folder name. For example, to create a folder named Games under the folder named Download, first click the **Download** folder. Then click the **File** menu, select **New**, and select **Folder** from the submenu that appears. The new folder will be created under Download, but its name will be New Folder. The name New Folder is automatically selected and highlighted for you to type a new name. Type **Games** to change the folder name, as shown in Figure 1-44. You can create folders within folders within folders, but there is a limitation as to the maximum depth of folders under folders, which depends on the length of the folder names. In Chapter 4, you will learn that you can also create a folder using the MD or MKDIR command from a command prompt.

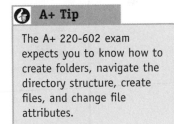

A+ Tip

The A+ 220-602 exam expects you to know how to create folders, navigate the directory structure, create files, and change file attributes.

DELETING A FOLDER

To delete a folder from Explorer, right-click the folder and select **Delete** from the shortcut menu. A confirmation dialog box asks if you are sure you want to delete the folder. If you click **Yes,** you send the folder and all its contents, including subfolders, to the Recycle Bin.

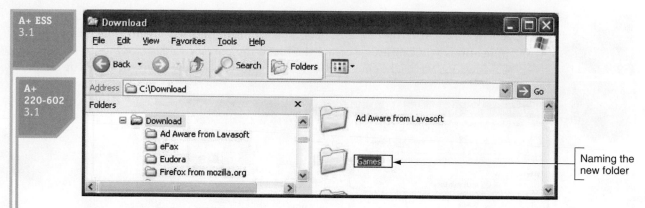

Naming the new folder

Figure 1-44   Edit the new folder's name

Emptying the Recycle Bin will free up your disk space. Files and folders sent to the Recycle Bin are not *really* deleted until you empty the bin. To do that, right-click the **bin** and select **Empty Recycle Bin** from the shortcut menu. In Chapter 4, you will learn that you can also delete a folder using the RD or RMDIR command from a command prompt.

CHANGING FILE ATTRIBUTES

Using Explorer or My Computer, you can view and change the properties assigned to a file; these properties are called the file attributes. Using these attributes, you can do such things as hide a file, make it a read-only file, or flag a file to be backed up. From Explorer or My Computer, right-click a file and select **Properties** from the shortcut menu. The Properties window shown in Figure 1-45 opens.

From the Properties window, you can change the read-only, hidden, and archive attributes of the file. The archive attribute is used to determine if a file has changed since the last backup. To change its value, click **Advanced** in the Properties window. In Chapter 4, you will learn that you

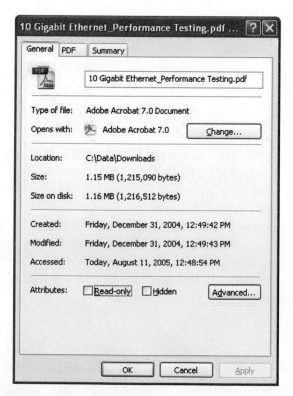

Figure 1-45   Properties of a file in Windows

A+ ESS
3.1

A+
220-602
3.1

can also change these attributes of a file or folder using the Attrib command from a command prompt. There is one other attribute of a file, called the system attribute, that says a file belongs to the OS. This attribute can be changed with the Attrib command, but not by using Explorer.

CHANGING FOLDER OPTIONS

You can also view and change options assigned to folders, which can control how users view the files in the folder and what they can do with these files.

Windows identifies file types primarily by the file extension. In Windows Explorer, by default, Windows has an annoying habit of hiding the extensions of files if it knows which application to use to open or execute the file. For example, just after installation, it hides .exe, .com, .sys, and .txt file extensions, but does not hide .doc, .ppt, or .xls files until the software to open these files has been installed. Also, Windows really doesn't want you to see its own system files, and hides these files from view until you force it to show them.

To view hidden files and file extensions, do the following:

1. Select the folder where system files are located.

2. Click **Tools** and then click **Folder Options**. The Folder Options window opens (see Figure 1-46).

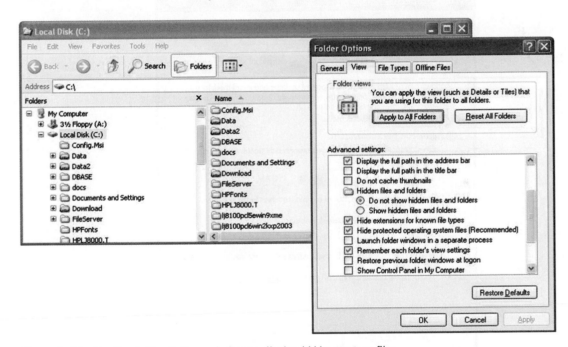

Figure 1-46 Use the Folder Options window to display hidden system files

3. Click the **View** tab. Select **Show hidden files and folders**. Uncheck **Hide extensions for known file types**. Uncheck **Hide protected operating system files**. Windows complains it doesn't want to show you these files. Click **Yes** to confirm that you really want to see them.

4. Click **Apply**. Click **OK** to close the Folder Options window.

SYSTEM PROPERTIES

The System Properties window can be used to view information about the system and manage several Windows tools and features. To open the System Properties window, right-click **My Computer** and select **Properties**. Another way to open the window is to click the **System** applet in Control Panel.

Here is a list of things you can do with System Properties:

- ◢ On the General tab, view information about the system, including the installed OS, the amount of RAM installed, and registration information.
- ◢ For Windows XP, on the Computer Name tab, change the name of the computer on the network. For Windows 2000, this is done on the Network Identification tab.
- ◢ On the Hardware tab, access Device Manager and create new hardware profiles.
- ◢ On the Advanced tab, control computer performance and decide how system failures will be handled.
- ◢ For Windows XP, on the System Restore tab, turn this feature on or off. System Restore is covered in Chapter 3, and is not available for Windows 2000.
- ◢ For Windows XP, on the Automatic Updates tab, control how Windows Updates will work (see Figure 1-47). Automatic Updates is not available for Windows 2000.
- ◢ For Windows XP, on the Remote tab, manage how outside users can control your computer.

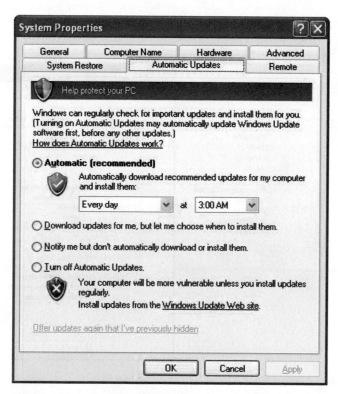

Figure 1-47 Control Automatic Updates of Windows XP using the System Properties window

CONTROL PANEL

A+ ESS
3.1

The Control Panel is a window containing several small utility programs called applets that are used to manage hardware, software, users, and the system. For Windows XP, to access the Control Panel, click **Start** and then click **Control Panel**. For Windows 2000 and Windows 9x/Me, to open Control Panel, click **Start**, **Settings**, and **Control Panel**.

Figure 1-48 shows the Windows XP Control Panel in Category View. Select a category to see the applets in that category, or click **Switch to Classic View** to see the applets when you first open Control Panel, as they are displayed in earlier versions of Windows.

A+ ESS
3.1

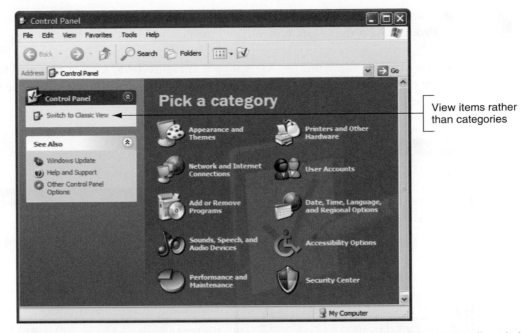

View items rather
than categories

Figure 1-48 The Windows XP Control Panel is organized by category, although you can easily switch
to Classic View

Besides accessing the several applets in Control Panel
from the Control Panel window, each applet can be
accessed directly. You will learn how to do this as you learn
to use these applets later in the book. For all the applets, if
you know the name of the applet program file, you can
launch the applet by using the Run dialog box. For
example, to open the Mouse Properties applet, type
Main.cpl in the Run dialog box, and then press **Enter**.

 A+ Tip

The A+ Essentials exam
expects you to be familiar
with the Control Panel and
its applets.

Notes

Use the Windows Search
utility to search for all files
that end with the file
extension .cpl to see a list of
Control Panel applets. Not all
applets displayed in the
Search Results window will
be currently installed in
Control Panel.

A+
220-602
3.1
3.3

DEVICE MANAGER

Device Manager is your primary Windows tool when
solving problems with hardware. It gives a graphical view
of hardware devices configured under Windows and the
resources and drivers they use. Using Device Manager, you
can make changes, update drivers, and uninstall device
drivers. For instance, when a device driver is being
installed, Windows might inform you of a resource conflict,
or the device simply might not work. You can use Device
Manager as a useful fact-finding tool for resolving the problem. You can also use Device
Manager to print a report of system configuration.

Here is how to access Device Manager under Windows 2000/XP and Windows 9x/Me
(Windows NT does not have a Device Manager):

▲ *Using Windows XP.* Click **Start**, right-click **My Computer**, and then select **Properties** on
the shortcut menu. The System Properties dialog box appears. Click the **Hardware** tab
and then click **Device Manager**. Or you can enter **Devmgmt.msc** in the Run dialog box.

▲ *Using Windows 2000.* Right-click the **My Computer** icon on the desktop, select
Properties on the shortcut menu, click the **Hardware** tab, and then click the **Device
Manager** button. You can also enter **Devmgmt.msc** in the Run dialog box.

A+
220-602
3.1
3.3

◢ *Using Windows 9x/Me.* Right-click the **My Computer** icon on the desktop, select **Properties** on the shortcut menu, and then click the **Device Manager** tab.

Device Manager for Windows XP is shown in Figure 1-49. Click a plus sign to expand the view of an item, and click a minus sign to collapse the view. Also notice the three-forked symbol near the bottom of the window representing a USB device.

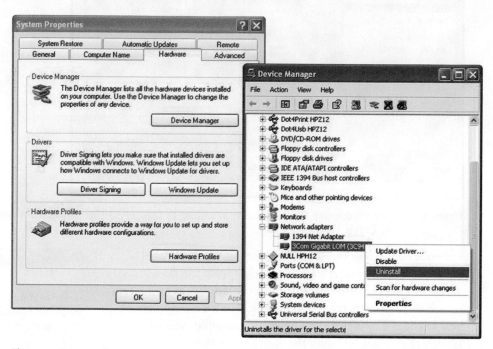

Figure 1-49 Windows XP Device Manager gives information about devices and allows you to uninstall a device

One thing you can do if you have a problem with an installed device is to use Device Manager to uninstall the device. Right-click the device and click **Uninstall** on the shortcut menu also showing in Figure 1-49. Then reboot and reinstall the device, looking for problems during the installation that point to the source of the problem. Sometimes reinstalling a device is all that is needed to solve the problem.

To find out more information about a device, right-click the device and select Properties on the shortcut menu. You can see the Properties dialog box for a network card in Figure 1-50. Many times, the source of a problem shows up in this window.

Figure 1-51 shows Device Manager under Windows 98 reporting a problem with a device using an exclamation point. In Device Manager, symbols that indicate a device's status are:

◢ A red X through the device name indicates a disabled device.
◢ An exclamation point on a yellow background indicates a problem with the device. (The device might still be functioning, but not in the way that Windows likes.)
◢ A blue I on a white field indicates that automatic settings were not used and resources have been manually assigned. It does not indicate a problem with the device.
◢ For Windows Me, a green question mark indicates a compatible driver is installed (not the driver designed for the device), which means the device might not be fully functional.

A+
220-602
3.1
3.3

Figure 1-50 The Properties window for a device helps you solve problems with the device

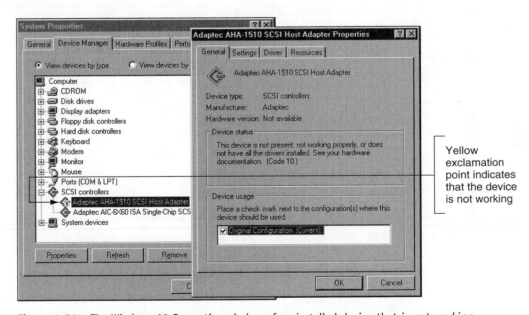

Figure 1-51 The Windows 98 Properties window of an installed device that is not working

A+
220-602
3.1
3.3

When a device is giving problems, check the Properties dialog box of that device for information. The Device Properties dialog box that opens can give you helpful information about solving problems with the device. From this window, you can update the driver for a device, enable or disable a device, and uninstall a device. How to do all this is covered in later chapters.

Using Device Manager, you can get a printed report of system information, which can be useful to document the status of a system. To print the report using Windows XP, click the

A+
220-602
3.1
3.3

printer icon on the Device Manager toolbar. For Windows 2000, click **View** and then click **Print**. For Windows 9x/Me, click **Print**. There are three options for the report: System summary, Selected class or device, and All devices and system summary.

SYSTEM INFORMATION

The System Information utility gives information similar to that given by Device Manager plus more. For example, it tells you the BIOS version you are using, the directory where the OS is installed, how system resources are used, information about drivers and their status, and much information about software installed on the system that is not included in Device Manager. This information is especially useful when talking with a technical support person on the phone who needs to know exactly what system and configuration is in front of you.

To run System Information using Windows 2000/XP or Windows 9x/Me, click **Start**, and then click **Run**. In the Run dialog box, enter **Msinfo32.exe**, and then click **OK**. The System Information dialog box opens (see Figure 1-52).

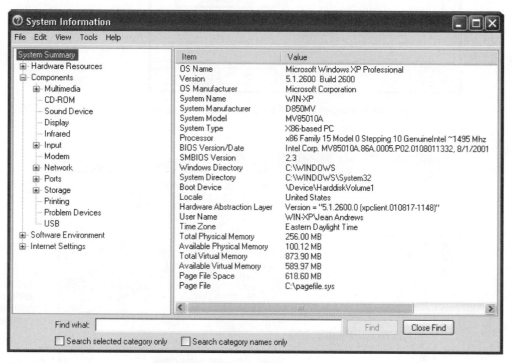

Figure 1-52   Use the Windows System Information utility to examine your system

System Information can be useful when strange error messages appear during startup. Use it to get a list of drivers that loaded successfully. If you have saved the System Information report when the system was starting successfully, comparing the two reports can help identify the problem device.

WINDOWS HELP AND THE MICROSOFT WEB SITE

Windows Help might provide useful information when you try to resolve a problem. To access Windows XP Help, click **Start**, and then click **Help and Support**. For Windows 2000 and Windows 9x/Me, click **Start**, and then click **Help**.

In many cases, the Help information includes suggestions that can lead you to a solution. For example, suppose you were trying to connect to the Internet using a phone line, but can't make the call. You check the phone connection, the modem lights, and all the obvious things, but still can't get it to work. When you turn to the Help tool and search for help with a dial-up connection, the window in Figure 1-53 appears, which suggests you delete all dial-up networking connections and re-create them. Although doing this doesn't guarantee the solution, it's certainly worth trying.

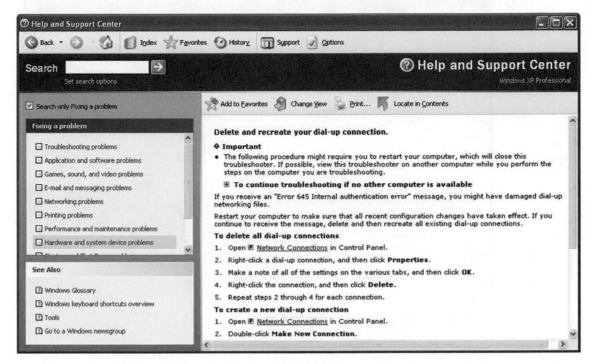

Figure 1-53 Troubleshooter making a suggestion to resolve a problem with using the modem to connect to the Internet

Also, the Microsoft Web site (*http://support.microsoft.com*), which is shown in Figure 1-54, has lots of information on troubleshooting. Search for the device, an error message, a Windows utility, a symptom, a software application, an update version number, or key words that lead you to articles about problem and solutions. You can also go to *www.microsoft.com* to browse for links on hardware and software compatibility. Other sources of help are application and device user and installation manuals, training materials, and the Web sites of application and device manufacturers. You can also use a search engine such as Google (*www.google.com*). Enter the error message, software application, symptom or Windows utility in the search box to search the Web for answers, suggestion, and comments.

> **Notes**
>
> If you are serious about learning to provide professional support for Windows, each OS has a resource kit, including support software and a huge reference book containing inside information about the OS. Check out *Microsoft Windows XP Professional Resource Kit* or *Microsoft Windows 2000 Professional Resource Kit*. Both are put out by Microsoft Press.

Beware, however, that you don't bump into a site that does more harm than good. Some sites are simply guessing, offering incomplete and possibly wrong solutions, and even offering a utility it claims will solve your problem but really contains only pop-up ads or spyware. Use only reputable sites you can trust. You'll learn about several of these excellent sites in this book.

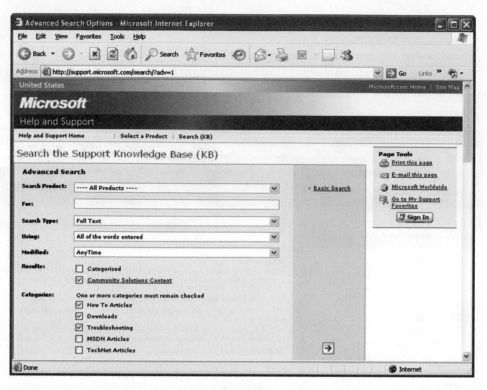

Figure 1-54   Microsoft Technical Support Web site

KEYSTROKE SHORTCUTS IN THE OS

Table 1-3 lists a few handy keystrokes to use when working with Windows, including the function keys you can use during startup. You can also use the mouse to do some of these same things, but keystrokes are sometimes faster. Also, in some troubleshooting situations, the mouse is not usable. At those times, knowing these keystrokes can get you out of a jam.

General Action	Keystrokes	Description
While loading Windows	F8	For Windows 2000/XP, to start in Safe Mode (covered in Chapter 5).
	Shift + F8	For Windows 2000/XP, start with Step-by-step confirmation (covered in Chapter 5).
	F4	For Windows 9x/Me, load previous version of DOS (covered in Chapter 7).
	F5	For Windows 98/Me, start in Safe Mode (covered in Chapter 7).
	F8 or Ctrl	For Windows 98/Me, display startup menu (covered in Chapter 7).
Managing Windows and applications	Alt + Tab	Hold down the Alt key and press Tab to move from one loaded application to another.
	Ctrl + Tab and Ctrl + Shift + Tab	Move through tabbed pages in a dialog box.
	Alt + ESC	Hold down the Alt key and press Esc to cycle through items in the order they were opened.

Table 1-3   Keystrokes that make working with Windows easier

General Action	Keystrokes	Description
	F6	In Windows 2000/XP, cycle through screen elements in a window or on the desktop.
	Win or Ctrl + Esc	Display Start menu. Use arrow keys to move over the menu. (The Win key is the one labeled with the Windows flag icon.)
	Win + E	Start Windows Explorer.
	Win + M	Minimize all windows.
	Win + Tab	Move through items on the taskbar.
	Win + R	Display the Run dialog box.
	Win + Break	Display the System Properties window.
	F5	Refresh the contents of a window.
	Alt + F4	Close the active application window, or, if no window is open, shut down Windows.
	Ctrl + F4	Close the active document window.
	Alt + Spacebar	In Windows 2000/XP, display the System menu for the active window. To close this window, you can then use the arrow key to step down to Close.
	Alt + M	First put the focus on the Start menu (use Win or Ctrl + Esc) and then press Alt + M to minimize all windows and move the focus to the desktop.
	F10 or Alt	Activate the menu bar in the active program.
	F1	Display help.
	Ctrl + Alt + Del	Display the Task List, which you can use to switch to another application, end a task, or shut down Windows.
	Application	When an item is selected, display its shortcut menu. (The Application key is labeled with a box and an arrow.)
Working with text anywhere in Windows	Ctrl + C	Shortcut to Copy.
	Ctrl + V	Shortcut for Paste.
	Ctrl + A	Shortcut for selecting all text.
	Ctrl + X	Shortcut for Cut.
	Ctrl + Z	Shortcut for Undo.
	Ctrl + Y	Shortcut for Repeat/Redo.
	Shift + arrow keys	Hold down the Shift key, and use the arrow keys to select text, character by character.
Managing files, folders, icons, and shortcuts	Ctrl + Shift while dragging a file	Create a shortcut.
	Ctrl while dragging a file	Copy a file.
	Shift + Delete	Delete a file without placing it in the Recycle Bin.
	F2	Rename an item.

Table 1-3 Keystrokes that make working with Windows easier (continued)

General Action	Keystrokes	Description
	Alt + Enter	Display an item's Properties window.
Selecting items	Shift + click	To select multiple entries in a list (such as filenames in Explorer), click the first item, hold down the Shift key, and click the last item you want to select in the list. All items between the first and last are selected.
	Ctrl + click	To select several nonsequential items in a list, click the first item to select it. Hold down the Ctrl key and click other items anywhere in the list. All items you click are selected.
Using menus	Alt	Press the Alt key to activate the menu bar.
	Alt, letter	After the menu bar is activated, press a letter to select a menu option. The letter must be underlined in the menu.
	Alt, arrow keys, Enter	In a window, use the Alt key to make the menu bar active. Then use the arrow keys to move over the menu tree and highlight the correct option. Use the Enter key to select that option.
	Esc	Press Esc to exit a menu without making a selection.
Copying to the Clipboard	Print Screen	Copy the desktop to the Clipboard.
	Alt + Print Screen	Copy the active window to the Clipboard.

Table 1-3 Keystrokes that make working with Windows easier (continued)

>> CHAPTER SUMMARY

▲ Operating systems used for desktop computers include DOS, Windows 9x/Me, Windows NT/2000/XP, Unix, a version of Unix called Linux, OS/2, and the Mac OS. The Windows Server 2003 operating systems are only used on servers. Windows Vista is the next Microsoft operating system.

▲ An operating system manages hardware, runs applications, provides an interface for users, and stores, retrieves, and manipulates files.

▲ Every OS is composed of two main internal components: a shell portion to interact with users and applications and a kernel portion to interact with hardware.

▲ An OS provides an interface for the user that is command driven or icon and menu driven.

▲ An OS manages files and folders using a file system. Two Windows file systems are FAT and NTFS.

▲ A hard drive is organized into partitions that contain one or more logical drives or volumes.

▲ Three types of software are BIOS (firmware) and device drivers, operating systems (OSs), and application software. Sometimes, device drivers are considered part of the OS.

▲ Application software relates to the OS, which relates to BIOS and device drivers to control hardware.

▲ Most processors can operate in real or protected mode. In real mode, a CPU processes 16 bits at a time, and in protected mode, it processes 32 bits at a time. Some high-end processors operate in 64-bit mode (long mode).

◢ Device drivers are written using either 16-bit, 32-bit, or 64-bit code. Most drivers today are 32-bit, protected-mode drivers that Windows loads from the registry.

◢ Windows Me and Windows NT/2000/XP use only 32-bit drivers, except for Windows XP Professional x64 Edition, which uses 64-bit drivers.

◢ Software manages memory by means of memory addresses that point to locations in RAM.

◢ Virtual memory uses hard drive space as memory to increase the total amount of memory available. In Windows, virtual memory is stored in the swap file. The Windows 9x/Me swap file is Win386.swp, and the Windows 2000/XP swap file is Pagefile.sys.

◢ From the Windows desktop, you can launch programs from the Start menu, a shortcut icon on the desktop, the Run dialog box, Windows Explorer, or My Computer.

◢ Windows utilities useful for maintaining and customizing a system, gathering information about the system and troubleshooting are the Display Properties window, the Taskbar and Start Menu Properties window, Windows Explorer, My Computer, System Properties, Control Panel, Device Manager, and System Information.

◢ Use Windows Help and the Microsoft Web site to resolve problems and find useful information.

◢ A computer technician needs to know how to troubleshoot the OS using keystrokes when the mouse is not available.

>> KEY TERMS

For explanations of key terms, see the Glossary near the end of the book.

boot record	graphical user interface (GUI)	registry
boot sector	initialization files	root directory
child directory	kernel	sector
cluster	logical drive	service
CMOS setup	long mode	shell
desktop	multitasking	shortcut
device driver	New Technology file system	startup BIOS
directory table	(NTFS)	subdirectory
FAT12	operating system (OS)	system BIOS
file allocation table (FAT)	partition	system tray
file extension	path	taskbar
file system	preemptive multitasking	track
filename	protected mode	volume
folder	real mode	

>> REVIEWING THE BASICS

1. List four major functions of an OS.

2. Which operating system is only used on Apple Macintosh computers?

3. Which operating system was developed by Microsoft using core components of OS/2 and was meant to replace OS/2?

4. What is the next Microsoft operating system for desktop computers to be released in 2006 and 2007?

5. Which operating system often used for server applications is a scaled-down version of Unix?

6. Why did many users choose not to upgrade to Windows Me?

7. What Microsoft OS is an upgrade of Windows 2000?

8. What are three possible interfaces an OS provides to the user? Briefly explain the functions of each.

9. Which file system is used by floppy disks?

10. What are two file systems used by hard drives?

11. Real mode operates using a(n) _____ -bit data path, and protected mode uses a(n) _____ -bit data path.

12. Which Microsoft operating system(s) support 16-bit device drivers or 32-bit device drivers?

13. Real mode allows programs direct access to _____, but protected mode does not.

14. List three types of information that are kept in the Windows registry.

15. List four ways to launch an application from the Windows desktop.

16. Give two situations in which Windows keystroke shortcuts might be useful.

17. How do you access the Display Properties window? What are two settings you can change from this window?

18. What Windows 2000/XP and Windows 9x utility allows you to update the device driver for a device?

19. Users and applications depend on what to relate to all hardware components?

20. Every operating system has two main internal components. The _____ relates to the user and to applications and provides a command, menu, or icon interface, whereas the _____ is responsible for interfacing with the hardware.

21. What command can you enter in the Run dialog box to launch Device Manager?

22. Applets in the Control Panel are stored as program files with what file extension?

23. What Windows 2000/XP tool can you use to reduce the number of partitions used by a hard drive?

24. What command can you enter in the Run dialog box to launch the Windows 2000/XP System Information utility?

25. Which Windows operating system(s) allow more than one user to be logged on simultaneously, each having their own open applications?

26. When using Linux, what is the purpose of an X Windows application?

27. What command can you enter in the Run dialog box of Windows 2000/XP to launch the Disk Management utility?

28. A floppy drive is divided into tracks, which are divided into sectors. How large is each sector?

29. What is the name of the file used by Windows 2000/XP to hold data and instructions in virtual memory?

30. Which of the two OS core components includes the Windows desktop? Which of the two OS core components includes the Windows memory manager?

31. What is the purpose of the Boot Camp software on a Mac?

32. What type of data is contained in files that have an .ini or .inf file extension?

33. In Windows XP Device Manager, how do you uninstall a device?

34. What is the Windows keyboard shortcut to move from one loaded application to another? To display the Start menu from the Windows desktop? To close the active application window? To shut down Windows when no applications are loaded?

>> THINKING CRITICALLY

1. Is a mouse more likely to be controlled by a device driver or by system BIOS?

2. Name one device that is likely to be controlled by system BIOS.

3. If your printer is giving you trouble, what is the best way to obtain an update for the device driver?

4. What Windows tool can you use to know how much RAM is installed on your system?

5. Why is 16-bit Windows software considered to be legacy software?

>> HANDS-ON PROJECTS

PROJECT 1-1: Using the Windows 2000/XP System Information Utility

Using Windows 2000/XP, do the following to run the System Information utility and gather information about your system:

1. Click **Start**, click **Run**, and then type **Msinfo32.exe** in the Run dialog box. Click **OK**. The System Information dialog box opens.

2. Browse through the different levels of information in this window and answer the following questions:

   a. What OS and OS version are you using?

   b. What is your CPU speed?

   c. What is your BIOS manufacturer and version?

   d. How much RAM is installed on your video card? Explain how you got this information.

   e. What is the name of the driver file that manages your parallel port? Your serial port?

   f. How is IRQ 10 used on your system? IRQ 4?

   g. Which DMA channels are used on your system and how are they used?

PROJECT 1-2: Using a Freeware Diagnostic Utility

You can download many freeware diagnostic utilities from the Internet and use them to examine, troubleshoot, and benchmark a system. Do the following to download and use one utility to examine your system:

1. Go to the CNET Networks Web site at *www.download.com* and use the Web site search box to search for Fresh Diagnose. Download the utility, saving it to a folder on your hard drive named **Downloads**.

2. Double-click the file to execute the program and install the software. When given the opportunity, choose to create a shortcut to the software on your desktop.

3. Double-click the shortcut to run the Fresh Diagnose program.

4. Browse through the Fresh Diagnose menus and answer the same questions listed in Project 1-1 for the Windows 2000/XP System Information utility.

5. Compare the two programs, Fresh Diagnose and System Information, by answering the following questions:

  a. Which product is easier to use and why?

  b. Which product gives more information about your system?

  c. What is one advantage that System Information has over Fresh Diagnose?

  d. What is one advantage that Fresh Diagnose has over System Information?

  e. Which product do you prefer and why?

PROJECT 1-3:   Using Device Manager

Using Device Manager under Windows 2000/XP or Windows 9x/Me, answer the following questions about your computer. To access Device Manager using Windows 2000/XP, open the System Properties dialog box, click the **Hardware** tab, and then click **Device Manager**. For Windows 9x/Me, right-click the **My Computer** icon on the desktop, select **Properties** on the shortcut menu, and click the **Device Manager** tab.

1. Does your computer have a network card installed? If so, what is the name of the card?

2. Name three settings that you can change under Device Manager.

3. What are all the hardware devices that Device Manager recognizes as present?

PROJECT 1-4:   Using Shortcuts

Create a shortcut on your desktop to Notepad (Notepad.exe), a text editor. Using a second method for creating shortcuts, add a shortcut to the Windows command prompt (Cmd.exe or Command.com). First, locate the two program files on your hard drive by clicking Start, Search (or Find for Windows 9x/Me), and using the Search or Find dialog box. Then create the shortcuts. List the steps you took to create each shortcut.

PROJECT 1-5:   Practicing Keystrokes

Disconnect your mouse and then practice using the keyboard in case you must troubleshoot a system when the mouse does not work. Do the following:

1. Open Explorer and display the files in the root directory of drive C. List the steps and keystrokes you used to do this.

2. Unhide all the files in this folder. For Windows 2000/XP, from the Tools menu, select Folder Options, select the View tab, and then select Show hidden files and folders. Also uncheck Hide extensions for known file types. And also uncheck Hide protected operating system files. For Windows 9x/Me, from the View menu, select Folder Options, select the View tab, and then select Show all files. List the steps and keystrokes you used.

3. If you are using Windows 2000/XP, what is the exact size of the file Boot.ini in bytes, and the date and time the file was last modified? If you are using Windows 9x/Me, what is the size of the file IO.SYS in bytes, and the date and time the file was last modified?

>> REAL PROBLEMS, REAL SOLUTIONS

REAL PROBLEM 1-1:   Becoming a PC Support Technician

You've just been hired as a PC support technician in the IT department of your university. At the job interview, you were promised a two-week training period, but by noon on your first day on the job it dawns on you that "training period" means you gotta train yourself *really quick*! Listed below are some problems you encounter that day. How do you solve these problems and what Windows tools do you use?

1. A history professor calls you into his office and tells you he thinks the memory on his computer needs upgrading. He wants you to tell him how much RAM is currently installed. What do you do?

2. A PE instructor discovers the history professor has Windows XP on his desktop. She thinks she has a version of Windows 9x/Me on her desktop and wants you to tell her exactly which OS she has installed. What do you do?

3. The Office Administrator for Career Education is working from home today. She calls you to say she must connect to the Internet but her dial-up connection is not working. Walk her through the steps to verify that Windows XP is recognizing her modem correctly. What are these steps?

4. A student in a computer lab is trying to answer a question in the lab about Windows XP Automatic Updates. She needs to know if the system is set to receive Windows updates automatically. What steps do you give her to find the answer?

5. A student in the Media Center complains that his monitor is flickering. You suspect the resolution is set too low under Windows XP. List the steps to find out the current resolution on your Windows XP system. What is the highest resolution possible for your monitor?

6. A student in a computer lab asks you how much space is free on her drive C using Windows XP. What steps do you use?

7. Your boss asks you to go down the hall to the Windows XP computer in the break room and find out the path and name of the device driver for the optical drive (CD drive or DVD drive) that is installed. What steps do you use? What is the path and name of the optical drive device driver on your Windows XP system?

Installing Windows 2000/XP

Windows 2000 and Windows XP share the same basic Windows architecture and have similar characteristics. Historically, Windows 2000 is the culmination of the evolution of Microsoft operating systems from the 16-bit DOS operating system to a true 32-bit, module-oriented operating system, complete with improved security, user-friendly Plug and Play installations, and other easy-to-use features. Windows XP includes additional support for multimedia, Plug and Play, and legacy software, making the final step for Microsoft to announce the merging of Windows 9x/Me and Windows NT operating systems into a single OS.

Windows XP is the current choice as a Windows OS for personal computers and it is the only Windows OS for which you can buy a license. (At the time this book went to print, Windows Vista was not yet available.) However, because many individual users and corporations still rely on Windows 2000, you need to know how to support it.

This chapter lays the foundation for understanding the architecture of Windows 2000/XP and then shows you how to plan a Windows XP and Windows 2000 Professional installation, the steps to perform the installations, and what to do after the OS is installed.

Notes

Some instructors and readers might prefer to study DOS and Windows 9x/Me before you study Windows 2000/XP. This book is designed so that you can cover Chapters 6 and 7 on DOS and Windows 9x/Me before you cover Chapters 2, 3, 4, and 5 on Windows 2000/XP; you can also cover all six chapters sequentially. Also, if you are studying this book in preparation for the A+ exams, know that content in Chapters 6 and 7 is not covered on the exams and can be skipped.

FEATURES AND ARCHITECTURE OF WINDOWS 2000/XP

In this section of the chapter, you'll learn about the features, versions, and architecture of Windows 2000/XP. First we'll look at the several Windows 2000/XP versions and when it is appropriate to use each. Then you'll learn about the operating modes used by Windows, its networking features, and how it handles hard drives and file systems on those drives. Finally, you'll learn about when it is appropriate to use Windows XP or Windows 2000.

VERSIONS AND FEATURES OF WINDOWS XP AND 2000

Windows XP comes in several varieties: Windows XP Professional, Windows XP Home Edition, Windows XP Media Center Edition, Windows XP Tablet PC Edition, and Windows XP Professional x64 Edition (formally called Windows XP 64-Bit Edition).

Windows XP Home Edition and Windows XP Professional have these features, among others, that are not included with Windows 2000:

◢ A new user interface, shown in Figure 2-1. Notice how different it looks from the desktops of earlier Windows versions such as Windows 98 and Windows 2000.

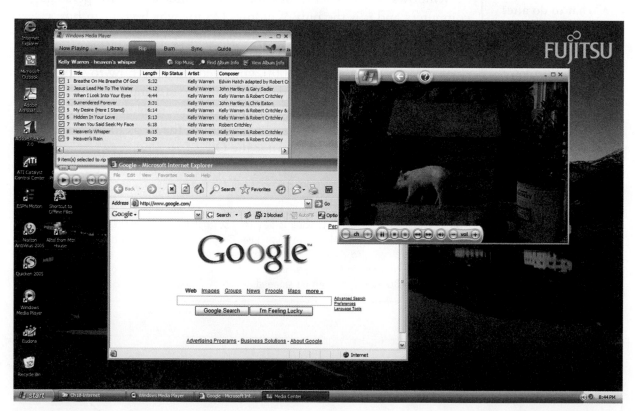

Figure 2-1   New user interface and sample windows

▲ The ability for two or more users to be logged on simultaneously. Each user has a separate profile, and Windows XP can switch between users, keeping a separate set of applications open for each user.

▲ Windows Media Player for Windows XP, a centralized application for working with digital media

▲ Windows Messenger for instant messaging, conferencing, and application sharing

▲ Windows Security Center was added with Windows XP Service Pack 2

▲ The ability to burn a CD simply by dragging and dropping a folder or file onto the CD-R device icon (see Figure 2-2)

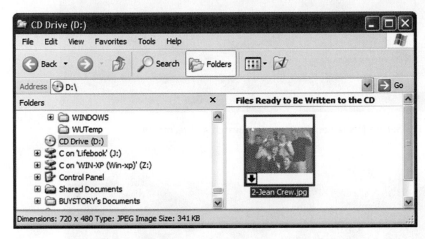

Figure 2-2   Files can be dragged and dropped to the CD folder for later burning to CD

▲ A way for someone to assist a user at the computer by remotely controlling the computer, called Remote Assistance

▲ An expanded Help feature

▲ Advanced security features

In addition to these features of Windows XP Home Edition, Windows XP Professional offers:

▲ A way for a user to control the computer from a remote location, called Remote Desktop

▲ A way for an administrator to manage user profiles from a server (roaming profiles)

▲ Additional security features

▲ Multilingual capabilities

▲ Support for new higher-performance processors

Windows XP Media Center Edition is an enhanced version of Windows XP Professional, and includes additional support for digital entertainment hardware such as video recording integrated with TV input. When you first launch Media Center (see Figure 2-3), it takes you through a wizard to configure how you will connect to TV (by satellite, cable, or set-top box) and if and how you want it to track TV listings available from your local cable company (see Figure 2-4). It's designed for the high-end PC home market and is only available when preinstalled on a high-end PC manufactured by a Microsoft partner. Windows XP Tablet PC Edition is also built on Windows XP Professional with additional support for tablet PCs.

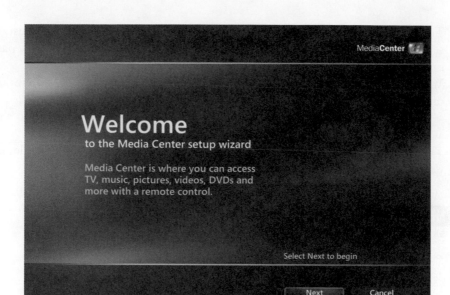

Figure 2-3   Set up Media Center so you can watch and record TV

Figure 2-4   Media Center is set to watch live TV, record TV, search your online
TV guide, and play movies

There is also Windows XP Professional x64 Edition, which used to be called Windows XP
64-Bit Edition. This version of Windows XP uses 64-bit code and is designed to be used with
64-bit processors such as the AMD Athlon 64 or Opteron or the Intel Itanium. The OS is
used for high-end gaming computers using AMD processors, for servers, or for heavily technical workstations that run scientific and engineering applications and need greater amounts
of memory and higher performance than standard desktop PCs. For example, an aircraft
designer who uses software to simulate how various conditions affect aircraft materials might
use Windows XP Professional x64 Edition on a system that supports resource-intensive
simulation and animation applications.

Windows XP has several built-in features to manage audio and video, including support for
inputting images from digital cameras and scanners, a Windows Movie Maker for editing

video, and Windows Media Player, Version 8. (Windows Me has Media Player, Version 7.) With Media Player, you can play DVDs, CDs, and Internet radio. There's a jukebox for organizing audio files, including MP3 files used on music CDs. You can also burn your own music CDs using Media Player with a CD-R or CD-RW drive. To access the Media Player, click Start, All Programs, and Windows Media Player. Figure 2-5 shows the Media Player window.

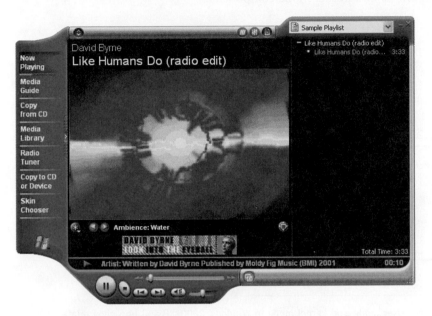

Figure 2-5 Windows Media Player

 Notes

Windows Internet Explorer, Windows Media Player, a firewall, and other Microsoft products are tightly integrated with the Windows XP operating system. Some users see this as a disadvantage, and others see it as an advantage. Tight integration allows applications to interact easily with other applications and the OS, but makes it more difficult for third-party software to compete with Microsoft applications and more difficult to remove or reinstall an integrated component that is giving problems.

Windows 2000 includes four operating systems:

- *Windows 2000 Professional* was designed to replace both Windows 9x and Windows NT Workstation as a personal computer desktop or notebook OS. It is an improved version of Windows NT Workstation, using the same new technological approach to hardware and software, and has all the popular features of Windows 9x, including Plug and Play.

- *Windows 2000 Server* is the improved version of Windows NT Server and is designed as a network operating system for low-end servers.

- *Windows 2000 Advanced Server* is a network operating system that has the same features as Windows 2000 Server but is designed to run on more powerful servers.

- *Windows 2000 Datacenter Server* is a network operating system that is a step up from Windows 2000 Advanced Server. It is intended for use in large enterprise operations centers.

A+ Exam Tip

Microsoft offers several operating systems designed to run on servers, including Windows 2000 Server and Windows Server 2003. None of the server operating systems is covered on the A+ exams.

WINDOWS 2000/XP ARCHITECTURE AND OPERATING MODES

Windows 2000/XP operates in two modes, user mode and kernel mode, which each take advantage of different CPU functions and abilities. (The Windows 2000/XP architecture was also used by Windows NT.) In Figure 2-6, you can see how OS components are separated into user mode and kernel mode components.

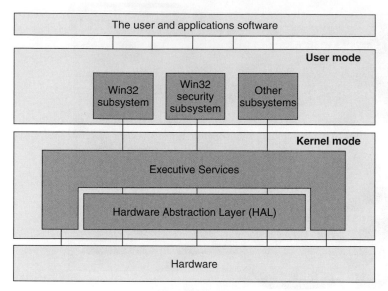

Figure 2-6 User mode and kernel mode in Windows 2000/XP and how they relate to users, application software, and hardware

USER MODE

User mode is a processor mode in which programs have only limited access to system information and can access hardware only through other OS services. The OS has several **subsystems,** or OS modules, that use this mode and interface with the user and with applications. The Windows tools you use, such as Windows Explorer, run primarily in user mode. In Figure 2-6, note the Win32 subsystem, which is probably the most important user mode subsystem because it manages and provides an environment for all 32-bit programs, including the user interface (such as the one for Explorer). The Win32 security subsystem provides logon to the system and other security functions, including privileges for file access.

All applications relate to Windows 2000/XP by way of the Win32 subsystem, either directly or indirectly. Figure 2-7 shows how various programs that run under Windows 2000/XP interact with subsystems. For instance, each legacy DOS application resides in its own NTVDM. An **NTVDM (NT virtual DOS machine)** is a carefully controlled environment that Windows 2000/XP provides. In it, a DOS application can interface with only one subsystem and cannot relate to anything outside the system. All 16-bit Windows 3.x applications reside in a **Win16 on Win32 (WOW)** environment. Within the WOW, these 16-bit applications can communicate with one another and the WOW, but that's as far as their world goes. Figure 2-7 shows three 16-bit Windows 3.x applications residing in a WOW that resides in one NTVDM. Because each DOS application expects to run as the only application on a PC, each has its own NTVDM.

You can see in Figure 2-7 that 32-bit applications do not require an NTVDM and can relate to the Win32 subsystem directly, because they are written to run in protected mode. They can also use a single line of communication (called single-threading) with the Win32 subsystem or multiple lines for interfacing (called **multithreading**) with the Win32 subsystem, depending on what the process requests. A **thread** is a single task that the process requests from the kernel,

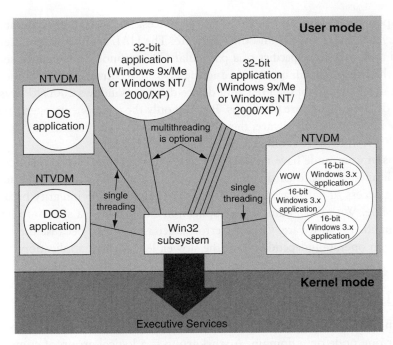

Figure 2-7 Environment subsystems in Windows 2000/XP user mode include NTVDMs for DOS and Windows 3.x applications and optional multithreading for 32-bit applications

such as the task of printing a file. A **process** is a program or group of programs that is running, together with the system resources assigned to it, such as memory addresses, environmental variables, and other resources. Figure 2-8 shows how the Microsoft Word program (msword.exe) is launched as a running process together with its resources and running threads.

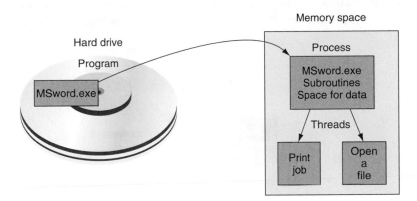

Figure 2-8 A process is a running program and its resources

Sometimes a process is called an instance, such as when you say, "Open two instances of Internet Explorer." Technically, you are saying to open two Internet Explorer processes. An example of multithreading is Microsoft Word requesting that the subsystem read a large file from the hard drive and print a job at the same time. Single-threading happens when the application does not expect both processes to be performed at the same time but simply passes one request followed by another.

KERNEL MODE

Kernel mode is the operating system mode in which programs have extensive access to system information and hardware. Kernel mode is used by two main components: the HAL and a group of components collectively called executive services. The **HAL (hardware abstraction layer)** is the layer between the OS and the hardware. The HAL is available in different versions, each designed to address the specifics of a particular CPU technology. **Executive services** interface between the subsystems in user mode and the HAL. Executive services components manage hardware resources by way of the HAL and device drivers. Windows 2000/XP was designed to port easily to different hardware platforms. Because only the components operating in kernel mode actually interact with hardware, they are the only parts that need to be changed when Windows 2000/XP moves from one hardware platform to another.

Applications in user mode have no access to hardware resources. In kernel mode, executive services have limited access to hardware resources, but the HAL primarily interacts with hardware. Limiting access to hardware mainly to the HAL increases OS integrity because more control is possible. With this isolation, an application cannot cause a system to hang by making illegal demands on hardware. Overall performance is increased because the HAL and executive services can operate independently of the slower, less efficient applications using them.

NETWORKING FEATURES

A+ ESS
5.1

A+
220-602
5.2

A workstation running Windows 2000/XP can be configured to work as one node in a workgroup or one node on a domain. A **workgroup** is a logical group of computers and users that share resources (Figure 2-9), where administration, resources, and security on a workstation are controlled by that workstation. Each computer maintains a list of users and their rights on that particular PC. A Windows **domain** is a group of networked computers that share a centralized directory database of user account information and security for the entire group of computers (Figure 2-10). A workgroup uses a **peer-to-peer** networking model, and a domain uses a **client/server** networking model. Using the client/server model, the directory database is controlled by a Network Operating System (NOS). Popular NOSs are Windows Server 2003, Windows 2000 Server, Novell NetWare, Unix, Linux, and Mac OS. Windows 2000 for the desktop has network client software built in for Windows

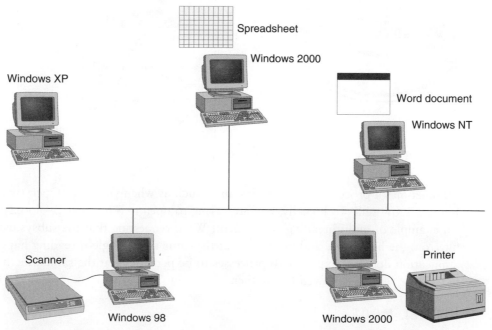

Figure 2-9 A Windows workgroup is a peer-to-peer network where no single computer controls the network and each computer controls its own resources

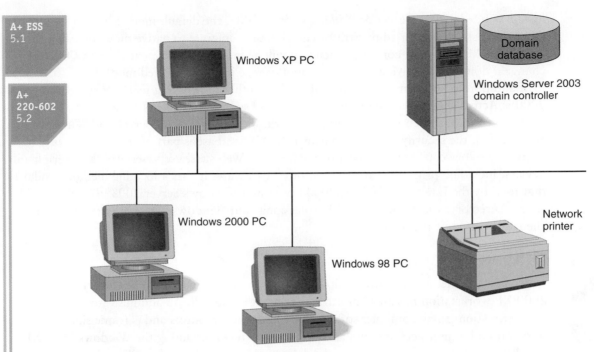

Figure 2-10 A Windows domain is a client/server network where security on each PC or other device is controlled by a centralized database on a domain controller

servers (Microsoft Client), Mac OS (AppleTalk Client), and Novell NetWare (Client for NetWare). Windows XP supports Microsoft Client and Client for NetWare. Alternately, for Novell NetWare, you can install Novell's version of its client software.

WINDOWS DOMAINS

In a Windows 2000 Server or Windows Server 2003 domain, a network administrator manages access to the network through a centralized database. In Figure 2-10, you see the possible different components of a Windows domain. Every domain has a **domain controller**, which stores and controls a database of (1) user accounts, (2) group accounts, and (3) computer accounts. This database is called the directory database or the **security accounts manager (SAM)** database.

Because the domain controller database is so important, Windows allows backup copies of the database to exist on more than one computer in the domain. Under Windows NT, a network can have a primary domain controller and one or more backup domain controllers. The **primary domain controller (PDC)** holds the original directory database, and read-only copies are stored on **backup domain controllers (BDCs)**. An administrator can update the database on the PDC from any computer on the network, and the BDCs later get a copy of the updated database.

With Windows 2000 Server and Windows Server 2003, a network can have any number of domain controllers, each keeping a copy of the directory that can be edited. An administrator can update the directory on any one of these domain controllers, which will then communicate the change to the other domain controllers.

When Windows NT and Windows 2000/2003 domain controllers are on the same network, conflicts can result because of the differences in the way the domain controllers work in each OS. For this reason, Windows 2000 runs in two modes: native mode and mixed mode. **Native mode** is used when no Windows NT domain controllers are present, and **mixed mode** is used when there is at least one Windows NT domain controller on the network. Mixed mode is necessary when a large network is being upgraded from Windows NT to Windows 2000/2003, and some servers have been upgraded but others have not. When you install Windows 2000 Server or Windows Server 2003, the default mode is mixed mode. After the installation, an administrator can choose to migrate to native mode by using the Computer Management console, which you will learn about in the next chapter. Once you change a domain to native mode, you cannot change it back to mixed mode.

In addition to native mode and mixed mode, another networking feature new to Windows 2000 is **Active Directory**, a directory database and service that allows for a single administration point for all shared resources on a network. In Windows 2000 Server and Windows Server 2003, the security accounts manager (SAM) database is part of Active Directory. Active Directory can track file locations, databases, Web sites, users, services, and peripheral devices, including printers, scanners, and other hardware. It uses a locating method similar to that used by the Internet. Windows 2000 Server and Windows Server 2003 versions provide Active Directory, and Windows 2000 Professional and Windows XP act as Active Directory clients, or users, of the directory.

WINDOWS 2000/XP LOGON

A+ ESS
5.1

A+
220-602
5.2

Regardless of whether Windows 2000/XP computers are networked or not, every Windows 2000/XP workstation has an **administrator account** by default. An administrator has rights and permissions to all computer software and hardware resources and is responsible for setting up other user accounts and assigning them privileges. During the Windows 2000/XP installation, you enter a password to the default administrator account. When the workstation is part of a Windows workgroup, you can log on as an administrator after the OS is installed and create local user accounts. If the workstation is part of a domain, a network administrator sets up global user accounts that apply to the entire domain, including giving access to the local workstations. Local user accounts, as well as other ways to secure a workstation, are covered in Chapter 4.

When Windows 2000/XP starts up, you must log on before you can use the OS. Windows XP displays a logon screen by default. For Windows 2000, you see the logon screen when you press Ctrl+Alt+Del. To log on, enter a user name and password, and click **OK**. Windows 2000/XP tracks which user is logged on to the system and grants rights and permissions according to the user's group or to specific permissions granted this user by the administrator. If you do not enter a valid account name and password, Windows 2000/XP does not allow you access to the system.

Using Windows XP, more than one user can be logged on at the same time. In Windows XP, if you are in a workgroup and want to log off or log on as another user, you can press **Ctl-Atl-Del** and the Log Off Windows dialog box appears (see Figure 2-11). If you belong to a domain, when you press Ctl-Atl-Del, the Windows Security dialog box appears. You can use this dialog box for logging on and off.

Figure 2-11 Switch users or log off in Windows XP

HOW WINDOWS 2000/XP MANAGES HARD DRIVES

A+ ESS
3.1

A+
220-602
3.1

A hard drive is divided into 512-byte sectors. These sectors on a hard drive are organized into partitions and logical drives. An OS manages a logical drive with a file system, and the OS itself is installed on one of these logical drives. When Windows 2000/XP is installed on a new hard drive, four steps are involved in logically organizing the drive:

1. Cylinders on the drive are divided into partitions, and a partition table at the beginning of the drive records where each partition begins and ends on the drive.

2. Each partition is divided into one or more logical drives, which are named drive C, D, E, and so forth. Creating these first two levels is called partitioning the drive.

3. Each logical drive (also called a volume) is formatted with a file system, FAT16, FAT32, or NTFS. This step is called formatting a drive (logical drive, that is).

4. If the hard drive is to be the boot device in a system, the last step of preparing the drive is to install an operating system on logical drive C. This step is called installing an OS.

We next explain how partitions, logical drives, and file systems look and work, and how to make good decisions when choosing how many and how big each logical drive on a hard drive will be; this process is called "slicing" your drive.

UNDERSTANDING PARTITIONS AND LOGICAL DRIVES

Recall that a hard drive can be organized into one or more partitions and that partitions contain logical drives. Figure 2-12 shows an example with the hard drive divided into two partitions.

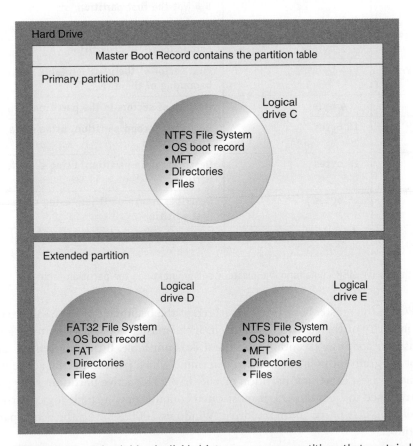

Figure 2-12   A hard drive is divided into one or more partitions that contain logical drives

A+ ESS
3.1

A+
220-602
3.1

The first partition contains one logical drive (drive C), and the second partition is divided into two logical drives (D and E). The first sector at the beginning of a hard drive (512 bytes located on head 0, track 0, sector 1) is called the master boot sector or, more commonly, the Master Boot Record (MBR), which contains two items:

▲ The master boot program (446 bytes), which loads the OS boot program stored in the OS boot record. (The OS boot program begins the process of loading the OS.)
▲ The partition table, which contains the description, location, and size of each partition on the drive (up to four).

Table 2-1 lists the contents of the MBR. The first item is the master boot program and the last five items in Table 2-1 make up the partition table.

Item	Bytes Used	Description
1	446 bytes	Master boot program that calls the OS boot program on the OS boot record
2	16-byte total	Description of the first partition
	1 byte	Is this the bootable partition? (Yes = 90h, No = 00h)
	3 bytes	Beginning location of the partition
	1 byte	System indicator; possible values are: 0 = Not a DOS partition 1 = DOS with a 12-bit FAT 4 = DOS with a 16-bit FAT 5 = Not the first partition 6 = Partition larger than 32 MB
	3 bytes	Ending location of partition
	4 bytes	First sector of the partition table relative to the beginning of the disk
	4 bytes	Number of sectors in the partition
3	16 bytes	Describes second partition, using same format as first partition
4	16 bytes	Describes third partition, using same format as first partition
5	16 bytes	Describes fourth partition, using same format as first partition
6	2 bytes	Signature of the partition table, always AA55

Table 2-1 Hard drive MBR containing the master boot program and the partition table

During POST, the master boot program stored at the beginning of the MBR executes and checks the integrity of the partition table itself. If the master boot program finds any corruption, it refuses to continue execution, and the disk is unusable. If the table entries are valid, the master boot program looks in the table to determine which partition is the active partition, which, in most cases, is the first partition on the drive. The **active partition** is the partition on the hard drive used to boot the OS. It most often contains only a single logical drive (drive C) and is usually the first partition on the drive. Windows 2000/XP calls the active partition the **system partition**.

The master boot program looks in the first sector of this active partition to find and execute the OS boot program. This first sector of the active partition is called the OS boot record, and, if the active partition is the first partition on the drive, this sector is physically the second sector on the drive, immediately following the MBR sector.

Using DOS or Windows 9x, a hard drive can have one or two partitions. Using Windows 2000/XP, a drive can have up to four partitions. A partition can be a **primary partition** (having only one logical drive in the partition, such as drive C, in which case it is sometimes called a logical partition) or an **extended partition** (having more than one logical drive, such as drive D and drive E). There can be only one extended partition on a drive. Therefore, with DOS and Windows 9x, the drive can have one primary and one extended partition. Under Windows 2000/XP, the drive can have four partitions, but only one of them can be an extended partition. The active partition is always a primary partition.

>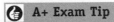
> **Notes**
>
> Suppose you try to boot your system and get the message, "Invalid drive specification." This error can be caused by a number of problems; a possibility is a **boot sector virus**. This type of virus attacks the MBR master boot program. To replace the MBR program with a fresh one, use the Windows 2000/XP Fixmbr command or the Windows 9x Fdisk /MBR command.

> **A+ Exam Tip**
>
> The A+ Essentials exam expects you to know the difference between these terms: active partition, primary partition, extended partition, and logical partition.

WINDOWS 2000/XP BOOT PARTITION AND SYSTEM PARTITION

Windows 2000/XP assigns two different functions to hard drive partitions holding the OS (see Figure 2-13). The **system partition**, normally drive C, is the active partition of the hard drive. This is the partition that contains the OS boot record. Remember that the MBR program looks to this OS boot record for the boot program as the first step in turning the PC over to an OS. The other partition, called the **boot partition**, is the partition where the Windows 2000/XP operating system is stored.

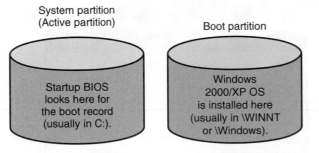

Figure 2-13 Two types of Windows 2000/XP hard drive partitions

For most installations, the system partition and the boot partition are the same (drive C) and Windows is installed in C:\Windows (for Windows XP) or C:\Winnt (for Windows 2000). An example of when the system partition and the boot partition are different is when Windows XP is installed as a dual boot with Windows 2000. Figure 2-14 shows how

> **Notes**
>
> Don't be confused by the terminology here. It is really true that, according to Windows 2000/XP terminology, the Windows OS is on the boot partition, and the boot record is on the system partition, although that might seem backward. The PC boots from the system partition and loads the Windows 2000/XP operating system from the boot partition.

A+ ESS
3.1

Windows XP is installed on drive E and Windows 2000 is installed on drive C. For Windows XP, the system partition is drive C and the boot partition is drive E. (For Windows 2000 on this computer, the system and boot partitions are both drive C.)

A+
220-602
3.1

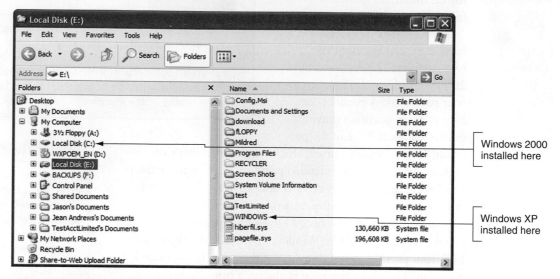

Figure 2-14   Windows XP and Windows 2000 installed on the same system

> **Notes**
>
> To know what file system a logical drive is using, in Windows Explorer, right-click the drive and select **Properties** from the shortcut menu (see Figure 2-15).

UNDERSTANDING FILE SYSTEMS

Each logical drive or volume must have a file system installed; the process is called formatting the drive. The file system is needed for the OS to track where on the drive it places files and folders.

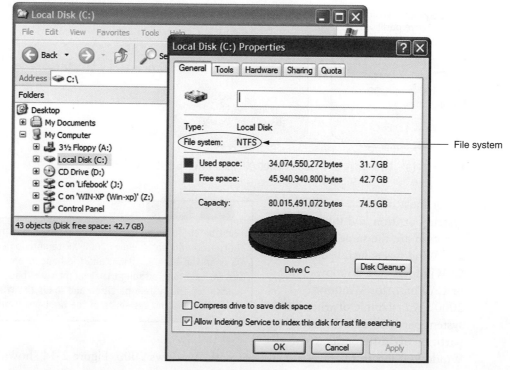

Figure 2-15   This drive C is using the NTFS file system

A+ ESS
3.1

A+
220-602
3.1

Recall that floppy disks use the FAT12 file system, which you learned about in Chapter 1. The only difference between FAT12 and FAT16 or FAT32 is the number of bits used for each entry in the FAT. The structure of the boot record, FAT, and root directory that makes up the FAT12 file system also applies to FAT16 and FAT32. Let's now look at how each file system is organized, the advantages of each file system, and what you need to know when slicing your drive.

FAT16

DOS and all versions of Windows support the FAT16 file system, which uses 16 bits for each cluster entry in the FAT. Using FAT16, the smallest cluster size is four sectors. Because each sector is 512 bytes, a cluster that contains four sectors is 2,048 bytes. Because an OS writes a file to a drive using one or more clusters, the least amount of space it uses for one file is 2,048 bytes. If a file contains less than 2,048 bytes, the remaining bytes in the cluster are wasted. This wasted space is called slack. If a drive contains many small files, much space is wasted.

This problem could be partially solved if the cluster size were smaller than four sectors. However, just the opposite is true: The more sectors assigned to the logical drive, the more sectors per cluster. This is because the OS is limited by the number of bits in the FAT that it uses to number the clusters. For FAT16, the FAT table has 16 bits for each cluster number. Using 16 bits, the largest possible number is 65,535 (binary 1111 1111 1111 1111). Therefore, it is not possible to have more than 65,535 clusters when using FAT16. Consequently, the number of sectors assigned to each cluster must be large in order to accommodate a large logical drive.

FAT32

Beginning with Windows 95 OSR2 (OS Release 2), Microsoft offered a FAT that contains 32 bits per FAT entry instead of the older 12-bit or 16-bit FAT entries. Only 28 bits are used to hold a cluster number; the remaining four bits are not used.

FAT32 is efficient for logical drives up to 16 GB. In this range, the cluster size is 8K. After that, the cluster size increases to about 16K for drives in the 16-GB to 32-GB range. Windows 2000/XP supports FAT32 only for drives up to 32 GB. For drives larger than 32 GB, the NTFS file system is used.

 Notes

Using Windows tools, changing the size of a partition or logical drive or changing a file system on a drive erases everything on the logical drive. If you want to resize a drive or partition or change file systems without losing your data, you can use a third-party utility. One very good utility is Norton PartitionMagic by Symantec (*www.symantec.com*). Figure 2-16 shows a Norton PartitionMagic screen from which you can resize a partition without disturbing data. This software also examines a hard drive and tells you how much of the drive is used for slack space. Knowing this can help you decide if a file system change will yield more usable drive space.

A+ ESS
3.1

A+
220-602
3.1

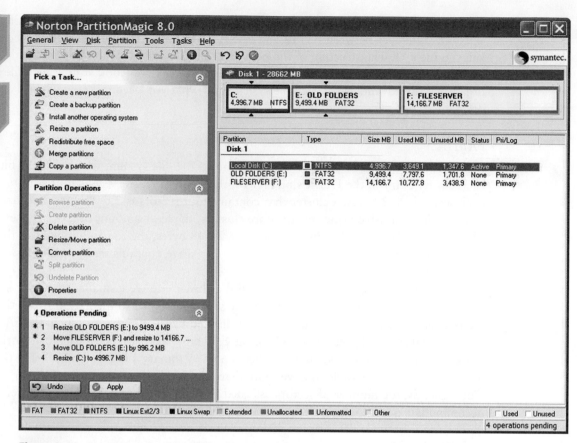

Figure 2-16   Use Norton PartitionMagic to create, resize, and merge partitions and redistribute free space on partitions

NTFS

Windows 2000/XP supports NTFS (New Technology file system). NTFS is designed to provide more security and be more efficient than the FAT file system. NTFS uses a database called the **master file table (MFT)** to hold information about files and directories and their locations on the hard drive. For Windows 2000/XP, in most situations, use NTFS, but use FAT32 if you have Windows 9x/Me installed on the drive as a second OS.

When a logical drive is formatted for NTFS, each cluster can range from 512 bytes on smaller disks to 4K on larger disks. Clusters are numbered sequentially by logical cluster numbers (LCN) from the beginning to the end of the drive. Each cluster number is stored in a 64-bit entry, compared to either 16 bits for FAT16 or 32 bits for FAT32.

The MFT tracks the contents of a logical drive by using one or more rows for each file or directory on the drive, and, if a data file is small, the entire file is contained in the MFT. As shown in Figure 2-17, the MFT information about each file is contained in one record, or row, including header information (abbreviated H in Microsoft documentation); standard information (SI) about the file, including date and time; filename (FN); data about the location of the file; and security information about the file, called the security descriptor (SD). Entries in the MFT are ordered alphabetically by filename to speed up a search for a file listed in the table.

A+ ESS
3.1

A+
220-602
3.1

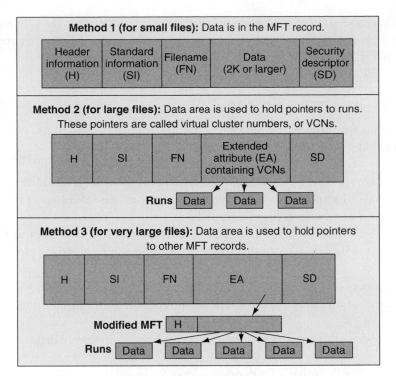

Figure 2-17 The NTFS file system uses a master file table to store files using three methods, depending on the file size

Also notice in Figure 2-17 that the data area in the MFT record is 2K for small logical drives but can be larger for larger logical drives. For small files (generally about 1500 bytes or less), if the data can fit into the 2K area, the file description and the file's data are fully contained within the MFT.

> **Notes**
>
> When upgrading from Windows 9x/Me to Windows 2000/XP, it is best to install NTFS at the same time you install the OS from the setup CD, though you can convert a FAT file system to NTFS after Windows 2000/XP is installed. To convert a FAT32 volume to an NTFS volume, first back up all important data on the drive and then use this command at a command prompt: **convert D: /FS:NTFS**, where D: is the drive to be converted. Keep in mind that the program requires some free space on the drive. If it doesn't find enough free space, the program terminates.

On the other hand, if the file is moderately large and the data does not fit into the MFT, the data area in the MFT becomes an extended attribute (EA) of the file, which only points to the location of the data. The data itself is moved outside the table to clusters called runs. The record in the MFT for this moderately large file contains pointers to these runs. Each data run, or cluster, assigned to the file is given a 64-bit virtual cluster number (VCN). The MFT maps the VCNs for the file onto the LCNs for the drive. This mapping is stored in the area of the MFT record that would have contained the data if the file had been small enough.

> **Notes**
>
> Windows NT Workstation 4.0 uses NTFS Version 4.0 (NTFS4) file system. Windows 2000/XP uses the latest version of NTFS, the one introduced by Windows NT Server 4.0, called the NTFS Version 5.0 (NTFS5) file system. The NTFS5 version includes numerous enhancements over previous versions but cannot be read by Windows NT Workstation 4.0 unless Windows NT 4.0 Service Pack 4 is applied.

In the third method shown in Figure 2-17, if the file is so large that the pointers to all the VCNs cannot be contained in one MFT record, then additional MFT records are used. The first MFT record is called the base file record and holds the location of the other MFT records for this file.

ADVANTAGES OF NTFS AND FAT

When choosing between the NTFS file system and the FAT16 or FAT32 file system, consider the advantages that NTFS offers over FAT:

▲ NTFS is a recoverable file system. NTFS retains copies of its critical file system data and automatically recovers a failed file system. It uses this information the first time the disk is accessed after a file system failure.
▲ NTFS under Windows 2000/XP supports encryption (encoding files so they can't be deciphered by others) and disk quotas (limiting the hard drive space available to a user).
▲ NTFS supports compression (reducing the size of files and folders). FAT32 supports compression of an entire logical drive but not compression of individual files or folders.
▲ NTFS provides added security in the event you boot from floppy disks:

- If you boot a PC using a DOS or Windows 9x boot disk, you can access the hard drive of a Windows 2000/XP system that uses the FAT file system, but you cannot access an NTFS file system.
- If you boot a PC using the Windows 2000/XP Recovery Console, you can access the NTFS file system only if you provide an administrator password. In fact, if the administrator forgets his or her password to the OS, the hard drive is not accessible from the Recovery Console. When using Windows tools, the only recourse is to reload the OS.

> **✎ Notes**
>
> Third-party utility software can sometimes help you recover a forgotten administrator password. For example, ERD Commander by Winternals (*www.winternals.com*) is a bootable operating system on CD that contains Locksmith, a utility that lets you reset a forgotten administrator password. Boot a Windows 2000/XP system from the ERD Commander CD to launch a Windows-like desktop from which you can use several recovery tools.

▲ NTFS supports mirroring or imaging drives, meaning that two copies of data can be kept on two different drives to protect against permanent data loss in case of a hard drive crash. This feature makes NTFS an important alternative for file servers.
▲ NTFS uses smaller cluster sizes than FAT16 or FAT32, making more efficient use of hard drive space when small files are stored.
▲ NTFS supports large-volume drives. NTFS uses 64-bit cluster numbers, whereas FAT16 uses 16-bit cluster numbers and FAT32 uses 32-bit cluster numbers. Because the number of bits assigned to hold each cluster number is so large, the cluster number itself can be large, and the table can accommodate very large drives with many clusters. Overall, NTFS is a more effective file system for drives larger than 1 GB, is more reliable, and offers more features.

The advantages of the FAT file system over NTFS include the following:

▲ The FAT file system has less overhead than the NTFS file system and, therefore, works best for hard drives that are less than 500 MB.

A+ ESS
3.1

A+
220-602
3.1

◢ The FAT file system is compatible with Windows 9x/Me and DOS operating systems. If you plan to use either DOS or Windows 9x/Me on the same hard drive as Windows 2000/XP, use the FAT file system so that DOS and Windows 9x/Me can access files used by Windows 2000/XP.

◢ Legacy applications designed for Windows 9x/Me, but installed on a Windows 2000/XP system, might not work with the NTFS file system. To support these applications, use the FAT file system.

After you have divided a hard drive into partitions and logical drives, each logical drive can be formatted using any file system the OS supports. For example, you can create two logical drives, drive C and drive D. Using Windows 2000/XP, drive C can be formatted using FAT32, and drive D can be formatted using NTFS.

HOW MANY PARTITIONS DO YOU NEED?

When you configure a new hard drive or install Windows 2000/XP, you must decide how many partitions you use and the size of each partition. You can leave some space unused that you might want to hold until a new need arises such as installing another OS on the drive.

Your first step is to remember that the active or primary partition has only one logical drive C. You can have up to three more partitions (one can be an extended partition). Each primary partition has one logical drive, and within the extended partition, you can put several logical drives. You determine how many logical drives and what portion of the extended partition is allotted to each.

For most situations using Windows 2000/XP, you will only use one primary partition containing drive C and format it using the NTFS file system. However, here are reasons to use more partitions and more logical drives:

◢ You plan to install more than one OS on the hard drive, creating what is called a dual-boot system. For example, you might want to install Windows 98 on one partition and Windows XP on another so you can test software under both operating systems. For this situation, create two partitions.

◢ Some people prefer to use more than one logical drive to organize data on their hard drives. For example, you might want to create a second partition on the drive to be used exclusively to hold a backup of data from another computer on the network. Another example is when you want to install Windows and all your applications on one partition and your data on another. Having your data on a separate partition makes backing up easier.

> **⚡ Caution**
>
> It's convenient to back up one partition (or logical drive) to another partition on a different hard drive. However, don't back up one partition (or logical drive) to another partition on the same hard drive, because when a hard drive fails, quite often all partitions on the drive are damaged and you will lose both your data and your backup.

◢ The larger the logical drive, the larger the cluster size, and the more slack or wasted space. For large drives, you might want to use two or more logical drives to optimize space by reducing the cluster size. In this situation, use as few logical drives as possible but still keep cluster size to a minimum.

◢ FAT16 and FAT32 have limitations on the size of a logical drive they support. For these file systems, you might have to use more than one logical drive to use all available space on the drive.

Table 2-2 gives the information you need to determine how to slice your drive. Notice that the largest logical drive possible using DOS or Windows 9x FAT16 is 2 GB. (This limitation is

A+ ESS
3.1

A+
220-602
3.1

rooted in the largest cluster number that can be stored in a 16-bit FAT entry.) For Windows 2000/XP, FAT16 logical drives can be no larger than 4 GB. However, you can see from the table that to make a drive that big, the cluster size must be huge. Also, the largest hard drive that FAT16 can support is 8.4 GB; if the drive is larger than that, you must use FAT32.

File System	Size of Logical Drive	Sectors Per Cluster	Bytes Per Cluster
FAT16	Up to 128 MB	4	2,048
	128 to 256 MB	8	4,096
	256 to 512 MB	16	8,192
	512 MB to 1 GB	32	16,384
	1 GB to 4 GB*	64	32,768
FAT32	512 MB to 8 GB	8	4,096
	8 GB to 16 GB	16	8,192
	16 GB to 32 GB	32	16,384
	More than 32 GB**	64	32,768
NTFS	Up to 512 MB	1	512
	512 MB to 1 GB	2	1,024
	1 GB to 2 GB	4	2,048
	More than 2 GB	8	4,096

*For DOS and Windows 9x, the largest FAT16 is 2 GB. For Windows NT/2000/XP, the largest FAT16 is 4 GB.
**Windows 2000/XP does not support FAT32 for drives larger than 32 GB.

Table 2-2 Size of some logical drives compared to cluster size for FAT16, FAT32, and NTFS

When a logical drive is first created, a drive letter is assigned to each logical drive. For a primary partition, drive C is assigned to the one volume, and drives D, E, and so forth are assigned to volumes in the other partitions. However, if a second hard drive is installed in a system, the program takes this into account when assigning drive letters. If the second hard drive has a primary partition, the program assigns it to drive D, leaving drive letters E, F, G, H, and so forth for the volumes in the other partitions of both hard drives. For example, in a two-hard-drive system in which each hard drive has a primary partition, an extended partition, and three logical drives, the drive letters for the first hard drive are C, E, and F, and the drive letters for the second hard drive are D, G, and H.

If the second hard drive is not going to be the boot device, it does not have to have a primary partition. If you put only a single extended partition on that drive, then the program assigns the drive letters C, D, and E to the first drive and F, G, H, and so forth to the second drive.

WHEN TO USE WINDOWS 2000 AND WINDOWS XP

If you're thinking of upgrading from Windows 2000 to Windows XP, know that Windows XP is generally more stable than Windows 2000. It was designed to avoid situations that occurred with Windows 2000, which caused drivers and applications to bring these systems down. Installing Windows XP should also be easier than installing Windows 2000. In addition, Windows XP has increased security, including a built-in Internet firewall designed to protect a home PC connected directly to the Internet by way of an always-on connection such as a cable modem or DSL. (Firewalls, cable modems, and DSL are covered in Chapters 9 and 10.) Also, many new hardware devices provide drivers only for Windows XP, and applications are written only for XP.

On the other hand, if you have a notebook computer, know that notebook computer manufacturers often create their own unique build for an operating system. If you are supporting an old notebook computer that was purchased with Windows 2000 on it, continue to use the notebook manufacturer's version of this OS. In general, it's best to not upgrade an OS on a notebook unless you want to use some feature the new OS offers.

For notebooks, follow the general rule, "If it ain't broke, don't fix it." If a notebook is working well with Windows 2000 installed and serving its purpose, leave it alone.

PLAN THE WINDOWS 2000/XP INSTALLATION

This section explains what you need to do before you begin an installation of Windows XP or Windows 2000. Careful planning and preparation before you begin the installation will help make sure Windows 2000/XP installs successfully and all your hardware and applications work under the newly installed OS.

Generally, before installing Windows 2000/XP, do the following:

◢ For Windows XP, verify that the system meets the minimum and recommended requirements shown in Table 2-3. For Windows 2000, you must have at least 650 MB of free space on your hard drive, at least 64 MB of RAM, and a 133-MHz Pentium-compatible CPU or higher. You'll also need to verify that all installed hardware components and software are compatible with Windows XP or Windows 2000 and you have Windows XP or Windows 2000 drivers for hardware devices. Also make sure your hard drive is large enough to hold the OS, applications, and data.

Component or Device	Minimum Requirement	Recommended Requirement
One or two CPUs	Pentium II 233 MHz or better	Pentium II 300 MHz or better
RAM	64 MB	128 MB up to 4 GB
Hard drive partition	2 GB	More than 2 GB
Free space on the hard drive partition	1.5 GB (bare bones)	2 GB or more
CD-ROM drive or DVD-ROM drive	12x	12x or faster
Video	Super VGA (800 x 600)	Higher resolutions are nicer
Input devices	Keyboard and mouse or other pointing device	Keyboard and mouse or other pointing device

Table 2-3 Minimum and recommended requirements for Windows XP Professional

◢ Decide about Windows 2000/XP installation options. Your choices are a clean install (gives you a fresh start), an upgrade (picks up previous Windows settings and installed software), or dual boot (install Windows 2000/XP to work alongside the currently installed OS).

◢ Decide how you will partition your hard drive and what file system you will use.

◢ Decide how your computer will connect to a network, including whether the PC will be configured as a workstation in a workgroup or as part of a domain.

◢ Decide how the installation process will work. You can install the OS from the original Windows 2000/XP setup CD, from setup files stored on your hard drive, or from across the network. In addition, you can perform an attended or unattended installation.

▲ Make a final checklist to verify that you have done all of the and are ready to begin the installation.

> **Notes**
>
> Remember that the requirements of an OS vary depending on which version you have installed and what applications and hardware you have installed with it. Also, occasionally Microsoft will adjust a minimum or recommended requirement.

MINIMUM REQUIREMENTS AND HARDWARE COMPATIBILITY

Before you begin the Windows 2000/XP installation, ask yourself the following to verify your system qualifies and gather up what you'll need to get it going under Windows 2000/XP:

▲ **What CPU *and how much* RAM *is installed?*** Recall from Chapter 1 that you can use the My Computer icon on the Windows desktop to determine the current CPU and available RAM (see Figure 2-18).

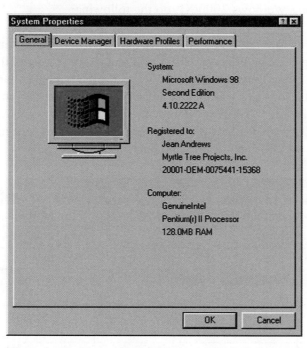

Figure 2-18 Windows 98 reports how much RAM is available; an important factor when deciding to upgrade to Windows 2000/XP

▲ *How much hard drive space is available?* To see how much hard drive space is available on a logical drive, open Windows Explorer, right-click the drive letter, and select **Properties** from the shortcut menu (see Figure 2-19). Part of the installation process for an upgrade is to clean up the hard drive, which might free some hard drive space. Even though Windows XP requires only 1.5 GB to install, you cannot achieve acceptable results unless you have at least 2.0 GB of free hard drive space on the volume that holds Windows XP. (Windows 2000 requires a minimum of 650 MB of free space to install.) However, for best results, use a hard drive partition with at least 10 GB of free space so your key applications can be installed on the same partition. For best results for users that have many applications, make the partition about 15 GB. To know how many and how large are the partitions on the drive, in Windows 9x/Me, use the Fdisk command and, in Windows 2000/XP, use the Disk Management utility from the Windows desktop. Figure 2-20 shows the

A+ ESS
3.2

A+
220-602
3.2

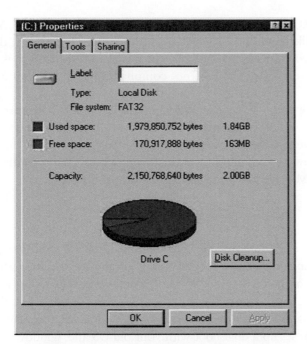

Figure 2-19 Make sure you have enough free hard drive space for Windows 2000/XP

Figure 2-20 Use Windows 98 Fdisk command to find out how a hard drive is partitioned

Fdisk utility displaying partition information for a Windows 98 hard drive. (You'll learn more about Fdisk in Chapter 6.) To install Windows 2000/XP on this drive, you'll most likely need to repartition the drive into one large partition.

A+ ESS
1.1
3.2

◢ *Does my motherboard BIOS qualify?* Your motherboard BIOS should meet the **Advanced Configuration and Power Interface (ACPI)** standards developed by Intel, Microsoft, and Toshiba, which apply to system BIOS, the OS, and certain hardware devices and software to control when a device goes into an inactive state in order to conserve power. To take full advantage of Windows 2000/XP power management abilities, your system BIOS must be ACPI-compliant. If your BIOS is not ACPI-compliant and you install Windows, Windows does not install ACPI support but installs a legacy HAL that does not support ACPI. If you later flash your BIOS to make it ACPI-compliant, you have to reinstall

A+ ESS
1.1
3.2

A+
220-602
3.2

A+ ESS
3.2

Windows to include ACPI support. A BIOS made after January, 1999, is ACPI compliant, and most likely you'll never be called on to upgrade a system that old. However, to know if your BIOS is compliant, enter CMOS setup and look for ACPI information and features. If your BIOS is not compliant, maybe you can flash the BIOS with an upgrade.

▲ *Will my software work under Windows 2000/XP?* For Windows XP, most software written for Windows 2000 or Windows 98/Me will work under Windows XP. However, there are several ways you can make sure. One way is to run the Readiness Analyzer. Use the following command from the Windows XP CD, substituting the drive letter of your CD-ROM drive for D in the command line, if necessary:

```
D:\I386\Winnt32 /checkupgradeonly
```

Depending on the release of Windows XP, your path might be different. The process takes about 10 minutes to run and displays a report that you can save and later print. The default name and path of the report is C:\Windows\compat.txt. The report is important if you have software you are not sure will work under Windows XP. If the analyzer reports that your software or hardware will not work under Windows XP, you might choose to upgrade the software or set up a dual boot with your old OS and Windows XP. (Dual-boot setup is covered later in the chapter.) For Windows 2000, to find out if your system qualifies, you can run the Check Upgrade Only mode on the Windows 2000 setup CD.

▲ *Will my hardware devices work under Windows 2000/XP?* If you can find Windows XP or Windows 2000 drivers for your device, then you can assume the device will install and work under Windows 2000/XP. To find the drivers, first look on the device's setup CD. If you don't find them there, go to the hardware manufacturer Web site and search for Windows XP drivers or Windows 2000 drivers for the device. If you find Windows XP or Windows 2000 drivers, then download them and you're good to go.

> **Notes**
>
> When upgrading to Windows 2000/XP, if the Windows 2000/XP Setup cannot find a critical driver such as the driver to control a hard drive, it cancels the upgrade.

If you plan to erase the hard drive as part of the installation, store these drivers on floppy disks, burn a CD, or put them on a network drive until you're ready to install them under Windows 2000/XP. If you cannot find an upgrade, sometimes a device will work if you substitute a Windows driver written for a similar device. Check the documentation for your device, looking for information about other devices it can emulate. It is especially important to know that you have Windows XP or Windows 2000 drivers for your network card or modem card before you install the OS, because you need the card to access the Internet to get upgrades.

> **Notes**
>
> Microsoft offers the Windows Marketplace of tested products page at *testedproducts.windowsmarketplace.com*. Click the Hardware tab to see a list of hardware device categories. Figure 2-21 shows the beginning of the list of qualifying modem cards. However, if you find your device listed, you still have to locate the Windows XP or Windows 2000 drivers. Also, just because a device is not listed doesn't mean it won't work under Windows 2000/XP.

▲ *What if I can't find the drivers?* If you are not sure you have the right Windows XP or Windows 2000 drivers for your hardware components, then install Windows 2000/XP as a dual boot with your current OS. Later, when you get the component working under Windows 2000/XP, you can uninstall the other OS.

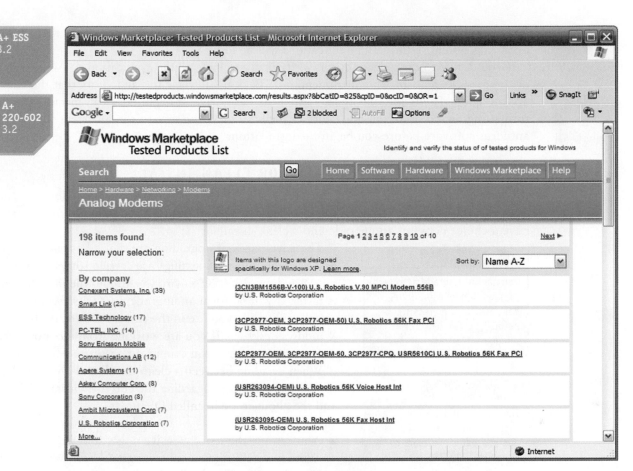

Figure 2-21 Use the Microsoft Web site to verify that your computer, peripheral devices, and applications all qualify for Windows 2000/XP

UPGRADE, CLEAN INSTALL, OR DUAL BOOT?

If you are installing Windows 2000/XP on a new hard drive, then you are doing a clean install. If Windows 9x/Me or Windows NT/2000 is already installed on the hard drive, then you have three choices:

▲ You can perform a clean install, overwriting the existing operating system and applications.
▲ You can perform an upgrade installation.
▲ You can install Windows 2000/XP in a second partition on the hard drive and create a dual-boot situation.

Each of these options has advantages and disadvantages.

CLEAN INSTALL—ERASING EXISTING INSTALLATIONS

A clean install that overwrites the existing installation has some advantages; one advantage is that you get a fresh start. With an upgrade, problems with applications or the OS might follow you into the Windows 2000/XP load. If you erase everything (format the hard drive), then you are assured that the registry as well as all applications are as clean as possible. The disadvantage is that, after Windows 2000/XP is installed, you must reinstall application software on the hard drive and restore the data from backups. If you do a clean install, you can choose to format the hard drive first, or simply do a clean install on top of the existing installation. If you don't format the drive, the data will still be on the drive, but the previous operating system settings and applications will be lost.

If you decide to do a clean install, verify that you have all the application software CDs or floppy disks and software documentation. Back up all the data, and verify that the back-ups are good. Then, and only then, format the hard drive or begin the clean install without formatting the drive. If you don't format the hard drive, be sure to run a current version of antivirus software before you begin the installation.

DECIDE BETWEEN AN UPGRADE OR CLEAN INSTALL

If you plan to set up a dual boot, then you will perform a clean install for Windows 2000/XP. If you already have an OS installed and you do not plan a dual boot, then you have a choice between an upgrade and a clean install.

> **Notes**
>
> You cannot upgrade a compressed Windows 9x drive. You must uncompress it before you can upgrade to Windows 2000/XP.

The advantages of upgrading are that all applications and data and most OS settings are carried forward into the new Windows 2000/XP environment, and the installation is faster. If you perform an upgrade, you must begin the installation while you are in the current OS (from the Windows desktop). If you are working from a remote location on the network, you cannot do an upgrade.

When deciding between a clean install and an upgrade, consider these issues regarding the currently installed OS and the about-to-be installed OS:

> **A+ Exam Tip**
>
> The A+ Essentials exam expects you to know the upgrade paths available to Windows 2000/XP.

◢ You can use the less expensive upgrade version of Windows XP Professional to upgrade from Windows 98, Windows Me, Windows NT 4.0, and Windows 2000 to Windows XP Professional.

◢ You can use the less expensive upgrade version of Windows XP Home Edition to upgrade from Windows 98 or Windows Me to Windows XP Home Edition.

◢ If you currently have Windows 95 installed, you must do a clean install using the more expensive "For a New PC" version of Windows XP Professional or Windows XP Home Edition.

◢ If you have Windows 9x/Me installed, know that upgrading to Windows 2000/XP requires that you have Windows 2000/XP drivers for all your hardware and many times applications must also be reinstalled. Therefore, little time and effort is saved with upgrading over a clean install.

◢ Upgrading from Windows 2000 to Windows XP is usually more successful because drivers, applications and registry entries are more likely to carry forward into the new OS than when upgrading from Windows 9x/Me.

◢ All versions of Windows 9x/Me and Windows NT Workstation 3.51 and higher can be upgraded to Windows 2000.

◢ If you are upgrading from Windows NT using NTFS, Setup automatically upgrades to the Windows 2000/XP version of NTFS.

◢ If you are upgrading from Windows NT using FAT16 or Windows NT with third-party software installed that allows Windows NT to use FAT32, Setup asks you whether you want to upgrade to NTFS.

CREATING A DUAL BOOT

The ability to boot from both Windows XP and Windows 2000 on the same machine or to boot Windows 2000/XP and another OS, such as DOS or Windows 98, is called a **dual boot**.

2

A+ ESS
3.2

A+
220-602
3.2

Don't create a dual boot unless you need two operating systems, such as when you need to verify that applications and hardware work under Windows 2000/XP before you delete the old OS. Windows 2000/XP does not support a second operating system on the same partition, so you must have at least two partitions on the hard drive.

Recall that Windows 2000/XP can support up to four partitions on a hard drive. All four can be primary partitions (which can have only one logical drive), or one of the partitions can be an extended partition (which can have several logical drives). For the first primary partition, the active partition, that drive is drive C. For a dual boot with Windows 2000/XP, one OS is installed in the active partition on drive C, and the other OS is installed on another partition's logical drive.

Because of the incompatibility problems between the Windows NT NTFS file system and the Windows 2000/XP NTFS file system, a dual boot between Windows NT and Windows 2000/XP is not recommended.

A+ ESS
3.1
3.2

A+
220-602
3.1
3.2

HARD DRIVE PARTITIONS AND FILE SYSTEMS

For Windows XP, this OS needs at least a 2-GB partition for the installation (but use a larger partition if at all possible) and should have about 1.5 GB of free space on that partition. Windows 2000 needs a minimum of 650 MB, but use at least a 2-GB partition. You can install Windows 2000/XP on the same partition as another OS, but Windows 2000/XP overwrites the existing OS on that partition. If you do not have a free 2-GB partition for the installation, you must delete smaller partitions and repartition the drive. Deleting a partition erases all data on it, so be sure to create backups first. Follow these general directions to ensure that partitions on the hard drive are adequate to install Windows 2000/XP:

- ◢ For Windows 9x/Me, use Fdisk at the command prompt, and for Windows 2000, use Disk Management to determine what partitions are on the drive, how large they are, what logical drives are assigned to them, and how much free space on the drive is not yet partitioned.
- ◢ If existing partitions are too small, look at the free space on the drive. If there is enough free space that is not yet partitioned, use that free space to create a new partition that is at least 2 GB.
- ◢ If you cannot create a 2-GB or larger partition, back up your data, delete the smaller partitions, and create a 2-GB or larger active partition on the drive.
- ◢ If you have free space on the drive for other partitions, don't partition them at this time. First install Windows XP and then use Disk Management under Windows XP to partition the remaining free space on the drive.

Before you start the installation, decide which file system you will use. The file systems supported by Windows 2000/XP are FAT16, FAT32, and NTFS. Here are the general directions for selecting a file system:

- ◢ Use the NTFS file system if you are interested in file and folder security, file compression, control over how much disk space a user is allowed, or file encryption.
- ◢ Use the FAT32 file system if you are setting up a dual boot with Windows 9x/Me and each OS must access all partitions.
- ◢ Use the FAT16 file system if you are setting up a dual boot with MS-DOS or Windows NT and each OS must access all partitions.
- ◢ For a dual boot between Windows 2000 and Windows XP, you can use either the FAT32 or NTFS file system.

A+ ESS
3.2

A+
220-602
3.2

WILL THE PC JOIN A WORKGROUP OR A DOMAIN?

If you are installing Windows 2000/XP on a network, you must decide how you will access the network. If you have fewer than 10 computers networked together, Microsoft recommends that you join these computers in a workgroup, in which each computer controls its own resources. In this case, each user account is set up on the local computer, independently from user accounts on other PCs. There is no centralized control of resources. For more than 10 computers, Microsoft recommends that you use a domain controller running a network operating system such as Windows Server 2003 to control network resources. (Windows 2000 or Windows XP Professional installed on a workstation can then be a client on this Windows network.) You will also want to use a domain controller if you want to administer and secure the network from a centralized location, or if several centralized resources on the network are shared by many users. How to manage workgroups is covered in Chapter 4, but managing a domain controller is beyond the scope of this book.

> **Notes**
>
> Windows XP Home Edition does not support joining a domain. If you plan to use a domain controller on your network, install Windows XP Professional.

You need to know how to configure the computer to access the network. You should know these things before you begin the installation:

- The computer name and workgroup name for a peer-to-peer network
- The username, user password, computer name, and domain name for a domain network
- For TCP/IP networks, how the IP address is assigned, either dynamically (gets its IP address from a DHCP server when it first connects to the network) or statically (IP address is permanently assigned to the workstation). If the network is using static IP addressing, you need the IP address for the workstation. (DHCP servers, which are used to assign IP addresses when a computer connects to a network, are covered in Chapters 8 and 9.)

HOW WILL THE INSTALLATION PROCESS WORK?

If you are installing Windows 2000/XP on a networked PC, you have a choice where you'll store the Windows 2000/XP installation files. Without a network, you can install the OS from a CD in the computer's CD drive, but with a network, you can store the files on a file server on the network and perform the installation from the file server. If you will be doing multiple installations on the network, consider using a file server. Copy all the files from the \i386 folder on the Windows 2000/XP CD to a folder on the file server and then share that folder on the network. During the installation, when you are ready for the CD, point the setup program to the file server folder instead.

> 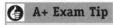 **A+ Exam Tip**
>
> The A+ Essentials exam expects you to know about unattended installations and about the convenience of putting the Windows setup files in the \i386 directory on a file server. A server used in this way is called a **distribution server**.

A+ ESS
3.2

A+
220-602
3.2

> ✎ **Notes**
>
> For a Windows 2000/XP installation on a single computer, before the installation, you might want to copy the Windows 2000/XP installation files to the hard drive into a folder named \i386. You can do this if the hard drive is already formatted and you don't intend to format it during the installation. Having the installation files stored on the hard drive is handy later when you want to install additional Windows 2000/XP components.

If you are installing Windows 2000/XP on a desktop or notebook computer that does not have a CD drive, consider using an external CD drive that connects to a USB port. If you need to boot from the Windows 2000/XP setup CD, keep in mind that most computers allow you to boot from a USB device. If you can't boot from a USB device, you can boot from a floppy disk and start the Windows installation from a command prompt.

Windows 2000/XP offers a number of options for installation that can be automated so you don't need to sit at the computer responding to the questions that setup asks during installation. One method, called an **unattended installation**, is performed by storing the answers to installation questions in a text file or script that Windows 2000/XP calls an **answer file**. A sample answer file is stored on the Windows 2000/XP CD. If you must perform many installations on computers that have the same Windows 2000/XP setup, it might be worth your time to develop an answer file to perform unattended installations. You can perform unattended installations for both upgrades and clean installs. How to set up unattended installations is beyond the scope of this chapter.

> ✎ **Notes**
>
> To learn how to create an unattended installation of Windows XP, go to the Microsoft Support Web site (*support. microsoft.com*) and search for the Microsoft Knowledge Base article 314459. For unattended Windows 2000 installations, search for article 216258. You can also search the Web site for other articles on this subject.

Another option is **drive imaging**, sometimes called **disk cloning** or disk imaging, which replicates the drive to a new computer or to another drive on the same computer. All contents of the drive, including the OS, applications, and data, get duplicated to the new drive. To clone a drive after the installation, use the Sysprep.exe utility to remove configuration settings such as the computer name that uniquely identifies the PC. Then clone the entire hard drive to a new PC using third-party drive-imaging software. Examples of drive-imaging software are Drive Image and Norton Ghost by Symantec Corp (*www.symantec.com*) and ImageCast by Phoenix Technologies (*www.phoenix.com*).

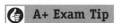 **A+ Exam Tip**

The A+ Essentials exam expects you to know about drive imaging.

Another option you must decide upon is how you will proceed through the installation process. When you first start a Windows Setup program, it will offer you choices for how you want to step through the installation. Choices might be Custom, Typical, Express, or others. You have more control over a Custom installation, but a Typical or Express installation is easier to do and should be used in most situations. You'll learn more about these options later in the chapter.

FINAL CHECKLIST

Before you begin the installation, complete the final checklist shown in Table 2-4 to verify that you are ready.

Things to Do	Further Information
Does the PC meet the minimum or recommended hardware requirement?	CPU: RAM: Hard drive partition size: Free space on the partition:
Do you have in hand the Windows 2000/XP device drivers for your hardware devices?	List hardware and software that need to be upgraded:
Do you have the product key available?	Product key:
Have you decided how you will join a network?	Workgroup name: Domain name: Computer name:
Will you do an upgrade or clean install?	Current operating system: Does the old OS qualify for an upgrade?

For a clean install, will you set up a dual boot?	List reasons for a dual boot:
	For a dual boot
	    Size of the second partition:
	    Free space on the second partition:
	    File system you plan to use:

Have you decided on a file system?	File system you plan to use:
Have you backed up important data on your hard drive?	Location of backup:

Table 2-4   Checklist to complete before installing Windows 2000/XP

Notes

The Product Key is written on the CD cover of the Windows XP setup CD or affixed to the back of the Windows XP documentation booklet, as shown in Figure 2-22. Technicians sometimes mount the Product Key sticker on the side of a computer. Try looking for it there (see Figure 2-23). For notebook computers, look for the Product Key sticker on the bottom of the notebook. If you have lost the Product Key and are moving this Windows XP installation from one PC to another, you can use a utility to find out the Product Key. On the PC that has the old Windows XP installation, download and run the key finder utility from Magical Jelly Bean Software at *www.magicaljellybean.com/keyfinder.shtml*.

2

Figure 2-22 The Product Key is on a sticker on the back of the Windows XP documentation

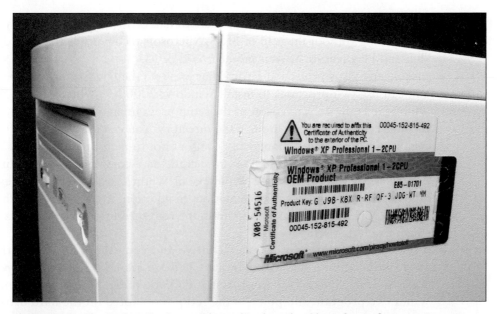

Figure 2-23 The Product Key is sometimes placed on the side or front of a computer case

STEPS TO INSTALL WINDOWS XP

A+ ESS
3.2

A+
220-602
3.2

This section explains the steps to install Windows XP as a clean install (with and without another OS already installed), as an upgrade, and in a dual-boot environment. Before we get into the step-by-step instructions, here are some general tips about installing XP:

◢ If you want to begin the installation by booting from the Windows CD in a CD drive or other media such as a USB device, verify that the boot sequence is first the CD drive or USB device, then the hard drive (see Figure 2-24).

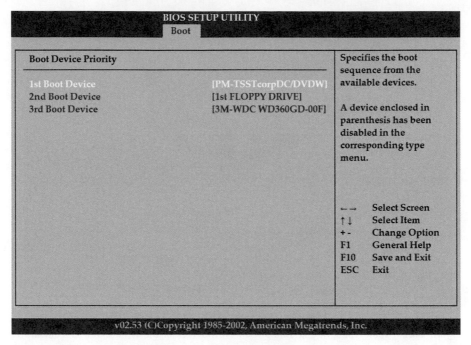

Figure 2-24   Use CMOS setup to verify the boot sequence looks to the optical drive before it checks the hard drive for an operating system

◢ Also, because Windows 2000/XP prefers to handle its own Plug and Play hardware installations without the help of BIOS, Microsoft recommends that you disable the Plug and Play feature of your motherboard BIOS.

◢ Disable any virus protection setting that prevents the boot sector from being altered.

◢ You can use two programs to install Windows 2000/XP: Winnt.exe and Winnt32.exe. Winnt.exe is the 16-bit version of the setup program and Winnt32.exe is the 32-bit version. Both are located in the \i386 directory. You can use Winnt.exe for a clean install on a computer running MS-DOS, but not to perform an upgrade. Use Winnt32.exe for a clean install or an upgrade on a computer running Windows. Regardless of whether you use Winnt.exe or Winnt32.exe, the program executed is called Setup in Windows documentation. In addition, if you boot from the Windows 2000/XP CD, the Setup.exe program in the root directory of the CD is launched, which displays a setup menu.

◢ If the computer does not have a CD drive and you cannot boot from the hard drive, you can boot from an external CD drive attached to the PC by way of a USB port. Another option is to boot from a DOS bootable floppy disk; then run the Winnt.exe program and point to the setup files stored on the hard drive or another device.

2

A+ ESS
3.2

▲ For a notebook computer, connect the AC adapter and use this power source for the complete OS installation, updates, and installation of hardware and applications. You don't want the battery to fail you part way through a process.

A+
220-602
3.2

WINDOWS XP CLEAN INSTALL WHEN AN OS IS NOT ALREADY INSTALLED

Follow these general directions to perform a clean install of Windows XP on a PC that does not already have an OS installed:

1. Boot from the Windows XP CD, which displays the menu shown in Figure 2-25. This menu might change slightly from one Windows XP release to another. Press **Enter** to select the first option. If your PC does not boot from a CD, go to a command prompt and enter the command **D:\i386\Winnt.exe**, substituting the drive letter of your CD-ROM drive for D, if necessary. (The path might vary depending on the release of Windows XP.) The End-User License agreement appears. Accept the agreement by pressing **F8**.

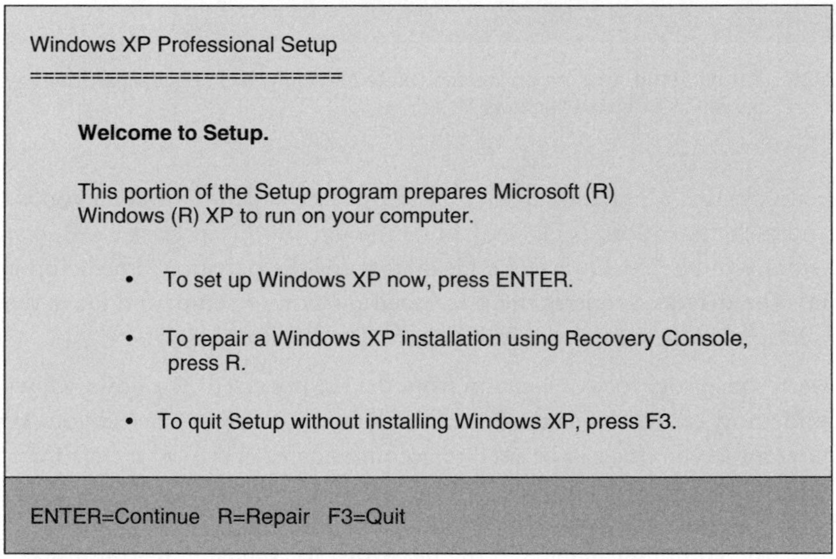

> **📝 Notes**
>
> When installing Windows from across the network to a remote PC, you can only do a clean install. In this situation, run Winnt32.exe on the local Windows computer to perform a clean install on the remote PC.

```
Windows XP Professional Setup
===========================

    Welcome to Setup.

    This portion of the Setup program prepares Microsoft (R)
    Windows (R) XP to run on your computer.

        •  To set up Windows XP now, press ENTER.

        •  To repair a Windows XP installation using Recovery Console,
           press R.

        •  To quit Setup without installing Windows XP, press F3.

ENTER=Continue   R=Repair   F3=Quit
```

Figure 2-25 Windows XP Setup opening menu

2. Setup lists all partitions that it finds on the hard drive, the file system of each partition, and the size of the partition. It also lists any unpartitioned free space on the drive. From this screen, you can create and delete partitions and select the partition on which you want to install Windows XP. If you plan to have more than one partition on the drive, create only one partition at this time. The partition must be at least 2 GB in size and have 1.5 GB free. However, if you have the space, make it much larger so all applications can be installed on this partition—say about 10 GB. After the installation, you can use Disk Management to create the other partitions. Figure 2-26 shows an example of the list provided by Setup when the entire hard drive has not yet been partitioned.

```
Windows XP Professional Setup
==========================

    The following list shows the existing partitions and
    unpartitioned space on this computer.

    Use the UP and DOWN ARROW keys to select an item in the list.

        •   To set up Windows XP on the selected item, press ENTER.

        •   To create a partition in the unpartitioned space, press C.

        •   To delete the selected partition, press D.


    ┌──────────────────────────────────────────────────────┐
    │  28663 MB Disk 0 at Id 0 on bus 0 on atapi [MBR]       │
    │                                                        │
    │     Unpartitioned space                  28663 MB      │
    │                                                        │
    │                                                        │
    └──────────────────────────────────────────────────────┘


    ENTER=Install      C=Create Partition      F3=Quit
```

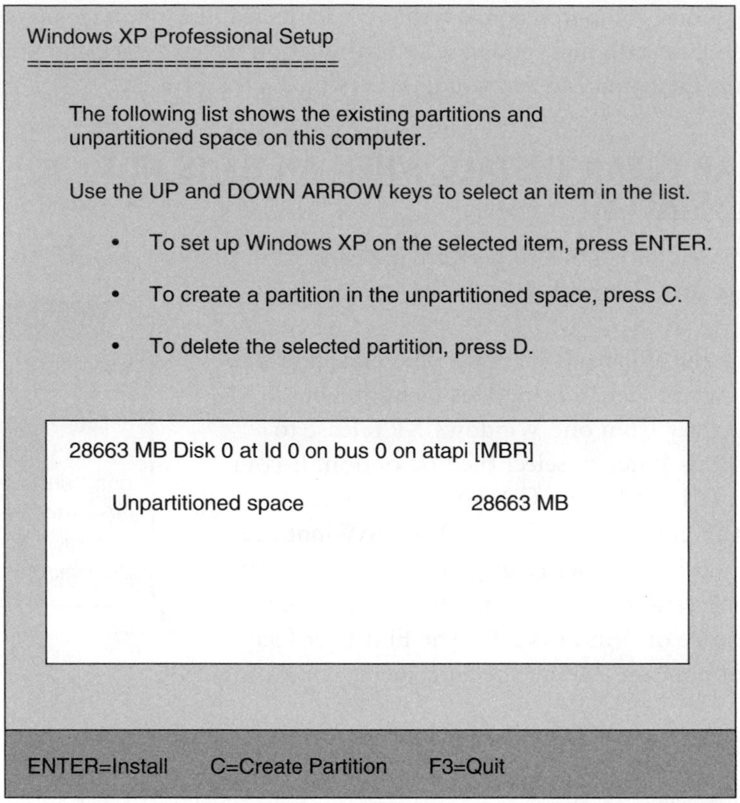

Figure 2-26 During Setup, you can create and delete partitions and select a partition on which to install Windows XP

3. If you created a partition in Step 2, Setup asks which file system you want to use to format the partition, NTFS or FAT. If the partition is at least 2 GB in size, the FAT file system will be FAT32. Select a file system for the partition. The Setup program formats the drive, completes the text-based portion of setup, and loads the graphical interface for the rest of the installation. The PC then restarts.

4. Select your geographical location from the list provided. Windows XP will use it to decide how to display dates, times, numbers, and currency. Select your keyboard layout. Different keyboards can be used to accommodate special characters for other languages.

5. Enter your name, the name of your organization, and your product key.

6. Enter the computer name and the password for the Administrator account. This password is stored in the security database on this PC. If you are joining a domain, the computer name is the name assigned to this computer by the network administrator managing the domain controller.

7. Select the date, time, and time zone. The PC might reboot.

8. If you are connected to a network, you will be asked to choose how to configure your network settings. The Typical setting installs Client for Microsoft Networks, File and Printer Sharing, and TCP/IP using dynamically assigned IP addresses. The Custom setting allows you to configure the network differently. If you are not sure which to use, choose the Typical settings. You can change them later. How networks are configured is covered in Chapter 8.

Notes

It is *very* important that you remember the Administrator password. You cannot log on to the system without it.

2

A+ ESS
3.2

A+
220-602
3.2

9. Enter a workgroup or domain name. If you are joining a domain, the network administrator will have
given you specific directions on how to configure user
accounts on the domain.

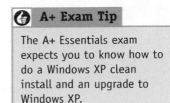

Notes

During a normal Windows XP
installation, setup causes the
system to reboot three times.

WINDOWS XP CLEAN INSTALL WHEN AN OS IS ALREADY INSTALLED

For a clean install on a PC that already has an OS installed,
follow these general directions:

1. Close any open applications. Close any boot management software or antivirus software that might be
running in the background.

2. Insert the Windows XP CD in the CD drive. Autorun launches the opening window
shown in Figure 2-27. Your screen might look different depending on the release of
Windows XP you are using. (If the menu does not, you can start the installation by
using this command in the Run dialog box: **D:\i386\winnt32.exe,** where you substitute the drive letter of your CD drive for D, if necessary.)

A+ Exam Tip

The A+ Essentials exam
expects you to know how to
do a Windows XP clean
install and an upgrade to
Windows XP.

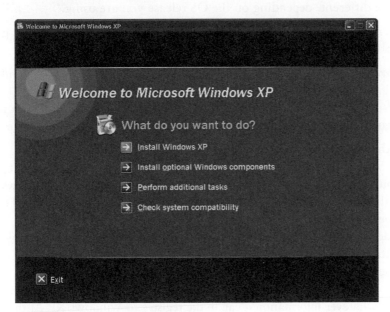

Figure 2-27   Windows XP Setup menu

3. Select the option to **Install Windows XP**. On the next screen, under Installation Type,
select **New Installation**. Read and accept the licensing agreement. The installation
process works the same as in the preceding procedure, picking up with Step 2.

UPGRADE TO WINDOWS XP

When performing an upgrade to Windows XP, follow these general directions:

1. Clean up the hard drive: erase unneeded or temporary files, empty the Recycle Bin,
defragment the drive (use Windows 9x/Me or Windows 2000 Disk Defragmenter), and
scan the drive for errors (use Windows 9x/Me ScanDisk or Windows 2000 Chkdsk).

A+ ESS
3.2

A+
220-602
3.2

2. If you have determined that you must upgrade hardware or software and that these upgrades are compatible with your old OS, perform the upgrades and verify that the hardware or software is working.

3. If you do not have the latest BIOS for your motherboard, flash your BIOS.

4. Back up important files.

5. Scan the hard drive for viruses using a current version of antivirus software.

6. If you have a compressed hard drive, uncompress the drive. The only exception is that if you are using Windows NT file compression on an NTFS drive, you do not need to uncompress it.

7. Uninstall any hardware or software that you know is not compatible with Windows XP and for which you have no available upgrade. Reboot the system.

8. You're now ready to do the upgrade. Insert the Windows XP Upgrade CD in the CD-ROM drive. The Autorun feature should launch the Setup program, with the menu shown in Figure 2-27. Select the option to **Install Windows XP**.

9. If the Setup menu does not appear, you can enter the Setup command in the Run dialog box. Use the command **D:\i386\winnt32.exe**, where you substitute the drive letter of your CD-ROM drive for D, if necessary. Also, the path on your setup CD might be different, depending on the OS release you are using.

10. On the next screen, under Installation Type, select **Upgrade**. The menu gives you two options:

   ▲ *Express Upgrade*. This upgrade uses existing Windows folders and all the existing settings it can.
   ▲ *Custom Upgrade*. This upgrade allows you to change the installation folder and the language options. Using this option, you can also change the file system to NTFS.

11. Select the type of upgrade, and accept the licensing agreement.

12. Select the partition on which to install Windows XP. If the drive is configured as FAT and you want to convert to NTFS, specify that now. Note that Windows XP has an uninstall utility that allows you to revert to Windows 98 if necessary. This uninstall tool does not work if you convert FAT to NTFS.

13. Setup does an analysis of the system and reports any compatibility problems. Stop the installation if the problems indicate that you will not be able to operate the system after the installation.

14. For an upgrade from Windows 98 or Windows Me to Windows XP, the Setup program converts whatever information it can in the registry to Windows XP. At the end of the installation, you are given the opportunity to join a domain. For Windows NT and Windows 2000 upgrades, almost all registry entries are carried forward into the new OS; the information about a domain is not requested because it is copied from the old OS into Windows XP.

DUAL BOOT USING WINDOWS XP

You can configure Windows XP to set up a dual boot with another operating system. Start the installation as you would for a clean install on a PC with another operating system already installed. When given the opportunity, choose to install Windows XP on a different partition than the other OS. Windows XP recognizes that another OS is installed and sets up the startup menu to offer it as an option for booting. After the installation, when you boot with a dual boot, the boot loader menu automatically appears and asks you to select an operating system, as shown in Figure 2-28.

A+ ESS
3.2

A+
220-602
3.2

Please select the operating system to start:

    Microsoft Windows XP Professional
    Microsoft Windows 98

Use the up and down arrow keys to move the highlight to your choice.
Seconds until highlighted choice will be started automatically: xx
Press ENTER to choose.

For troubleshooting and advanced startup options for Windows, press F8.

Figure 2-28 Menu displayed for a dual boot

The first active partition (drive C) must be set up with a file system that both operating systems understand. For example, for a dual boot with Windows 98, use the FAT32 file system. For a dual boot with Windows 2000, use either the FAT32 or the NTFS file system. You should install the other operating system first, and then you can install Windows XP in a different partition. When you install Windows XP on another partition, it places only the files necessary to boot in the first active partition, which it calls the system partition. This causes Windows XP to initiate the boot rather than the other OS. The rest of Windows XP is installed on a second partition, which Windows XP calls the boot partition. This is the same way that Windows NT and Windows 2000 manage a dual boot with an older OS.

 Notes

When setting up a dual boot, always install the older operating system first.

Earlier Windows operating systems were not aware of applications installed under the other OS in a dual boot. For example, in a dual boot with Windows 98 and Windows 2000, an application had to be installed twice, once under Windows 98 and once under Windows 2000. However, Windows XP is able to use an application installed under the other OS in a dual boot. For example, if you set up a dual boot with Windows XP and Windows 98, an application installed under Windows 98 can be executed from Windows XP. This application might be listed under the Start menu of Windows XP. If it is not, you can use Windows XP Explorer to locate the program file. Double-click the application to run it from Windows XP. This makes implementing a dual boot easier because you don't have to install an application under both OSs.

AFTER THE WINDOWS XP INSTALLATION

Immediately after you have installed Windows XP, there are several things to do to prepare the system for use and protect it against disaster. They include the following:

1. Activate Windows XP using Product activation (how to do that is coming up).

2. Verify you can access the network and the Internet. Then access the Internet and download and install all OS service packs, updates, and patches.

3. Verify that all hardware works and install additional devices, such as printers, as needed. (How to install hardware is covered in Chapter 3.)

4. Create user accounts for Windows XP. (Chapter 4 covers creating user accounts.)

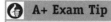

Notes

After you have set up user accounts, new users might want to transfer their data and settings from their old PC to the new Windows XP PC. How to do all this is covered in Chapter 4.

5. Install additional Windows components. To install Windows components, open the Add or Remove Programs applet in Control Panel. Click **Add/Remove Windows Components**, as shown in Figure 2-29. Then check a component you want to install and click **Next**. Follow the directions onscreen.

6. Install applications. (Don't attempt to install applications and components before you first download and install service packs and patches.)

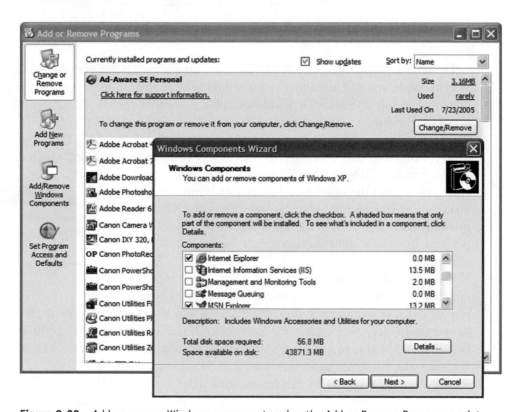

Figure 2-29   Add or remove Windows components using the Add or Remove Programs applet

A+ Exam Tip

The A+ Essentials exam expects you to know that after the Windows installation you need to apply service patches and updates, verify user data, and install additional Windows components.

7. Verify that the system functions properly, and back up the system state. This backup of the system can later help you recover the OS in the event of system failure. (How to back up the system state is covered in Chapter 3.)

8. You also might want to uninstall some Windows XP components or at least curtail how they function. For example, when Windows XP starts, it loads Windows Messenger by default, which consumes system resources even if you are not using it. To stop Windows Messenger from loading at startup, click **Start**, **All Programs**, and **Windows Messenger**. If the .NET Passport Wizard launches, close the wizard.

2

A+ ESS
3.2

A+
220-602
3.2

Click **Tools** on the menu bar, and then click **Options**. The Options window opens, as shown in Figure 2-30. Click the **Preferences** tab and uncheck **Run this program when Windows starts**. Click **OK**.

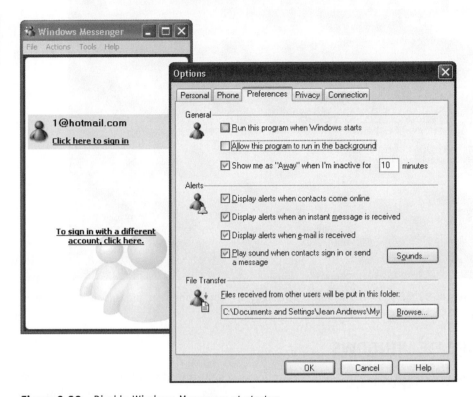

Figure 2-30 Disable Windows Messenger at startup

PRODUCT ACTIVATION

Product activation is a method used by Microsoft to prevent unlicensed use of its software so that you must purchase a Windows XP license for each installation of Windows XP. The license was introduced with Microsoft Office XP, and Microsoft says it will continue using product activation in all future Microsoft products. The first time you log on to the system after the installation, the Activate Windows dialog box appears with these three options (see Figure 2-31):

- Yes, let's activate Windows over the Internet now
- Yes, I want to telephone a customer service representative to activate Windows
- No, remind me to activate Windows every few days

If you choose to activate Windows over the Internet and are connected to the Internet at the time, the process is almost instant. Windows XP sends a numeric identifier to a Microsoft server, which sends a certificate activating the product on your PC. You have up to 30 days after installation to activate Windows XP; after that the system will not boot. If you install Windows XP from the same CD on a different computer and you attempt to activate Windows from the new PC, a dialog box appears telling you of the suspected violation of the license agreement. You can call a Microsoft operator and explain what caused the discrepancy. If your explanation is reasonable (for example, you uninstalled Windows XP from one PC and installed it on another), the operator can issue you a valid certificate. You can then type the certificate value into a dialog box to complete the boot process.

A+ ESS
3.2

A+
220-602
3.2

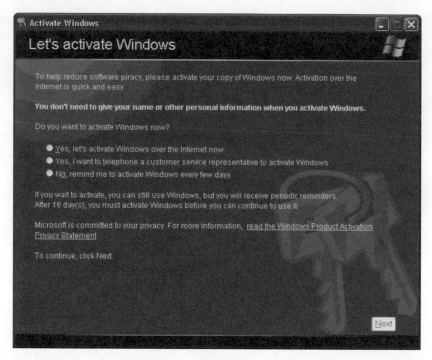

Figure 2-31 Product activation is a strategy used by Microsoft to prevent software piracy

A+ ESS
3.2
3.4

A+
220-602
3.2
3.4

UPDATE WINDOWS

The Microsoft Web site offers patches, fixes, and updates for known problems and has an extensive knowledge base documenting problems and their solutions. It's important to keep these updates current on your system to fix known problems and plug up security holes to keep viruses and worms out.

> **Notes**
>
> If you don't have an Internet connection, you can download Windows updates to another computer and then transfer them to the computer you are working on. Also, you can order a CD from Microsoft for Windows XP Service Pack 2, which contains improved security features (among other things).

HOW TO INSTALL UPDATES

To launch Windows Update, connect to the Internet and then click **Start**, point to **All Programs**, and click **Windows Update**. Or you can access Windows Update by going to the Microsoft site *windowsupdate.microsoft.com*. When you get to the site, click **Express Install (Recommended)** to begin the update process.

The Windows Update process uses ActiveX controls to scan your system, find your device drivers and system files, and compare these files to the ones on the Windows Update server. If you do not already have Active Setup and the ActiveX controls installed on your computer, a prompt to install them appears when you access the site. After Windows Update scans your system and locates update packages and new versions of drivers and system files, it offers you the option of selecting files for download. Click **Download and Install Now**, and the window on the right side of Figure 2-32 appears so you can watch the progress.

> **Notes**
>
> If you think you might later want to uninstall a critical update or service pack, select the option to Save uninstall information. Later, to uninstall the fix, again execute the downloaded file. When given the option, select "Uninstall a previously installed service pack."

2

A+ ESS
3.2
3.4

A+
220-602
3.2
3.4

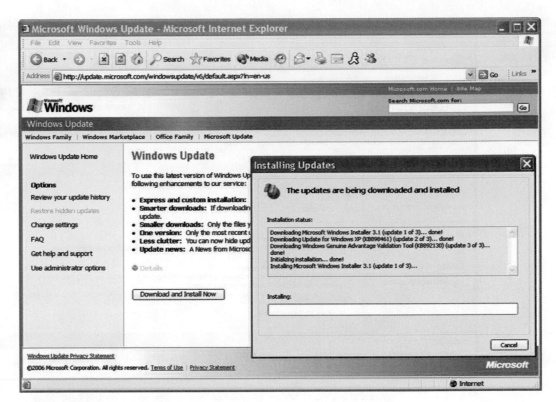

Figure 2-32 Installing updates to Windows XP

If your Windows setup CD is old or the PC hasn't been updated in a while, Windows selects the updates in the order you can receive them and will not necessarily list all the updates you need on the first pass. After you have installed the updates listed, go back and start again until Windows Updates tells you there is nothing left to update. It might take two or more passes to get the PC entirely up to date.

WINDOWS XP SERVICE PACK 2 (SP2)

So far, Microsoft has released two major service packs for Windows XP. The latest is Service Pack 2. Service Pack 2 offers some really great benefits, including Windows Firewall and Internet Explorer Pop-up Blocker. As you work your way through the Windows Update process, when the system is ready to receive Service Pack 2, you'll see it listed as the only update to download and install. It will take some time and a reboot to complete the process of installing Service Pack 2. You'll need at least 1.8 GB of free space on the drive for the installation. Alas, Figure 2-33 shows what will happen if the hard drive doesn't have enough free space for the SP2 installation.

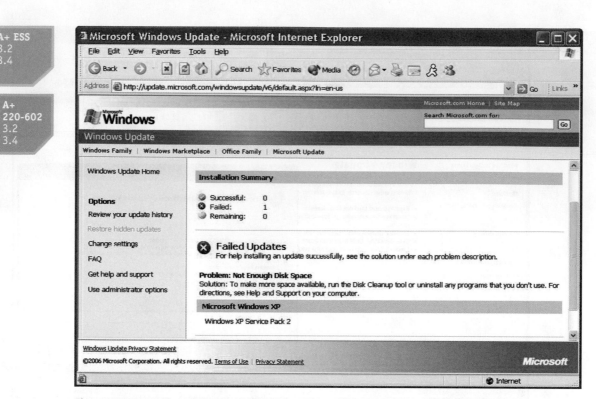

Figure 2-33 Service Pack 2 won't install because of lack of free space on the hard drive

AUTOMATIC UPDATES

After you've gotten Windows XP current with all its updates, set the system so that it will stay current. To do that, click **Start**, right-click **My Computer**, and click **Properties**. In the System Properties window, click the **Automatic Updates** tab (see Figure 2-34).

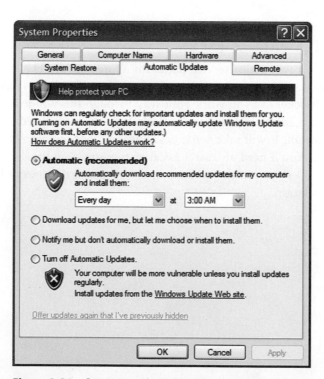

Figure 2-34 Set Automatic Updates for automatic and daily updating

2

A+ ESS
3.2
3.4

A+
220-602
3.2
3.4

You'll want to make these automatic update settings according to how the PC connects to the Internet and user habits. For an always-up broadband connection (such as cable modem or DSL), select **Automatic (recommended)** and choose to automatically download and install updates every day. If the PC doesn't have an always-up Internet connection (such as dial-up), you might want to select **Notify me but don't automatically download or install them.** This option works better if a user doesn't want to be bothered with a long and involved download when the PC first connects to the ISP using a slow dial-up connection. Discuss the options with the user. Make sure the user understands that if the update process is not fully automated, he or she needs to take the time to do the updates at least once a week.

STEPS TO INSTALL WINDOWS 2000

A+ ESS
3.2

A+
220-602
3.2

In this section, you'll learn about the difference in the installation processes between Windows XP and Windows 2000. A clean install, upgrade, and dual-boot installation of Windows 2000 use the same installation programs as does Windows XP: the 16-bit Winnt.exe program, or the 32-bit Winnt32.exe installation program.

> **Notes**
>
> If you are having problems with Windows Setup detecting your hard drive, the problem might be out-of-date BIOS. Try flashing BIOS and then attempting the Windows installation again. To flash the BIOS, download the BIOS update from the Web site of the motherboard manufacturer and carefully follow the directions on the site. However, be certain the update is the exact match for the BIOS on your motherboard.

> **A+ Tip**
>
> The A+ Essentials exam expects you. To know how to perform a clean install of Windows 2000 Professional.

CLEAN INSTALLATION

The Windows 2000 package comes with documentation and a CD. For United States distributions, the package includes a floppy disk to provide 128-bit data encryption. (This disk is not included in distributions to other countries because of laws that prohibit 128-bit data encryption software from leaving the United States.)

If your PC is capable of booting from a CD, then insert the CD and turn on the PC. The Welcome to Setup screen appears (see Figure 2-35). Press **Enter** to begin the installation. On the next screen, press **F8** to accept the end-user license agreement (EULA). Then skip to Step 6 in the following list of steps. However, if your PC does not boot from a CD and you have a clean, empty hard drive, first create a set of Windows 2000 setup disks to boot the PC and to begin the installation. The remaining installation is done from the CD.

To make the four setup disks, follow these directions:

1. Using a working PC, format four floppy disks.

2. Place the Windows 2000 CD in the CD-ROM drive and a formatted floppy disk in the floppy disk drive. For Windows 9x/Me, click **Start**, then **Run**, and enter this command in the Run dialog box (substitute the letter of the CD-ROM drive for D: and the letter of the floppy drive for A:, if necessary):

   ```
   D:\bootdisk\makeboot.exe A:
   ```

3. Insert new disks in the drive as requested. Label the disks Windows 2000 Setup Disks 1, 2, 3, and 4.

A+ ESS
3.2

A+
220-602
3.2

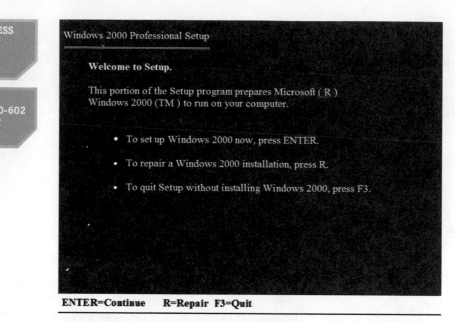

Figure 2-35 Windows 2000 setup screen after booting from the setup CD

4. Now begin the Windows 2000 installation. Boot the PC from the first setup disk created earlier. You will be asked to insert each of the four disks in turn and then asked to insert the Windows 2000 CD.

5. The Windows 2000 license agreement appears. Accept the agreement and the Welcome screen appears, as shown in Figure 2-36. Select **Install a new copy of Windows 2000** and click **Next**. On the next screen, accept the license agreement. The setup process is now identical to that of booting directly from the CD. Save the four setup floppy disks in case you have future problems with Windows 2000.

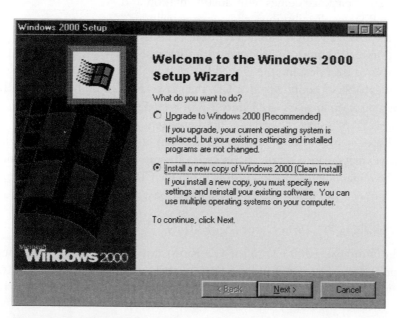

Figure 2-36 Using the Setup Wizard, you can do an upgrade, do a clean install, or create a dual boot

6. Windows 2000 searches the hard drive for partitions and asks which partition to use. If the partitions are not created, it creates them for you. You are asked to decide which file system to use. If the hard drive is already partitioned and contains a

2

A+ ESS
3.2

A+
220-602
3.2

partition larger than 2 GB, and you select the FAT file system, then Windows 2000 automatically formats the drive using the FAT32 file system.

7. During installation, you are given the opportunity to change your keyboard settings for different languages, enter your name and company name, and enter the product key found on the CD case. You are also given the opportunity to enter date and time settings and an administrator password.

8. If Setup recognizes that you are connected to a network, it provides the Networking Settings window to configure the computer to access the network. If you select Typical settings, then Setup automatically configures the OS for your network. If the configuration is not correct after the installation, you can make changes.

9. At this point in the installation, you are asked to remove the Windows 2000 CD and click **Finish**. The computer then restarts. After Windows 2000 loads, it completes the process of connecting to the network. You are asked questions about the type of network. (For example, does the network use a domain or workgroup?) When the configuration is complete, verify that you have access to the network if there is one.

CLEAN INSTALL WHEN THE HARD DRIVE HAS AN OPERATING SYSTEM INSTALLED

To do a clean install of Windows 2000, do the following:

1. Insert the Windows 2000 CD in the CD-ROM drive. If your PC detects the CD, a window opens with the message "This CD-ROM contains a newer version of Windows than the one you are presently using. Would you like to upgrade to Windows 2000?" Answer **No**. The Install Windows 2000 window appears (see Figure 2-37).

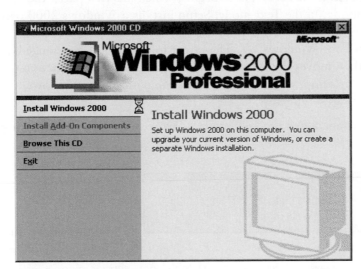

Figure 2-37   Windows 2000 Setup window

2. Click **Install Windows 2000**. The Windows Setup Wizard opens, as shown in Figure 2-36. Select **Install a new copy of Windows 2000 (Clean Install)**. Windows displays the license agreement and asks you to accept it. Enter the product key from the back of the CD case, and you will be given the opportunity to select special options. After a reboot, the installation continues as described earlier.

3. When you insert the setup CD, if the setup menu does not automatically, start the installation by entering the command **D:\i386\ winnt32.exe** in the Run dialog box. Substitute the drive letter of the CD drive for D:, if necessary.

UPGRADE INSTALLATION

To upgrade your operating system from Windows 9x/Me or Windows NT using the Windows 2000 CD, first prepare for the installation as described for a Windows XP upgrade earlier in the chapter. Then do the following:

1. Insert the Windows 2000 CD in the CD-ROM drive. If your system is set to detect the CD automatically, it runs the setup program and shows a message asking if you want to upgrade your computer to Windows 2000. Answer **Yes** and the installation begins. If Windows does not detect the CD, click **Start**, then **Run**, enter **D:\i386\winnt32.exe** in the Run dialog box, and then click **OK**. Substitute the drive letter of the CD-ROM drive for D:, if necessary. On the Welcome to Windows 2000 Setup Wizard window, select **Upgrade to Windows 2000 (Recommended)**. Follow the directions on the screen.

2. Windows 2000 Setup performs the upgrade in two major stages: the Report phase and the Setup phase. During the Report phase, Windows 2000 Setup scans the hardware, device drivers, current operating system, and applications for compatibility. In this phase, if Setup recognizes that the device driver or application will not work under Windows 2000, it gives you the opportunity to provide a new device driver or files that will update the application. Next, Setup generates a report of its findings. If its findings indicate that an unsuccessful installation is likely, you can abandon the installation. Then check with hardware and software manufacturers for fixes. In the Report phase, Setup also creates an answer file that it uses during the Setup phase, installs the Windows 2000 boot loader, and copies Windows 2000 installation files to the hard drive.

3. The PC reboots and the Setup phase begins, which has two parts: the Text mode and the GUI mode. In the Text mode, Setup installs a Windows 2000 base in the same folder that the old OS is in, usually C:\Windows for Windows 9x/Me and C:\WINNT for Windows NT. The target folder cannot be changed at this point. Setup then moves the Windows registry and profile information to %windir%\setup\temp, where %windir% is the path to the Windows folder, most likely C:\Windows\setup\temp.

4. The PC reboots again and the GUI mode of Setup begins. Setup reads information that it saved about the old Windows system and makes appropriate changes to the Windows 2000 registry. It then migrates application DLLs to Windows 2000 and reboots for the last time. The upgrade is complete.

> **Notes**
>
> During installation, Windows 2000 records information about the installation to a file called Setuplog.txt. This file is useful when troubleshooting any problems that occur during installation.

5. After the installation is complete, access the Internet and download all service packs, patches, and updates. To install updates, click **Start** and then click **Windows Update**. Make sure that Windows 2000 Service Pack 4 is installed. SP4 is the last service pack Microsoft made available for Windows 2000 before it stopped providing mainstream support for the OS. Also install any additional Windows components you need, hardware devices, and applications. You'll also need to set up user accounts. Verify that all applications and installed hardware devices work. After everything is done, make a backup of the system state to be used in the event of a system failure. How to back up the system state is covered in Chapter 3, and how to set up user accounts is covered in Chapter 4.

>> CHAPTER SUMMARY

▲ There are presently five versions of Windows XP: Windows XP Home Edition, Windows XP Professional, Windows XP Media Center Edition, Windows XP Tablet PC Edition, and Windows XP Professional x64 Edition.

▲ Windows 2000 is actually a suite of operating systems: Windows 2000 Professional, Windows 2000 Server, Windows 2000 Advanced Server, and Windows 2000 Datacenter Server.

▲ The two architectural modes of Windows 2000/XP are user mode and kernel mode. Kernel mode is further divided into two components: executive services and the hardware abstraction layer (HAL).

▲ A process is a unique instance of a program running together with the program resources and other programs it may use. A thread is one task that the process requests from the kernel, such as the task of printing a file.

▲ An NTVDM provides a DOS-like environment for DOS and Windows 3.x applications.

▲ Windows 3.x 16-bit applications run in a WOW.

▲ A workgroup is a group of computers and users sharing resources. Each computer maintains a list of users and their rights on that particular PC. A domain is a group of networked computers that share a centralized directory database of user account information and security.

▲ Of all Windows 2000/XP accounts, the administrator account has the most privileges and rights. It can create user accounts and assign them rights.

▲ Windows 2000 can run in native mode and mixed mode. Native mode is used when all domain servers are Windows 2000 servers. Mixed mode is used when a domain has both Windows 2000 and Windows NT servers controlling the domain.

▲ Windows 2000/XP supports FAT16, FAT32, and NTFS. NTFS under Windows 2000/XP is not compatible with NTFS under Windows NT.

▲ For the FAT file system, the DOS or Windows operating system views a hard drive through a FAT (file allocation table), which lists clusters, and a directory, which lists files.

▲ For the NTFS file system, information about files and directories is stored in the master file table (MFT).

▲ A hard drive is divided into partitions, which might also be divided into logical drives, or volumes. A Master Boot Record (MBR) at the beginning of the hard drive contains a table of partition information. Each logical drive contains a file system, either FAT16, FAT32, or NTFS.

▲ Windows 2000/XP supports four partitions, one of which can be an extended partition. The active partition, which Windows 2000/XP calls the system partition, is used to boot the OS.

▲ Windows 2000/XP offers a clean install and an upgrade installation. A clean install overwrites all information from previous operating system installations on the hard drive.

▲ You can install Windows XP as a dual boot with Windows 2000, because they both use the same version of NTFS. To dual boot Windows 2000/XP with Windows 9x/Me or Windows NT, you must use FAT32 or FAT16. Always install the older OS first, and install Windows 2000/XP on a different partition than another OS.

▲ Hardware and software must be compatible with Windows 2000/XP. Check the Microsoft Web site to verify compatibility with Windows 2000/XP before beginning an installation. If you need to flash BIOS, do it before you begin the installation.

▲ Unlike earlier versions of Windows, Windows XP is aware of applications installed under another OS when it is installed as a dual boot.

▲ Microsoft uses product activation to prevent the use of its software products, including Windows XP, on more than one computer.

▲ After the installation, install any Windows updates or service packs and any additional Windows components. Install all hardware and applications and verify everything is working.

>> KEY TERMS

For explanations of key terms, see the Glossary near the end of the book.

Active Directory
active partition
administrator account
Advanced Configuration and
    Power Interface (ACPI)
answer file
backup domain controllers
    (BDCs)
boot loader menu
boot partition
boot sector virus
client/server
disk cloning
distribution server
domain

domain controller
drive imaging
dual boot
executive services
extended partition
HAL (hardware abstraction layer)
kernel mode
master file table (MFT)
mixed mode
multithreading
native mode
NTFS (New Technology file
    system)
NTVDM (NT virtual DOS
    machine)

peer-to-peer
primary domain controller
    (PDC)
primary partition
product activation
security accounts manager
    (SAM)
slack
system partition
thread
unattended installation
Win16 on Win32 (WOW)
workgroup

>> REVIEWING THE BASICS

1. Name the five versions of Windows XP.

2. When installing Windows XP Service Pack 2 on a notebook computer, why is it important to use an AC adapter rather than a battery during the installation?

3. When you are trying to determine if your Windows 2000 computer can support Windows XP, list the steps to know how much RAM is currently installed.

4. Which version of Windows XP must be installed on a system that is using the Intel Itanium processor? Why?

5. How many processors in a system can Windows XP support?

6. How much free space on a partition does Windows XP require for installation? How much does it require for acceptable operation?

7. How much memory is required to install Windows XP? How much is recommended to run applications under Windows XP?

8. How long do you have to activate Windows XP? What happens if you don't?

9. What is the first Microsoft product to use product activation?

10. What is the path for the report file created when you run the Windows XP Readiness Analyzer?

11. What is the difference between joining a workgroup and joining a domain?

12. What layer of Windows 2000/XP is most responsible for interacting with hardware?

    What is one reason that interaction with hardware is limited to only one or two components of Windows 2000/XP?

13. What are the two modes of the Windows 2000/XP architecture?

14. Which of these two modes contains the NTVDM?

15. What is the name of the folder on the Windows 2000/XP CD where the installation files are stored?

16. Before you install Windows 2000/XP, how can you determine if the OS supports all the hardware on your PC?

17. What is one reason to use a clean install rather than an upgrade when migrating from Windows 98 to Windows 2000?

18. What file systems does Windows 98 support? Windows XP?

19. What is the file system that is common to DOS, Windows 9x, Windows NT, Windows 2000, and Windows XP?

20. Windows 2000/XP assumes a BIOS manufactured after what date is a good BIOS?

21. Which of the two Windows 2000/XP setup programs is a 32-bit program? A 16-bit program?

22. Windows 2000/XP is installed using a system partition and a boot partition. Which of these partitions must be the active partition of the hard drive?

23. In a Windows 2000/XP workgroup, where is access to an individual workstation on the network controlled?

24. In a Windows 2000 domain, where is access to an individual workstation on the network controlled?

25. What is required before Windows 2000/XP can provide full power management functionality?

26. Name three manufacturers responsible for the initial development of ACPI.

27. If you are installing Windows 2000 on a new hard drive and your system cannot boot from a CD, how do you begin the installation?

28. If you install Windows 2000 on an 8-GB hard drive, use a single partition for the drive, and choose not to use the NTFS file system, what file system will Windows 2000 automatically use?

29. What is the command to create a set of Windows 2000 boot disks?

30. If your BIOS is not ACPI-compliant, what should you do before you install Windows 2000?

31. If an administrator is concerned about security on a system, which file system is appropriate?

32. Can you perform an upgrade of Windows 2000 from a remote computer on the network? Explain your answer.

>> THINKING CRITICALLY

1. You are planning an upgrade from Windows 98 to Windows XP. Your system uses a modem card that you don't find listed on the Microsoft Windows XP list of compatible devices. What do you do next?

   a. Abandon the upgrade and continue to use Windows 98.

   b. Check the Web site of the modem manufacturer for a Windows XP driver.

   c. Buy a new modem card.

   d. Install a dual boot for Windows 98 and Windows XP and only use the modem when you have Windows 98 loaded.

2. You have just installed Windows XP and now attempt to install your favorite game that worked fine under Windows 98. When you attempt the installation, you get an error. What is your best next step?

   a. Purchase a new version of your game, one that is compatible with Windows XP.

   b. Download any service packs or patches to Windows XP.

   c. Reinstall Windows 98.

3. If you find out that one of your applications is not supported by Windows XP and you still want to use XP, what can you do to solve this incompatibility problem?

4. Is it possible to install Windows XP on a system that does not have a CD-ROM drive or other optical drive? Explain your answer.

>> HANDS-ON PROJECTS

PROJECT 2-1:   Preparing for Windows XP

Use the Microsoft Web site *testedproducts.windowsmarketplace.com* to research whether a home or lab PC that does not have Windows XP installed qualifies for Windows XP. Fill in the following table and print the Web pages showing whether each hardware device and application installed on the PC qualifies for Windows XP.

Hardware Device or Application	Specific Device Name or Application Name and Version	Does It Qualify for Windows XP?
Motherboard or BIOS		
Video card		
Modem card (if present)		
Sound card (if present)		
Printer (if present)		
Network card (if present)		
CD-ROM drive (if present)		
DVD drive (if present)		
SCSI hard drive (if present)		

Hardware Device or Application	Specific Device Name or Application Name and Version	Does It Qualify for Windows XP?
Other device		
Application 1		
Application 2		
Application 3		

PROJECT 2-2:   Preparing for an Upgrade

On a PC with Windows 2000 or an earlier version of Windows installed, run the Readiness Analyzer from the Windows XP CD to determine whether the PC is ready for Windows XP installation. Make a list of any hardware or software components found incompatible with Windows XP, and draw up a plan for getting the system ready for an XP upgrade.

PROJECT 2-3:   Updating Windows

On a Windows XP system connected to the Internet, click **Start, All Programs,** and **Windows Update.** This takes you to the Microsoft Web site, which searches your system and recommends Windows XP updates. Print the Web page showing a list of recommended updates. For a lab PC, don't perform the updates unless you have your instructor's permission.

PROJECT 2-4:   Installing Windows Components

Using Windows XP, log on with Administrator privileges and install a Windows component. What component did you install? List the steps you used to install the component.

PROJECT 2-5:   Using the Internet for Problem Solving

Access the *support.microsoft.com* Web site for Windows XP support. Print one example of an article from the Knowledge Base that addresses a problem when installing Windows XP.

PROJECT 2-6:   Installing Windows XP

Prepare your hard drive for a clean installation of Windows XP by formatting the hard drive. Follow the instructions in the chapter to install Windows XP. Write down each decision you had to make as you performed the installation. If you get any error messages during the installation, write them down and list the steps you took to recover from the error. How long did the installation take?

 Caution

This project will erase everything on your hard drive. Do not do it if you have important data on the hard drive.

>> *REAL PROBLEMS, REAL SOLUTIONS*

REAL PROBLEM 2-1:   A Corrupted Windows Installation

As a PC support technician for a small organization, it's your job to support the PCs, the small network, and the users. One of your coworkers, Jason, comes to you in a panic. His Windows XP system won't boot, and he has lots of important data files in several locations on the drive. He has no idea in which folder some of the files are located. Besides the applications data he's currently working on, he's especially concerned about losing e-mail addresses, e-mail, and his Internet Explorer Favorites links.

After trying everything you know about recovering Windows XP, you conclude the OS is corrupted beyond repair. Based on what you have learned in this chapter, list the steps you would take to reinstall Windows XP and recover all the data that Jason needs.

REAL PROBLEM 2-2:   Troubleshooting an Upgrade

Your friend, Thomas, has upgraded his Windows 2000 desktop computer to Windows XP. After the installation, he made many unsuccessful attempts to connect to the Internet using his dial-up modem. The modem just refuses to work, and he has turned to you for help. He tells you the internal modem came installed on the original PC and is a Smart Link 56K modem by Uniwill Computer Corporation. Do the following to plan your troubleshooting approach:

1. List the questions you should ask Thomas to help diagnose the problem.

2. List the steps you would take if you were sitting at the computer solving the problem.

3. What do you think is the source of the problem? Explain your answer.

Maintaining Windows 2000/XP

In the last chapter, you learned about the Windows 2000/XP architecture and how to install Windows 2000/XP. This chapter covers supporting and maintaining Windows 2000/XP, including installing and supporting hardware and applications, protecting and maintaining Windows system files, and optimizing the OS. As a support technician, because you might be called on to edit the Windows registry, you'll also learn about the registry and how to safely edit it manually. In the chapter, we use Windows XP as our primary OS, but, as you read, know that we'll point out any differences between Windows XP and Windows 2000 so that you can use this chapter to study both these operating systems. As you read, you might consider following the steps in the chapter first using a Windows XP system and then going through the chapter again using a Windows 2000 system.

SUPPORTING HARDWARE AND APPLICATIONS

This section discusses how to install hardware with Windows 2000/XP. Because hard drives are installed differently than other devices, you'll learn about the special tools and methods used to install hard drives. Then we'll discuss what to do when you have a problem with a hardware device using Windows. Next, you'll learn how to install applications including special considerations for legacy applications. You'll also learn about some additional Windows tools to monitor and manage hardware and applications. By the time you finish this section of the chapter, you should know how to support hardware and applications using Windows 2000/XP.

A+ ESS
3.2
3.3

A+
220-602
3.1

INSTALLING HARDWARE UNDER WINDOWS 2000/XP

Only administrators can install a hardware device if any type of user input is required. Any user can install a hardware device only if the following are true: the device drivers can be installed without user input, all files necessary for a complete installation are present, the drivers have been digitally signed (**digital signatures** are digital codes that can be used to authenticate the source of files), and there are no errors during installation. If one of these conditions is not met, someone logged onto the system with administrator privileges must do the installation. How to create a user account and assign administrative privileges to that account are covered in Chapter 4.

To install a hardware device, it's best to use the device drivers written specifically for the OS (Windows XP or Windows 2000). If your hardware device comes bundled with drivers for Windows 2000/XP on CD or floppy disk, use those drivers. If the drivers are not written for your specific OS (2000 or XP), go to the manufacturer's Web site to download the correct drivers. Look for a Download or Support link on the home page or search on the device. Figure 3-1 shows links on the Sound Blaster Web site (*www.soundblaster.com*).

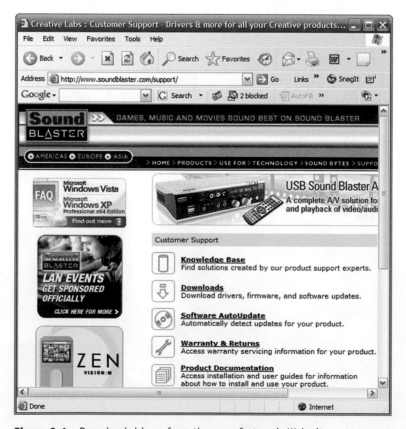

Figure 3-1   Download drivers from the manufacturer's Web site

A+ ESS
3.2
3.3

A+
220-602
3.1

If a driver is not available from the manufacturer, you can try these Web sites:

- ▲ *www.driverzone.com* by Barry Fanion
- ▲ *www.driverguide.com* by DriverGuide.com
- ▲ *www.helpdrivers.com* by Elsten Jerson
- ▲ *www.windrivers.com* by Jupitermedia Corporation
- ▲ *www.drivershq.com* by Drivers HeadQuarters
- ▲ *www.pcdrivers.com* by PCdrivers, Inc.

Here are general directions to install a hardware device using Windows 2000/XP:

1. If necessary, download the driver files to your hard drive. Don't forget which folder you put them in.

2. Read the instructions that come bundled with the device or that you downloaded from the Internet. It is especially important to find out if you need to install the device first or the drivers first. Always follow the specific instructions of a device manufacturer when installing a device (see Figure 3-2).

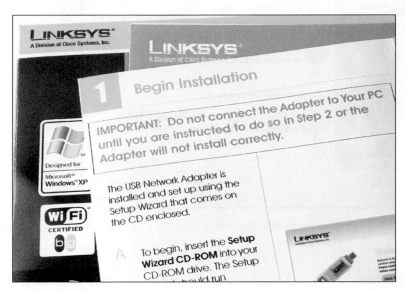

Figure 3-2 This documentation makes it clear to install the software before installing the device

3. If instructions that come bundled with your device say to install the software before you install the device, first run the setup CD that came bundled with the device. Sometimes the device setup program will tell you when in the process to plug in the device.

Next, let's look at specific directions for installing a device under Windows XP and then under Windows 2000.

STEPS TO INSTALL A HARDWARE DEVICE USING WINDOWS XP

Follow these steps to install a device using Windows XP:

1. If the installation begins by first installing the device, power down the computer and physically install the device. (For USB or FireWire devices, it is not necessary to power down the PC before you plug in the device.) After the device is installed and

Windows XP first starts, a bubble message appears on the system tray (see Figure 3-3) and the Found New Hardware Wizard opens (see Figure 3-4).

Figure 3-3   Windows XP detects new hardware is present

Figure 3-4   The Windows XP Found New Hardware Wizard steps you through a hardware installation

> **Notes**
>
> When Windows 2000/XP is searching for drivers, it is looking for a driver information file that has an .inf extension.

2. So that you can use the drivers on CD that came with the device or your downloaded drivers, click **Install from a list or specific location (Advanced)**. If you want to use drivers that come bundled with Windows, click **Install the software automatically (Recommended)**. Click **Next** to continue.

3. The next window in the wizard appears (see Figure 3-5). Click **Search for the best driver in these locations**. If your drivers are on CD, check **Search removable media**. If your drivers are on your hard drive, check **Include this location in the search**. Then click **Browse** and locate the folder on the hard drive where you put the drivers. Click **Next**.

4. Windows XP locates the driver files and installs them. On the final screen of the wizard, click **Finish**.

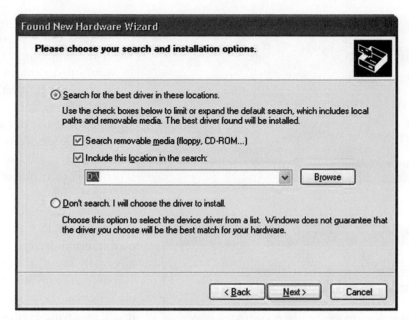

Figure 3-5 The Found New Hardware Wizard asks for directions to locate driver files

5. Go to Device Manager and make sure Windows recognizes the device with no errors. Figure 3-6 shows the properties window of a device that is working properly.

Figure 3-6 Device Manager reporting that the newly installed device is working properly

6. Now test the device to make sure it works. For example, if you have just installed a CD-RW drive, try burning a CD.

Sometimes Windows XP proceeds with a hardware installation using Microsoft drivers without displaying a dialog box that allows you to search for the driver files that

A+ ESS
3.2
3.3

A+
220-602
3.1

Notes

When a new device is being installed, if Windows recognizes the drivers were not digitally signed by Microsoft, it displays a dialog box similar to that in Figure 3-7 (which, in this particular case, is for a Netgear wireless adapter). Now you have a decision to make. You can stop the installation and go to the manufacturer's Web site to try to find approved drivers, or you can continue with the installations. For most devices, it is safe to continue the installation using unsigned drivers. To do that, click **Continue Anyway**.

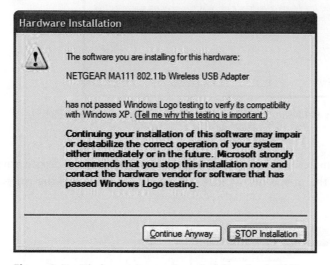

Figure 3-7 Windows asks you for a decision about using unsigned drivers

you want to use for the installation. To prevent this from happening, run the setup program on the manufacturer's CD that is bundled with the device before installing the device. Later, after the device is installed, Windows will use the manufacturer's installed drivers for the device.

For example, Windows XP normally installs a modem using its own internal drivers. After you physically install the modem, when you first start up Windows, it simply tells you the modem is installed, giving you no options. If that happens to you, use Device Manager to uninstall the modem. Then use the modem setup CD to install the modem drivers. Next time you start Windows, it will detect the new modem and use the drivers that you have already installed. Another way to install manufacturer drivers is to first allow Windows XP to install its own drivers. Then, after the installation, use Device Manager to update these drivers to the manufacturer drivers. How to update drivers is covered later in this chapter.

STEPS TO INSTALL A DEVICE USING WINDOWS 2000

To install a device using Windows 2000, do the following:

1. Follow specific manufacturer instructions to begin the installation by installing the setup CD or physically installing the device.

2. After you have installed the device, the Found New Hardware Wizard automatically launches (see Figure 3-8). Click **Next**.

A+ ESS
3.2
3.3

A+
220-602
3.1

Figure 3-8 The Found New Hardware Wizard automatically launches as soon as Windows 2000 recognizes a new device is installed

3. In the next window, which is shown in Figure 3-9, click **Search for a suitable driver for my device (recommended)** and click **Next**. This choice lets you select a driver provided by Windows 2000 or use the device manufacturer drivers.

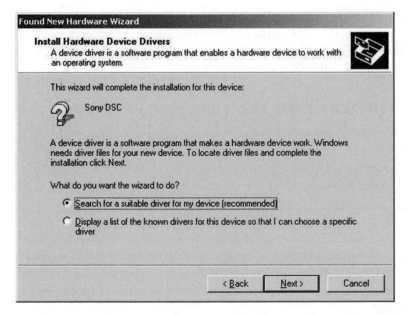

Figure 3-9 Tell the Found New Hardware Wizard how to select a driver for the device

4. On the next window, click **Specify a location,** if necessary, and then click **Next**. In the following window, shown in Figure 3-10, click the **Browse** button and locate the driver files you want to use, either on CD or stored on your hard drive. Click **OK** to complete the installation.

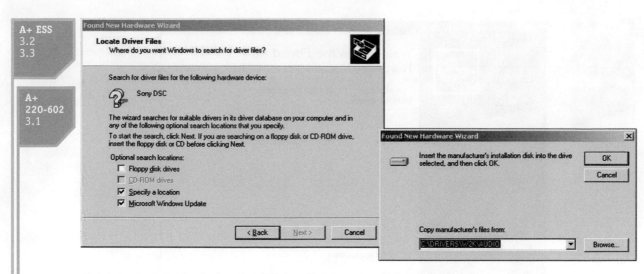

Figure 3-10   Point to the location of driver files for a new device

If the Found New Hardware Wizard does not automatically launch or you have a problem with the wizard, you can use the Add/Remove Hardware applet in the Control Panel to install the device. After the device is installed, use Device Manager to verify the device is working properly and then test the device.

PREPARING A HARD DRIVE FOR FIRST USE

Some hardware devices, such as a hard drive or memory, require special tools to set them up and manage them. In this part of the chapter, you'll learn to set up a new hard drive. Later in the chapter, you'll learn about the Windows tools to manage memory, which can help optimize a Windows 2000/XP system.

OS TOOLS TO PARTITION AND FORMAT A HARD DRIVE

Recall from the last chapter, that when Windows 2000/XP is first installed, it will create one or more partitions on a hard drive and install a file system (NTFS or FAT) on each logical drive in each partition. Creating partitions and logical drives and formatting logical drives can be done in the following ways:

◢ When installing Windows 2000/XP, the Windows setup process executed from the Windows setup CD creates partitions and logical drives, assigns letters to these drives, and formats them as you specify. During installation, you must use some or part of the hard drive to create the primary partition and format drive C. Partitioning and formatting the rest of the hard drive can wait until after Windows is installed.

◢ After Windows 2000/XP is installed, any partition or logical drive except the one on which Windows is installed can be created using Disk Management, available from the Windows desktop. You can use Windows Explorer, Disk Management, or the Format command to format each logical drive.

◢ Using Windows 2000/XP, the Diskpart command, which is part of the Recovery Console, can be used to partition a drive and create logical drives within these

A+ ESS
1.2
3.1
3.2
3.3

A+
220-602
3.1

partitions. In Windows XP, the Diskpart command is available at a command prompt as well. How to use the Recovery Console is covered in Chapter 5.

◢ You can also use third-party software such as PartitionMagic to partition a drive, create logical drives, and format them. This software can create, resize, move, split, or combine partitions and logical drives without erasing data. It can also convert one file system to another without losing data.

Notes

Original equipment manufacturers (OEMs), such as Dell and IBM, routinely create a hidden partition on a hard drive where they store recovery routines and a backup of the OS. For example, a Lenovo ThinkPad notebook computer has a hidden partition on the hard drive. To recover from a system failure, you can press a key at startup to access software on this partition. It displays a menu from which you can choose to reinstall the OS back to its state at the time the ThinkPad was purchased. If these recovery partitions are hidden, you can use PartitionMagic, which is partition management software by Symantec (*www.symantec.com*), to display these hidden partitions.

APPLYING | CONCEPTS

Windows Explorer or My Computer does not distinguish between logical drives stored on the same hard drive or on different hard drives. For example, Figure 3-11 shows three drives, C, D, and E, that are logical drives on one physical hard drive. If you right-click one drive, such as drive D in the figure, and select **Properties** on the shortcut menu, you can see the amount of space allotted to this logical drive and how much of it is currently used. Also note in the figure that drive D is formatted using the FAT32 file system. It is possible for one logical drive to be formatted with one file system and other logical drives on the same hard drive to be formatted with a different file system such as FAT16 or NTFS. To know what logical drives belong to what physical drives, use Disk Management.

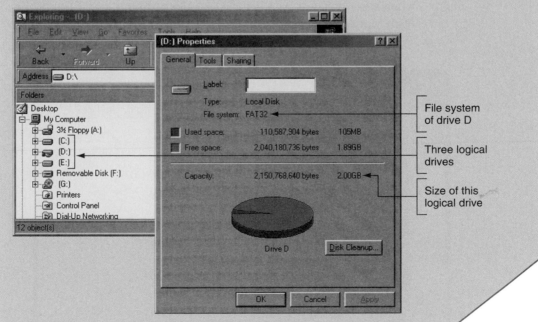

Figure 3-11 This hard drive contains three logical drives

There are several reasons to partition and format a drive:

▲ When you first install a new hard drive, you must partition it to prepare it for use.

▲ If an existing hard drive is giving errors, you can repartition the drive and reformat each logical drive to begin fresh. Repartitioning destroys all data on the drive, so back up important data first.

▲ If you suspect a virus has attacked the drive, you can back up critical data and repartition to begin with a clean drive.

▲ If you want to wipe a hard drive clean and install a new OS, you can repartition a drive in preparation for formatting it with a new file system. If you do not want to change the size or number of partitions, you don't have to repartition the drive.

Now let's look at how to use the Disk Management window.

DISK MANAGEMENT

Disk Management is a graphical, user-friendly utility that you can use to create partitions and format logical drives. Disk Management can also be used to create volumes on dynamic disks, and to convert a basic disk to a dynamic disk. Windows 2000/XP offers two ways to configure a hard drive: as a basic disk or a dynamic disk. A basic disk uses the same configuration used by Windows 9x/Me and DOS whereby a disk is divided into partitions, which are divided into logical drives. Dynamic disks don't use partitions or logical drives; instead they use dynamic volumes, which are called dynamic because you can change their size. Dynamic disks are mainly used when you want to implement RAID where files can be stored across more than one physical hard drive.

Here are two ways to access the Disk Management utility:

▲ In Control Panel, open the **Administrative Tools** applet and double-click **Computer Management**. The Computer Management window opens (see Figure 3-12). Click **Disk Management**.

▲ Type **Diskmgmt.msc** in the Run dialog box and press **Enter**.

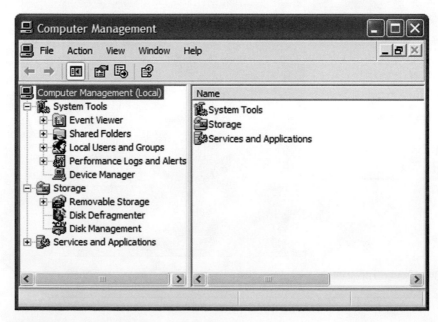

Figure 3-12   Computer Management window

3

A+ ESS
1.2
3.1
3.2
3.3

A+
220-602
3.1

When Disk Management first loads, it examines the drive configuration for the system and displays all installed drives in a graphical format so you can see how each drive is allocated. For example, the Disk Management window shown in Figure 3-13 shows one hard drive installed that has a single drive C formatted with the NTFS file system. Compare this figure to Figure 3-14, which shows a system that has one hard drive installed that is sliced into three partitions. Notice in Figure 3-14 the color coding at the bottom of the window: dark blue for the primary partition (drive C), green for an extended partition (none in the figure), and light blue for logical drives (drive E and drive F).

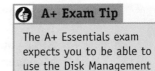

A+ Exam Tip

The A+ Essentials exam expects you to be able to use the Disk Management window.

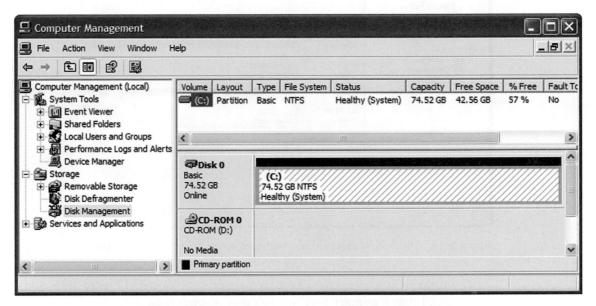

Figure 3-13   Disk Management shows installed drives, partitions, and file systems

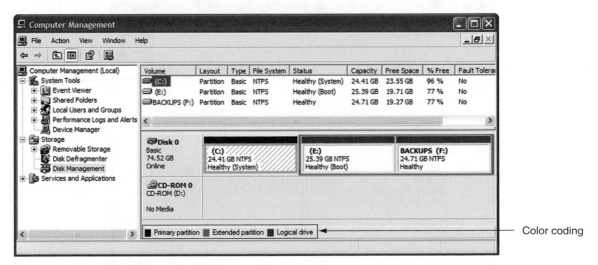

Color coding

Figure 3-14   This one hard drive has three partitions

You can now do the following to partition and format the new drive:

1. After you install a new second hard drive in the system and then access Disk Management, you'll see the new drive in the window. Right-click the new drive and select **New Partition** from the shortcut menu, as shown in Figure 3-15. The New Partition Wizard launches. Click **Next**.

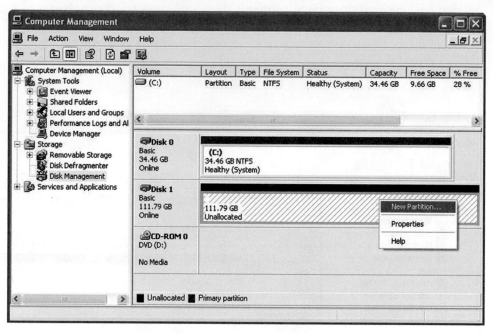

Figure 3-15   The Disk Management window shows a new drive not yet partitioned

2. On the next screen, chose **Primary partition**, as shown in Figure 3-16, and click **Next**. Recall that a primary partition has only a single logical drive.

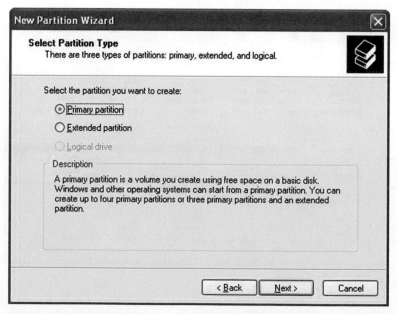

Figure 3-16   The first partition on a hard drive should be the primary partition

3

A+ ESS
1.2
3.1
3.2
3.3

A+
220-602
3.1

3. On the next screen, you can decide to include all the available space on the drive in this one partition or leave some for other partitions. Enter the amount of available space for this partition and click **Next**. On the next screens, you must decide the drive letter to be assigned to the logical drive, the file system (**NTFS** is the best choice), and the volume name. When the wizard finishes partitioning and formatting the drive, it will look similar to the drive shown in Figure 3-17.

4. Make sure you can use the drive space by using Explorer to create a folder in the new partition and copy some files to it.

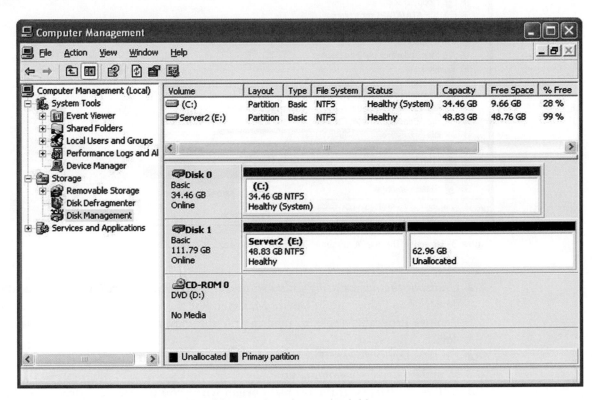

Figure 3-17   One partition created and formatted on the new hard drive

A+ ESS
1.3
3.2
3.3

SOLVING HARDWARE PROBLEMS USING WINDOWS 2000/XP

As with all computer problems, begin solving the problem by questioning the user, identifying recent changes to the system, and making an initial determination of the software or hardware problem. After you've solved the problem, don't forget to document the initial

A+
220-602
3.1
3.2
3.3

symptoms, what actions you took, and the outcome. When a device won't work under Windows 2000/XP or gives errors, you can try these things to solve the problem:

◢ *Try a simple reboot.* Reboot the system; many times that alone solves your problem.

◢ *Check Device Manager.* Use Device Manager to search for useful information about problems with the device.

◢ *Uninstall the device using Device Manager.* Use Device Manager to uninstall the device. Then reboot and reinstall the drivers. To uninstall the device, right-click the device in Device Manager and select **Uninstall** from the shortcut menu (see Figure 3-18).

> **Notes**
>
> You must be logged on with administrator privileges to make changes from Device Manager.

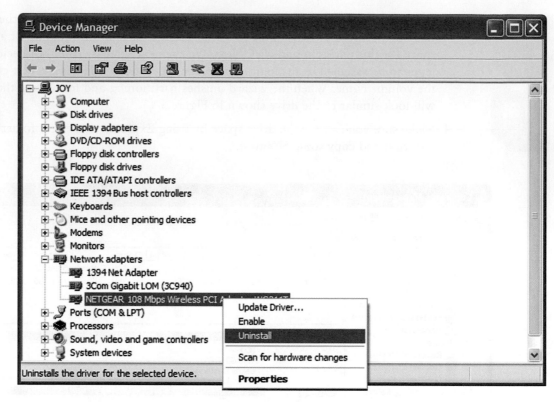

Figure 3-18   Use Device Manager to uninstall a device

▲ *Uninstall the device using utility software.* Some USB or FireWire devices and other devices don't show up in Device Manager. For these devices, you can use the Add or Remove Programs applet to uninstall the software for the device, which includes its device drivers.

▲ *Update device drivers.* For some situations, you can update the existing drivers. How to update drivers is coming up.

▲ *Roll back drivers.* If the problem began when you updated the drivers, roll back the drivers to the previous version. You can use Device Manager to do the rollback.

▲ *Check CMOS setup for errors.* Some devices, such as motherboard ports and expansion slots, hard drives, optical drives, floppy drives, and tape drives, are detected by the system BIOS and reported on the CMOS setup screens. On these screens, you can disable or enable some of these devices (see Figure 3-19). Know that, for ports and expansion slots, CMOS setup recognizes the port or slot, but not the device or expansion card using that slot. Any device that shows up in CMOS setup should also be listed in Device Manager. To access CMOS setup, press a key at startup before Windows loads. A message displays onscreen early in the startup process such as "Press F2 for setup" or "Press Del for BIOS setup."

▲ *Check Event Viewer for errors.* Use Event Viewer to check for hardware errors recorded in a Windows log that might help give you clues. How to use Event Viewer is covered later in the chapter.

▲ *Return to an earlier restore point.* For Windows XP, try using System Restore to return the system to an earlier point in time before the device installation. System Restore is also covered later in the chapter.

▲ *Verify device drivers.* If you suspect the drivers might be the source of the problem, you can verify the drivers are certified by Microsoft. How to do that is coming up.

▲ *Use utilities that come bundled with the device.* When you use the device setup CD to install the device drivers, many times the setup also installs utilities to manage the device.

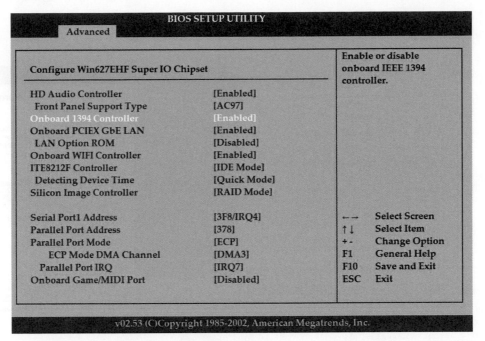

Figure 3-19 In CMOS setup, you can disable and enable motherboard ports and other components

Look for such a utility listed under the Start, All Programs menu. When you have problems with a device, look for this utility and any diagnostic or testing software the utility might offer. For problems with hard drives, you can most likely download a diagnostic utility from the hard drive manufacturer Web site.

Now that you have a good feel for the general approach to solving hardware problems, let's look at how to update drivers, roll back drivers, and verify that a particular driver has been certified.

UPDATING AND ROLLING BACK DRIVERS

Suppose you install a new application on your computer and the function keys on your keyboard don't work the way the application says they should. Or suppose you read that your sound card manufacturer has just released a driver update for your card and you want to try them out. Both of these situations are good reasons to try the Update Driver process. Here's how to use Device Manager to update the drivers for a device:

1. Locate drivers for your device and have the CD handy or download the driver files from the manufacturer's Web site to your hard drive.

2. Using Device Manger, right-click the device and select **Properties** from the shortcut menu. The Properties window for that device appears (see Figure 3-20).

3. Select the **Driver** tab and click **Update Driver**. The Hardware Update Wizard opens. On the first screen of the wizard, you are asked permission for Windows to look for drivers on the Windows Update Web site. If you are providing the drivers, select **No, not this time** and click **Next**. However, if you are trying to update drivers for a component that uses Windows drivers (such as a Microsoft keyboard, mouse, or fingerprint reader), then give permission. In this situation, the wizard goes to the Microsoft Web site, searches for updates to the driver, informs you if there is an update, and asks permission to install the update. Windows XP only suggests an update if the hardware

A+ ESS
1.3
3.2
3.3

A+
220-602
3.1
3.2
3.3

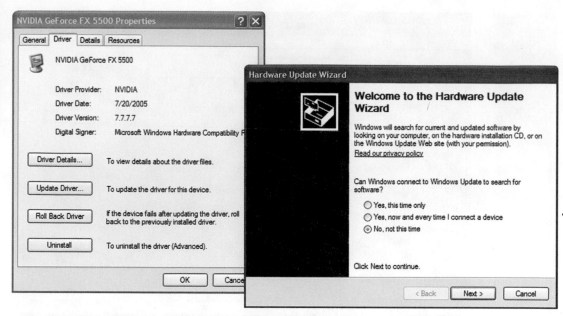

Figure 3-20 Use Device Manager to update drivers for a device

ID of the device exactly matches the hardware ID of the update. A hardware ID is a number the manufacturer assigns to a device that uniquely identifies the product.

4. If you are providing the drivers, on the next wizard screen, click **Install from a list or specific location (Advanced)**. On the next screen, click **Search for the best driver in these locations** and then check **Include this location in the search** check box. You can then click **Browse** to locate the driver files. Remember, Windows is looking for an .inf file to identify the drivers. Continue to follow directions onscreen to complete the installation.

> **Notes**
>
> If you do not have an always-on connection to the Internet and you want Windows to search for driver updates on the Windows Update site, connect to the Internet before you launch the Update Device Driver Wizard.

If you update a driver and the new driver does not perform as expected, you can revert to the old driver by using the Driver Rollback feature. To revert to a previous driver, open the Properties window for the device (see Figure 3-20), and click **Roll Back Driver**. If a previous driver is available, it will be installed. In many cases, when a driver is updated, Windows saves the old driver in case you want to revert to it. Keep in mind that Windows does not save printer drivers when they are updated and does not save drivers that are not functioning properly at the time of an update.

> **Notes**
>
> By default, Device Manager hides legacy devices that are not Plug and Play. To view installed legacy devices, click the **View** menu of Device Manager, and check **Show hidden devices** (see Figure 3-21).

You can also copy an older driver from another PC or a backup medium to this PC for a rollback. Two files are needed: a .sys file and an .inf file. The .sys file is the actual driver, and the .inf file contains information about the driver. Put these files in the C:\Windows\system32\reinstall-backups\ folder, and then perform the rollback.

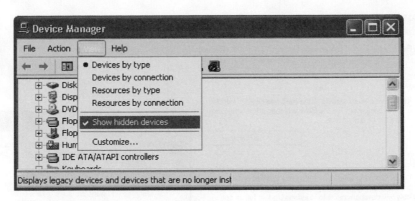

Figure 3-21 By default, Windows XP does not display legacy devices in Device Manager; you show these hidden devices by using the View menu

VERIFY THAT DRIVERS ARE CERTIFIED BY MICROSOFT

Windows 2000/XP supports the verification of digital signatures assigned to device drivers and application files, which certifies that the driver or other software has been tested and approved by Microsoft's Windows Hardware Quality Labs (WHQL) for Windows 2000 or Windows XP. If you suspect a problem with a driver, do one of the following to verify that it is digitally signed by Microsoft:

▲ *Use the File Signature Verification tool.* Type the **Sigverif.exe** command in the Run dialog box. This command displays information about digitally signed files, including device driver files and application files, and logs information to *systemroot*\Sigverif.txt (most likely *systemroot* is C:\).

▲ *Use the Driver Query tool.* To direct output to a file, including information about digital signatures, enter this command in the Run dialog box:

```
Driverquery/si > myfile.txt
```

▲ *Use Device Manager.* In a device's Properties dialog box, click the **Driver** tab and then click **Driver Details**. In the Driver File Details window under Digital Signer, look for Microsoft Windows XP Publisher (for Microsoft drivers) or Microsoft WHQL (for manufacturer drivers).

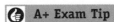

> 🔔 **A+ Exam Tip**
>
> The A+ Essentials exam expects you to be familiar with methods to verify that drivers and applications are signed.

As a Windows administrator, you might want to control what happens when you or someone else attempts to install a device that is not digitally signed. To do that, open the System Properties window and then click the **Hardware** tab (see Figure 3-22). Then click the **Driver Signing** button. The Driver Signing Options window opens, also shown in Figure 3-22. Select how you want Windows to handle unsigned driver installations and click **OK**.

A+ ESS
1.3
3.2
3.3

A+
220-602
3.1
3.2
3.3

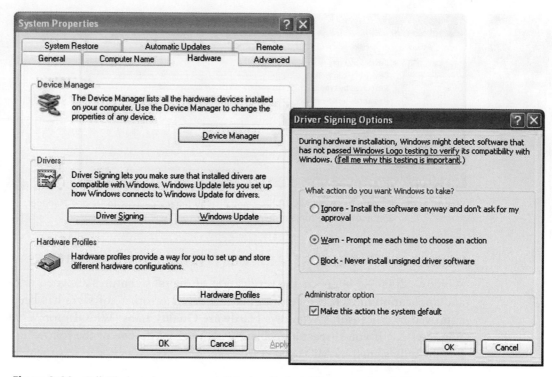

Figure 3-22 Tell Windows how you want it to handle installing an unsigned driver

A+ ESS
3.2

A+
220-602
3.2
3.3

Notes

Use the Driver Query tool to save information about your system to a file when the system is healthy. Later, if you have a problem with drivers, you can compare reports to help identify the problem driver.

INSTALLING AND SUPPORTING APPLICATIONS

To install applications and other software under Windows 2000/XP, you can use the Add or Remove Programs applet in the Control Panel, or you can run the application's setup program from the Run dialog box. You can install software only if you have Administrator privileges. An installed program is normally made available to all users when they log on. If a program is not available to all users, try installing the program files in the C:\Documents and Settings\All Users folder.

From the Windows 2000/XP Add or Remove Programs window, shown in the background of Figure 3-23, you can change or remove presently installed programs; add new programs from a CD, a floppy disk, or from Microsoft over the Internet; and add or remove Windows components.

Notes

To uninstall software, select the software to uninstall, and then click the **Change/Remove** icon. If other users are logged on to the system, the Warning message in Figure 3-23 appears. Log everyone off and then uninstall the software.

Notes

The Windows 2000 Add/Remove Programs utility, shown in Figure 3-24, looks and works the same as the Windows XP utility. In the figure, note the expanded drop-down menu in the upper-right corner, which shows how you can sort the view of presently installed programs.

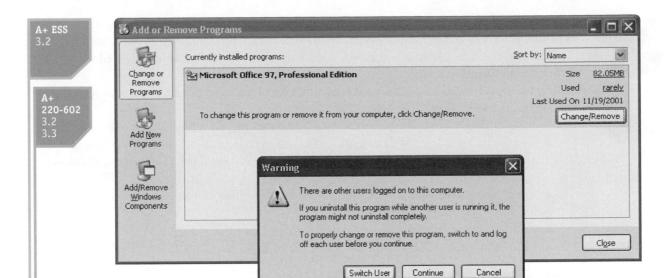

A+ ESS
3.2

A+
220-602
3.2
3.3

Figure 3-23 To uninstall software using the Add or Remove Programs applet, only one user, an administrator, should be logged on to the system

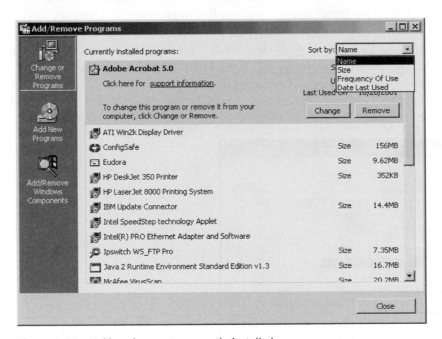

Figure 3-24 Making changes to currently installed programs

HOW TO INSTALL LEGACY SOFTWARE UNDER WINDOWS XP

Legacy applications written for DOS, Windows 9x/Me, or Windows NT might work under Windows 2000 or Windows XP, might not work at all, or might be sluggish. Legacy applications that don't work under Windows 2000 are more likely to work under

> **Notes**
>
> You can cause a program to launch automatically each time you start Windows by putting a shortcut to the program in the Startup menu folder for the user. For each user, this folder is C:\Documents and Settings*Username*\Start Menu\Programs \Startup. If you want the software to start up automatically for all users, put the shortcut in this folder: C:\Documents and Settings\All Users\Start Menu\Programs\Startup.

Windows XP. Some legacy applications that you should not attempt to run under Windows XP are older versions of antivirus software, and maintenance and cleanup utilities. In these cases, it is best to upgrade your software to versions designed to work under Windows XP.

If a legacy application does not start up and run successfully after you have installed it, try the following:

◢ Check the Microsoft Web site for updates to Windows 2000/XP or the Microsoft application (*windowsupdate.microsoft.com*). You learned how to perform Windows updates in the last chapter.
◢ Check the software manufacturer's Web site for updates or suggestions on how to run the software under Windows 2000/XP.
◢ Consider upgrading the software to a later version.
◢ Use the Windows XP Compatibility Mode utility.

The **Compatibility Mode utility** provides an application with the environment it expects from the operating system for which it was designed, including Windows 95, Windows 98, Windows Me, Windows NT, and Windows 2000. (Compatibility mode does not apply to DOS applications.) There is more than one way to use the utility, but the easiest way is to create a shortcut on the desktop to an installed application and then set the properties of the shortcut to use compatibility mode. After you create the shortcut to the application, right-click it and select **Properties** from the shortcut menu. The Properties window appears (see Figure 3-25). Select the **Compatibility** tab, check **Run this program in compatibility mode for,** and then select the operating system that you want Windows XP to emulate. Click **Apply** to apply the change. Run the software to find out whether the problem is solved.

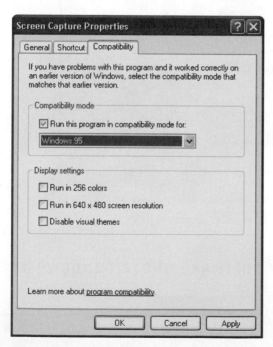

Figure 3-25 Setting Windows XP to run a legacy program in compatibility mode

If it is not solved, you can provide Microsoft with information that might help it fix the problem in some future Windows XP update. To provide the information, run the Program Compatibility Wizard. Click **Start, All Programs, Accessories,** and **Program Compatibility**

3

A+ ESS
3.2

A+
220-602
3.2
3.3

Wizard. Follow directions on the wizard screen to locate the program file. After you locate the program file, you are asked to test the application and then respond to the questions shown in Figure 3-26.

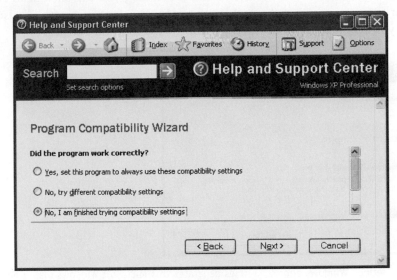

Figure 3-26 Using the Program Compatibility Wizard

If you answer, **No, I am finished trying compatibility settings,** then the screen in Figure 3-27 appears. If you respond **Yes** to the question, "Would you like to send this information to Microsoft?", then the information needed to help Microsoft solve problems with the application is transmitted to the Microsoft Web site over the Internet.

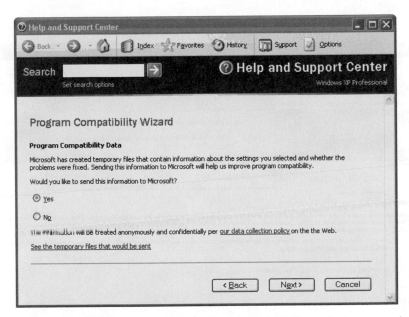

Figure 3-27 If running a legacy program in compatibility mode does not solve the problem, you can send helpful information to Microsoft

A+ ESS
3.2
3.3

A+
220-602
3.2
3.3

HOW TO SOLVE PROBLEMS WITH APPLICATIONS

When Windows XP encounters a problem with an application, it uses the Error Reporting service to collect information about the problem and display a message similar to the one shown in Figure 3-28. If you are connected to the Internet, you can click **Send Error Report** to get suggestions about the problem from Microsoft. Microsoft will also use the information you send to help with future Windows updates and patches.

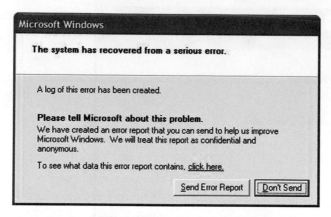

Figure 3-28   A serious Windows error sometimes generates this Microsoft Windows dialog box

After the information is sent, a dialog box similar to the one in the foreground in Figure 3-29 appears. Click **More information** to see Microsoft's insights and suggestions about the problem. Your browser will open and display information from Microsoft. If the problem is caused by a Microsoft product such as Internet Explorer or Microsoft Office, sometimes the Web site will point you to a patch you can download to fix the problem. An example of this available patch is showing in the background in Figure 3-29.

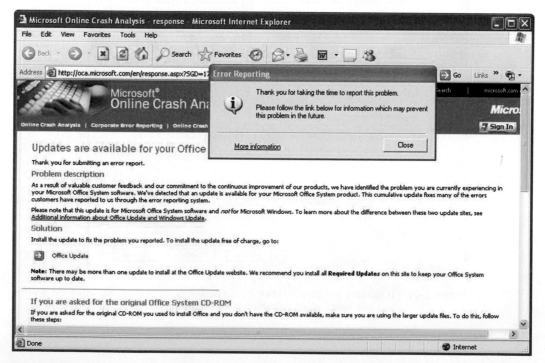

Figure 3-29   Click More information to see Microsoft's insights into a problem

A+ ESS
3.2
3.3

A+
220-602
3.2
3.3

Windows 2000 does not offer the Error Reporting service, but both Windows 2000 and Windows XP have Dr. Watson, a similar utility that automatically launches when an application problem occurs. It generates a report that you can then send to the software developers to help them solve the problem. By default, Dr. Watson stores the log file, Drwtsn32.log, in this folder for Windows XP: C:\Documents and Settings\All Users.WINNT\Application Data\Microsoft\DrWatson. For Windows 2000, the file is stored here: C:\Documents and Settings\All Users\Documents\DrWatson folder. To change the location of the file, use the Drwtsn32 command, which launches the Dr. Watson window shown in Figure 3-30.

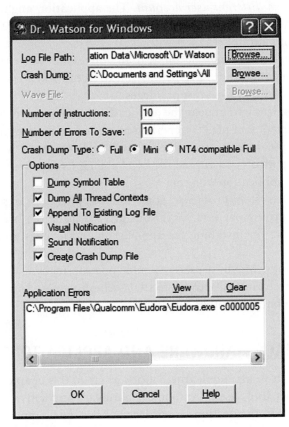

Figure 3-30 Change settings for a Dr. Watson log file and crash dump

Here are some other useful tips for solving problems with applications:

- ▲ *Try a reboot.* Reboot the system and see if that doesn't solve the problem.
- ▲ *Suspect a virus is causing a problem.* Scan for viruses and check Task Manager to make sure some strange process is not interfering with your applications. How to use Task Manager to identify a bad process is covered later in the chapter.
- ▲ *Windows update might solve the problem.* When Microsoft is aware of application problems caused by Windows, it sometimes releases a patch to solve the problem. Make sure Windows updates are current.
- ▲ *You might be low on system resources.* Close all other applications. Check Task Manager to make sure you have unnecessary processes closed. If you must run more than one application at a time, you can increase the priority level for an application that is not getting its fair share of resources. To do that, on the **Processes** tab of Task Manager, right-click the application and click **Set Priority**.

A+ ESS
3.2
3.3

A+
220-602
3.2
3.3

Then increase the priority level. (Know that this works only for the current session.)

▲ *Download Updates or Patches for the Application.* Software manufacturers often publish updates or patches for their software to address known problems. You can go to the software Web site to download these updates and get information about known problems.

▲ *Uninstall and reinstall the application.* Sometimes an application gives problems because the installation gets corrupted. You can try uninstalling and reinstalling the application. However, in doing so you might lose any customized settings, macros, or scripts.

▲ *Run the application under a different user account.* The application might require that the user have privileges not assigned to the current account. Try running the application under an account with administrator privileges.

▲ *Install the application under a different account.* If an application will not install, the user account you are using might not have permission to install software. Install software using an account with administrative privileges.

▲ *Consider data corruption.* It might appear the application has a problem when the problem is really a corrupted data file. Try creating an entirely new data file. If that works, then suspect that previous errors might be caused by corrupted data. You might be able to recover part of a corrupted file by changing its file extension to .txt and importing it into the application as a text file.

▲ *Consider hard drive or file system problems.* Some older applications expect the file system used on the hard drive to be FAT32. If your drive is using the NTFS file system, problems might occur. Try installing the application and its data on a FAT32 partition.

▲ *Try restoring default settings.* Maybe a user has made one-too-many changes to the application settings. Try restoring all settings to their default values. This might solve a problem with missing toolbars and other functions.

A+ ESS
3.2

TOOLS USEFUL TO MANAGE HARDWARE AND APPLICATIONS

Besides the Windows utilities you've already learned about so far in this chapter, you also need to be aware of several other tools useful to monitor hardware and software and solve problems when they occur. In this section, you'll learn about the Computer Management console, the Microsoft Management Console, Event Viewer, and the Windows 2000/XP Support Tools, including Dependency Walker.

COMPUTER MANAGEMENT

Computer Management is a window that consolidates several Windows 2000/XP administrative tools that you can use to manage the local PC or other computers on the network. To use most of these tools, you must be logged on as an administrator, although you can view certain settings and configurations in Computer Management if you are logged on with lesser privileges.

To access Computer Management, open **Control Panel**, open the **Administrative Tools** window, and then double-click the **Computer Management** icon. The Computer Management window opens (see Figure 3-31). Using this window, you can access Event Viewer, Device Manager, Disk Management, Disk Defragmenter (covered in Chapter 4), Services Console, and manage user groups (also covered in Chapter 4). You can also monitor problems with hardware, software, and security. Several tools available from the Computer Management window are covered in this chapter.

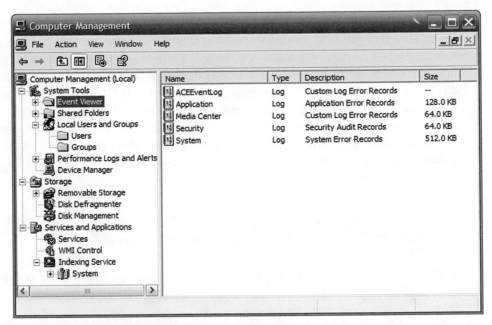

Figure 3-31 Windows 2000/XP Computer Management combines several administrative tools into a single easy-to-access window

---

Notes

By default, the Administrative Tools group is found in Control Panel, but you can add the group to the All Programs menu. To do that for Windows XP, right-click the taskbar and select **Properties** from the shortcut menu. The Taskbar and Start Menu Properties window opens. Select the **Start Menu** tab and then click **Customize** (as shown on the left side of Figure 3-32). Click the **Advanced** tab, as shown on the right side of Figure 3-32. Scroll down through the list, select **Display on the All Programs Menu**, and click **OK**. Now, to use the Administrative Tools group, click **Start, All Programs**, and **Administrative Tools**. (To add the tool to the Start menu in Windows 2000, in the Taskbar and Start Menu Properties window, click the **Advanced** tab.)

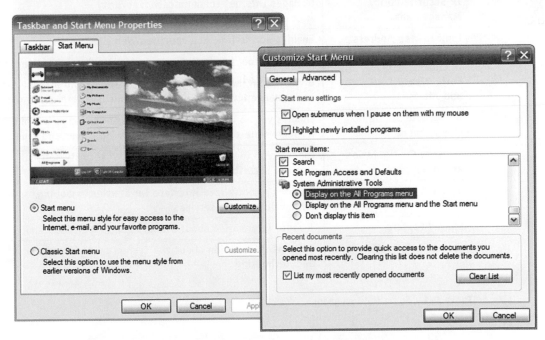

Figure 3-32 Use the Taskbar and Start Menu Properties window to change items on the Start menu

A+ ESS
3.2

MICROSOFT MANAGEMENT CONSOLE

Microsoft Management Console (MMC) is a Windows utility that can be used to build your own customized console windows. A **console** is a single window that contains one or more administrative tools such as Device Manager or Disk Management. In a console, these individual tools are called **snap-ins**. An example of a console is Computer Management, which has a filename of Compmgmt.msc. (Event Viewer and Disk Defragmenter are two snap-ins in that console.) A console is saved in a file with an .msc file extension, and a snap-in in a console can itself be a console. When you use MMC to build a console, you can use any of the snap-ins listed in Table 3-1. To use all the functions of MMC, you must be logged on with administrator privileges.

Snap-in	Description
Active X Control	Enables you to add ActiveX controls to your system
Certificates	Provides certificate management at the user, service, or computer level
Component Services	Links to the Component Services management tool, which is located in Control Panel
Computer Management	Links to the Computer Management tools in Control Panel
Device Manager	Lets you see what hardware devices you have on your system and configure device properties
Disk Defragmenter	Links to the Disk Defragmenter utility (Defrag.exe)
Disk Management	Links to the Disk Management tool
Event Viewer	Links to the Event Viewer tool, which displays event logs for the system
Fax Service Management	Enables you to manage fax settings and devices
Folder	Enables you to add a folder to manage from MMC
Group Policy	Provides a tool to manage group policy settings
Indexing Service	Searches files and folders using specified parameters
IP Security Policy Management	Manages Internet communication security
Link to Web Address	Enables you to link to a specified Web site
Local Users and Groups	Provides a tool to manage settings for local users and groups
Performance Logs and Alerts	Gives you an interface from which to set up and manage logs of performance information and alerts about system performance
Removable Storage Management	Enables you to manage settings and configuration information for removable storage devices such as Zip drives and tape backup drives
Security Configuration and Analysis	Enables you to manage configuration of security settings for computers that use security template files
Services	Provides a centralized interface for starting, stopping, and configuring system services
Shared Folders	Provides information about shared folders, open files, and current sessions
System Information	Contains information about the system that you can use when troubleshooting

Table 3-1   Some MMC snap-ins

3

A+ ESS
3.2

You can use MMC to create a console that contains some popular utility tools. Follow these steps for Windows XP (differences for Windows 2000 are noted) to create one console:

1. Click **Start**, click **Run**, enter **MMC** in the Run dialog box, and then click **OK**. An empty console window appears, as shown in Figure 3-33.

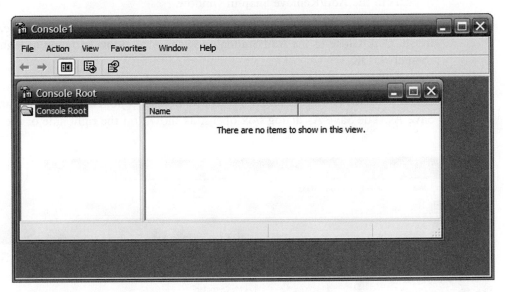

Figure 3-33 An empty console

2. Click **File** on the menu bar (in Windows 2000, click **Console**), and then click **Add/Remove Snap-in**. The Add/Remove Snap-in window opens, as shown on the left side of Figure 3-34. This window on the left is empty because no snap-ins have been added to the console.

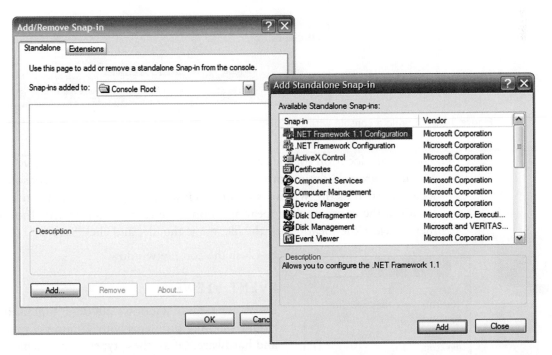

Figure 3-34 The Add/Remove Snap-in window

3. Click **Add**. You see a list of snap-ins that can be added to a console, as shown on the right side of Figure 3-34. Select a snap-in and then click **Add**.

4. If parameters for the snap-in need defining, a dialog box opens that allows you to set up these parameters. The dialog box offers different selections, depending on the snap-in being added. When you have made your selections, click **Finish**. The new snap-in appears in the Add/Remove Snap-in window.

5. Repeat Steps 3 and 4 to add all the snap-ins that you want to the console. When you finish, click **Close** in the Add Standalone Snap-in window showing in Figure 3-34, then click **OK**.

6. The left side of Figure 3-35 shows a console with four snap-ins added. To save the console, click File on the menu bar (for Windows 2000, click **Console**), and then click **Save As**. The Save As dialog box opens, as shown on the right side of the figure.

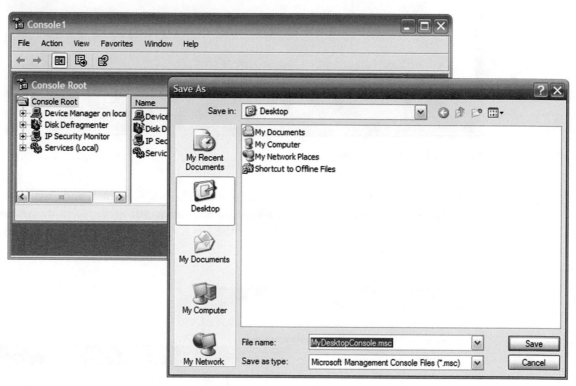

Figure 3-35 Saving a console with four snap-ins

7. The default location for the console file is C:\Documents and Settings*username*\Start Menu\Programs\Administrative Tools. However, you can save the console to any location, such as the Windows desktop. However, if you save the file to its default location, the console will appear as an option under Administrative Tools on the Start menu. Select the location for the file, name the file, and click **Save**.

> **Notes**
>
> After you create a console, you can copy the .msc file to any computer or place a shortcut to it on the desktop.

8. Close the console window.

EVENT VIEWER

Event Viewer is a Windows 2000/XP tool useful for troubleshooting problems with Windows, applications, and hardware. Of all these types of problems, it is most useful when troubleshooting problems with hardware.

A+ ESS
3.2
3.3

A+
220-602
3.1
3.3

Event Viewer displays logs of significant events such as a hardware or network failure, OS error messages, a device or service that has failed to start, or General Protection Faults.

Event Viewer (Eventvwr.msc) is a Computer Management console snap-in. You can open it by using the Computer Management window, by entering **Eventvwr.msc** in the Run dialog box, or by clicking **Start**, **All Programs** (for Windows 2000, **Programs**), **Administrative Tools**, **Event Viewer**. Either way, the window in Figure 3-36 opens.

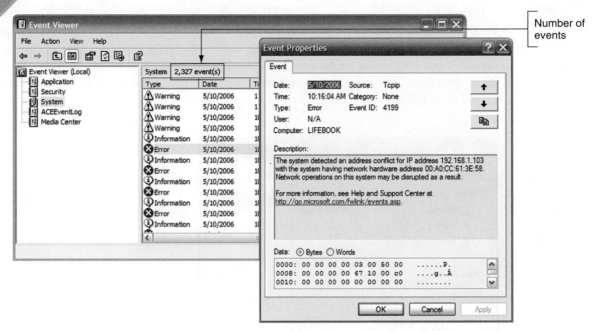

Figure 3-36 Use Event Viewer to see information about events with applications, security, and the system

Depending on the OS version and original equipment manufacturer (OEM) features, Event Viewer shows three or more logs. The first three logs in Figure 3-36 are standard to all systems. They are described next:

- ▲ *The application log* records application events. The events recorded depend on what the developer of the application set to trigger a log entry. One type of event recorded in this log is an Error Reporting event, which you learned about earlier in the chapter.
- ▲ *The security log* records events based on audit policies, which an administrator sets to monitor user activity such as successful or unsuccessful attempts to access a file or log on to the system. Only an administrator can view this log.
- ▲ *The system log* records events triggered by Windows components, such as a device driver failing to load during the boot process. Windows 2000/XP sets which events are recorded in this log. All users can access this log file.

The security log records security audit events. You'll learn more about these audit events in Chapter 10. The system and application logs can record three types of events:

- ▲ *Information* events are recorded when a driver, service, or application functions successfully.
- ▲ *Warning* events are recorded when something happens that may indicate a future problem but does not necessarily indicate that something is presently wrong with the system. For example, low disk space might trigger a warning event.

A+ ESS
3.2
3.3

A+
220-602
3.1
3.3

◢ *Error* events are recorded when something goes wrong with the system, such as a necessary component failing to load, data getting lost or becoming corrupted, or a system or application function ceasing to operate.

To view a log within Event Viewer, click the log that you want to view in the left pane. This generates a summary of events that appears in the right pane. Double-click a specific event to see details about it (refer back to Figure 3-36).

Notice in the figure that over 2,000 events are listed in the system log. That can be a lot of events to read! To save time, you might want to view only certain events and not the entire list to find what you're looking for. Fortunately, you can filter events so only certain ones are listed. To do that, right-click a log in the left pane and select **Properties** from the shortcut menu. The log's Properties window appears. Click the **Filter** tab (see Figure 3-37).

Figure 3-37   Criteria to filter events in Event Viewer

To filter events, you can use several event characteristics to build these filters, which are listed in Table 3-2.

Event Characteristics	Description
Event type	The type of event, such as information, error, or warning
Event source	The application, driver, or service that triggered the event
Category	The category that the event falls under, such as an attempt to log on to the system or access a program
Event ID	A number that identifies the event and makes tracking events easier for support personnel

Table 3-2   Event characteristics that can be used to filter events

3

A+ ESS
3.2
3.3

A+
220-602
3.1
3.3

Event Characteristics	Description
User	The logon name for a user
Computer	The name of a computer on the system
From: To:	The range of events that you want to view. You can view the events from first to last event, or you can view all events that occurred on a specific date and in a specific time range.

Table 3-2 Event characteristics that can be used to filter events (continued)

Another way you can avoid a ballooning log file is to set a size limit and specify what happens when the log reaches this limit. If you right-click a log, select **Properties** on the shortcut menu, and click the **General** tab, you can set the maximum size of the log in megabytes (as well as view general information about the log). You can set the log to over-write events as needed, overwrite events that are more than a specified number of days old, or not overwrite events at all. Select this last option when system security is high and you do not want to lose any event information. If you select this option, the system simply stops recording events when the log file reaches the maximum size (see Figure 3-38).

Figure 3-38 View information about a log, including maximum size of the log file, in the System Log Properties dialog box

To allow the system to record events in the log after a log reaches maximum size, you have to review the events and clear the log manually, either by clicking the **Clear Log** button in the Properties dialog box or selecting **Clear All Events** from the Action menu. Before clearing the log, Event Viewer gives you a chance to save it.

Event Viewer can be useful when you suspect someone is attempting to illegally log onto a system and you want to view login attempts. But Event Viewer is most useful in solving intermittent hardware problems. For example, on our network we have a file server and

A+ ESS
3.2
3.3

A+
220-602
3.1
3.3

A+ ESS
3.2

several people in the office update Microsoft Word documents stored on the server. For weeks people complained about these Word documents getting corrupted. We downloaded the latest patches for Windows and Microsoft Office and scanned for viruses thinking that the problem might be with Windows or the application. Then we suspected a corrupted template file for building the Word documents. But nothing we did solved our problem of corrupted Word documents. Then one day someone thought to check Event Viewer on the file server. The Event Viewer had faithfully been recording errors when writing to the hard drive. What we had suspected to be a software problem was, in fact, a failing hard drive, which was full of bad sectors. We replaced the drive and the problem went away.

WINDOWS 2000/XP SUPPORT TOOLS AND DEPENDENCY WALKER

Windows 2000/XP offers several support tools that you can install. They are located in the \Support\Tools folder on the Windows 2000/XP CD. To install them, you can run the Setup program located in that folder (see Figure 3-39). To start the Setup program, enter this command in the Run dialog box (but don't include the ending period): **D:\Support\Tools\Setup.exe**. If necessary, substitute the drive letter of your CD-ROM drive for D in the command line. In this folder, you can also find some documentation files about the support tools.

Figure 3-39 The \Support\Tools folder on the Windows XP CD

Notes

A file with an .htm or .html file extension is a hypertext markup language (HTML) file. A **hypertext** file is a text file that contains hypertext tags to format the file and create hyperlinks to different points in the file or to other files. Hypertext files are used on the Web and are read and displayed using a Web browser such as Microsoft Internet Explorer or Netscape Navigator. To read a hypertext file using Windows Explorer, double-click the filename; your default browser will open the file.

One Support Tool utility is Dependency Walker (Depends.exe), which lists all the files used by an application. It can be useful when you've installed an application, but the application doesn't work correctly. Go to a computer that has the application

**A+ ESS
3.2**

installed correctly and use Dependency Walker to get a report of files used by the application. Then use Dependency Walker to get the same report on the computer with the problem. You can then compare the two reports, looking for DLL files that are missing on the bad installation, are not the correct size, or are incorrectly date-stamped. A DLL file is a Windows file with a .dll file extension that an application uses to relate to Windows. Dependency Walker can also be useful if an application is giving General Protection Fault errors. Compare a report of files the application uses on a good computer to files used on the computer giving errors.

To use Windows XP Dependency Walker, click **Start**, point to **All Programs** and **Windows Support Tools**, and then click **Command Prompt**. A Command Prompt window opens showing the current directory as C:\Program Files\Support Tools. To see a list of tools, type the command **Dir** and press **Enter**. To use Dependency Walker, type the command **Depends** and press **Enter**. The Dependency Walker window opens. When you click **File** and **Open** and then navigate to a program file and click **Open**, the Dependency Walker window displays a list of files on which this program is dependent. Figure 3-40 shows the dependencies for the Notepad.exe program.

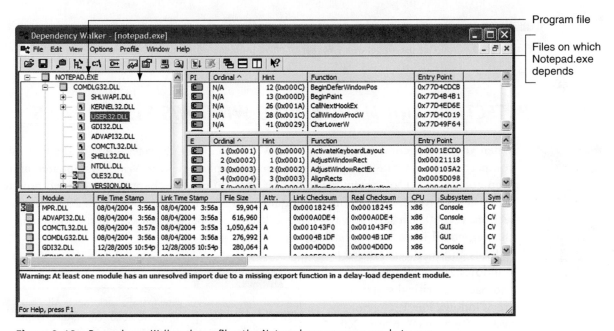

Figure 3-40 Dependency Walker shows files the Notepad.exe program needs to run

To use Windows 2000 Dependency Walker, click **Start**, point to **Programs, Windows 2000 Support Tools**, and **Tools**, and then click **Dependency Walker**. Figure 3-41 shows a Dependency Walker window. Click **File** on the menu bar, click **Open**, and then select the main executable file for an application. In the figure, Apache.exe is selected. Apache is a popular Web server application. The window lists all supporting files that Apache.exe uses and how they depend on one another.

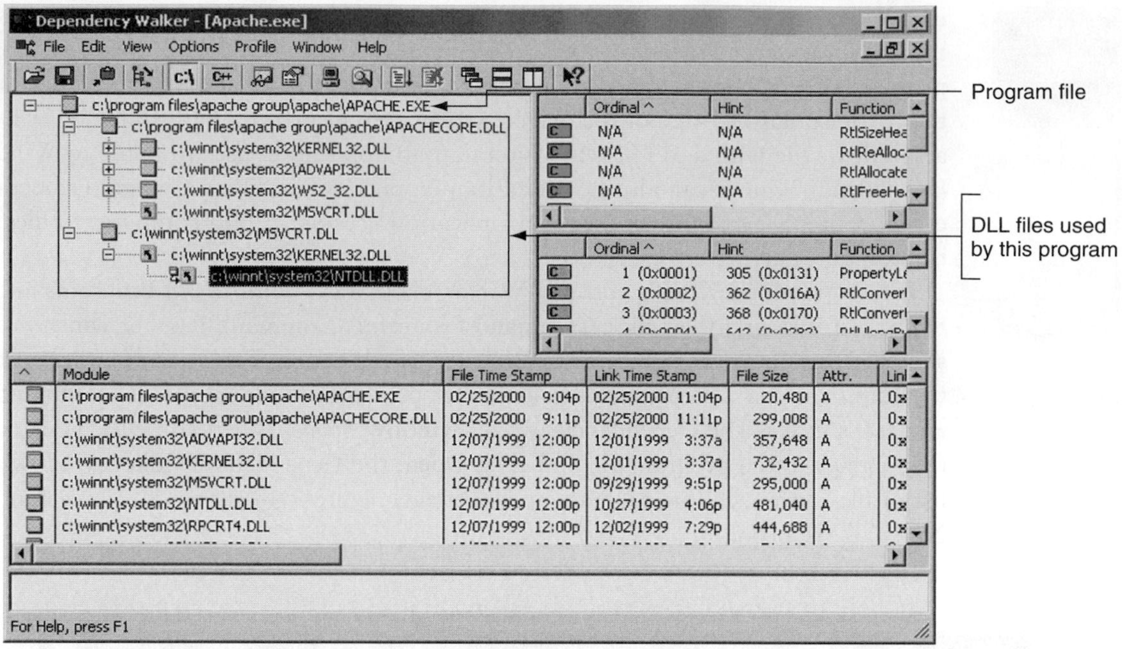

Figure 3-41 You can use Dependency Walker to solve problems with applications

PROTECTING AND MAINTAINING WINDOWS SYSTEM FILES

When you first become responsible for a Windows 2000/XP system, one of the first things you need to do is make sure procedures are set in place to keep Windows updated and to keep good backups of system files and user data. In the last chapter, you learned how to set Windows XP to perform automatic updates and how to update Windows 2000. In this section, you'll learn several ways you can keep good backups of system files. In the next chapter, you'll learn how to back up user data.

Tools and methods offered by Windows 2000/XP to protect and back up critical system files are Windows File Protection, System Restore (Windows XP only), backing up the system state, and Automated System Recovery (Windows XP only). All these tools are covered in the following sections. You need to know how to make the necessary backups and then how to use these backups in the event a problem arises.

Windows 2000/XP calls the files critical to a successful operating system load the **system state data**. This includes all files necessary to boot the OS, the Windows 2000/XP registry, and all system files in the *%SystemRoot%* folder, the folder in which Windows 2000/XP is installed.

> **Notes**
>
> Recall that to update Windows XP, click **Start, All Programs, Windows Update**. For Windows 2000, click **Start, Windows Update**. Another way to update either OS is to open your browser and go to the *windowsupdate.microsoft.com* Web site to download and install updates.

> **Notes**
>
> Windows XP is most likely installed in C:\Windows. Windows 2000 is likely to be installed in C:\WINNT. Microsoft documentation sometimes calls the folder in which Windows is installed \winnt_root or %SystemRoot%. To help you become comfortable with both names, we use them both in this chapter.

A+ ESS
1.3
3.4

A+
220-602
3.1
3.3
3.4

WINDOWS FILE PROTECTION

Windows 2000/XP provides a feature called Windows File Protection (WFP) to protect system files from being accidentally changed or deleted. When applications are installed, the installation program might attempt to overwrite a Windows system file with a version that the application knows it needs. Applications tend to use the same Windows system files, so if an application changes one of these shared system files, another application that depends on the file might give errors or the system might even become unstable. Also, users might attempt to accidentally delete an important Windows system file, or malicious software might attempt to overwrite a system file with an infected version. For all these reasons, Windows File Protection does not allow system files to be altered or deleted. System files protected have a .sys, .dll, .ttf, .fon, .ocs, or .exe file extension.

Notes

As Windows File Protection protects system files, it does allow legitimate updates to those files, when necessary.

Windows File Protection protects system files by keeping copies of good system files in the C:\Windows\system32\dllcache folder shown in Figure 3-42 (for Windows 2000, the folder is C:\WINNT\system32\dllcache). When WFP wants to validate a system file, it compares it to one in this folder and uses the one in the folder to replace a questionable system file. If it doesn't have a good system file in the Dllcache folder, it requests that you insert the Windows 2000/XP setup CD so it can get a fresh copy.

Figure 3-42 Windows File Protection stores good copies of system files in the C:\Windows\system32\dllcache folder

Windows File Protection works by using two processes. One is a background process that notifies WFP when a protected file is modified. WFP then checks the file signature to see whether it is the correct Microsoft version of the file. If the file version is not

A+ ESS
1.3
3.4

A+
220-602
3.1
3.3
3.4

correct, WFP looks in the Dllcache folder, which contains cached copies of system files, or asks that the Windows 2000/XP CD be inserted so that WFP can find the file and restore it from the CD. Replacing incorrect system files with correct ones from the Windows 2000/XP CD requires administrative permissions. If a non-administrator user is logged on when WFP activates, WFP does not prompt that user to insert the Windows 2000/XP CD, but waits until an administrator logs on to request the CD and replace the file.

Notes

If a file has been modified, is correctly signed as a Microsoft-approved version, and is not present in the Dllcache folder, WFP adds it to that folder to be used as the correct version on future scans.

When WFP restores a file, it shows the following message by default, replacing *file_name* with the name of the system file it restored:

```
A file replacement was attempted on the protected system file
file_name. To maintain system stability, the file has been restored
to the correct Microsoft version. If problems occur with your
application, please contact the application vendor for support.
```

If you see this message, carefully note what application was working at the time and what happened just before the message. Maybe an application is being installed, a virus is present, a corrupted application is performing an illegal operation, or a user has made a mistake. It is important to have as much information as possible to figure out which applications might need to be scanned for viruses or replaced altogether.

The other tool that WFP uses is the **System File Checker (SFC)**. (The program filename is Sfc.exe.) This tool can be used in several situations. If the administrator set the system to perform an unattended installation, the SFC checks all protected system files after Setup is completed to see whether they were modified during the installation. If any incorrect modifications have been made or if any important system files are unsigned, WFP retrieves a copy of the file from the Dllcache folder or requests it from the Windows 2000/XP CD.

An administrator can also use the SFC command to verify that the system is using correct versions of all protected system files, either as a preventative maintenance measure or when he or she suspects that system files have become corrupted or deleted. For example, if more than one application gives errors or Windows gives errors after the boot, you might suspect system files have been corrupted. To use System File Checker, you can type **sfc.exe** or **sfc** in a Command Prompt window or in the Run dialog box. When you type this command, you need to include one of the switches listed in Table 3-3. For example, to perform an immediate scan of protected system files, you would use this command line: **sfc /scannow**. Figure 3-43 shows the result of using this command and switch.

Switch	Function
/cachesize=x	Sets the size of the file cache, in megabytes
/cancel	Discontinues scans of protected system files
/enable	Enables normal operation of WFP
/purgecache	Empties the file cache and immediately scans all protected system files, populating the Dllcache folder with confirmed correct versions of system files (may require insertion of the Windows 2000/XP CD as the source for correct versions)

Table 3-3   Switches for the SFC utility

A+ ESS
1.3
3.4

A+
220-602
3.1
3.3
3.4

Switch	Function
/quiet	Replaces incorrect versions of system files with correct ones without prompting the user
/scanboot	Performs a scan of protected system files every time the system boots
/scannow	Performs an immediate scan of protected system files
/scanonce	Performs a scan of protected system files the next time the system boots
/?	Displays a list of available switches for the sfc command

Table 3-3   Switches for the SFC utility (continued)

Figure 3-43   Use the SFC utility to scan the system for corrupted system files

A+
220-602
3.1
3.4

WINDOWS XP SYSTEM RESTORE

The **System Restore** utility is new to Windows XP. System Restore can be set to routinely make snapshots of critical Windows system files necessary to load the OS. When Windows XP is giving problems, you can use System Restore to restore the system state to its condition at the time a snapshot was taken.

The restore process does not affect user data on the hard drive but can affect installed software and hardware, user settings, and OS configuration settings. Also, the restore process cannot help you recover from a virus or worm infection unless the infection is launched at startup. The restoration is taken from a snapshot of the system state, called a **restore point**, that was created earlier. The system automatically creates a restore point before you install new software or hardware or make other changes to the system. You can also manually create a restore point at any time.

> **Notes**
>
> System Restore only works to recover from errors if the registry is somewhat intact because restore points replace certain keys in the registry but cannot completely rebuild a totally corrupted registry. On the other hand, restoring the system state from a previous backup completely restores the registry from the backup.

A+ ESS
1.3
3.4

A+
220-602
3.1
3.4

APPLYING CONCEPTS

By default, Windows XP System Restore is turned on when the OS is first installed. To be on the safe side, when you first become responsible for a system, do the following to verify that Windows XP System Restore is turned on:

1. Right-click **My Computer** and select **Properties** from the shortcut menu. The System Properties window opens.

2. Click the **System Restore** tab, as shown in Figure 3-44. Make sure **Turn off System Restore** is not checked. On this window, you can also see how much disk space is allotted to keeping restore points.

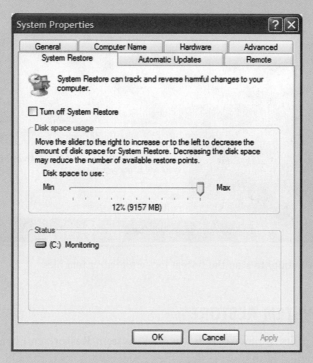

Figure 3-44   System Restore is turned on and off using the System Properties window

3. If you have made changes to this window, click **Apply**. Click **OK** to close the window.

   To manually create a restore point:

1. Click **Start, All Programs, Accessories, System Tools**, and **System Restore**. The System Restore window appears, as shown in Figure 3-45.

2. The System Restore window gives you two choices: Restore my computer to an earlier time and Create a restore point. Select **Create a restore point**, and then click **Next**.

3. Type a description of the restore point, such as **Just before I updated the video driver**. The system automatically assigns the current date and time to the restore point.

4. Click **Create** and then **Close**. The restore point is saved in the System Volume Information folder on drive C. (Users cannot access this folder.)

   If your system is giving you problems, for example, if errors occur after you have installed a hardware device, first try to use Driver Rollback to fix the problem so that as few changes as possible to the system are lost. If Driver Rollback does not work or is not appropriate, do the following to revert the system to the restore point:

A+ ESS
1.3
3.4

A+
220-602
3.1
3.4

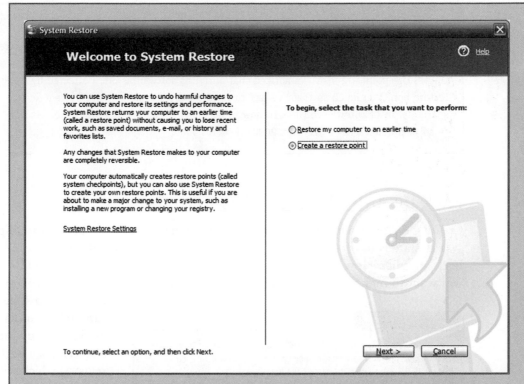

Figure 3-45 Use System Restore to manually create a restore point before making major changes to the system

1. Click **Start, All Programs, Accessories, System Tools**, and **System Restore**.

2. If necessary, click **Restore my computer to an earlier time**, and then click **Next**. A window appears, as shown in Figure 3-46. Notice the two restore points in the figure, one created by the system and one created manually.

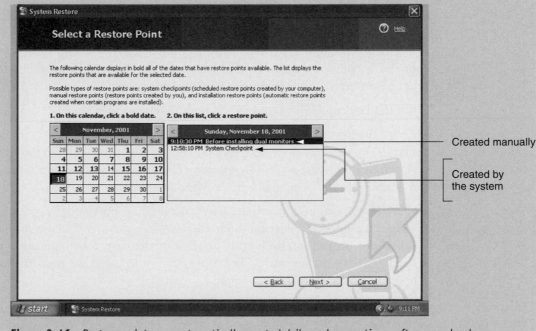

Figure 3-46 Restore points are automatically created daily and every time software or hardware is installed

A+ ESS
1.3
3.4

A+
220-602
3.1
3.4

3. Select the date and time and the specific restore point. Click **Next** twice.

Windows XP reboots and restores the system state to the settings saved in the restore point. Changes to user data are not affected, but any installation or configuration changes made after the restore point are lost. I've noticed that antivirus software is often affected by using a restore point; so much so that I've had to reinstall the software, so use System Restore sparingly. In Chapter 5, you'll learn how to use System Restore and other tools to solve problems when Windows 2000/XP won't boot.

BACK UP AND RESTORE THE SYSTEM STATE

Creating restore points can help in some situations, but an even better way to protect the system state is to make a backup of all system state files using the Windows 2000/XP Backup utility. How to back up and restore the system state is covered in this section. You will want to make a habit of always backing up the system state before you make major changes to a system so that you can undo your changes if need be. Backing up the system state also creates a backup of the registry, which will be useful when you need to manually edit the registry.

 Notes

The Windows 2000/XP Backup utility is not normally installed in Windows XP Home Edition. For this OS, however, you can install it by double-clicking the Ntbackup.msi file in the D:\Valueadd\ MSFT\Ntbackup folder on the Windows XP setup CD.

BACK UP THE SYSTEM STATE

When you back up the system state data, you cannot select which files you want to back up because Windows 2000/XP always backs up all of them. Here is the process for backing up the system state:

1. Click **Start,** point to **All Programs** (**Programs** in Windows 2000), **Accessories, System Tools,** and then click **Backup.** (Or you can enter **Ntbackup.exe** in the Run dialog box.) Depending on how the utility is configured, the Backup Utility window opens or the Backup or Restore Wizard launches (see Figure 3-47). If the wizard launches, click **Advanced Mode** to see the Backup Utility window.

2. On the Backup Utility window, click the **Backup** tab (see Figure 3-48).

3. Check the **System State** box in the list of items you can back up. Notice in Figure 3-48 that the system state includes the boot files and the registry. It also includes the COM+ (Component Object Model) Registration Database, which contains information about applications and includes files in the Windows folders.

4. Click **Browse** to point to where you want the backup saved. You can back up to any media, including a folder on the hard drive, Zip drive, tape drive, or network drive. For better protection, back up to another media than your hard drive, such as another hard drive on the network. Click **Start Backup** to begin the process. A dialog box appears. Click **Start Backup** again.

3

Figure 3-47 Backup or Restore Wizard

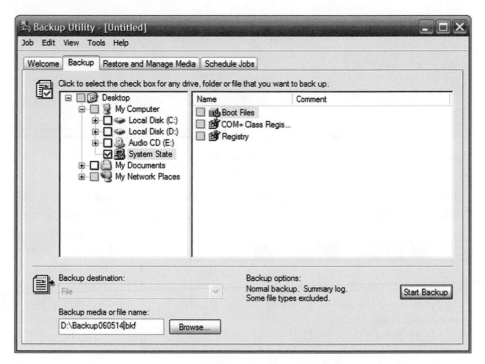

Figure 3-48 Back up the Windows 2000/XP registry and all critical system files

RESTORE THE SYSTEM STATE

If Windows gives errors or the registry gets corrupted, you can restore the system to the state it was in when the last System State backup was made. To do that, launch the Windows

 Notes

When you back up the system state, the registry is also backed up to the folder *%SystemRoot%*\repair\RegBack. If you later have a corrupted registry, you can copy files from this folder to the registry folder, which is *%SystemRoot%*\System32\Config.

A+ ESS
1.3
3.4

A+
220-602
3.1
3.4

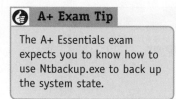

A+ Exam Tip

The A+ Essentials exam expects you to know how to use Ntbackup.exe to back up the system state.

Backup tool by clicking **Start**, pointing to **All Programs** (**Programs** in Windows 2000), **Accessories**, and **System Tools**, and then clicking **Backup**. Or you can type **Ntbackup.exe** in the Run dialog box and press **Enter**. Either way, the Backup window opens showing the Backup tab. You then need to click the **Restore and Manage Media** tab (**Restore** tab in Windows 2000), which is shown in Figure 3-49.

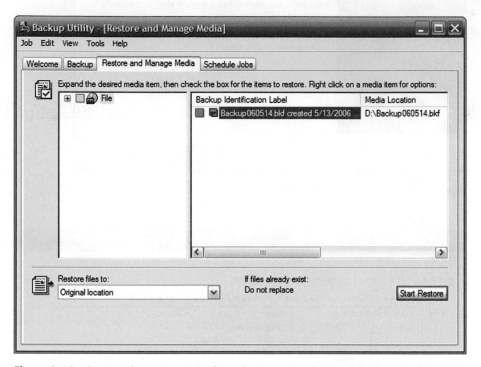

Figure 3-49   Restore the system state from the Restore and Manage Media tab of the Backup dialog box

From the Restore and Manage Media tab, first select the backup you want to restore. Then, in the list box in the lower-left corner, select the location to which the backup is to be restored. Click the **Start Restore** button in the lower-right corner to start the process. Remember that you can restore the system state as a way of restoring the registry.

Notes

If you ever need to manually edit the Windows registry, it's a good idea to make a backup of the registry first. The easiest and safest way to do that is to back up the entire system state. Later, if you need to undo your changes to the registry, use the Backup utility to restore the system state.

The biggest limitation to using the Backup utility to restore the system state is that, in order to use the utility, you must be able to boot to the Windows desktop. How to deal with problems when you can't boot to the Windows desktop is covered in Chapter 5.

A+ ESS
3.3
3.4

A+
220-602
3.3
3.4

WINDOWS XP AUTOMATED SYSTEM RECOVERY

You can use the Windows XP Automated System Recovery (ASR) tool to back up the entire drive on which Windows is installed (most likely drive C). Later, if Windows gets corrupted, you can recover the system from the last time you made an ASR backup. Keep in mind, however, that everything on the drive since the ASR backup was made is lost,

3

A+ ESS
3.3
3.4

A+
220-602
3.3
3.4

including installed software and device drivers, user data, and any changes to the system configuration.

In this section, you will learn how to make the ASR backup, how to restore the system from the backup, and about best practices when using the ASR tool.

CREATING THE ASR BACKUP AND ASR DISK

The ASR backup process creates two items: a full backup of the drive on which Windows is installed and an ASR floppy disk on which information that will help Windows use Automated System Recovery is stored. The ASR backup process places the location of the backup file on the floppy. The backup file will be just as large as the contents of the hard drive volume, so you will need a massive backup medium, such as another partition on a different hard drive, a tape drive, or a writeable CD-R or CD-RW drive.

 Caution

Do not back up drive C to a folder on drive C. The ASR backup process allows you to do this, but restoring later from this backup does not work. In addition, when a hard drive partition fails, most likely other partitions on the drive will also be lost, and so will your backup if you've put it on one of these other partitions. Therefore, to better protect your installation, back up to a different hard drive or other media.

Follow these directions to create the backup and the ASR floppy disk:

Notes

To use Automated System Recovery in Windows XP Home Edition, the Backup utility must first be installed.

1. Click **Start, All Programs, Accessories, System Tools,** and **Backup.** The Backup or Restore Wizard appears (see Figure 3-50).

Figure 3-50 Use the Backup or Restore Wizard to back up the hard drive partition after the Windows XP installation is complete

2. Click the **Advanced Mode** link. The Backup Utility window appears. On the Welcome tab, click **Automated System Recovery Wizard.** On the following screen, click **Next.**

3. The Backup Destination window appears. Select the location of the medium to receive the backup and insert a disk into the drive. This disk will become the ASR disk. Click **Next**.

4. Click **Finish**. The backup process shows its progress, as seen in Figure 3-51.

5. When the backup is finished, label the ASR disk with the name of the disk, the date it was created, and the computer's name, and put the disk in a safe place.

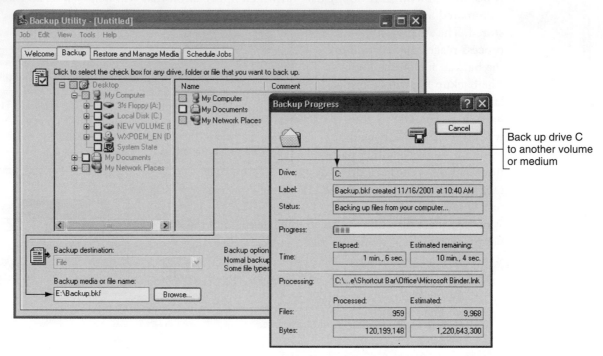

Figure 3-51   The Backup utility can create a backup of drive C and an ASR disk to be used later for the Automated System Recovery utility

RESTORING THE SYSTEM USING AN ASR BACKUP

To restore the logical drive to its state when the last ASR disk set was made, do the following:

1. Insert the Windows XP CD in the CD-ROM drive, and hard boot the PC.

2. You will see a message that says "Press any key to boot from CD." Press any key.

3. A blue screen appears with the message "Press F6 to load RAID or SCSI drivers." If your system uses RAID or SCSI, press **F6**. If your system does not use RAID or SCSI, ignore the message.

4. At the bottom of the blue screen, a message says, "Press F2 to run the Automated System Recovery process." Press **F2**.

5. The screen shown in Figure 3-52 appears, instructing you to insert the ASR floppy disk. Insert the disk and then press **Enter**.

Windows XP Setup then does the following:

1. Loads files it needs to run

2. Repartitions and reformats the drive (see Figure 3-53)

```
Windows Setup
=============




          Please insert the disk labeled:

   Windows Automated System Recovery Disk

             Into the floppy drive.



            Press any key when ready.
```

Figure 3-52   Automatic System Recovery process must have the ASR floppy disk

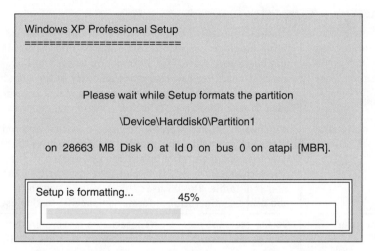

```
Windows XP Professional Setup
=============================




       Please wait while Setup formats the partition

              \Device\Harddisk0\Partition1

    on  28663  MB  Disk  0  at  Id 0  on  bus  0  on  atapi  [MBR].

   ┌──────────────────────────────────────────────────────┐
   │ Setup is formatting...            45%                 │
   │                                                       │
   │ ▓▓▓▓▓▓▓▓▓▓▓▓▓▓▓▓▓▓                                    │
   └──────────────────────────────────────────────────────┘
```

Figure 3-53   As part of the Automatic System Recovery process, Windows XP Setup repartitions and reformats the volume holding Windows XP

3. Installs Windows from the Windows XP CD

4. Launches the Automatic System Recovery Wizard to restore the Windows system state, applications, and data to what they were at the time of the last ASR backup

As the ASR recovery process progresses, it erases everything on the volume being restored and reformats the logical drive just before the Windows XP installation process begins.

PLANNING AHEAD FOR AUTOMATED SYSTEM RECOVERY

As you have seen, Automated System Recovery is a drastic step in recovering a failed Windows XP startup. All software and hardware installations, user data, and user settings on the Windows XP volume made after the backup are lost. For this reason, it's a good idea to carefully plan how best to use Automated System Recovery. Here's one suggestion: When you install Windows XP, create a partition for Windows XP that will hold Windows XP and all installed software, but not the user data. Use a second partition on the drive for user data, say drive D. After you have installed all applications and devices, make an ASR backup of drive C to a different hard drive or other media. Then use Ntbackup to schedule daily or weekly backups of the user data on drive D. In the event of a total system failure, you can recover drive C from the ASR backup media and then recover the user data from your daily or weekly backups of that data.

A+ ESS
3.3
3.4

A+
220-602
3.3
3.4

A+ ESS
3.1

A+
220-602
3.1

To set your advance planning in place, partition the hard drive so that drive C is large enough for Windows and other software, but the bulk of the hard drive space is devoted to user data. Make drive C about 5 to 15 GB in size, which should be plenty of room for Windows and other software.

THE WINDOWS 2000/XP REGISTRY

The Windows 2000/XP registry is a hierarchical database containing information about all the hardware, software, device drivers, network protocols, and user configuration needed by the OS and applications. Many components depend on this information, and the registry provides a secure and stable location for it. Table 3-4 lists ways in which some components use the registry.

Component	Description
Setup programs for devices and applications and Windows Update programs	Setup programs can record configuration information in the registry and query the registry for information needed to install drivers and applications. They can also make an entry in the registry to cause a program to run the next time Windows starts, a technique often used to complete an installation process that requires a reboot.
User profiles maintained and used by the OS	Windows maintains a profile for each user that determines the user's environment. User profiles are kept in files, but, when a user logs on, the profile information is written to the registry, where changes are recorded, and then later written back to the user profile file. The OS uses this profile to control user settings and other configuration information specific to this user.
Files active when Ntldr is loading the OS	During the boot process, NTDetect.com surveys present hardware devices and records that information in the registry. Ntldr loads and initializes device drivers using information from the registry, including the order in which to load them.
Device drivers	Device drivers read and write configuration information from and to the registry each time they load. The drivers write hardware configuration information to the registry and read it to determine the proper way to load.
Hardware profiles	Windows can maintain more than one set of hardware configuration information (called a hardware profile) for one PC. The data is kept in the registry. An example of a computer that has more than one hardware profile is a notebook that has a docking station. Two hardware profiles describe the notebook, one docked and the other undocked. This information is kept in the registry.
Application programs	Many application programs read the registry for information about the location of files the program uses and various other parameters.

Table 3-4   Components that use the Windows 2000/XP registry

Most users never see or care about the registry, its organization, or contents. However, as a PC support technician, you need to be familiar with the registry and know how to protect it from corruption. Occasionally, you might need to manually edit the registry to solve a problem that cannot be solved any other way. The following sections look at how the registry is organized, how to back up and recover the registry, and how you can manually edit the registry.

HOW THE REGISTRY IS ORGANIZED

When studying how the registry is organized, keep in mind that there are two ways to look at this organization: physical and logical. To fully understand the nature of the registry, you need to be familiar with both.

LOGICAL ORGANIZATION OF THE REGISTRY

Logically, the organization of the registry looks like an upside-down tree with six branches, called keys or subtrees (see Figure 3-54), which are categories of information stored in the registry. Each key is made up of several subkeys that may also have subkeys, and subkeys hold, or contain, values. Each value has a name and data assigned to it. Data in the registry is always stored in values, the lowest level of the tree.

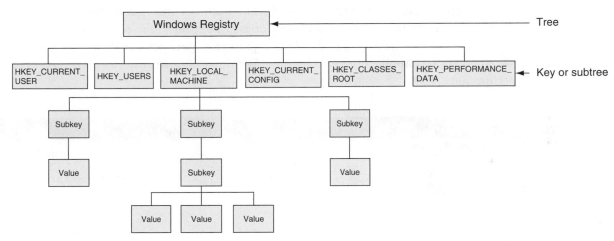

Figure 3-54 The Windows 2000/XP registry is logically organized in an upside-down tree structure of keys, subkeys, and values

The six subtrees shown in Figure 3-54 are listed in Table 3-5 together with their primary functions. As the table shows, the HKEY_LOCAL_MACHINE subtree is the mainstay key of the registry.

Subtree (Main Keys)	Primary Function
HKEY_CLASSES_ROOT	Contains information about software and the way software is configured. It contains one key for every file extension for which the OS has an associated application.
HKEY_CURRENT_USER	Contains information about the currently logged-on user. This key points to data stored in HKEY_USERS
HKEY_LOCAL_MACHINE	Contains all configuration data about the computer, including information about device drivers and devices used at startup. The information in this key does not change when different users log on.
HKEY_USERS	Contains information used to build the logon screen and the ID of the currently logged-on user.

Table 3-5 The six subtrees of the Windows 2000/XP registry

Subtree (Main Keys)	Primary Function
HKEY_CURRENT_CONFIG	Contains information about the active hardware configuration, which is extracted from the data stored in the HKEY_LOCAL_ MACHINE subkeys called SOFTWARE and SYSTEM
HKEY_PERFORMANCE_DATA	Does not contain data, but is used as a pass-through for performance data from Windows to programs that monitor performance. Because this key cannot be edited, it does not show up in the Registry Editor window.

Table 3-5 The six subtrees of the Windows 2000/XP registry (continued)

When you first open the Windows Registry Editor to view and edit the registry, you see a window similar to that in Figure 3-55. In the figure, there are five high levels showing, one for each key or subtree that can be edited. (The sixth key showing in Figure 3-54, the HKEY_PERFORMANCE_DATA key, does not appear in the editor because data isn't stored in this key. The key is used only as a pointer to performance data provided by Windows so that applications that monitor Windows performance can easily access this performance data.)

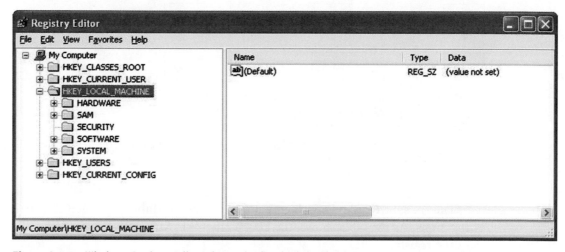

Figure 3-55 Windows Registry Editor shows the five high-level subtrees in the Windows 2000/XP registry that can be edited

PHYSICAL ORGANIZATION OF THE REGISTRY

The physical organization of the registry is quite different from the logical organization. Physically, the registry is stored in five files called hives. Figure 3-56 shows the way the five subtrees that hold data are stored in hives. (Remember, one subtree does not hold data and does not use a hive.)

 Tip

> Notice in Figure 3-55 that the HKEY_LOCAL_MACHINE subtree has been opened to show subkeys under it; several subkeys have their own subkeys. If you click a subkey that has values assigned to it, those values appear on the right side of the window. Later in this section, you will see how to edit values in the registry.

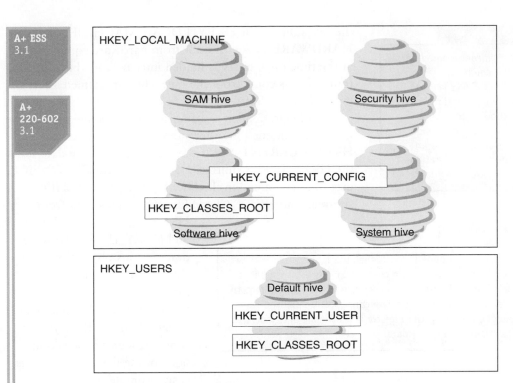

Figure 3-56 The relationship between registry subtrees (keys) and hives

Here is the breakdown:

- ◢ HKEY_LOCAL_MACHINE (abbreviated HKLM) data is kept in four hives: the SAM hive, the Security hive, the Software hive, and the System hive. In addition, the HARDWARE subkey of the HKLM key is built when the registry is first loaded, based on data collected about the current hardware configuration.
- ◢ HKEY_USERS (abbreviated HKU) data is partly kept in the Default hive and partly gathered from these two files:

  - \Documents and Settings*username*\Ntuser.dat
  - \Documents and Settings*username*\Local Settings\Application Data\Microsoft\Windows\Usrclass.dat

- ◢ HKEY_CURRENT_CONFIG (abbreviated HKCC) data is gathered when the registry is first loaded into memory. Data is taken from the HKLM keys, which are kept in the Software hive and the System hive.
- ◢ HKEY_CLASSES_ROOT (abbreviated HKCR) data is gathered when the registry is built into memory. It gathers data from these locations:

  - HKLM keys that contain system-wide data stored in the Software hive
  - For the currently logged on user, data is taken from the HKCU keys, which gather current user data from the file \Documents and Settings*username*\Local Settings\Application Data\Microsoft\Windows\Usrclass.dat.

- ◢ HKEY_CURRENT_USER (abbreviated HKCU) data is built at the time the registry is loaded into memory when a user logs on. Data is taken from HKEY_USERS data kept in the Default hive and data kept in the Ntuser.dat and Usrclass.dat files of the current user.

As you can see, only two main keys have associated hives, HKEY_LOCAL_MACHINE (four hives) and HKEY_USERS (the Default hive). Looking back at Figure 3-55, you can see

> **Notes**
>
> Device Manager reads data from the combined HKLM\HARDWARE key to build the information it displays about hardware configurations. You can consider Device Manager to be an easy-to-view presentation of this HARDWARE key data.

> **Notes**
>
> Also important to understand is that the registry as we know it with its six subtrees doesn't really exist as such until it is built in memory. Because so much of what we call the registry depends on the current hardware configuration and the currently logged on user, the registry is a dynamic entity dynamically built from changing data.

the five subkeys for HKEY_LOCAL_MACHINE. The HARDWARE subkey is built from hardware configuration at the time the registry is loaded into memory, but the other four subkeys come from the hives they are named after (Sam, Security, Software, and System).

From Figure 3-56, you can also see that some subtrees use data contained in other subtrees. For instance, the HKEY_CURRENT_USER data is a subset of the data in the HKEY_USERS subtree. HKEY_CURRENT_CONFIG uses data contained in the HKEY_LOCAL_MACHINE subtree. And HKEY_CLASSES_ROOT uses data from HKEY_LOCAL_MACHINE and HKEY_USERS. However, don't let this physical relationship cloud your view of the logical relationship among these subtrees. Although data is shared among the different subtrees, logically speaking, none of the five main subtrees is subordinate to any other.

The five registry hives are stored in the \%*SystemRoot*%\system32\config folder as a group of files. In a physical sense, each hive is a file. Each hive is backed up with a log file and a backup file, which are also stored in the \%*SystemRoot*%\system32\config folder.

BACKING UP AND RECOVERING THE REGISTRY

Before you the edit the registry, it's very important you first make a backup so that if you make a mistake or your changes cause a problem, you can backtrack your changes. There are basically two ways to back up the registry: the safest way is to back up the entire system state including the registry, or you can back up only keys in the registry that you expect to change.

BACKING UP THE SYSTEM STATE ALSO BACKS UP THE REGISTRY

Earlier in the chapter, you learned how to use the Windows 2000/XP Backup utility to back up the system state. When the system state is backed up, the Backup utility also puts a copy of the registry files in these locations:

◢ **C:\Windows\repair\.** Backups are placed here at the end of the Windows 2000 and Windows XP installations. Also, Windows XP places backups here whenever the system state is backed up using the Windows Backup utility.
◢ **C:\Windows\repair\RegBack\.** Windows 2000 places backups here whenever the system state is backed up using the Windows Backup utility.

Later, if you need to recover the registry or the entire system state, you can use the Ntbackup routine to restore the system state or you can copy the backed-up registry files into the C:\Windows\system32\config folder.

BACKING UP INDIVIDUAL KEYS IN THE REGISTRY

A less time-consuming method of backing up the registry is to back up a particular key that you plan to edit. However, know that if the registry gets corrupted, having a backup of only a

3

A+ ESS
3.1

A+
220-602
3.1

particular key will most likely not help you much when trying a recovery. Also, don't use this technique to back up the entire registry or an entire tree within the registry. Use this method only to back up a subkey and all the subkeys within it. Before you edit a subkey, back it up first.

To back up a key along with its subkeys in the registry, follow these steps:

1. Open the registry editor. To do that, click **Start, Run**, type **Regedit** in the Run dialog box and then press **Enter**.

2. For Windows XP, select the key you want to back up and right-click it. Click **Export** in the shortcut menu, as shown in Figure 3-57. The Export Registry File dialog box appears, as shown in Figure 3-58.

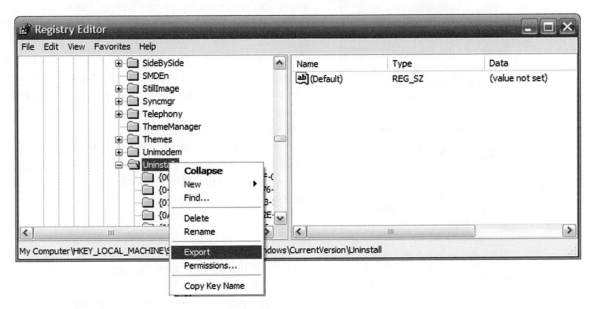

Figure 3-57 Using the Windows XP registry editor, you can back up a key and its subkeys using the Export command

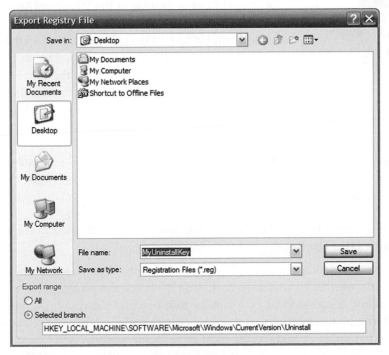

Figure 3-58 Save the exported key to the Windows desktop

A+ ESS
3.1

A+
220-602
3.1

3. Select the location to save the export file and name the file. A convenient place to store an export file while you edit the registry is the desktop. Click **Save** when done. The file saved will have a .reg file extension. (To export a registry key using Windows 2000, select the key, click **Registry** on the menu bar, and then click **Export Registry File.**)

4. You can now edit the key. Later, if you need to undo your changes, exit the registry editor and double-click the saved export file. The key and its subkeys saved in the export file will be restored. After you're done with an export file, delete it.

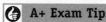 Notes

Changes to the registry take effect immediately and are permanent. Therefore, before you edit the registry, you should use one of the two backup methods just discussed so that you can restore it if something goes wrong.

🔘 **A+ Exam Tip**

The A+ Essentials exam expects you to know the difference between Windows 2000 Regedit.exe and Regedt32.exe, and when to use each. You should also know that Windows XP has only a single registry editor.

Notes

With Windows XP, typing either Regedt32 or Regedit in the Run dialog box launches the Regedit.exe program.

EDITING THE REGISTRY

When you make a change in Control Panel, Device Manager, or many other places in Windows 2000/XP, the registry is modified automatically. This is the only way most users will ever change the registry. However, on rare occasions you might need to edit the registry manually, for example, when you uninstall an application and registry entries are not completely removed and these orphan entries are giving startup errors.

Windows XP has only a single registry editor, Regedit.exe. Windows 2000 offers two registry editors, each with a slightly different look and feel, and with some slight differences, as follows:

▲ Regedt32.exe is located in the \%*SystemRoot*%\system32 folder. It shows each key in a separate window. Under the Options menu, you have the option to work in read-only mode. Regedt32.exe has a Security menu that allows you to apply permissions to keys and subkeys to control which user accounts have access to these keys.

▲ Regedit.exe is located in the \%*SystemRoot*% folder and shows all keys in the same window. It has a look and feel similar to Explorer. Regedit.exe has the advantages that you can export the registry to a text file and use a more powerful search tool than the one in Regedt32.exe, but has the disadvantage that it cannot display registry values longer than 256 characters. Use Regedit.exe to export registry keys before you edit them.

Let's look at a sample situation in which you might need to edit the registry: changing the name of the Recycle Bin on the Windows XP desktop for a currently logged on user. To make the change, do the following:

1. To open Registry Editor, click **Start, Run**, and then type **Regedit** in the Run dialog box. Click **OK**. The Registry Editor window appears.

2. Locate the subkey that is listed after this paragraph. This subkey is the name of the Recycle Bin on the Windows desktop. You can click the plus sign (+) to the left of the yellow folder icon of each subkey to move down through the tree. As you click through the hierarchy to get to this key, note that if the currently selected subkey has a value, that value appears in the right pane of the window.

HKEY_CURRENT_USER\Software\Microsoft\Windows\CurrentVersion\Explorer\
CLSID\645FF040-5081-101B-9F08-00AA002F954E

3

A+ ESS
3.1

A+
220-602
3.1

3. For Windows XP, right-click the subkey and select **Export** from the shortcut menu (see Figure 3-59). Name the export file **RecycleKey.reg** and save the file to the Windows desktop. Click **Save**. For Windows 2000, select the key, click **Registry** on the menu bar, click **Export Registry File**, and save the file to the Windows desktop.

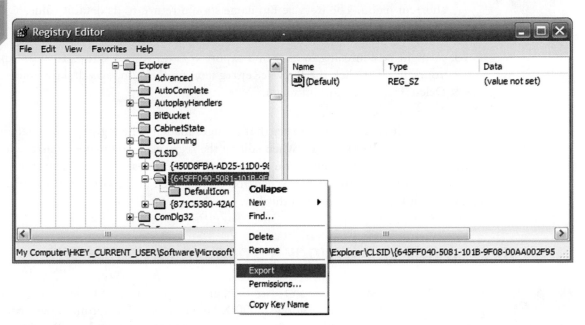

Figure 3-59 Export the key before you edit it

4. In Figure 3-60, notice in the right pane that "(value not set)" is listed under Data. This means that no value is set and the default value will be used. The default value for this name is Recycle Bin. Position the window on the screen so that you can see the Recycle Bin icon. In the right pane, double-click (**Default**), the name of the value. The Edit String dialog box appears, also shown in Figure 3-60. The Value data should be empty in the dialog box. If a value is present, you selected the wrong value. Check your work and try again. To help you find the right key, notice the current key is displayed at the bottom of the Registry Editor window.

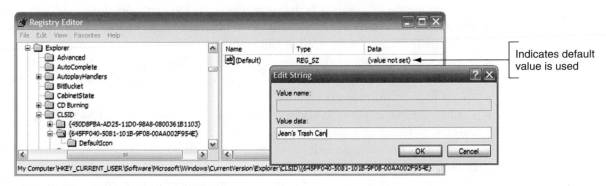

Figure 3-60 Editing a registry subkey value

5. Enter a new name for the Recycle Bin. For example, in Figure 3-60, the new name is "Jean's Trash Can." Click **OK**.

6. To see your change, right-click the desktop and select **Refresh** on the shortcut menu. The name of the Recycle Bin changes.

A+ ESS
3.1

A+
220-602
3.1

7. To restore the name to the default value, in the Registry Editor window, again double-click the name of the value. The Edit String dialog box appears. Delete your entry and click **OK**.

8. To verify the change is made, right-click the desktop and select **Refresh** on the shortcut menu. The Recycle Bin name should return to its default value.

9. To exit the Registry Editor window, click **File, Exit**.

10. It might be confusing to later find export keys on your desktop. To clean up after yourself, right-click the **RecycleKey.reg** icon on the Windows desktop and select **Delete** from the shortcut menu.

From these directions, you can see that changes made to the registry take effect immediately. Therefore, take extra care when editing the registry. If you make a mistake and don't know how to correct a problem you create, then you can restore the system state or double-click the exported key to recover. When you double-click an exported key, the registry is updated with the values stored in this key.

OPTIMIZING THE WINDOWS 2000/XP ENVIRONMENT

A+ ESS
3.2

A+
220-602
3.3

Sluggish Windows systems are so frustrating, and as a PC support technician, you need to know how to configure the Windows 2000/XP environment for optimum performance and how to teach users to do the necessary routine maintenance to keep Windows running smoothly. Here is a summary of the tasks you need to do when you first become responsible for a Windows 2000/XP system:

▲ Put procedures in place to back up Windows system files after you have made major changes to a system such as installing software or hardware or adding a new user account. You can use the Backup Utility to back up just the system state, or, for Windows XP, you can use Automated System Recovery to back up the entire drive C. In some cases, it's appropriate to use both methods. Also make sure Windows XP System Restore is turned on.

▲ Set Windows XP so that it automatically downloads updates, and, for Windows 2000, put in place the necessary schedule and procedures to manually download these updates.

▲ Use a firewall and antivirus software to protect the system from attack. (Firewalls and antivirus software are covered in Chapter 1.)

▲ Create user accounts so that users can do their jobs and perform routine maintenance, but cannot make major changes to the system that you have not authorized. (How to set up user accounts is covered in Chapter 4.)

▲ Put procedures in place to keep current backups of user data. (How to do that is covered in Chapter 4.)

▲ Teach users how to routinely clean up the hard drive and how to verify that their data backups are current and the data recovery routines work (covered in Chapter 4).

▲ Check the Windows 2000/XP operating environment to be certain that unneeded software and services are not clogging up the works and that memory settings are optimized.

This last item in the bulleted list is the subject of this section of the chapter. We'll first look at some tools to manage software and then how to uninstall unwanted software. Finally, you'll learn how to optimize memory settings.

A+ ESS
3.2

A+
220-602
3.3

When you first become responsible for a sluggish Windows 2000/XP system and you do all the tasks described in this and the next two chapters, but the system is still sluggish, you might want to consider that the problem is related to hardware. There might not be enough installed RAM or the processor might need upgrading. In general, upgrading an existing PC is recommended as long as the cost of the upgrade stays below half the cost of buying a new machine.

A+ ESS
1.1
3.2
3.3

A+
220-602
3.1
3.2
3.3

TOOLS TO MANAGE SOFTWARE

In this section, we'll look at three tools to help you manage startup and running software: Windows 2000/XP Task Manager, the Windows XP System Configuration Utility (commonly called Msconfig), and the Services console.

Viruses, adware, worms, and other malicious software can use Windows resources and pull a system down. Keep anti-virus software running in the background. If you see a marked decrease in Windows performance, scan the hard drive for viruses, worms, and adware. Chapter 1 gives more information on how to protect from malicious software.

TASK MANAGER

Task Manager (Taskman.exe) lets you view the applications and processes running on your computer as well as performance information for the processor and memory. There are three ways you can access Task Manager:

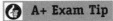

A+ Exam Tip

The A+ Essentials exam expects you to know how to use Task Manager, Msconfig.exe, and the Services Console.

- Press **Ctrl+Alt+Delete**. Depending on your system, Task Manager appears or the Windows Security window opens. If the security window opens, click the **Task Manager** button.
- Right-click a blank area on the taskbar, and then select **Task Manager** on the shortcut menu.
- Press **Ctrl+Shift+Esc**.

Windows 2000 Task Manager has three tabs: Applications, Processes, and Performance. Windows XP Task Manager adds two additional tabs, Networking and Users. (The Users tab shows only when a system is set for Fast User Switching and lets you monitor other users logged onto the system.) On the Applications tab (see Figure 3-61), each application loaded can have one of two states: Running or Not Responding. If an application is listed as Not Responding, you can end it by selecting it and clicking the End Task button at the bottom of the window. You will lose any unsaved information in the application.

The second tab, the Processes tab, lists system services and other processes associated with applications, together with how much CPU time and memory the process uses. This information can help you determine which applications are slowing down your system. Figure 3-62 shows the list of processes for a Windows XP system immediately after the installation was completed with no applications installed. Figure 3-63 shows a similar window for Windows 2000.

A+ ESS
1.1
3.2
3.3

A+
220-602
3.1
3.2
3.3

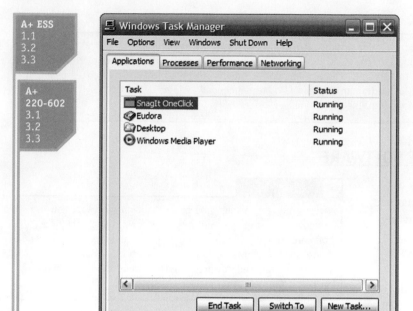

Figure 3-61   The Applications tab in Task Manager shows the status of active applications

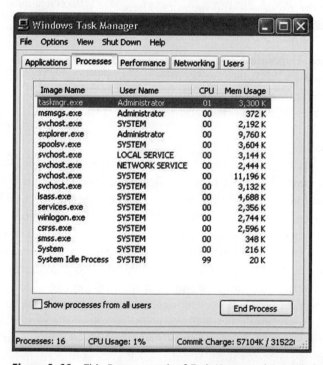

Figure 3-62   This Processes tab of Task Manager shows Windows processes running
in the background of a barebones Windows XP system

When you have a sluggish Windows system, close all open applications and open **Task Manager**. Check the **Applications** tab to make sure no applications are running. Then click the **Processes** tab. Compare the list in Figure 3-62 (for Windows XP) or Figure 3-63 (for Windows 2000) with the list of processes running on the sluggish system. Any extra processes you see might be caused by unwanted applications running in the background or malicious software running. If you see a process running that you are not familiar with, search the Microsoft web site (*support.microsoft.com*) to verify the process is legitimate.

A+ ESS
3.1
3.2

A+
220-602
3.2

APPLYING CONCEPTS

To change memory settings and page file sizes in Windows 2000/XP, do the following:

1. Right-click **My Computer** and select **Properties** on the shortcut menu.

2. The System Properties dialog box opens. Click the **Advanced** tab.

3. For Windows XP, click **Settings** under Performance. For Windows 2000, click the **Performance Options** button.

4. The Performance Options dialog box opens. Click the **Advanced** tab (see Figure 3-81). Notice in this window how you can decide the priorities for processor scheduling, and for Windows XP, memory usage. Unless you're using this computer as a Web server or other server on the network, for Windows XP, select **Programs** for both Processor scheduling and Memory usage, and, for Windows 2000, select **Applications**.

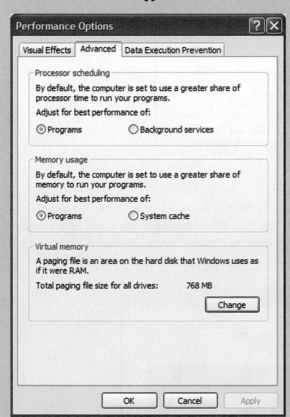

Figure 3-81 Setting performance options for Windows XP

5. Click the **Change** button.

6. The Virtual Memory dialog box opens (see Figure 3-82). In this dialog box, you can change the size of the paging file and select the drive for the file. If you select more than one drive, the file will be spread over these drives.

Upgrading memory can sometimes greatly improve Windows performance. If a system routinely runs memory-hungry applications such as video-editing software (for example, Adobe Creative Suite), drafting software (for example, Autodesk AutoCAD), or database

> **Notes**
>
> You can also access the Windows 2000/XP Performance Options dialog box from the Computer Management window. To do so, open the Computer Management window, right-click **Computer Management (Local)**, and select **Properties** on the shortcut menu.

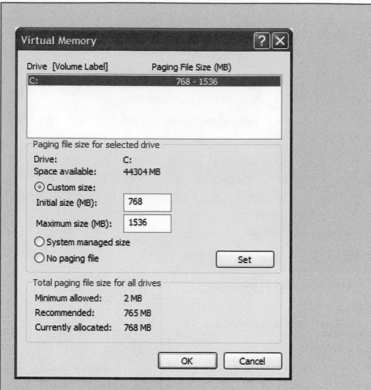

Figure 3-82   Use the Virtual Memory dialog box to change paging file settings

management software (for example, Microsoft SQL Server), you need to install as much RAM in the system as it will hold. However, for normal use, to know if your system would benefit from an upgrade, open **Task Manager** and click the **Performance** tab. If the Total Physical Memory is less than the Total Commit Charge, Windows is having to use the page file excessively. Therefore, more RAM is needed. Figure 3-83 shows an example of a system that is in need of an upgrade.

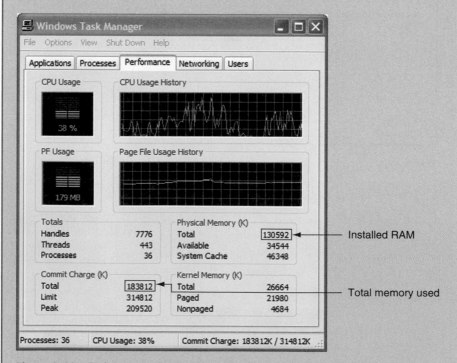

Figure 3-83   Task Manager indicates more memory is needed

A+ ESS
3.1
3.2

Compare this figure to Figure 3-64 earlier in the chapter. In the system shown in Figure 3-64, 1 GB of RAM is installed, and the Performance tab shows that this memory is more than sufficient.

A+
220-602
3.2

In addition to the information in this chapter, other important sources of information about Windows 2000 are the Microsoft Web site at *support.microsoft.com* and the *Windows 2000 Professional Resource Kit* by Microsoft Press. The *Resource Kit* includes a CD that contains additional Windows 2000 utilities. These resources can further help you understand Windows 2000 and solve problems with the OS. Also remember that user manuals, the Web, training manuals, and product installation documentation are all excellent sources of information.

>> CHAPTER SUMMARY

▲ Any user can install a hardware device if the device can be installed without user input, all files necessary for a complete installation are present, the drivers have been digitally signed, and there are no errors during installation.

▲ When a second hard drive is installed, Disk Management in Windows 2000/XP is used to prepare the disk for use. Diskpart can also be used from the Recovery Console.

▲ Windows XP offers processes to help find updates for a driver, roll back a driver if an update fails, and verify that a driver is certified by Microsoft. Generally, hardware devices are mostly managed by Windows 2000/XP Device Manager.

▲ You can install software in Windows 2000/XP only if you have Administrator privileges.

▲ Compatibility mode in Windows XP provides an application written for Windows 9x/Me or later with the environment for which it was designed.

▲ Windows XP uses the Error Reporting service to report application problems to Microsoft and perhaps suggest a fix.

▲ The Computer Management window is a console that includes several useful Windows utilities.

▲ Microsoft Management Console (MMC) can be used to create customized consoles to manage the OS.

▲ Event Viewer is used to view system, application, and security events.

▲ Windows 2000/XP Support Tools can be installed from the Windows 2000/XP CD and include several utilities to support hardware and applications.

▲ Windows File Protection (WFP) protects the system files against an application, a virus, or a user changing or deleting them. System File Checker is part of the WFP system.

▲ Windows XP System Restore maintains a list of restore points that can be used to restore the system state to a previous point in time before a problem occurred.

▲ Back up the Windows 2000/XP system state on a regular basis using the Backup utility. This backup includes system files, files to load the OS, and the registry. Back up the system state before editing the registry.

▲ Windows XP Automated System Recovery can be used to back up the entire drive C to prepare for a corrupted Windows installation.

- When solving problems with a sluggish Windows 2000/XP system, remove unwanted software, scan for viruses, clean up the hard drive, and consider the possibility you might need to upgrade memory or some other hardware component.

- The Windows registry should always be backed up before you edit it. Only edit it when other methods of solving a problem have failed.

- Task Manager and Msconfig (for Windows XP only) can be used to determine if a process is launched at startup that you can remove or disable to improve Windows performance.

- Task Manager is used to manage processes and measure performance, giving information about the processor, memory, the hard drive, and virtual memory.

- Virtual memory uses hard drive space as memory to increase the total amount of memory available. In Windows 2000/XP, virtual memory is stored in a swap file named Pagefile.sys.

- Virtual memory is managed in Windows 2000/XP from the System Properties dialog box.

>> KEY TERMS

For explanations of key terms, see the Glossary near the end of the book.

console	hypertext	System Restore
digital signatures	restore point	system state data
Disk Management	snap-ins	
hardware profile	System File Checker (SFC)	

>> REVIEWING THE BASICS

1. What does *%SystemRoot%* mean?

2. What are the normal path and the filename of the Windows 2000/XP virtual memory file?

3. In what folder does Windows 2000 store a backup of the registry when backing up the system state?

4. What is the command to install the Windows 2000/XP Support Tools?

5. What type of user account must you be using to install a hardware device that is using drivers that are not digitally signed by Microsoft?

6. What Windows utility can you use to help you decide if the system needs more RAM?

7. What tool can you use to create a console containing Device Manager and Event Viewer?

8. What is the file extension assigned to a console file?

9. Name one snap-in contained in a Computer Management console.

10. What is the program filename for System File Checker?

11. List three ways to access the Task Manager.

12. List the steps used to end an application when it refuses to respond to keystrokes or the mouse action.

13. What are the three logs kept by Event Viewer?

14. In what folder do you put a console file that you want displayed when you are logged on as an administrator and then click Start, Programs, and Administrative Tools?

15. Before clearing the Event Viewer log, explain how you can save the log for later viewing.

16. By default, Windows 2000/XP makes the paging file how large compared to the amount of RAM installed?

17. What Windows utility lists all the applications set to load at Windows startup?

18. What Windows utility can you use to list all the currently running applications?

19. In what folder does Windows XP File Protection store an extra copy of system files?

20. What SFC command sets the system to scan system files at the next reboot?

21. What SFC command sets the system to scan system files at every reboot?

22. What two files are used to build the HKEY_CLASSES_ROOT key of the registry?

23. What two files are used to build the HKEY_USERS key of the registry?

24. What Windows XP program file is used to edit the registry?

25. What registry key is used to record installed software?

26. In what folder do you install a program so that it starts up each time any user logs onto the system?

27. Looking at a program filename and file extension, how can you tell if the program is a MMC snap-in or a command-line program?

28. Which Windows registry subtree gets its information from the four registry files, Sam, Security, Software, and System?

29. In Windows 2000/XP, a file that contains part of the Windows registry is called a(n) _____.

30. To which registry key does the HKEY_CURRENT_USER key point for information?

31. What two components are created when you back up a system using the Automated System Recovery process?

>> THINKING CRITICALLY

1. You installed a hardware device that does not work. Then you updated the device drivers. Now Windows gives an error when it first starts up. What do you do first?

   a. Use System Restore to undo the installation.

   b. Use Automated System Recovery to undo the installation.

   c. Use Driver Rollback to undo the driver update.

   d. Use Device Manager to uninstall the device.

2. You need to install a customized console on 10 computers. What is the best way to do that?

   a. When installing the console on the first computer, write down each step to make it easier to do the same chore on the other nine.

   b. Create the console on one computer and copy the .mmc file to the other nine.

   c. Create the console on one computer and copy the .msc file to the other nine.

3. Can an application or device driver specify if it will use physical memory or the swap file for its data? Why or why not?

4. You are attempting to upload images from your digital camera to your Windows XP system using a USB connection, but you get errors. Select the appropriate task or tasks to solve the problem.

   a. Update Windows XP with service packs or patches.

   b. Reinstall the digital camera software.

   c. Reboot your system.

   d. Verify that the camera is turned on.

>> HANDS-ON PROJECTS

PROJECT 3-1: Problem-Solving Using the Microsoft Knowledge Base

Your hard drive has been attacked by a malicious virus, and you have decided to restore it from the last backup made by the ASR backup process. You cannot find the ASR floppy disk required for the restore process. Search the Microsoft Knowledge Base for the steps to re-create the ASR floppy disk when the ASR backup is available. Print the Knowledge Base article.

PROJECT 3-2: Editing and Restoring the Registry

Practice editing and restoring the registry by doing the following:

1. Export the registry key HKEY_CURRENT_USER\Software\Microsoft\Windows\CurrentVersion\Explorer to an export file stored on the desktop.

2. Change the name of the Recycle Bin and refresh your desktop. Verify the name was changed on the desktop. Exit the registry editor.

3. Restore the registry to its original state using the export file you created. Refresh your desktop and verify the Recycle Bin is restored to its original name.

4. Delete the desktop icon and export file.

PROJECT 3-3: Using System Restore

Create a restore point. Make a change to the display settings. Restore the system using System Restore. Are the changes still in effect? Why or why not?

PROJECT 3-4: Restoring the System State

Understanding the importance of making backups is essential to learning to support Windows. Do the following to examine the power and limitations of backing up the system state data:

1. Back up the Windows 2000/XP system state to a folder on your network or hard drive. What is the path to your backup?

2. Make several changes to the Windows environment: Using the Display Properties window, change the wallpaper background of the desktop, the screen resolution, and the Windows Theme. What are these new settings?

3. Using the Add or Remove Programs applet in Control Panel, remove and add a Windows component. Which component did you remove? Which component did you add?

4. Reboot your system and verify your changes were all implemented.

5. Now restore the system state from the backup you made. Which of your changes were undone and which (if any) were left untouched?

PROJECT 3-5:   Using the ASR Process

Create an ASR backup following directions in the chapter. Add a few data files to the hard drive. Restore the system using the ASR process. Do the data files still exist on the hard drive? Why or why not?

PROJECT 3-6:   Using the Microsoft Management Console

Using the Microsoft Management Console, follow the step-by-step directions in the chapter to create a customized console in Windows 2000/XP. Put two snap-ins in the console: Device Manager and Event Viewer.

PROJECT 3-7:   Using the Microsoft Knowledge Base

Using the Microsoft support Web site (*support.microsoft.com*), print information about the following:

▲ Troubleshooting IEEE 1394 devices running under Windows XP

▲ How to set up Windows XP to support multiple CPUs

▲ How to set up and troubleshoot multiple monitors with Windows XP

PROJECT 3-8:   Using Windows 2000 DiskProbe to Back Up the MBR

Windows 2000 DiskProbe edits individual sectors on a hard drive and can edit the MBR, boot sectors, and the FAT16, FAT32, and NTFS file system tables, as well as data files. Research DiskProbe and find directions that show you how to back up the MBR, which contains the partition table. Follow these directions and answer these questions:

1. In the C:\ProgramFiles\Support Tools folder, find the document Dskprtrb.doc, which describes how to use DiskProbe. Print the page from the document that describes how to save the MBR record on a floppy disk.

2. If the Windows 2000 Support Tools are not installed, install them now.

3. Run DiskProbe (click **Start**, point to **Programs, Windows 2000 Support Tools**, and **Tools**, and then click **DiskProbe**).

4. Follow the directions to save the MBR, including the partition table, to a floppy disk.

5. How many bytes of data are included in the MBR? What is the file size?

6. What is the disadvantage of using DiskProbe to restore the MBR in the event it becomes corrupted?

7. Research the Microsoft Web site. Is DiskProbe available in Windows XP? Where can you find it?

<u>**PROJECT 3-9:**</u>   Using Dependency Walker

Follow these steps to use Dependency Walker to list the files used by Internet Explorer:

1. If the Windows 2000/XP Support Tools are not installed, install them now.

2. Using directions in the chapter, run Dependency Walker.

3. Set Dependency Walker to show all supporting files used by Internet Explorer.

4. List the files or print the screen showing them.

<u>**PROJECT 3-10:**</u>   Finding Windows 2000/XP Utilities

The following table lists some important Windows utilities covered in this chapter. Fill in the right side of the table with the filename and path of each utility. (*Hint*: You can use Windows Explorer or Search to locate files.)

Utility	Filename and Path
System File Checker	
System Configuration Utility	
Command window	
Windows Backup	
System Information	
Task Manager	

>> REAL PROBLEMS, REAL SOLUTIONS

<u>**REAL PROBLEM 3-1:**</u>   Problems Starting Windows XP

Tim, a coworker who uses many different applications on his Windows XP system, complains to you that his system is very slow starting up and responding when he loads and unloads applications. You suspect the system is loading too many services and programs during startup that are sucking up system resources. What do you do to check for startup processes and eliminate the unnecessary ones? If you have access to a Windows XP system that needs this type of service, test your answers on this system. Write down at least 10 things you should do or try that were discussed in the chapter to speed up a sluggish Windows XP installation.

Supporting Windows 2000/XP Users and Their Data

In the last chapter, you learned how to support and maintain the Windows 2000/XP operating system. This chapter focuses on meeting user needs and supporting their data. In Windows 2000/XP, everything a user is allowed or not allowed to do is determined by the privileges assigned to the currently active user account. Therefore, the first step in learning how to support users is to learn how to set up and support a user account that meets the user's needs. Next, you'll learn about some Windows tools that can help you support users so that they can effectively do their jobs.

Last in the chapter, we'll focus on supporting the hard drive. The hard drive normally holds most user data and all user preferences and settings. Keeping the hard drive working well and keeping good backups are essential to maintaining the system and its data so that users don't have to be concerned about having to deal with a sluggish system or corrupted or lost data.

MANAGING USER ACCOUNTS

A+ ESS
3.1
3.2
6.1
6.2
6.3

A+
220-602
3.1
5.2
5.3
6.1
6.2

Windows 2000/XP requires a user to log onto the system with a valid user account before he or she can use Windows. If you are responsible for managing these accounts, you need to know how to set up a user account and how to help the user transfer files and settings that belong to his or her account from one computer to another.

UNDERSTANDING AND SETTING UP USER ACCOUNTS

In this section, you'll learn how to create and manage user accounts. If several users need access to a computer, to save time, you'll find it easier to manage user accounts and their profiles at the group level rather than individually. Let's first look at the different types of user accounts, the different groups to which a user account can belong, and how an account's user profile can be managed. Then you'll see how to create accounts and control how a user logs on and how to deal with a forgotten password.

> **Notes**
>
> Windows XP Professional supports a multilingual environment. For non-English speaking users, consider downloading and installing the Multilingual User Interface (MUI) components for Windows XP. To know more about these options, their benefits, and limitations, go to the Microsoft Web site and search on the TechNet article with the title "Comparing Windows XP Professional Multilingual Options."

TYPES OF USER ACCOUNTS

A **user account** defines a user to Windows and records information about the user, including the user name, the password used to access the account, groups to which the account belongs, and the rights and permissions assigned to the account. Permissions assigned to a user account control what the user can and cannot do and access in Windows.

There are two types of user accounts in Windows 2000/XP:

- **Global user accounts**, sometimes called domain user accounts, are used at the domain level, created by an administrator using Windows 2000 Server or Windows Server 2003, and stored in the SAM (security accounts manager) database on a Windows domain controller. A user can log on to any computer on the networked domain using a global user account, and the information about a global user account's rights and permissions apply to each workstation in the domain. The centralized SAM database is part of Active Directory, which is a repository of information used to manage a Windows network that is itself managed by Windows 2000 Server or Windows Server 2003. When a user logs on, the domain controller on the network manages the user account logon (see Figure 4-1). How to set up and manage global user accounts in a Windows domain is not covered in this book.

- A **local user account** is created on a local computer and allows a user access to only that one computer. An administrator creates a local user account, assigns a user name and password to the account, and gives the account rights and permissions. As a general rule, a user account should have no more rights than a user needs to do his or her job. For example, an administrator who is responsible for setting up and maintaining user accounts in an office workgroup can set the permissions on a user account to deny the user the right to install a printer, install software, or do any other chores that change the PC software or hardware environment.

Local user accounts are set up and managed at each individual workstation. When Windows 2000/XP is first installed, it automatically creates two local accounts, called **built-in user accounts**, as follows:

A+ ESS
3.1
3.2
6.1
6.2
6.3

A+
220-602
3.1
5.2
5.3
6.1
6.2

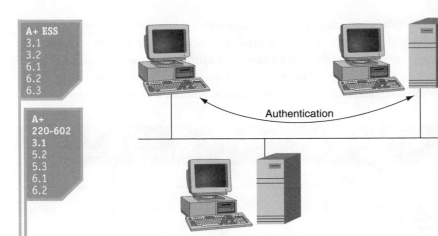

Figure 4-1 On a domain, a user account login is managed by the domain controller

▲ *The built-in administrator account.* An administrator has rights and permissions to all computer software, data, and hardware resources. Under Windows 2000/XP, the administrator can create other user accounts and assign corresponding rights and permissions to individual accounts, to groups of selected accounts, or to all accounts that use the computer.

▲ *The built-in guest account.* The built-in guest account has very limited privileges and gives someone who does not have a user account access to a computer. The guest account is useful in a business environment where many people use a single computer for limited purposes and it is not practical for all of them to have unique user accounts. For example, a hotel might provide a computer in the lobby for its guests who would log onto Windows using the built-in guest account.

USER GROUPS

A user group is a predefined set of permissions and rights assigned to user accounts, and is an efficient way for an administrator to manage multiple user accounts that require these same permissions and rights. When installed, Windows 2000/XP sets up several user groups, including the following:

▲ Administrator. An account that is a member of the Administrator group can install or uninstall devices and applications and can perform all administrative tasks. When Windows 2000/XP is first installed, one user account is created in this group and the account is called the Administrator.

▲ Backup Operators. An account that is a member of the Backup Operator group can back up and restore any files on the system regardless of their access privileges to these files.

▲ Power Users. A Power User account can read from and write to parts of the system other than their own local drive, install applications, and perform limited administrative tasks.

▲ Limited Users group (also known as Limited account or Users account). An account that is a member of the Limited Users group has read-write access only on its own folders, read-only access to most system folders, and no access to other users' data. Using a Limited account, a user cannot install applications or carry out any administrative responsibilities.

▲ Guests group. An account that is a member of the Guests group is intended to be used by people who use a workstation only once or occasionally and have limited access to files and resources. A guest account has permission to shut down a computer. When Windows 2000/XP is first installed, one Guest account is created.

A+ ESS
3.1
3.2
6.1
6.2
6.3

A+
220-602
3.1
5.2
5.3
6.1
6.2

With most Windows 2000/XP systems, an administrator can manage user accounts using only the administrator, limited account, and guest accounts. When an account is first created, the only available choices are administrator and limited. After the account is created, an administrator can assign an account to a group other than these two. Table 4-1 summarizes the permissions granted to the three account types: administrator, limited, and guest account.

Action Permitted	Administrator Account	Limited Account	Guest Account
Create user accounts	Yes		
Change system files	Yes		
Read other user account files	Yes		
Add or remove hardware	Yes		
Change other user account passwords	Yes		
Change your own user account password	Yes	Yes	
Install any software	Yes		
Install most software	Yes	Yes	
Save documents	Yes	Yes	Yes
Use installed software	Yes	Yes	Yes

Table 4-1   Actions permitted for three account types

ACCESS CONTROL

One of the main reasons for using account types that limit certain activities is so that an administrator can control what data files a user can access. For example, suppose a group of users in the Accounting Department works together in a workgroup. Some of these users need access to all payroll data, but other users are only allowed access to accounts payable and accounts receivable. In order to provide for this type of access control, an administrator will decide which type of user account an employee needs.

Suppose Danielle needs to use the local network to access payroll data that is stored on Kelly's computer. In order to provide for that access, the administrator must set up a user account for Danielle on Kelly's computer. Figure 4-2 shows what happens if a user tries to use

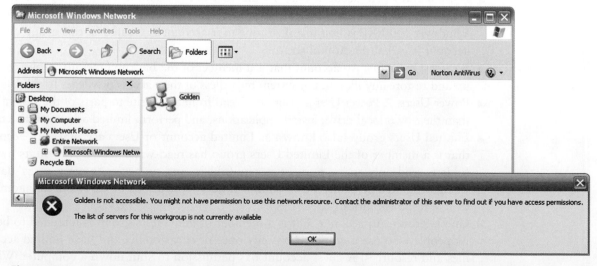

Figure 4-2   A user cannot access a networked computer unless he or she has an account on that computer

A+ ESS
3.1
3.2
6.1
6.2
6.3

A+
220-602
3.1
5.2
5.3
6.1
6.2

My Network Places to access a remote computer on the network without proper permissions. To keep this error from happening, an administrator needs to create an account on each individual computer in the workgroup that the user needs to access.

Also notice in Table 4-1 that a user account with limited or guest privileges cannot view the folders belonging to another account. Figure 4-3 shows the error displayed when a limited-account user attempted to view the files belonging to another user.

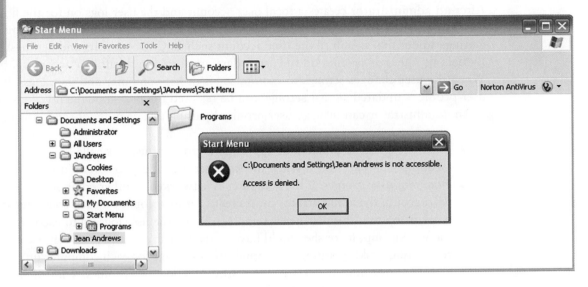

Figure 4-3　This user does not have access to another user's folders

Even though a limited or guest account cannot normally access files belonging to another account, an administrator can make exceptions as needed. The Cacls (change access control lists) command can be used to view and change the access control for files and folders.

Suppose, for example, an administrator wants to give permission for a user account, JSmith, to have access to a file, Myfile.txt. Figure 4-4 shows the use of five Cacls commands that can be used. The first, third, and fifth commands display access information for the Myfile.txt file (Cacls Myfile.txt). The second command grants read-only access for the

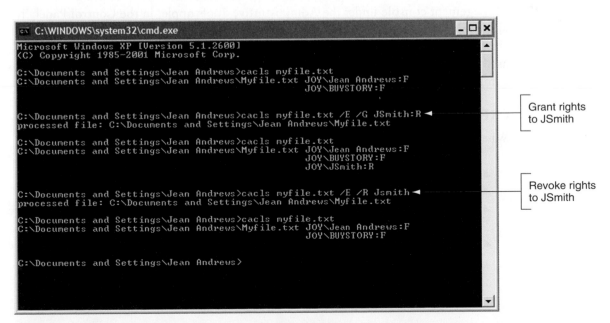

Figure 4-4　Use the Cacls command to change user permissions for files and folders

A+ ESS
3.1
3.2
6.1
6.2
6.3

user JSmith. (In the command line, the /E parameter says to edit the list and the /G parameter says to grant permission to the following user. The :R parameter says the permission is read-only.) The fourth command revokes JSmith's access permission. In Chapter 10, you'll learn how you can take more control over which user account has access to which files and folders.

USER PROFILES

A+
220-602
3.1
5.2
5.3
6.1
6.2

After an administrator creates a local user account and the user logs on for the first time, the system creates a **user profile** for that user. A folder is created in the C:\Documents and Settings folder that is named the user account such as C:\Documents and Settings\JSmith. By default, the user profile and the user's data are stored in this folder and its subfolders. When the user changes settings to customize his or her computer and then logs off, the user profile is updated so that settings can be restored the next time the user logs on.

An administrator can manage user profiles by using one or more of the following:

- ▲ *Group profiles*. A profile that applies to a group of users is called a **group profile**. Group profiles are useful when the same settings apply to several users.
- ▲ *Roaming user profiles*. If the computer is networked to other computers in a Windows workgroup, the administrator must create a user account on each computer in the workgroup that this user needs to access. When the user logs on to each computer in the workgroup, he or she would have to reestablish the user profile at each computer, re-creating desktop settings and application settings for each computer unless the administrator implements a feature called roaming user profiles. With **roaming user profiles**, settings established by a user at one computer are stored in a file on a file server on the network and shared with all computers in the workgroup. When a user moves from one computer to another computer in the workgroup, the roaming profile follows the user so that he or she does not have to redo settings at each computer.
- ▲ *Mandatory user profiles*. Another type of profile used with workgroups is a **mandatory user profile**. This profile is a roaming user profile that applies to all users in a user group, and individual users cannot change that profile. It is used in situations where users perform only specific job-related tasks.

An administrator creates group, roaming, and mandatory profiles using the Computer Management console under the Administrative Tools applet in the Control Panel. To view all profiles stored on a Windows XP computer, use the System Properties window. Click **Start** and then right-click **My Computer**. Select **Properties** and then click the **Advanced** tab, as shown in Figure 4-5. Under User Profiles, click the **Settings** button. For a Windows 2000 computer, in the System Properties window, click the **User Profiles** tab.

CREATING LOCAL USER ACCOUNTS

When setting up accounts for users, you need to be aware of these restrictions:

- ▲ User names for Windows 2000/XP logon can consist of up to 15 characters.
- ▲ Passwords can be up to 127 characters.
- ▲ User accounts can be set up with or without passwords. Passwords provide greater security. Where security is a concern, always set a password for the Administrator account.
- ▲ Passwords can be controlled by the administrator, but generally, users should be allowed to change their own passwords.

A+ ESS
3.1
3.2
6.1
6.2
6.3

A+
220-602
3.1
5.2
5.3
6.1
6.2

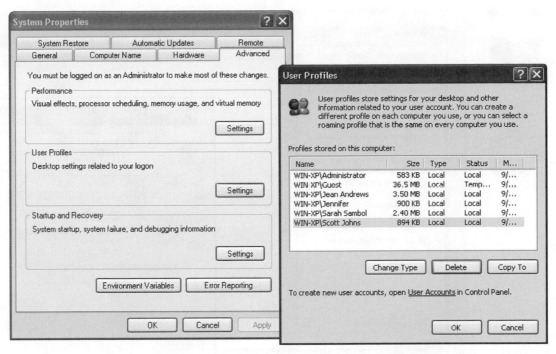

Figure 4-5 View all user profiles stored on this PC using the System Properties window

Where security is a concern, follow these guidelines to make passwords as secure as possible:

Notes

In Chapter 10, you'll learn more about how to create the most secure passwords.

- ◢ Do not use a password that is easy to guess, such as one consisting of real words, your telephone number, or the name of your pet.
- ◢ Use a password that is a combination of letters, numbers, and even non-alphanumeric characters.
- ◢ Use at least seven characters in a password.

APPLYING CONCEPTS As an administrator, you can create a user account using the Computer Management console or the User Accounts applet in the Control Panel. If the account is created in Computer Management, the account will automatically be added to the Limited group. If it is created using the Control Panel, the new account will be a member of the Administrator group.

To create a local user account using Computer Management, follow these steps:

1. Log on to the computer as an administrator.

2. Right-click **My Computer**. Select **Manage** on the shortcut menu. The Computer Management console window opens. (Note that you can also access Computer Management by way of the **Control Panel**, **Administrative Tools** applet.)

3. Expand **Local Users and Groups** by clicking the plus sign to its left. Right-click **Users** and then select **New User** on the shortcut menu. The New User window opens (see Figure 4-6). Enter the User name, enter the password twice, and check the boxes to decide how and when the password can be changed. You can also enter values for the Full name and Description to help identify the user. Click **Create**.

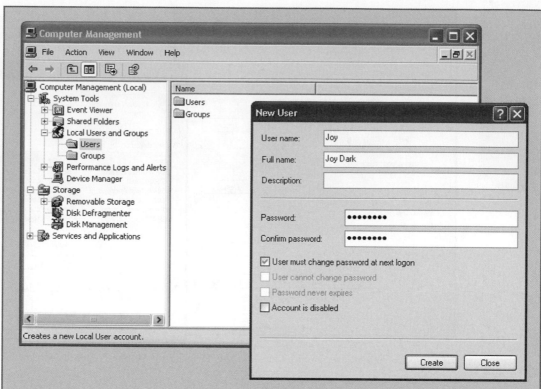

Figure 4-6 Create a user account using either Computer Management or the User Account applets in Control Panel

4. The account is created with the default type Limited, which means the account cannot create, delete, or change other accounts; make system-wide changes; or install software. If you want to give the account Administrator privileges, then open the **Control Panel** and double-click the **User Accounts** applet.

5. The User Accounts window opens, listing all accounts. To make changes to an account, click **Change an account**, and then click the account you want to change.

6. In the next window, you can choose to change the name of the account, change the password, remove a password, change the picture icon associated with the account, change the account type, or delete the account. Click **Change the account type**.

7. In the next window, select **Computer administrator** and click **Change Account Type**. Click **Back** twice on the menu bar to return to the opening window.

When you set up a user account, the account can be put into the Administrator group or the Limited Group. However, if you want to put the account into another user group, you must use the Computer Management console, as follows:

1. In the Computer Management windows, under Local Users and Groups, click **Groups**. The list of groups appears in the right pane (see Figure 4-7).

2. Right-click the group you want to assign a user and select **Add to Group** from the shortcut menu. The group's Properties window appears. For example, in Figure 4-8, the Power Users Properties window is showing. Listed in this window are all users assigned to this group.

4

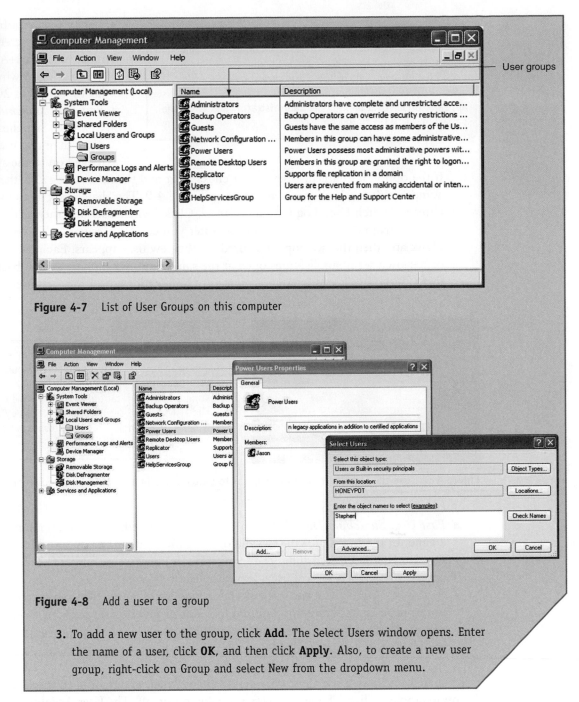

Figure 4-7 List of User Groups on this computer

Figure 4-8 Add a user to a group

3. To add a new user to the group, click **Add**. The Select Users window opens. Enter the name of a user, click **OK**, and then click **Apply**. Also, to create a new user group, right-click on Group and select New from the dropdown menu.

CONTROLLING HOW A USER LOGS ON

With Windows 2000, there is only one way to log on to the system: pressing the Ctrl+Alt+Del keys to open the logon window. Also, with Windows 2000, one user must log off before another can log on. However, Windows XP allows more than one user to be logged on at the same time (called multiple logons), and, in a Windows XP workgroup, you have some options as to how logging on works:

▲ *Welcome screen*. The default option is a Welcome screen that appears when the PC is first booted or comes back from a sleep state. All users are listed on the Welcome screen along with a picture (which can be the user's photograph); a user clicks his or her user name and enters the password.

> **Notes**
>
> When Windows XP lists the user accounts on the Welcome screen, it does not show the built-in administrator account in the list. If you want to log onto the system using this account, press Ctrl-Alt-Del. The Log On to Windows dialog box appears. Under User name, type **administrator**, and enter the password. Click **OK** to log on.

▲ *Logon window.* Instead of the Welcome screen, the user must press **Ctrl+Alt+Del** to get to a logon window similar to Windows 2000.

▲ *Fast User Switching Enabled.* Fast User Switching enables more than one user to be logged on to the system.

If the option is enabled, when a user clicks Start and then clicks Log Off, the Log Off Windows dialog box opens, as shown in Figure 4-9. This dialog box gives three choices: Switch User, Log Off, and Cancel. Click **Switch User** and then select a new account from the list of user accounts. After you enter a password, the screen goes blank and then the desktop configured for the new user appears. Each user can have his or her own set of applications open at the same time. When users switch back and forth, Windows keeps separate instances of applications open for each user.

> **Notes**
>
> When you log off, all your documents are closed. If you need to step away from your computer leaving your documents open, to secure or lock your Windows XP workstation, press the Windows key and L. For added security, in the Display Properties window, you can also require a password-protected screensaver.

Figure 4-9   Use the Log Off Windows dialog box to switch users in a multiple logon environment

▲ *Fast User Switching Disabled.* If this option is disabled, only one user can log on at a time. In the Log Off Windows dialog box, the Switch User option does not appear. Disable Fast User Switching when you want to conserve resources because performance is poor when several users leave applications open.

▲ *Automatic logon.* You can use automatic logon so that the Welcome screen does not appear and you are not required to select or enter a user account or enter its password. This method is like leaving your front door wide open when you leave home; it's not recommended because anyone can access your system.

To change the way a user logs on, open Control Panel, and then open the **User Accounts** applet. Click **Change the way users log on or off**. The User Accounts window opens as shown in Figure 4-10. If you want to require users to press Ctl-Alt-Del to get a logon window, then uncheck **Use the Welcome screen**. If you want to allow only one user logged on at a time, then uncheck **Use Fast User Switching**. When you're done with your changes, click **Apply Options** to close the window.

> **Notes**
>
> For a computer that belongs to a domain, you can enable automatic logon by editing the registry. How to do that is covered in the Microsoft Knowledge Base Article 315231.

To use automatic logon and bypass logging on altogether, for a standalone computer or one that is networked in a workgroup, enter **control userpasswords2** in the Run dialog box and press **Enter**. The User Accounts window shown in Figure 4-11 appears. Uncheck **Users must enter a user name and password to use this computer** and then click **Apply**.

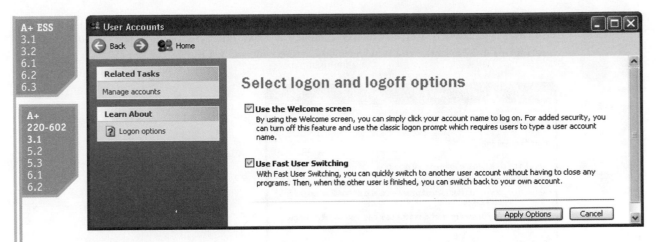

Figure 4-10 Options to change the way users log on or off

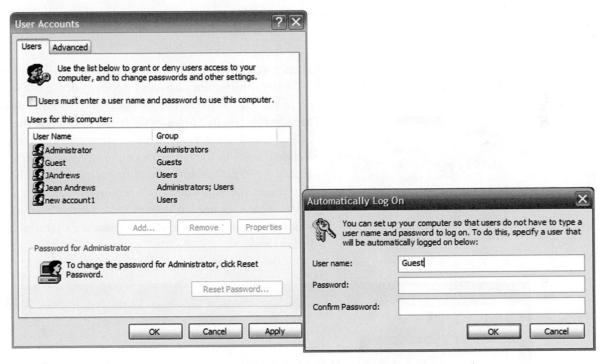

Figure 4-11 Configure Windows to automatically log on a user without a required password

A dialog box appears asking that you enter the user account and password that you want to use to automatically log on. Enter the account and password, and click **OK** twice to close both windows. Later, if you want to log onto the computer using a different user account, hold down the **Shift** key while Windows is starting.

FORGOTTEN PASSWORD

Sometimes a user forgets his or her password or the password is compromised. If this happens and you have Administrator privileges, you can reset the password.

Keep in mind, however, that resetting a password causes the OS to lock the user out from using encrypted email or files or from using Internet passwords stored on the computer. You can reset a password using the Computer Management console or the User Accounts applet. In the Computer Management console, right-click the user account and select **Set Password**

A+ ESS
3.1
3.2
6.1
6.2
6.3

A+
220-602
3.1
5.2
5.3
6.1
6.2

in the shortcut menu. A dialog box appears warning you of the danger of losing data when you reset a password. Click **Proceed** to close the box. The Set Password dialog box appears (see Figure 4-12). Enter the new password twice and click **OK**.

Figure 4-12 An administrator can reset a user account password

Because of the problem of losing encrypted data and Internet passwords when a user password is reset, each new user should create a **forgotten password floppy disk** for use in the event the user forgets the password. To create the disk, open the **User Accounts** applet in Control Panel, click the account, and select **Prevent a forgotten password** under Related Tasks in the left pane of the window shown in Figure 4-13. Follow the wizard to create the disk. Explain to the user the importance of keeping the disk in a safe place in case it's needed later. If a user enters a wrong password at logon, he or she will be given the opportunity to use the disk.

> **Notes**
>
> The forgotten password floppy disk should be kept in a protected place so that others cannot use it to gain unauthorized access to the computer.

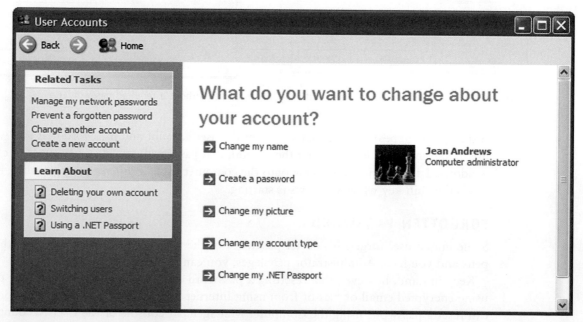

Figure 4-13 Create a forgotten password floppy disk

A+ ESS
3.1
3.2
6.1
6.2
6.3

A+
220-602
3.1
5.2
5.3
6.1
6.2

TRANSFERRING USER FILES AND PREFERENCES TO A NEW PC

When you're setting up a new user on a Windows XP computer, the user might want to move user files and preferences from another PC to this new PC. There are two tools to do that: the Files and Settings Transfer Wizard and the User State Migration Tool (USMT). These tools can help make a smooth transition because a user who is moving from one PC to another does not have to manually copy files and reconfigure OS settings.

Both utilities transfer files in the Documents and Settings folder as well as user preferences. Settings transferred include settings for Display Properties, Internet Explorer, MS Messenger, Netmeeting, Microsoft Office, Outlook Express, Media Player, and others. The transfer tools work if the old computer's OS is Windows 95, Windows 98, Windows 98SE, Windows ME, Windows NT 4.0, Windows 2000, or Windows XP (32-bit). Both transfer tools are discussed in this section.

 Notes

> Before using either of these tools, install antivirus software on the destination computer in case transferring user files also transfers a virus. You don't want the new PC to get infected. Also, make sure to apply all service packs and updates to Windows XP on the new computer before you perform the transfer. These service packs solved some problems with the tools that we'll be discussing in this section.

WINDOWS XP FILES AND SETTINGS TRANSFER WIZARD

The Windows XP **Files and Settings Transfer Wizard** is intended to be used by the user rather than the administrator. There is more than one way to use the wizard, but the steps listed below are the easiest method:

1. On the old computer, insert the Windows XP setup CD and open Windows Explorer. Locate on the CD the \Support\Tools folder and double-click the Files and Settings Transfer Wizard program, **Fastwiz.exe**. The wizard launches. Click **Next**.

2. On the next screen, you are asked if this is the new or old computer. Select **Old computer** and click **Next**.

3. The screen in Figure 4-14 appears, asking you to select a transfer method. Select **Other (for example, a removable drive or network drive)**. Click **Browse** and point to a

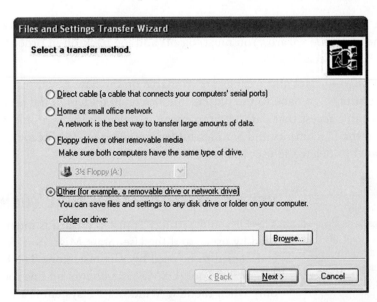

Figure 4-14 The Files and Settings Transfer Wizard is asking where to save data to be transferred

A+ ESS
3.1
3.2
6.1
6.2
6.3

A+
220-602
3.1
5.2
5.3
6.1
6.2

location to save the files and settings. If both the old and new computers are on the same network, it's convenient to point to a folder on the new computer. Click **OK** and then click **Next**.

4. Follow the wizard instructions on the next screens to select the files and settings you want to transfer. Then the wizard saves all the files and settings to the location you have specified. Click **Finish** to close the wizard.

5. Now go to the new computer and log onto your user account that is to receive the files and settings. Click **Start, All Programs, Accessories, System Tools,** and **Files and Settings Transfer Wizard**. The wizard's Welcome window opens. When you click **Next**, the wizard asks if this is the New computer or Old computer. Select **New computer** and then click **Next**. Figure 4-15 shows the next screen. Select **I don't need the Wizard Disk. I have already collected my files and settings from my old computer** and click **Next**.

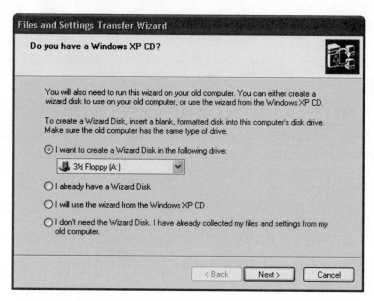

Figure 4-15   On the new computer, the Files and Settings Transfer Wizard can be used to point to the location of saved files and settings

6. Follow the wizard instructions onscreen to point to the location of the saved files and settings and close the wizard. You must log off and log back on in order for the changes to take effect.

7. Verify that all your data and settings are available on the new PC. If security is a concern, be sure to go back to the old PC and delete all folders in the user profile so that others can't access that data. A simple way to delete the user profile and all user data kept in the Documents and Settings folder is to use the User Accounts applet in Control Panel to delete the user account on the old PC.

Notes

Note the first option in Figure 4-15. You can use this option to put the wizard program on a floppy disk. This disk can then be used to run the wizard on the old computer if the old computer does not have a CD-ROM drive.

USER STATE MIGRATION TOOL (USMT)

The Files and Settings Transfer Wizard is intended to be used by users, and the User State Migration Tool (USMT) is designed to be used by administrators. The **User State Migration Tool (USMT)** is a command-line tool that works only when the new Windows XP system is a member of a Windows domain.

4

A+ ESS
3.1
3.2
6.1
6.2
6.3

A+
220-602
3.1
5.2
5.3
6.1
6.2

A+ ESS
3.1

A+
220-602
3.1

An administrator uses two commands at the command prompt of this tool: the scanstate command, which is used to copy the information from the old computer to a server or removable media, and the loadstate command, which is used to copy the information to the new computer. These two commands can be stored in batch files and executed automatically when installing Windows XP over a large number of computers in an enterprise. For details on how to use the command lines in a batch file, see the *Windows XP Resource Kit* by Microsoft Press.

TOOLS FOR SUPPORTING USERS AND THEIR DATA

In this part of the chapter, you'll learn about some tools that can help you support users. The tools covered are the Command Prompt window and its commands, Task Scheduler, Group Policy, Start menu, and Remote Assistance.

THE COMMAND PROMPT WINDOW

For all versions of Windows, you can open a Command Prompt window and use it to enter command lines to perform a variety of tasks, such as deleting a file or running the System File Checker utility. To open the window, click **Start**, click **Run**, and enter **Cmd** or **Cmd.exe** in the Run dialog box. When you're working in a Command Prompt window, to clear the window, type **Cls** and press **Enter**. To close the window, type **exit** and press **Enter**, as shown in Figure 4-16.

Figure 4-16 Use the exit command to close the Command Prompt window

Many of the commands you will learn about in this section can also be used from the Recovery Console. The Recovery Console is a command-line OS that you can load from the Windows 2000/XP setup CD to troubleshoot a system when the Windows desktop refuses to load. How to use the Recovery Console is covered in the next chapter.

FILE NAMING CONVENTIONS

When using the Command Prompt window to create a file, keep in mind that filename and file extension characters can be the letters a through z, the numbers 0 through 9, and the following characters:

In a Command Prompt window, if a filename has spaces in it, it is sometimes necessary to enclose the filename in double quotes.

> **Notes**
>
> As you work through the following list of commands, keep in mind that if you enter a command and want to terminate its execution before it is finished, you can press Ctrl+Break to do so.

> **A+ Exam Tip**
>
> The A+ Essentials exam expects you to know how to use the Cmd command to get a Command Prompt window.

WILDCARD CHARACTERS IN COMMAND LINES

> **A+ Exam Tip**
>
> The A+ 220-602 exam expects you to know how to use the Help, Dir, Attrib, Edit, Copy, Xcopy, Format, MD, CD, RD, Defrag, and Chkdsk commands, which are all covered in this section.

As you work at the command prompt, you can use two wildcard characters in a filename to execute a command on a group of files, or in an abbreviated filename if you do not know the entire name. The question mark (?) is a wildcard for one character, and the asterisk (*) is a wildcard for one or more characters. For example, if you want to find all files in a directory that start with A and have a three-letter file extension, you would use the following command:

```
dir a*.???
```

HELP

Use this command to get help about any command. Table 4-2 lists some sample applications of this command:

Command	Result
Help Xcopy	Gets help about the Xcopy command
Help	Lists all commands
Help |More	Lists information one screen at a time

Table 4-2 Sample Help commands

DIR

Use this command to list files and directories. Table 4-3 lists some examples using additional parameters, wildcards, and a filename:

Command	Result
DIR /P	Lists one screen at a time
DIR /W	Presents information using wide format, where details are omitted and files and folders are listed in columns on the screen
DIR *.txt	Lists all files with a .txt file extension
DIR Myfile.txt	Checks that a single file is present

Table 4-3 Sample Dir commands

DEL OR ERASE

The Del or Erase command erases files or groups of files. If the command does not include drive and directory information, the OS uses the default drive and directory when executing the command. The default drive and directory, also called the current drive and directory, shows in the command prompt. Note that in the command lines in this section, the command prompt is not bolded, but the typed command is in bold.

To erase all files in the A:\DOCS directory, use the following command:

```
C:\> ERASE A:\DOCS\*.*
```

A+ ESS
3.1

A+
220-602
3.1

To erase all files in the current default directory, use the following command:

```
A:\DOCS> DEL *.*
```

To erase all files in the current directory that have no file extensions, use the following command:

```
A:\DOCS> DEL *.
```

To erase the file named Myfile.txt, use the following command:

```
A:\> DEL MYFILE.TXT
```

COPY *[DRIVE:\PATH\]FILENAME [DRIVE:\PATH\]FILENAME*

The Copy command copies a single file or group of files. The original files are not altered. To copy a file from one drive to another, use a command similar to this one:

```
A:\> COPY C:\Data\Myfile.txt A:\mydata\Newfile.txt
```

The drive, path, and filename of the source file immediately follow the Copy command. The drive, path, and filename of the destination file follow the source filename. If you do not specify the filename of the destination file, the OS assigns the file's original name to this copy. If you omit the drive or path of the source or the destination, then the OS uses the current default drive and path.

To copy the file Myfile.txt from the root directory of drive C to drive A, use the following command:

```
C:\> COPY MYFILE.TXT A:
```

Because the command does not include a drive or path before the filename Myfile.txt, the OS assumes that the file is in the default drive and path. Also, because there is no destination filename specified, the file written to drive A will be named Myfile.txt.

To copy all files in the C:\DOCS directory to the floppy disk in drive A, use the following command:

```
C:\> COPY C:\DOCS\*.* A:
```

To make a backup file named System.bak of the System file in the \Windows\system32\config directory of the hard drive, use the following command:

```
C:\WINDOWS\system32\config> COPY SYSTEM SYSTEM.BAK
```

If you use the Copy command to duplicate multiple files, the files are assigned the names of the original files. When you duplicate multiple files, the destination portion of the command line cannot include a filename.

Notes

When trying to recover a corrupted file, you can sometimes use the Copy command to copy the file to new media, such as from the hard drive to a floppy disk. During the copying process, if the Copy command reports a bad or missing sector, choose the option to ignore that sector. The copying process then continues to the next sector. The corrupted sector will be lost, but others can likely be recovered. For Windows 2000/XP, the Recover command can be used to accomplish the same thing.

A+ ESS
3.1

A+
220-602
3.1

RECOVER

Use the Recover command to attempt to recover a file when parts of the file are corrupted. To use it, you must specify the name of a single file in the command line, like so:

```
C:\Data> Recover Myfile.doc
```

XCOPY /C /S /Y /D:

The Xcopy command is more powerful than the Copy command. It follows the same general command-source-destination format as the Copy command, but it offers several more options. For example, you can use the /S parameter with the Xcopy command to copy all files in the directory \DOCS, as well as all subdirectories under \DOCS and their files, to the disk in drive A, like so:

```
C:\> XCOPY C:\DOCS\*.* A: /S
```

To copy all files from the directory C:\DOCS created or modified on March 14, 2006, use the /D switch, as in the following command:

```
C:\> XCOPY C:\DOCS\*.* A: /D:03/14/06
```

Use the /Y parameter to overwrite existing files without prompting, and use the /C parameter to keep copying even when an error occurs.

MKDIR *[DRIVE:]PATH* OR MD *[DRIVE:]PATH*

The Mkdir command (abbreviated MD, for "make directory") creates a subdirectory under a directory. To create a directory named \Game on drive C, you can use this command:

```
C:\> MD C:\Game
```

The backslash indicates that the directory is under the root directory. To create a directory named Chess under the \Game directory, you can use this command:

```
C:\> MKDIR C:\Game\Chess
```

Note that the OS requires that the parent directory Game already exist before it creates the child directory Chess.

Figure 4-17 shows the result of the Dir command on the directory \Game. (Remember that it makes no difference if you use uppercase or lowercase in a command line.) Note the two initial entries in the directory table, the . (dot) and the .. (dot, dot) entries. The Mkdir command creates these two entries when the OS initially sets up the directory. You cannot edit these entries with normal OS commands, and they must remain in the directory for the directory's lifetime. The . entry points to the subdirectory itself, and the .. entry points to the parent directory, in this case, the root directory.

CHDIR *[DRIVE:]PATH* OR CD *[DRIVE:]PATH* OR CD..

The Chdir command (abbreviated CD, for "change directory") changes the current default directory. Using its easiest form, you simply state the drive and the entire path that you want to be current, like so:

```
A:\> CD C:\GAME\CHESS
```

4

```
C:\WINDOWS\system32\cmd.exe

C:\GAME>dir
 Volume in drive C has no label.
 Volume Serial Number is DCB8-611B

 Directory of C:\GAME

05/16/2006  02:07 PM    <DIR>          .
05/16/2006  02:07 PM    <DIR>          ..
               0 File(s)              0 bytes
               2 Dir(s)  45,675,298,816 bytes free

C:\GAME>md CHESS

C:\GAME>dir
 Volume in drive C has no label.
 Volume Serial Number is DCB8-611B

 Directory of C:\GAME

05/16/2006  02:07 PM    <DIR>          .
05/16/2006  02:07 PM    <DIR>          ..
05/16/2006  02:07 PM    <DIR>          CHESS
               0 File(s)              0 bytes
               3 Dir(s)  45,675,298,816 bytes free

C:\GAME>
```

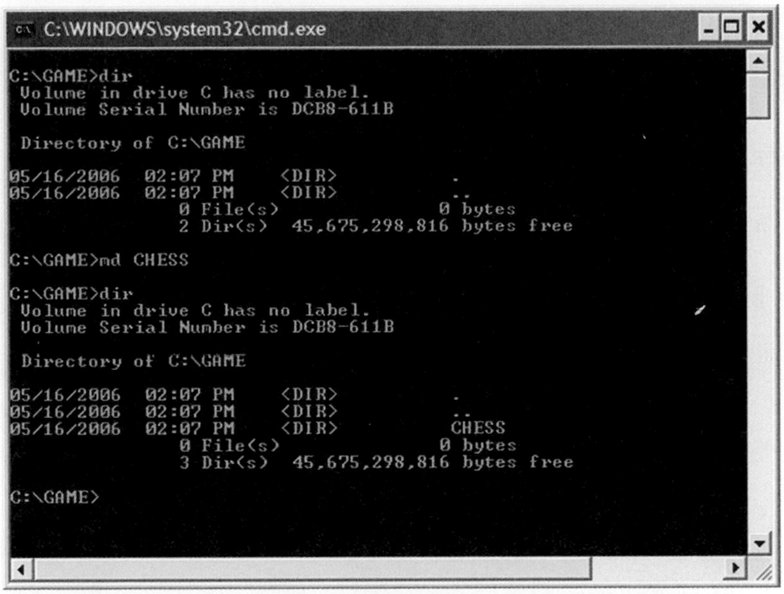

Figure 4-17   Results of the Dir command on the \Game directory

The command prompt now looks like this:

C:\GAME\CHESS>

To move from a child directory to its parent directory, use the .. variation of the command:

C:\GAME\CHESS> **CD..**

C:\GAME>

Remember that .. always means the parent directory. You can move from a parent directory to one of its child directories simply by stating the name of the child directory:

C:\GAME> **CD CHESS**

C:\GAME\CHESS>

   Remember to not put a backslash in front of the child directory name; doing so tells the OS to go to a directory named Chess that is directly under the root directory.

RMDIR *[DRIVE:]PATH* OR RD *[DRIVE:]PATH*

The Rmdir command (abbreviated RD, for "remove directory") removes a subdirectory. Before you can use the Rmdir command, three things must be true:

- ◢ The directory must contain no files.
- ◢ The directory must contain no subdirectories.
- ◢ The directory must not be the current directory.

The . and .. entries are present when a directory is ready for removal. For example, to remove the \Game directory in the preceding example, the Chess directory must first be removed, like so:

```
C:\> RMDIR C:\GAME\CHESS
```

Or, if the \GAME directory is the current directory, you can use this command:

```
C:\GAME> RD CHESS
```

After you remove the CHESS directory, you can remove the \GAME directory. However, it's not good to attempt to saw off a branch while you're sitting on it; therefore, you must first leave the \GAME directory like this:

```
C:\GAME> CD..
```

```
C:\> RD \GAME
```

ATTRIB

The Attrib command displays or changes the read-only, archive, system, and hidden attributes assigned to files. To display the attributes of the file Myfile.txt, you can use this command:

```
C:\> ATTRIB MYFILE.TXT
```

To hide the file, you can use this command:

```
C:\> ATTRIB +H MYFILE.TXT
```

To remove the hidden status of the file, you need to use this command:

```
C:\> ATTRIB -H MYFILE.TXT
```

To make the file a read-only system file, use this command:

```
C:\> ATTRIB +R +S MYFILE.TXT
```

When you put more than one parameter in the Attrib command, the order doesn't matter. This command works the same way as the one above:

```
C:\> ATTRIB +S +R MYFILE.TXT
```

To remove the read-only system status of the file, use this command:

```
C:\> ATTRIB -R -S MYFILE.TXT
```

The archive bit is used to determine if a file has changed since the last backup. To turn on the archive bit, use this command:

```
C:\> ATTRIB +A MYFILE.TXT
```

A+ ESS
3.1
3.3

A+
220-602
3.1

A+ ESS
3.1

To turn off the archive bit, use this command:

```
C:\> ATTRIB -A MYFILE.TXT
```

CHKDSK [DRIVE:] /F /R

Using Windows 2000/XP, the Chkdsk command fixes file system errors and recovers data from bad sectors. Used without any parameters, the Chkdsk command only reports information about a drive and does not make any repairs. However, used with the /F parameter, Chkdsk fixes file system errors it finds. These errors include those in the FAT or MFT caused by clusters marked as being used but not belonging to a particular file (called lost allocation units) and clusters marked as belonging to more than one file (called cross-linked clusters). A lost cluster is one that has no FAT or MFT entry pointing to it, and a cross-linked cluster is one that has two or more FAT or MFT entries pointing to it. (In the sample commands following, we're not showing the command prompt because the default drive and directory are not important.) To check the hard drive for these types of errors and repair them, use this command:

```
CHKDSK C: /F
```

To redirect a report of the findings of the Chkdsk command to a file that you can later print, use this command:

```
CHKDSK C: >Myfile.txt
```

Use the /R parameter of the Chkdsk command to fix file system errors and also examine each sector of the drive for bad sectors, like so:

```
CHKDSK C: /R
```

If Chkdsk finds bad sectors, it attempts to recover the data; it cannot actually repair bad sectors. The Chkdsk command will not fix anything unless the drive is locked, which means the drive has no open files. If you attempt to use Chkdsk with the /F or /R parameter when files are open, Chkdsk tells you of the problem and asks permission to run the next time Windows is restarted.

For Windows 2000/XP, Chkdsk can be used in a Command Prompt window, in the Recovery Console, or from the Windows desktop. (How to use Chkdsk from the Windows 2000/XP desktop is covered later in the chapter along with an expanded explanation of what the utility does and how it works.)

DEFRAG [DRIVE:]/S

The Defrag command examines a hard drive or disk for **fragmented files** (files written to a disk in noncontiguous clusters) and rewrites these files to the disk or drive in contiguous clusters. You use this command to optimize a hard drive's performance.

Use the /S:N parameter to sort the files on the disk in alphabetical order by filename, like so:

```
DEFRAG C: /S:N
```

Use the /S:D parameter to sort the files on the disk by date and time, as shown here:

```
DEFRAG C: /S:D
```

If Defrag discovers a drive does not need defragging, it gives that report and stops. The Defrag command works under Windows 9x/Me and Windows XP. It is not available from the Windows 2000/XP Recovery Console, and the command is not included with Windows 2000. You can also defrag a drive using the Disk Defragmenter utility from the Windows 2000/XP desktop. This utility is covered later in the chapter.

EDIT *[DRIVE:PATH]FILENAME*

The Edit program (Edit.com) is a handy, "quick and dirty" way to create and edit text files while working at a command prompt. For example, to create a file named Mybatch.bat in the C:\Data folder, use this command (a discussion of .bat files is coming up):

`C:\> ` **EDIT C:\Data\Mybatch.bat**

If the file does not already exist, Edit creates an empty file. Later, when you exit the Edit editor, changes you made are saved to the newly created file. Figure 4-18 shows the Mybatch.bat file being edited.

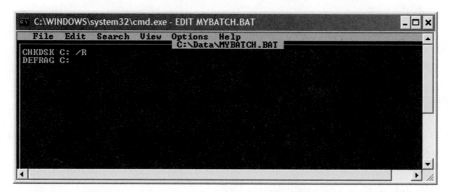

Figure 4-18 Using the Edit editor to create and edit the Mybatch.bat file

After you have made changes in this window, you can exit the editor this way: Press the **Alt** key to activate the menus, select the **File** menu, and then choose **Exit**. When asked if you want to save your changes, respond **Yes** to exit the editor and save changes. (You can also use your mouse to point to menu options.)

A file with a .bat file extension is called a **batch file**. You can use a batch file to execute a group of commands from a command prompt. To execute the commands stored in the Mybatch.bat file, enter the command Mybatch.bat at a command prompt, as shown in Figure 4-19.

Notice in Figure 4-19 that the Chkdsk command could not run because the system is currently in use. Later in the chapter, you'll learn how to schedule a batch routine to run in the middle of the night when it is unlikely the system will be in use.

> **Notes**
>
> Do not use word-processing software, such as Word or WordPerfect, to edit a batch file unless you save the file as a text (ASCII) file. Word-processing applications use control characters in their document files; these characters keep the OS from interpreting commands in a batch file correctly.

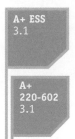

```
C:\WINDOWS\system32\cmd.exe - mybatch.bat                    _ □ X

C:\Data>EDIT MYBATCH.BAT

C:\Data>mybatch.bat

C:\Data>CHKDSK C: /R
The type of the file system is NTFS.
Cannot lock current drive.

Chkdsk cannot run because the volume is in use by another
process.  Would you like to schedule this volume to be
checked the next time the system restarts? (Y/N) n

C:\Data>DEFRAG C:
Windows Disk Defragmenter
Copyright (c) 2001 Microsoft Corp. and Executive Software Interna

Analysis Report
     74.52 GB Total,  42.53 GB (57%) Free,  7% Fragmented (15% fil
>
_
```

Figure 4-19   Executing the batch file

FORMAT *DRIVE:*/V:*LABEL*/Q /FS: *FILESYSTEM*

Recall that you can format a floppy disk using Windows Explorer and you can format a hard drive using Disk Management. In addition, you can use the Format command from a Command Prompt window and from the Windows 2000/XP Recovery Console. Table 4-4 lists various sample uses of the Format command.

Command	Description
Format A: /V:mylabel	Allows you to enter a volume label only once when formatting several disks. The same volume label is used for all disks. A volume label appears at the top of the directory list to help you identify the disk.
Format A: /Q	Re-creates the root directory and FATs if you want to quickly format a previously formatted disk that is in good condition. /Q does not read or write to any other part of the disk.
Format D: /FS:NTFS	Formats drive D using the NTFS file system.
Format D: /FS:FAT32	Formats drive D using the FAT32 file system.

Table 4-4   Sample usages of the Format command

TASK SCHEDULER

With the Windows 2000/XP Task Scheduler utility, you can schedule a batch routine, script, or program to run daily, weekly, monthly or at certain events such as startup. Scheduled tasks are stored in the C:\Windows\Tasks folder.

In the following steps, we'll schedule the Mybatch.bat file that you saw created earlier in the chapter to run at 11:59 p.m. every Monday. Recall that we created the Mybatch.bat file using the Edit command. You can also create a batch file using Notepad.

1. Click **Start, All Programs (Programs** for Windows 2000), point to **Accessories, System Tools,** and click **Scheduled Tasks.** The Scheduled Tasks window opens, as shown in Figure 4-20.

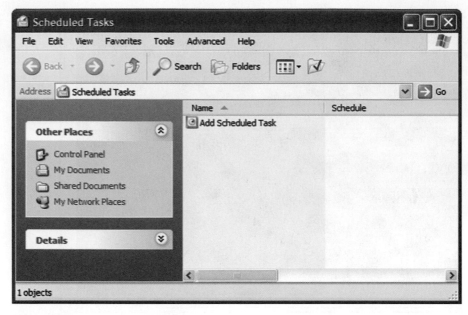

Figure 4-20   Use the Scheduled Tasks window to add, delete, or change a scheduled task

2. Double-click **Add Scheduled Task**. The Scheduled Task Wizard opens. Click **Next**. To select the program to schedule, click **Browse** and find and click the program file. In our example, we're using the **Mybatch.bat** file in the \Data folder. Click **Open**.

3. Enter a name for the scheduled task and select how often to perform the task, as shown in Figure 4-21, and then click **Next**.

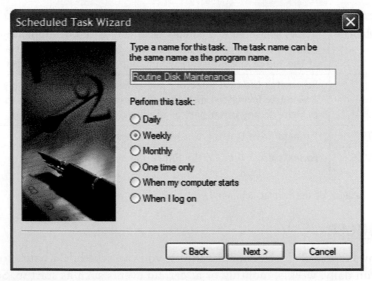

Figure 4-21   Name the task and select when it will be performed

4. Enter the start time and select the day of the week for the task to execute. For example, enter **11:59 PM every Monday**. Click **Next**.

5. Enter your or another username and the password to this user account. The task will run under this account name. Click **Next**.

6. The wizard reports the scheduled task parameters. Click **Finish**.

A+ ESS
3.4

7. To change settings for a scheduled task, right-click the task and select **Properties** from the shortcut menu. The properties window opens with the name of the task in the title bar of the window, as shown in Figure 4-22. You can use this window to change the initial and advanced settings for a task.

Figure 4-22 Advanced settings for a scheduled task

Later, to get a listing of information about scheduled tasks that have already run, open the Scheduled Tasks utility. If the details of previously run tasks are not shown in the window, you can click **View**, **Details**, to display these details.

> **Notes**
>
> Notice in Figure 4-22 the power management options to not run the task when a notebook computer is running on batteries and also the option to power up a system to run the task. This feature requires a motherboard that supports the option for software to power up the PC and the feature is enabled in CMOS setup. To learn if your motherboard supports the feature, see CMOS setup or the motherboard documentation. If not, the PC must be turned on for the scheduler to work.

GROUP POLICY

A+ ESS
6.1
6.2
6.3

A+
220-602
5.2
5.3
6.1
6.2
6.3

Another way to manage what users can do and how the system can be used is by applying settings from the **Group Policy** console (Gpedit.msc) under Windows XP Professional and Windows 2000 Professional.

Group Policy works by making entries in the registry, applying scripts to the Windows startup, shutdown, and logon processes, and affecting security settings. Group Policy is intended to be used on a domain where group polices are managed by Active Directory, although you can use it on a standalone computer or a computer in a work-

> **Notes**
>
> Windows XP Home Edition does not have the Group Policy console.

group. Group Policy can be applied to your computer, regardless of the currently logged-on user (called Computer Configuration in the Group Policy console) or can be applied to each

A+ ESS
6.1
6.2
6.3

A+
220-602
5.2
5.3
6.1
6.2
6.3

user who logs on (called User Configuration in the Group Policy console). Computer-based policies are applied just before the logon window is displayed, and user-based policies are applied after a user logs on. For a standalone computer or a computer in a workgroup, to control the computer for all users, use Computer Configuration instead of User Configuration to implement Group Policy settings.

To access the Group Policy console, enter **gpedit.msc** in the Run dialog box. Notice in the Group Policy window (see Figure 4-23) the two main groups of policies: Computer Configuration and User Configuration.

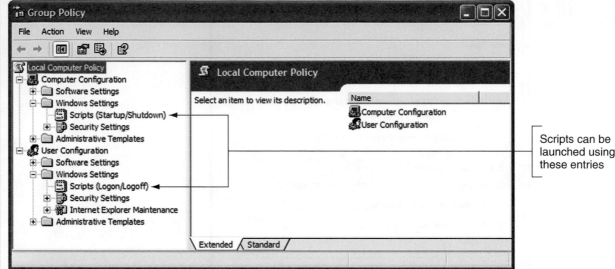

Scripts can be launched using these entries

Figure 4-23 Using the Group Policy console, you can control many Windows events and settings, including the startup process

Also in Figure 4-23, you can see four ways a script can be launched using Group Policy: at startup, shutdown, when a user logs on, or when a user logs off. Because a script can launch a program, Group Policy can be used to launch a program. These scripts are stored in one of these four folders:

▲ C:\WINDOWS\System32\GroupPolicy\Machine\Scripts\Startup
▲ C:\WINDOWS\System32\GroupPolicy\Machine\Scripts\Shutdown
▲ C:\WINDOWS\System32\GroupPolicy\User\Scripts\Logon
▲ C:\WINDOWS\System32\GroupPolicy\User\Scripts\Logoff

It's important to know about these four folders because malicious software has been known to hide in them. When trying to solve a problem with startup or shutdown, one thing you can do is look in these four folders for any unwanted scripts or programs. You'll learn more about startup and shutdown problems in Chapter 5 and about ridding your system of malicious software in Chapter 10.

To see what Group Policies are currently applied to the system, you can enter the Windows 2000/XP command, **Gpresult.exe**, at a command prompt, or you can use the Windows XP Help and Support Center. To use the Help and Support center, click **Start**, **Help and Support**. On the right side of the window, click **Use Tools to view your computer information and diagnose problems**. Then, in the left pane, click **Advanced System Information**. Next click **View Group Policy settings applied**. Information is first collected and then the window in Figure 4-24 appears.

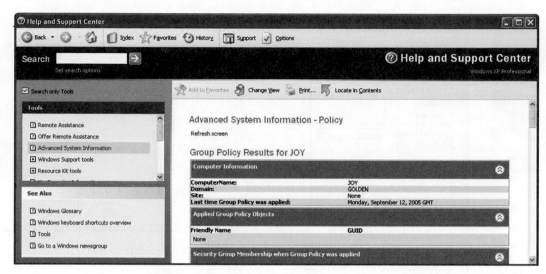

Figure 4-24 Use the Help and Support Center to view Group Policies currently applied to your system and environment

To add or remove a Group Policy that is executed at startup, open the Group Policy console (Gpedit.msc) and do the following:

1. In the Group Policy window, under either Computer Configuration or User Configuration, open **Administrative Templates**, open **System**, and then open **Logon** (see Figure 4-25).

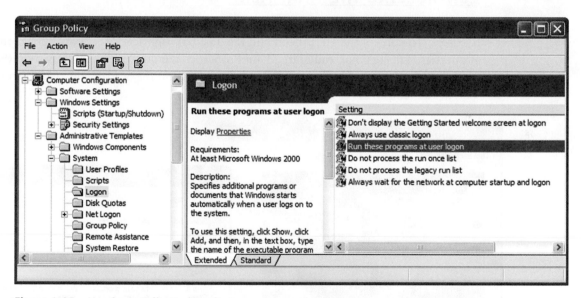

Figure 4-25 Use Group Policy to launch a program or script at logon

2. In the right pane, double-click **Run these programs at user logon,** which opens the properties window shown on the left side of Figure 4-26. Select **Enabled** and then click **Show**. The Show Contents dialog box opens, which is shown on the right side of Figure 4-26.

3. To add a script or executable program to the list of items to run at logon, click **Add**. In the figure, a batch file has been added so that you can see a sample of a program that will launch at logon. To remove an item from the list, select it and click **Remove**. Click **OK** to close the dialog box and **Apply** to apply the changes. Click **OK** to close the Properties window.

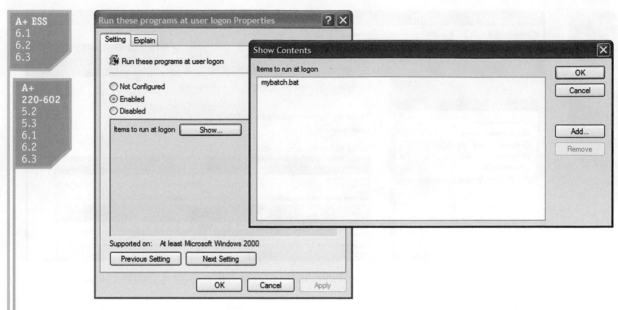

Figure 4-26 Group Policy items to run at logon

4. To put into effect the changes you have made, reboot the system or enter the command **Gpupdate.exe** at the command prompt.

CONTROLLING THE START MENU

An administrator might want to control the programs that appear on the Start menu for all users. To control the Start menu and the Taskbar, right-click the **Start** button and select **Properties**. The Taskbar and Start Menu Properties window opens, as shown on the left side of Figure 4-27. Click **Customize** to change the items on the Start menu, as shown on the right side of the figure.

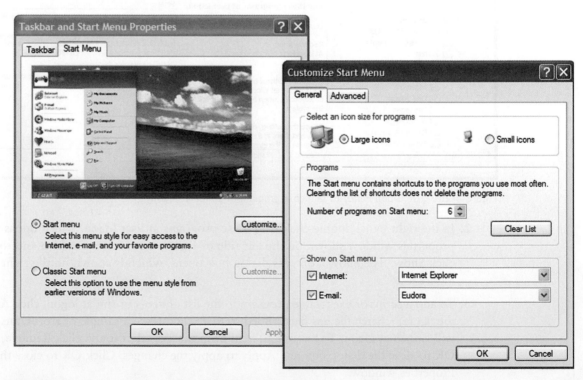

Figure 4-27 Customize the taskbar and Start menu

4

A+ ESS
3.1

You can also control items that appear in the Windows XP All Programs menu or the Windows 2000 Programs menu. To do that, right-click the **Start** button and select **Open All Users** from the shortcut menu, as shown in Figure 4-28. The Start Menu folder opens as shown in Figure 4-29. Items in this folder appear at the top of the All Programs or Programs menu. Open the **Programs** folder to view and change items that appear in the lower part of the All Programs or Programs menu.

Figure 4-28   Shortcut menu available on the Start button

Figure 4-29   The Start Menu folder

A+
220-602
3.4

WINDOWS XP REMOTE ASSISTANCE

Windows XP also offers two new features called Remote Desktop and Remote Assistance. **Remote Desktop** allows a user to connect to and use their Windows XP computer from anywhere on the Internet. You will learn to use Remote Desktop in Chapter 9. Using **Remote Assistance**, a user sitting at the PC can give a support technician at a remote location full access to the desktop. Let's first look at how you as a technician can use Remote Assistance, and then we'll look at what has to be in place before you can use it.

HOW TO USE REMOTE ASSISTANCE

As a PC support technician, you might be called on to help a Windows XP user over the phone. If you've ever had to work with a novice user in this situation, you know how frustrating this can be. Remote Assistance can help both you and the user through this situation by allowing the user to give you remote control of his or her desktop. As you work, the user can watch the desktop as you solve the problem at hand. As the user watches, it's a good idea to explain what you are doing and why you are doing it so that the user can learn from the experience and be comfortable with what you are doing. As you use Remote Assistance, you can talk with the user over the phone or by a chat window that is part of Remote Assistance.

To use Remote Assistance, the user sends you an invitation to help, and then you accept the invitation and initiate the session. The user then agrees to allow you to connect and must also agree to give you control of his desktop. The user can also require you to enter a password to connect and can put a time limit on when the invitation will expire. In this section, we're assuming that Remote Assistance has already been set up for first use. How to set up Remote Assistance for first use is covered in the next section.

Have the user do the following to send you an invitation:

1. Click **Start, Help and Support**. The Help and Support Center opens (see Figure 4-30). Click **Invite a friend to connect to your computer with Remote Assistance**. On the next window, click **Invite someone to help you**.

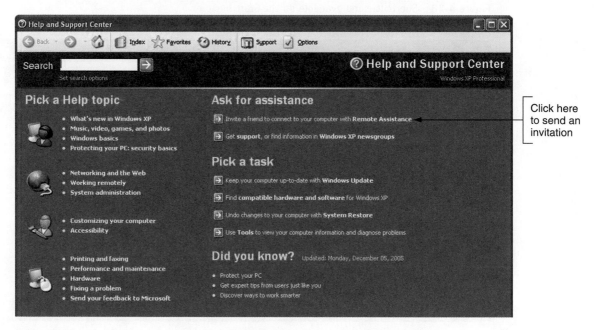

Figure 4-30 The first step in using Remote Assistance is a user sends an invitation

2. In the next window, shown in Figure 4-31, the user must select how the invitation will be sent. The invitation is actually an encoded file named RcBuddy.MsRcIncident. The user can send the file to you in one of three ways: by using Windows Messenger, by using e-mail, or by saving the file to some location such as a floppy disk or shared folder on a file server. Either way, you must have the file in order to accept the invitation. For the e-mail invitation, the user enters your e-mail address and then clicks **Invite this person**. A box appears allowing the user to enter a text message. The user can enter any text message and then clicks **Continue**.

3. On the next screen, shown in Figure 4-32, the user can set a time limit on the invitation and enter a password that you must use in order to make the connection. The user can tell you the password over the phone. The user then clicks **Send Invitation**.

4. When you receive the e-mail, the invitation is an attached file.

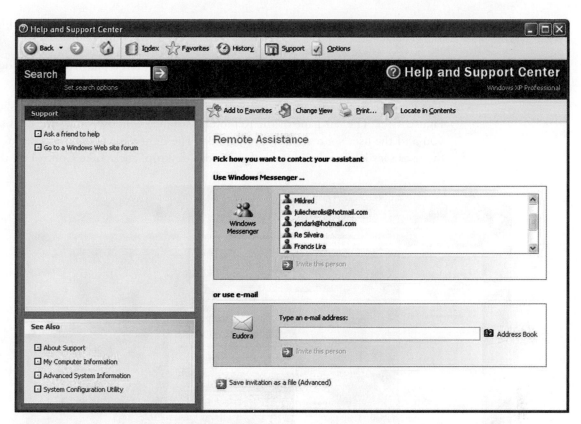

Figure 4-31   The user decides how the invitation will be sent

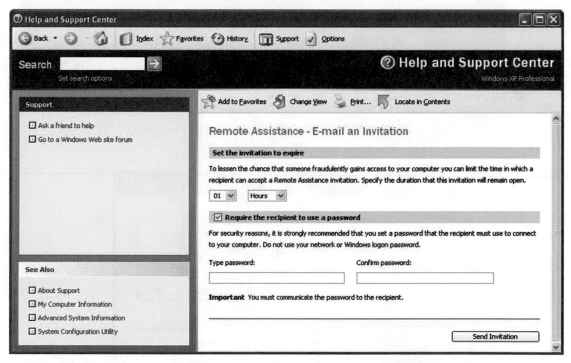

Figure 4-32   The user can require a password and set a time limit on the invitation

A+
220-602
3.4

The next step is for you to accept the invitation and initiate the session, as follows:

1. Double-click the invitation file. If the user has required a password, a dialog box appears asking for it. Enter the password and click **Yes**.

2. The Remote Assistance window opens on your desktop, similar to the one shown in Figure 4-33. The left pane of the Remote Assistance window shows the chat session that you and the user share for communication. The right pane is the user's desktop just as the user sees it. To take control of the user's desktop, click **Take Control** on the menu.

Chat session between you and the user

Your desktop

User's desktop

Figure 4-33 The Remote Assistance window on the technician's desktop

3. A dialog box appears on the user's screen, as shown in Figure 4-34. When the user clicks **Yes**, you can control the desktop.

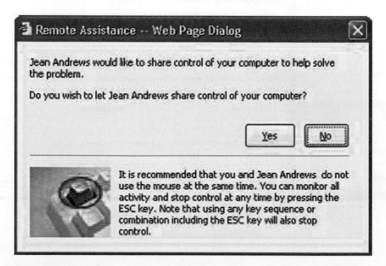

Figure 4-34 The user must perform this final step of the invitation

4

A+
220-602
3.4

4. The user's desktop looks like the one in Figure 4-35. The Remote Assistance window is displayed with a white chat box on the left side that can be used for the two of you to chat.

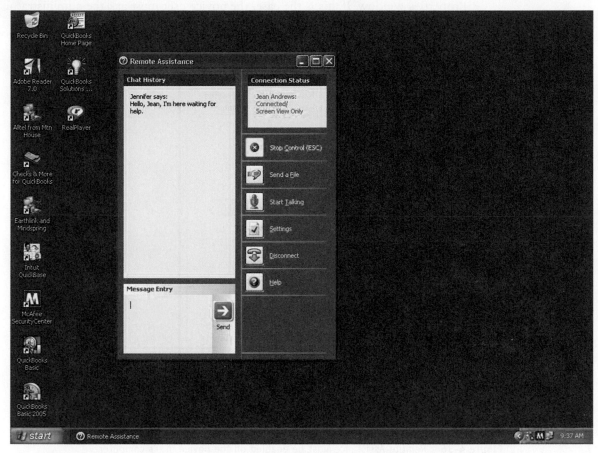

Figure 4-35 The Remote Assistance window on the user's desktop

5. As you work, the user can watch every keystroke and action that you execute on the user's desktop. If the user presses any key, control returns to the user. Either one of you can end the session by clicking **Disconnect**. The invitation can be used more than once until the time limit has expired.

HOW TO SET UP REMOTE ASSISTANCE FOR FIRST USE

As you have just seen, Remote Assistance is a nifty little tool that can make life easy when it works. It's an especially useful tool in a corporate environment where technical support staff within the company have expected and prepared for Remote Assistance sessions to be used when they support their in-house customers. However, as you're about to see, Remote Assistance is awkward and difficult to use when preparations have not been made in advance and when the user and the technician are connected only by the Internet.

Here is what must happen before Remote Assistance can be used for the first time:

▲ Unless both computers are on the same domain, the technician must have the same user account set up on both computers and this account must have the same password.

A+
220-602
3.4

◢ Remote Assistance must be enabled on the user's computer. To do that, open the System Properties box on the user's computer and select the **Remote** tab (see Figure 4-36). Check **Allow Remote Assistance invitations to be sent from this computer**, and then click **OK**. Some user accounts don't have the privilege of making changes on the System Properties window. If this is the case, the novice user must ask the administrator to enable Remote Assistance on the user's computer.

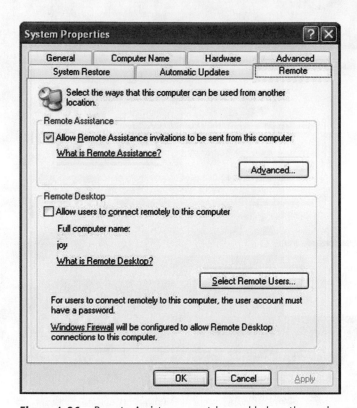

Figure 4-36 Remote Assistance must be enabled on the novice user's computer

If you and the user are both on the same local network, you are now ready to create a Remote Assistance session, which should happen with ease. However, if you are connected by way of the Internet, things can get complicated. Here are the concerns:

◢ If the user is behind a hardware or software firewall, the firewall might have to be told to allow a Remote Assistance session. For hardware firewalls, the user must know how to do this, which is different for each device. The user can find the directions in the user manual that came with the firewall and follow these directions.

◢ If you are sitting behind a firewall, you also might have to configure your firewall to allow the Remote Assistance session. How to configure firewalls is covered in Chapter 9.

For a novice user who is already frustrated with a Windows XP problem and is not able to follow directions given by a technician, all this preparation might be too much. You have to judge when Remote Assistance helps and when it just further complicates your situation.

> **Notes**
>
> Several alternatives to Remote Assistance are available. One excellent product is Control-F1 by Blueloop (www.ctrl-f1.co.uk). Using Control-F1, when a technician is in a chat session with a customer somewhere on the Internet, a remote control session can easily be established with a few clicks.

4

SUPPORTING HARD DRIVES

A+ ESS
3.1
3.2
3.3
3.4

A+
220-602
3.1
3.2
3.4

Hard drives that are heavily used over time tend to fill up with outdated and unneeded software and data over time. Therefore, they tend to slow down because they are not properly optimized. And inevitably, something is going to go wrong with Windows or the drive itself, and backups will be your only salvation. For all these reasons, a PC support technician needs to know how to perform routine maintenance on a hard drive and show users how to do it, how to configure a hard drive to conserve space, how to keep good backups of user data, and how to recover data when it gets lost or corrupted. All these skills are covered in the following sections of the chapter.

HARD DRIVE ROUTINE MAINTENANCE TASKS

We now look at three important routine maintenance tasks for hard drives: deleting temporary files, defragging the drive, and scanning it for errors.

DISK CLEANUP

Temporary or unneeded files accumulate on a hard drive for a variety of reasons. For instance, an installation program might not clean up after itself after it finishes installing an application, and cached Web pages can take up a lot of disk space if you don't have the Internet settings correct. In addition, don't forget about the Recycle Bin; deleted files sit there taking up space until you empty it.

Microsoft says that Windows XP needs at least 318 MB of free hard drive space for normal operation, and the Defrag utility needs at least 15 percent of the hard drive to be free before it can completely defrag a drive. So, it's important to occasionally delete unneeded files. Disk Cleanup (Cleanmgr.exe) is a convenient way to delete temporary files on a hard drive. To access Disk Cleanup under Windows 2000/XP, use one of these two methods:

▲ Enter **Cleanmgr.exe C:** in the Run dialog box and press **Enter.**
▲ Right-click the drive in My Computer or Windows Explorer and select **Properties** from the shortcut menu. The Disk Properties window opens, as shown in Figure 4-37. On the General tab, click **Disk Cleanup.**

Regardless of how you launch the utility, the window in Figure 4-38 opens. From this window, you can select nonessential files to delete in order to save drive space. In addition, Disk Cleanup tells you how much total space you can save and how much space each type of removable file is taking; it also describes each type of file. Included in the list are temporary files created by applications that the applications no longer need.

DEFRAG AND WINDOWS DISK DEFRAGMENTER

Another problem that might slow down hard drive performance is fragmentation. Recall that a cluster is the smallest unit of space on a hard drive that can hold a file. An OS views a hard drive as a long list of clusters that it can use to hold its data. When several clusters are used to hold a single file, this group of clusters is called a **chain.** **Fragmentation** occurs when a single file is placed in clusters that are not right next to each other.

After many files have been deleted and added to a drive, files become fragmented. On a well-used hard drive, it is possible to have a file stored in clusters at 40 or more locations. Fragmentation is undesirable because when the OS has to access many different locations on the drive to read a file, access time slows down. In addition, if the file becomes corrupted, recovery utilities are less likely to be able to find all the clusters of this file if the file is fragmented rather than located on the drive in one continuous chain.

Figure 4-37 The Disk Properties window

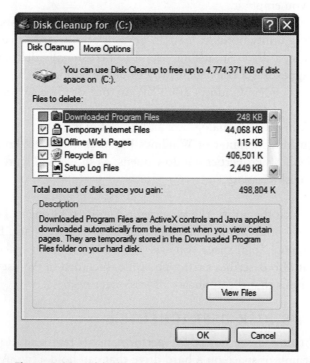

Figure 4-38 Disk Cleanup is a quick-and-easy way to delete temporary files on a hard drive

To reduce fragmentation of the drive, you can **defragment** the hard drive periodically. You should defragment your hard drive at a minimum of every six months, and ideally every month, as part of a good maintenance plan.

Here are the different ways to defrag a drive:

▲ For Windows 2000 or Windows XP, to use Disk Defragmenter, first close all open applications. Then choose **Start, All Programs** (**Programs** for Windows 2000),

A+ ESS
3.1
3.2
3.3
3.4

A+
220-602
3.1
3.2
3.4

Accessories, and **System Tools**. Then click **Disk Defragmenter**. From the Disk Defragmenter window (see Figure 4-39), you can select a drive and defragment it.

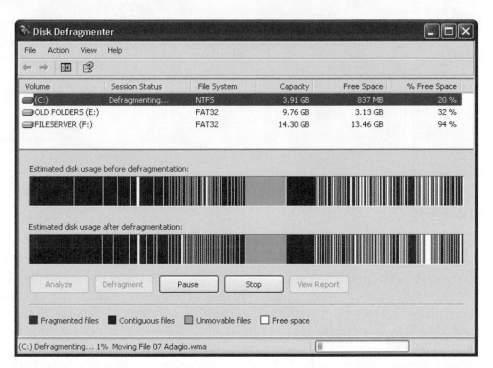

Figure 4-39 Windows XP defragmenting a volume

◢ Enter **Dfrg.msc** in the Run dialog box and press **Enter**.
◢ For Windows XP, recall from earlier in the chapter, the Defrag command (**Defrag.exe**) can be used from a command prompt. Enter Defrag X:, where X: is the logical drive you want to defrag.

> **Notes**
>
> Defragmenting a large hard drive might take a long time, even several days for a very large drive with millions of files, so plan for this before you begin.

Generally, defragmenting a hard drive should be done when the hard drive is healthy; that is, it should be done as part of routine maintenance. If you get an error message when attempting to defrag, try the utilities discussed in the following sections to repair the hard drive and then try to defrag again.

CHKDSK AND ERROR CHECKING

Recall from earlier in the chapter that you can use the Chkdsk command to repair hard drive errors. The utility is also available from the Windows 2000/XP desktop. Before we see how to use the desktop utility, you might be interested in knowing exactly what the utility is doing.

Recall that a directory or folder on a floppy disk or hard drive contains a list of all the files in that directory or folder. Also recall that for the FAT file system, the FAT contains a long list of cells, one cell for each cluster on the drive. For each file in a directory, the directory entry contains the cluster number for the first cluster used to hold the file. For example, in Figure 4-40, a directory contains four files. File 1 starts in cluster 4 on the drive and uses eight clusters (clusters 4, 5, 6, 7, 22, 23, 24, and 25). In the figure, you can see the directory entry for File 1 contains a 4 that indicates the file begins in cluster 4.

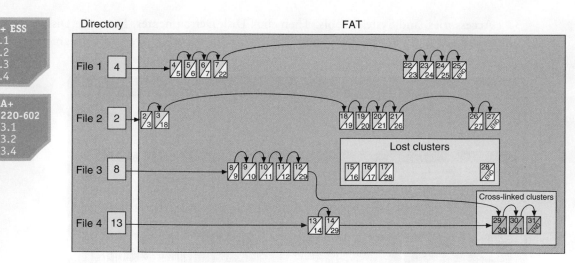

Figure 4-40   Lost and cross-linked clusters

To know which other clusters are used for the file, you would have to turn to the FAT because each cell in the FAT contains a pointer to the next cluster used by the file, forming a cluster chain. In Figure 4-40, each box in the FAT represents a cluster on the drive. The top number in the box represents the position of the cell in the FAT and, therefore, the cluster on the drive. For example, for the first box of File 1, the 4 says this box is in the fourth position in the FAT and represents the fourth cluster on the drive. The bottom number in the box is what is actually written in the FAT cell and is a pointer to the next cluster on the drive in the file chain. In the first box of File 1, the bottom number is a 5, indicating the next cluster used by the file is the fifth cluster on the drive. The fifth cell contains a 6, meaning the next cluster used by the file is the sixth cluster on the drive. The sixth cell entry contains a 7. The seventh cluster entry contains a 22 and so forth, until the 25th cell contains an end-of-file marker indicating the file ends with cluster 25. Therefore, the FAT holds the map or chain to all the other clusters in the file.

Occasionally, the chain of entries in the FAT becomes corrupted, resulting either in lost clusters or cross-linked clusters, as shown in Figure 4-40. In the figure, the chain of FAT entries for File 3 has lost track of its clusters and points to a cluster chain that belongs to File 4. Clusters 29 through 31 are called **cross-linked clusters** because more than one chain points to them, and clusters 15 through 17 and 28 are called **lost clusters** or **lost allocation units** because no chain in the FAT points to them. Using the NTFS file system, the same types of errors—cross-linked and lost clusters—can occur inside the master file table (MFT).

Another problem that can occur with hard drives is bad sectors. Bad sectors are caused by a corrupted area on the hard drive that is not able to consistently keep data. If Event Viewer reports many read or write errors to a drive, suspect many sectors are going bad and it's time to replace the drive. Chkdsk cannot actually repair a bad sector, but it might be able to recover the data stored in one.

Using Windows 2000/XP, searching for and repairing file system errors and bad sectors can be done using two different methods. Both methods launch the same utility, Chkdsk.exe, and are described in the following list:

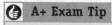 **A+ Exam Tip**

The A+ Essentials exam expects you to know how to check a disk for errors using Windows 2000/XP Chkdsk.

▲ *Error Checking from the Windows desktop.* Open Windows Explorer or My Computer, right-click the drive, and select **Properties** from the shortcut menu.

4

A+ ESS
3.1
3.2
3.3
3.4

A+
220-602
3.1
3.2
3.4

Click the **Tools** tab, as shown in the left window in Figure 4-41, and then click **Check Now**. The Check Disk dialog box opens, as shown on the right side of Figure 4-41. Check the **Automatically fix file system errors** and **Scan for and attempt recovery of bad sectors** check boxes, and then click **Start**. For the utility to correct errors on the drive, it needs exclusive use of all files on the drive, which Windows calls a locked drive. If files are open, a dialog box opens telling you about the problem and asking your permission to scan the drive the next time Windows starts.

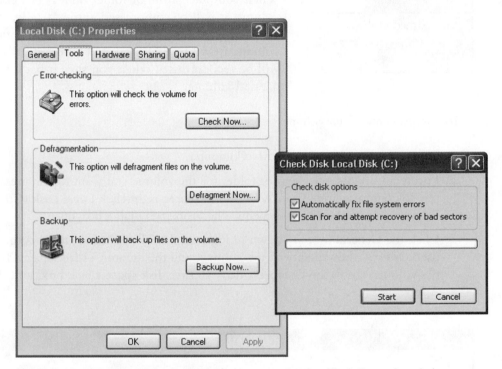

Figure 4-41   Windows XP repairs hard drive errors under the drive's Properties window using Windows Explorer

▲ *The Windows 2000/XP Chkdsk command.* You learned how to use the Chkdsk command earlier in the chapter. You can use it from a Command Prompt window or from the Recovery Console.

Scanning the entire hard drive for bad sectors can take a long time and must be done when the computer is not in use so that the hard drive can be locked down (that is, have no files open) for the entire process. In other words, start the job and then expect a long wait until it's done.

CONSERVING HARD DRIVE SPACE

A+
220-602
3.1
3.2
3.4
5.2
6.1

Besides cleaning the hard drive of unneeded files, two other ways to conserve hard drive space are to implement disk, folder, or file compression and to use disk quotas. Both conservation methods are discussed in this section.

DISK, FOLDER, AND FILE COMPRESSION

Compressing files, folders, or entire volumes reduces the hard drive space required for data and software. As such, using compression can help meet the ever-increasing demand for

A+ ESS
3.1
3.2
3.3
3.4

A+
220-602
3.1
3.2
3.4
5.2
6.1

more space on hard drives. For instance, software packages requiring 200 to 250 MB of hard drive space were unheard of three or four years ago, but these space requirements are now quite common. Although hard drive sizes have increased as well, we often seek ways to cram still more data onto nearly full hard drives.

Compression software works under Windows 2000/XP at the file, folder, or volume level by rewriting data in files in a mathematically coded format that uses less space. Using the NTFS file system in Windows 2000/XP, you can compress a single file or folder or you can compress the entire NTFS volume. When you place a file or folder on a NTFS compressed volume, it will be compressed automatically. When you open a compressed file that is stored on a compressed volume, it will be decompressed automatically and then will be recompressed when you save it back to the compressed volume.

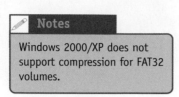

Notes

Windows 2000/XP does not support compression for FAT32 volumes.

To compress an NTFS volume:

1. Open Windows Explorer or My Computer.

2. Locate and right-click the root folder for the volume you want to compress. For example, to compress drive C, in Windows Explorer, right-click **Local Disk (C:)** and select **Properties** from the shortcut menu. The Properties dialog box opens.

3. Click the **General** tab, as shown in Figure 4-42. This window displays the file system used (NTFS), the capacity of the volume, and the amount of free space. To compress the volume, check the **Compress drive to save disk space** check box, and then click **Apply**.

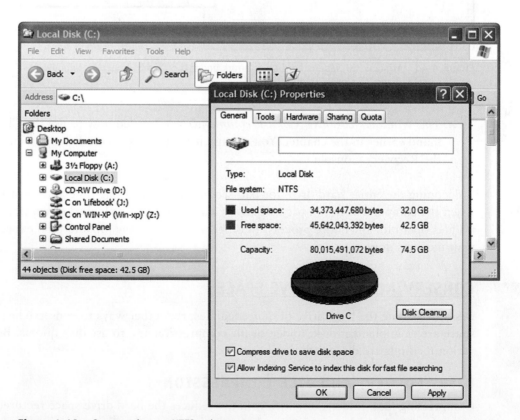

Figure 4-42 Compressing an NTFS volume

4

A+ ESS
3.1
3.2
3.3
3.4

A+
220-602
3.1
3.2
3.4
5.2
6.1

4. The Confirm Attribute Changes dialog box opens. Indicate whether you want to compress only the root folder or the entire volume, and then click **OK** to begin compression.

To compress a single folder or file on a Windows 2000/XP NTFS volume, right-click the folder or file and select **Properties** from the shortcut menu. Click the **General** tab, and then click **Advanced**. In the Advanced Attributes dialog box, check the **Compress contents to save disk space** check box (see Figure 4-43).

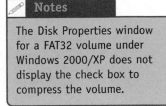

Notes

The Disk Properties window for a FAT32 volume under Windows 2000/XP does not display the check box to compress the volume.

Figure 4-43   Compress a folder using the Advanced Attributes dialog box for the folder

DISK QUOTAS

To limit how much disk space a user account can access, an administrator can set **disk quotas**. This is important when two or more users are using a single computer and need to share its storage capacity. A disk quota does not specify where a user's files must be located; it just specifies how much total space the user can take up on a volume. The disk quota set applies to all users accounts. You can only set disk quotas if you are using NTFS.

Notes

For a FAT32 volume, files and folders cannot be compressed; as such, the General tab does not have an Advanced button. For these volumes, you can use a third-party file compression utility such as WinZip.

Notes

Windows 2000/XP volume, folder, and file compression can also be done using the Compact command at the command prompt, which executes the program file, Compact.exe.

A+ ESS
3.1
3.2
3.3
3.4

A+
220-602
3.1
3.2
3.4
5.2
6.1

APPLYING|CONCEPTS

To set disk quotas so that users cannot exceed the specified disk space, do the following:

1. Log on as an administrator, and open **My Computer** or **Windows Explorer**.

2. Find the partition on which you want to set a disk quota. Right-click it and select **Properties** on the shortcut menu.

3. Click the **Quota** tab and the **Enable quota management** check box, as shown in Figure 4-44.

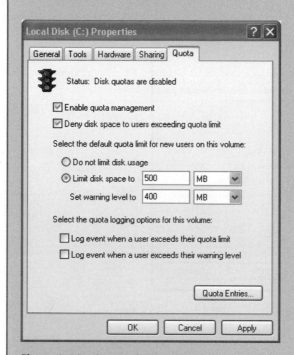

Figure 4-44   Setting disk quotas

4. To stop a user from using space beyond the quota, check **Deny disk space to users exceeding quota limit**.

5. To set the quota for disk space used, click the **Limit disk space to** radio button, and then enter the value in the two boxes next to it. (In our example, disk space is limited to 500 MB.)

6. In the box next to **Set warning level to**, enter the warning level value (**400 MB** in our example). This warns users when they have used 400 MB of their allotted 500 MB of storage space.

7. So that you can monitor disk drive use and know when users have reached their warning levels, check **Log event when a user exceeds their quota limit** and check **Log event when a user exceeds their warning level**. Later, you can click **Quota Entries** to view these logged entries.

8. Click **OK**. You are prompted to enable disk quotas, as shown in Figure 4-45. Click **OK** to respond to the prompt.

A+ ESS
3.1
3.2
3.3
3.4

A+
220-602
3.1
3.2
3.4
5.2
6.1

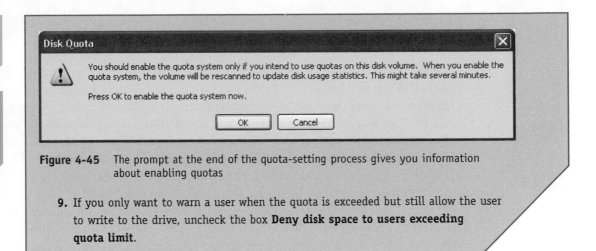

Figure 4-45 The prompt at the end of the quota-setting process gives you information about enabling quotas

9. If you only want to warn a user when the quota is exceeded but still allow the user to write to the drive, uncheck the box **Deny disk space to users exceeding quota limit**.

A+ ESS
3.1
3.2
3.3
3.4
6.1
6.2
6.3

A+
220-602
3.1
3.2
3.4

MAKING BACKUPS

A backup is an extra copy of a data or software file that you can use if the original file becomes damaged or destroyed. Losing data due to system failure, a virus, file corruption, or some other problem really makes you appreciate the importance of having backups. In the last chapter, you learned how to back up system files and even the entire hard drive. This section of the chapter focuses on backing up data files and other user files.

> **Notes**
>
> With data and software, here's a good rule of thumb: If you can't get along without it, back it up.

APPLYING CONCEPTS Dave was well on his way to building a successful career as a PC repair technician. His PC repair shop was doing well and he was excited about his future. But one bad decision changed everything. He was called to repair a server at a small accounting firm. The call was on the weekend when he was normally off, so he was in a hurry to get the job done. He arrived at the accounting firm and saw that the problem was an easy one to fix, so he decided not to do a backup before working on the system. During his repairs, the hard drive crashed and all data on the drive was lost—four million dollars worth! The firm sued, Dave's business license was stripped, and he was ordered to pay the money the company lost. A little extra time to back up the system would have saved his whole future. True story!

Because most of us routinely write data to the hard drive, in this section, we focus on backing up from the hard drive to another media. However, when you store important data on any media such as a flash drive, external hard drive, or floppy disk, always keep a second copy of the data on another media. Never trust important data to only one media.

The following sections cover how to devise a disaster recovery plan, how to make backups, and how to restore data from those backups.

PLANNING FOR DISASTER RECOVERY

The time to prepare for disaster is before it occurs. If you have not prepared, the damage from a disaster will most likely be greater than if you had made and followed disaster plans. Suppose the hard drive on your PC stopped working and you lost all its data. What would

A+ ESS
3.1
3.2
3.3
3.4
6.1
6.2
6.3

A+
220-602
3.1
3.2
3.4

be the impact? Are you prepared for this to happen? Consider these points and tips when making your backup and recovery plans:

- Decide on the backup media (tape, CD, DVD, flash drive, another hard drive, or other media). Even though it's easy to do, don't make the mistake of backing up your data to another partition or folder on your same hard drive. When a hard drive crashes, most likely all partitions go down together and you will have lost your data and your backup. Back up to another media and, for extra safety, store it at an off-site location.

- Windows 2000/XP offers the Ntbackup.exe program to back up files and folders. However, you can purchase third-party backup software that might be easier to use and offer more features. Also, you can purchase an external hard drive like the one by Kanguru (*www.kanguru.com*) shown in Figure 4-46 that comes with its own backup software. External hard drives use a USB, Firewire, or eSATA port. You can schedule the software to automatically back up to the drive on a regular basis or you can manually create a backup at any time. However, before you decide to use an all-in-one backup system such as this one, be certain you understand the risks of not keeping backups at an off-site location and keeping all your backups on a single media.

Figure 4-46 This external hard drive by Kanguru uses a USB port and comes bundled with backup software

- Because backing up data takes time and backup media is expensive, you can use a selective backup plan where you only back up data that changes often. For example, you might ask users to store all their data in certain folders and then you only maintain current backups of these folders rather than back up an entire hard drive. Also, scheduled backups that run during the night are the least disruptive for users.

- Data should be backed up after about every four to ten hours of data entry. This might mean you back up once a day, once a week, or once a month.

- So that you'll have the right information when you need to recover data from your backups, always record your regular backups in a log with the following information:
  - Folders or drives backed up
  - Date of the backup
  - Type of backup
  - Label identifying the tape, disk, or other media

If you discover that data has been lost days or weeks ago, you can use this backup log or table to help you recover the data. Keep the records in a notebook. You can also store the records in a log file (a file where events are logged or recorded) each time you back up. Store the file on a floppy disk or another PC. Figure 4-47 shows one example of a backup log table.

Folder backed up	Date	Type of backup	Tape label
C:\Payroll	2006-06-02	Full	June, First Friday
C:\Payroll	2006-06-05	Incremental	Monday
C:\Payroll	2006-06-06	Incremental	Tuesday
C:\Payroll	2006-06-07	Incremental	Wednesday
C:\Payroll	2006-06-08	Incremental	Thursday
C:\Payroll	2006-06-09	Full	June, Second Friday
C:\Payroll	2006-06-12	Incremental	Monday

Figure 4-47 Keeping backup logs can help you know how to recover data

▲ When you perform a backup for the first time or set up a scheduled backup, verify that you can use the backup tape or disks to successfully recover the data. This is a very important step in preparing to recover lost data. After you create a backup, erase a file on the hard drive, and use the recovery procedures to verify that you can re-create the file from the backup. This verifies that the backup medium works, that the recovery software is effective, and that you know how to use it. After you are convinced that the recovery works, document how to perform it.

> **Notes**
>
> If you travel a lot and your organization doesn't provide online backup, keeping good backups of data on your notebook computer might be a problem. Several Internet companies have solved this backup-on-the-go problem by providing remote backup services over the Internet. In a hotel room or other remote location, connect to the Internet and back up your data to a Web site's file server. If data is lost, you can easily recover it by connecting to the Internet and logging into your backup service Web site.
> If security is a concern, be sure you understand the security guarantees of the site. Two online backup services are @Backup (*www.backup.com*) and Remote Backup Systems (*www.remote-backup.com*).

HOW TO BACK UP DATA

To perform a backup using Ntbackup.exe under Windows 2000/XP, follow these steps:

1. Click **Start**, point to **All Programs** (**Programs** for Windows 2000), point to **Accessories**, point to **System Tools**, and then click **Backup**. The Backup Wizard appears. Click **Advanced Mode**.

2. The Backup utility opens. Click the **Backup** tab. Your screen should look like Figure 4-48. If you want to perform a backup immediately, check the drive and subfolders to back up.

3. In the lower-left corner of the Backup Utility window, note the text box labeled Backup media or filename, which specifies where to back up to. To change this location, click the **Browse** button. The Save As dialog box appears. Navigate to the drive and path where you'd like to save the backup file and enter a name for the file. Click **Save**. The new path and name for the backup file appear in the text box.

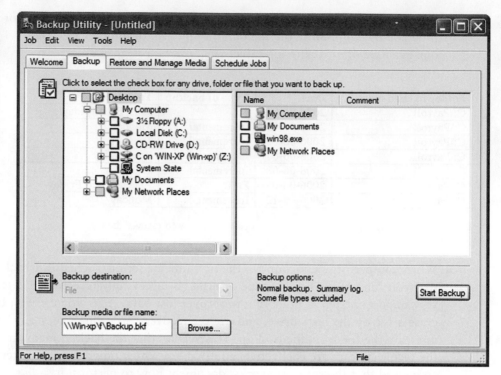

Figure 4-48 You can perform an immediate backup from the Backup tab

4. Click the **Start Backup** button in the lower-right corner to perform the backup.

You can schedule a single backup to be done at a later time or repeated on a schedule until you terminate the schedule. When planning routinely scheduled backups, you have some options so that you don't have to back up everything at each backup. It's a lot less expensive and less time-consuming to only back up what's changed since the last backup. Windows 2000/XP offers these options for scheduled backups:

▲ *Full backup (also called a normal backup).* All files selected for backup are copied to the backup media. Each file is marked as backed up by clearing its archive attribute. Later, if you need to recover data, this full backup is all you need. (After the backup, if a file is changed, its archive attribute is turned on to indicate the file has changed since its last backup.)

▲ *Copy backup.* All files selected for backup are copied to the backup media, but files are not marked as backed up (meaning file archive attributes are not cleared). A Copy backup is useful if you want to make a backup apart from your regularly scheduled backups.

▲ *Incremental backup.* All files that have been created or changed since the last backup are backed up, and all files are marked as backed up (meaning file archive attributes are cleared). Later, if you need to recover data, you'll need the last full backup and all the incremental backups since this last full backup.

▲ *Differential backup.* All files that have been created or changed since the last full or incremental backup are backed up, and files are not marked as backed up. Later, if you need to recover data, you'll need the last full backup and the last differential backup.

▲ *Daily backup.* All files that have been created or changed on this day are backed up. Files are not marked as backed up. Later, if you need to recover data, you'll need the last full backup and all daily backups since this last full backup.

A+ ESS
3.1
3.2
3.3
3.4
6.1
6.2
6.3

A+
220-602
3.1
3.2
3.4

The two best ways to schedule backups are a combination of full backups and incremental backups, or a combination of full backups and differential backups. When using incremental backups, because they are smaller than differential backups, you save time and money when backing up. On the other hand, recovering data is less time-consuming when using differential backups because you only need two backups to perform a full recovery (the last full backup and the last differential backup.)

For a business with heavy data entry, suppose you decide you need to back up every night at 11:55. To implement this backup plan, you might decide to schedule two backups: A full backup each Friday at 11:55 P.M., and a differential backup each Monday, Tuesday, Wednesday, and Thursday at 11:55 P.M. In a project at the end of this chapter, you'll learn how you can reuse tapes on a rotating basis for a backup plan similar to this one.

> **Notes**
>
> When making your backup plan, for extra protection, take into account that you might want to keep several generations of backups on hand. If you always overwrite the backup with a new backup, you only have one generation of backups. However, sometimes a file gets corrupted or accidentally deleted and you don't discover the problem for several weeks. If you don't keep several generations of backups, you will have no chance of recovering the data. On the other hand, if you back up weekly and keep the last 10 weeks of backups, you can go back and search previous backups to recover the file.

To schedule a backup, do the following:

1. Begin by clicking the **Schedule Jobs** tab, as shown in Figure 4-49. Select a date on which you want to schedule a backup, and then click the **Add Job** button.

2. The Backup Wizard opens. On the first screen, click **Next**. Select **Back up selected files, drives, or network data**, and then click **Next**.

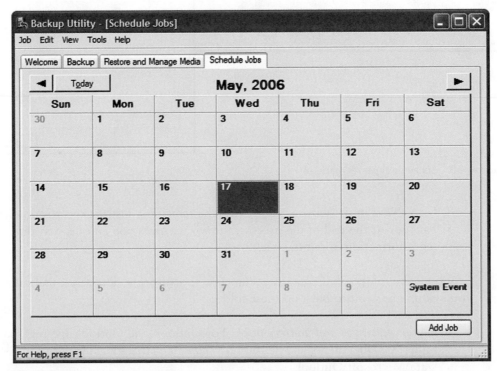

Figure 4-49 The Schedule Jobs tab of the Windows 2000/XP Backup Utility window

3. On the next screen, select the drives, folders, or files you want to back up, and then click **Next**.

4. Follow the steps through the wizard to choose where you want to save your backup, give a name to the backup, and select the type of backup (Normal, Copy, Incremental, Differential, or Daily). Note that a Normal backup is a full backup.

5. Then you are asked if you want to verify the data after backup and compress the data. Next, you must decide if you want to append the data to an existing backup or replace an existing backup. Your decision largely depends on how much space you have available for backups.

6. When asked if you want to perform the backup now or later, select **Later** and give the backup a name, as shown on the left side of Figure 4-50. Click the **Set Schedule** button.

7. The Schedule Job window appears, as shown on the right side of Figure 4-50. Schedule how often the backup is to occur, and then click **OK**. Notice in the figure, a backup is scheduled for each Monday, Tuesday, Wednesday, and Thursday at 11:55 P.M.

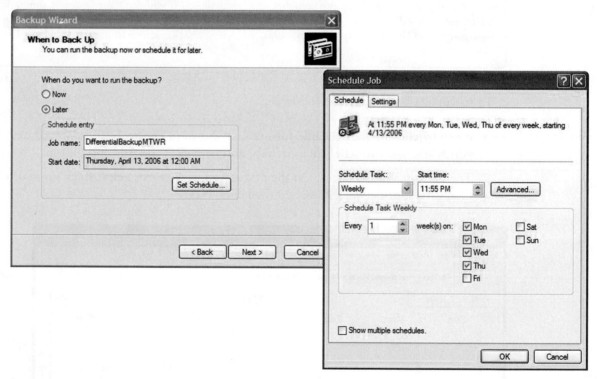

Figure 4-50 Schedule repeated backups

8. Click **Next** in the wizard, and follow the remaining instructions to complete the backup. At the end of the process, the wizard gives you an onscreen report summarizing information about the backup.

Besides the folders that contain documents, spreadsheets, databases, and other data files, you also might want to back up these folders:

▲ *E-mail messages and address book.* For Outlook and Outlook Express, back up this folder: C:\Documents and Settings*username*\Local Settings\Application Data\Microsoft\Outlook.

▲ *Internet Explorer favorites list.* To back up an IE favorites list, back up this folder: C:\Documents and Settings*username*\Favorites.

A+ ESS
3.1
3.2
3.3
3.4
6.1
6.2
6.3

A+
220-602
3.1
3.2
3.4

RESTORING DATA FROM BACKUPS

To recover files, folders, or the entire drive from backup using the Windows 2000/XP Backup utility, click the **Restore and Manage Media** tab on the Backup Utility window, and then select the backup job to use for the restore. The Backup utility displays the folders and files that were backed up with this job. You can select the ones that you want to restore. When you restore from backup, you'll lose all the data you've entered in restored files since the backup,

 Notes

By default, Windows XP Home Edition does not include the Backup utility. To install it manually, go to the \VALUEADD\ MSFT\NTBACKUP folder on your Windows XP setup CD and double-click **Ntbackup.msi**. The installation wizard will complete the installation.

so be sure to use the most recent backup and then re-enter the data that's missing.

If you are faced with the problem of lost or corrupted data and you don't have a current backup, you still might be able to recover the lost data. Some available options are discussed next.

A+ ESS
1.3
3.3

A+
220-602
3.3

SOLVING HARD DRIVE PROBLEMS

Although the hard drive itself is a hardware component, problems with hard drives can be caused by software as well. Problems can also be categorized as those that prevent the hard drive from booting and those that prevent data from being accessed. In this section, you will learn about hardware and software problems that prevent data from being accessed. In the next chapter, you'll learn about what to do when you cannot boot from the hard drive.

START WITH THE END USER

When an end user brings a problem to you, begin the troubleshooting process by interviewing the user. When you interview the user, you might want to include these questions:

- Can you describe the problem and show me how to reproduce it?
- Was the computer recently moved?
- Was any new hardware or software recently installed?
- Was any software recently reconfigured or upgraded?
- Did someone else use your computer recently?
- Does the computer have a history of similar problems?
- Can you show me how to reproduce the problem?

After you gather this basic information, you can begin diagnosing and addressing the hard drive problems.

PRIORITIZE WHAT YOU HAVE LEARNED

If a hard drive is not functioning and data is not accessible, setting priorities helps focus your work. For most users, data is the first priority unless they have a recent backup. Software can also be a priority if it is not backed up. Reloading software from the original installation disks or CD can be time-consuming, especially if the configuration is complex or you have written software macros or scripts but did not back them up.

If you have good backups of both data and software, hardware might be your priority. It could be expensive to replace, but downtime can be costly, too. The point is, when trouble arises, determine your main priority and start by focusing on that. If your first priority is solving the problem at hand, as with all computer problems, begin troubleshooting by making an initial determination that the problem is software or hardware related.

A+ ESS
1.3
3.3

A+
220-602
3.3

USE ALL AVAILABLE RESOURCES

A smart technician is aware of the resources available to help solve a problem. As you are troubleshooting a PC problem, consider the following:

◢ You can use Disk Management to check partitions or Task Manager to look for a process that is a bottleneck for hard drive, memory, or CPU activity. To check for excessive reads and writes to the hard drive, in Task Manager, select the **Processes** tab and click **View, Select Columns**. The Select Columns dialog box appears (see Figure 4-51).

Figure 4-51 Selecting columns for the Processes tab of Task Manager

Check the four I/O read and write entries and click **OK**. You can then search for applications that are causing excessive reading and writing to the drive, as shown in Figure 4-52.

◢ Documentation often lists error messages and their meanings.

◢ The Internet can also help you diagnose hardware and software problems. Go to the Microsoft Web site for help with Windows or another Web site of a product manufacturer, and search for the FAQs (frequently asked questions) list or bulletin board. It's likely that others have encountered the same problem and posted the question and answer. If you search and cannot find your answer, you can post a new question.

◢ Technical support from the hard drive manufacturer can help you interpret an error message, or it can provide general support in diagnosing a problem. Most technical support is available during working hours by telephone. Check your documentation for telephone numbers. An experienced computer troubleshooter once said, "The people who solve computer problems do it by trying something and making phone calls,

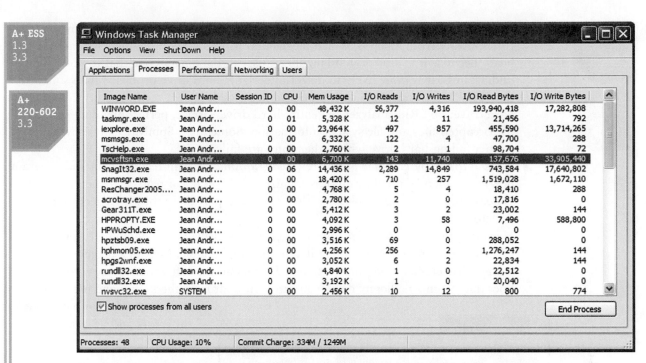

Figure 4-52 Look for an application that might be causing slow drive performance by excessive reading and writing to the hard drive

trying something else and making more phone calls, and so on, until the problem is solved."

Third-party utility software can be a great help when solving hard drive problems. The following list describes some of those utility programs and tells you what to expect from them when a hard drive fails. Note that these are *not* complete listings of the utility software functions, nor of all available software. See specific software documentation for more details.

◢ *Norton Utilities* by Symantec (*www.symantec.com*) offers several easy-to-use tools to prevent damage to a hard drive, recover data from a damaged hard drive, and improve system performance. Many functions of these tools have been taken over and improved by utilities included with recent versions of Windows. The most commonly used Norton Utilities tools now are the recovery tools. Two examples are Norton Disk Doctor, which automatically repairs many hard drive and floppy disk problems, and UnErase Wizard, which allows you to retrieve accidentally deleted files. When using Norton Utilities, be certain you use the version of the software for the operating system you have installed. Using Norton with the wrong OS can do damage.

◢ *PartitionMagic* by Symantec (*www.symantec.com*) lets you manage partitions on a hard drive more quickly and easily than with Fdisk for Windows 9x/Me or Disk Management for Windows NT/2000/XP. You can create new partitions, change the size of partitions, and move partitions without losing data or moving the data to another hard drive while you work. You can switch file systems without disturbing your data, and you can hide and show partitions to secure your data.

◢ *SpinRite* by Gibson Research (*www.grc.com*) is hard drive utility software that has been around for years. Still a DOS application without a sophisticated GUI interface, SpinRite has been updated to adjust to new drive technologies. It supports FAT32,

NTFS, SCSI, Zip drives, and Jaz drives. You can boot your PC from a floppy disk and run SpinRite from a floppy, which means that it doesn't require much system overhead. Because it is written in a language closer to the binary code that the computer understands, it is more likely to detect underlying hard drive problems than software that uses Windows, which can stand as a masking layer between the software and the hard drive. SpinRite analyzes the entire hard drive surface, performing data recovery of corrupted files and file system information. Sometimes, SpinRite can recover data from a failing hard drive when other software fails.

▲ *GetDataBack* by Runtime Software (*www.runtime.org*) can recover data and program files even when Windows cannot recognize the drive. It can read FAT and NTFS file systems and can solve problems with a corrupted partition table, boot record, or root directory.

▲ *Hard drive manufacturer's diagnostic software* is available for download from the Web site of many hard drive manufacturers. For example, Maxtor's diagnostic software is PowerMax (*www.maxtor.com*). Download the software and use it to create a bootable diagnostic floppy disk. You can then boot from the floppy and use it to examine a Maxtor hard drive for errors and, if necessary, low-level format the drive.

✎ Notes

Always check compatibility between utility software and the operating system with which you plan to use it. One place you can check for compatibility is the service and support section of the software manufacturer's Web site.

HOW TO RECOVER LOST DATA

If a hard drive is giving problems, and you need to recover lost data, don't write anything to the drive until you have copied the data to another media. If the file system is giving errors, it can write to the very area where the lost data is stored. Once the data is overwritten, it is almost impossible to recover it unless you pay for very expensive data recovery services. If a data file is lost, accidentally deleted, or corrupted, but you can still boot to the Windows desktop, do the following to recover the data:

▲ *Try treating a corrupted file as a text file.* If a data file that is used by an application is corrupted, try changing its file extension to .txt and importing the file into the application as a text file. Using this method, if the file header is damaged, you might be able to recover at least part of the file.

▲ *Restore the file from backups.* Do you have a backup of the file? How to restore files from backups is covered earlier in the chapter.

▲ *Check the Recycle Bin.* The file might be there. If you find it, right-click the file and select Restore from the shortcut menu.

▲ *Use commands from a Command Prompt window.* Use the CD command to go to the folder where the file is supposed to be. Then try using the Windows XP Recover command to recover the file. For Windows 2000, try to use the Copy command to copy the file to another media.

▲ *Try data recovery software.* If you are still not able to recover the file, go to the Web site of a data recovery service. Sometimes you can run a utility on the Web site to search for the file and tell you if the software on the site can help you. If the utility says it can recover your file, you can purchase the software to do the job. On the Internet, do a search on "data recovery" for lots of examples.

A+ ESS
1.3
3.3

A+
220-602
3.3

▲ *Consider a data recovery service.* These services are expensive, but might be worth the expense for important data. To find a service, do a Google search on "data recovery." Before engaging a service, be sure to get good recommendations and read some reviews about the service. Before you agree to the service, understand the guarantees and expenses.

If the hard drive will not boot and your first priority is to recover the data, do the following:

▲ Use the Recovery Console to boot the system and copy the data from the hard drive to another media. The Recovery Console is covered in the next chapter.

▲ Following safety procedures to protect the computer against static electricity, carefully remove the hard drive from the computer case. Use a USB to IDE converter to connect the drive to the USB port on a working computer (see Figure 4-53). You can then use Windows Explorer on the working computer to locate and copy the data to the primary hard drive.

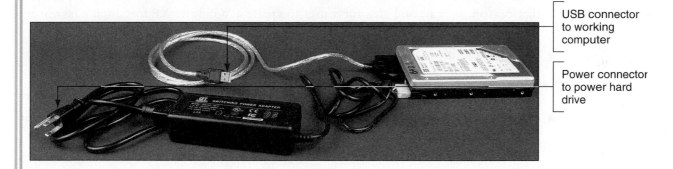

USB connector
to working
computer

Power connector
to power hard
drive

Figure 4-53 Connect the hard drive to a working computer using its USB port

▲ If Windows Explorer can't find the data, try using data recovery software to recover the data.

▲ If the hard drive is so damaged that data recovery software doesn't help, try downloading diagnostic software from the hard drive manufacturer's Web site to test the drive and possibly repair it.

▲ Consider a data recovery service. As said earlier, be sure to use a reliable one and understand the expenses and guarantees before you agree to the service.

As you work on a problem, keep notes as to what you've tried and the outcome. The documentation will be useful the next time you face a similar problem.

>> CHAPTER SUMMARY

▲ Windows 2000/XP requires a valid user account before you can use Windows. The user account identifies the user to Windows. Permissions assigned to a user account control what the user can and cannot do and access in Windows.

▲ Local user accounts apply to a single standalone computer or a single computer in a workgroup, and global user accounts are managed from a domain controller and apply to every computer in the domain.

▲ When using Windows in a domain, global user account information is stored in the SAM, which is part of Active Directory in Windows 2000 Server and Windows Server 2003.

▲ When a user makes changes to the system, the changes are often recorded in the user profile so the next time the user logs on, these changes automatically take effect.

▲ Methods that administrators can use to manage and secure multiple computers and users include roaming user profiles, mandatory user profiles, and group profiles.

▲ Passwords on user accounts are needed to secure computers and their resources. Passwords should not be easy to guess and should be a combination of letters, numbers, and non-alphanumeric characters.

▲ An administrator can create a user account using the Computer Management console or the User Accounts applet in Control Panel.

▲ Resetting a password under Windows XP causes the OS to lock out the user from using encrypted e-mail or files or using Internet passwords stored on the computer. For that reason, it is a good idea for a user to create a Windows XP forgotten password floppy disk.

▲ In Windows 2000, you can only log on to the system by pressing Ctrl+Alt+Del to open the logon window. In a Windows XP workgroup, you can use the logon window, Welcome screen, or Fast User Switching.

▲ Windows user groups include Administrators, Backup Operators, Power Users, Limited Users, and Guests. In this list, each group has fewer permissions and rights than the previous group.

▲ The Windows XP Files and Settings Transfer Wizard and the User State Migration Tool (USMT) enable a user to make a smooth transition from one computer to another by transferring user files and settings. The first tool is intended to be used by the user in a workgroup, and the second tool is intended to be used by an administrator in a domain.

▲ Commands useful to managing data and hard drives are Help, Dir, Del, Copy, Recovery, Xcopy, MD, CD, RD, Attrib, Chkdsk, Defrag, Edit, and Format.

▲ Windows XP looks to certain folders to find scripts and programs to launch at startup. Group Policy and Scheduled Tasks can be used to set startup scripts.

▲ Remote Assistance can be used for a technician to take control of a user's desktop to solve Windows XP problems.

▲ Show users how to routinely clean up, defrag, and check a hard drive for errors.

▲ Using disk quotas, an administrator can limit the amount of hard drive space a user can use.

▲ File, folder, and volume compression can only be used with the NTFS file system.

▲ For disaster recovery, it is important to create and test a plan that includes keeping records of backups and recovery procedures.

▲ Back up data after about every four to ten hours of data entry. For best security, store the backup media at an off-site location.

▲ When data is lost on a hard drive, don't write anything to the drive if you intend to try to recover the data.

>> KEY TERMS

For explanations of key terms, see the Glossary near the end of the book.

Administrator	forgotten password floppy disk	lost clusters
Backup Operators	fragmentation	mandatory user profile
batch file	fragmented files	Power Users
built-in user accounts	global user accounts	Remote Assistance
chain	Group Policy	Remote Desktop
compression	group profile	roaming user profiles
cross-linked clusters	Guests	scanstate
defragment	Limited Users	user account
disk quotas	loadstate	User State Migration Tool
Files and Settings Transfer	local user account	(USMT)
Wizard	lost allocation units	wildcard

>> REVIEWING THE BASICS

1. What are the two basic differences between the Files and Settings Transfer Wizard and the USMT utility?

2. What are the two commands in the USMT?

3. When is the local user profile created?

4. How are a roaming profile and a mandatory profile the same? How are they different?

5. What are two important criteria that make for a good password?

6. What can a user do to keep from having the administrator reset a forgotten password?

7. Which user group has more rights, Power Users or Administrators?

8. When using Group Policy on a computer in a workgroup, which type of configuration do you use?

9. What do you implement to control how much disk space a user can take up?

10. What is the difference between a cross-linked cluster and a lost cluster? What can cause them?

11. What Windows 2000/XP utility program checks for cross-linked and lost clusters?

12. What file system is necessary to use if a volume is to be compressed under Windows 2000?

13. What is the difference between an incremental backup and a differential backup?

14. What must you do before you can use the Windows Backup utility on a Windows XP Home Edition PC?

15. Why should you create a disaster recovery plan? What type of information would you include in it?

16. List three third-party utility programs used to support hard drives.

17. When Windows XP is first installed, what two built-in user accounts are also installed?

18. If you want to log onto a Windows XP system using the administrator account, what keys do you first press?

19. How do you change the way a user can log onto Windows XP?

20. The _____ command erases files or groups of files.

21. What command is used to create a subdirectory? To change the current directory? To remove a subdirectory?

22. The _____ command displays or changes the read-only, archive, system, and hidden characteristics of files.

23. What is the command to check drive C for errors, repair these file system errors, and recover data from bad sectors?

24. What is the command to move data on drive C so that all clusters of a file are in contiguous locations on the drive?

25. What is the command to format drive D, using the NTFS file system?

>> THINKING CRITICALLY

1. Your Windows XP system locks up occasionally. What are some probable causes and solutions? (*Note:* This question combines skills learned in this and other chapters.)

   a. The hard drive has errors. Run _____ to correct file system errors.

   b. An application might not be compatible with Windows XP. To find out if you have applications installed that are not certified by Microsoft for Windows XP, run the _____ utility.

   c. The hard drive might be full. To find out use _____.

   d. The system might have a virus. To eliminate that possibility, use _____.

2. You have an important FoxPro database stored on your hard drive. The drive has been giving bad sector errors for several weeks. You kept meaning to back up the data, but have not gotten around to it. Now you attempt to access the database and FoxPro tells you it cannot open the file. What do you try first? Second? Third?

   a. Reenter all the data and promise yourself you'll be more faithful about backups.

   b. Use SpinRite software to attempt to recover the file.

   c. Use Chkdsk to recover data from bad sectors.

   d. Change the file extension of the database file to .txt and tell FoxPro to attempt to open the file as an ASCII text file.

3. A virus has attacked your hard drive and now when you start up Windows, instead of seeing a Windows desktop, the system freezes and you see a blue screen of death (an error message on a blue background). You have extremely important document files on the drive that you cannot afford to lose. What do you do first?

   a. Try a data recovery service even though it is very expensive.

   b. Remove the hard drive from the computer case and install it in another computer.

   c. Try GetDataBack to recover the data.

   d. Use Windows utilities to attempt to fix the Windows boot problem.

>> HANDS-ON PROJECTS

PROJECT 4-1: Join a Windows XP Newsgroup

When researching a specific problem with Windows XP or just to learn more about troubleshooting this OS, one thing you can do is join a newsgroup. To join up, do the following:

1. Click **Start,** and then **Help and Support.** On the Help and Support window, click **Get support, or find information in Windows XP newsgroups.** Click **Go to a Windows Web site forum,** and then click **Go to Windows Newsgroups.**

2. After you're in the forum, you can post a question or read questions and answers posted by other users. Microsoft does not support this forum, so be careful about following the advice of users posting answers to questions on the forum.

3. Print one question and answer from the newsgroup.

PROJECT 4-2: Managing User Accounts

Using Windows XP, do the following to experiment with managing user accounts:

1. Create a Limited user account and add it to the group of Backup Operators. Log on as the Backup Operator. Can you view the contents of the My Documents folder for an account with Administrator privileges?

2. As a Backup Operator, try to install a new Windows component. What error message do you receive?

3. Create a user account with Limited privileges. Log on using this account. Can you view the contents of the My Documents folder for an account with Administrator privileges?

4. What is the error message you receive if you try to create a new account while logged in under an account with Limited privileges?

PROJECT 4-3: Researching a Backup Plan

You are responsible for the data on the file server of a small company. Currently, the file server hard drive is 120 GB, but only 35 GB of data is stored on the drive. You are investigating what backup media to use and have decided to compare the cost of backing up to tapes and to external USB removable storage. Research both media and answer the following questions:

1. Research tape drives and tapes. What tape drive do you recommend? How much will it cost? Print the Web page showing the drive.

2. What tapes will you use on the drive? How much will each tape cost? Print the Web page showing the tapes for sale.

3. How many tapes will it require to back up the current 35 GB of data? How many tapes will be required when the drive is full of data? If you make a backup each night and rotate tapes using the system described in Table 4-5, how much will it cost to use this tape backup system for one year?

4. Research external USB hard drives or other USB removable storage devices as your backup media. What removable storage media do you recommend? How much will it cost? Print the Web page showing the drive or other device.

5. Now answer this Hands-On Project's Question 3 for the removable storage media.

6. Which storage solution is less expensive? Other than cost, what other factors should you consider when selecting a backup media?

PROJECT 4-4:   Scheduling Backups

Using Table 4-5 as your guide, set up Windows XP backup schedules to create the backups of data and the Windows XP system state. Assume all data for all users is stored in the C:\Documents and Settings folder. Print the details of each scheduled backup.

Name of Backup	How Often Performed	Storage Location	Description
Child backup	Daily	On-site	Keep four daily backup tapes of data that has changed that day, and rotate the tapes each week. Label the four tapes Monday, Tuesday, Wednesday, and Thursday. A Friday daily (child) backup is not made, because on Friday you make the parent backup.
Parent backup	Weekly	Off-site	Perform a full backup each week on Friday. Keep five weekly backup tapes, one for each Friday of the month, and rotate them each month. Label the tapes Friday 1, Friday 2, Friday 3, Friday 4, and Friday 5.
Grandparent backup	Monthly	Off-site, in a fireproof vault	Perform the monthly backup on the last Friday of the month. Make a full backup of data and the system state. Keep 12 tapes, one for each month. Rotate them each year. Label the tapes January, February, and so on.

Table 4-5   The child, parent, grandparent backup method

PROJECT 4-5:   Scheduling a Batch Job

Create a batch file that contains commands to delete all files in the C:\Windows\Temp folder, defrag drive C, and check the drive for errors. Test the batch file by running it from the command prompt. After you know it works correctly, schedule the batch job to run every Wednesday at 10:00 P.M. Print the contents of the file.

4

PROJECT 4-6: Using Windows to Back Up Files and Folders

This exercise lets you practice using Windows Backup and see how the Backup utility manages several situations.

PART I

1. Using Windows Explorer, create a folder called **Backtest** on a hard drive.

2. Use Explorer to find a .txt file, and copy it to the new folder. Copy two other files to the Backtest folder. Make a subfolder called **Subfolder** in Backtest and copy a fourth file to C:\backtest\subfolder.

3. Right-click the .txt file and rename it **Overwrite.txt**. Right-click the second file and rename it **Delete.txt**. Rename the third file **NoChange.txt**. Leave the fourth file alone for now. Use Explorer and write down the file sizes before the backup.

4. Click **Start, All Programs** (**Programs** for Windows 2000), **Accessories, System Tools**, and **Backup**.

5. Use the directions provided in this chapter to back up the Backtest folder to a floppy disk. Use Explorer and compare the backup file sizes to the original file sizes. How are they different?

6. Delete the file **Delete.txt**. Edit and change the contents of Overwrite.txt. Make no changes to NoChange.txt. Delete **Subfolder**.

7. Using Windows Backup, restore the files from the backup to their original folder.

   a. What did Backup do with the Delete.txt file?

   b. What did Backup do with the Overwrite.txt file?

   c. What did Backup do with the NoChange.txt file?

   d. What did Backup do with the missing subfolder and missing file?

   e. What is the name of the backup file on the floppy disk?

   f. What are the name and path to the error log created by Backup?

   g. Print the error log.

PART II

1. Use Windows Explorer to copy the Backtest folder to a second floppy disk.

2. Delete all files in the Backtest folder on the hard drive.

3. Use Windows Explorer to copy the three files back to the Backtest folder.

4. Delete the files in the Backtest folder on the hard drive.

5. Open the Recycle Bin and restore the three files to the Backtest folder by highlighting them and using the **File, Restore** option. Did they return to the correct folder?

6. Once again, delete the files in the Backtest folder on the hard drive.

7. Highlight the three files in the Recycle Bin, and click **File, Delete**. Can you still restore the files?

>> REAL PROBLEMS, REAL SOLUTIONS

REAL PROBLEM 4-1: A Corrupted Windows Installation

As a PC support technician for a small organization, it's your job to support the PCs, the small network, and the users. One of your coworkers, Jason, comes to you in a panic. His Windows XP system won't boot, and he has lots of important data files in several locations on the drive. He has no idea in which folder some of the files are located. Besides the applications data on which he's currently working, he's especially concerned about losing e-mail addresses, e-mail, and his Internet Explorer Favorites links.

After trying everything you know about recovering Windows XP, you conclude the OS is corrupted beyond repair. Based on what you have learned in this and previous chapters, list the steps you would take to reinstall Windows XP and recover all the data that Jason needs.

CHAPTER 5

Troubleshooting Windows 2000/XP Startup

In the last three chapters, you have been learning about supporting and maintaining Windows 2000/XP, its users, and their data. In this chapter, we complete that discussion of Windows 2000/XP by looking at when Windows 2000/XP will not load the Windows desktop or loads the desktop with errors.

When a computer refuses to boot or the Windows desktop refuses to load, it takes a cool head to handle the situation gracefully. What helps more than anything else is to have a good plan so you don't feel so helpless. This chapter is designed to give you just that—a plan with all the necessary details so that you can determine just what has gone wrong and what to do about it. Knowledge is power. When you know what to do, the situation doesn't seem nearly as hopeless.

To begin the chapter, you'll see what happens when Windows 2000/XP starts and loads the Windows desktop. Next, you'll see a survey of all the tools and utilities you can use to solve boot problems. Finally, you'll learn the strategies and step-by-step approaches to solving boot problems with Windows 2000/XP.

UNDERSTANDING THE WINDOWS 2000/XP BOOT PROCESS

A Windows 2000/XP system has started up when the user has logged on, the Windows desktop is loaded, and the hourglass associated with the pointer has disappeared. To know how to support the boot process, it's not necessary to understand every detail of this process, but it does help to have a general understanding of the more important steps. In this section, you learn what happens during the boot process, what files are needed to boot, and how to change some settings that affect Windows 2000/XP startup.

WHAT HAPPENS WHEN WINDOWS 2000/XP STARTS UP

Table 5-1 outlines the steps in the boot sequence for Intel-based computers up to the point that the boot loader program, Ntldr, turns control over to the Windows core component program, Ntoskrnl.exe.

Step Number	Step Performed by	Description of Step
1	Startup BIOS	Startup BIOS runs the POST (power-on self test).
2	Startup BIOS	Startup BIOS turns to the hard drive to find an OS. It first loads the MBR (Master Boot Record) and runs the master boot program within the MBR. (The master boot program is at the very beginning of the hard drive, before the partition table information.)
3	MBR program	The MBR program uses partition table information to find the active partition. It then loads the OS boot sector (also called the OS boot record) from the active partition and runs the program in this boot sector.
4	Boot sector program	This boot sector program launches Ntldr (NT Loader).
5	Ntldr, the Windows 2000/XP boot strap loader program	Ntldr changes the processor from real mode to 32-bit flat memory mode, in which 32-bit code can be executed.
6	Ntldr, the Windows 2000/XP boot strap loader program	Ntldr launches the minifile system drivers so files can be read from either a FAT or NTFS file system on the hard drive.
7	Ntldr, the Windows 2000/XP boot strap loader program	Ntldr reads the Boot.ini file, a hidden text file that contains information about installed OSs on the hard drive. Using this information, Ntldr builds the boot loader menu described in the file. The menu is displayed if Ntldr recognizes a dual boot system or sees a serious problem with the boot (see Figure 5-1). Using the menu, a user can decide which OS to load or accept the default selection by waiting for the preset time to expire.
8	Ntldr, the Windows 2000/XP boot strap loader program	If the user chooses an OS other than Windows 2000/XP, then Ntldr runs Bootsect.dos and Ntldr is terminated. Bootsect.dos is responsible for loading the other OS.

Table 5-1 Steps in the Windows 2000/XP boot process for systems with Intel-based processors

5

Step Number	Step Performed by	Description of Step
9	Ntldr, the Windows 2000/XP boot strap loader program	If the user chooses Windows 2000/XP, then the loader runs Ntdetect.com, a 16-bit real mode program that queries the computer for time and date (taken from CMOS RAM) and surveys hardware (buses, drives, mouse, ports). Ntdetect passes the information back to Ntldr. This information is used later to update the Windows 2000/XP registry concerning the Last Known Good hardware profile used.
10	Ntldr, the Windows 2000/XP boot strap loader program	Ntldr then loads Ntoskrnl.exe, Hal.dll, and the System hive. Recall that the System hive is a portion of the Windows 2000/XP registry that includes hardware information used to load the proper device drivers for the hardware present. Ntldr then loads these device drivers.
11	Windows 2000/XP loader (the last step performed by Ntldr)	Ntldr passes control to Ntoskrnl.exe; Ntoskrnl.exe continues to load the Windows desktop and the supporting Windows environment.

Table 5-1 Steps in the Windows 2000/XP boot process for systems with Intel-based processors (continued)

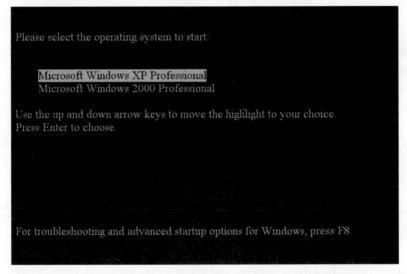

Figure 5-1 The Windows 2000/XP boot loader menu allows the user to choose which OS to load

FILES NEEDED TO START WINDOWS 2000/XP

The files needed to boot Windows 2000/XP successfully are listed in Table 5-2. Several of these system files form the core components of the Windows OS architecture, which you can see diagrammed in Chapter 2 in Figure 2-6.

 A+ Tip

The A+ Essentials exam expects you to know about these system files: Boot.ini, Ntldr, Ntdetect.com, and Ntbootdd.sys.

A+ ESS
3.1
3.3

A+
220-602
3.3

File	Location and Description
Ntldr	▲ Located in the root folder of the system partition (usually C:\) ▲ Boot strap loader program
Boot.ini	▲ Located in the root folder of the system partition (usually C:\) ▲ Text file contains boot parameters
Bootsect.dos	▲ Located in the root folder of the system partition (usually C:\) ▲ Used to load another OS in a dual boot environment
Ntdetect.com	▲ Located in the root folder of the system partition (usually C:\) ▲ Real-mode program detects hardware present
Ntbootdd.sys	▲ Located in the root folder of the system partition (usually C:\) ▲ Required only if a SCSI boot device is used
Ntoskrnl.exe	▲ Located in *winnt_root*\system32 folder of the boot partition (usually C:\Windows\system32) ▲ Core component of the OS executive and kernel services
Hal.dll	▲ Located in *winnt_root*\system32 folder of the boot partition (usually C:\Windows\system32) ▲ Hardware abstraction layer
Ntdll.dll	▲ Located in *winnt_root*\system32 folder of the boot partition (usually C:\Windows\system32) ▲ Intermediating service to executive services; provides many support functions
Win32k.sys Kernel32.dll Advapi32.dll User32.dll Gdi32.dll	▲ Located in *winnt_root*\system32 folder of the boot partition (usually C:\Windows\system32) ▲ Core components of the Win 32 subsystem
System	▲ Located in *winnt_root*\system32\config folder of the boot partition (usually C:\Windows\system32\config) ▲ Registry hive that holds hardware configuration data including which device drivers need loading at startup
Device drivers	▲ Located in *winnt_root*\system32\drivers folder of the boot partition (usually C:\Windows\system32\drivers) ▲ Windows and third-party drivers needed for startup
Pagefile.sys	▲ Located in the root folder of the system partition (usually C:\) ▲ Virtual memory swap file

Table 5-2   Files needed to boot Windows 2000/XP successfully

5

A+ ESS
3.1
3.3

A+
220-602
3.3

IMPORTANT FOLDERS USED IN THE STARTUP PROCESS

As you can see from Table 5-2, most Windows system files are stored in the C:\Windows\System 32 folder. Here is a list of the key folders used by Windows 2000/XP:

Notes

When repairing a corrupted hard drive, a support person often copies files from one PC to another. However, the Bootsect.dos file contains information from the partition table for a particular hard drive and cannot be copied from another PC.

- *C:\Windows* – Contains the Windows 2000/XP installation and includes several subfolders
- *C:\Windows\System32* – The most important subfolder in C:\Windows, which contains core Windows system files and subfolders
- *C:\Windows\System32\config* – Contains the registry hives
- *C:\Windows\System32\drivers* – Contains device driver files
- *C:\Documents and Settings* – Contains information for each user. Each user account has a subfolder by that name, which contains these important subfolders: My Documents, Desktop, Start Menu.
- *C:\Program Files* – Contains installed applications

THE BOOT.INI FILE

One key file used by Windows 2000/XP startup is Boot.ini. Recall that the Boot.ini file is a hidden text file stored in the root directory of the active partition that Ntldr reads to see what operating systems are available and how to set up the boot. You can view and edit the Boot.ini file, which might be necessary when you are trying to solve a difficult boot problem. Figure 5-2 shows an example of a Boot.ini file for Windows XP. Figure 5-3 shows a similar file for a system that uses a Windows 2000 and Windows XP dual boot.

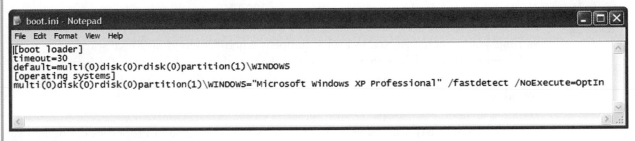

Figure 5-2 A sample Windows XP Boot.ini file

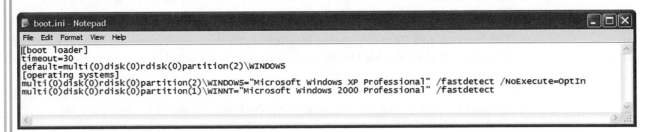

Figure 5-3 A sample Boot.ini file on a dual-boot system

A+ ESS
3.1
3.3

A+
220-602
3.3

Before you can view or edit the Boot.ini file using a text editor such as Notepad, you must first change the folder options to view hidden system files. To do so, open **Windows Explorer**, select the root directory, click **Tools** on the menu bar, click **Folder Options**, and then select the **View** tab. Uncheck the option to **Hide protected operating system files**.

There are two main sections in Boot.ini: the [boot loader] section and the [operating systems] section. The [boot loader] section contains the number of seconds the system gives the user to select an operating system before it loads the default operating system; this is called a timeout. In Figure 5-2, the timeout is set to 30 seconds. If the system is set for a dual boot, the path to the default operating system is also listed in the [boot loader] section. In Figure 5-3, you can see the default OS is loaded from the \Windows folder in the second partition.

The [operating systems] section of the Boot.ini file provides a list of operating systems that can be loaded, including the path to the boot partition of each operating system. Here is the meaning of each entry in Figure 5-2:

- *Multi(0)*. Use the first hard drive controller.
- *Disk(0)*. Use only when booting from a SCSI hard drive.
- *Rdisk(0)*. Use the first hard drive.
- *Partition(1)*. Use the first partition on the drive.

Switches are sometimes used in the [operating systems] section. In Figure 5-2, the first switch used in this Boot.ini file is /fastdetect, which causes the OS not to attempt to inspect any peripherals connected to a COM port (serial port) at startup.

The second switch is /NoExecute = OptIn. This switch is new with Windows XP Service Pack 2 and is used to configure Data Execution Prevention (DEP). DEP stops a program if it tries to use a protected area of memory, which some viruses attempt to do.

CUSTOMIZING THE WAY WINDOWS 2000/XP STARTS UP

A+ ESS
3.3

You might want to change the way Windows 2000/XP starts up. In Chapter 4, you learned how to change the way users can log onto the system. In this section, you'll see some other settings you can change to affect what happens when Windows 2000/XP starts up.

It's interesting to know that many of the changes that you learn to make here are implemented in Windows by making a change to the Boot.ini file. Do the following to change Windows startup options:

1. Right-click **My Computer** and select **Properties**. The System Properties dialog box opens. Click the **Advanced** tab, as shown in Figure 5-4.

2. For Windows XP, under Startup and Recovery, click **Settings**. For Windows 2000, click the **Startup and Recovery** button.

3. The Startup and Recovery dialog box opens, as shown in Figure 5-5. Change settings as desired and then click **OK** to save them (or click **Cancel** if you do not want to save them).

Recall that the Boot.ini file can contain the /NoExecute switch to configure Data Execute Prevention (DEP) that stops a program if it oversteps its boundaries in memory. To configure DEP (which changes the /NoExecute switch), select the **Advanced** tab of the Windows XP System Properties window. Then, under Performance, click **Settings**. The Performance Options window opens. Click the **Data Execution Prevention** tab. The default setting is *Turn on DEP for essential Windows programs and services only*.

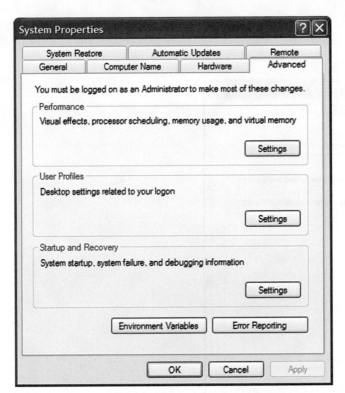

Figure 5-4 You can access startup and recovery options from the System Properties dialog box

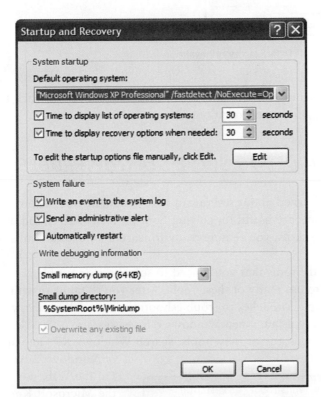

Figure 5-5 Changing the default operating system and timeout value in the Startup and Recovery dialog box

A+ ESS
3.3

For added protection, select **Turn on DEP for all programs and services except those I select,** as shown in Figure 5-6. Then, click **Apply** and reboot the system.

A+
220-602
3.3

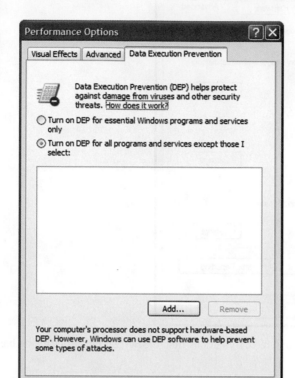

Figure 5-6   Configure Windows XP Data Execution Prevention

Later, if DEP stops a program that you know is legitimate, you can go back to this window and add the program to the exceptions list.

TROUBLESHOOTING TOOLS TO SOLVE STARTUP PROBLEMS

A+
220-602
3.1
3.3

In previous chapters, you learned about several support and maintenance tools for Windows 2000/XP. Some of those tools are useful for solving boot problems. To round out your Windows 2000/XP support skills, you're now ready to learn about some similar tools useful to solve startup problems.

Table 5-3 lists many of the tools that you'll need to solve startup problems. Later in the chapter, you'll learn how to use many of these tools. After you're familiar with the tools, we'll tackle the step-by-step approaches to troubleshooting, and at that time, you'll see how these tools can get you out of a jam when Windows refuses to start.

For more information about any of these tools, search Windows XP Help and Support or Windows 2000 Help. On the Web, you can search the Microsoft Knowledge Base at *support.microsoft.com*, or use the book, *Microsoft Windows XP Professional Resource Kit Documentation*

> 🖉 **Notes**
>
> Many technical people use the terms "boot" and "startup" interchangeably. However, in general, the term "boot" refers to the hardware phase of starting up a computer. Microsoft consistently uses the term "startup" to refer to how its operating systems are booted, well, started, I mean.

A+ ESS 3.3 / A+ 220-602 3.1 3.3	Tool	Available in Win XP	Available in Win 2000	Description
	Add or Remove Programs	X	X	▲ Accessed from the Control Panel ▲ Use it to uninstall, repair, or update software or certain device drivers that are causing a problem.
	Advanced Options Menu	X	X	▲ Accessed by pressing the F8 key when Windows first starts to load ▲ Use several options on this menu to help you troubleshoot boot problems.
	Automated System Recovery (ASR)	X		▲ Accessed from the Windows setup CD ▲ Use ASR as a last resort because the logical drive on which Windows is installed is formatted and restored from the most recent backup. All data and applications written to the drive since the last backup are lost.
	Backup (Ntbackup.exe)	X	X	▲ Enter Ntbackup.exe in the Run dialog box. ▲ Use it to restore the system state, data, and software from previously made backups.
	Boot logging	X	X	▲ Press F8 at startup and select from the Advanced Options menu. ▲ Log events to the Ntbtlog.txt file to investigate the source of an unknown startup error.
	Bootcfg (Bootcfg.exe)	X	X	▲ Enter Bootcfg at a command prompt. ▲ Use it to view the contents of the Boot.ini file.
	Cacls.exe	X	X	▲ At a command prompt, enter Cacls with parameters. ▲ Use it to gain access to a file when permissions to the file are in error or corrupted. The utility can change the access control list (ACL) assigned to a file or group of files to control which users have access to a file.
	Chkdsk (Chkdsk.exe)	X	X	▲ At a command prompt, enter Chkdsk with parameters. ▲ Use it to check and repair errors on a logical drive. If critical system files are affected by these errors, repairing the drive might solve a startup problem.
	Cipher.exe	X	X	▲ At a command prompt, enter Cipher with parameters.

Table 5-3 Windows 2000/XP maintenance and troubleshooting tools

A+ ESS
3.3

A+
220-602
3.1
3.3

Tool	Available in Win XP	Available in Win 2000	Description
			◢ Log in as an administrator and use this command to decrypt a file that is not available because the user account that encrypted the file is no longer accessible.
Compact.exe	X	X	◢ At a command prompt, enter Compact with parameters. ◢ Use it with an NTFS file system to display and change the compressions applied to files and folders.
Computer Management (Compmgmt.msc)	X	X	◢ Accessed from Control Panel or you can enter Compmgmt.msc at a command prompt. ◢ Use it to access several snap-ins to manage and troubleshoot a system.
Defrag.exe	X		◢ At a command prompt, enter Defrag with parameters. ◢ Use it to defragment a drive to improve drive performance and access time.
Device Driver Roll Back	X	X	◢ Accessed from Device Manager ◢ Use it to replace a driver with the one that worked before the current driver was installed.
Device Manager (Devmgmt.msc)	X	X	◢ Accessed from the System Properties window ◢ Use it to solve problems with hardware devices, to update device drivers, and to disable and uninstall a device.
Disk Cleanup (Cleanmgr.exe)	X	X	◢ Accessed from a drive's properties window or by entering Cleanmgr in the Run dialog box ◢ Use it to delete unused files to make more disk space available. Not enough free hard dive space can cause boot problems.
Disk Defragmenter (Dfrg.msc)	X	X	◢ Accessed from a drive's properties window ◢ Use it to defragment a logical drive or floppy disk.
Disk Management (Diskmgmt.msc)	X	X	◢ Accessed from the Computer Management console or, at a command prompt, enter Diskmgmt.msc. ◢ Use it to view and change partitions on hard drives and to format drives.
Driver Signing and Digital Signatures (Sigverif.exe)	X	X	◢ At a command prompt, enter Sigverif with parameters.

Table 5-3   Windows 2000/XP maintenance and troubleshooting tools (continued)

5

A+ ESS 3.3	Tool	Available in Win XP	Available in Win 2000	Description
				▲ When a device driver or other software is giving problems, use it to verify that the software has been approved by Microsoft.
A+ 220-602 3.1 3.3	Error Reporting	X		▲ This automated Windows service displays error messages when an application error occurs
				▲ Follow directions onscreen to produce an error report and send it to Microsoft. Sometimes the Microsoft Web site responds with suggestions to solve the problem.
	Event Viewer (Eventvwr.msc)	X	X	▲ Accessed from the Computer Management console
				▲ Check the Event Viewer window for error messages to help you investigate all kinds of hardware, security, and system problems.
	Expand.exe	X	X	▲ At a command prompt, enter Expand with parameters.
				▲ Use it to extract a file from a cabinet file or compressed file. This command is useful from the Recovery Console when you're trying to restore a system file.
	Group Policy (Gpedit.msc)	X	X	▲ At a command prompt, enter Gpedit.msc.
				▲ Use it to display and change policies controlling users and the computer.
	Last Known Good Configuration	X	X	▲ Press F8 at startup and select from the Advanced Options menu.
				▲ Use this tool when Windows won't start normally and you want to revert the system to before a driver or application that is causing problems was installed.
	Performance Monitor (Perfmon.msc)	X	X	▲ At a command prompt, enter Perfmon.msc.
				▲ Use it to view information about performance to help you identify a performance bottleneck.
	Program Compatibility Wizard	X		▲ Accessed by way of a desktop shortcut to a legacy application
				▲ Use it to resolve issues that prevent legacy software from working in Windows XP.

Table 5-3 Windows 2000/XP maintenance and troubleshooting tools (continued)

A+ ESS
3.3

A+
220-602
3.1
3.3

Tool	Available in Win XP	Available in Win 2000	Description
Recovery Console	X	X	▲ Accessed from the Windows setup CD ▲ Boot up this command-driven OS when you cannot boot from the hard drive. Use it to troubleshoot the Windows problem and recover data from the hard drive.
Registry Editor (Regedit.exe)	X	X	▲ At a command prompt, enter Regedit. ▲ Use it to view and edit the registry.
Runas.exe	X	X	▲ At a command prompt, enter Runas with parameters. ▲ Use it to run a program using different permissions than those assigned to the currently logged-on user.
Safe Mode	X	X	▲ At startup, press F8 and select the option from the Advanced Options menu. ▲ Use it when Windows does not start or starts with errors. Safe Mode loads the Windows desktop with a minimum configuration. In this minimized environment, you can solve a problem with a device driver, display setting, or corrupted or malicious applications.
SC (Sc.exe)	X	X	▲ At a command prompt, enter Sc with parameters. ▲ Use it to stop or start a service that runs in the background.
Services (Services.msc)	X	X	▲ Enter Services.msc in the Run dialog box. ▲ Graphical version of SC
System Configuration Utility (Msconfig.exe)	X		▲ Enter Msconfig in the Run dialog box. ▲ Troubleshoot the startup process by temporarily disabling startup programs and services.
System File Checker (Sfc.exe)	X	X	▲ At a command prompt, enter Sfc with parameters. ▲ Use it to verify the version of all system files when Windows loads. Useful when you suspect system files are corrupted, but you can still access the Windows desktop.
System Information (Msinfo32.exe)	X	X	▲ At a command prompt, enter Msinfo32.

Table 5-3 Windows 2000/XP maintenance and troubleshooting tools (continued)

Tool	Available in Win XP	Available in Win 2000	Description
			◢ Use it to display information about hardware, applications, and Windows that is useful when troubleshooting. Figure 5-7 shows a view of the System Information window.
System Information (Systeminfo.exe)	X	X	◢ At a command prompt, enter Systeminfo. ◢ A version of System Information to be used from a command-prompt window. Information is listed onscreen as text only. To direct that information to a file, use the command Systeminfo.exe >Myfile.txt. Later the file can be printed and used to document information about the system.
System Restore	X		◢ Accessed from the Start menu or when loading Safe Mode ◢ Use it to restore the system to a previously working condition; it restores the registry, some system files, and some application files.
Task Killing Utility (Tskill.exe)	X	X	◢ At a command prompt, enter Tskill with parameters. ◢ Use it to stop or kill a process or program currently running. Useful when managing background services such as an e-mail server or Web server.
Task Lister (Tasklist.exe)	X	X	◢ At a command prompt, enter Tasklist. ◢ Use it to list currently running processes similar to the list provided by Task Manager.
Task Manager (Taskman.exe)	X	X	◢ Right-click the taskbar and select Task Manager. ◢ Use it to list and stop currently running processes. Useful when you need to stop a locked-up application.
Windows File Protection	X	X	◢ Windows background service ◢ Runs in the background to protect system files and restore overwritten system files as needed.
Windows Update (Wupdmgr.exe)	X	X	◢ Accessed from the Start menu ◢ Use it to update Windows by downloading the latest patches from the Microsoft Web site.

Table 5-3 Windows 2000/XP maintenance and troubleshooting tools (continued)

A+ ESS
3.3

A+
220-602
3.1
3.3

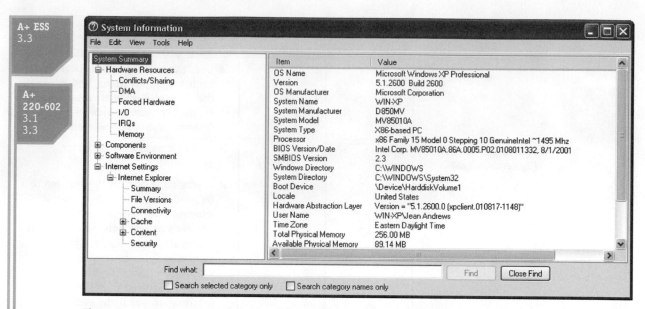

Figure 5-7 The System Information window displays important information about the system's hardware, software, and environment

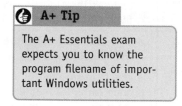

A+ Tip

The A+ Essentials exam expects you to know the program filename of important Windows utilities.

by Microsoft Press or *Microsoft Windows 2000 Professional Resource Kit* by Microsoft Press. In addition, to get help about a command-line tool, from a command prompt, enter the Help command followed by the tool name. For example, to get help about Defrag, enter **Help defrag**. For some commands not supported by Help, type the command followed by /?. For example, for help with the Cipher command, enter **Cipher /?**.

Now let's see how to use the options on the Advanced Options Menu and how to use the Recovery Console.

A+
220-602
3.3

ADVANCED OPTIONS MENU

As a PC boots and the "Starting Windows" message appears at the bottom of the screen, press the F8 key to display the Windows XP **Advanced Options menu**, which is shown in Figure 5-8, or the Windows 2000 Advanced Options menu, which is shown in Figure 5-9. This menu can be used to diagnose and fix problems when booting Windows 2000/XP. The purpose of each menu option is outlined in the following sections.

A+ Tip

The A+ Essentials and A+ 220-602 exams expect you to be able to select the appropriate next step in troubleshooting a failed boot when given a specific scenario. As you study the tools in this section, pay attention to how a tool affects the installed OS, applications, and data. The idea is to fix the problem by using the tool that least affects the OS, applications, and data.

SAFE MODE

Safe Mode boots the OS with a minimum configuration and can be used to solve problems with a new hardware installation or problems caused by user settings. Safe Mode boots with the mouse, monitor (with basic video), keyboard, and mass storage drivers loaded. It uses the default system services (it does not load any extra

```
Windows Advanced Options Menu
Please select an option:

        Safe Mode
        Safe Mode with Networking
        Safe Mode with Command Prompt

        Enable Boot Logging
        Enable VGA Mode
        Last Known Good Configuration (your most recent settings that worked)
        Directory Services Restore Mode (Windows domain controllers only)
        Debugging Mode
        Disable automatic restart on system failure

        Start Windows Normally
        Reboot
        Return to OS Choices Menu


Use the up and down arrow keys to move the highlight to your choice.
```

Figure 5-8   Press the F8 key at startup to display the Windows XP Advanced Options menu

```
Windows 2000 Advanced Options Menu
Please select an option:

        Safe Mode
        Safe Mode with Networking
        Safe Mode with Command Prompt

        Enable Boot Logging
        Enable VGA Mode
        Last Known Good Configuration
        Directory Services Restore Mode (Windows 2000 domain controllers only)
        Debugging Mode

        Boot Normally

Use ↑ and ↓ to move the highlight to your choice.
Press Enter to choose.
```

Figure 5-9   The Windows 2000 Advanced Options menu

services) and does not provide network access. It uses a plain video driver (Vga.sys) instead of the video drivers specific to your video card.

When you boot in Safe Mode, you will see "Safe Mode" in all four corners of your screen. In addition, you have a GUI interface in Safe Mode. The screen resolution is 600 x 800 and the desktop wallpaper (background) is black. Figure 5-10 shows Windows XP in Safe Mode. In the figure, you can see the running processes as reported by Task Manager.

After the OS loads in Safe Mode, you can disable any problem device, scan for viruses, use System Restore to restore the system to an earlier restore point, restore the system to a previously saved system state, run diagnostic software, or take other appropriate action to diagnose and solve problems. When you load Windows 2000/XP in Safe Mode, all files used for the load are recorded in the Ntbtlog.txt file. Use this file to identify a service, device driver, or application loaded at startup that is causing a problem.

If you boot into Safe Mode and Windows XP recognizes System Restore has previously been used to create restore points, Windows XP will give you the opportunity to launch the System Restore Wizard (see Figure 5-11). The wizard gives you the opportunity to choose a restore point from those previously saved. Recall that when Windows is restored to a restore point, all Windows settings are returned to the way they were when the restore point was created.

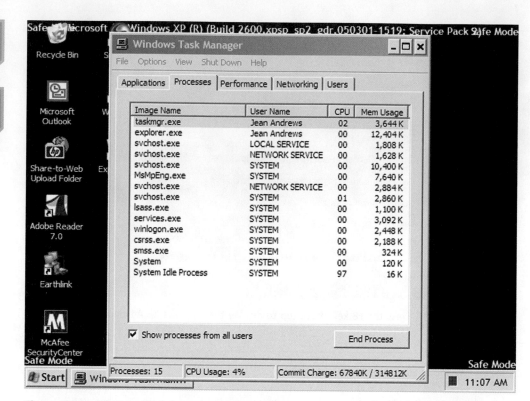

Figure 5-10 Windows XP Safe Mode with Task Manager

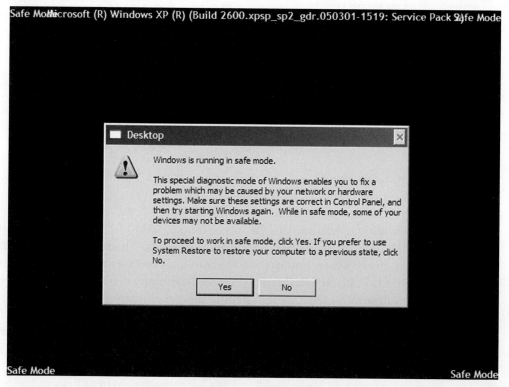

Figure 5-11 Windows XP gives you the opportunity to launch System Restore before it loads Safe Mode

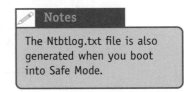

SAFE MODE WITH NETWORKING

Use this option when you are solving a problem with booting and need access to the network to solve the problem. For example, if you have just attempted to install a printer, which causes the OS to hang when it boots, and the printer drivers are downloaded from the network, boot into Safe Mode with Networking. Uninstall the printer and then install it again from the network. Also use this mode when the Windows 2000/XP installation files are available on the network, rather than the Windows 2000/XP setup CD, and you need to access these files.

SAFE MODE WITH COMMAND PROMPT

If the first Safe Mode option does not load the OS, then try this option. This Safe Mode option does not load a GUI desktop automatically. You would use it to get a command prompt only.

ENABLE BOOT LOGGING

When you boot with this option, Windows 2000/XP loads normally and you access the regular desktop. However, all files used during the load process are recorded in a file, C:\Windows\Ntbtlog.txt (see Figure 5-12). Thus, you can use this option to see what did and did not load during the boot. For instance, if you have a problem getting a device to work, check Ntbtlog.txt to see what driver files loaded. Boot logging is much more effective if you have a copy of Ntbtlog.txt that was made when everything worked as it should. Then you can compare the good load to the bad load, looking for differences.

> ✎ **Notes**
>
> The Ntbtlog.txt file is also generated when you boot into Safe Mode.

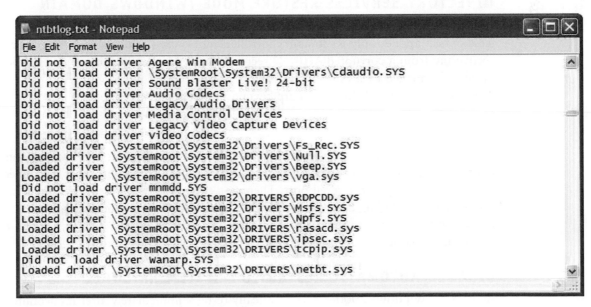

Figure 5-12 Sample C:\Windows\Ntbtlog.txt file

A+ ESS
3.3

A+
220-602
3.3

📝 **Notes**

If Windows hangs during the boot, try booting using the option Enable Boot Logging. Then look at the last entry in the Ntbtlog.txt file. This entry might be the name of a device driver causing the system to hang.

ENABLE VGA MODE

Use this option when the video setting does not allow you to see the screen well enough to fix a bad setting. This can happen when a user creates a desktop with black fonts on a black background, or something similar. Booting in this mode gives you a very plain, standard VGA video. You can then go to the Display settings, correct the problem, and reboot normally. You can also use this option if your video drivers are corrupted and you need to update, rollback, or reinstall your video drivers.

LAST KNOWN GOOD CONFIGURATION

Each time the system boots completely and the user logs on, the Last Known Good configuration is saved. Windows 2000/XP keeps the Last Known Good configuration in the registry. Use this option if you suspect the system was configured incorrectly. It restores Windows 2000/XP to the settings of the last successful boot, and all system setting changes made after this last successful boot are lost.

📝 **Notes**

The Last Known Good configuration is saved after the user logs on in normal mode. When booting in Safe Mode, the Last Known Good configuration is not saved. Therefore, if you have a Windows problem you're trying to solve, boot using Safe Mode so that you can log on without overwriting the Last Known Good configuration.

In some situations, the Last Known Good will not help you recover from the problem. If you have booted several times since a problem started, all the saved versions of the Last Known Good reflect the problem.

DIRECTORY SERVICES RESTORE MODE (WINDOWS DOMAIN CONTROLLERS ONLY)

This option applies only to domain controllers and is used as one step in the process of recovering from a corrupted Active Directory. Recall that Active Directory is the domain database managed by a domain controller that tracks users and resources on the domain. The details of how all this works are beyond the scope of this chapter.

DEBUGGING MODE

This mode gives you the opportunity to move system boot logs from the failing computer to another computer for evaluation. To use this mode, both computers must be connected to each other by way of the serial port. Then, you can reboot into this mode and Windows 2000/XP on the failing computer will send all the boot information through the serial port and on to the other computer. For more details, see the *Windows XP Professional Resource Kit* or the *Windows 2000 Professional Resource Kit* (Microsoft Press).

DISABLE AUTOMATIC RESTART ON SYSTEM FAILURE

By default, Windows 2000/XP automatically restarts immediately after it encounters a system failure, which is also called a stop error or a blue screen of death (BSOD). This type of error can be especially troublesome if you're trying to shut down a system and it encounters an error. The error can cause the system to continually reboot rather than shut down. For Windows XP, choose **Disable automatic restart on system failure** to stop the rebooting. (The option is not on the Windows 2000 Advanced Options menu.)

5

A+ ESS
3.3

A+
220-602
3.3

From the Windows 2000/XP desktop, you can modify this same setting using the System Properties window. Click the **Advanced** tab. For Windows XP, under Startup and Recovery, click **Settings**, and, for Windows 2000, click **Startup and Recovery**. On the Startup and Recovery window, uncheck **Automatically restart**, as shown in Figure 5-13. Next time the system encounters a stop error, it will shut down and not automatically restart. You'll learn more about stop errors later in the chapter.

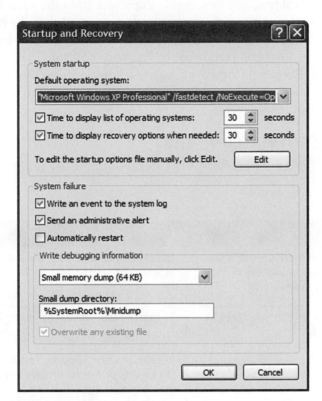

Figure 5-13   Control what happens after a stop error

RECOVERY CONSOLE

A+
220-602
3.1
3.3

The Advanced Options menu can help if the problem is a faulty device driver or system service. However, if the problem goes deeper than that, the next tool to use is the Recovery Console. Use it when Windows 2000/XP does not start properly or hangs during the load. It works even when core Windows system files are corrupted. The Recovery Console is a command-driven operating system that does not use a GUI. With it, you can access the FAT16, FAT32, and NTFS file systems.

> **Notes**
>
> Experienced techies remember the days when the Windows 9x/Me startup disk with tried-and-true DOS was the tool to use when Windows would not boot. Today that command-line OS is the Recovery Console. Many Recovery Console commands work and look much like DOS commands.

Using the Recovery Console, you can:

▲ Repair a damaged registry, system files, or file system on the hard drive.
▲ Enable or disable a service or device driver.
▲ Repair the master boot program on the hard drive or the boot sector on the system partition.

◢ Repair a damaged Boot.ini file.

◢ Recover data when the Windows installation is beyond repair.

The Recovery Console is designed so that someone can't maliciously use it to gain unauthorized access. You must enter the Administrator password in order to use the Recovery Console and access an NTFS volume. Unless you first set certain parameters, you are not allowed into all folders, and you cannot copy files from the hard drive to a floppy disk or other removable media. If the registry is so corrupted that the Recovery Console cannot read the password in order to validate it, you are not asked for the password, but you are limited in what you can do at the Recovery Console.

Now let's look at a list of Recovery Console commands, how to access the Recovery Console, how to use it to perform several troubleshooting tasks, and how to install the Recovery Console on the boot loader menu.

LIST OF RECOVERY CONSOLE COMMANDS

As a summary reference, Table 5-4 lists Recovery Console commands and their descriptions.

Command	Description	Examples
Attrib	Changes the attributes of a file or folder, and works the same as the DOS version	To remove the read-only, hidden, and system attributes from the file: `C:\> Attrib -r -h -s filename`

Batch	Carries out commands stored in a batch file	To execute the commands in File1:
		
		`C:\> Batch File1.bat`
		
		To execute the commands in File1 and store the results of the commands to File2:
		
		`C:\> Batch File1.bat File2.txt`

Cd	Displays or changes the current folder. It cannot be used to change drives.	To change folders to the C:\Windows\system folder:
		
		`C:\> Cd C:\windows\system`
		
		`C:\windows\system>`

Chkdsk	Checks a disk and repairs or recovers the data	To check drive C: and repair it: `C:\> Chkdsk C: /r`
Cls	Clears the screen	`C:\> cls`
Copy	Copies a single file. Use the command to replace corrupted system files or save data files to another media when the hard drive is failing.	To copy the file File1 on the CD to the hard drive's Winnt folder, naming the file File2: `C:\> Copy D:\File1 C:\Winnt\File2`
Del	Deletes a file	To delete File2: `C:\Winnt> Del File2`
Dir	Lists files and folders. Wildcard characters are allowed.	To list all files with a .exe file extension: `C:\> Dir *.exe`

Table 5-4 Commands available from the Recovery Console

5

A+ ESS
3.3

A+
220-602
3.1
3.3

Command	Description	Examples
Disable	Disables a service or driver. Use it to disable a service or driver that starts and prevents the system from booting properly. After you disable the service, restart the system to see if your problem is solved.	To disable the Event Log service: `C:\> Disable eventlog`
Diskpart	Creates and deletes partitions on the hard drive	Enter the command with no arguments to display a user interface: `C:\> Diskpart`
Enable	Displays the status and enables a Windows system service or driver	To display the status of the Event Log service: `C:\> Enable eventlog`
Exit	Quits the Recovery Console and restarts the computer	`C:\> Exit`

Expand	Expands compressed files and extracts files from cabinet files and copies the files to the destination folder	To extract File1 from the Drivers.cab file:
		`C:\> Expand D:\i386\Drivers.cab -f:File1`
		
		To expand the compressed file, File1.cp_:
		`C:\> Expand File1.cp_`

Fixboot	Rewrites the OS boot sector on the hard drive. If a drive letter is not specified, the system drive is assumed.	To repair the OS boot sector of drive C: `C:\> Fixboot C:`
Fixmbr	Rewrites the Master Boot Record boot program. This command is the same as the Windows 9x/Me Fdisk/MBR command.	To repair the Master Boot Record boot program: `C:\> Fixmbr`

Format	Formats a logical drive. If no file system is specified, NTFS is assumed.	To format using the NTFS file system:
		`C:\> Format D:`
		
		To format using the FAT32 file system:
		`C:\> Format D:/fs:FAT32`
		
		To format using the FAT16 file system:
		`C:\> Format D:/fs:FAT`

Help	Help utility appears for the given command	To get help with the Fixboot command: `C:\> Help fixboot`
Listsvc	Lists all available services. This command has no parameters.	`C:\> Listsvc`
Logon	Allows you to log on to an installation with the Administrator password. Use it to log onto a second installation of Windows in a dual-boot environment.	When logged onto the first Windows installation, use this command to log onto the second installation: `C:\> logon 2` If you don't enter the password correctly after three tries, the system automatically reboots.

Table 5-5 Commands available from the Recovery Console (continued)

A+ ESS
3.3

A+
220-602
3.1
3.3

Command	Description	Examples
Map	Lists all drive letters and file system types	`C:\> Map`
Md or Mkdir	Creates a folder	`C:\> MD C:\TEMP`
More or Type	Displays a text file onscreen	`C:\> Type filename.txt`
Rd or Rmdir	Deletes a directory	`C:\> RD C:\TEMP`
Rename or Ren	Renames a file	`C:\> Rename File1.txt File2.txt`
Set	Displays or sets Recovery Console environmental variables	To turn off the prompt when you are overwriting files: `C:\> Set nocopyprompt=true`
Systemroot	Sets the current directory to the directory where Windows 2000/XP is installed	`C:\> Systemroot` `C:\WINDOWS>`
Type	Displays contents of a text file	`C:\> Type filename.txt`

Table 5-5 Commands available from the Recovery Console (continued)

APPLYING|CONCEPTS   HOW TO ACCESS THE RECOVERY CONSOLE

The Recovery Console software is on the Windows 2000/XP setup CD and the four Windows 2000 setup disks. You can launch the Recovery Console from the CD or four disks, or manually install the Recovery Console on the hard drive and launch it from there.

How to access the Recovery Console using Windows XP. For Windows XP, to use the Recovery Console, insert the Windows XP setup CD in the CD drive and restart the system. When the Windows XP Setup opening menu appears (see Figure 5-14), press **R** to load the Recovery Console.

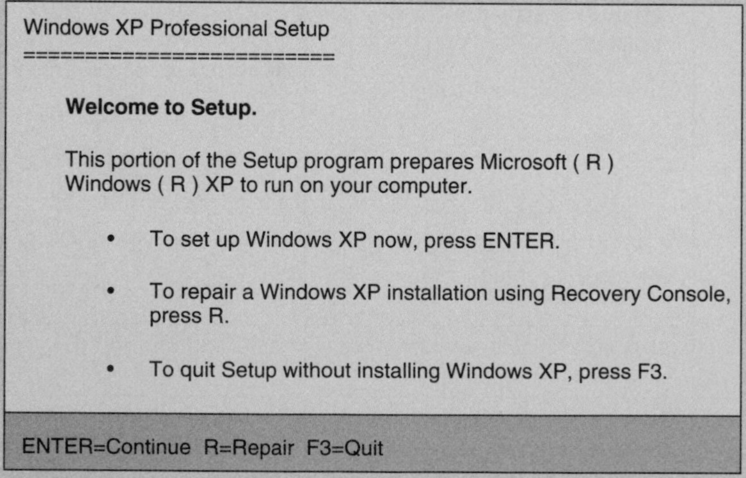

```
Windows XP Professional Setup
=========================

   Welcome to Setup.

   This portion of the Setup program prepares Microsoft ( R )
   Windows ( R ) XP to run on your computer.

      •   To set up Windows XP now, press ENTER.

      •   To repair a Windows XP installation using Recovery Console,
          press R.

      •   To quit Setup without installing Windows XP, press F3.

 ENTER=Continue  R=Repair  F3=Quit
```

Figure 5-14 Windows XP Setup opening menu

A+ ESS
3.3

A+
220-602
3.1
3.3

Access the Recovery Console using Windows 2000. For Windows 2000, you can boot from the Windows 2000 setup CD or you can boot from the four setup disks. Use the four setup disks if the computer will not boot from a CD drive. If you have not already created the Windows 2000 setup disks, you can go to a working Windows 2000 PC and create the disks by following the directions given in Chapter 2. Follow these steps to load Windows 2000 from the disks or from the setup CD and access the Recovery Console:

1. Insert the first of the four setup disks, and restart the PC. You are directed to insert each of the four disks in turn, and then the Setup screen appears, as shown in Figure 5-15. If you boot from the Windows 2000 setup CD, the same screen appears.

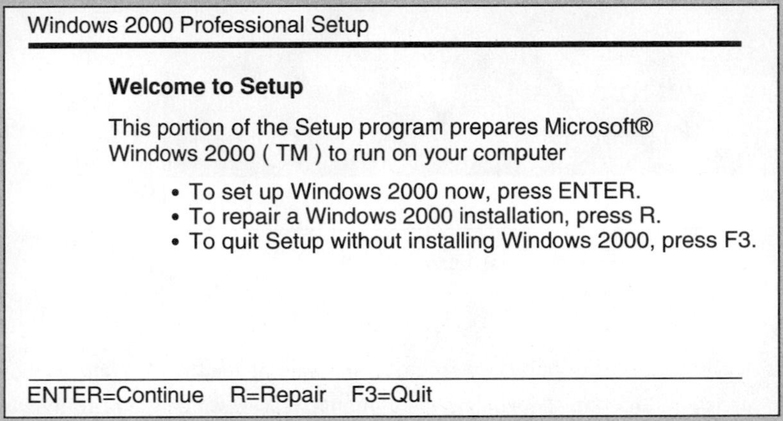

Windows 2000 Professional Setup

Welcome to Setup

This portion of the Setup program prepares Microsoft®
Windows 2000 (TM) to run on your computer

- To set up Windows 2000 now, press ENTER.
- To repair a Windows 2000 installation, press R.
- To quit Setup without installing Windows 2000, press F3.

ENTER=Continue   R=Repair   F3=Quit

Figure 5-15   Use this Windows 2000 Setup screen to access the Recovery Console

2. Type **R** to select the "To repair a Windows 2000 installation" option. The Windows 2000 Repair Options window opens (see Figure 5-16). Type **C** to select the Recovery Console.

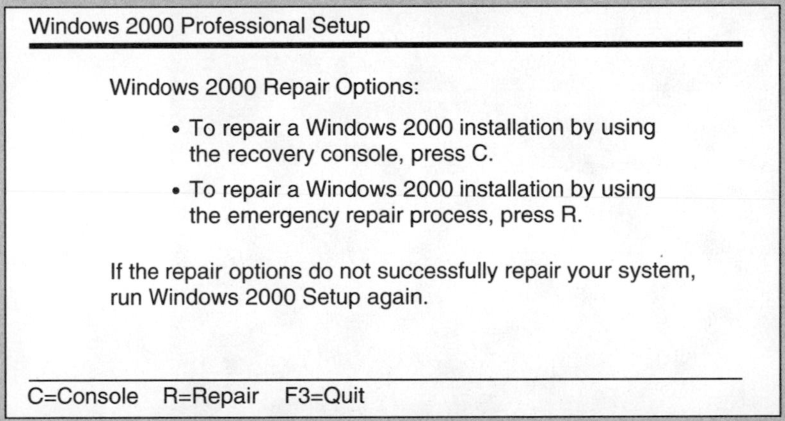

Windows 2000 Professional Setup

Windows 2000 Repair Options:

- To repair a Windows 2000 installation by using
  the recovery console, press C.

- To repair a Windows 2000 installation by using
  the emergency repair process, press R.

If the repair options do not successfully repair your system,
run Windows 2000 Setup again.

C=Console   R=Repair   F3=Quit

Figure 5-16   Windows 2000 offers two repair options

3. Note that as the Recovery Console attempts to load and give you access to the hard drive, it will display one of the following screens depending on the severity of the problem with the drive:

▲ If the Recovery Console cannot find the drive, the window in Figure 5-17 appears. Consider the problem hardware related. You might have a totally dead drive.

A+ ESS
3.3

A+
220-602
3.1
3.3

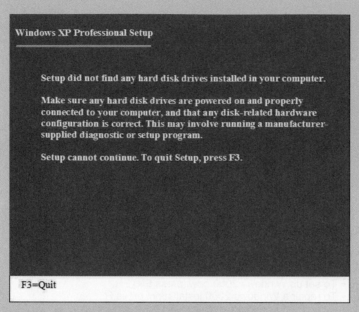

Figure 5-17   Windows setup cannot find a hard drive

▲ If the Console can find the hard drive, but cannot read from it, the window in Figure 5-18 appears. Notice in the window the C prompt (C:\>), which seems to indicate that the Recovery Console can access the hard drive, but the message above the C prompt says otherwise. When you try the DIR command, as shown in Figure 5-18, you find out that drive C: is not available. The Fixmbr and Fixboot commands might help.

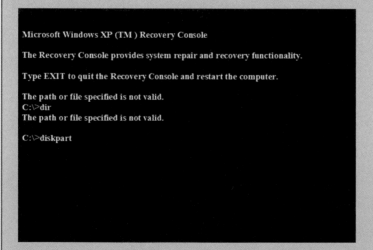

Figure 5-18   The Recovery Console cannot read from the hard drive

▲ If the Console is able to read drive C, but Windows is seriously corrupted, the window in Figure 5-19 appears. Use the DIR command to see what files or folders are still on the drive. Is the \Windows folder present? If not, then you might need to reformat the drive and reinstall Windows. But first try to find any important data that is not backed up.

A+ ESS
3.3

A+
220-602
3.1
3.3

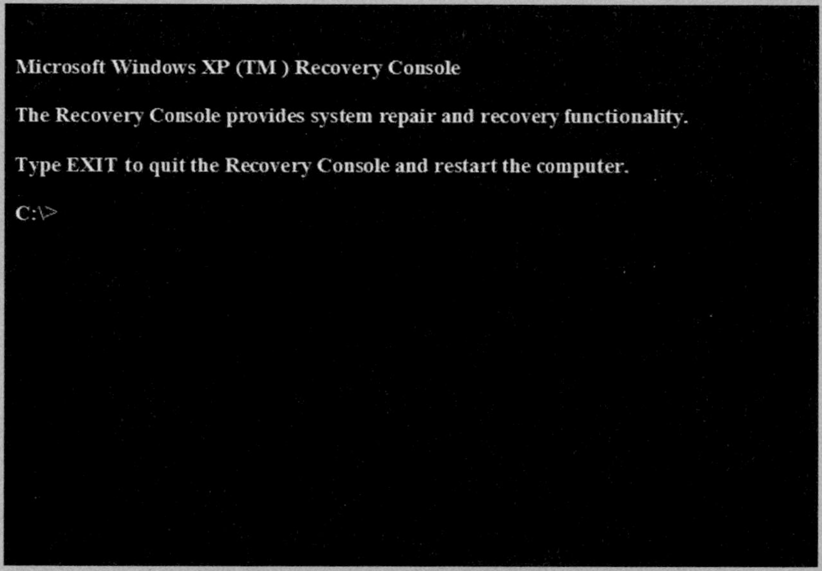

> Microsoft Windows XP (TM) Recovery Console
>
> The Recovery Console provides system repair and recovery functionality.
>
> Type EXIT to quit the Recovery Console and restart the computer.
>
> C:\>

Figure 5-19   The Recovery Console can read drive C, but cannot find a Windows installation

4. If the Console is able to determine that one or more Windows installations is on the drive, it gives you a choice of with which installation you want to work. If only one installation is showing, as in Figure 5-20, type **1** and press **Enter**. Next, you will be asked for the Administrator password. Enter the password and press **Enter**. The command prompt shows the Windows folder is the current working directory. You can now use the Recovery Console to try to find the problem and fix it. How to do that is coming up.

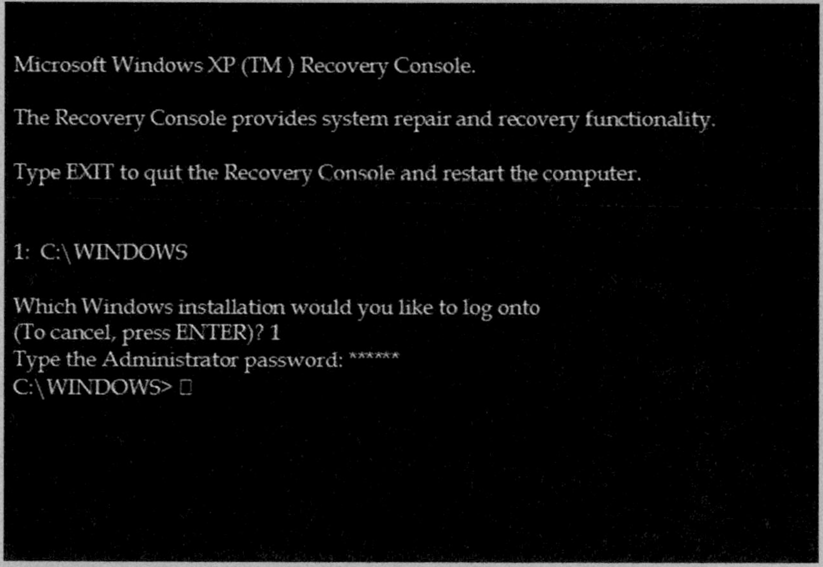

> Microsoft Windows XP (TM) Recovery Console.
>
> The Recovery Console provides system repair and recovery functionality.
>
> Type EXIT to quit the Recovery Console and restart the computer.
>
> 1: C:\WINDOWS
>
> Which Windows installation would you like to log onto
> (To cancel, press ENTER)? 1
> Type the Administrator password: ******
> C:\WINDOWS> □

Figure 5-20   The Recovery Console has found a Windows installation

5. To exit the Recovery Console, type **Exit** and press Enter. The system will attempt to boot to the Windows desktop.

> **Notes**
>
> Here are two useful tips to help you when using the Recovery Console: To retrieve the last command, press F3 at the command prompt. To retrieve the command one character at a time, press the F1 key.

USE THE RECOVERY CONSOLE TO FIX HARD DRIVE PROBLEMS

Here are the commands you can use to examine the hard drive structure for errors and possibly fix them:

◢ *Fixmbr and Fixboot.* The Fixmbr command restores the master boot program in the MBR, and the Fixboot command repairs the OS boot record. As you enter each command, you're looking for clues that might indicate at what point the drive has failed. For example, Figure 5-21 shows the results of using the Fixmbr command, which appears to have worked without errors, but the Fixboot command has actually failed. This tells us that most likely the master boot program is healthy, but drive C is not accessible. After using these commands, if you don't see any errors, exit the Recovery Console and try to boot from the hard drive.

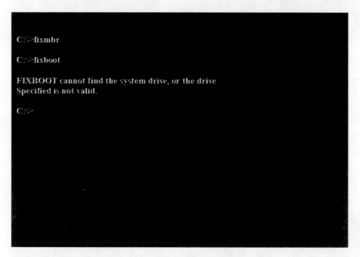

Figure 5-21 Results of using the Fixmbr and Fixboot commands in the Recovery Console

◢ *Diskpart.* Use the Diskpart command to view, create, and delete partitions on the drive. Type **Diskpart** and press **Enter** and a full screen appears listing the partitions the Console sees on the drive. See Figure 5-22.

◢ *Chkdsk.* Use this command to repair the file system and recover data from bad sectors: **chkdsk C: /r**.

USE THE RECOVERY CONSOLE TO RESTORE THE REGISTRY

You can use the Recovery Console to restore registry files with those saved at the last time the system state was backed up. Follow the six steps listed in Table 5-5 to restore the registry.

A+ ESS
3.3

A+
220-602
3.1
3.3

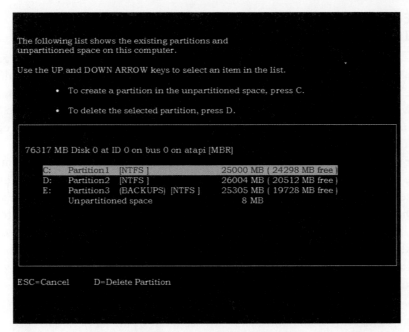

```
The following list shows the existing partitions and
unpartitioned space on this computer.

Use the UP and DOWN ARROW keys to select an item in the list.

        •  To create a partition in the unpartitioned space, press C.

        •  To delete the selected partition, press D.


   76317 MB Disk 0 at ID 0 on bus 0 on atapi [MBR]

        C:    Partition1   [NTFS ]                25000 MB ( 24298 MB free )
        D:    Partition2   [NTFS ]                26004 MB ( 20512 MB free )
        E:    Partition3   (BACKUPS)  [NTFS ]     25305 MB ( 19728 MB free )
              Unpartitioned space                    8 MB




 ESC=Cancel        D=Delete Partition
```

Figure 5-22   Using the Diskpart screen, you can view, delete, and create partitions

Step	Command	Description
1.	Systemroot	Makes the Windows folder the current folder
2.	CD System32\Config	Makes the Windows registry folder the current folder
3.	Ren Default Default.save Ren Sam Sam.save Ren Security Security.save Ren Software Software.save Ren System System.save	Renames the five registry files
4.	Systemroot	Returns to the Windows folder
5.	CD repair (for Windows XP) or CD repair\regback (for Windows 2000)	Makes the Windows registry backup folder the current folder
6.	Copy Default C:\Windows\ system32\config Copy Sam C:\Windows\ system32\config Copy Security C:\Windows\ system32\config Copy Software C:\Windows\ system32\config Copy System C:\Windows\ system32\config	Copies the five registry files from the backup folder to the registry folder. For hardware problems, first try copying just the System hive and reboot. For software problems, first try copying just the Software hive and then reboot. If you still have problems, try copying all five hives.

Table 5-5   Steps to restore the Windows 2000/XP registry

USE THE RECOVERY CONSOLE TO DISABLE A SERVICE OR DEVICE DRIVER

Sometimes when Windows fails, it first displays a stop error on a blue background (called a BSOD). The stop error might give the name of a service or device driver that caused the problem. If the service or driver is critical to Windows operation, booting into Safe Mode won't help because the service or driver will be attempted in Safe Mode. The solution is to boot the system using the Recovery Console and copy a replacement program file from the Windows 2000/XP setup CD to the hard drive.

In order to know what program file to replace, you'll need to know the name or description of the service or driver causing the problem. If an error message doesn't give you the clue you need, you might try to boot to the Advanced Options Menu (press **F8** while booting) and then select **Enable Boot Logging**. Then compare the Ntbtlog.txt file to one generated on a healthy system. You might be able to find the driver or service that caused the boot to halt.

If you know the service causing the problem, use these commands to list services and disable and enable a service:

▲ *Listsvc*. Enter the command Listsvc to see a list of all services currently installed, which includes device drivers. The list is really long, showing the name of each service, a brief one-line description and its status (disabled, manual, or auto). To find the service giving the problem, you'll have to have more information than what this list shows.

▲ *Disable*. Use the Disable command to disable a service. For example, to disable the service SharedAccess, which is the Windows Firewall service, use this command: **disable sharedaccess**. Before you enter the command, be sure to write down the current startup type that is displayed so you'll know how to enable the service later. For services that are auto-started like this one, the startup type is service_auto_start.

▲ *Enable*. Use the Enable command followed by the name of the service to show the current status of a service. To enable the service, use the startup type in the command line. For example, to reinstate the Firewall service, use this command:

```
enable sharedaccess service_auto-start
```

If you think you've found the service that is causing the problem, disable it and reboot the system. If the problem disappears or the error message changes, you might have found the right service to replace. The next step is to replace the program file with a fresh copy.

USE THE RECOVERY CONSOLE TO RESTORE SYSTEM FILES

Based on error messages and your research about them, if you think you know which Windows system file is corrupted or missing, you can use the Recovery Console to copy a new set of system files from the Windows setup CD to the hard drive. For example, suppose you get an error message that Ntldr is corrupted or missing. To replace the file, you could execute the commands in Figure 5-23.

Here are other commands to use to restore system files:

▲ *Map*. Displays the current drive letters. This command is useful to find your way around the system, such as when you need to know the drive letter for the CD drive.

▲ *Systemroot*. Use this command to make the Windows directory the default directory (refer to Figure 5-23 for an example of its use).

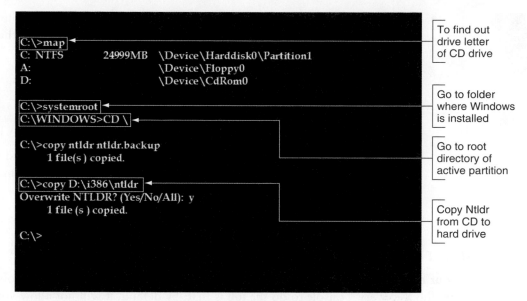

Figure 5-23 Recovery Console command to repair Ntldr

▲ *CD*. Change directory. For example, to make the root directory the default directory, use **CD **.

▲ *Delete*. Deletes a file. For example, to delete Ntldr in the Temp directory, use this command: **Delete C:\temp\ntldr**.

▲ *Copy*. To make a backup of the current Ntldr file, use this command:

```
copy ntldr ntldr.backup
```

▲ To copy the Ntldr file from the Windows setup CD to the root directory of the hard drive, use this command:

```
copy D:\i386\ntldr C:\
```

Substitute the drive letter for the CD drive in the command line.

A compressed file uses an underscore as the last character in the file extension; for example, Netapi32.dl_. When you use the Copy command, the file will automatically uncompress. For example, use this command to copy Netapi32.dl_ from the setup CD:

```
copy D:\i386\netapi32.dl_ netapi32.dll
```

▲ *Bootcfg*. This command lets you view and edit the Boot.ini file. Here are useful parameters:

- **bootcfg /list**   Lists entries in Boot.ini
- **bootcfg /copy**   Makes a copy of Boot.ini before you rebuild it
- **bootcfg /rebuild**   Rebuilds the Boot.ini file

▲ *Expand*. When you're looking for a certain file on the Windows 2000/XP setup CD, you'll find cabinet files that hold groups of compressed files (cabinet files have a .cab file extension). Use the Expand command to extract these files. Here are some useful parameters of the Expand command:

- To list all files in the driver.cab cabinet file:

```
expand D:\i386\driver.cab -f:* /d
```

A+ ESS
3.3

A+
220-602
3.1
3.3

- To extract the file Splitter.sys, in the Driver.cab file and copy it from the setup CD to the hard drive, first make the folder where you want the file to go the current folder. Then use the Expand command like this:

```
cd C:\windows\system32\drivers

expand D:\i386\driver.cab /f:splitter.sys
```

You can also use the Expand command to uncompress a compressed file. For example, to expand a file and copy it to the current folder, use this command:

```
expand D:\i386\netapi32.dl_
```

USE THE RECOVERY CONSOLE TO RECOVER DATA

If your hard drive is corrupted, you still might be able to recover data. The problem with using the Recovery Console to do the job is that, by default, it will not allow you to go into folders other than the system folders or to copy data onto removable media. To do these things, you first need to change some Recovery Console settings. Then you can use the Copy command to copy data from the hard drive to other media.

Here are the commands you'll need to change the settings:

- To allow access to all files and folders on all drives:

```
set allowallpaths = true
```

- To allow you to copy any file to another media such as a jump drive or floppy disk:

```
set allowremovablemedia = true
```

- To allow the use of wildcard characters * and ?:

```
set allowwildcards = true
```

OPTIONAL INSTALLATION OF THE RECOVERY CONSOLE

Although the Recovery Console can be launched from the Windows setup CD to recover from system failure, you can also install it on your working system so it appears on the OS boot loader menu. You can then use it to address less drastic problems that occur when you can boot from the hard drive.

To install the Recovery Console:

1. Open a command window.

2. Change from the current directory to the \i386 folder on the Windows 2000/XP CD.

3. Enter the command **winnt32 /cmdcons**. The Recovery Console is installed.

4. Restart your computer. Recovery Console should now be shown with the list of available operating systems on the OS boot loader menu.

STRATEGIES FOR TROUBLESHOOTING WINDOWS 2000/XP STARTUP

A+ ESS
1.3
3.3

A+
220-602
3.3

Now that you know how the Windows 2000/XP boot process works and about the different tools you can use to solve boot problems, you're ready to move on and actually tackle real startup problems that might plague even the best-run and best-maintained computer. In this section of the chapter, you'll learn the general guidelines for troubleshooting, how to respond to startup errors, how to clean up a sluggish startup, and how to restore system files. We'll then wrap up the chapter with some methods to use when you have abandoned all hope of fixing a few Windows errors and are ready to do a major overhaul of the entire Windows installation.

Ready? Let's get started!

GUIDELINES FOR TROUBLESHOOTING BOOT PROBLEMS

Here are some general guidelines to help you address boot problems:

- Interview the user to find out what has recently changed, what happened just before the problem started, and how to reproduce the problem. Ask what has recently happened. Has new hardware or software been installed? Don't forget to ask about any important data that is not backed up.
- If important data is not backed up, make every effort to copy the data to another media before you try to solve the Windows problem. Don't risk the data without the user's permission. If the system is giving so many errors that you cannot copy data, try booting into Safe Mode. If Safe Mode doesn't load, you can use the Recovery Console to access the data. If Recovery Console cannot access the hard drive, consider the problem related to hardware. The hard drive data cable might be loose, or the drive might be physically damaged.
- Next, determine at what point in the boot the system fails. Decide if you think the problem is hardware or software related.
- If you think the problem is related to hardware, check the simple things first. Turn off the power and restart the system. Check for loose cables, switches that are not on, stuck keys on the keyboard, a wall outlet switch that has been turned off, and similar easy-to-solve problems.
- If an error message is displayed onscreen, start by addressing it. You will learn several ways to address error messages later in the chapter. As you work to correct the problem and restore the system, always keep in mind to use the least drastic solution that will change as little of the system as possible.
- If you think the problem is software related and you cannot boot to the Windows desktop, try booting to the Advanced Options menu (hold down **F8** while Windows loads) and select the **Last Known Good Configuration**. If you want to use this option, it's important to use it early in the troubleshooting process before you accidentally overwrite the last known good.
- If you can load the Windows desktop, but the system is giving many errors or is extremely slow, suspect a virus is present. Run antivirus software to scan the entire hard drive for malicious software. If the antivirus software won't work or is not installed, boot into Safe Mode and install and run the software there. You will learn more about using antivirus software in Chapter 10.
- If the system has recently been changed, such as installing software or hardware, assume the installation is the guilty party until it's proven innocent. Use Device Manager to disable or uninstall the device. If this solves the problem, then try to find

updated device drivers for the device. Search the Microsoft Web site for known problems with the device or search the device manufacturer Web site. Try updating or rolling back the device drivers.

▲ If a new application or utility program has just been installed, go to the Add or Remove Programs applet in Control Panel and uninstall the software. Reboot the system. If the problem goes away, then try reinstalling the software. If the problem comes back, go to the software manufacturer's Web site and download and install any updates or fixes.

▲ The hard drive might be full or the file system corrupted. Use Disk Cleanup to clean up the hard drive, deleting unwanted files. Use Defrag and Chkdsk to optimize and repair the drive. If the system is slow while trying to do this, boot into Safe Mode and do these maintenance tasks from there. How to do these maintenance tasks is covered in Chapter 4.

▲ If you think unknown software is bogging down startup, you can do the following to clean up startup:

1. Boot into Safe Mode. To do that, while Windows is loading, press **F8** and select **Safe Mode with Networking** from the Advanced Options menu.

2. Use up-to-date antivirus software to scan for viruses. If you find a virus, clean it and reboot to see if the problem is solved. Rerun the AV software to make sure it caught everything.

3. Using the Add or Remove Programs applet in Control Panel, remove any unwanted software. Be sure to stop the software first. If necessary, you can use Task Manager to end a process and then you can uninstall it.

4. Check all folders that contain startup entries and move or delete any startup programs and scripts that might be bogging down the system or causing errors.

5. Use the Windows XP System Configuration utility (Msconfig) to temporarily disable processes that might cause problems.

6. Use the Services Console to permanently disable any services that might be causing a problem. If an error message tells you which service is causing the problem, you can uninstall that software.

▲ If you think Windows system files are missing or corrupted, you can do the following to restore system files:

1. Use the System File Checker utility to recover Windows system files. If SFC won't work, you can restore system files using the Recovery Console.

2. For Windows XP, try using System Restore to return the system to a previously saved restore point. If you can't boot to the normal Windows desktop, boot into Safe Mode and use System Restore from there.

3. If you have a backup of the system state, use Ntbackup to restore the system state using this backup.

▲ If the problem is still not solved, it's time to assume that the Windows installation is corrupted. Here are the tools used to restore a Windows installation:

1. For Windows XP, try using a Windows XP boot disk to find out if the boot files in the root directory of drive C are missing or corrupted. If necessary, you can restore these files using the Recovery Console.

5

A+ ESS
1.3
3.3

A+
220-602
3.3

A+ ESS
3.3

2. For Windows 2000, use the Emergency Repair Process to restore Windows 2000 to its state immediately after it was installed.

3. For Windows XP, use Automated System Recovery to restore the system to the last ASR backup.

4. Perform an in-place upgrade of Windows 2000/XP.

5. Perform a clean install of Windows 2000/XP.

As you work to solve a Windows problem, keep in mind that many tools are at your disposal. As you decide which tool to use to correct a problem, always use the least drastic solution to make the fewest possible changes to the system. For example, if you know a driver is giving a problem, even though you can use System Restore to restore the system before the driver was installed, doing so is more drastic than simply rolling back the driver. Always choose the method that makes as few changes to the system as possible and still solves the problem.

When you think the problem is solved, be sure to restart the system one last time to make sure all is well. Verify that everything is working and then ask the user to also verify that the problem is solved and all is working. And don't forget the paperwork. As you work, keep notes about the original symptoms, what you're doing, and the outcome. This paperwork will be a great help the next time you're faced with a similar problem.

RESPOND TO ANY STARTUP ERRORS

Recall that Windows 2000/XP system has successfully started when you can log onto Windows, the Windows desktop is loaded, and the hourglass associated with the pointer has disappeared. If an error message appears before the system startup is completed, the obvious first step is to address the error message. Table 5-6 lists different types of error messages and what to do about them. Most of the errors in the table will cause the system to lock up and the boot to fail.

Now let's see exactly what to do when an error occurs as Windows is loading, when a stop error causes Windows to lock up, when a program is not found, and when a device or service has failed to start.

Error Message	What It Means and What to Do About It
Errors that occur before the Windows load begins:	
Hard drive not found **Fixed disk error** **Disk boot failure, insert system disk and press enter** **No boot device available**	**Startup BIOS cannot find the hard drive.**
Invalid boot disk **Inaccessible boot device** **Invalid partition table** **Error loading operating system** **Missing operating system** **No operating system found** **Error loading operating system**	**The program in the MBR displays these messages when it cannot find the active partition on the hard drive or the boot sector on that partition. Use the Diskpart command from the Recovery Console to check the hard drive partition table for errors. Sometimes Fixmbr solves the problem. Third-party recovery software such as PartitionMagic might help. If a setup program came bundled with the hard drive (such as Data Lifeguard from Western Digital or MaxBlast from Maxtor), use it to examine the drive. Check the hard drive manufacturer's Web site for other diagnostic software.**

Table 5-6 Startup error messages and their meanings

A+ ESS
3.3

A+
220-602
3.3

Error Message	What It Means and What to Do About It
Black screen with no error messages	This is likely to be a corrupted MBR, partition table, boot sector, or Ntldr file. Boot the PC using a Windows 2000/XP boot disk and then try the fixmbr and fixboot commands from the Recovery Console. You might have to reinstall Windows.
When you first turn on the computer, it continually reboots.	This is most likely a hardware problem. Could be the CPU, motherboard, or RAM. First disconnect or remove all nonessential devices such as USB or FireWire devices. Inside the case, check all connections using safety precautions to protect the system against static electricity as you work. Try reseating RAM. Check for fans that are not working, causing the CPU to quickly overheat.
A disk read error occurred Missing NTLDR NTLDR is missing NTLDR is compressed	A disk is probably in the floppy disk drive. Remove the disk and reboot. When booting from the hard drive, these errors occur if Ntldr has been moved, renamed, or deleted, or is corrupted, if the boot sector on the active partition is corrupted, or you have just tried to install an older version of Windows such as Windows 98 on the hard drive. First try replacing Ntldr. Then check Boot.ini settings.
When you first turn on a system, it begins the boot process, but then powers down.	The CPU might be quickly overheating. Check for fans not running. Is this a new CPU installation? If so, make sure the cooler assembly on top of the CPU is correctly installed.
Stop errors that cause Windows to lock up:	
A text error message appears on a blue screen and then the system halts. Some stop errors follow:	Stop errors are usually caused by viruses, errors in the file system, a corrupted hard drive, or a hardware problem. Search the Microsoft Web site for information about an unidentified stop error.
Stop 0x00000024 or NTFS_File_System	The NTFS file system is corrupt. Immediately boot into the Recovery Console, and copy important data files that have not been backed up to another media before attempting to recover the system.
Stop 0x00000050 or Page_Fault_in_Nonpaged_Area	Most likely RAM is defective.
Stop 0x00000077 or Kernel_Stack_Inpage_Error	Bad sectors are on the hard drive, there is a hard drive hardware problem, or RAM is defective. Try running Chkdsk.
Stop 0x0000007A or Kernel_Data_Inpage_Error	There is a bad sector on the hard drive where the paging file is stored; there is a virus or defective RAM. Try running Chkdsk.
Stop 0x0000007B or Inaccessible_Boot_Device	There is a boot sector virus or failing hardware. Try Fixmbr.
While running Windows, a stop error appears and then the system reboots. The reboot happens so fast you can't read the error message.	For Windows XP, boot to the Advanced Options menu and choose Disable automatic restart on system failure.
Startup errors that occur because a program is corrupted or not found:	
A device has failed to start Service failed to start Program not found	A registry entry or startup folder is referencing a startup program it cannot find. Use Msconfig or the Services Console to find the entry and then replace the missing program. These errors are sometimes caused by uninstall routines that left behind these orphan entries. Depending on the error, the system might or might not halt.

Table 5-6 Startup error messages and their meanings (continued)

ERRORS THAT OCCUR BEFORE THE WINDOWS LOAD BEGINS

If an error occurs before Windows starts to load, you'll see a screen similar to Figure 5-24. Startup BIOS is still in control at this point. The error in the figure was caused when BIOS could not find a hard drive.

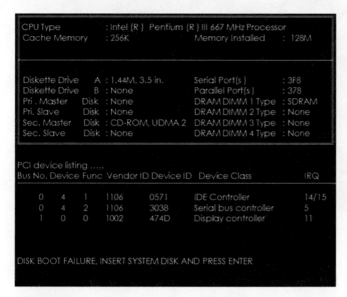

Figure 5-24   A startup error before the Windows load begins

To successfully boot, a computer needs the bare-bones minimum of hardware and software. If one of these hardware or software components is missing, corrupted, or broken, the boot fails. Also, when you are trying to solve a boot program, you can reduce the hardware and software to a minimum to help you isolate the source of a problem. For example, unplug USB devices, printers, a second monitor, or other peripheral devices. If you know how to work inside the computer case, you can disconnect data and power connectors to all drives except the hard drive that contains the OS.

Here is the list of essential hardware components:

- ◢ CPU, motherboard, memory, keyboard, and video card or onboard video
- ◢ A boot device such as a CD drive with bootable CD, a floppy drive with bootable floppy, or a hard drive with an OS installed
- ◢ A power supply with electrical power

How to troubleshoot hardware problems that cause the boot to fail is not covered in this book.

STOP ERRORS

One type of error message is a **stop error**, which is an error so drastic it causes Windows to hang or lock up. Figure 5-25 shows one example of a stop error. Look on the screen for information similar to that marked in the figure. For help with the problem, search the Microsoft support site (*support.microsoft.com*) on the exact text of the error message. This particular stop error in Figure 5-25 was caused by a USB device that had gone bad. When the device was unplugged, the system booted with no problems.

A+ ESS
3.3

A+
220-602
3.3

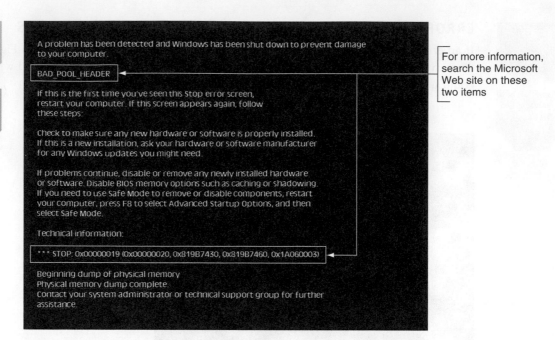

A problem has been detected and Windows has been shut down to prevent damage to your computer.

BAD_POOL_HEADER

For more information, search the Microsoft Web site on these two items

If this is the first time you've seen this Stop error screen, restart your computer. If this screen appears again, follow these steps:

Check to make sure any new hardware or software is properly installed. If this is a new installation, ask your hardware or software manufacturer for any Windows updates you might need.

If problems continue, disable or remove any newly installed hardware or software. Disable BIOS memory options such as caching or shadowing. If you need to use Safe Mode to remove or disable components, restart your computer, press F8 to select Advanced Startup Options, and then select Safe Mode.

Technical information:

*** STOP: 0x00000019 (0x00000020, 0x819B7430, 0x819B7460, 0x1A060003)

Beginning dump of physical memory
Physical memory dump complete.
Contact your system administrator or technical support group for further assistance.

Figure 5-25 A BSOD might be caused by hardware or software

PROGRAM NOT FOUND ERROR

Sometimes when software is uninstalled, the uninstall routine leaves behind an entry in the registry or a startup folder. When the registry entry tries to launch a program and the program has been deleted, an error is displayed. For example, Figure 5-26 shows an error message that appeared on the first boot after antivirus software had found and removed a virus. The antivirus software did not completely remove all parts of the virus, and somewhere in the system, the command to launch 0sis0ijw.dll is still working even though this program has been deleted. One way to find this orphan entry point is to use Msconfig. The Msconfig window in Figure 5-27 is showing us that the DLL is launched from a registry key.

RUNDLL

Error loading 0sis0ijw.dll

The specified module could not be found.

OK

Figure 5-26 Startup error indicates malware has not been completely removed

The next step is to back up the registry and then use Regedit to find and delete the key, as shown in Figure 5-28.

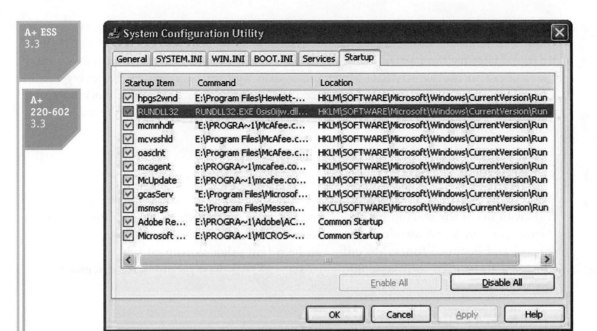

Figure 5-27 Msconfig shows how the DLL is launched during startup

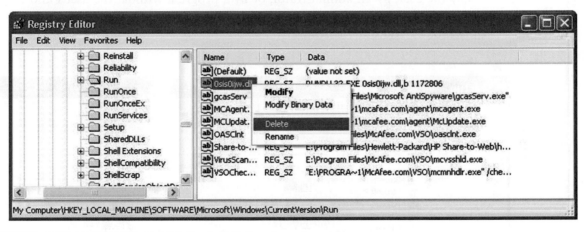

Figure 5-28 Delete orphan registry entry left there by malware

ERRORS FROM WHEN A DEVICE OR SERVICE HAS FAILED TO START

Error messages might be caused by a device driver, a service, or other software that is missing or corrupted. If the service or device is critical for Windows to run, the startup fails. Otherwise, the error message appears and you can still continue to the Windows desktop.

If you can get to the Windows desktop and the startup error indicates the problem is with a device driver, use Device Manager to update the driver. If that doesn't work, uninstall and reinstall the device. If the error message indicates a service has failed to start, use Msconfig to temporarily disable some or all services until you discover which service is causing the problem. You can then reinstall the application or restore the program from backup or from the Windows 2000/XP setup CD. For Windows services, use System File Checker to restore the system files.

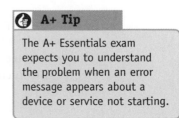

A+ Tip

The A+ Essentials exam expects you to understand the problem when an error message appears about a device or service not starting.

If the error causes the system to lock up so that the desktop does not load, try using tools that make the least changes to your system as possible before you use the more drastic tools. First try the Last Known Good Configuration on the Advanced Options menu. If that doesn't work, then try Safe Mode and System Restore. Next, try the Recovery Console to identify the service and replace the system file. If none of these work, then you'll need to consider restoring the Windows installation from backup or reinstalling Windows 2000/XP.

CLEANING UP STARTUP

When Windows startup is slow or gives errors, one thing you can do is perform a general clean up of the startup processes. For starters, you can check startup folders for startup processes and also look for undesired scheduled tasks, Group Policy startup entries, and installed fonts. Msconfig can help find other startup entries, and the Services Console can be used to disable unneeded services. All these methods are discussed in this section.

CHECK STARTUP FOLDERS

Certain folders are designated as startup folders for all user accounts or a particular user account. Scripts, programs, or shortcuts to programs can be placed in these startup folders by the user, by an administrator, or by a program without the user's knowledge. For example, Figure 5-29 shows a startup folder with all kinds of services placed there by Windows and other software.

Figure 5-29 This startup folder holds several unneeded services that appear in the system tray and take up system resources

To clean up startup, look in each startup folder mentioned in this section. If you find a program or shortcut there that you don't think you want, unless you know it's something you need, move it to a different folder rather than deleting it. Later, if you like, you can return it to the startup folder, or you can start the program manually from the new folder.

5

A+ ESS
3.2
3.3

A+
220-602
3.2
3.3

> ✎ **Notes**
>
> To keep programs kept in startup folders from executing as you start Windows, hold down the Shift key just after you enter your account name and password on the Windows logon screen. Keep holding down the Shift key until the desktop is fully loaded and the hourglass has disappeared. To permanently disable a startup item, remove it from its startup folder.

Your first step is to check these startup folders for any program file or a shortcut that is not needed:

▲ C:\Documents and Settings*username*\Start Menu\Programs\Startup
▲ C:\Documents and Settings\All Users\Start Menu\Programs\Startup

Your next step is to consider if Windows 2000/XP has been installed as an upgrade from Windows NT. If so, the C:\Winnt\Profiles folder will exist. Programs and shortcuts to programs might be in these folders:

C:\Winnt\Profiles\All Users\Start Menu\Programs\Startup
C:\Winnt\Profiles*username*\Start Menu\Programs\Startup

LOOK FOR UNWANTED SCHEDULED TASKS

Tasks scheduled to launch at startup are placed in this folder: C:\Windows\Tasks. The folder might contain a desired task, such as a utility to run a background service to keep software updated. However, it might also contain unwanted or even malicious tasks. When looking for unnecessary programs that slow down startup, be sure to check this folder.

The easiest way to view and change this folder is to open the Scheduled Tasks applet in Control Panel. When the Scheduled Tasks folder appears, click **View, Details**. The left side of Figure 5-30 shows that two tasks are scheduled. One task was placed there by an

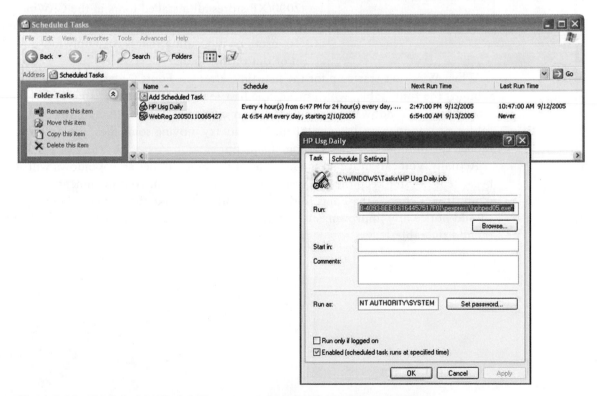

Figure 5-30 The Scheduled Task folder can contain tasks that launch at startup

A+ ESS
3.2
3.3

A+
220-602
3.2
3.3

HP printer installation program, and another was placed there by an administrator. The right side of the figure shows the details of the HP program task.

> **Notes**
>
> Tasks can be hidden in the Scheduled Tasks folder. To be certain you're viewing all scheduled tasks, unhide them by clicking **Tools**, **Folder Options**. In the Folder Options window, click the **View** tab, select **Show hidden files and folders**, and then uncheck **Hide protected operating system files**.

CHECK GROUP POLICY FOR UNWANTED STARTUP EVENTS

When an administrator uses Group Policy to cause a script to run, Group Policy places that script in one of the folders in the following list. Also, malicious software is sometimes placed in these same folders. Writers of malicious software pick these folders because many users aren't aware of them and don't know to look here for unwanted programs. When cleaning up a system, be sure to take a look at these folders for unwanted program files:

- C:\WINDOWS\System32\GroupPolicy\Machine\Scripts\Startup
- C:\WINDOWS\System32\GroupPolicy\Machine\Scripts\Shutdown
- C:\WINDOWS\System32\GroupPolicy\User\Scripts\Logon
- C:\WINDOWS\System32\GroupPolicy\User\Scripts\Logoff

> **Notes**
>
> Don't forget that we are using C:\Windows as the folder in which Windows is installed. Depending on where the OS is installed, your folder might be different, such as C:\Winnt or E:\Windows.

CHECK FOR TOO MANY INSTALLED FONTS

Windows comes with a group of fonts that can be used for the Windows desktop and in a variety of other places. Some applications install additional fonts and you can purchase and manually install other fonts. All installed fonts are loaded at startup, so if a system has had many new fonts installed, these can slow down startup. Windows 2000/XP stores all installed fonts in the C:\Windows\Fonts folder. (See Figure 5-31 for a few samples of those fonts). To install or uninstall a font is to simply move the fonts file in or out of this folder.

When Windows starts up for the first time after the Fonts folder has been changed, it rebuilds the fonts table, which means the first reboot after a font change is slowed down. Check the C:\Windows\Fonts folder on your computer. If you see more than 260 files in this folder, new fonts have been installed. You can try moving some files to a different folder to reduce the number of fonts loading at startup.

Actually, you can move all the files out of the Fonts folder and Windows will still work because it doesn't keep the one system font here. But then, your documents will look pretty plain. If you change the Fonts folder, don't forget it'll take the second reboot before you should notice any improvement in startup, because the first reboot must take the time to rebuild the table.

A+ ESS
3.2
3.3

A+
220-602
3.2
3.3

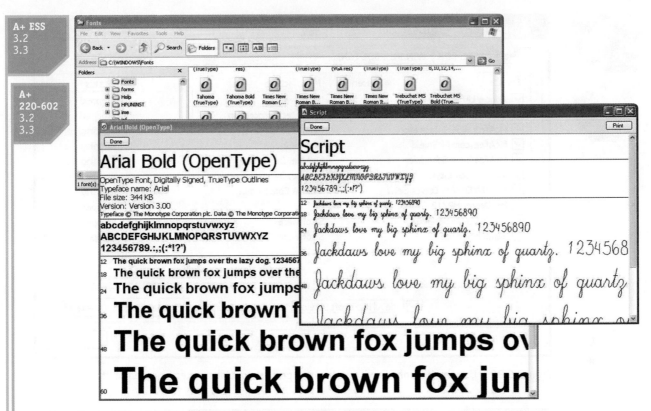

Figure 5-31 Fonts are kept in the C:\Windows\Fonts folder

USE WINDOWS XP MSCONFIG TO LIMIT STARTUP EVENTS

Recall from Chapter 3 that the Windows XP System Configuration Utility (Msconfig.exe) can be used to temporarily disable startup services and other programs and help you find the one causing a problem. To use it, enter Msconfig.exe in the Run dialog box. In the Msconfig window, click the **Services** tab to view all services that are set to start (see Figure 5-32).

At the bottom of this window, if you check **Hide All Microsoft Services**, the list of non-Microsoft services is displayed. Check the ones you want to start and uncheck the ones you want to temporarily disable.

Next, select the **Startup** tab showing in Figure 5-33. Listed are all the programs that Windows expects to start during the startup process. You'll be surprised how many there are after you've used a system for some time. Freeware, antivirus software, games, printer drivers, and all sorts of programs put entries in the registry or in startup folders to cause themselves to be launched at startup. Cleaning up this mess can make Windows XP work like new again. Uncheck any program you want to disable at the next startup or click **Disable All** to stop them all. Click **Apply**. Choose **Selective Startup** on the General tab and reboot. If your problem is solved or Windows starts much faster, you can permanently remove the program from startup.

To permanently remove the program from startup, first try to use the program's menus to set the program to not automatically launch at startup or remove the program file or shortcut from the startup folders. If you don't need the program, use the Add or Remove Programs applet to uninstall the program. As a last resort, you can search the registry for the key that is used to start the program. In Figure 5-33, you can see which programs are started because of an entry in a certain key of the registry. Editing the registry is dangerous and should only be done if other methods have failed.

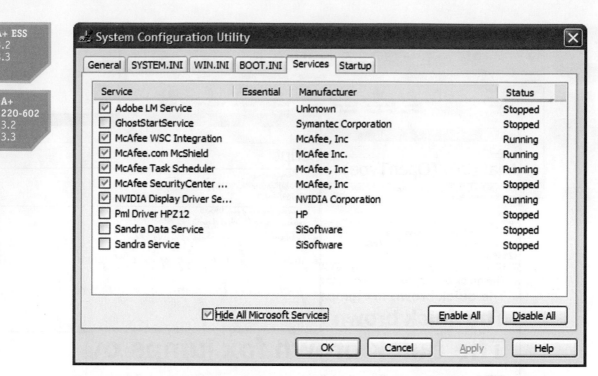

Figure 5-32 Use the Msconfig Services tab to temporarily control services launched at startup

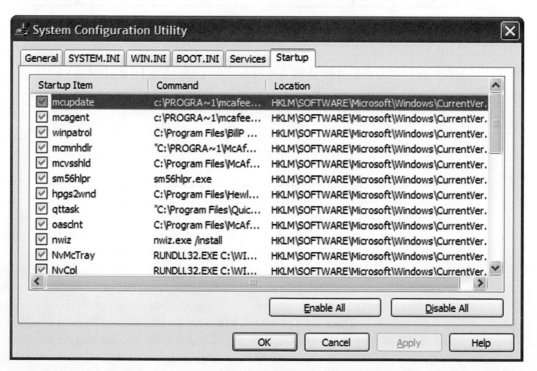

Figure 5-33 Use the Msconfig Startup tab to control programs launched at startup

5

A+ ESS
3.2
3.3

A+
220-602
3.2
3.3

Once you have permanently stopped unwanted programs and services from launching at startup and all problems have been resolved, return to the Msconfig window and select **Normal Startup** on the **General** tab.

> **Notes**
>
> If you are not familiar with a startup program, Google the Web on the program filename. If you suspect a Windows system service is causing a problem, you can use Msconfig to disable the service. If this works, then replace the service file with a fresh copy from the Windows setup CD.

CHECK FOR CORRUPTED OR UNNEEDED SERVICES

Recall that a service is a program that runs in the background to support other programs. Services are managed by the Services console (Services.msc). Use the Services console to see what services have been set to automatically start when Windows loads. To launch the Services console, type **Services.msc** in the Run dialog box and press **Enter**. The Services window opens, as shown on the left side of Figure 5-34.

To learn more about a service, right-click it and select **Properties** from the shortcut menu. In the resulting Properties window, which is shown on the right side of Figure 5-34 for one selected service, you can see the name of the program file and its path.

When investigating a service, try using a good search engine on the Web to search on the name of the service or the name of the program file that launches the service. Either can give you information you need to snoop out unwanted services. If you're not sure you want to keep a certain service, use Msconfig to temporarily disable it at the next boot so you can see what happens.

> **Notes**
>
> Recall from Chapter 3 that you can use Task Manager to investigate processes that are using too much of system resources, including CPU time, memory, and hard drive access.

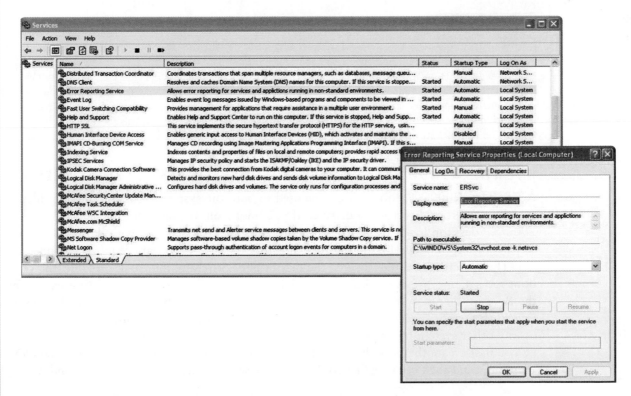

Figure 5-34 The Services console is used to start, stop, and schedule services

RESTORE SYSTEM FILES

If Windows startup is so corrupted you cannot identify a single service or program causing the problem, you can take a shotgun approach and just do a general restoration of system files. Tools that can help you do this are System Restore, backups of the system state, System File Checker, the Windows 2000/XP boot disk, and the Recovery Console. In this part of the chapter, we'll look at System Restore, the Windows 2000/XP boot disk, and the Recovery Console.

> **Notes**
>
> When using System Restore and system state backups, you run the risk of undoing *desired* changes to the Windows environment and software installations. Before using one of the fixes in this section, consider what desired changes will be lost when you apply the fix.

RETURN TO A PREVIOUS WINDOWS XP RESTORE POINT

Recall from Chapter 3 that the Windows XP **System Restore** utility can be used to restore the system state to its condition at the time a restore point was made. Before using System Restore to undo a change, if the change was made to a hardware device, first try Driver Rollback so that as few changes as possible to the system are lost. If Driver Rollback does not work or is not appropriate, then use System Restore to revert the system to the restore point. When selecting a restore point, select a point as close to the present as you can so that as few changes to the system as possible are lost.

If you can't boot to the Windows desktop, try booting into Safe Mode. When you do that, Windows XP asks if you want to go directly to System Restore rather than to Safe Mode. Choose to go directly to System Restore.

> **A+ Exam Tip**
>
> The A+ Essentials exam expects you to know how to boot to a system restore point.

> **Notes**
>
> To roll back the system to a Windows XP restore point using Windows XP requires that you can boot from the hard drive. However, there are other options using third-party utility software. For example, ERD Commander 2003 by Winternals (*www.winternals.com*) is an operating system that can be loaded from CD. Boot from the ERD Commander CD, which loads a GUI interface that looks like Windows XP. Using this Winternals desktop, you can access the registry, event logs, and Disk Management Console and reset a forgotten administrator password. You can also roll back the Windows XP system to a restore point.

USE THE WINDOWS 2000/XP BOOT DISK TO VERIFY BOOT FILES

A Windows 2000/XP boot disk can be used to boot the system bypassing the boot files stored in the root directory of drive C. If you boot from the disk and the Windows 2000/XP desktop loads successfully, then the problem is associated with damaged sectors or missing or damaged files in the root directory of drive C that are required to boot the OS. These sectors and files include the master boot program, the partition table, the OS boot record, and the boot files, Ntldr file, Ntdetect.com file, Ntbootdd.sys (if it exists), and the Boot.ini file. In addition, the problem can be caused by a boot sector virus. However, a boot disk cannot be used to troubleshoot problems associated with unstable device drivers or any other system files stored in the \Windows folder or its subfolders.

You first create the boot disk by formatting the disk using a working Windows 2000/XP computer and then copying files to the disk. These files can be copied from a Windows

5

A+ ESS
3.3

A+
220-602
3.3

2000/XP setup CD, or a Windows 2000/XP computer that is using the same version of Windows XP or Windows 2000 as the problem PC. Do the following to create the disk:

1. Obtain a floppy disk and format it on a Windows 2000/XP computer.

2. Using Explorer, copy Ntldr and Ntdetect.com from the \i386 folder on the Windows 2000/XP setup CD or a Windows 2000/XP computer to the root of the floppy disk.

3. If your computer boots from a SCSI hard drive, then obtain a device driver (*.sys) for your SCSI hard drive, rename it **Ntbootdd.sys**, and copy it to the root of the floppy disk. (If you used an incorrect device driver, then you will receive an error after booting from the floppy disk. The error will mention a "computer disk hardware configuration problem" and that it "could not read from the selected boot disk." If this occurs, contact your computer manufacturer or hard drive manufacturer for the correct version of the SCSI hard drive device driver for your computer.)

4. Look at Boot.ini on the problem computer, and then obtain an identical copy from another known good computer (or create your own) and copy it to the root of the floppy disk.

5. If you can't find a good Boot.ini file to copy, you can use the lines listed below to create a Boot.ini file. These lines work for a Boot.ini file if the problem computer is booting from an IDE hard drive:

```
[boot loader]

timeout=30

default=multi(0)disk(0)rdisk(0)partition(1)\WINDOWS

[operating systems]

multi(0)disk(0)rdisk(0)partition(1)\WINDOWS="Microsoft
Windows XP Professional" /fastdetect
```

6. Write-protect the floppy disk so it cannot become infected with a virus.

7. You have now created the Windows 2000/XP boot disk. Check CMOS setup to make sure the first boot device is set to the floppy disk, and then insert the boot disk and reboot your computer.

> **Tip**
>
> If you are creating your own Boot.ini file, be sure to enter a hard return after the /fastdetect switch in the last line of the file.

 Notes

> To learn more about the Windows XP boot disk, see the Microsoft Knowledge Base Articles 305595 and 314503 at the Microsoft Web site *support.microsoft.com*. To learn more about the Windows 2000 boot disk, see the Microsoft Knowledge Base Article 301680.

If the Windows 2000/XP desktop loads successfully, then do the following to attempt to repair the Windows 2000/XP installation:

1. Load the Recovery Console and use the Fixmbr and Fixboot commands to repair the MBR and the boot sector.

A+ ESS
3.3

A+
220-602
3.3

2. Run anti-virus software.

3. Use Disk Management to verify that the hard drive partition table is correct.

4. Defragment your hard drive.

5. Copy Ntldr, Ntdetect.com, and Boot.ini from your floppy disk to the root of the hard drive.

6. If you're using a SCSI hard drive, copy Ntbootdd.sys from your floppy disk to the root of the hard drive.

If the Windows 2000/XP desktop did not load by booting from the boot disk, then the next tool to try is the Recovery Console.

USE THE RECOVERY CONSOLE TO RESTORE SYSTEM FILES

If you are not able to boot from the hard drive, your next step is to use the Windows 2000/XP setup CD to boot to the Recovery Console using the instructions given earlier in the chapter. Then, try one or more of the following:

▲ Get a directory listing of files in the root directory. If you see garbage on the screen instead of a clean directory list, most likely the hard drive file system is corrupted or the hard drive is physically damaged.
▲ Use the Chkdsk command to scan the hard drive for errors.
▲ Try copying the backup copies of the registry files from the \Windows\repair folder to the \Windows\system32\config folder. Directions are given earlier in the chapter. Reboot to see if the problem is solved.
▲ If you have previously identified a key Windows service that is causing the problem, you can locate the file in the \Windows folder and replace it with a fresh copy from the Windows 2000/XP setup CD.
▲ To see a list of all services you can disable, use the Listsvc command. Use the Disable and Enable commands to try disabling each service one by one until you find the one causing the problem.

Looking for a failed Windows system file can sometimes be like looking for a needle in a haystack. At some point, you just decide it's time to take more drastic measures and restore the Windows installation to when it was last backed up. That's the subject of the next section.

RECOVER OR REPAIR THE WINDOWS 2000/XP INSTALLATION

If the Windows installation is so corrupted that none of the previous tools and methods have helped, you need to decide how best to repair the installation. For a notebook computer or a brand name computer such as a Dell or Gateway, the hard drive most likely has a recovery partition that you can use to recover the Windows installation. These computers might also have a recovery CD. For Windows XP, you can use Automated System Recovery, and for Windows 2000, you can use the Emergency Repair Process. You can also perform an in-place upgrade or you can reinstall Windows 2000/XP. All these methods are discussed in this section.

RECOVERY PARTITIONS AND RECOVERY CDS

In this chapter, we often refer to the Windows 2000/XP setup CD. If you have a notebook computer or a brand name computer such as a Dell, IBM, or Gateway, be sure to use the manufacturer's recovery CD (also called a restore CD) instead of a regular Windows 2000/XP setup CD (see Figure 5-35 for samples of both). This recovery CD has drivers specific to your system and the Windows 2000/XP build might be different from that of an off-the-shelf Windows 2000/XP setup CD. For example, Windows XP Home Edition installed on a notebook computer might have been built with all kinds of changes made to it by the notebook manufacturer making it different from the Windows XP Home Edition that you can buy in a retail store.

Figure 5-35   Brand name recovery CDs and a Windows XP setup CD

The manufacturer might have also put a hidden partition on the hard drive that can be used to recover the Windows installation. During startup, you'll see a message onscreen such as "Press F2 to recover the system" or "Press F11 to start recovery." When you press the appropriate key, a menu should appear that gives you two options: one repairs the Windows installation, saving user data, and the other reformats drive C and restores your system to the way it was when purchased. First, try to save user data before you attempt the destructive recovery. If neither method works, the hidden partition might be corrupted or the hard drive might be physically damaged.

If the recovery process doesn't work, try to use the recovery CD that came bundled with your computer to repair the installation. If you don't have the recovery CD, you might be able to buy one from the computer manufacturer. For notebook computers, you really must have this recovery CD to reinstall Windows because the device drivers on the CD are specific to your notebook. If you cannot buy a recovery CD, you might be able to download the drivers from the notebook manufacturer's Web site. Download them to another computer and burn them to a CD that you can use on the notebook to install drivers.

WINDOWS XP AUTOMATED SYSTEM RECOVERY

Recall from Chapter 3 that you can use the Automated System Recovery (ASR) tool to recover a system from the last time you made a full backup of drive C. To restore a system using the ASR backup, begin by booting from the Windows XP setup CD and pressing **F2**

A+ ESS
3.3

A+
220-602
3.3

Notes

When you use the ASR tool, everything written to drive C since the ASR backup was made will be lost, including software and device drivers, user data, and any changes to the system configuration.

when you see the message, "Press F2 to run the Automated System Recovery process." Then, follow the directions on the screen to restore drive C.

WINDOWS 2000 EMERGENCY REPAIR PROCESS

The Windows 2000 **Emergency Repair Process** should be used only as a last resort because it restores the system to the state it was in immediately after the Windows 2000 installation. All changes made since the installation are lost. The process uses an Emergency Repair Disk (ERD), which contains information about your current installation. The Windows 2000 ERD points to a folder on the hard drive where the registry was backed up when Windows 2000 was installed. This folder is *%SystemRoot%*\repair, which, in most systems, is C:\Winnt\repair.

APPLYING | CONCEPTS

Using the Windows 2000 ERD to recover from a corrupted registry returns you to the installation version of the registry, and you lose all changes to the registry since that time. Because of the way the ERD works, you do not need to update the disk once you've created it. Before a problem occurs, follow these directions to create the disk:

1. Click **Start**, point to **Programs**, **Accessories**, and **System Tools**, and then click **Backup**. The Backup window appears with the Welcome tab selected (see Figure 5-36). Select **Emergency Repair Disk**.

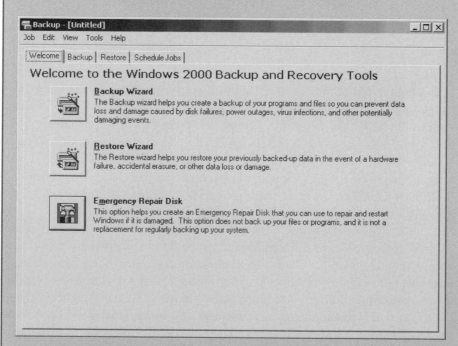

Figure 5-36   Use the Backup window to back up the registry and create an emergency repair disk

2. The Backup tab and the Emergency Repair Diskette dialog box open. If you check the box shown in Figure 5-37, the system backs up your registry to a folder under the Repair folder, *%SystemRoot%*\repair\RegBack.

A+ ESS
3.3

A+
220-602
3.3

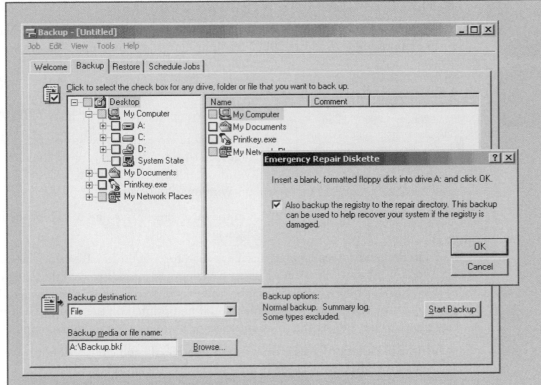

Figure 5-37 Create an ERD and back up the registry to the hard drive

3. Click **OK** to create the disk. Label the disk "Windows 2000 Emergency Repair Disk," and keep it in a safe place.

If your hard drive fails, you can use the ERD to restore the system, including system files, boot files, and the registry, to its state at the end of the Windows 2000 installation. Follow these steps:

1. Boot the PC from the four Windows 2000 setup disks. The Setup menu appears (refer back to Figure 5-15). Select option **R**.

2. When the Windows 2000 Repair Options window opens (refer back to Figure 5-16), select option **R**.

3. You are instructed to insert the Emergency Repair Disk. Follow the instructions on the screen to repair the installation.

4. If this process does not work, then your next option is to reinstall Windows 2000. If you don't plan to reformat the drive, you need to scan the drive for errors before you reinstall Windows. To do that, you can boot to the Recovery Console and use the Chkdsk command to scan the drive for errors. If you suspect that a virus damaged the file system, also use the Fixmbr command to replace the master boot program in case it has been corrupted by the virus.

Notes

Sometimes recovering the data on a hard drive is more important than fixing a Windows problem. If Windows is so corrupted it will not boot, but your first priority is to save the data on the drive, consider removing the hard drive and installing it in a working computer as a second drive. You can then copy all data from the drive to the primary drive in the working system. After your data is safe, then reinstall the hard drive in the first computer. At that point, you might want to solve your corrupted Windows problem by formatting the hard drive and reinstalling Windows to get a fresh, clean start.

IN-PLACE UPGRADE OF WINDOWS 2000/XP

An in-place upgrade installs Windows over the same existing installation. When you do an in-place upgrade of Windows 2000/XP, all installed applications and hardware must be reinstalled, but user data should not be lost.

Do the following to perform an in-place upgrade:

> **Tip**
>
> There are two ways to reinstall Windows 2000/XP: an in-place upgrade and a clean install. First try the in-place upgrade and if that doesn't work, then try a clean install.

1. Boot the computer from the Windows 2000/XP setup CD.

2. The Welcome to Setup screen appears, as shown back in Figure 5-14 (for Windows XP) or Figure 5-15 (for Windows 2000). Press **Enter** to select the option to set up Windows 2000/XP now.

3. On the next screen, press **F8** to accept the license agreement.

4. On the next screen, shown in Figure 5-38 for Windows XP, verify that the path to your Windows folder (most likely C:\Windows) is selected and then press **R** to repair Windows 2000/XP. Follow the instructions onscreen. During the installation, you'll be asked for the product key, which you'll find printed on the setup CD sleeve or case or stuck to the side of the computer case or bottom of a notebook computer.

5. If the installation gives problems or the original problem is still not solved after you finish the in-place upgrade, then try a clean installation of Windows.

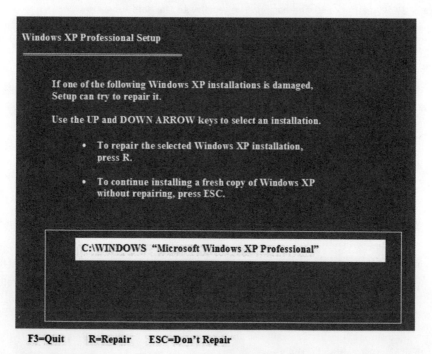

Figure 5-38   Windows XP Setup can repair the selected Windows installation

CLEAN INSTALLATION OF WINDOWS 2000/XP

A clean installation of Windows 2000/XP gives you a fresh start with the OS. First make sure you've copied important data files to a safe place. Then do the following to reinstall Windows 2000/XP:

You need to completely destroy the current Windows 2000/XP installation so that the Windows 2000/XP setup process won't think it is installing Windows as a second OS on the

A+ ESS
3.3

A+
220-602
3.3

drive (called a dual boot). One way to do that is to delete the partition used for drive C:. The Windows setup program will then create a new partition. A less drastic way is to delete the C:\Windows folder. Using this last method, data on the drive will be saved. Here is how to use either method:

1. Boot from the Windows 2000/XP setup CD and launch the Recovery Console.

2. If you decide you want to delete only the C:\Windows folder, type **del C:\windows** and then press **Enter**.

3. If you decide you want to totally wipe out the C: partition, type **diskpart** and then press **Enter**. Then select and delete the partition for drive C:.

4. Boot again from the Windows 2000/XP setup CD.

5. The Welcome to Setup screen appears, as shown in Figure 5-39 for Windows XP. Press **Enter** to select the default option to set up Windows XP.

6. Follow the directions onscreen to install the OS. You'll need the product key.

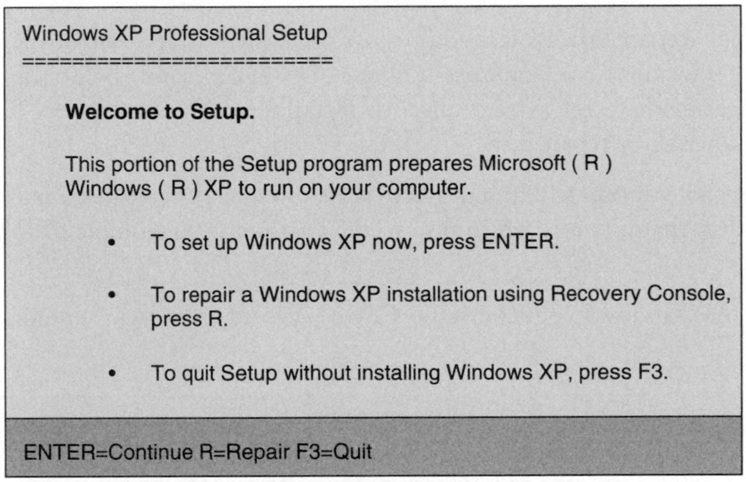

```
Windows XP Professional Setup
===========================

    Welcome to Setup.

    This portion of the Setup program prepares Microsoft ( R )
    Windows ( R ) XP to run on your computer.

        •   To set up Windows XP now, press ENTER.

        •   To repair a Windows XP installation using Recovery Console,
            press R.

        •   To quit Setup without installing Windows XP, press F3.


ENTER=Continue R=Repair F3=Quit
```

Figure 5-39 Windows XP Setup opening menu

>> CHAPTER SUMMARY

▲ The boot process for Windows 2000/XP uses files stored in the root directory of the hard drive and the C:\Windows\system32 folder.

▲ The boot process can be customized with entries in Boot.ini. The Boot.ini file can be edited with a text editor, but it is best to change the file using the System Properties dialog box.

▲ Tools to use to troubleshoot problems with loading Windows 2000/XP are the Advanced Options menu and the Recovery Console.

▲ To access the Advanced Options menu, press F8 when starting Windows 2000/XP.

▲ The Advanced Options menu includes Safe Mode, Safe Mode with networking, Safe Mode with command prompt, enable boot logging, enable VGA mode, Last Known Good configuration, directory services restore mode, debugging mode, and disable automatic restart on system failure. This last option is available only in Windows XP.

▲ The Recovery Console is a command interface with a limited number of commands available to troubleshoot a failing Windows 2000/XP load. The console requires that you enter the Administrator password.

▲ Access the Recovery Console by first booting from the Windows 2000/XP CD, or the four Windows 2000 setup disks or install the console under the boot loader menu and access it from there.

▲ When solving problems with a sluggish or failing Windows 2000/XP startup, you might need to respond to any startup error messages, clean up the startup process, restore system files, and perhaps repair the Windows 2000/XP installation.

▲ Programs can be loaded during Windows startup by storing files in startup folders, using Task Scheduler, Group Policy, or the Services console, or by making entries in the registry. When cleaning up the startup process, be sure to check all these locations and to scan for viruses and other malicious software.

▲ When you cannot load the Windows desktop, tools to use to check for errors with Windows system files and restore these files include System Restore, a boot disk, and the Recovery Console.

▲ The Emergency Repair Process lets you restore the system to its state at the end of the Windows 2000 installation. Don't use it unless all other methods fail, because you will lose all changes made to the system since the installation. The Emergency Repair Process requires the emergency repair disk.

▲ The Windows XP Automated System Recovery (ASR) process creates a backup and an ASR floppy disk that can be used to restore the backup of the volume or logical drive holding Windows XP.

▲ You can use the Windows 2000/XP setup CD to perform an in-place upgrade of Windows.

>> KEY TERMS

For explanations of key terms, see the Glossary near the end of the book.

32-bit flat memory mode	Boot.ini	Recovery Console
Advanced Options menu	Emergency Repair Process	stop error
blue screen of death (BSOD)	minifile system	System Restore

>> REVIEWING THE BASICS

1. In the Windows 2000/XP boot process, what program reads and loads the boot menu?

2. Where is the Boot.ini file stored?

3. What does *%SystemRoot%* mean?

4. Under what circumstances would you use the Enable VGA Mode option on the Advanced Options menu?

5. What key do you press to display the Advanced Options menu during startup?

6. When you look at a Windows desktop, how can you tell if the system has been booted into Safe Mode?

7. What is the purpose of Safe Mode with networking under the Advanced Options menu?

8. What is the name of the log file that Windows 2000/XP uses when booting in Safe Mode?

9. List the steps to load the Recovery Console when using the four Windows 2000 rescue disks.

10. Which Windows 2000/XP folder contains one subfolder for every user account?

11. What two subfolders in the C:\Windows\system32 folder contain files needed for Windows startup?

12. What Recovery Console command is used to extract a file from a .cab file?

13. Which option on the Windows XP Advanced Options menu is not available on the Windows 2000 menu?

14. Which Recovery Console command can be used to examine the partitions on a hard drive for errors?

15. On the Windows setup CD, what type of file uses an underscore as the last character in the file extension?

16. Under what circumstances is the Administrator password not required when launching the Recovery Console?

17. What is the purpose of the Systemroot command under the Recovery Console?

18. Under the Recovery Console, what is the command to rewrite the Master Boot Program?

19. What is the command line to install the Recovery Console on the boot loader menu?

20. Before you can perform the Windows 2000 Emergency Repair Process, what disk must you have? What is contained on the disk?

21. When would you use System File Checker? What is the command to execute it?

22. What is the program filename for System File Checker?

23. What are the names of two utility programs that allow you to view the contents of the Boot.ini file?

24. What is the Windows XP recovery tool that is similar to the Windows 2000 Emergency Repair Process?

25. Place these tools in the order in which you should try them when troubleshooting the boot process: Recovery Console, Advanced Options Menu, System Restore.

>> THINKING CRITICALLY

1. Your Windows XP system boots to a blue screen and no desktop. What do you do first?

   a. Reinstall Windows XP.

   b. Attempt to boot into the Advanced Options menu.

   c. Attempt to boot into the Recovery Console.

   d. Attempt to use the Automated System Recovery.

2. You tried to use the Automated System Recovery to restore a failed Windows XP system. The process failed with errors, but there is a very important data file on the hard drive that you need to recover. The hard drive is using the NTFS file system. What do you do?

   a. Most likely the file is toast. The ASR process probably destroyed the file if it were not already destroyed.

   b. Boot to the Recovery Console using the Windows XP setup CD and attempt to recover the file.

c. Reinstall Windows XP and then recover the file.

d. Boot to the Advanced Options menu and use Safe Mode to recover the file.

3. When you start Windows XP, you see an error message about a service that has failed to start, and then the system locks up. You think this service is related to a critical Windows process. What do you try first? Second?

   a. Boot into Safe Mode and run System Restore.

   b. Select the Last Known Good Configuration on the Advanced Options menu.

   c. Perform an in-place upgrade of Windows XP.

   d. Use the Recovery Console to restore the system file.

4. While cleaning up the Windows XP startup process, you discover a program in this folder: C:\WINDOWS\System32\GroupPolicy\Machine\Scripts\Startup. You know that this program is not one that an administrator or other user placed there. What is your next step?

   a. Delete the program file and move on to the next step in cleaning up startup.

   b. Assume the file is malicious and run antivirus software.

   c. Assume the file is malicious, delete the file, and run antivirus software.

   d. Move the file to another folder.

5. Which statement(s) are true about the Windows 2000/XP boot disk?

   a. The boot disk can be used to boot the system to the Windows 2000/XP desktop when Ntldr is missing from the hard drive.

   b. The boot disk can be used to boot to the desktop even when the C:\Windows folder is corrupted.

   c. The boot disk can be used in place of the boot files in the root directory of the active partition.

   d. The boot disk can be used to boot to the desktop even when the partition table is corrupted.

>> HANDS-ON PROJECTS

PROJECT 5-1:   Practice Using the Recovery Console

To get some practice using the Recovery Console, first boot from your Windows 2000/XP setup CD and load the Recovery Console. Then do the following:

1. Get a directory listing of C:\. Are files normally hidden in Windows Explorer displayed in the list?

2. Create a folder on your hard drive named C:\Temp.

3. List the files contained in the Drivers.cab cabinet file.

4. Expand one of these files and put it in the C:\Temp folder.

5. Exit the Recovery Console and reboot.

PROJECT 5-2: Using Ntbtlog.txt

Compare an Ntbtlog.txt file created during a normal boot to one created when booting into Safe Mode. Note any differences you find.

PROJECT 5-3: More Practice with Recovery Console

Using Windows Explorer, rename the Ntldr file in the root directory of drive C. Reboot the system. What error message do you see? Now use Recovery Console to restore Ntldr without using the renamed Ntldr file on drive C. Copy the file from the Windows setup CD to drive C. List the commands you used to do the job.

PROJECT 5-4: Sabotage a Windows XP System

In a lab environment, follow these steps to find out if you can corrupt a Windows XP system so that it will not boot, and then repair the system.

1. Looking at Figure 5-40, make a list of the user-mode processes critical to Windows XP.

Figure 5-40 Processes that launch when Windows XP is newly installed

2. Rename or move one of these program files shown in Figure 5-40. Which program file did you select? In what Windows folder did you find it?

3. Restart your system. Did an error occur? Check in Explorer. Is the file restored? What Windows feature repaired the problem?

4. Try other methods of sabotaging the Windows XP system, but carefully record exactly what you did to sabotage the boot. Can you make the boot fail?

5. Now recover the Windows XP system. List the steps you took to get the system back to good working order.

PROJECT 5-5:   Using a Windows 2000/XP Boot Disk

Create a Windows 2000/XP boot disk and use it to boot your computer. Describe how the boot worked differently from booting entirely from the hard drive.

>> REAL PROBLEMS, REAL SOLUTIONS

REAL PROBLEM 5-1:   Problems Starting Windows XP

Tim, a coworker who uses many different applications on his Windows XP system, complains to you that his system is very slow starting up and responding when he loads and unloads applications. You suspect the system is loading too many services and programs during startup that are sucking up system resources. What do you do to check for startup processes and eliminate the unnecessary ones? If you have access to a Windows XP system that needs this type of service, test your answers on this system. Write down at least 10 things you should do or try, as discussed in the chapter, to speed up a sluggish Windows XP installation.

CHAPTER 6

Windows 9x/Me Commands and Startup Disk

In this chapter, you will learn:

- **What happens when you first turn on your PC and DOS and Windows 9x/Me start**

- **About the commands DOS and Windows 9x/Me use to manage memory**

- **To use different commands at the command prompt**

- **How to use a Windows 9x/Me startup disk to prepare a hard drive for first use and to troubleshoot a failed boot**

Even though DOS and Windows 9x/Me are no longer supported by Microsoft, there is much to gain in understanding how these legacy OSs work. Just as knowing how to drive a manual-shift car can help you be a better driver when driving an automatic, so can understanding old operating systems help you better support the newer ones. Using DOS and Windows 9x/Me utilities and commands, you can sometimes get a better understanding of how a hardware device works and how an OS interacts with it than you can with the Windows 2000/XP operating system. That's because many times the older the technology, the less complicated it is and the more control you have over it.

Having worked in the computer industry for many years, I can personally tell you that I can see a greater depth of understanding among technicians who support Windows 2000/XP if they have had the benefit of first studying DOS and Windows 9x/Me. In fact, if you are given the opportunity, you might find it helpful to study this chapter and Chapter 7 before you turn your attention to the chapters on Windows 2000/XP (Chapters 2, 3, 4, and 5). Because this chapter is written so that it can be studied before these Windows 2000/XP chapters, you'll find a few short instances where material is duplicated, for example, the commands used at the command prompt to manage files and directories.

In this chapter, you'll learn what happens when DOS and the DOS-core portion of Windows 9x/Me are loaded, how DOS and Windows 9x/Me manage memory, how to use the command line, and how to use the Windows 9x/Me startup disk. You'll then have all the background knowledge you need to begin your study of Windows 9x/Me in the next chapter.

301

UNDERSTANDING DOS AND WINDOWS 9X/ME STARTUP

The Windows 9x/Me operating system is built on a DOS core. In this section, you'll learn what first happens during booting when only the MS-DOS core of Windows 9x/Me is loaded, which provides a command prompt for you to enter commands. This command-driven, real-mode OS environment first discussed in Chapter 1 allows you to use commands useful when troubleshooting a system that cannot boot to a Windows desktop.

You can load the MS-DOS core in two ways: from the Windows 9x/Me hard drive or from a Windows 9x/Me startup disk. If the hard drive is healthy enough, it's easier to load from it, but in situations where the hard drive is really messed up, you can boot to a command prompt from a startup floppy disk.

> **Notes**
>
> Windows 9x/Me is fast being outdated by Windows XP. However, the Windows 9x/Me startup disk is still a popular troubleshooting tool and well worth your time to learn how it works. In many situations, you can use it when other more sophisticated tools fail you.

You'll learn how to use both methods later in the chapter. Now let's turn our attention to the steps involved in getting the MS-DOS core OS loaded. As you read, refer to Figure 6-1, which outlines the process.

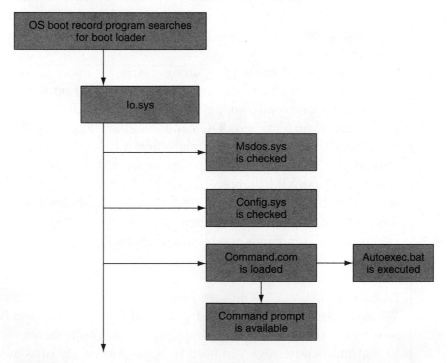

Figure 6-1 Steps to load the MS-DOS core

OS BOOT RECORD PROGRAM LOCATES AND EXECUTES IO.SYS

When a computer is first turned on, startup BIOS stored on the motherboard is in charge and begins by testing essential hardware present. This process is called POST (power-on self test). After POST, startup BIOS looks to CMOS RAM to know which storage media to search for an OS. (CMOS RAM is a small amount of memory on the motherboard used to hold configuration settings for the system.) When startup BIOS turns to a hard drive or floppy disk for an OS, the little program in the OS boot record is found. This program then searches for the boot loader program. For Windows 9x/Me or MS-DOS, it searches for a hidden file named Io.sys. (A hidden file is a file that does not appear in the directory list.) The Io.sys file contains the basic I/O software for real mode. Once Io.sys is loaded into memory, the boot record program is no longer needed, and control is turned over to Io.sys.

MSDOS.SYS IS CHECKED

Io.sys requires that the Msdos.sys file be present. Msdos.sys is a text file that contains some parameters and switches you can set to affect the way the OS boots. You will learn about the contents of Msdos.sys and how to change it to affect the boot process in Chapter 7. Io.sys reads Msdos.sys and uses the settings in it.

CONFIG.SYS IS CHECKED

Io.sys then looks on the hard drive or floppy for a file named Config.sys. This configuration file contains several commands. Some more important commands are:

▲ How many files it can open at any one time. An example of this command is:

```
Files=99
```

▲ How many file buffers to create. A buffer is a temporary holding area for files. A sample command is:

```
Buffers=40
```

▲ What 16-bit (real mode) device drivers to load. Each device driver requires one command line. The sample command below loads the device driver for a mouse. The name of the driver file is Mouse.sys and should be stored in the root directory of the floppy disk or hard drive.

```
Device=mouse.sys
```

Several 16-bit drivers can be loaded into memory from commands in Config.sys. Io.sys puts these programs in memory wherever it chooses. However, a program can request that it be put in a certain memory location. Know that protected mode (32-bit) drivers are not loaded from Config.sys, but from the registry.

Sometimes Config.sys is used to create a RAM drive. A RAM drive is an area of memory that looks and acts like a hard drive, but because it is memory, it is much faster. (Memory is faster than a hard drive mainly because a hard drive has mechanical moving parts and memory is an electronic device with no moving parts.) When booting from the Windows 9x/Me startup disk, DOS creates a RAM drive to hold files after they have been uncompressed. This eliminates the need for hard drive access, and there is no room for the files on the floppy disk. An example of a command in Config.sys to create a RAM drive is:

> **Notes**
>
> Under MS-DOS, a program such as a device driver that stays in memory until the CPU needs it is called a **terminate-and-stay-resident (TSR)** program. The term is seldom used today, except when talking about real-mode programs.

```
device=ramdrive.sys 2048
```

The command tells the OS to create a RAM drive that is 2048K in size.

COMMAND.COM IS EXECUTED

Next Io.sys looks for another OS file, named Command.com. This file has three parts: more code to manage I/O, programs for internal OS commands such as Copy and Delete, and a short program that looks for the Autoexec.bat file.

> **Notes**
>
> Some OS commands, such as Dir and Copy, are **internal commands**, meaning they are embedded in the Command.com file, and others are **external commands**, meaning they have their own program files. An example of an external command is Format, stored in the file Format.com.

AUTOEXEC.BAT IS EXECUTED

Command.com looks for Autoexec.bat and, if found, executes it. The filename Autoexec.bat stands for "automatically executed batch file." A **batch file** is a text file that contains a series of commands that are executed in order. Autoexec.bat lists OS commands that execute automatically each time the OS is loaded.

The following commands are examples of commands that might be found in the Autoexec.bat file:

- The Path command, shown in the following command line, lists two paths, separated by semicolons. The OS later uses the paths listed in the Path command to locate program files.

```
PATH C:\;C:\Windows;
```

- The Set command is used to create and assign a value to an environmental variable. Once the assignment has been made using the Set command, an application can later read and use the value. When an application is installed, the installation program might add a Set command to your Autoexec.bat file. For example, this Set command assigns a value to the variable Mypath:

```
Set Mypath = C:\VERT
```

Later, when the application loads, it can read the value assigned to Mypath, which is C:\VERT, to know where to look to find data it needs.

- The Restart command, as shown in the following command line, causes the system to reboot.

```
Restart.com
```

- The Temp command lets applications know where to store temporary files. Add the Temp command to Autoexec.bat if applications are putting temporary files in strange locations. An example of a Temp command is:

```
Temp=C:\Temp
```

> **Notes**
>
> By default, DOS stores temporary files in C:\Temp, Windows 9x/Me uses C:\Windows\Temp, Windows 2000 uses C:\Winnt\Temp, and Windows XP uses C:\Windows\Temp.

- The Echo command, shown below, turns on and off the displaying of commands and messages. Use it in a batch file to control output to the screen.

```
Echo off
```

Booting into real mode with a command prompt is completed after Autoexec.bat has finished executing. At this point, Command.com is the program in charge, displaying a command prompt and waiting for a command. On the other hand, if a program or menu was executed from Autoexec.bat, it might ask you for a command.

The command prompt indicates the drive that loaded the OS. If the OS files were loaded from a floppy disk, the command prompt is A:\> (called the A prompt). If the OS was loaded from the hard drive, the command prompt is C:\> (the C prompt). The colon following the letter identifies the letter as the name of a drive, and the backslash identifies the directory on the drive as the root or main directory. The > symbol is the prompt symbol that the OS uses to say, "Enter your command here." This drive and root directory are now the default drive and directory, sometimes called the current or working drive or directory.

> **Notes**
>
> Note that commands used at a command prompt are not case sensitive; that is, you can enter *WIN*, *Win*, or *win*.

If you want to load the Windows 9x/Me desktop, use the Win command, which executes the program Win.com. Enter this command at the C prompt:

```
C:\> WIN
```

COMMANDS TO MANAGE MEMORY

Memory management under DOS and Windows 9x/Me can seem complicated because of the way the process has evolved over the past 20 years or so. Like an old house that has been added to and remodeled several times, the present-day design is not as efficient as that of a brand-new house. Decisions made by IBM and Microsoft in the early 1980s still significantly affect, and in some cases limit, the way memory is used under Windows 9x/Me. We'll first look at how DOS and Windows 9x/Me divide up the memory address space, and then we'll look at the commands and utilities DOS and Windows 9x/Me use to manage these addresses.

HOW DOS AND WINDOWS 9X/ME DIVIDE MEMORY

Early CPUs had only 20 lines on the bus available to handle addresses, so the largest memory address the CPU could use was 11111111111111111111 in binary, which is 1,048,575, or 1024K, or 1 MB of memory. This 1 MB of memory was used by DOS and divided up according to the scheme shown in Table 6-1. Then newer CPUs and motherboards were developed with 24 address lines and more, so that memory addresses above 1024K became available. Memory addresses above 1024K are called **extended memory**. And, memory addresses are often expressed using hexadecimal notation.

Range of Memory Addresses	Range Using Hex Terminology	Type of Memory
0 to 640K	0 to A0000	Conventional or base memory
640K to 1024K	A0000 to FFFFF	Upper memory (A through F ranges)
Above 1024K	100000 and up	Extended memory

Table 6-1 Division of memory under DOS and Windows 9x/Me

When a PC is first booted, many programs demand memory addresses, including the ROM BIOS programs on the motherboard and some circuit boards, device drivers, the OS, and applications. This process of assigning memory addresses to programs is called memory mapping.

Sometimes older ROM BIOS programs and device drivers expect to be assigned certain memory addresses and will not work otherwise. Windows 9x/Me is committed to maintain backward compatibility with these old programs. This fact is probably the greatest limitation of Windows 9x/Me today.

To get a clear picture of how memory addresses are mapped, look at the memory map shown in Figure 6-2. The first 640K of memory addresses are called **conventional memory**, or base memory. The memory addresses from 640K up to 1024K are called **upper memory**. Memory above 1024K is called extended memory. The first 64K of extended memory is called the **high memory area (HMA)**. Now let's look at each type of memory address.

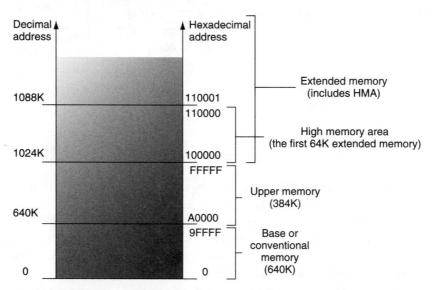

Figure 6-2 Memory address map (not to scale) showing the starting and ending addresses of conventional, upper, and extended memory, including the high memory area

CONVENTIONAL MEMORY

In the early 1980s, when IBM and Microsoft were designing the original PCs, they decided to make 640K of memory addresses available to the user, thinking that this was plenty for anything the user would ever want to do. This 640K of addresses was intended to hold the OS, the application software, and the data being processed. At that time, 640K of memory addresses was more than enough to handle all the applications available. Today, 640K of memory addresses is grossly inadequate.

The problem caused by restricting the number of memory addresses available to the user to only 640K could have been solved by simply providing more addresses to the user in future versions of DOS. However, another original design decision ruled this out. The next group of memory addresses is 384K above conventional memory and called upper memory. This group was assigned to utility operations for the system. The system requires memory addresses to communicate with peripherals. The programs (such as BIOS on a video card or on the motherboard) and data are assigned memory addresses in this upper memory area. For example, the video BIOS and its data are placed in the very first part of upper memory, the area from 640K to 768K. All video ROM written for DOS-based computers assumes that these programs and data are stored in this area. Also, many DOS and Windows applications interact directly with video ROM and RAM in this address range.

Programs almost always expect data to be written into memory directly above the addresses for the program itself, an important fact for understanding memory management.

Thus, if a program begins storing its data above its location in conventional memory, eventually it will "hit the ceiling," the beginning of upper memory assigned to video ROM. The major reason that applications have a 640K memory limit is that video ROM begins at 640K. If DOS and Windows 9x/Me allowed applications into these upper memory addresses, all DOS-compatible video ROM would need to be rewritten, and many DOS applications that access these video addresses would not work. The 32-bit device drivers and applications under Windows 9x/Me don't have this problem because they can run from extended memory and turn to the OS to access video.

UPPER MEMORY

The memory map in Figure 6-2 shows that the memory addresses from 640K up to (but not including) 1024K are called upper memory. This area of memory is used by BIOS and device drivers. In the hexadecimal number system, upper memory begins at A0000 and goes through FFFFF. Because the hex numbers in upper memory begin with A through F, the divisions of upper memory are often referred to as the A range, B range, and so on, up to the F range. Video ROM and RAM are stored in the first part of upper memory, hex A0000 through CFFFF (the A, B, and C areas of memory). Sixteen-bit BIOS programs for other legacy expansion boards are assigned memory addresses in the remaining portions of upper memory. BIOS on the motherboard (the system BIOS) is assigned the top part of upper memory, from F0000 through FFFFF (the F area of upper memory). Upper memory often has unassigned addresses, depending on which boards are present in the system. Managing memory effectively involves gaining access to these unused addresses in upper memory and using them to store device drivers and TSR (terminate-and-stay-resident) programs.

> **Notes**
>
> For more information about how the hexadecimal number system is used with memory addressing, see "The Hexadecimal Number System and Memory Addressing" in the online content.

EXTENDED MEMORY AND THE HIGH MEMORY AREA

Memory above 1 MB is called extended memory. The first 64K of extended memory is called the high memory area, which exists because a bug in the programming for the older Intel 286 CPU (the first CPU to use extended memory) produced this small pocket of unused memory addresses. Beginning with DOS 5, the OS capitalized on this bug by storing portions of itself in the high memory area, thus freeing some conventional memory where DOS had been stored. This method of storing part of DOS in the high memory area is called "loading DOS high." You will see how to do this later in the chapter.

Extended memory is actually managed by the OS as a device (the device is memory) that is controlled by a device driver. To access extended memory, you need the device driver (called a memory extender) that controls it, and you must use applications that have been written to use extended memory. The amount of extended memory you can have on your computer is limited by the amount of RAM that can be installed on your motherboard and the number of memory addresses the CPU and the memory bus can support.

APPLYING|CONCEPTS Using Windows 9x/Me Device Manager, you can see how the first 1 MB of memory addresses are assigned (see Figure 6-3). To view the list on the Device Manager window, select **Computer**, click **Properties**, and then click **Memory**. Notice in the figure that the system BIOS has been assigned memory addresses in the F range of upper memory. This F range is always reserved for motherboard BIOS and is never requested by other programs. When the CPU is first turned on and needs a program in order to know how to boot up, it begins with the instructions stored on the ROM BIOS chip that are assigned to these memory addresses.

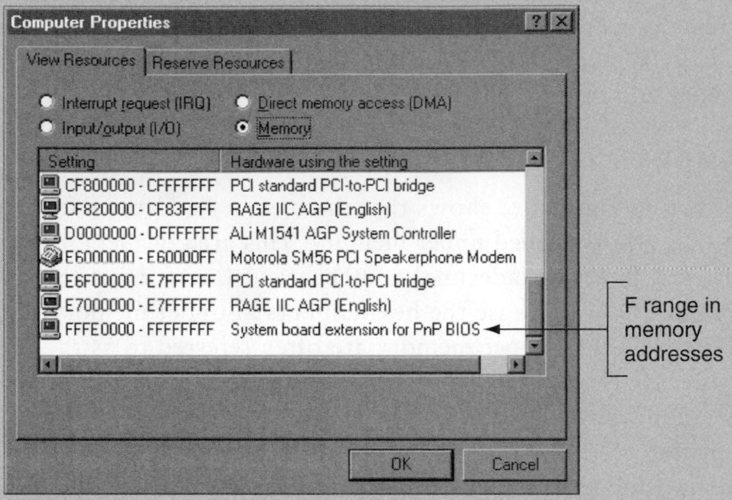

Figure 6-3   Computer Properties dialog box shows how the first megabyte of memory addresses is assigned

WINDOWS 9X/ME AND DOS UTILITIES THAT MANAGE MEMORY

The two utilities used by DOS and Windows 9x/Me to manage memory above 640K are Himem.sys and Emm386.exe. **Himem.sys** is the device driver for all memory above 640K. The program file **Emm386.exe** contains the software that loads device drivers and other programs into upper memory. Himem.sys is automatically loaded by Windows 9x/Me during the boot process, but can also be loaded by an entry in Config.sys. Emm386.exe is not loaded automatically by Windows 9x/Me, but you can load it by an entry in Config.sys.

USING HIMEM.SYS

Himem.sys is considered a device driver because it manages memory as a device. It can be executed by the Device= command in Config.sys. Figure 6-4 shows an example of a very simple Config.sys file on a floppy disk that loads Himem.sys. The Config.sys file is being edited by the Edit.com text editor utility.

To create the file on a floppy disk, at a command prompt, you can use either of these two methods:

▲ Make drive A the default drive and enter this command:

```
A:\> Edit Config.sys
```

▲ Make drive C the default drive and enter this command:

```
C:\> Edit A:Config.sys
```

The second line in the Config.sys file, device=A:\util\mouse.sys, tells DOS to load into memory a device driver from the \Util directory on the floppy disk. This driver allows you to use the mouse while in MS-DOS mode.

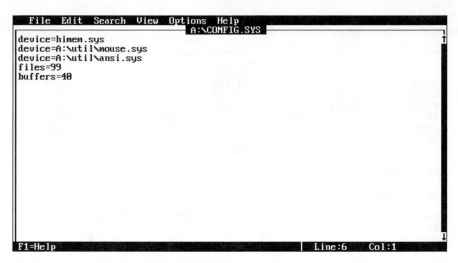

```
  File  Edit  Search  View  Options  Help
                        A:\CONFIG.SYS
device=himem.sys                                                    ↑
device=A:\util\mouse.sys
device=A:\util\ansi.sys
files=99
buffers=40




                                                                    ↓
  F1=Help                                    Line:6     Col:1
```

Figure 6-4 Config.sys set to use memory above 640K

The third line in the Config.sys file, device=A:\util\ansi.sys, tells DOS to load the device driver Ansi.sys into memory. Ansi.sys helps control the keyboard and monitor, providing color on the monitor and an additional set of characters to the ASCII character set. For more information about ASCII and ANSI, see "ASCII Character Set and Ansi.sys" in the online content.

USING EMM386.EXE

In DOS and Windows 9x/Me, Emm386.exe manages the memory addresses in upper memory. Before we see how to use it, let's begin by examining memory when upper memory addresses are not available. To do that, we use the MEM command, which lets us view how memory is currently allocated. You can use the /C option to get a complete list and include the |MORE option to page the results on your screen. Figure 6-5 was produced using this command:

MEM /C |MORE

In Figure 6-5, the first column shows the programs currently loaded in memory. The second column shows the total amount of memory used by each program. The columns labeled Conventional and Upper Memory show the amount of memory being used by each program in each of these categories. This PC is not making use of upper memory for any of its programs. At the bottom of the screen is the total amount of free conventional memory (544,720 bytes) that is available to new programs to be loaded. In this section, we are trying to make this value as high as possible.

```
Modules using memory below 1 MB:

    Name        Total            Conventional        Upper Memory
    --------   ----------        --------------       -------------
    MSDOS      18,672   (18K)    18,672   (18K)          0    (0K)
    HIMEM       1,168    (1K)     1,168    (1K)          0    (0K)
    DBLBUFF     2,976    (3K)     2,976    (3K)          0    (0K)
    IFSHLP      2,864    (3K)     2,864    (3K)          0    (0K)
    WIN         3,616    (4K)     3,616    (4K)          0    (0K)
    COMMAND     8,416    (8K)     8,416    (8K)          0    (0K)
    SAVE       72,768   (71K)    72,768   (71K)          0    (0K)
    Free      544,720  (532K)   544,720  (532K)          0    (0K)

Memory Summary:

    Type of Memory       Total          Used           Free
    --------------      -----------    -----------    -----------
    Conventional          655,360        110,640        544,720
    Upper                       0              0              0
    Reserved                    0              0              0
    Extended (XMS)    133,156,864         69,632    133,087,232
    --------------      -----------    -----------    -----------
-- More --
```

Figure 6-5   MEM report with /C option on a PC not using upper memory

CREATING AND USING UPPER MEMORY BLOCKS

Figure 6-6 shows an example of a Config.sys file that is set to use upper memory addresses. The first line loads the Himem.sys driver. The second line loads the Emm386.exe file. Emm386.exe assigns addresses in upper memory to memory made available by the Himem.sys driver. The NOEMS switch at the end of the command line says to Windows, "Do not create any simulated expanded memory." Expanded memory is an older type of memory above 1 MB that is no longer used by software. The command to load Emm386.exe must appear after the command to load Himem.sys in the Config.sys file.

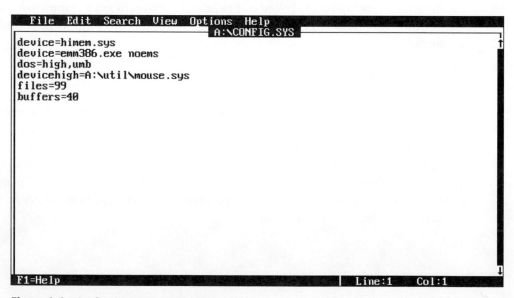

Figure 6-6   Config.sys set to use upper memory

The command DOS=HIGH,UMB serves two purposes. The one command line can be broken into two commands like this:

```
DOS=HIGH

DOS=UMB
```

The DOS=HIGH portion tells the OS to load part of the DOS core into the high memory area ("loading DOS high"). Remember that the high memory area is the first 64K of extended memory. This memory is usually unused unless we choose to store part of DOS in it with this command line. Including this command in Config.sys frees some conventional memory that would have been used by the OS.

The second part of the command, DOS=UMB, creates upper memory blocks. An **upper memory block (UMB)** is a group of consecutive memory addresses in the upper memory area that has had physical memory assigned to it. The OS identifies blocks that are not currently being used by system ROM or expansion boards, and the memory manager makes these blocks available for use. This command, DOS=UMB, enables the OS to access these upper memory blocks. After the UMBs are created, they can be used in these ways:

▲ Devicehigh= command in Config.sys
▲ Loadhigh command in Autoexec.bat
▲ Loadhigh command at the command prompt (explained in the next section)

The fourth line in the Config.sys file in Figure 6-6 uses a UMB. The command Devicehigh=A:\Util\Mouse.sys tells the OS to load the mouse device driver into one of the upper memory blocks created and made available by the previous three lines. This process of loading a program into upper memory addresses is called loading high.

LOADING DEVICE DRIVERS HIGH

Using the Devicehigh= command in Config.sys, rather than the Device= command, causes the driver to load high. With the Devicehigh= command, the OS stores these drivers in UMBs using the largest UMB first, then the next largest, and so on until all are loaded. Therefore, to make sure there is enough room to hold them all in upper memory, order the Devicehigh= command lines in Config.sys so that the largest drivers are loaded first.

You can determine the amount of memory a device driver allocates for itself and its data by using the MEM command with the /M filename option:

MEM /M filename

The filename is the name of the device driver without the file extension.

You can also use a UMB from Autoexec.bat using the Loadhigh (LH) command. For example, to load high Mscdex.exe, a utility to access a CD-ROM drive, use either of the following commands:

LH Mscdex.exe

Loadhigh Mscdex.exe

In either case, the program is loaded into the largest UMB available and does not use up more precious conventional memory. Note that before the Loadhigh command will work, the program files Himem.sys and Emm386.exe must be available to the OS, and these three lines must be added to Config.sys and executed by booting the computer:

Device=HIMEM.SYS

Device=EMM386.EXE NOEMS

DOS=UMB

If the Himem.sys and Emm386.exe files are not in the root directory of the boot device, you must include the path to the filename in the Device= line, like this:

```
Device=C:\DOS\HIMEM.SYS
```

 Notes

> When a program is loaded high, two things can go wrong. Either the program might not work from upper memory, causing problems during execution, or there might not be enough room in upper memory for the program and its data. If the program causes the computer to hang when you attempt to run it, or if it simply refuses to work correctly, remove it from upper memory.

Windows 9x/Me, which is mostly a 32-bit OS, "lives" in extended memory together with its device drivers and applications, and uses only base and upper memory for 16-bit components. Managing base and upper memory can get pretty sticky, but the good news is if you are using all 32-bit drivers and applications in a Windows 9x/Me environment, you do not need to be concerned about managing base and upper memory.

USING THE COMMAND PROMPT

As a PC technician, your tools and skills are not complete until you are comfortable building and using command lines. In this section, you will first learn how to access a command prompt, about file and directory (also called folders) naming conventions, about wildcard characters used in command lines, and how to launch programs from the command prompt. Then you will learn to use several commands to manage files and directories and perform many useful utility tasks when managing an OS, applications, and data. Finally, you'll learn how to create and use batch files. Some of the commands in this section are also found in Chapter 4 where they can also be used in Windows 2000/XP.

ACCESSING A COMMAND PROMPT

There are several ways to get to a command prompt using Windows 9x/Me and DOS:

◢ To access a command prompt window, sometimes called a **DOS box**, from a Windows 9x/Me desktop, click **Start, Programs,** and **MS-DOS Prompt**. A Command Prompt window opens, as shown in Figure 6-7. Using a command prompt window, you can enter the DOS-like commands discussed in this chapter. To exit the window, type **Exit** at the command prompt.

◢ Click **Start,** click **Run,** and enter **Command.com** in the Run dialog box.

◢ When you boot from the Windows 9x/Me startup disk or any bootable floppy disk, you get a command prompt instead of the Windows desktop. This method does not require access to the hard drive or the Windows desktop to load.

◢ Using Windows 95 or Windows 98 (not Windows Me), click **Start,** click **Shutdown,** and select **Restart in MS-DOS mode** from the Shutdown dialog box. Using this method, you get a command prompt provided by the DOS real-mode core of Windows 95/98.

◢ Using Windows 9x/Me, hold down the **Ctrl** key or the **F8** key while booting, which causes the OS to display a startup menu. From the menu, select **Command prompt only**. This method requires access to the hard drive, but works even when the Windows desktop cannot load.

Figure 6-7 A Command Prompt window can be used to practice the commands given in this section

For convenience, you can add a command prompt icon to your Windows desktop for easy access. To do that, locate the program file (Command.com) in Windows Explorer and, while holding down the Ctrl key, drag the icon to your desktop. Another way to create the shortcut is to click **Start**, point to **Programs, Accessories,** and **Command Prompt**. Then, right-click **Command Prompt** and select **Create Shortcut** on the shortcut menu.

APPLYING CONCEPTS   For practice, try all the preceding methods of accessing a command prompt. Then create a command prompt icon on your desktop.

A command prompt provides information about the current drive and directory. For example, if you booted a Windows 98 PC from a bootable floppy disk into command prompt mode, you would see the A prompt (A:\>). Recall that the A: indicates the current drive. (A drive letter is always followed by a colon.) The backslash indicates the root directory, and the > symbol indicates that you can enter a new command.

To make the hard drive (drive C) the default drive, enter C: at the A prompt. The prompt then changes to indicate the current directory and drive in the root directory of drive C. It looks like this on your screen:

C:\>

FILE AND DIRECTORY NAMING CONVENTIONS

When working with a command prompt, it is important to understand how to name directories and files, and how to type directory names and filenames in the command line. Under DOS, a filename can contain up to eight characters, a separating period, and a file extension of up to three characters, like this: *filename.ext*. This is called the 8.3 format. Characters can be the letters a through z, the numbers 0 through 9, and the following characters:

_ ^ $ ~ ! # % & - { } ( ) @ ' `

Under MS-DOS, be sure to not use a space, period, *, ?, or \ in a filename or file extension. Acceptable file extensions for program files are .com, .sys, .bat, and .exe. For example, the DOS utility program that displays information about the system is Msd.exe.

Under Windows, directory names and filenames can be as long as 255 characters and can contain spaces. When creating subdirectories under directories, know that the maximum depth of directories you can create is dependent on the length of the directory names. When working from a command prompt and using long directory names or filenames, put double quotation marks around the name, like this: "My long filename.doc".

When using long filenames in Windows 9x/Me, remember that the DOS portion of the system can understand only eight-character filenames with three-character extensions. When the DOS part of the system is operating, it truncates long filenames and assigns new eight-character names. For example, under DOS, the filename Mydocument.doc is displayed with the first seven letters and a tilde (~) character:

```
Mydocum~.doc
```

If you have two documents that would have the same name when truncated in this manner, DOS also adds an identifying number. For example, if you have a document named Mydocument.doc and one named Mydocumentnew.doc, DOS truncates these as:

```
Mydocu~1.doc
```

```
Mydocu~2.doc
```

When you boot using a Windows 9x/Me startup disk or some other MS-DOS disk, be aware of this file-naming convention.

USING WILDCARD CHARACTERS IN COMMAND LINES

As you work at the command prompt, you can use two wildcard characters in a filename to execute a command on a group of files, or in an abbreviated filename if you do not know the entire name. The question mark (?) is a wildcard for one character, and the asterisk (*) is a wildcard for more than one character. For example, if you want to find all files in a directory that start with A and have a three-letter file extension, you would use the following command:

```
dir a*.???
```

LAUNCHING A PROGRAM USING THE COMMAND PROMPT

In Chapter 1, you learned how to launch a program from the Windows desktop. You can also launch a program from a command prompt window. At the command prompt, when you type a single group of letters with no spaces, the OS assumes that you typed the filename of a program file you want to execute, which is stored in the current directory (the directory showing in your command prompt). The OS attempts to find the program file by that name, copy the file into RAM, and then execute the program.

As an example of launching a program, let's use the program Mem.exe, a program that displays how memory is currently allocated. For Windows 9x/Me, the program file Mem.exe is stored on the hard drive in the C:\Windows\Command folder. Note what happens in

Figure 6-8 when you type the first command shown in the figure, *mem*, at the A: prompt, and then press Enter, like this:

```
A:\>mem
```

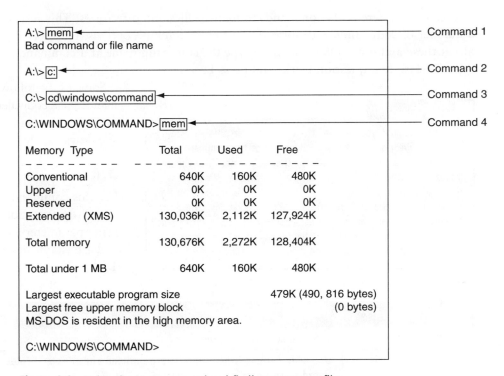

Figure 6-8 that the prompt changes to C:\>, indicating that the logical drive C

Figure 6-8 Using the Mem command and finding a program file

The OS says it cannot find the program to execute. It looked only on the floppy disk (drive A) for Mem.com, Mem.exe, or Mem.bat, the three file extensions that the OS recognizes for programs. If the OS finds none of these files in the current directory, it stops looking and displays this error message:

```
Bad command or file name
```

Now look at the second command in the figure. To help the OS locate the program file, you must change the default drive to the hard drive by giving this command:

```
A:\> C:
```

Notice in Figure 6-8 that the prompt changes to C:\>, indicating that the logical drive C on the hard drive is the default drive. In the third command in the figure, you change the default directory on the hard drive to \Windows\Command using the CD (**change directory**) **command**, like this:

```
C:\>CD\windows\command
```

(Remember that DOS and Windows commands are not case sensitive, so it makes no difference whether you type CD, Cd, or cd.) The prompt now looks like this:

```
C:\WINDOWS\COMMAND>
```

You can now enter the mem command again, which is showing as the fourth command in the figure. The OS locates and executes the program file.

COMMANDS TO MANAGE FILES AND DIRECTORIES

You can use different OS commands to manage files and directories. This section describes a number of commands with some of their more common options. For more information about these and other OS commands, type the command name at a command prompt, type /? (slash and question mark) and press **Enter**.

> ✎ **Notes**
>
> If you think that you've seen the commands in this section before, you're right! Chapter 4 covers all of the commands that you are expected to know for the A+ exams. However, this book is also designed so that you can cover the Windows 2000/XP chapters (Chapters 2, 3, 4, and 5) before *or* after you cover Chapters 6 and 7 on DOS and Windows 9x/Me. Thus, the duplicated commands are included in this chapter so that you can study this chapter without having first covered Chapter 4, if that's what you choose to do.

Some of the following commands have equivalent Windows tools that are available from the Windows 9x/Me desktop.

DIR

Use this command to list files and directories. Some examples using parameters, wildcards, and a filename are shown in Table 6-2:

Sample Command	Effect
DIR /P	List one screen at a time.
DIR /W	Use wide format, where details are omitted and files and folders are listed in columns on the screen.
DIR *.txt	Use a wildcard character, listing all files with a .txt file extension.
DIR Myfile.txt	Check that a single file is present.

Table 6-2 Examples of the Dir command

RENAME OR REN

The Rename command renames a file or folder. For example, to change the name of Myfile.txt to Mybackup.txt, use this command:

```
Ren Myfile.txt Mybackup.txt
```

TYPE

The Type command displays the contents of a text file on your screen. Some examples are shown in Table 6-3:

Sample Command	Effect
Type Myfile.txt	Displays file contents
Type My file.txt >PRN	Redirects output to printer
Type Myfile.txt |More	Displays output one screen at a time

Table 6-3 Examples of the Type command

DEL OR ERASE

The Del or Erase command erases files or groups of files. If the command does not include drive and directory information, like the following examples, the OS uses the default drive and directory when executing the command.

In the sample command lines that follow, the typed command is in bold and the command prompt is not bold. To erase all files in the A:\DOCS directory, use the following command:

```
C:\> ERASE A:\DOCS\*.*
```

To erase all files in the current default directory, use the following command:

```
A:\DOCS> DEL *.*
```

To erase all files in the current directory that have no file extension, use the following command:

```
A:\DOCS> DEL *.
```

To erase the file named Myfile.txt, use the following command:

```
A:\> DEL MYFILE.TXT
```

COPY

The Copy command copies a single file or group of files. The original files are not altered. To copy a file from one drive to another and to rename the file, use a command similar to this one:

```
A:\> COPY C:\data\myfile.txt A:\mydata\newfile.txt
```

The drive, path, and filename of the source file immediately follow the Copy command. The drive, path, and filename of the destination file follow the source filename. If you do not specify the filename of the destination file, the OS assigns the file's original name to this copy. If you omit the drive or path of the source or the destination, then the OS uses the current default drive and path.

To copy the file Myfile.txt from the root directory of drive C to drive A, use the following command:

```
C:\> COPY MYFILE.TXT A:
```

Because the command does not include a drive or path before the filename Myfile.txt, the OS assumes that the file is in the default drive and path. Also, because there is no destination filename specified, the file written to drive A will be named Myfile.txt.

To copy all files in the C:\DOCS directory to the floppy disk in drive A, use the following command:

```
C:\>COPY C:\DOCS\*.* A:
```

To make a backup file named System.bak of the System.ini file in the \Windows directory of the hard drive, use the following command:

```
C:\WINDOWS>COPY SYSTEM.INI SYSTEM.BAK
```

If you use the Copy command to duplicate multiple files, the files are assigned the names of the original files. When you duplicate multiple files, the destination portion of the command line cannot include a filename.

> **Notes**
>
> When trying to recover a corrupted file, you can sometimes use the Copy command to copy the file to new media, such as from the hard drive to a floppy disk. During the copying process, if the Copy command reports a bad or missing sector, choose the option to ignore that sector. The copying process then continues to the next sector. The corrupted sector will be lost, but others can likely be recovered.

XCOPY /C /S /Y /D:

The Xcopy command is more powerful than the Copy command. It follows the same general command-source-destination format as the Copy command, but it offers several more options. For example, you can use the /S parameter with the Xcopy command to copy all files in the directory \DOCS, as well as all subdirectories under \DOCS and their files, to the disk in drive A, like so:

```
C:\>XCOPY C:\DOCS\*.* A: /S
```

To copy all files from the directory C:\DOCS created or modified on March 14, 2006, use the /D switch, as in the following command:

```
C:\>XCOPY C:\DOCS\*.* A: /D:03/14/06
```

Use the /Y parameter to overwrite existing files without prompting, and use the /C parameter to keep copying even when an error occurs.

DELTREE *[DRIVE:]PATH*

The Deltree command deletes the directory tree beginning with the subdirectory you specify, including all subdirectories and all files in all subdirectories in that tree. Use it with caution! As an example of deleting a directory tree, you can delete the C:\DOCS folder and all its contents by using this command:

```
C:\>DELTREE C:\DOCS
```

MKDIR *[DRIVE:]PATH* OR MD *[DRIVE:]PATH*

The Mkdir command (abbreviated MD, for make directory) creates a subdirectory under a directory. To create a directory named \GAME on drive C, you can use this command:

```
MKDIR C:\GAME
```

The backslash indicates that the directory is under the root directory. To create a directory named CHESS under the \GAME directory, you can use this command:

```
MKDIR C:\GAME\CHESS
```

The OS requires that the parent directory GAME already exist before it creates the child directory CHESS.

Figure 6-9 shows the result of the Dir command on the directory \GAME. Note the two initial entries in the directory table, the . (dot) and the .. (dot, dot) entries. The Mkdir command creates these two entries when the OS initially sets up the directory. You cannot edit these entries with normal OS commands, and they must remain in the directory for the directory's lifetime. The . entry points to the subdirectory itself, and the .. entry points to the parent directory, in this case, the root directory.

```
C:\>DIR \GAME

 Volume in drive C has no label
 Volume Serial Number is 0F52-09FC
 Directory of C:\GAME

 .            <DIR>      02-18-93    4:50a
 ..           <DIR>      02-18-93    4:50a
 CHESS        <DIR>      02-18-93    4:50a
 NUKE         <DIR>      02-18-93    4:51a
 PENTE        <DIR>      02-18-93    4:52a
 NETRIS       <DIR>      02-18-93    4:54a
 BEYOND       <DIR>      02-18-93    4:54a
         7 file(s)             0 bytes
                        9273344 bytes free

C:\>
```

Figure 6-9   Results of the Dir command on the \GAME directory

CHDIR *[DRIVE:]PATH* OR CD *[DRIVE:]PATH* OR CD..

The Chdir command (abbreviated CD, for change directory) changes the current default directory. Using its easiest form, you simply state the drive and the entire path that you want to be current, like so:

CD C:\GAME\CHESS

The command prompt now looks like this:

C:\GAME\CHESS>

To move from a child directory to its parent directory, use the .. variation of the command:

C:\GAME\CHESS> **CD..**

C:\GAME>

Remember that .. always means the parent directory. You can move from a parent directory to one of its child directories simply by stating the name of the child directory:

C:\GAME>**CD CHESS**

C:\GAME\CHESS>

Remember, do not put a backslash in front of the child directory name; doing so tells the OS to go to a directory named CHESS that is directly under the root directory.

RMDIR *[DRIVE:]PATH* OR RD *[DRIVE:]PATH*

The Rmdir command (abbreviated RD, for remove directory) removes a subdirectory. Before you can use the Rmdir command, three things must be true:

- ◢ The directory must contain no files.
- ◢ The directory must contain no subdirectories.
- ◢ The directory must not be the current directory.

The . and .. entries are present when a directory is ready for removal. For example, to remove the \GAME directory in the preceding example, the CHESS directory must first be removed, like so:

C:\>**RMDIR C:\GAME\CHESS**

Or, if the \GAME directory is the current directory, you can use this command:

C:\GAME>**RD CHESS**

Once you remove the CHESS directory, you can remove the \GAME directory. It's not good to attempt to saw off a branch while you're sitting on it; you must first leave the \GAME directory like this:

C:\GAME>**CD..**

C:\>**RD \GAME**

ATTRIB

The Attrib command displays or changes the read-only, archive, system, and hidden attributes assigned to files. To display the attributes of the file MYFILE.TXT, you can use this command:

ATTRIB MYFILE.TXT

To hide the file, you can use this command:

ATTRIB +H MYFILE.TXT

To remove the hidden status of the file, you need only use this command:

ATTRIB -H MYFILE.TXT

To make the file a read-only system file, use this command:

ATTRIB +R +S MYFILE.TXT

When you put more than one parameter in the Attrib command, the order doesn't matter. This command works the same way as the one above:

ATTRIB +S +R MYFILE.TXT

To remove the read-only system status of the file, use this command:

ATTRIB -R -S MYFILE.TXT

The archive bit is used to determine if a file has changed since the last backup. To turn on the archive bit, use this command:

ATTRIB +A MYFILE.TXT

To turn off the archive bit, use this command:

```
ATTRIB -A MYFILE.TXT
```

EXTRACT *FILENAME.CAB FILE1.EXT* /D

The Extract command extracts files from a cabinet file such as the Ebd.cab file on the Windows 98 startup disk. To list the files contained in the cabinet file, use this command:

```
EXTRACT EBD.CAB /D
```

To extract the file Debug.exe from the Ebd.cab file, use this command:

```
EXTRACT EBD.CAB DEBUG.EXE
```

To extract all files from the Ebd.cab cabinet file, use this command:

```
EXTRACT EBD.CAB *.*
```

This command is available under Windows 9x/Me. For Windows 2000/XP, use the Expand command, which is available under the Recovery Console.

EDIT *[PATH][FILENAME]*

The Edit program (Edit.com) is a handy, "quick and dirty" way to edit text files while working at a command prompt. To edit the Autoexec.bat file on a floppy disk, use this command:

```
EDIT A:\AUTOEXEC.BAT
```

If the file does not already exist, Edit creates an empty file. Later, when you exit the Edit editor, changes you made are saved to the newly created file.

If you opened the Autoexec.bat file on the Windows 98 startup disk, your screen should be similar to the one shown in Figure 6-10. (Know that the Autoexec.bat file located on the hard drive will not have much in it because Windows 9x/Me on the hard drive doesn't use it except to support legacy applications and devices.) After you have made changes in this window, you can exit the editor this way: Press the **Alt** key to activate the menus, select the **File** menu, and then choose **Exit**. When asked if you want to save your changes, respond **Yes** to exit the editor and save changes.

If you make a mistake when editing Autoexec.bat or Config.sys, you can cause a boot problem. Before editing these files on your hard drive, always make a rescue disk. If you are editing one of these files on a rescue disk, you can make a backup copy of the file before you edit it or have a second rescue disk ready just in case.

Do not use word-processing software, such as Word or WordPerfect, to edit Autoexec.bat or Config.sys, unless you save the file as a text (ASCII) file. Word-processing applications place control characters in their document files that prevent the OS from interpreting the file correctly.

> **Notes**
>
> When working from a command prompt, you can reboot your computer (Ctrl+Alt+Del) to execute the new Autoexec.bat file, or you can type Autoexec.bat at the command prompt. If the computer stalls during the boot, use another startup disk to reboot. You can also press the F5 key to bypass the startup files during the boot.

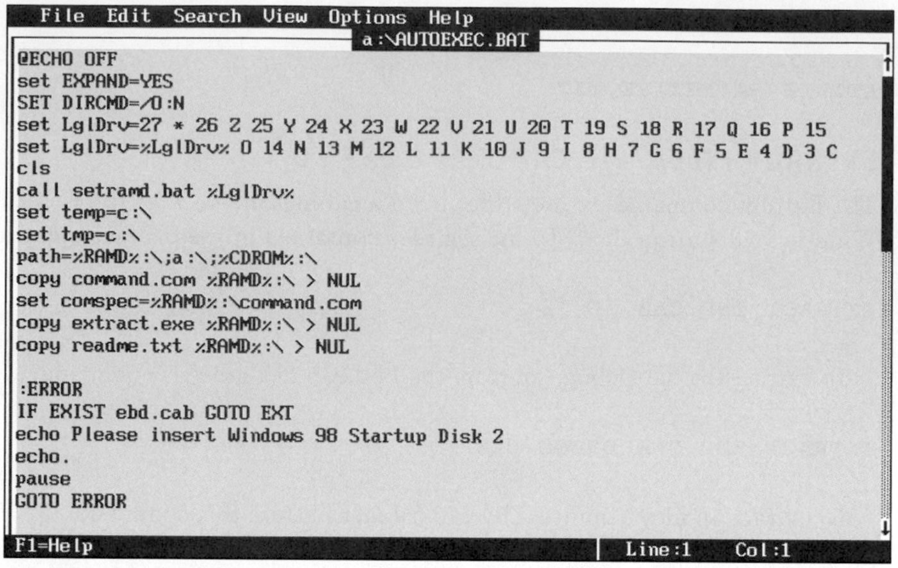

```
 File  Edit  Search  View  Options  Help
                    a:\AUTOEXEC.BAT
@ECHO OFF
set EXPAND=YES
SET DIRCMD=/O:N
set LglDrv=27 * 26 Z 25 Y 24 X 23 W 22 V 21 U 20 T 19 S 18 R 17 Q 16 P 15
set LglDrv=%LglDrv% O 14 N 13 M 12 L 11 K 10 J 9 I 8 H 7 G 6 F 5 E 4 D 3 C
cls
call setramd.bat %LglDrv%
set temp=c:\
set tmp=c:\
path=%RAMD%:\;a:\;%CDROM%:\
copy command.com %RAMD%:\ > NUL
set comspec=%RAMD%:\command.com
copy extract.exe %RAMD%:\ > NUL
copy readme.txt %RAMD%:\ > NUL

 :ERROR
IF EXIST ebd.cab GOTO EXT
echo Please insert Windows 98 Startup Disk 2
echo.
pause
GOTO ERROR

 F1=Help                                    Line:1     Col:1
```

Figure 6-10   Using the Edit editor to make changes to Autoexec.bat

COMMANDS TO MANAGE HARD DRIVES AND DISKS

Next, we'll look at some commands used to manage the hard drive and floppy disks. Using the following commands, you can prepare a drive or disk for first use, optimize a drive or disk, repair a damaged file system, and view and edit file system entities.

CHKDSK [DRIVE:] /F /R

Using MS-DOS and Windows 9x/Me, the Chkdsk command fixes file system errors, and the Scandisk command discussed next corrects problems with bad sectors on a drive. Using Windows 2000/XP, both these functions are combined in the one command, Chkdsk; therefore, Windows 2000/XP does not have a Scandisk command.

For all these OSs, used without any parameters, the Chkdsk command reports information about a drive. Use the /F parameter to have Chkdsk fix file system errors it finds, including errors in the FAT or MFT caused by clusters marked as being used but not belonging to a particular file (called lost allocation units) and clusters marked in the FAT or MFT as belonging to more than one file (called cross-linked clusters). To check the hard drive for these types of errors and repair them, use this command:

CHKDSK C: /F

To redirect a report of the findings of the Chkdsk command to a file that you can later print, use this command:

CHKDSK C: >Myfile.txt

If it finds bad sectors, it attempts to recover the data. The Chkdsk command will not fix anything unless the drive is locked, which means there can be no hard drive activity at the time. Therefore, run Chkdsk with the /F parameters when the drive is not in use.

SCANDISK DRIVE: /A /P

The Scandisk command scans a hard drive for errors and repairs them if possible. Scandisk checks the FAT, long filenames, lost and cross-linked clusters, directory tree structure, bad sectors, and compressed structure, if the drive has been compressed using DriveSpace or

6

DoubleSpace (these are drive compression utilities). The /A parameter is used to scan all non-removable local drives. Use this command only to display information without fixing the drive:

`SCANDISK C: /P`

Use this command to display information and fix errors:

`SCANDISK C:`

DEFRAG *DRIVE*: /S

The Defrag command examines a hard drive or disk for fragmented files (files written to a disk in noncontiguous clusters) and rewrites these files to the disk or drive in contiguous clusters. Use this command to optimize a hard drive's performance.

 Notes

In effect, Scandisk C: in Windows 9x/Me is equivalent to Chkdsk C: /R in Windows 2000/XP with one exception. Scandisk can check each sector and, if it finds a sector is not readable, it can mark the sector as bad in the FAT so it won't be used again. Windows 2000/XP Chkdsk only attempts to recover the data from a bad sector but doesn't mark new sectors as bad. Know that neither Scandisk or Chkdsk can actually fix a bad sector.

Use the /S:N parameter to sort the files on the disk in alphabetical order by filename.

`DEFRAG C: /S:N`

Use the /S:D parameter to sort the files on the disk by date and time.

`DEFRAG C: /S:D`

FDISK /STATUS /MBR

The Fdisk command is used to prepare a hard drive for first use. It creates partitions and logical drives on the hard drive, displays partition information, and restores a damaged Master Boot Record. Table 6-4 shows parameters for this command.

Fdisk Command Parameter	Description
FDISK /MBR	Repairs a damaged MBR program stored at the beginning of the hard drive just before the partition table
FDISK /Status	Displays partition information for all hard drives in the system

Table 6-4 Examples of the Fdisk command

Fdisk works under Windows 9x/Me and is useful when booting from a Windows 9x/Me startup disk to examine the partition table on a malfunctioning hard drive, or to prepare a hard drive for first use. You will learn more about the Fdisk command later in this chapter.

FORMAT *DRIVE*: /S /V: *VOLUMENAME* /Q /U /AUTOTEST

Recall that the Format command is used to format a disk or a hard drive. For a hard drive using Windows 9x/Me, first run Fdisk to partition the drive and create each logical drive. Then use Format to format each logical drive. Table 6-5 shows parameters for this command.

Format Command Parameter	Description
/V	Allows you to enter a volume label only once when formatting several disks. The same volume label is used for all disks. A volume label appears at the top of the directory list to help you identify the disk.
/S	Stores the system files on the disk after formatting. Writes the two hidden files and Command.com to the disk, making the disk bootable. Not available under Windows 2000/XP or Windows Me.
/Q	Re-creates the root directory and FATs if you want to quickly format a previously formatted disk that is in good condition. /Q does not read or write to any other part of the disk.

Table 6-5   Parameters for the Format command

UNFORMAT

The Unformat command might be able to reverse the effect of an accidental format. To unformat a disk, use this command:

`UNFORMAT C:`

DEBUG

The Debug program is an editor with few boundaries. Whereas a text editor such as Notepad or WordPad can only edit the contents of a text file, Debug can do so much more. It can view and manipulate the components of a file system on floppy disks and hard drives, including the FAT, directories, boot records, and any other area of the drive or disk. You can also use Debug to view the contents of memory and hexadecimal memory addresses. In fact, its ability to step into any area of a drive, disk, or memory makes it an extremely dangerous tool. To access Debug, enter the command Debug at the command prompt. For an example of using Debug to view contents of memory, see the online content section, "Behind the Scenes with DEBUG."

COMMANDS TO MANAGE THE OPERATING SYSTEM

Commands that can help you diagnose OS problems and/or repair them include Sys, Scanreg, Ver, and MSD, all discussed next.

SYS *DRIVE*:

Using Windows 9x/Me, the Sys command copies the Windows 9x/Me system files needed to boot to a disk or hard drive. (The Sys command is not used with Windows 2000/XP.) Use the command if the system files on a drive are corrupt—you can access the drive, but you cannot boot from it. The command to copy system files to the hard drive is:

`SYS C:`

SCANREG /RESTORE /FIX /BACKUP

The Scanreg command restores or repairs the Windows 98/Me registry. (Scanreg is not available under Windows 2000/XP.) Scanreg uses backups of the registry that Windows 98/Me

Registry Checker automatically makes each day. To restore the registry from a previous backup, use this command:

`SCANREG /RESTORE`

A menu appears asking you which backup to use.

To repair a corrupted registry, use this command:

`SCANREG /FIX`

To create a new backup of the registry, use this command:

`SCANREG /BACKUP`

Don't use this last command if you are having problems with the registry because you might overwrite a good backup of the registry with a corrupted one.

VER

Use the Ver command to display the version of the operating system in use.

MICROSOFT DIAGNOSTIC UTILITY (MSD)

DOS and Windows 9x/Me offered the Microsoft Diagnostic Utility (MSD), a utility useful for viewing information about the system, including information about memory, video, ports, device drivers, and system resources.

To load MSD using Windows 9x/Me, click **Start**, click **Run**, enter **MSD.EXE** in the Run dialog box, and then click **OK**. The MSD window appears (see Figure 6-11). Because MSD is a DOS-based 16-bit utility program, it does not always get the full picture of the Windows environment, so beware. Sometimes information on the MSD screen conflicts with information given by Device Manager or System Information. Its most actuate results are given when you execute it from a command prompt provided by the Windows 9x/Me startup disk, which you'll learn to use later in the chapter. You will practice using MSD in a project at the end of this chapter.

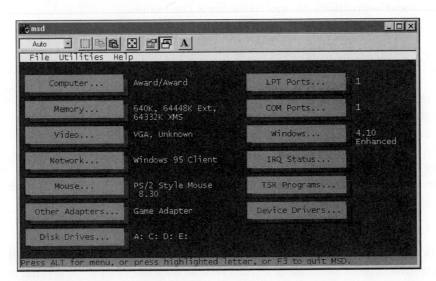

Figure 6-11   MSD opening screen

USING BATCH FILES

Recall from earlier in the chapter that Autoexec.bat is a batch file. Batch files can be used in many other ways than just helping with the boot. Suppose, for example, you have a list of OS commands that you want to execute several times. Perhaps you have some data files to distribute to several PCs in your office, but your network is down, so you must walk from one PC to another, repeatedly doing the same job. This kind of task can get real old, real quick. Fortunately, to make life easier, you can store the list of commands in a batch file on disk, and then execute the batch file at each PC. This will save you time and reduce errors.

When using batch files, create the batch file as a text file and give it a .bat file extension. For example, you can store these five OS commands on a disk in a file named MYLOAD.BAT:

```
C:

MD\UTILITY

MD\UTILITY\TOOLS

CD\UTILITY\TOOLS

COPY A:\TOOLS\*.*
```

In the batch file, the first command makes drive C the default drive. Then a new directory and subdirectory on drive C are created. Next, you make the new \Tools directory the default directory and copy files from the floppy disk to it.

From the command prompt, you execute the batch file just as you do other program files, by entering the filename, with or without the file extension:

```
A:\>MYLOAD
```

All commands listed in the file will execute, beginning at the top of the list. Any good book on DOS or DOS Web site provide examples of the very useful ways you can implement batch files, including adding user menus. One excellent site with tons of information about MS-DOS and batch files is by Computer Hope at *www.computerhope.com/msdos.htm*. Also, the Windows XP Help and Support Center has a list of commands you can use in batch files and instructions on how to use these commands.

USING THE WINDOWS 9X/ME STARTUP DISK

A floppy disk with enough software to load an operating system is called a bootable disk, or system disk. A bootable disk with some utility programs to troubleshoot a failed hard drive is called a rescue disk, emergency startup disk (ESD), or startup disk. Having a rescue disk available for an emergency is very important, and a PC technician should always have one or more on hand. In this section, you'll learn to create a Windows 9x/Me startup disk and use it to prepare a hard drive or disk for first use and to troubleshoot a failed boot.

CREATING A WINDOWS 9X/ME STARTUP DISK

A Windows 9x/Me startup disk has everything you need to prepare a new hard drive for use and to troubleshoot a failed hard drive. The disk does not need to be created on the same computer that will use it, although in most cases you should use the same version of

6

Windows as used by the computer that will be using the disk. Follow these instructions to create a startup disk for Windows 9x/Me:

1. Click **Start** on the taskbar, point to **Settings**, and then click **Control Panel**.

2. In the Control Panel window, double-click the **Add/Remove Programs** icon.

3. Click the **Startup Disk** tab, and then click the **Create Disk** button (see Figure 6-12).

4. Windows might need the Windows CD to create the disk. Insert the CD if it is requested. Windows then creates the startup disk.

5. Write protect the disk so that later when you use it, an infected system cannot put a virus on the disk. Label the disk and keep it in a safe place.

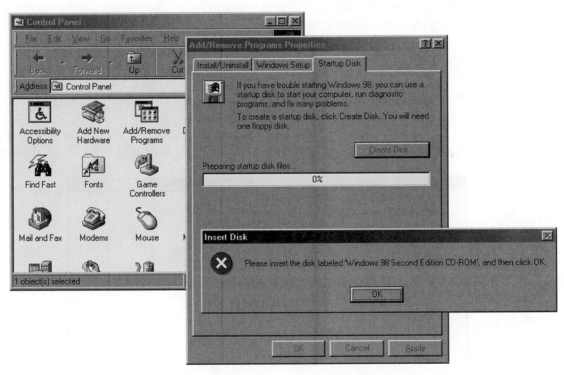

Figure 6-12 Windows might use the Windows CD to create a startup disk

Windows places many utility programs on the disk that you will learn to use in the next sections. Because there is so much content on the disk, Windows compresses the program files and then stores them all in one large file. This large file is called a **cabinet file**, and is named Ebd.cab. During startup, a RAM drive is created and the contents of the cabinet file are uncompressed and copied to the RAM drive. This RAM drive is necessary because there is not enough space for the cabinet file on the floppy disk, and the startup disk assumes the hard drive might not be accessible. You can also use the Extract command to extract specific files when the RAM drive is not active.

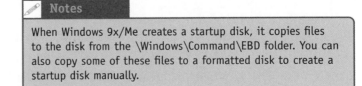

Notes

When Windows 9x/Me creates a startup disk, it copies files to the disk from the \Windows\Command\EBD folder. You can also copy some of these files to a formatted disk to create a startup disk manually.

APPLYING|CONCEPTS   Using Windows 9x/Me, create a startup disk and boot from the disk. What messages and questions do you see on the screen when you boot from the disk? If you have access to a Windows 2000 or Windows XP computer, boot it using the Windows 9x/Me startup disk. What messages or questions do you see? Are there any differences?

USING A STARTUP DISK TO PARTITION AND FORMAT A NEW DRIVE

If you have just installed a new hard drive and you are not ready to install an OS, you can use a Windows 9x/Me startup disk to partition and format the drive. As a hardware technician, you are often called on to install a hard drive and verify that it's in good working order, although you are not expected to install an OS. By partitioning and formatting the drive and then using Scandisk to check each sector, you know all is well. This method also works when you are installing a second hard drive in a system, and this second drive will not hold the OS.

USE FDISK TO PARTITION A DRIVE

To use Fdisk to partition the drive, do the following:

1. Boot from a startup disk that has the Fdisk.exe utility on it and enter **Fdisk** at the command prompt. The Fdisk opening menu shown in Figure 6-13 appears.

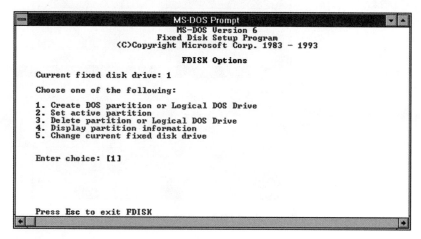

Figure 6-13   Fixed disk setup program (Fdisk) menu

2. Select option **1** to create the first partition. The menu in Figure 6-14 appears.

3. Use option 1 to create the primary DOS partition. If you plan to install Windows 9x, be sure this partition is at least 150 MB, preferably more. Make this first partition the active partition, which is the partition used to boot the OS. Fdisk automatically makes this partition drive C.

4. Next, use either option 1 or 2 to create other DOS partitions using the remainder of the hard drive. If you created an extended partition, use option 3 to create logical drives in the extended partition.

5. When you create logical drives using Fdisk, you need to decide how large you want each drive to be. If you have at least 512 MB available for the drive, a message appears asking, "Do you wish to enable large disk support (Y/N)?" If you respond **Y**, then Fdisk assigns the FAT32 file system to the drive. Otherwise, it uses FAT16.

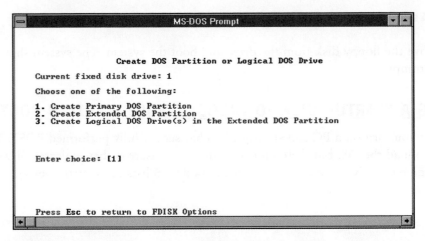

Figure 6-14 Fdisk menu to create partitions and logical drives

6. When Fdisk is completed, the hard drive has a partition table, an active partition, perhaps other partitions, and logical drives within these partitions, as shown in Figure 6-15.

7. Exit the Fdisk window and reboot the PC before you format the logical drives.

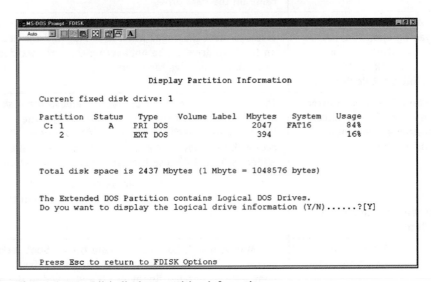

Figure 6-15 Fdisk displays partition information

FORMAT EACH LOGICAL DRIVE

Now that the hard drive is partitioned and logical drives are created and assigned drive letters, the next step is to format each logical drive. The three commands used to format logical drives C, D, and E are as follows:

```
Format C:/S

Format D:

Format E:
```

In the Format command line, the /S option makes the drive bootable, and the drive letter tells the OS which drive to format. Then, as a last step to verify the drive is in good working order, use Scandisk to check the drive for bad sectors, as shown below.

```
Scandisk C:
```

Remove the floppy disk from the drive and boot the system. The system should boot to the C prompt.

USING A STARTUP DISK TO TROUBLESHOOT A FAILED BOOT

Suppose you turn on a PC and startup BIOS has successfully performed POST. The next step is to load the OS, but there's an error message onscreen that indicates BIOS cannot access the hard drive or find an OS to load. Table 6-6 lists some error messages that might appear in this situation.

Error Message	Meaning of the Error Message
Invalid drive specification	The BIOS is unable to find a hard drive or a floppy drive that setup tells it to expect. Look for errors in CMOS setup, or use Fdisk to examine the partition table on the hard drive.
No boot device available	The hard drive is not formatted, or the format is corrupted, and there is no disk in drive A. Use Fdisk to examine the partition table on the hard drive.
Invalid partition table Error loading operating system Missing operating system Invalid boot disk Inaccessible boot device	The Master Boot program at the beginning of the hard drive displays these messages when it cannot find the active partition on the hard drive or the boot record on that partition. Use Fdisk to examine the drive for errors.
Non-system disk or disk error Bad or missing Command.com No operating system found Can't find NTLDR	The disk in drive A is not bootable. Remove the disk in drive A and boot from the hard drive. If you still get the error, use Fdisk to examine the partition table on the hard drive. If you can access drive C, look for missing system files on the drive. For Windows 9x or DOS, use the Sys command to restore system files.
Not ready reading drive A: Abort, Retry, Fail? General failure reading drive A: Abort, Retry, Fail?	The disk in drive A is missing, is not formatted, or is corrupted. Try another disk or remove the disk to boot from the hard drive.
Missing operating system Error loading operating system	The MBR is unable to locate or read the OS boot sector on the active partition, or there is a translation problem on large drives. Boot from a bootable floppy or CD and examine the hard drive file system for corruption.
Error in Config.sys line xx	In a Windows 9x/Me environment, an entry in Config.sys is incorrect or is referencing a 16-bit program that is missing or corrupted.

Table 6-6   Error messages that appear after the PC has passed POST and before an OS has successfully loaded

> **Notes**
>
> In this chapter, we're assuming you are using Windows 9x/Me. When troubleshooting a failed boot in a Windows 2000/XP environment, you can use the Recovery Console on the Windows 2000/XP setup CD instead of the Windows 9x/Me startup disk. In the Recovery Console, rather than Fdisk, use the Diskpart command to examine the partition table on the hard drive.

In isolating the root cause of these problems, the first question to ask is "Can I boot from another device other than the hard drive?" If so, then you have proven that all essential subsystems except the hard drive subsystem are

6

functioning. In effect, you have isolated the problem to the hard drive. At this point, ask the question, "Can I use commands on the startup disk to read the hard drive?"

Here are commands to try and things to do:

1. Place a Windows 9x/Me startup disk in the floppy drive. Turn off the PC and reboot.

2. When given the opportunity, enter CMOS setup and verify the boot sequence is first drive A and then drive C. Save any changes you made to CMOS and allow the boot to continue. (How to access CMOS setup is covered in a project at the end of this chapter.)

3. The OS loads from the startup disk and a startup menu appears (see Figure 6-16).

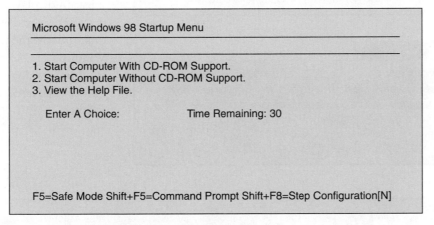

Figure 6-16   Windows 98 rescue disk startup menu

4. Select the **Start Computer With CD-ROM Support** option. The OS then examines the system for problems. For a hard drive formatted with the NTFS file system, a message is displayed: "Windows 98 has detected that drive C does not contain a valid FAT or FAT32 partition." It then provides an A prompt where you can enter commands.

5. For a Windows 9x/Me system, type **DIR C:** at the A prompt and then press **Enter**. If this step displays a list of files and folders on the hard drive, then the partition table and file system on the drive are intact. You then know that the problem has to do with the OS boot record, OS hidden files, and command interface files. Try this command to restore these files: **SYS C:**.

6. To examine the partition tables of all installed hard drives, type **Fdisk /status** at the A prompt and press **Enter**. Figure 6-17 shows the results for a system that has two hard drives installed.

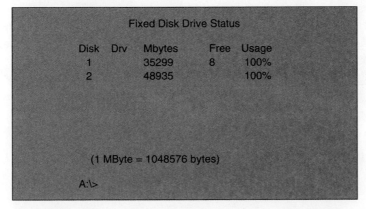

Figure 6-17   Results of the Fdisk /status command for a system with one 36 GB hard drive and one 49 GB drive

7. If the partition table is corrupted an error message is displayed. Type the command **Fdisk /MBR** at the A prompt and press **Enter**. If the MBR program on the master boot record is corrupted, this will solve the problem.

 Notes

At any time after you have booted from the startup disk, at the A prompt, type **C:** and press **Enter** to get a C prompt. If you successfully get a C prompt, then you can try to load the Windows desktop. To do that, at the C prompt, type **C:\Windows\win** and press **Enter**, which executes Win.com on the hard drive. Win.com and the supporting files needed to load the Windows desktop take up too much room to be stored on a floppy disk, so the only way this last command will work is if the hard drive is accessible and healthy.

Notes

You have just seen how you can use a Windows 98 startup disk to examine the partition table on a Windows 2000/XP system, proving that the boot problem is a Windows problem, and not a hardware problem. However, know that when attempting to solve a Windows problem, always use the disks, CDs, and recovery tools native to the installed OS.

If you still cannot use Fdisk to display the partition information, the problem is with the partition table, the hard drive, its cabling, or its power source. If you have successfully used Fdisk to display partition information on the drive, then it's time to treat the problem as a Windows problem. How to troubleshoot loading Windows 9x/Me is covered in the next chapter.

APPLYING | CONCEPTS

Many PC technicians use a Windows 9x/Me startup disk when troubleshooting Windows 2000/XP computers, because the Windows 9x/Me startup disk has a useful set of tools and resources that are not as easily available under Windows 2000/XP. Here are three situations in which you might choose to use a Windows 9x/Me startup disk:

- You are helping someone solve a problem with their Windows 2000/XP system, which refuses to boot. You have your Windows 98 startup disk handy, so you boot from it and get to an A prompt. In order to get to an A prompt successfully, many subsystems in the computer must be functioning, including the motherboard, processor, memory, floppy disk drive, power supply, and video system. In fact, you have just proven that the problem is isolated to the hard drive.
- A Windows XP computer comes to you for repair with a failed hard drive. You install a new hard drive, but you do not have the Windows XP setup CD to install Windows XP on the drive. In this situation, you can use a Windows 9x/Me startup disk to boot the system and create a partition table on the drive. This assures you that the drive is functioning properly even without installing an OS.
- Your Windows 2000 system will not boot, and your term paper is stored on the hard drive! If the hard drive is using the FAT file system, you might be able to use the Windows 98 startup disk to recover the file.

>> *CHAPTER SUMMARY*

▲ During the boot, the ROM BIOS startup program searches secondary storage for an OS.

▲ When the OS loads from a hard drive, the BIOS first executes the Master Boot Record (MBR) program, which turns to the partition table to find the OS boot record. The program in the OS boot record attempts to find a boot loader program for the OS, which for Windows 9x/Me, is the program Io.sys.

▲ Io.sys, which uses Msdos.sys, and Command.com, form the core of real-mode Windows 9x/Me. These three files are necessary to boot to a command prompt. Config.sys and Autoexec.bat are not required but are used if they are present. Other files are needed to load the GUI desktop and run GUI applications.

▲ Autoexec.bat and Config.sys are two files that contain commands used to customize the 16-bit portion of the Windows 9x/Me load process.

▲ A RAM drive is an area of memory that looks and acts like a hard drive, only it performs much faster. The Windows 9x/Me startup disk uses a RAM drive to hold program files, assuming the hard drive is not accessible.

▲ Typical commands in the Autoexec.bat file include Path, Set, Restart, Temp, and Echo.

▲ Windows 9x/Me uses Command.com to provide a command prompt window.

▲ DOS and Windows 9x/Me divide memory addresses into conventional (0 to 640K), upper (640K to 1024K), and extended memory (above 1024K).

▲ Conventional memory is used to hold the OS, applications, and data. Upper memory holds BIOS and device drivers. Extended memory can be used only by applications, the OS, and device drivers, if Himem.sys and Emm386.exe are managing it.

▲ The Del or Erase command deletes files or groups of files.

▲ The Copy command copies a single file or group of files. More powerful than the Copy command, the Xcopy command supports copying subdirectories.

▲ Mkdir creates a subdirectory, Chdir changes the current directory, and Rmdir removes a subdirectory.

▲ The Attrib command displays or changes the read-only, archive, system, and hidden attributes assigned to files.

▲ The Fdisk command is used to partition a hard drive and display partition information.

▲ The Format command is used to format floppy disks and logical drives. The /S parameter with the Format command makes a drive bootable. The Unformat command attempts to reverse the effect of an accidental format.

▲ Chkdsk and Scandisk both check drives for errors and repair them. Scandisk does a more thorough scan for Windows 9x/Me and basically replaces Chkdsk.

▲ The Defrag command rewrites files on a hard drive in contiguous clusters to improve hard drive performance.

▲ The Sys command copies the system files needed to boot to a disk or drive.

▲ The Scanreg command restores or repairs the Windows 98/Me registry.

▲ Batch files can be used to execute a group of commands using only a single command.

◢ A floppy disk with enough software to load an operating system is called a bootable disk, or system disk. A bootable disk with some utility programs to troubleshoot a failed hard drive is called a rescue disk, emergency startup disk (ESD), or startup disk.

◢ Create a startup disk in Windows 9x/Me using the Add/Remove Programs applet in the Control Panel.

>> KEY TERMS

For explanations of key terms, see the Glossary near the end of the book.

Autoexec.bat	extended memory	rescue disk
batch file	external commands	startup disk
bootable disk	fragmented files	system disk
CD (change directory) command	hidden file	terminate-and-stay-resident
conventional memory	high memory area (HMA)	(TSR)
DOS box	Himem.sys	upper memory
emergency startup disk (ESD)	internal commands	upper memory block (UMB)
Emm386.exe	RAM drive	wildcard

>> REVIEWING THE BASICS

1. What three OS files are necessary to boot to MS-DOS mode? What is the function of each? What additional two files are not required but are used if they are present?

2. Why is it important not to edit Autoexec.bat with word-processing software such as Microsoft Word or WordPerfect?

3. What is the purpose of the command Device = himem.sys in the Config.sys file?

4. Give two ways to access a command prompt from Windows 95/98.

5. What Windows 9x/Me program file provides a Command Prompt window?

6. What are the two wildcard characters that can be used in command lines?

7. What is the /S switch used for with the Format command? The /V switch?

8. What is the name of the single directory created when a floppy disk or logical drive is first formatted?

9. What command is used to partition a hard drive?

10. The _____ command erases files or groups of files.

11. What command is used to create a subdirectory? To change the current directory? To remove a subdirectory?

12. The _____ command displays or changes the read-only, archive, system, and hidden characteristics of files.

13. What is a hidden file? Name a Windows 9x/Me file that is hidden.

14. What is the command to copy Myfile.dat from the root directory of drive A to the \Data folder on drive C?

15. What is the command to delete all files in the A:\data folder that begin with the letter A and have the .txt file extension?

16. What is the command to make the file Myfile.txt a hidden system file?

6

17. What is the command to copy all data and subfolders from the A:\data folder to the C:\data folder?

18. What is the purpose of the Ebd.cab file on the Windows 98 startup disk?

19. What applet in the Windows 98 Control Panel is used to create a startup disk?

20. List the steps to add a shortcut to your Windows desktop to access a command prompt window.

21. At a command prompt, how must you type long filenames that contain spaces?

22. When using a real-mode command prompt, how will DOS display the filename Mydocument.doc?

23. What is the batch file used by Windows 98 to control the boot process?

24. What command used on a startup disk can you use to demonstrate the master boot record is healthy but which does not validate the file system on the drive?

25. If you suspect Io.sys or Msdos.sys is missing on the hard drive, what command can you use to refresh these files?

>> **THINKING CRITICALLY**

1. If a PC boots first to the hard drive before checking the floppy disk for an OS, how do you change this boot sequence so that it first looks on the floppy disk for an OS?

2. A PC continues to reboot. You try to solve the problem by booting from a Windows 98 startup disk. You boot to the A prompt and look on the hard drive. You discover an unwanted command in the Autoexec.bat file on the hard drive. Explain the source of the problem and describe how to fix it.

3. Explain the difference between the Copy command and the Xcopy command.

4. Explain the difference between the Chkdsk and Scandisk commands.

5. You need to make 10 duplicates of one floppy disk. Describe how to do this using two different methods. Which method is better and why?

>> **HANDS-ON PROJECTS**

PROJECT 6-1:   Practicing Commands

Go to a command prompt and do the following. Write down the commands you use to accomplish each step:

1. Create a folder on your hard drive named /testme.

2. Make that folder the current folder.

3. Select a file in the Program Files folder on your hard drive. What is the name of the file? What is its size in bytes?

4. Copy the file to the /testme folder.

5. Format a floppy disk, making it bootable.

6. Display on the screen the amount of free bytes on the floppy disk. How many bytes are free?

7. Copy the file from the /testme folder to the floppy disk.

8. Make the floppy disk the current drive. What prompt do you now see?

9. Make the file on the floppy disk a hidden file.

10. Display on the screen the amount of free bytes on the floppy disk. How many bytes are free? Calculate how many bytes were used on the floppy disk to hold the file.

11. Unhide the hidden file on the floppy disk.

12. Rename the file **myfile.xxx**. What message appears when you rename the file?

13. Display a list of all files on the floppy disk that begin with the letter M.

PROJECT 6-2   Using Microsoft Diagnostics with Windows 9x/Me

DOS and Windows offer the Microsoft Diagnostics utility. This utility examines your system, displaying useful information about ports, devices, memory, and the like. You can find the MSD.EXE utility in the \TOOLS\OLDMSDOS directory on your Windows 9x/Me installation CD.

1. Using Windows Explorer, copy the utility to your hard drive and store it in a folder named \Tools.

2. Boot your PC to an MS-DOS prompt in real mode. To boot into real mode, press **Ctrl** or **F8** as you start the system. The Windows Startup menu appears. Select **Command prompt only**. From the DOS prompt, execute this command: **C:\TOOLS\MSD**. The MSD window appears (shown earlier in Figure 6-11).

3. Browse carefully through all menu options of this utility and answer the following questions about your system:

    a. List the following information or print the appropriate MSD screen that contains it: manufacturer; version number; and date of your system BIOS, video BIOS, and mouse device driver.

    b. What kind of video card is installed?

    c. How much memory is currently installed on this PC?

    d. What version of the OS is the PC running?

    e. What CPU is the PC using?

4. Exit MSD. Save the information you noted to compare with the information that you will obtain from MSD in Windows 2000/XP.

You need Windows 2000 or Windows XP installed on a PC to do the rest of this project:

1. Copy the **MSD.exe** program to a folder on your Windows 2000/XP PC named \Tools.

2. From within Windows 2000/XP, open a command prompt. (Click **Start**, **Programs** (**All Programs** for Windows XP), **Accessories**, and **Command Prompt**.)

3. From the command prompt, start MSD using this command: **C:\Tools\MSD**.

4. Browse through all menu options and answer the same questions about your system as you did for Windows 9x/Me. Record any errors you get.

PROJECT 6-3: Creating a Startup Disk Using Windows 9x/Me

Using directions in the chapter, create a startup disk in Windows 9x/Me, and then test it by rebooting the computer with the disk still in the drive. Answer these questions using the Readme.txt file on the startup disk:

1. What command line is recommended to check your hard drive for errors?

2. At what point in the boot process is the RAM drive created?

3. If you reboot your PC after booting from the startup disk, will the RAM drive remain in memory?

A system disk is bootable but has no troubleshooting programs on it. Using a second disk, create a system disk using Windows Explorer. Compare the contents of the two disks. (*Hint*: To create a system disk, insert a blank disk in the floppy drive, and, in Explorer, right-click drive A and select Format from the shortcut menu.)

PROJECT 6-4: Changing the Boot Sequence and Using the Windows 9x/Me Startup Disk

Recall that BIOS looks to CMOS RAM settings to find out which secondary storage device should have the OS. You can change the boot sequence on your PC by using CMOS setup unless another technician responsible for the system has password protected it. Do the following:

1. Shut down your PC. Turn it back on and look for keystrokes to enter CMOS setup displayed somewhere on the screen during startup in a statement such as "Press the Del key to enter setup" or "Press F8 for setup."

2. Browse through the CMOS setup menus looking for the option to change the boot sequence. If necessary, change the boot sequence so that the BIOS looks to the floppy drive before it looks to the hard drive for an OS.

3. Exit CMOS setup, saving your changes, and continue to the Windows desktop.

4. Shut down the system, insert your Windows 9x/Me startup disk in the floppy drive, and turn on the PC.

5. Use the Ver command at the command prompt. What OS and version are you using?

6. Use the Fdisk /status command. How many and what size partitions are on the hard drive?

PROJECT 6-5: Long Filenames at a Command Prompt

Recall that DOS does not recognize long filenames, including the DOS used on the Windows 9x/Me startup disk. Suppose your hard drive has failed and you boot your PC using a Windows 98 startup disk. You get to the C prompt and go to the directory containing your term paper: C:\Data\My Term Paper.doc. How will the filename appear on your screen? Find out by using Windows Explorer to create the folder and file on your hard drive. Then boot from a Windows 98 startup disk and use the CD and DIR commands to display the filename.

PROJECT 6-6:   Challenge Project

Using Windows 9x/Me, create your own bootable disk that loads the 16-bit real-mode drivers to use a mouse. Test the mouse by booting from the disk and using the mouse with the EDIT text editor.

(*Hint*: First locate a 16-bit mouse driver file such as Mouse.sys. Load the driver file using a Device= command in Config.sys.)

>> REAL PROBLEMS, REAL SOLUTIONS

REAL PROBLEM 6-1:   Using Batch Files

Your friend, Dennis, has asked for your help writing a batch file. He keeps a Word document on his Windows XP desktop named MyList.doc, which is a list of things to do. He wants another icon on the desktop that represents a batch file with a single command in the file. The purpose of the batch file is to put a copy of his to-do list document in this location: C:\data\mylist.doc. Do the following:

1. On your desktop, create a Word document file named **MyList.doc**. What is the path to this file?

2. Create a folder named **C:\Data**.

3. Use Notepad to create a batch file with a single Copy command, and store the batch file on your desktop.

4. After you have tested the batch file, print its contents. What is the path to your batch file?

Supporting Windows 9x/Me

As a PC support technician, you need to know how to install, use, and troubleshoot the Windows OSs commonly used today. Microsoft considers Windows 9x/Me a legacy OS and no longer supports it. However, it's a great learning tool to prepare you to understand the more sophisticated operating systems such as Windows XP and Windows Vista, and many individual and corporate users still use Windows 9x/Me. This chapter covers how Windows 9x/Me is structured, how it works with various software programs and hardware devices, and how to troubleshoot it.

WINDOWS 9X/ME ARCHITECTURE

Windows 9x/Me has had several releases, including Windows 95, Windows 95 Service Release 2 (also known as Windows 95 SR2, Windows 95 Rev B, Windows 95B, and

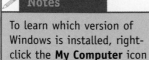

To learn which version of Windows is installed, right-click the **My Computer** icon and select **Properties** from the shortcut menu. The System Properties window opens. Click the **General** tab.

Windows 95 OSR2), Windows 98, Windows 98 Second Edition (SE), and Windows Me (Millennium Edition). Each of these OSs uses the same basic architecture, and each release improved on previous versions and added new features.

Like other OSs, Windows 9x/Me has a shell and a kernel. Recall from Chapter 1 that the shell is the component of the OS that relates to the user and to applications, and the kernel interacts with hardware. Because the kernel has more power to communicate with hardware devices than the shell, applications operating under the OS cannot get to hardware devices without the shell passing those requests to the kernel. This structure provides for a more stable system.

The two most important parts of the shell are the user component and the GDI. The **user component** manages input from the keyboard and other user devices, output from the user interface, and the **GDI (Graphics Device Interface)**. The GDI is a component of the OS responsible for presenting the graphical interface to the user and providing graphics support to output devices. Table 7-1 lists the purpose of each component.

Component Name	Main Files Holding the Component	Functions
Kernel	Kernel32.dll, Krnl386.exe	Handles the basic OS functions, such as managing memory, file I/O, and loading and executing programs
User	User32.dll, User.exe	Controls the mouse, keyboard, ports, and desktop, including the position of windows, icons, and dialog boxes
GDI	GDI32.dll, GDI.exe	Draws screens, graphics, and lines, and manages printing

Table 7-1   Core components of Windows 9x/Me

A BRIDGING OF TWO WORLDS

Windows 9x/Me is a compromise OS that bridges the world of 16-bit processing with the world of 32-bit processing. In Figure 7-1, you can see that DOS was a 16-bit OS, used only 16-bit device drivers, and managed base, upper, and extended memory. In contrast, Windows NT/2000/XP is a true 32-bit OS.

Windows 9x/Me is a mix of 16-bit processing and 32-bit processing. In bridging these two worlds, the core components of Windows 9x/Me (kernel, user, and GDI) are compiled as a combination of 16-bit and 32-bit code, and Windows 95/98 accepts both 16-bit and 32-bit drivers. (Windows Me accepts only 32-bit drivers.) In Chapter 6, you learned that it manages memory the same way that DOS does. In this chapter, you'll learn that it uses memory paging and virtual memory as does Windows NT/2000/XP.

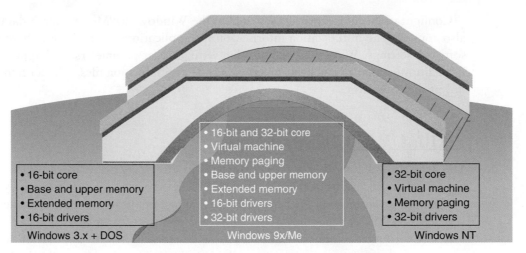

Figure 7-1 Windows 9x/Me is the bridge from DOS to Windows NT/2000/XP

The Windows 9x/Me core relates to users, software, and hardware by way of several components, as shown in Figure 7-2. The core components (user, GDI, and kernel) stand in the middle between interface tools for the user and applications and the four main components in the figure that manage hardware. These four hardware-related components are as follows:

▲ The **VMM (Virtual Machine Manager)** is responsible for managing memory, virtual machines, and all the resources needed by each application. Virtual machines are discussed later in the chapter.

▲ The **IFS (Installable File System)** manager takes care of all disk access.

▲ The **Configuration Manager** configures all legacy and Plug and Play devices and communicates these configurations to devices.

▲ The **WDM (Win32 Driver Model)** driver manager, first used with Windows 98, is responsible for managing device drivers.

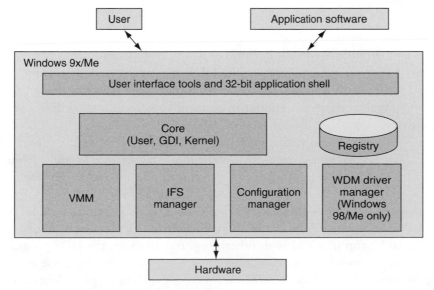

Figure 7-2 The Windows 9x/Me architecture as it relates to the user, software, and hardware

Configuration data is primarily stored in the Windows 9x/Me registry, a database that also contains the initialization information for applications, a database of hardware and software settings, Windows configuration settings, user parameters, and application settings. In addition, some data is kept in text files called initialization files, which often have an .ini or .inf file extension.

VIRTUAL MACHINES

You need to understand how the components in Figure 7-2 relate to applications and hardware. Applications call on the OS to access hardware or other software by using an **application programming interface (API) call**. When applications are first loaded by Windows 9x/Me, the methods to access hardware and software are made available to the software through an interface called a **virtual machine (VM)**. An application sees a virtual machine as a set of resources made available to it through these predefined APIs, as shown in Figure 7-3.

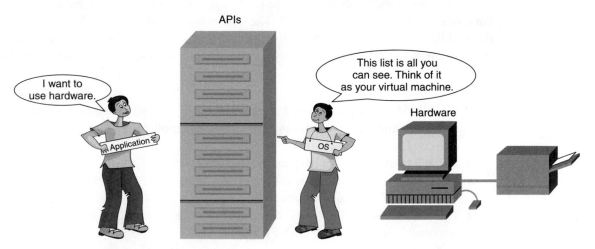

Figure 7-3 An application is not allowed direct access to hardware but is allowed access to a list of predefined APIs

An OS can provide a virtual machine to a single application that commands all the resources of that virtual machine, or the OS can assign a virtual machine to be shared by two or more applications. Think of virtual machines as multiple logical machines within one physical machine, similar in concept to several logical drives within one physical drive.

Figure 7-4 shows several virtual machines that Windows 9x/Me can provide. In the figure, the system virtual machine (system VM) is the most important VM under Windows 9x/Me, and is where all OS processes run. It can also support 32-bit and 16-bit Windows applications.

In contrast to Windows applications that expect to share resources, a DOS program expects to directly control the hardware of the entire PC, memory included. If a DOS program were to be run in a VM with other programs running, the DOS program might attempt to use memory addresses not assigned to it, which would cause errors in a multitasking environment. Windows 9x/Me solves this problem by providing each DOS program with its own virtual machine. In effect, the DOS program says, "I want all of the memory and all of this and all of that," and Windows 9x/Me says, "OK, here they are,"

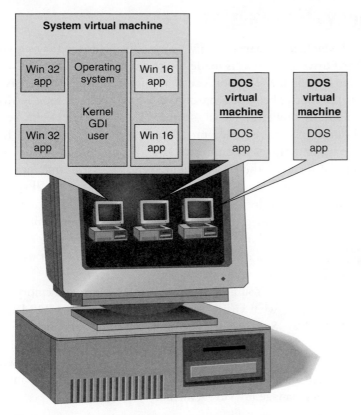

Figure 7-4 Windows 9x/Me uses the virtual machine concept

and gives the program its own virtual machine, including all the virtual memory addresses it wants from 0 to 4 GB as well as its own virtual hardware! As far as the DOS program is concerned, it can go anywhere and do anything within its own PC. The DOS program does not try to communicate with any other application or to access the data of another program, because it thinks there are no other programs; it controls its entire world, and is the only program in it. That's a virtual machine.

Windows 16-bit applications offer a slightly different challenge to Windows 9x/Me. These programs make some of the same mistakes that DOS programs do and can cause the system to hang. However, they also sometimes expect to access other programs and their data. Fortunately, the 16-bit Windows programs don't expect to control the hardware directly and are content to route their requests to Windows. Because they communicate with hardware through the OS, Windows 9x/Me places these programs within the system virtual machine. In addition, Windows 9x/Me puts these programs together in their own memory space so they can share memory addresses, which means they can also share data.

The result of all 16-bit programs sharing the same memory space also means that when a 16-bit Windows program causes an error called a Windows Protection Error or a **General Protection Fault**, the error can disturb other 16-bit programs, causing them to fail. However, this error does not disturb DOS programs in their own virtual machines or 32-bit programs that don't share their virtual memory addresses.

> **Notes**
>
> One important result of running DOS programs in individual virtual machines is that when a DOS program makes an error, the virtual machine it is using hangs, but other programs and the OS are isolated from the problem and, thus, in theory are not affected.

VIRTUAL MEMORY

The Windows Virtual Machine Manager (VMM) is responsible for managing virtual memory, which is hard drive space that is made to act like memory. The VMM stores virtual memory in a file called a swap file. The purpose of virtual memory is to increase the amount of memory available. Of course, because a hard drive is much slower than RAM, virtual memory works considerably slower than real memory. The VMM moves 4K segments, called **pages,** in and out of physical RAM, a process called **memory paging.** If RAM is full, the manager takes a page and moves it to the swap file.

If RAM is full much of the time, the VMM might spend excessive time moving pages in and out of RAM. That can cause excessive hard drive use, decrease overall system performance, and even cause the system to lock up or applications to fail. This situation, sometimes called **disk thrashing,** can cause premature hard drive failure. If you are experiencing very slow system response and observe the hard drive is in constant use, suspect excessive memory paging.

Notes

To avoid excessive memory paging, leave fewer applications open at the same time or install more RAM.

You have some control over virtual memory settings. To see what virtual memory settings Windows 9x/Me offers, click **Start,** point to **Settings,** click **Control Panel,** double-click **System,** and then select the **Performance** tab. Click **Virtual Memory** and the Virtual Memory dialog box shown in Figure 7-5 opens. These settings are used to tell Windows how to manage the swap file. Unless you have good reason to do otherwise, select the **Let Windows manage my virtual memory settings** option.

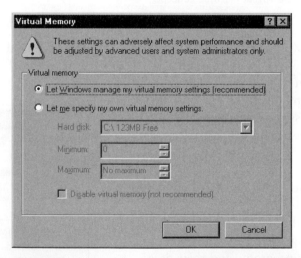

Figure 7-5   Options for managing virtual memory in Windows 9x/Me

One reason you might want to change a virtual memory setting is to make the file size permanent to prevent Windows from resizing the file, which can slow down performance. To improve performance, first defragment the hard drive so there is plenty of unfragmented space for the file. Then set the maximum and minimum file sizes to the same value, which forces the size not to change. If you have the available hard drive space, set the size to about 2.5 times the amount of RAM.

Notice in Figure 7-5 that you can specify the location of the swap file. The name of the swap file in Windows 9x/Me is **Win386.swp,** and its default location is C:\Windows. You can choose to put the swap file on a compressed drive, but Windows does not compress the swap file itself. You'll learn more about compressed drives later in the chapter.

INSTALLING WINDOWS 9X/ME, HARDWARE, AND SOFTWARE

In this section, you will learn how to install Windows 9x/Me and how to install hardware and applications with Windows 9x/Me. Because you can't purchase a new license for Windows 9x/Me, you'll never be called on to install Windows 9x/Me on a new computer. However, when a hard drive fails on an older computer, you'll need to install the OS on the replacement drive. Also, if an existing Windows 9x/Me installation gets corrupted, you might need to reinstall the OS.

INSTALLING WINDOWS 9X/ME

Before installing Windows 9x/Me, verify that your system meets requirements for the OS. Check the following:

▲ Verify that the minimum and recommended hardware requirements for Windows 9x/Me are met. Table 7-2 lists these requirements. For Windows 9x/Me to perform satisfactorily, the PC should meet the recommended requirements.

▲ Windows 95/98 claims that it supports legacy hardware devices, but Windows Me does not. To check whether a particular hardware product has been tested for use with Windows Me, go to *www.microsoft.com/whdc/hcl/default.mspx*.

▲ You also need to check software packages and programs for compatibility. You can do this by checking the documentation or the manufacturer's Web site for each program.

Description	Windows 95	Windows 98	Windows Me
Processor	486–25 MHz or higher	486DX–66 MHz (Pentium is recommended)	Pentium 150 MHz
RAM	4 MB (8 MB is recommended)	16 MB (24 MB is recommended)	32 MB
Free hard drive space	50 MB	195 MB (315 MB is recommended)	320 MB

Table 7-2 Minimum and recommended hardware requirements for Windows 9x/Me

Now let's turn our attention to the two types of Windows 9x/Me setup CDs and decisions you must make about the installation before you begin. Then we'll look at the details of installing the OS.

TWO TYPES OF SETUP CDs

Two kinds of Windows 9x/Me setup CDs exist: Windows 9x/Me for a New PC that can be used to install the OS on a drive that has no previous OS installed, and Windows 9x/Me Upgrade that requires an earlier version of Windows already be installed. When Microsoft was still selling these CDs, the CD for installing Windows on a new PC was significantly more expensive than the upgrade CD.

You have some freedom as to how you can use either CD:

> **Notes**
>
> Windows Me does not support 16-bit legacy drivers that work under Windows 95/98, so it's important to verify that your hardware devices are compatible with Windows Me.

▲ If you begin the installation with a hard drive that has no Windows installed, you can use either the upgrade CD or the CD for a new PC. If you use the upgrade CD, during the installation you must prove you have a Windows setup CD or floppy disk for an earlier version of Windows by providing that CD or floppy when the Setup program asks for it. If you cannot provide the CD or floppy, the upgrade installation terminates. If you use the setup CD for a new PC, that step is skipped during the installation. Using either setup CD, you're performing a new installation of the OS, which is called a **clean install**.

▲ If an older version of Windows is already installed on the hard drive, you can use either the upgrade CD or the CD for a new PC. Using either CD, you can perform an upgrade or you can perform a clean install. However, if you choose to perform a clean install using the upgrade CD, you'll need the setup CD or floppy for the previous version of Windows in hand to use when the Setup program asks for it.

The point is that the two CDs differed in cost, not in how they can be used, with one exception: If you are using the upgrade CD, you must prove you have the right to use it by providing a setup CD or floppy from an older version of Windows, or you must start with an older version of Windows already installed.

CLEAN INSTALL OR UPGRADE

Two ways you can install Windows are a clean install or an upgrade. Remember you can perform an upgrade or a clean install with either the Windows 9x/Me for a New PC CD or the Windows 9x/Me Upgrade CD. If no previous version of Windows is installed, your only option is a clean install. If Windows is already installed, you can choose between a clean install or an upgrade. Consider these advantages and disadvantages when making your decision:

▲ A clean install ignores any settings in the currently installed OS, including information about installed hardware or software. Therefore, after the clean install, you must reinstall all hardware and applications.

▲ An **upgrade install** carries forward as much information as it can about what the current OS knows concerning installed hardware and software, user preferences, and other settings. If you don't encounter any problems along the way, an upgrade is much faster than a clean install.

▲ If you are having problems with your current operating system and applications, consider doing a clean install rather than an upgrade so that you can get a fresh start. Any unsolved problems with corrupted applications or system settings will not cause you problems in the new installation.

▲ If the old OS is not in good enough shape to boot up successfully, you have no choice: Perform a clean install.

▲ With a clean install, because you're starting over, it's important you verify that you have all the application software installation CDs or floppy disks and then back up all data on the drive. Also take time to verify that the backups are good and that you have all device driver software.

▲ If the PC is on a network, it is possible to install the OS from another computer on the network. However, if you want to do an upgrade, you must begin the upgrade from within the current OS. Therefore, if you are performing an installation across a network, you are forced to do a clean install.

> **Tip**
>
> For an upgrade or a clean install, to speed up the installation, you can copy the files and folders on the Windows 9x/Me setup CD to a folder on your hard drive (see Figure 7-6) and run the Setup program from that folder. Also, having the Windows 9x/Me CD files on your hard drive makes it easier to access the files later when adding Windows components or updating drivers.

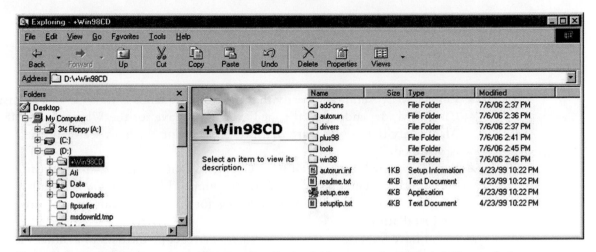

Figure 7-6 Having Windows set up files stored on the hard drive can make the installation go faster and later be an ongoing convenience

CHOOSING A FILE SYSTEM

One decision you must make when you install Windows 9x/Me is which file system you will use for the drive that will hold the Windows installation. Your choices are FAT16 and FAT32.

FAT16

DOS and all versions of Windows support the FAT16 file system, which uses 16 bits for each cluster entry in the FAT. Using 16 bits, the largest possible number is 65,535 (binary 1111 1111 1111 1111). Therefore, it is not possible to have more than 65,535 clusters when using FAT16. Therefore, the number of sectors assigned to each cluster must be large in order to accommodate a large logical drive.

With FAT16, the smallest possible cluster size is four sectors. Each sector is 512 bytes, which means the smallest cluster size is 2,048 bytes. Because an OS writes a file to a drive using one or more clusters, the least amount of space it uses for one file is 2,048 bytes. If a file contains fewer than 2,048 bytes, the remaining bytes in the cluster are wasted. This wasted space is called slack. If a drive contains many small files, much space is wasted.

FAT32

Beginning with Windows 95 OSR2 (OS Release 2), Microsoft offered a FAT that contains 32 bits per FAT entry instead of the older 12-bit or 16-bit FAT entries. Only 28 bits are used to hold a cluster number; the remaining four bits are not used. Because FAT32 has more bits to hold a cluster number, the number of clusters can be larger, which means the size of a cluster can be smaller. Smaller clusters mean the drive is likely to have less slack than when using FAT16. For these reasons, choose FAT32 for your file system unless the same PC will also be running Windows NT, which does not support FAT32.

After you have installed Windows 9x/Me, you can convert a FAT16 volume to FAT32 using Drive Converter. To access the Converter, after Windows is installed, click **Start**, **Programs**, **Accessories**, **System Tools**, and **Drive Converter (FAT32)**. As an alternative, you can use the Run dialog box. For the 16-bit version, enter **cvt.exe**, and for the 32-bit version, enter **cvt1.exe**, and then click **OK**. The Drive Converter Wizard steps you through the process.

INSTALLING WINDOWS 9X/ME AS A CLEAN INSTALLATION

After you have verified that the system qualifies and decided to perform a clean installation, do the following to prepare your system:

- ◢ Enter CMOS setup and verify that the boot sequence is first the floppy disk or CD-ROM, depending on the media that you have for the Windows 9x/Me setup. Also verify that any feature that prevents editing the boot sector of the hard drive is disabled.
- ◢ For a new hard drive, recall from Chapter 6 that the drive can be partitioned using Fdisk and formatted using the Format command before an OS is installed. The Windows 9x/Me installation will do this for you, or you can do it before you do the installation.
- ◢ If you have important data on your hard drive, copy the data to another medium.
- ◢ If you are performing a clean install and Windows is already installed on the drive (such as when the current installation is corrupted and you want to reinstall the OS), you do not need to format the hard drive before you begin the installation, although you should delete all folders on the hard drive used for the OS or applications, including the \Windows folder, files, and subfolders. This forces Setup to perform a clean install and makes certain that no corrupted system files or applications remain, but still keep any data files that might be on the drive.
- ◢ If you want, you can also format the hard drive. Do this if you suspect a virus is present. If you suspect a boot sector virus is present, you can use the Fdisk/MBR command (discussed in Chapter 6) to rewrite the master boot sector program.

 Caution

> Many CMOS setups have an option that can protect against some boot sector viruses. It prevents writing to the boot sector of the hard drive. This feature must be turned off before installing Windows, which must write to the boot sector during installation. Windows 9x/Me does not tell you that you must turn the feature off and start the installation over until about halfway through the installation.

You are now ready to perform the installation. Windows 9x/Me comes on a CD or set of floppy disks (yes, floppy disks are still around). Do one of the following to begin the installation:

- ◢ If you are installing Windows 98 or Windows Me from a CD (and your PC can boot from a CD-ROM drive), insert the CD in the drive and reboot.
- ◢ If your PC cannot boot from a CD, boot from a floppy disk or hard drive, then insert the CD in the CD-ROM drive, and enter the command **D:\Setup.exe**, substituting the drive letter of your CD-ROM drive for *D* if necessary. The Windows 95 setup CD is not bootable, so you will need a bootable floppy disk to begin the Windows 95 installation.
- ◢ If you are installing the OS from floppy disks, you can boot from the hard drive or floppy disk. To boot from the floppy disk, insert the Windows 9x/Me Disk 1, which is bootable, and boot the PC. At the A prompt, enter the command **Setup.exe**. You can also boot from a hard drive; to do so, go to a C prompt, insert the Windows 9x/Me Disk 1 in the floppy disk drive, and then enter the command **A:\Setup** to execute the Setup program on the floppy disk.

However you begin, the Windows 9x/Me setup screen appears. Then, a dialog box opens, as shown in Figure 7-7. Click **Continue** and then follow the directions onscreen.

Figure 7-7 Exit setup or continue with the Windows installation

INSTALLING WINDOWS 9X/ME AS AN UPGRADE

It's unlikely you'll ever be called on to upgrade a computer to Windows 9x/Me. However, here's what you need to know just in case the need arises. Before you begin the installation, in addition to the items listed previously, do the following:

- ◢ Verify that you have enough space on the hard drive. Delete files in the Recycle Bin and temporary directories.
- ◢ Run ScanDisk to check and repair errors on the hard drive. From Windows 95/98, click **Start, Programs, Accessories, System Tools**, and **ScanDisk**, and then scan each logical drive in the system. From a Windows startup disk, enter the command **Scandisk** at the command prompt.
- ◢ Run a current version of antivirus software to check for viruses.
- ◢ Check Config.sys and Autoexec.bat for potential problems. Verify that any hardware devices using device drivers loaded from these files work under the old OS so that you know your starting point if problems occur under the new OS.
- ◢ The Windows 9x/Me upgrade process moves commands in Autoexec.bat that are used to load terminate-and-stay-resident programs (TSRs) required for 16-bit Windows drivers and applications to Winstart.bat. Look for the Winstart.bat file in the root directory after the installation is done. If setup does not find any TSRs to put in the file, it will not be created.
- ◢ If TSRs such as QEMM386 (a memory manager by Quarterdeck) are loaded from Config.sys or Autoexec.bat, and problems arise because they run during the installation, disable them. To disable a command line, type **REM** at the beginning of the command line; this turns the line into a remark or comment. Later, after the installation, you can activate these lines again by removing the REMs.
- ◢ If you are connected to a network, verify that the connection works. If it does, Windows setup should be able to reestablish the connection correctly at the end of the installation.
- ◢ Create a Windows 9x/Me rescue disk for use in the event that the installation fails.
- ◢ Decide if you want to use FAT16 or FAT32 for your file system. Remember that you can choose FAT16 and then later convert to FAT32 using the Windows Drive Converter.

◢ If you are installing Windows 98 on a compressed drive, be aware that the registry can reside on any compressed drive, but the swap file can reside on a compressed drive only if the drive is compressed using protected-mode software such as DriveSpace. **DriveSpace** marks the area for the swap file as uncompressible. If your drive is compressed with real-mode compression software, such as DoubleSpace, then know that you cannot put the swap file on this compressed drive. The best practice is to back up the data and then uncompress the drive. You can later compress it using Windows 98 DriveSpace.

◢ Windows Me will not install on a compressed drive, so you must uncompress any portions of your hard drive that are compressed. If you are not sure whether your hard drive is compressed, run ScanDisk, which will tell you.

◢ Uninstall power management tools and disk management tools.

Sometimes Microsoft releases last-minute documentation on the setup CD. Check the Readme.txt file for any setup information provided. Then, after everything is ready for the installation, do the following to get to the setup screen:

1. Start the PC, loading the current operating system.

2. Close all open applications, including any antivirus software that is running. Close any icons that are open in the system tray.

3. Insert the CD in the CD-ROM drive or the floppy disk in the floppy drive. Your CD-ROM drive might be configured to run a CD automatically when it is first inserted. This Autoplay feature causes the Setup opening menu to appear without your entering the Setup command (see Figure 7-8). To disable the feature, hold down the Shift key while inserting the CD.

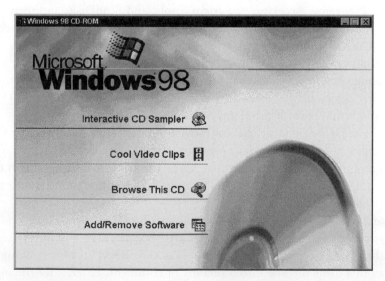

Figure 7-8   The opening screen of the Windows 98 CD provides links you can use to navigate the CD

4. Open the Run dialog box and enter the command **D:\Setup.exe**, substituting the drive letter for your CD-ROM drive or floppy drive for D if necessary. Click **OK**.

5. Follow the instructions on the setup screen. When you have the opportunity to select the folder to install Windows, select the folder in which the current OS is installed; most likely that is \Windows. If you use the same folder, Setup uses whatever settings it finds there.

INSTALLATION PROCESS FROM THE SETUP SCREEN FORWARD

After you get to the setup screen, the installation process is the same, no matter whether you are doing an upgrade or a clean install. During the installation, you are asked to choose from four setup options:

▲ *Typical*. This option installs all components that are usually installed with Windows 9x/Me. Most often, this is the option to choose.

▲ *Portable*. Use this option when installing Windows 9x/Me on a notebook computer.

▲ *Compact*. Use this option if you are short on hard drive space and want the smallest possible installation. No optional components are installed. After the installation, if you need a component, you can install it by double-clicking the **Add/Remove Programs** applet in Control Panel.

> **Notes**
>
> When installing Windows 9x/Me, you have the option of creating the startup disk, as discussed earlier. Be sure to create this disk to help in emergencies.

▲ *Custom*. Use this option if you know you need components not normally installed under the Typical installation. You have the opportunity to select any group of components to include in the installation.

During the installation, Setup records information in log files. The primary log file is Setuplog.txt, a hidden text file that Setup uses when recovering from a crash to determine how far it got in the installation. Figure 7-9 shows a portion of Setuplog.txt in which the system ran a virus check on CMOS and began checking drives.

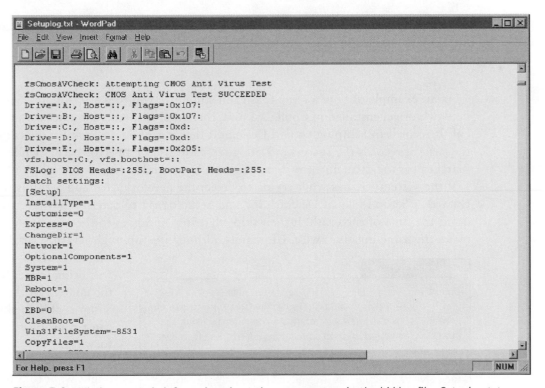

Figure 7-9 Windows records information about the setup process in the hidden file, Setuplog.txt

If the system fails to respond during the hardware detection phase, an entry is recorded in Detcrash.log, which is a binary file Setup uses to help recover from a crash caused by a hardware problem. Setup does not use the contents of the hidden Detlog.txt file; it is created only for the benefit of the user. The Detection Log (Detlog.txt) keeps a record of hardware detected, as shown in Figure 7-10.

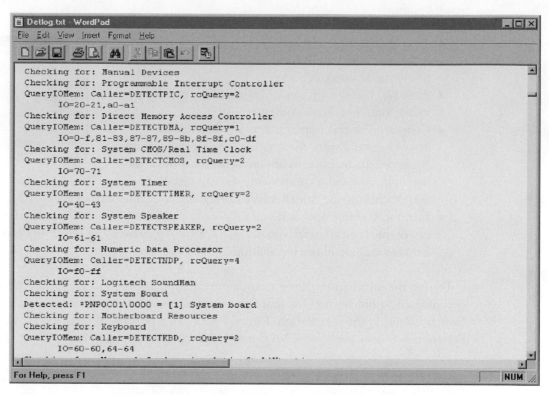

Figure 7-10 The hidden Detlog.txt file shows what hardware has been detected

As an example of how a setup crash can still move you forward, suppose Setup sees a network driver installed in Config.sys and, therefore, suspects that a network card is present. It records in Setuplog.txt and Detlog.txt that it is about to look for the card. If it finds the card, it records the success in Detlog.txt. However, if an error occurs while Setup searches for the card, an entry is made in the Detcrash.log file.

If the system crashes while trying to detect the network card and Setup is then restarted, Setup looks at Detcrash.log and Setuplog.txt to determine what it was trying to do at the time of the crash. It then skips that step and goes to the next step, so it doesn't make the same mistake twice. Ultimately, although Setup might crash several times during the installation, progress is still being made. By reading the content of the log files, Setup is able to skip steps that cause a problem and move forward.

In certain situations, you might want to force Setup to begin installation at the beginning instead of looking to Setuplog.txt for the entry point; for example, when you think you might have resolved a problem with hardware and want Setup to attempt to find the hardware again. To do this, delete Setuplog.txt to force a full restart.

> **Notes**
>
> Unless you've fixed the problem, be careful not to delete the log files during the installation, especially if you've just experienced a crash. Also, always restart the computer by using the power on/power off method so that the ISA bus is fully initialized, which does not always happen during a warm boot. When this ISA bus is fully initialized, errors encountered in the previous boot are less likely to follow you into this boot.

After the installation is complete, do the following:

1. Go to Control Panel and verify that the system date and time are correct. If they are not correct, make the change in CMOS setup.

2. Access the Internet and go to the Microsoft Web site (*windowsupdate.microsoft.com*). Download and install any available **service packs** or **patches**, which are updates and fixes to the OS released by Microsoft.

3. Using Control Panel, open the **Add/Remove Programs** applet, click the **Windows Setup** tab, and install any additional Windows components.

4. If this is an upgrade installation, open and test the applications you already had installed under Windows 9x/Me. Any problem you have with a particular application might be solved by uninstalling and then reinstalling it, or installing any patches necessary to make it work with the new OS. Check the application manufacturer's Web site for available updates.

DOWNLOADING AND INSTALLING UPDATES FOR WINDOWS 9X/ME

Microsoft is no longer updating Windows 9x/Me. However, you can download all the previously published updates from the Microsoft Web site, *windowsupdate.microsoft.com*. In Windows 98 and Windows Me, you can access this page by clicking **Windows Update** on the Start menu. The update process examines your system and recommends available updates for you to select, download, and install following directions on the screen (see Figure 7-11). Download all the available updates immediately after you have installed Windows 9x/Me. Because no more updates will be published, you should not have to update this legacy OS again.

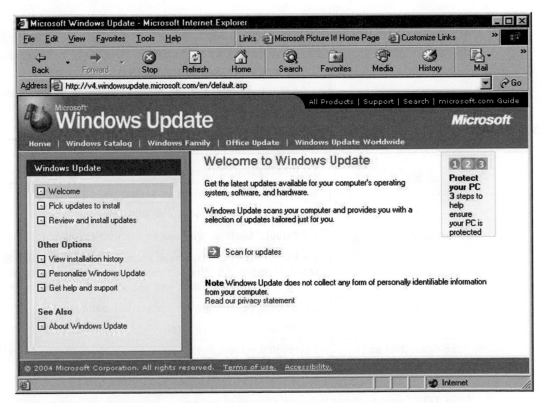

Figure 7-11 Download Windows updates from the Microsoft Web site

CONFIGURING THE WINDOWS 9X/ME STARTUP WITH MSDOS.SYS

In Windows 9x/Me, the text file Msdos.sys contains several parameters that affect how the OS boots. You can change some entries in this file to customize the boot process.

The file is a hidden, read-only, system file, so before you can edit it, you must first use the Attrib command at the command prompt to make the file available for editing. (Note that you can change the hidden and read-only attributes using Windows Explorer, but not the system attribute.)

> **Tip**
>
> Make a backup copy of Msdos.sys in case you want to revert to the form it was in before changes were made.

Follow these steps to change the options in Msdos.sys:

1. Go to an OS command prompt.

2. Go to the root directory of your hard drive by entering the following:
   CD

3. Make the file available for editing by entering the following:
   ATTRIB -R -H -S MSDOS.SYS

4. Make a backup copy of the file by entering the following:
   COPY MSDOS.SYS MSDOS.BK

5. Use Edit.com to edit the file by entering the following:
   EDIT MSDOS.SYS

6. Exit the editor, saving your changes. Then return the file to a hidden, read-only, system file by entering the following:
   ATTRIB +R +H +S MSDOS.SYS

Table 7-3 lists each entry in the Msdos.sys file and its purpose. You can refer to this table as

Command-Line Variable Name	Purpose of the Values That Can Be Assigned to the Variable
AutoScan	0 = Computer does not scan hard drive.
	1 = Default. Prompts the user before running ScanDisk on the hard drive when booting up after the computer was not shut down properly.
	2 = Automatically scans without prompting the user.
BootMulti	0 = Default. Boot only to Windows 9x/Me.
	1 = Allows for a dual boot.
BootWin	1 = Default. Boots to Windows 9x/Me.
	0 = Boots to previous version of DOS.
BootGUI	1 = Default. Boots to Windows 9x/Me with the graphical user interface.
	0 = Boots only to the command prompt for DOS 7.0 (the DOS core of Windows 95) or 7.1 (the DOS core of Windows 98). Autoexec.bat and Config.sys will be executed, and you will be in real-mode DOS.
BootMenu	0 = Default. Doesn't display the startup menu.
	1 = Displays the startup menu.
BootMenuDefault	1 through 8 = The value selected on the startup menu by default. (Normally this value should be 1.)

Table 7-3 Contents of the Msdos.sys file options section

Command-Line Variable Name	Purpose of the Values That Can Be Assigned to the Variable
BootMenuDelay	*n* = Number of seconds delay before the default value in the startup menu is automatically selected.
BootKeys	1 = Default. The function keys work during the boot process (F4, F5, F6, F8, Shift+F5, Ctrl+F5, Shift+F8). 0 = Disables the function keys during the boot process. (This option can be used to help secure a workstation.)
BootDelay	*n* = Number of seconds the boot process waits (when it displays the message "Starting Windows 95" or "Starting Windows 98") for the user to press F8 to get the startup menu (default is 2 seconds).
Logo	1 = Default. Displays the Windows 9x/Me logo screen. 0 = Leaves the screen in text mode.
Drvspace	1 = Default. Loads Drvspace.bin, used for disk compression, if it is present. 0 = Doesn't load Drvspace.bin.
DoubleBuffer	1 = Default. When you have a SCSI drive, enables double buffering for the drive. (See the drive documentation.) 0 = Doesn't use double buffering for the SCSI drive.
Network	1 = If network components are installed, includes the option "Safe Mode with networking support" in the startup menu. 0 = Doesn't include the option on the startup menu. (This is normally set to 0 if the PC has no network components installed. The startup menu is renumbered from this point forward in the menu.)
BootFailSafe	1 = Default. Includes Safe Mode in the startup menu. 0 = Doesn't include Safe Mode in the startup menu.
BootWarn	1 = Default. Displays the warning message when Windows 9x/Me boots into Safe Mode. 0 = Doesn't display the warning message.
LoadTop	1 = Default. Loads Command.com at the top of conventional memory. 0 = Doesn't load Command.com at the top of conventional memory. (Use this option when there is a memory conflict with this area of memory.)

Table 7-3   Contents of the Msdos.sys file options section (continued)

you read about the different options available when installing and configuring Windows 9x/Me.

Figure 7-12 shows a sample Msdos.sys file. The lines containing Xs at the bottom of the file are used to ensure that the file size is compatible with other programs.

```
[Paths]
WinDir=C:\WIN95
WinBootDir=C:\WIN95
HostWinBootDrv=C

[Options]
BootMulti=1
BootGUI=1
BootMenu=1
Network=0
;
;The following lines are required for compatibility with other programs.
;Do not remove them (MSDOS.SYS needs to be >1024 bytes).
;xxxxxxxxxxxxxxxxxxxxxxxxxxxxxxxxxxxxxxxxxxxxxxxxxxxxxxxxxxxxxxxxxa
;xxxxxxxxxxxxxxxxxxxxxxxxxxxxxxxxxxxxxxxxxxxxxxxxxxxxxxxxxxxxxxxxb
;xxxxxxxxxxxxxxxxxxxxxxxxxxxxxxxxxxxxxxxxxxxxxxxxxxxxxxxxxxxxxxxxc
;xxxxxxxxxxxxxxxxxxxxxxxxxxxxxxxxxxxxxxxxxxxxxxxxxxxxxxxxxxxxxxxxd
;xxxxxxxxxxxxxxxxxxxxxxxxxxxxxxxxxxxxxxxxxxxxxxxxxxxxxxxxxxxxxxxxe
;xxxxxxxxxxxxxxxxxxxxxxxxxxxxxxxxxxxxxxxxxxxxxxxxxxxxxxxxxxxxxxxf
;xxxxxxxxxxxxxxxxxxxxxxxxxxxxxxxxxxxxxxxxxxxxxxxxxxxxxxxxxxxxxxg
;xxxxxxxxxxxxxxxxxxxxxxxxxxxxxxxxxxxxxxxxxxxxxxxxxxxxxxxxxxxxxxh
;xxxxxxxxxxxxxxxxxxxxxxxxxxxxxxxxxxxxxxxxxxxxxxxxxxxxxxxxxxxxxi
;xxxxxxxxxxxxxxxxxxxxxxxxxxxxxxxxxxxxxxxxxxxxxxxxxxxxxxxxxxxxj
;xxxxxxxxxxxxxxxxxxxxxxxxxxxxxxxxxxxxxxxxxxxxxxxxxxxxxxxxxxxk
;xxxxxxxxxxxxxxxxxxxxxxxxxxxxxxxxxxxxxxxxxxxxxxxxxxxxxxxxxxl
;xxxxxxxxxxxxxxxxxxxxxxxxxxxxxxxxxxxxxxxxxxxxxxxxxxxxxxxxxxm
;xxxxxxxxxxxxxxxxxxxxxxxxxxxxxxxxxxxxxxxxxxxxxxxxxxxxxxxxxn
;xxxxxxxxxxxxxxxxxxxxxxxxxxxxxxxxxxxxxxxxxxxxxxxxxxxxxxxxo
;xxxxxxxxxxxxxxxxxxxxxxxxxxxxxxxxxxxxxxxxxxxxxxxxxxxxxxxp
;xxxxxxxxxxxxxxxxxxxxxxxxxxxxxxxxxxxxxxxxxxxxxxxxxxxxxxq
;xxxxxxxxxxxxxxxxxxxxxxxxxxxxxxxxxxxxxxxxxxxxxxxxxxxxxr
;xxxxxxxxxxxxxxxxxxxxxxxxxxxxxxxxxxxxxxxxxxxxxxxxxxxxs
```

Figure 7-12   A sample Msdos.sys file

INSTALLING AND MANAGING HARDWARE WITH WINDOWS 9X/ME

After a hardware device is physically installed in a system, the next step is to install the software necessary to interface with it. This software, called a device driver, is written to interface with a specific device and operating system. Knowing how to install and manage hardware is an essential skill of a PC support technician.

Here are three ways to begin the process of installing a device driver:

▲ When a new device is installed and you power up the PC, Windows recognizes it and immediately launches the Found New Hardware Wizard. If the wizard does not launch automatically, you can start it manually. Go to Control Panel and double-click the **Add New Hardware** icon, which launches the wizard.

▲ You can run an installation setup program on the floppy disk or CD that came bundled with the device. Look for and run a setup program named Setup.exe or Install.exe.

▲ If you downloaded a driver file from the Internet, double-click the file to launch the setup program.

One step in the Found New Hardware wizard is to select the hardware device from a list of devices (see Figure 7-13). If you click **OK**, Windows uses a Windows driver for the device, or you can click **Have Disk** to use your own drivers. If you have a driver on a floppy disk or CD or you downloaded a driver from the Internet to a folder on your hard drive, click **Have Disk** and point the wizard to the disk, CD, or folder that contains the driver. Sometimes you must select a folder on the disk or CD for the operating system to use. For example, if the disk or CD has three folders named \Win9x, \Win2k, and \Winxp, select the \Win9x folder.

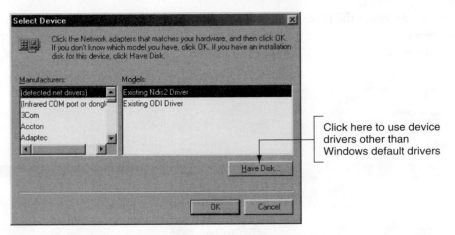

Figure 7-13 To use device drivers supplied by the device manufacturer, click Have Disk

VIEWING AND CHANGING CURRENT DEVICE DRIVERS

You can view and change current device drivers from Control Panel. For example, to view the current video driver in Windows 98, click **Start, Settings, Control Panel**, and then double-click **Display**. Click the **Settings** tab to view the currently installed display driver, as shown in Figure 7-14.

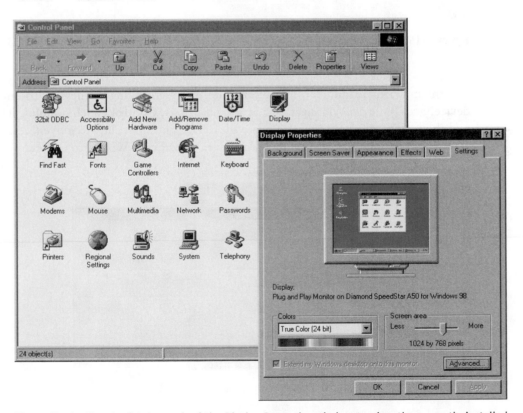

Figure 7-14 Use the Settings tab of the Display Properties window to view the currently installed display driver

To change the video card driver, click **Advanced**, click the **Adapter** tab, and then click the **Change** button. You see the Windows 98 Update Device Driver Wizard. Click **Next** to see the dialog box in Figure 7-15, which includes options to let Windows 98 search for a new driver from its list of Windows drivers or to display a list of all the drivers in a specific location, so that you can select the driver you want. To provide your own driver, click the second option and then click **Next**. Then click **Have Disk** to provide the new driver from a floppy disk, a CD, or a file downloaded from the Internet.

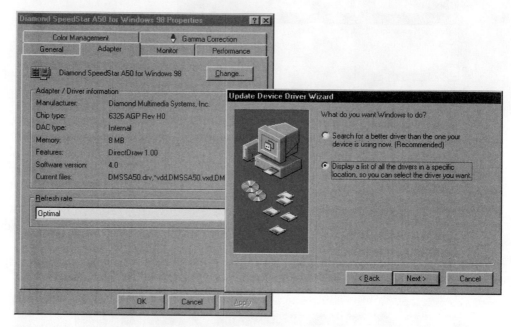

Figure 7-15 The Windows 98 Update Device Driver Wizard enables you to install a new device driver for a previously installed device

If the new driver fails, try uninstalling and then reinstalling the device. To uninstall a device, access Device Manager. (Click **Start, Settings, Control Panel**, double-click **System**, and then click **Device Manager**.) Select the device and then click **Remove** (see Figure 7-16). Then reboot the PC and allow the Found New Hardware Wizard to launch.

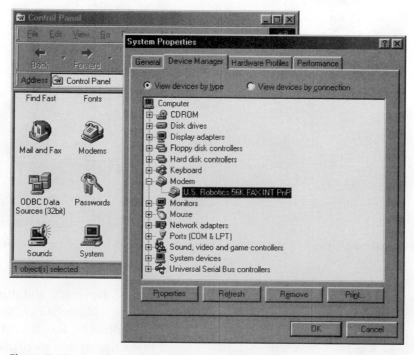

Figure 7-16 Use Device Manager to uninstall a device

PLUG AND PLAY AND HARDWARE INSTALLATIONS

Remember that Plug and Play (PnP) is a set of design specifications for both hardware and software that works to make hardware installations supposedly effortless. For a system to be truly Plug and Play, it must meet these criteria:

▲ The system BIOS must be PnP. (To know if your BIOS is PnP, you can use MSD, a 16-bit command-line diagnostic utility, or you can check the CMOS setup screen.)
▲ All hardware devices and expansion cards must be PnP-compliant. (All PCI expansion cards are PnP.)
▲ The OS must be Windows 9x/Me or another OS that supports PnP.
▲ A 32-bit device driver must be available (from the device manufacturer or Windows).

If all these things are true, hardware installation should be just a matter of installing the new hardware device, turning on the PC, and perhaps providing the 32-bit driver, if it is not included with Windows 9x/Me. During the boot process, Windows 9x/Me surveys the devices and their needs for resources and allocates resources to each device. Windows 9x/Me is free to assign these resources to the devices and avoids assigning the same resource to two devices. For PnP to work, each device in the system must be able to use whatever resources the OS assigns to it.

Although it supports 16-bit device drivers and applications, Windows 95/98 works better using 32-bit drivers and 32-bit applications. If you are using older 16-bit drivers under Windows 95/98, search for 32-bit drivers to replace them. Look on the device manufacturer's Web site or the Microsoft Web site. Windows Me does not support 16-bit drivers, but does support 16-bit applications.

To learn whether a driver is 16-bit or 32-bit, look at how Windows loads it. If the driver is a 32-bit driver written for Windows 9x/Me, it is loaded from the registry. System.ini can contain both 16-bit and 32-bit drivers. If the driver is loaded from Autoexec.bat or Config.sys, it is a 16-bit driver written for DOS. Also look in Device Manager for an exclamation point beside the device, which indicates that the driver has a problem. For instance, this exclamation point might indicate that the driver is a 16-bit driver and, as such, might need updating to a 32-bit driver.

During the Windows 95/98 installation, Windows Setup tries to substitute 32-bit drivers for all 16-bit drivers it finds in use, and, if it can, eliminates the Autoexec.bat and Config.sys files altogether. However, if it can't substitute a 32-bit driver for an older 16-bit driver, it puts (or keeps) the proper lines in the Config.sys file and sets itself up to use the older driver. Because Windows Me does not support 16-bit drivers, it does not allow them to be loaded from Autoexec.bat or Config.sys.

DISK COMPRESSION IN WINDOWS 95/98

If you run short on hard drive space on a Windows 95/98 system, one thing you can do is compress the drive. Windows 95 and Windows 98 support disk and drive compression (Windows Me does not) using the DriveSpace utility on a FAT16 volume. A compressed volume under Windows 9x is slower to access and somewhat unstable and should not be used if important data is on the volume. Use it with caution!

Notes

Windows 95/98 does not compress FAT32 volumes.

To compress a FAT16 volume in Windows 95/98 using DriveSpace, first back up the data on the volume. Next, click **Start, Programs, Accessories,** and **System Tools.** Then select **DriveSpace** and follow the steps to select and compress the drive. After the drive is compressed, never trust important data to it. Figure 7-17 shows the error message you receive if you attempt to compress a FAT32 drive.

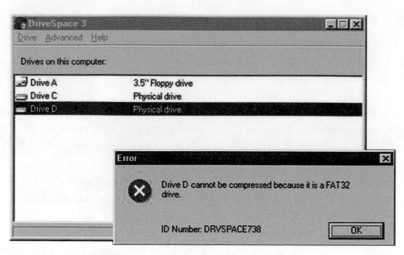

Figure 7-17   DriveSpace can compress only FAT16 drives

HARD DRIVE PREVENTIVE MAINTENANCE

To keep a hard drive clean, optimized, and error free, you can use these utilities from the Windows 9x/Me desktop:

◢ *Disk Cleanup*. To access Disk Cleanup, right-click the drive in Windows Explorer and select **Properties** from the shortcut menu. The Disk Properties window opens, as shown on the left side of Figure 7-18. On the General tab, click **Disk Cleanup**. From this window, as shown on the right side of Figure 7-18, you can select nonessential files to delete in order to save drive space.

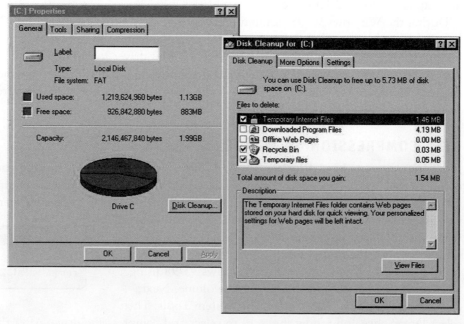

Figure 7-18   The Disk Properties window provides Disk Cleanup, a quick-and-easy way to delete temporary files on a hard drive

▲ *Disk Defragmenter*. To use Disk Defragmenter, choose **Start, Programs, Accessories, System Tools**, and then **Disk Defragmenter**. Select the drive to defrag and click **OK** (see Figure 7-19). If you want to watch the defragmenting progress as it moves through the FAT, click **Show Details** in the Disk Defragmenter window. Recall from Chapter 6 that you can also defrag a drive using the Defrag command from a command prompt.

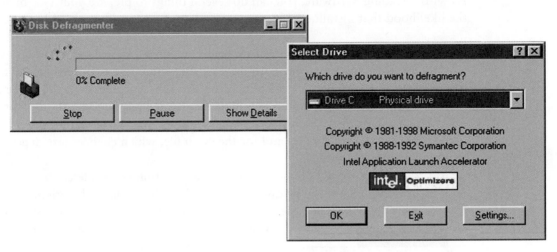

Figure 7-19   Windows 98 Disk Defragmenter windows

▲ *ScanDisk*. To use ScanDisk from the Windows 9x/Me desktop, click **Start, Programs, Accessories, System Tools**, and then **ScanDisk**. The ScanDisk utility first asks which drive you want to scan and gives you the choice of a Standard or Thorough scan. The Standard scan checks files and folders for errors. The Thorough scan does all that the Standard scan does and also checks the disk surface for bad sectors. Click **Start** to begin the scan. Figure 7-20 shows the results of a scan. Recall from Chapter 6 that you can also use the Scandisk command from a command prompt.

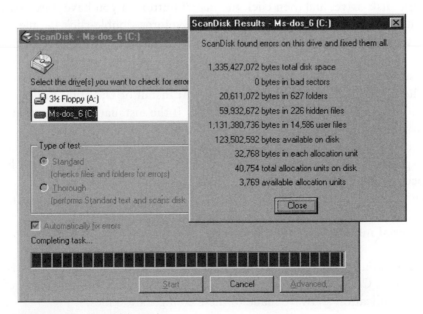

Figure 7-20   ScanDisk results

INSTALLING AND MANAGING SOFTWARE IN WINDOWS 9X/ME

As the bridge between earlier and later versions of Windows, Windows 9x/Me can use both 16-bit and 32-bit software. This section shows you how to install and manage both.

PREPARING FOR SOFTWARE INSTALLATION

As with installing hardware, you can do several things to prepare your system and to increase the likelihood that installing software on Windows 9x/Me will work without a snag:

- ◢ *Check available resources.* Check your computer resources to make sure you have (1) enough space on your hard drive, (2) the minimum requirements for memory, and (3) the proper CPU and video monitor. Read the documentation to make sure your system meets the minimum requirements. Remember that you should not completely fill your hard drive with software and data because the operating system needs extra space for temporary files and for the swap file, which changes size depending on how much space is needed.
- ◢ *Protect the original software.* After the installation is complete, put the original software setup CD or floppy disks in a safe place. If you have the original software handy, reinstalling it will be easier should something go wrong with the installed software.

 Notes

For best performance with Windows 9x/Me, allow a minimum of 100 MB of unused hard drive space for working with temporary files used by applications.

- ◢ *Back up the registry and system configuration files.* Many older software setup programs edit Config.sys, Autoexec.bat, Win.ini, and System.ini files during the installation. Newer software might add its own entries to the Windows registry. Before you begin the installation, make backup copies of all these files so that you can backtrack if you want to. (You will learn more about backing up the registry later in the chapter.)

INSTALLING SOFTWARE

To install software designed for Windows 9x/Me, access Control Panel and double-click the **Add/Remove Programs** icon. Insert the software CD in the CD drive or the floppy disk in the floppy disk drive, and then click the **Install** button. If you have downloaded a software file from the Internet, using Windows Explorer, double-click the file. Follow directions on the setup screen. If the CD-ROM drive is set to Autorun, a setup screen might appear automatically as soon as you insert the software installation CD in the drive. For older software, click **Start** and **Run** to display the Run dialog box. Enter the drive and name of the installation program, for example, **A: Install** or **D: Setup**. Either way, the installation program loads and begins executing. If the installation program asks you a question you cannot answer, you can always abandon the installation and try again later.

Most software asks you for a serial number unique to your copy of the software. The number is probably written on the CD or on the first floppy disk, or it might be stamped on the documentation. If necessary, write the serial number on the floppy disk, on the label side of the CD, or on the CD case, so that you have it if you lose the documentation later. Copyright agreements often allow you to install the software on only one computer at a time. This serial number identifies the copy of the software that you have installed on this machine.

After the installation is complete and the software is working, update your backup copies of Autoexec.bat, Config.sys, System.ini, Win.ini, and the registry so that they reflect the changes the application software made to these configuration files.

TROUBLESHOOTING SOFTWARE INSTALLATIONS

If you have problems installing software in Windows 9x/Me, try the following:

- ◢ If an application locks up when you first open it, try deleting all files and folders under \Windows\Temp. A software installation sometimes leaves files and folders in the Windows temporary directories.
- ◢ Look at the Readme.htm hypertext file in the \Windows directory, which will point you to the Programs.txt file, also in the \Windows directory. If there is a software problem that was known when Windows shipped, information about the problem and what to do about it might be in these text files. You can also check the Web site of the software manufacturer or the Microsoft Web site for help.

SUPPORTING DOS APPLICATIONS UNDER WINDOWS 9X/ME

Windows 3.x used **PIF (program information file)** files to manage the virtual machine environment for DOS applications and provided a PIF editor to alter these files. Each application had its own PIF file that was used to specify the DOS environment that Windows 3.x created for it. If an application had no PIF file, Windows 3.x used the settings in the _Default.pif file in the \Windows\System folder. Windows 9x/Me manages the environment for DOS applications in a slightly different way. The Apps.inf file has a section named [PIF95] that contains a master list of settings to be used for all DOS applications listed in the file.

To customize the settings for any one DOS application, use the Properties feature of the DOS program file, which creates an individual PIF for the program file and serves as the PIF editor. Right-click the program filename, and select **Properties** from the shortcut menu. Windows searches for the program's PIF file and, if none is found, creates one using default values. If Windows 9x/Me was installed over Windows 3.x, then _Default.pif still exists in the \Windows\System directory and default values are read from it. Regardless of where the default values come from, any changes are stored in the PIF for the application. To make changes, from the Properties window of the program file, click the **Program** tab, and then click the **Advanced** button (see Figure 7-21). (Note that the Program tab will not be present for Windows applications. This fact can help you know that Windows recognizes a program to be a DOS program.)

If you select the **Use current MS-DOS configuration** option, Windows executes the contents of Dosstart.bat, which is stored in the Windows folder. **Dosstart.bat** is a type of Autoexec.bat file that executes in two situations: when you select "Restart the computer in MS-DOS mode" from the Shutdown menu, or when you run a program in MS-DOS mode. This file can be used to load real-mode device drivers, but Set commands are not executed.

If you select the **Specify a new MS-DOS configuration** option, you can then change the Autoexec.bat and Config.sys files used for this MS-DOS mode only. For example, if the application runs slowly in DOS mode and does a lot of disk accessing, you can add entries to run real-mode SmartDrive here. SmartDrive is a 16-bit driver used to manage disk caching. It is not normally run under Windows 9x/Me, having been replaced by the faster 32-bit Vcache, which is built into Windows 9x/Me. In this situation of excessive disk accessing, because Windows 9x/Me does not manage disk access in MS-DOS mode, loading SmartDrive from the Advanced Program Settings window is appropriate, because Vcache will not be running.

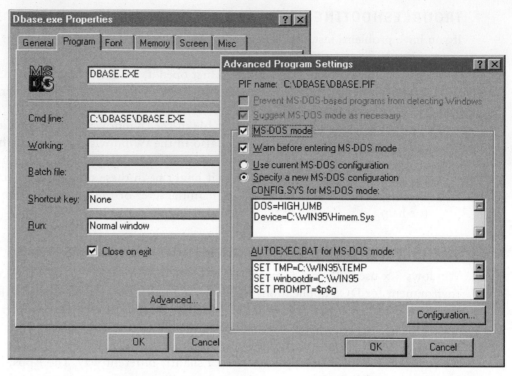

Figure 7-21   Properties sheets for a DOS application affect the way Windows 9x/Me provides an environment for the application

BOOTING WINDOWS 9X/ME

In Chapter 6, we discussed how to boot to a command prompt. In this section, we cover the startup process in Windows 9x/Me, including the differences between booting Windows 95 and booting Windows 98/Me. We'll also discuss how an application loads at startup. First, however, let's look at important files that Windows 9x/Me uses when booting.

FILES USED TO CUSTOMIZE THE STARTUP PROCESS

Windows 9x/Me uses several files to control the startup process. Autoexec.bat and Config.sys are text files that can contain settings for environmental variables and commands to load 16-bit drivers and TSRs. Windows 9x/Me supports Autoexec.bat and Config.sys for backward compatibility with DOS. If Autoexec.bat or Config.sys files are present in the root directory, the command lines in them are executed during the boot, and they are used to customize the loading process.

Just as DOS uses text files to hold information about what is loaded, Windows 3.x also uses text files to hold custom settings that help control the loading process. These files are called **initialization files**, and some entries in them are read and used by Windows 9x/Me. However, most Windows 9x/Me settings are stored in the Windows registry rather than in text files.

You can edit these text files with the Edit.com program from the command prompt or any text editor from within Windows. The Windows System Configuration Editor (**Sysedit**) is a handy Windows text editor designed to be used with these files. To use Sysedit, type **sysedit** in the Run dialog box, and then press **Enter**. These files then automatically appear for editing: Autoexec.bat, Config.sys, **Win.ini**, **System.ini**, and **Protocol.ini** (see Figure 7-22).

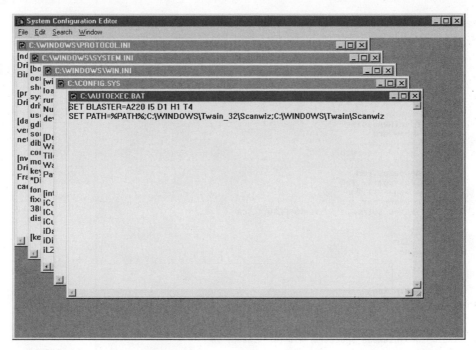

Figure 7-22 Sysedit can be used to edit Windows system files

Recall that an initialization file, which has a .ini file extension, is used by Windows and application software to store configuration information needed when they are first loaded. An application can have its own .ini files and registry, and can also store its information in the Windows .ini files and the Windows registry. Table 7-4 shows Windows .ini files, which Windows 9x/Me supports for backward compatibility with Windows 3.x.

Windows Initialization File	General Purpose of the File
System.ini	Contains hardware settings and multitasking options; older protected mode (32-bit) drivers loaded from the [386Enh] section can cause problems
Progman.ini	Contains information about Program Manager groups
Win.ini	Contains information about user settings, including printer, fonts, file associations, and settings made by applications
Control.ini	Contains information about the user's desktop, including color selections, wallpaper, and screen saver options
Mouse.ini	Contains settings for the mouse
Protocol.ini	Contains information about the configuration of the network

Table 7-4 Windows .ini files

System.ini and Win.ini are used by both Windows 3.x and Windows 9x/Me. A sample Windows 98 System.ini file is shown in Figure 7-23. The two sections required for the boot process are [boot] and [386Enh]. Windows 3.x kept many more entries in these sections than does Windows 9x/Me, which really uses these files only for backward compatibility with older applications.

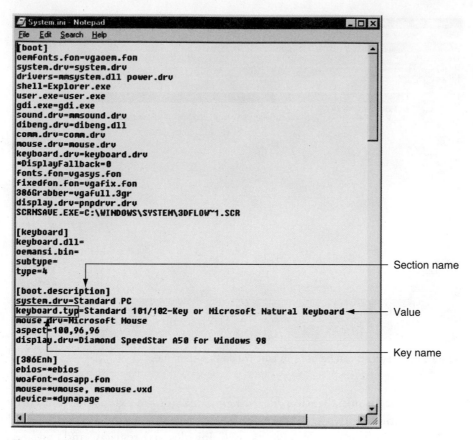

Figure 7-23   A sample Windows 98 System.ini file

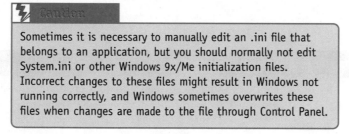

Sometimes it is necessary to manually edit an .ini file that belongs to an application, but you should normally not edit System.ini or other Windows 9x/Me initialization files. Incorrect changes to these files might result in Windows not running correctly, and Windows sometimes overwrites these files when changes are made to the file through Control Panel.

Initialization files are only read when Windows or an application using .ini files starts up. If you change the .ini file for an application, you must restart the software for the change to take effect. If you want the application to ignore a line in the .ini file, you can turn the line into a comment line by putting a semicolon or the letters REM at the beginning of the line.

We now turn our attention to the Windows 9x/Me startup process, in which these and other files are used.

THE WINDOWS 9X/ME STARTUP PROCESS

Windows 9x/Me first loads in real mode and then switches to protected mode. With DOS, the two core real-mode system files responsible for starting up the OS, Io.sys and Msdos.sys, remain in memory, running even after the OS is loaded. With Windows 9x/Me, Io.sys is responsible only for the initial startup process performed in real mode. Then, control is turned over to Vmm32.vxd, which works in protected mode, and Io.sys is terminated. Recall that Windows 9x/Me includes a file named Msdos.sys, but it is only a text file that contains some parameters and switches you can set to affect the way the OS boots.

Startup in Windows 9x/Me is a five-phase process, as shown in Figure 7-24. We will look at each phase in the following sections.

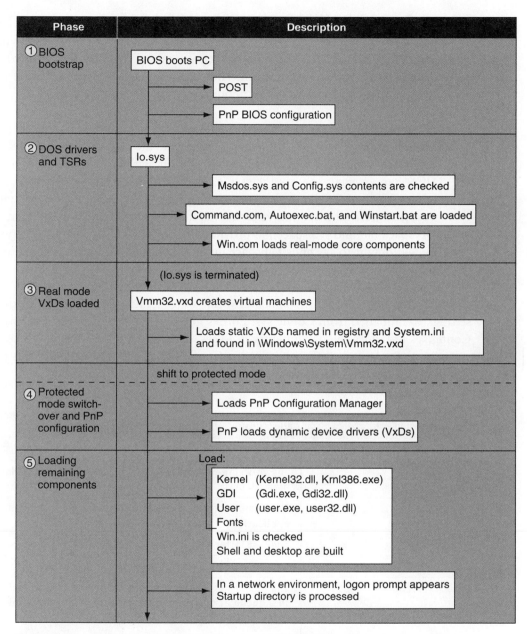

Figure 7-24 Windows 9x/Me core components and the loading process

PHASE 1: STARTUP BIOS BOOTSTRAP AND POST

Startup BIOS begins the process by performing POST (power-on self test). Then, BIOS examines the devices on the system and determines which ones are PnP-compliant. BIOS first enables the devices that are not PnP and then tries to make the PnP devices use the leftover resources. It also looks to permanent RAM for information about hardware, and uses that information to help configure PnP devices that have their configuration information recorded there. It saves information that Windows uses later to complete the hardware configuration.

The BIOS then looks for a device (hard drive, floppy disk, CD drive, or other drive) containing the OS. The bootstrap loader program is executed, and it looks for the initial hidden file of Windows 9x/Me (Io.sys). Io.sys is loaded.

PHASE 2: DOS DRIVERS AND TSRs ARE LOADED

In Phase 2, Io.sys is in control, and it creates a real-mode operating system environment. Io.sys checks the text file Msdos.sys for boot parameters. Then, Io.sys automatically loads the following drivers if they are present: Himem.sys, Ifshlp.sys, Setver.exe, and Drvspace.bin (or Dblspace.bin). Note the following about these files:

- Himem.sys provides access to extended memory.
- Sixteen-bit programs use Ifshlp.sys to access the file system.
- Setver.exe is included for backward compatibility with DOS applications that expect all DOS components to be from the same version. Setver.exe "asks" the DOS application what version of DOS it expects to use and presents DOS components to that application as if they were all from that version, even if they are actually from different versions.
- Drvspace.bin and Dblspace.bin provide disk compression. One of these two files is loaded only if Io.sys finds Dlbspace.ini or Drvspace.ini in the root directory of the boot drive.

Io.sys also sets several environmental variables to default settings. In DOS, these default settings were loaded from Config.sys. Entries in Io.sys cannot be edited, but an entry in Config.sys overrides the default entry in Io.sys. Therefore, if you want to use settings different from the default, put the command in Config.sys, which is executed at this point in the load. Table 7-5 lists the default Io.sys entries.

Entry	Description
Buffers=30	The number of file buffers to create
DOS=HIGH	The DOS core of Windows 9x/Me is loaded into the high memory area (HMA)
Files=60	The number of files that can be open at one time under 16-bit applications
Lastdrive=Z	The last letter that can be assigned to a logical drive
Shell=Command.com /P	Loads Command.com and executes Autoexec.bat
Stacks=9,256	The number of frames of instructions that can be held in memory in a queue at one time; used for backward compatibility with older applications

Table 7-5 Entries in Io.sys that once were in Config.sys

Next, Io.sys loads Command.com and follows instructions stored in Autoexec.bat and Winstart.bat. The default assignments made to environmental variables that were stored in Autoexec.bat in DOS are shown in the following list:

- Tmp=c:\windows\temp
- Temp=c:\windows\temp
- Prompt=pg
- Path=c:\windows;c:\windows\command

The Tmp and Temp variables are used by some software to locate where to put their temporary files. You can change any of these variables by making an entry in Autoexec.bat. Next, Io.sys loads Win.com. Then, Win.com loads other real-mode core components.

PHASE 3: REAL-MODE VxDs ARE LOADED

In Phase 3, Io.sys relinquishes control to the Virtual Machine Manager (VMM) component housed in Vmm32.vxd along with some virtual device drivers. A **virtual device driver (VxD)** creates and manages virtual machines to provide access to hardware for software running in the VM. Under Windows 3.x, these VxDs were loaded from System.ini and had a .386 file extension. Under Windows 9x/Me, if stored in individual files, they have a .vxd file extension. They are called **static VxDs** because after they are loaded into memory, they remain there. (Conversely, **dynamic VxDs** are loaded into and unloaded from memory as needed.)

Vmm32.vxd is built specifically for a particular computer when Windows 9x/Me is installed and contains some VxDs critical for a successful boot. Therefore, each installation of Windows will have a different build of this file. (The VxD drivers now included in Vmm32.vxd were listed in the [386Enh] section of System.ini under Windows 3.x.) Vmm32.vxd terminates Io.sys and, while still in real mode, loads static VxD device drivers as identified in four different locations. They can be embedded in Vmm32.vxd, named in the registry or System.ini, or stored in the .vxd files in the \Windows\System\Vmm32 directory.

If you suspect a problem with a VxD that is part of the Vmm32.vxd file, you can put a new version of the .vxd file in the \Windows\System\Vmm32 directory. If Windows finds a VxD driver there, it uses that driver instead of the one embedded in Vmm32.vxd. Also, VxD drivers are listed in the registry and in System.ini. Normally, the entries are the same, and entries are only listed in System.ini for backward compatibility. However, if an entry in System.ini differs from an entry in the registry, the value in System.ini is used.

PHASE 4: PROTECTED-MODE SWITCHOVER AND PnP CONFIGURATION

At the beginning of Phase 4, Vmm32.vxd switches to protected mode and loads Configuration Manager. Configuration Manager configures legacy and PnP devices. It uses any information that PnP BIOS might have left for it and loads the 32-bit dynamic device drivers (VxDs) for the PnP devices.

PHASE 5: LOADING THE REMAINING COMPONENTS

In Phase 5, with Vmm32.vxd still in control, the three core components are loaded, and then fonts and other associated resources are loaded. Win.ini is checked and commands stored there are executed to allow backward compatibility. The shell and user desktop are loaded. If the computer is working in a networked environment, a logon dialog box is displayed, and the user can log on to Windows 9x/Me and the network. Finally, any processes stored in the Startup directory are performed.

DIFFERENCES BETWEEN THE WINDOWS 95 AND WINDOWS 98/ME BOOT PROCESS

Windows 98 made some minor changes in what happens during startup to speed up the boot process. For instance, Windows 95 waits two seconds, displaying "Starting Windows 95" so that you can press a key to alter the boot process. Windows 98 eliminated this two-second wait and, in its place, allows you to press and hold the Ctrl key as it loads. If you do, you see the startup menu that is also available with Windows 95.

APPLYING | CONCEPTS   If you want an application to load automatically at startup, you can:

▲ Place a shortcut in the folder C:\Windows\All Users\Startup Menu\Programs\StartUp.

▲ Put the name of the program file in the Load= or Run= line in Win.ini.

▲ Manually edit the registry key HKEY_LOCAL_MACHINE\SOFTWARE\ Microsoft\Windows\CurrentVersion\Run.

Try one of the first two methods yourself.

TROUBLESHOOTING TOOLS FOR WINDOWS 9X/ME

Now let's look at some support tools that are useful for troubleshooting problems with the OS during or after the boot. Table 7-6 lists tools that monitor and improve system performance, control the OS, and help with troubleshooting. Several of these major tools are covered in detail in this section; in the next section, you will see how to use these tools in troubleshooting situations.

Notes

Tools new with Windows Me are System Restore and System File Protection. System Restore automatically backs up the registry and other system files when the system is idle. System File Protection is similar to Windows 2000/XP System File Protection; it prevents system files from being accidentally deleted and prevents application installations from overwriting newer DLL files with older or nonstandard versions.

Tool	Windows 95	Windows 98/Me	Description
System Monitor Filename: Sysmon.exe Location: \Windows		X	Tracks the performance of some important system components. To run, click Start, Programs, Accessories, System Tools, and System Monitor.
System Configuration Utility Filename: MsConfig.exe Location: \Windows\ System		X	Allows you to temporarily modify the system configuration to help with troubleshooting. To run, select System Configuration Utility from the Tools menu of the System Information window or type Msconfig in the Run dialog box.
Dr. Watson Filename: Drwatson.exe Location: \Windows		X	Traps errors in log files created by applications and takes a snapshot of the system to use for troubleshooting.
Registry Checker Filename: Scanreg.exe Location: \Windows\ Command		X	Backs up, verifies, and recovers the registry from the command prompt. To use the Windows version of Registry Checker (Scanregw.exe), select Registry Checker from the Tools menu of the System Information window.

Table 7-6   Windows 9x/Me system performance and troubleshooting tools

7

Tool	Windows 95	Windows 98/Me	Description
Automatic Skip Driver Agent Filename: Asd.exe Location: \Windows		X	Automatically skips drivers that prevent Windows from loading and records problems encountered in the log file Asd.log. To run, select Automatic Skip Driver Agent from the Tools menu of the System Information window.
Microsoft System Information Filename: MSInfo32.exe Location: \Program Files\ Common files\Microsoft shared\Msinfo	X	X	Displays system information, including installed hardware and device drivers. To run, click Start, Programs, Accessories, System Tools, and System Information, or type Msinfo32.exe in the Run dialog box.
Hardware Diagnostic tool (Hwinfo.exe)		X	Displays the same information as System Information, but in text form. Enter hwinfo/ui in the Run dialog box.
Windows Update Filename: lexplore.exe Location: www.microsoft.com/ windowsupdate	X	X	Downloads service packs (fixes) for Windows from the Microsoft Web site.
System options in Control Panel (example: System Properties)	X	X	Several applets in Control Panel can be used to monitor and tweak system performance.
System File Checker Filename: Sfc.exe Location: \Windows\ System		X	Verifies system files. This tool scans for changed, deleted, or corrupted system files and restores them from the originals on the Windows CD. To run, select System File Checker from the Tools menu of the System Information window.
Microsoft Backup Filename: Msbackup.exe Location: \Program Files\ Accessories\ Backup	X	X	Backs up files and folders to prevent loss when your hard drive fails. To run, click Start, Programs, Accessories, System Tools, and Backup.
System Recovery Filename: pcrestor.bat Location: On the Windows 98/Me CD in \Tools\Sysrec		X	Uses a full system backup created by Microsoft Backup to reinstall Windows and restore the system to its state as of the last backup.

Table 7-6 Windows 9x/Me system performance and troubleshooting tools (continued)

Tool	Windows 95	Windows 98/Me	Description
Scheduled Task Wizard Filename: Mstask.exe Location: \Windows\System	X	X	Schedules tasks such as MS Backup to run at predetermined times.
Version Conflict Manager Filename: Vcmui.exe Location: \Windows		X	Replaces an older Windows file with a newer file that was saved when Windows or an application was installed.
System Configuration Editor Filename: Sysedit.exe Location: \Windows\System	X	X	Text editor to edit files that configure how Windows loads. To run it, enter Sysedit.exe in the Run dialog box. Sysedit automatically opens Protocol.ini, System.ini, Win.ini, Config.sys, and Autoexec.bat for editing.
Task Manager Filename: Taskman.exe Location: \Windows	X	X	Runs, switches, and ends applications, and accesses the Shutdown menu. To run it, type Taskman in the Run dialog box.
Signature Verification Tool Filename: sigverif.exe Location: \Windows		X	Checks device drivers for digital signatures given to them by Microsoft, which ensures they have been tested by Microsoft. To run it, use the System Information window.
Digital Signature Check		X	Identifies drivers that have been digitally signed by Microsoft to verify their integrity. To use it, enable this key in the registry: HKEY_LOCAL_MACHINE\Software\Microsoft\Driver Signing.

Table 7-6　Windows 9x/Me system performance and troubleshooting tools (continued)

SYSTEM MONITOR

System Monitor allows you to monitor how system resources are being used by applications. It can monitor the file system, memory, the kernel, printer sharing services, and network performance data.

APPLYING CONCEPTS　System Monitor is not automatically installed in a typical installation. To install it, go to Control Panel, and select **Add/Remove Programs**. Click **Windows Setup**, and then select **System Tools**. Click the **Details** button, select **System Monitor**, and click **OK**. To run System Monitor, click **Start**, point to **Programs**, **Accessories**, **System Tools**, and then click **System Monitor**.

Figure 7-25 shows System Monitor tracking the kernel and disk cache hits and misses. Under the File menu, you can add and delete items the monitor is tracking. Use System Monitor to help determine if an application is using an inordinate amount of resources or has a memory leak. A memory leak occurs when you exit software and it unloads from memory, but it does not release the memory addresses that it was using for its data back to the OS. Memory leaks can occur when software is corrupted, poorly written, or plagued with a virus. You notice memory leaks when your system gets sluggish after you have launched and exited an application several times before rebooting the system. A reboot releases all memory addresses.

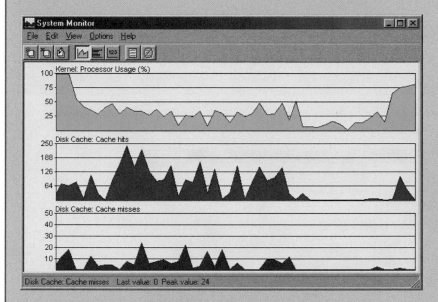

Figure 7-25 System Monitor can track the performance of several system resources

SYSTEM CONFIGURATION UTILITY (MSCONFIG)

Similar to the way Safe Mode works, the System Configuration Utility (Msconfig.exe) reduces the startup process to its essentials. If starting Windows in this condition eliminates the problem you are troubleshooting, you can use this utility to add items back one at a time until the problem occurs; the source of the problem is related to the last item you added. To use the utility, do the following:

1. To access the utility, click **Start,** point to **Programs, Accessories, System Tools,** and then click **System Information.** The Microsoft System Information window opens.

2. From the **Tools** menu, select **System Configuration Utility** (see Figure 7-26). The System Configuration Utility dialog box opens, as shown in Figure 7-27. Another way to access the utility is to type **Msconfig** in the Run dialog box, and then press **Enter.**

3. To diagnose a problem, select **Diagnostic startup–interactively load device drivers and software,** and then click **OK** to restart your computer.

4. If this solves the problem, then the clean start was successful. Next, select **Selective startup** from the dialog box shown in Figure 7-27 and methodically select first one item and then another to restore, until the problem reappears. Begin by restoring all entries in Autoexec.bat and Config.sys, to determine if real-mode drivers and programs loaded from these files are the source of the problem.

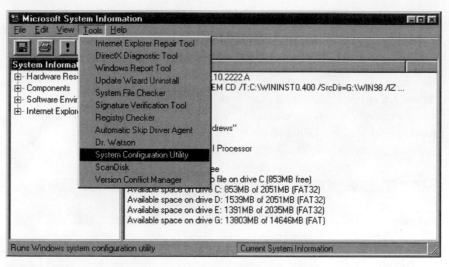

Figure 7-26 The System Information window provides access to many Windows support tools

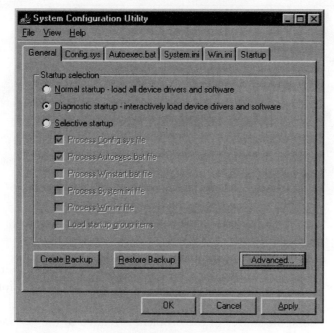

Figure 7-27 The Windows 98 System Configuration Utility helps troubleshoot Windows configuration problems

5. If the problem still occurs, even with the clean boot, then try the following:

▲ If you have not already done so, scan for a virus, using a current version of antivirus software.

▲ Use Registry Checker to check for corrupted system files.

▲ Use System File Checker to check for corrupted system files.

▲ Check the CMOS setup screen for incorrect settings.

DR. WATSON

Dr. Watson is a troubleshooting tool you can use when you have problems running an application. Dr. Watson is a Windows utility that can record detailed information about the system, errors that occur, and the programs that caused them in a log file named \Windows\Drwatson\Watson*XX*.wlg, where *XX* is an incrementing number. Each log file is created as it is needed to record errors. To learn about the benefits of Dr. Watson, start the program (see Figure 7-28), reproduce the application error, and then look at the events logged in the Dr. Watson window under the Diagnosis tab. When you click **View** on the menu bar, you will see the Standard View is selected. To see additional information about the system and programs currently running, select **Advanced View**.

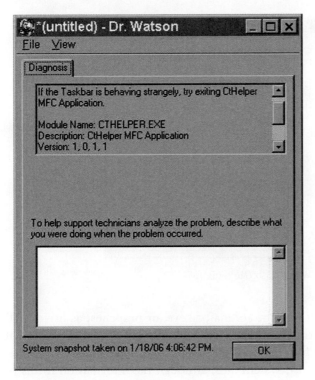

Figure 7-28 The Dr. Watson opening window

Information on the Diagnosis tab can be cross-checked to the Microsoft Web site, *support.microsoft.com*, for possible solutions. Also, software developers can sometimes use the information provided by Dr. Watson to help get to the bottom of an application error.

Notes

For errors that you cannot reproduce at will, consider having Windows load Dr. Watson each time Windows starts. You can do this by creating a shortcut to Drwatson.exe in the Startup folder.

THE WINDOWS 9X/ME REGISTRY AND REGISTRY CHECKER

In supporting and troubleshooting Windows 9x/Me, you need to understand the role of the registry and .ini files. The registry is a database of configuration information and settings for users, hardware, applications, and the OS. Starting with Windows 9x/Me, the registry takes over the essential functions of .ini files. However, Windows 9x/Me still supports .ini files for compatibility with Windows 3.x and legacy software and hardware devices.

Note that entries that 7-bit Windows applications make in Win.ini and System.ini are not added to the registry because these applications cannot access the registry. Entries made in .ini files by applications that can access the registry are copied into the registry. In this section, we'll examine how the registry is organized, how to recover from a corrupted registry, and how and why you might modify the registry.

HOW THE REGISTRY IS ORGANIZED

The registry organizes information in a hierarchical database with a treelike, top-to-bottom design. The Windows 9x/Me registry allows for keys to cascade to several levels on the tree. Figure 7-29 shows a portion of a Windows 9x/Me registry. Names in the left pane of the window are called keys. The values assigned to the selected key are listed in the right pane of the window. Each value has a name such as ScreenSaveTime, and to the right of each name is the value data assigned to that name, such as "60."

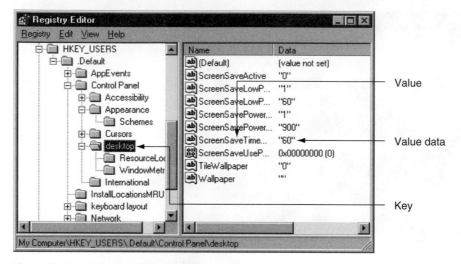

Figure 7-29   Structure of the Windows 9x/Me registry

The registry is organized into the six major keys, or branches, as listed in Table 7-7. The Windows 95/98 registry is contained in two files, System.dat and User.dat. Windows Me added a third registry file, Classes.dat. The registry files are located in the Windows directory as hidden, read-only, system files, although the information forms only a single database, which is built in memory each time Windows starts.

Key	Description
HKEY_CLASSES_ROOT	Contains information about file associations and OLE data. (This branch of the tree is a mirror of HKEY_LOCAL_MACHINE\ Software\Classes.)
HKEY_USERS	Includes user preferences, including desktop configuration and network connections.
HKEY_CURRENT_USER	Contains information about the current user preferences for a multiuser system. If there is only one user of the system, this is a duplicate of HKEY_USERS.
HKEY_LOCAL_MACHINE	Contains information about hardware and installed software.
HKEY_CURRENT_CONFIG	Contains the same information in HKEY_LOCAL_MACHINE\ Config and has information about printers and display fonts.
HKEY_DYN_DATA	Keeps information about Windows performance and Plug and Play information.

Table 7-7   Six major branches, or keys, of the Windows 9x/Me registry

RECOVERING FROM A CORRUPTED REGISTRY

Windows 95 has a way to recover from a corrupted registry that is different from the method used by Windows 98/Me. These methods are discussed next.

Windows 95 Backup of the Registry

Windows 95 maintains a backup copy of the two registry files and names the backup files System.da0 and User.da0. Each time Windows 95 boots successfully, it makes a new backup of the two registry files. If Windows 95 has trouble loading and must start in Safe Mode, it does not back up the registry.

If Windows 95 does not find a System.dat file when it starts, it automatically replaces it with the backup System.da0. If both System.dat and User.dat are missing, or if the WinDir= command is missing in Msdos.sys, Windows 95 tells you that the registry files are missing and starts in Safe Mode. It then displays the Registry Problem dialog box. If you see this dialog box, click the **Restore From Backup** and **Restart** buttons to restore the registry files from System.da0 and User.da0. If these files are also missing, the registry cannot easily be restored. You can either restore the files from your own backups or run Windows 95 Setup. There is also another option: Look for the file System.1st in the root directory of the hard drive. This is the System.dat file created when Windows 95 was first installed. In an emergency, you can revert to this file.

Windows 98/Me Registry Checker

Windows 98/Me offers a utility called the Registry Checker, which is not available with Windows 95. It automatically backs up the registry each day, and by default, it keeps the last five days of backups. In an emergency, you can recover the registry from one of these backups. You can also tell Registry Checker to make an additional backup on demand, for example, when you make changes to the registry and want to back them up before you make new changes. There are two versions of Registry Checker: Scanreg.exe is executed from the command prompt and is a 16-bit real-mode program, and Scanregw.exe is the 32-bit, protected mode, GUI version executed from within Windows.

To access Registry Checker from within Windows, select **Start**, point to **Programs, Accessories, System Tools,** and then click **System Information**. The Microsoft System Information window opens. From the menu bar, select **Tools** and then **Registry Checker** (see Figure 7-30). (Alternately, you can click **Start**, click **Run**, and type **Scanregw** in the Run dialog box, and then press **Enter**.) Registry Checker tells you if the registry is corrupted and fixes it, if allowed. You can also create a new backup at this time.

Backups are kept in cabinet files in the \Windows\Sysbckup folder as rb001.cab, rb002.cab, and so on. To revert to one of these backups, you must first be in MS-DOS mode. For Windows Me, boot from a bootable disk. For Windows 98, boot from a bootable disk or boot to an MS-DOS prompt from the Windows 98 startup menu. (Windows Me does not have this option on the startup menu.) From the MS-DOS prompt (not a DOS box within a Windows session), use the commands in Table 7-8 to repair or recover the registry.

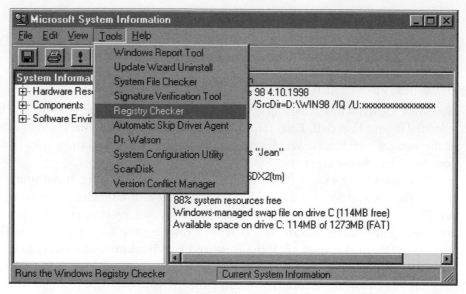

Figure 7-30 The Registry Checker is available under Programs, Accessories, System Tools, System Information; it is used to back up, restore, and repair the Windows 98/Me registry

Command	Purpose
Scanreg /Restore	Restores the registry from a previous backup. A screen appears asking you which backup to use.
Scanreg /Fix	Repairs the corrupted registry. If the problem is inherent to the registry itself, this might work. If you want to undo a successful change to the registry, use the Restore option instead.
Scanreg /Backup	Creates a new backup of the registry at the DOS prompt. Don't do this if the registry is giving you problems.
Scanreg /Opt	Optimizes the registry. ScanReg looks for and deletes information in the registry that is no longer used. This reduces the size of the registry, which might speed up booting.
Scanreg /?	Opens the Help feature of ScanReg.

Table 7-8 Commands used to repair or recover the Windows 98 or Windows Me registry

MODIFYING THE REGISTRY

When you make a change in Control Panel, Device Manager, or many other places in Windows 9x/Me, the registry is modified automatically. This is the only way most users will ever change the registry. However, on rare occasions you might need to edit the registry manually. For example, if a virus infected your registry, you might be instructed to edit the registry by an antivirus technical staff person or by directions downloaded from an antivirus Web site. Following these directions, you might edit a key or delete an entry added by the virus. The first step in editing the registry is to back up the registry. The simplest way to do that is to click **Start**, click **Run**, and type **Scanregw** in the Run dialog box, and then press **Enter**. When the Registry Checker asks if you want to back up the registry, click **Yes**. When you see the "Backup Complete" message, click **OK**.

The next step is to use Regedit.exe, located in the Windows folder. You can use Explorer to locate the file, then double-click it, or you can click **Start**, then **Run**, type **Regedit** in the

Run dialog box, and then press **Enter**. When you do, the window in Figure 7-31 opens. Open one branch of the tree by clicking the + sign to the left of the key, and close the branch by clicking the – sign. To search for an entry in the registry, click the **Edit** menu and then click **Find**.

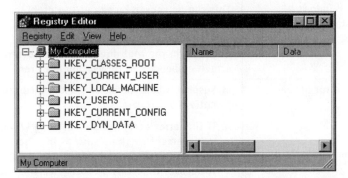

Figure 7-31 The six major keys, or branches, of the registry seen in the Registry Editor

TROUBLESHOOTING WINDOWS 9X/ME

This section covers Windows 9x/Me troubleshooting. It is important for you to know how to troubleshoot problems that occur during a Windows installation, problems that occur during the startup process, and problems that occur during normal Windows operations.

> **Notes**
>
> For specific error messages that occur during installation and what to do about them, go to the Microsoft Web site *support.microsoft.com* and search for the error message.

TROUBLESHOOTING WINDOWS 9X/ME INSTALLATIONS

Table 7-9 lists some problems that might occur while installing Windows 9x/Me and what to do about them.

Symptom	Description and Solution
An error message about BIOS appears during installation.	This is most likely caused by BIOS not allowing changes to the boot sector to protect it from viruses. Disable the feature in CMOS setup.
Windows 9x/Me stalls during the first restart after installation.	This is probably caused by legacy hardware that is not configured correctly. Try the following: ◢ Remark (REM) out all entries in Config.sys and Autoexec.bat. ◢ Disable the ISA enumerator by commenting out this line in System.ini: Device=ISAPNP.386.
During the first restart after installation, an error message appears with information about a bad or missing file.	This is probably caused by an error in Config.sys or Autoexec.bat. Try renaming both files so they are not executed. If this solves the problem, then comment out each line in the file, one at a time, until you know which line caused the problem.

Table 7-9 Some problems and solutions when installing Windows 9x/Me

Symptom	Description and Solution
During the first restart after the installation, you get an error message about a missing or damaged VxD file.	This is most likely caused by a missing or corrupted VxD file. Run Windows setup again and select the option to Verify or replace the missing or corrupted VxD (virtual device driver).
After upgrading from Windows 95 to Windows 98, the startup screen still says Windows 95.	This can be caused by one of two problems. First, the Io.sys file might not have been updated. If so, use the Sys C: command to replace it. Second, the file Logo.sys might be in the root directory, which overrides the logo screen embedded in Io.sys. Delete or rename the file.
"Invalid system disk" error appears during setup.	◢ Suspect a boot sector virus. Run a current version of antivirus software. ◢ If this error occurs while installing Windows when disk management software such as DiskPro is running, Windows might have damaged the hard drive MBR. To recover from this problem, see the documentation for the disk management software.

Table 7-9 Some problems and solutions when installing Windows 9x/Me (continued)

TROUBLESHOOTING WINDOWS 9X/ME STARTUP

When Windows 9x/Me does not start up correctly, you can go through these basic steps to troubleshoot it:

1. Check and address any error messages that occur during a normal boot.

2. If you cannot boot to a normal desktop, boot in Safe Mode and begin troubleshooting there. If you can boot to Safe Mode but cannot boot normally, you probably have a driver problem of some kind because the main difference between Safe Mode and normal booting is the drivers that are loaded.

3. If you cannot boot using Safe Mode, the GUI portion of the OS is not functioning. Boot to the command prompt using the startup menu. Use commands at the C prompt for troubleshooting.

4. If the startup menu is not accessible, the MS-DOS core of the OS is not functioning. Boot from an emergency startup disk, and try to access drive C.

5. If you cannot access drive C, then the hard drive is not accessible. Try Fdisk. If Fdisk does not work, treat the problem as a hardware problem.

ERROR MESSAGES RECEIVED WHILE LOADING WINDOWS 9X/ME

Error messages during startup can be used to help you zero in on the problem and its solution. Table 7-10 shows error messages that Windows 9x/Me might give, and it lists advice about what to do when you see them. Specific errors are covered later in this section. If you get an error not listed in the table, search the Microsoft Web site (*support.microsoft.com*) for the message and what to do about it.

Error Message or Problem	What to Do
MS-DOS compatibility mode	▲ Windows is using real-mode drivers to access the hard drive rather than the preferred 32-bit drivers. After backing up the Config.sys and System.ini files, remove any references to real-mode drivers for the hard drive in these files. ▲ The problem might be due to an outdated motherboard BIOS. Consider updating the BIOS.
Bad or missing file Real-mode driver missing or damaged	▲ Verify that Config.sys, Autoexec.bat (root directory of the hard drive), and System.ini (Windows folder) are present and in the right location. ▲ Check Config.sys and Autoexec.bat for errors using the step-by-step confirmation option from the Windows 9x/Me startup menu. To check System.ini, rename the file so that it will not be used and boot with a bare-bones version of the file. ▲ Look in the Win.ini file for applications that are attempting to load at startup but have been deleted or uninstalled. Check the Load= or Run= lines.
Error in config.sys line xx	There is a problem loading a device driver or with the syntax of a command line. Check the command line for errors. Verify that the driver files are in the right directory. Reinstall the driver files.
Cannot open file *.inf	▲ This error is most likely caused by insufficient memory. Disable any TSRs running in Autoexec.bat. ▲ Close any applications that are running or remove them from the StartUp folder.
Invalid directory	A command issued in the Autoexec.bat file is referencing a working directory that does not exist. Check the Autoexec.bat file for errors.
Bad command or file not found	A command in Autoexec.bat cannot be interpreted, or the OS cannot find the program file specified in the command line. Check the spelling of the filename and the path to the program file.
Insufficient disk space	Run ScanDisk and Defragmenter. Check free space on the hard drive.
Invalid system disk	Suspect a boot sector virus. Run a current version of antivirus software.
Bad or missing command.com	Io.sys could be missing or corrupted. Restore the file from a backup or an emergency startup disk. To restore all real-mode files needed to begin loading Windows 9x/Me, do the following: (1) Boot from a Windows 9x/Me emergency startup disk; (2) restore Io.sys, Msdos.sys, Drvspace.bin, and Command.com by executing the command SYS C:, and (3) remove the floppy disk and reboot.
Invalid VxD dynamic link call from IFSMGR	This error is caused by a missing or corrupted Msdos.sys file. Restore the file from a backup or from an emergency startup disk.
Missing system files	Run the SYS C: command.

Table 7-10 Error messages received while loading Windows 9x/Me

Error Message or Problem	What to Do
System registry file missing	System.dat, User.dat, and/or Classes.dat (for Windows Me) is corrupted or missing. For Windows 95, restore them by using either System.da0 or User.da0. For Windows 98/Me, run ScanReg.
VxD error returns to command prompt	A VxD file is missing or corrupted. Run Windows Setup from the Windows 9x/Me CD, and choose Verify installed components.
Error containing the text "Kernel32.dll"	An error that contains this text probably indicates a corrupted kernel. Try restoring system files. If that doesn't work, reinstall Windows. Note that this error might appear at other times, not just during the boot process.
Himem.sys not loaded, missing or corrupt Himem.sys	Himem.sys is corrupted, not in the right directory, or not the right version for the currently loaded OS. Compare Himem.sys in the \Windows folder to the copies in the \Windows\command\ebd folder or on the Windows setup CD.
Device not found	Errors are in System.ini, Win.ini, or the registry. Look for references to devices or attempts to load device drivers. Use Device Manager to remove a device or edit System.ini or Win.ini.
Device/Service has failed to start	A hardware device or driver necessary to run the device or critical software utility is causing problems. If the device is non-essential, try using Device Manager to remove it. Then reinstall the device. If the device is an essential device, try using System File Checker to restore system files.

Table 7-10 Error messages received while loading Windows 9x/Me (continued)

Windows has several tools you can use to help troubleshoot problems with booting:

▲ Use the System Configuration Utility (Msconfig.exe) to limit what loads during the boot in order to attain the cleanest possible boot.
▲ Use Device Manager to disable a device that you think is causing a problem.
▲ Use Automatic Skip Driver Agent (ASDA) to keep Windows from installing a driver that might be corrupted, including built-in Windows drivers.
▲ Use the Windows 9x/Me startup menu to try Safe Mode, the command prompt, and other troubleshooting options.

WINDOWS 9X/ME STARTUP MENU OPTIONS

Normally, when you load Windows, the message "Starting Windows" appears and then the OS loads. However, you can force the startup menu to appear rather than the "Starting Windows" message by pressing the F8 key or holding down the Ctrl key during the boot.

The Windows 95/98 startup menu options are listed below. Note that the Windows Me startup menu does not offer options 6 and 7:

1. Normal
2. Logged (\BOOTLOG.TXT)
3. Safe Mode
4. Safe Mode with network support
5. Step-by-step confirmation

6. Command prompt only

7. Safe Mode command prompt only

8. Previous version of MS-DOS

What to expect when you select each menu option is described next. Option 4 appears if the OS is configured for a network, and Option 8 appears if a previous version of DOS was retained during the Windows 9x/Me installation.

Normal

In Msdos.sys, if BootGUI=1, this option starts Windows 9x/Me. If BootGUI=0, this option boots to the DOS 7.0 or DOS 7.1 prompt (the DOS core of Windows 9x/Me). Either way, the commands in Autoexec.bat and Config.sys are executed.

If a problem appears when you boot in normal mode but does not appear when you boot in Safe Mode, then suspect that Config.sys, Autoexec.bat, System.ini, and Win.ini are the sources of your problem. To eliminate Config.sys or Autoexec.bat as the source of the problem, boot using the Step-by-step confirmation option on the startup menu. To eliminate Win.ini or System.ini as the source of the problem, do the following:

1. Change the name of the System.ini file in the Windows folder to System.sav.

2. Find the System.cb file in the Windows folder, and make a copy of it. Rename the copy System.ini. Don't rename the original System.cb file because you might need it at another time.

3. In the [boot] section of the System.ini file, add this line and then save the file: **drivers=mmsystem.dll**

4. Change the name of the Win.ini file in the Windows folder to Win.sav.

5. Restart your computer.

If this works, the problem was in the Win.ini or System.ini files, and you can reexamine these files in detail to determine the exact source of the problem.

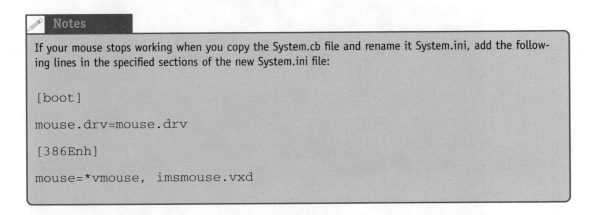

> **Notes**
>
> If your mouse stops working when you copy the System.cb file and rename it System.ini, add the following lines in the specified sections of the new System.ini file:
>
> ```
> [boot]
>
> mouse.drv=mouse.drv
>
> [386Enh]
>
> mouse=*vmouse, imsmouse.vxd
> ```

Logged (\Bootlog.txt)

This option is the same as Normal, except that Windows 9x/Me tracks the load and startup activities and logs them to the Bootlog.txt file. A portion of a sample Bootlog.txt file is shown in Figure 7-32. This file contains information about which components loaded successfully and which did not. The file can be a helpful tool when troubleshooting.

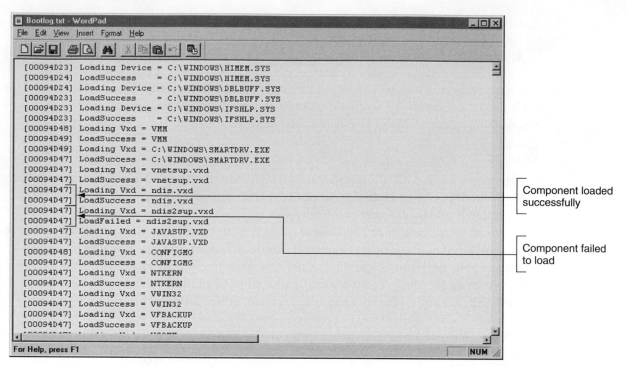

Figure 7-32 The Bootlog.txt file contains information about successful and unsuccessful boot activities

Safe Mode (Press the F5 Key While Loading)

When you have problems with the Windows 9x/Me boot process but no error message appears during the boot, you can use Safe Mode to troubleshoot the problems. You can get to Safe Mode either from the startup menu or by pressing the F5 key while Windows is loading. Figure 7-33 shows Windows 98 booted into Safe Mode.

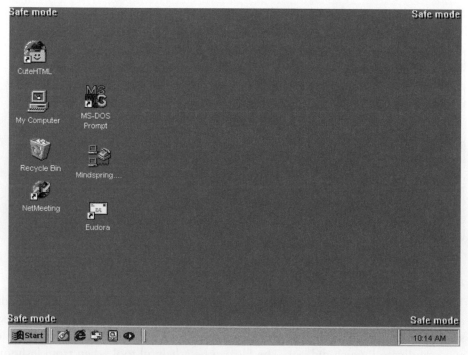

Figure 7-33 Windows 98 Safe Mode desktop

Safe Mode starts Windows 9x/Me with a minimum default configuration to give you an opportunity to correct an error in the configuration. Safe Mode does not execute entries in the registry that load device drivers and bypasses Config.sys, Autoexec.bat, and the [boot] and [386Enh] sections of System.ini. Therefore, devices such as the CD-ROM drive won't work in Safe Mode. Safe Mode does load basic keyboard and mouse drivers and loads standard VGA display drivers. It sets the display resolution to 640 x 480. Also, when you enter Safe Mode, Windows 98/Me includes support for networks, but Windows 95 does not.

For example, if you selected a video driver that is incompatible with your system, Windows 9x/Me detects the problem when it starts and enters Safe Mode with a standard VGA driver selected. You can then go to Device Manager, select the correct driver, and restart Windows.

From the startup menu, you can choose to enter Safe Mode if you know of a problem you want to correct. For example, if you selected a group of background and foreground colors that makes reading the screens impossible, you can reboot and choose Safe Mode. Safe Mode gives you the standard color scheme along with the VGA mode. You then can go to Display Properties, make the necessary corrections, and reboot.

Sometimes you will use Safe Mode for troubleshooting when you don't know exactly what the problem is. In that situation, after you are in Safe Mode, use the following checklist:

- Use a current version of antivirus software to scan for a virus.
- Sometimes loading in Safe Mode is all that is needed. Try to reboot the PC in normal mode.
- If the Safe Recovery dialog box opens, select the option of Use Safe Recovery. Windows 9x/Me then attempts to recover from previous boot problems. Try to boot again.
- If you were having problems installing a device before the Windows problem started, disable or remove the device in Device Manager. Reboot after disabling each device that you suspect to be a problem.
- If you have just made configuration changes, undo the changes and reboot.
- Look for real-mode drivers or TSRs (programs loaded in Config.sys, Autoexec.bat, or System.ini) that might be causing a problem, and disable them by putting a semicolon or an REM at the beginning of the command line.
- Try to boot again. If the problem is still not solved, restore the registry. For Windows 95, make backups of System.dat and User.dat. Then overwrite them with System.da0 and User.da0. For Windows 98/Me, use ScanReg to restore the registry from backups. (ScanReg was covered earlier in the chapter.)
- Run ScanDisk to repair errors on the hard drive and optimize it. While in Safe Mode, select **Start, Programs, Accessories, System Tools,** and **ScanDisk.** Under Type of Test, click **Thorough** (as shown in Figure 7-34).
- Run the Defragmenter utility to optimize the drive.
- For Windows 98, run System File Checker to verify system files.
- For Windows 98/Me, run Automatic Skip Driver Agent to skip loading any driver that causes a problem. Reboot and examine the Asd.log file for recorded errors.
- For Windows 98/Me, use the System Configuration Utility to reduce the system to essentials and reboot. If the problem goes away, restore one item at a time until the problem returns. Then you can identify the item that is the source of the problem.
- Using Explorer, search for files in system folders that have changed recently. To sort file and folder names by date last modified using Explorer, click the Modified column

heading. To reverse the sort order, hold down the Ctrl key while clicking the Modified column heading. If software or drivers have been installed recently, suspect that they might be the source of the problem.

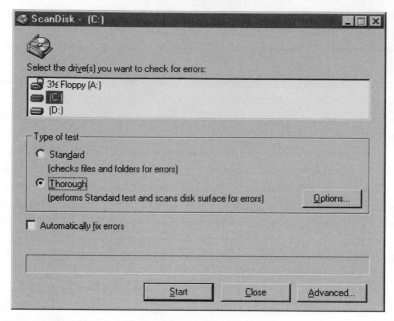

Figure 7-34 Use ScanDisk to check the hard drive for errors

Safe Mode with Network Support

This option allows you access to the network when booting into Safe Mode. It is useful if Windows 95 is stored on a network server and you need to download changes to your PC in Safe Mode. This option is not available on the startup menu in Windows 98/Me, which automatically includes network support.

For Windows 95, to eliminate the network connection as a source of a boot problem you are troubleshooting, first boot in Safe Mode without network support and then boot in Safe Mode with network support. If the boot without network support succeeds but the boot with network support gives errors, then suspect that the network drivers might be the source of the problem. For Windows 98/Me, disable the network card in Device Manager to eliminate the network drivers as the source of the problem.

Step-by-Step Confirmation

This option asks for confirmation before executing each command in Io.sys, Config.sys, and Autoexec.bat. You can accomplish the same thing by pressing Shift+F8 when the message "Starting Windows 95/98" appears.

Command Prompt Only

This option is not available with Windows Me. Under Windows 95/98, it executes the contents of Autoexec.bat and Config.sys but doesn't start Windows 95/98. You get a DOS prompt instead. Type **WIN** to load Windows 95/98. This command executes the file Win.com. You can use several switches with the WIN command when troubleshooting the OS. Table 7-11 lists these switches.

In a troubleshooting situation, try each switch until you find one that works. You can then identify the source of the problem, and can sometimes put entries in the System.ini file to make the switch a permanent part of the load.

Command/Switch	Purpose
WIN /D:M	Starts Windows in Safe Mode
WIN /D:F	Turns off 32-bit disk access; use this option if there appears to be a problem with hard drive access
WIN /D:S	Instructs Windows not to use memory address F000:0, which is used by BIOS
WIN /D:V	Instructs Windows that the system BIOS should be used to access the hard drive rather than the OS
WIN /D:X	Excludes all upper memory addresses from real-mode drivers

Table 7-11 Switches used with the WIN command

Safe Mode Command Prompt Only

This option is not available with Windows Me. Under Windows 95/98, this option does not execute the commands in Autoexec.bat or Config.sys. On the screen, you see only the DOS prompt.

Previous Version of MS-DOS

This option loads a previous version of DOS if one is present. You can get the same results by pressing the F4 key when the message "Starting Windows 95/98" appears. This option is not available in Windows 98 SE or Windows Me.

TROUBLESHOOTING WITH THE STARTUP MENU

If you tried using the tools recommended in the previous sections, but have not yet identified the source of the problem, use the following checklist to troubleshoot using the startup menu:

- Try a hard boot. A soft boot might not do the trick, because TSRs are not always kicked out of RAM with a soft boot.
- If you have not already done so, try Safe Mode next.
- Try the Step-by-step confirmation option next. Look for error messages caused by a missing or corrupted driver file. Try not allowing real-mode drivers to load. After the problem command within Autoexec.bat or Config.sys is identified, you can eliminate the command or troubleshoot it. Specific commands in these files and their purposes are covered in Chapter 6.
- Use the Logged option next, and examine the Bootlog.txt file that is created to see if it identifies the problem. Try comparing the log file to one created on a working PC to find out what was happening when the error occurred.
- Try booting using the Command prompt only option. From the command prompt, run the real-mode version of ScanDisk, which you can find in the \Windows\Command folder, to scan the hard drive for errors. From a command prompt, enter this command: **C:\Windows\Command\Scandisk**. If the Scandisk.exe program on the hard drive is corrupted, use the one on the emergency startup disk.
- From the command prompt in Windows 98/Me, type **Scanreg/Fix** and try to reboot.
- Next, type **Scanreg/Restore** and select the latest known good backup of the Windows 9x/Me registry. Try to reboot.
- From the command prompt, you can use the **WIN** command with the switches listed in Table 7-11. If one of these commands solves the problem, look for real-mode drivers that might be in conflict, eliminating those that you can. Examine Bootlog.txt for errors and try booting from Safe Mode again.

◢ Try booting with the Safe Mode command prompt only. Remember that when you are in Safe Mode, the registry is not executed. If you suspect a corrupted registry, restore it to its last saved version as you learned to do earlier. Then try the WIN command with or without the switches, as necessary.

USING THE STARTUP DISK FOR TROUBLESHOOTING

If you cannot solve the startup problems by using the troubleshooting utilities within Windows or on the startup menu, use an emergency startup disk to recover from the failed boot. If you do not have an emergency startup disk, create one on another computer and use it to work with the computer that has the problem. How to create this emergency startup disk is covered in Chapter 6.

Before You Use the Startup Disk

Before using the startup disk, it is a good idea to check it for viruses on a working computer by scanning it with antivirus software. If you find a virus on the emergency startup disk, destroy the disk and use a working computer to create a new one. Chapter 6 gives you some tips and things to try after booting from the disk.

Using the Fdisk command on the disk, you can determine if the partition table on the hard drive is intact. If the partition table is good, the next step is to run the Windows 9x/Me Setup program stored on the Windows setup CD. When given the opportunity, select **Verify installed components**. Setup then restores damaged or missing system files. If you cannot use Fdisk to verify the partition table, you might be faced with a hardware problem or the entire hard drive might need to be repartitioned and Windows reinstalled.

Accessing the CD-ROM Drive When Booting from a Floppy Disk

Because the Windows setup program and files are normally stored on a CD, your emergency startup disk should include the drivers necessary to access the CD drive. When you are recovering from a failed hard drive, you will not have access to the 32-bit Windows CD-ROM drivers on the hard drive. Windows 98 and later versions of Windows automatically add the real-mode CD-ROM device drivers to their rescue disks, but Windows 95 does not. This section explains how to add this function to a Windows 95 rescue disk.

Two files are required to access a CD-ROM drive while in real mode: the 16-bit device driver provided by the manufacturer of the CD-ROM drive (or a generic real-mode driver that works with the drive) and the 16-bit real-mode OS interface to the driver, Mscdex.exe. The device driver is loaded from Config.sys, and Mscdex.exe is loaded from Autoexec.bat.

For example, suppose your CD-ROM drive comes with a floppy disk that includes the following files:

◢ *Install.exe.* CD-ROM installation program
◢ *Cdtech.sys.* CD-ROM device driver
◢ Instruction files and documentation

To make your Windows 95 rescue disk capable of accessing the CD-ROM drive when you boot from this disk, first you need to copy two files to the root directory of the rescue disk: Mscdex.exe from the C:\Windows\Command folder and Cdtech.sys from the floppy disk bundled with your CD-ROM drive. Then add the following command or a similar one to the Config.sys file (the parameters in the command lines are explained in the following list):

```
DEVICE = A:\CDTECH.SYS /D:MSCD001
```

Put the following command or a similar one in your Autoexec.bat file on the floppy disk:

```
MSCDEX.EXE /D:MSCD001 /L:E /M:10
```

The explanations of these command lines are as follows:

- When the program Mscdex.exe executes, it uses the MSCD001 entry as a tag back to the Config.sys file to learn which device driver is being used to interface with the drive. In this case, it is Cdtech.sys.
- To Mscdex.exe, the drive is named MSCD001 and is being managed by the driver Cdtech.sys.
- Mscdex.exe uses Cdtech.sys as its "go-between" to access the drive.
- Mscdex.exe also assigns a drive letter to the drive. If you want to specify a drive letter, use the /L: option in the command line. In this example, the CD-ROM drive is drive E. If you don't use the /L: option, then the next available drive letter is used.
- The /M: option controls the number of memory buffers.
- If the files referenced in these two commands are stored on the floppy disk in a different directory from the root directory, then include the path to the file in front of the filename.

TROUBLESHOOTING PROBLEMS AFTER WINDOWS 9X/ME STARTUP

Troubleshooting a PC problem begins with isolating it into one of two categories: problems that prevent the PC from booting and problems that occur after a successful startup. In this section, we look at problems that occur after the boot that might be caused by hardware, applications, or Windows. Begin by asking the user questions such as the following to learn as much as you can:

- When did the problem start?
- Were there any error messages or unusual displays on the screen?
- What programs or software were you using?
- Did you move your computer system recently?
- Has there been a recent thunderstorm or electrical problem?
- Have you made any hardware, software, or configuration changes?
- Has someone else been using your computer recently?
- Can you show me exactly what you did when this problem occurred? (Have the user reproduce the problem and watch each step.)
- Next, ask whether the PC boots properly. If not, then begin troubleshooting the failed boot.

Here are some general tips for troubleshooting hardware:

- Try rebooting the computer. The problem with the device may disappear when Windows redetects it.
- Frequent system lockups and General Protection Faults might indicate corrupted memory modules. Try using memory-testing software to check for intermittent memory errors, which indicate the module needs replacing. An example of memory-testing software is DocMemory by CST, Inc. (*www.docmemory.com*).
- For external devices such as monitors, printers, and scanners, try turning on the device before turning on the computer. If your computer is on and you are rebooting, leave the device on and online.

▲ If a device doesn't work with one application, try it with another. If the problem occurs only with one application, the problem is probably not with the hardware device but with that application.

▲ Check Device Manager for errors it reports about the device. If it reports errors, use the Hardware Troubleshooter in Device Manager to help resolve the problem or go to the Microsoft Web site and search for the error message.

▲ The driver might be corrupted or need updating. Look on the Web for updated device drivers. Search the device manufacturer's Web site or the Microsoft Web site for information about problems with the device and solutions.

▲ Use Device Manager to uninstall the device and then reinstall it. If you uninstall the device and then reboot, Windows should recognize an uninstalled device and automatically launch the Found New Hardware Wizard. If it doesn't launch, then chances are the device is not working or is not PnP.

▲ For PnP devices on expansion cards such as sound cards, modems, and network cards, if you uninstall the device in Device Manager and Windows does not recognize the device when you reboot, the device might not be working. The expansion card needs to be reseated or moved to a different expansion slot. If that doesn't work, the card needs replacing.

▲ If none of these things work, ask yourself what changed since the device last worked. For example, maybe you added another hardware device that conflicts with the one you are using, or maybe you have added software that conflicts with the software that the problem device is using. Try disabling other devices or try uninstalling software that you suspect is causing the problem. Use Automatic Skip Driver Agent to eliminate other devices that might prevent the problem driver from working.

For application software problems, try the following:

▲ Address any error messages that appear when using the software.

▲ If you don't understand the error message, write it down or print it, and then look it up on the Microsoft support Web site or the product manufacturer's Web site. Follow the directions given on the Web sites to solve the problem.

▲ Read the documentation that came with the application and documents on the manufacturer Web site. Perhaps you are using a function incorrectly.

▲ A virus might be the source of the problem. Run current antivirus software.

▲ Consider that data files might be corrupted. Try creating new data files used by the software.

▲ Consider that the hardware the software is using might have a problem. For the hard drive, run ScanDisk and Defrag and check for free disk space. Delete files in the \Windows\Temp folder. For a device other than the hard drive, try using another application to access the device.

▲ Try uninstalling and reinstalling the software. Back up the data first.

▲ Launch Dr. Watson and then try to reproduce the error with the application. Look in the Dr. Watson log files for clues and search the Microsoft Web site.

▲ Perhaps the application depends on OS files that are corrupted. Try restoring Windows system files. Check the Microsoft Web site for Windows 9x/Me service packs that might resolve the problem. Install all Windows service packs. You might have to reinstall Windows.

▲ Ask yourself, "When was the last time the software worked?" What happened differently then? Did you get an error message that seemed insignificant at the time? What has happened to your computer since the software last worked? Have you added more software or changed the hardware configuration?

▲ A configuration file, which contains software settings, might be corrupted. Look for a file with a file extension of .ini, .inf, or .cfg.

If a shortcut on the Windows desktop does not work or gives errors, try the following:

▲ Icons on the desktop are created by putting files in the \Windows\Desktop folder. First decide if the icon on the desktop is actually a shortcut. An icon might represent a file stored in the Desktop folder or it might be a shortcut to a file stored anywhere on the drive. If the icon has a small, bent-arrow shortcut symbol on the icon, it is a shortcut. For example, the icon in Figure 7-35 on the right represents the document file MyLetter1.doc stored in the \Windows\Desktop folder, and the icon on the left is a shortcut to the file MyLetter2.doc, which can be stored anywhere on the drive.

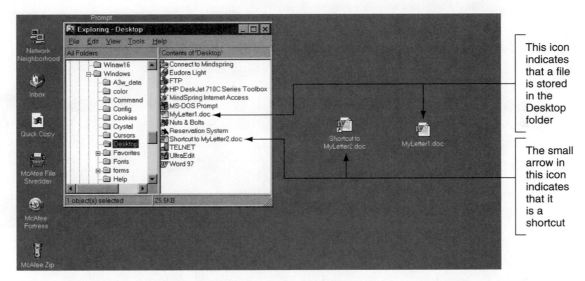

Figure 7-35 One icon is a shortcut, and the other icon represents a file stored in the Desktop folder

▲ If the icon is a shortcut, right-click the shortcut and select **Properties** from the drop-down menu. Look for the name and location of the target file for the shortcut. Now search for this file to see if it's still in the same location and named the same.

If the system is performing slowly, try the following:

▲ The problem might be caused by lack of resources. If your system is running low on memory or has too many applications open, it might not be able to support a device. A corrupted Windows system file or registry can also cause problems with hardware devices. Try verifying system files or restoring the registry from backup.

▲ Check the hard drive. Run ScanDisk and Defrag. Delete unneeded files and empty the Recycle Bin. Generally clean up the hard drive, making plenty of room for the swap file and temporary files used by applications.

▲ Suspect a virus. Run a current version of antivirus software. Clean or delete all files that contain viruses. Restore system files.

▲ Check for applications loaded at startup that use system resources. Close applications not currently in use.

▲ Look for icons in the **system tray**, the small area on the right side of the taskbar at the bottom of the screen. These icons represent small applets that are loaded at startup and take up system resources. Keep these icons to a minimum.

◢ Clean up the registry using the Scanreg /opt command.

◢ Remove extraneous software such as fancy screen savers and desktop wallpaper and photos.

◢ Verify that Windows is using optimum caching on the hard drive and CD-ROM drive. Go to the System Properties window and click the **Performance** tab. Click **File System**. The File System Properties window opens (see Figure 7-36). On the Hard Disk tab, select Full Read-ahead optimization, and on the CD-ROM tab, select Large cache size.

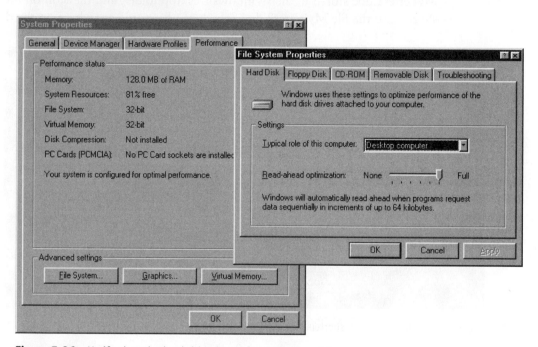

Figure 7-36 Verify that the hard drive is set for optimal caching

ERROR MESSAGES USING WINDOWS 9X/ME

Table 7-12 lists some error messages that might appear when using Windows 9x/Me and what to do about them.

Error Message	What to Do
Bad command or file not found	The OS command just executed cannot be interpreted, or the OS cannot find the program file specified in the command line. Check the spelling of the filename and the path to the file.
Insufficient memory	This error happens during or after the boot under Windows when too many applications are open. Close some applications. A reboot might help.
Incorrect DOS version	In real-mode DOS, when you execute a DOS external command, the OS looks for a program file with the same name as the command. It finds that this file belongs to a different version of the OS than the one that is now running. Use the Setver command at the command prompt or in Autoexec.bat.

Table 7-12 Error messages when using Windows 9x/Me

WINDOWS HELP AND THE MICROSOFT WEB SITE

Windows Help might provide useful information when you try to resolve a problem. To access the Troubleshooting tool of Windows Help, click **Start,** click **Help,** and then click **Troubleshooting.** The Help information includes suggestions that can lead you to a solution. For example, in Figure 7-37, the Hardware Troubleshooter suggests that you check to see that the device is not listed twice in Device Manager. If this is the case, you should remove the second occurrence of the device.

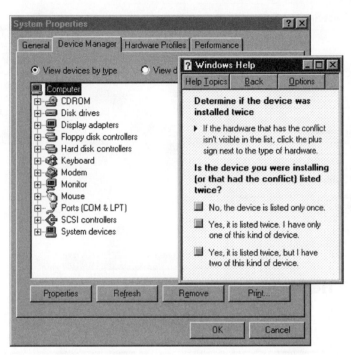

Figure 7-37 Troubleshooter making a suggestion to resolve a hardware conflict

Also, the Microsoft Web site (*support.microsoft.com*; see Figure 7-38) has lots of information on troubleshooting. Search for the device, an error message, a Windows utility, a symptom, a software application, an update version number, or keywords that lead you to articles about problems and solutions. You can also go to *www.microsoft.com* to browse for links on hardware and software compatibility. Other sources of help are application and device user and installation manuals, training materials, and the Web sites of application and device manufacturers.

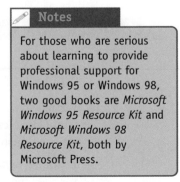

Notes

For those who are serious about learning to provide professional support for Windows 95 or Windows 98, two good books are *Microsoft Windows 95 Resource Kit* and *Microsoft Windows 98 Resource Kit*, both by Microsoft Press.

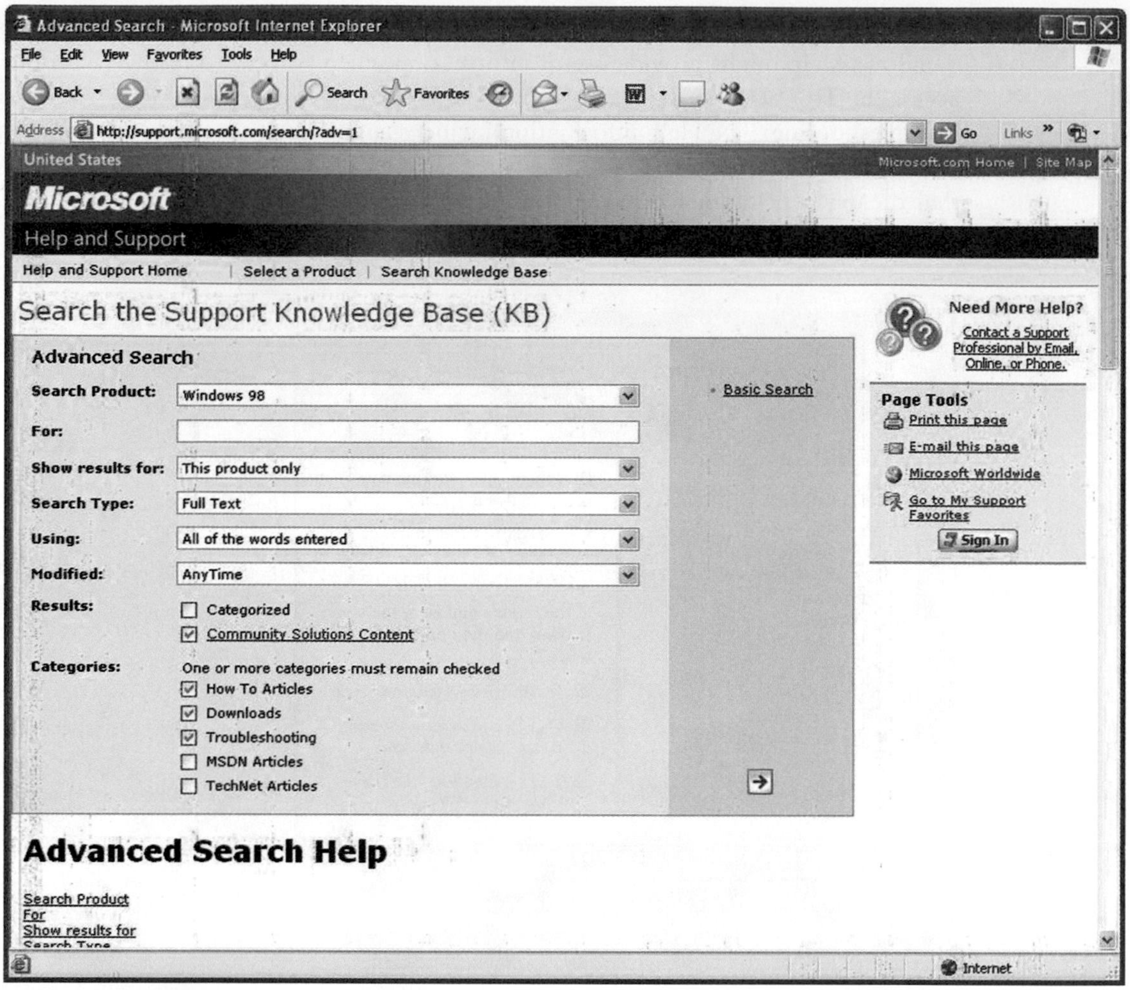

Figure 7-38 Microsoft Technical Support Web site

>> CHAPTER SUMMARY

▲ Windows 9x/Me has a shell and kernel; the Windows 9x/Me core consists of the kernel, the user, and the GDI.

▲ Virtual machines (VMs) are multiple logical machines within one physical machine. If an application crashes or produces another type of error within a VM, only that VM is affected, instead of the entire system.

▲ Although Windows 95/98 supports 16-bit drivers, using 32-bit drivers whenever possible is better. Windows Me does not use 16-bit drivers.

▲ If Windows is already installed and you want to do a clean install, delete the \Windows folder or use the setup screen to install the new OS in a different folder.

▲ Before performing a Windows 98/Me upgrade, check hardware and software compatibility, run antivirus software, and back up your system. The Setup Wizard on the Windows 98 CD will guide you through the setup process. After Setup is complete, test installed applications and back up your system again.

▲ When adding new hardware to Windows 9x/Me, use the Add New Hardware Wizard. Select the hardware from a list of devices to use a Windows driver, or click Have Disk to use your own drivers (from a manufacturer's disk or downloaded from the Internet to a folder on your hard drive). Alternately, you can run the Setup program provided by the device manufacturer.

▲ For a Windows 9x/Me system to be truly Plug and Play (PnP), the system BIOS must be PnP, all hardware devices and expansion cards must be PnP-compliant, and a 32-bit device driver must be available for any installed hardware device.

▲ Dosstart.bat is a type of Autoexec.bat file that executes when you restart the computer in MS-DOS mode or when you run a program in MS-DOS mode.

▲ An OS that supports protected mode can create a virtual real mode for a 16-bit application so that the application thinks it is the only program running, has all memory available to it, and accesses data using a 16-bit data path. Windows 9x/Me ordinarily runs a 16-bit DOS application in a virtual DOS machine.

▲ Starting with Windows 9x/Me, the Windows registry takes over the essential functions of .ini files. However, Windows 9x/Me still supports System.ini and Win.ini for backward compatibility with legacy hardware devices and legacy software applications.

▲ The registry is contained in two files, System.dat and User.dat, for Windows 95/98 and in three files, System.dat, User.dat, and Classes.dat, for Windows Me. Windows 95 maintains backups of these files, called System.da0 and User.da0, that you can use when troubleshooting. Windows 98/Me keeps compressed backups of the registry and system files in cabinet files named rb000.cab, rb001.cab, and so forth.

▲ Changes in Control Panel, Device Manager, and other locations in Windows 9x/Me can change the registry automatically. The Regedit utility is used to edit the registry manually.

▲ The Registry Checker (Scanreg.exe or Scanregw.exe) backs up, verifies, and recovers the registry. It automatically backs up the registry every day and keeps the last five days of backups.

▲ The five phases of the Windows 9x/Me boot process are: (1) BIOS POST and bootstrap; (2) loading the OS real-mode operating environment; (3) loading of real-mode VxDs; (4) protected-mode switchover and PnP configuration; and (5) loading remaining components.

▲ Applications are loaded at startup by a shortcut in the StartUp folder, the name of the program file in the Load= or Run= line in Win.ini, or an entry in the registry.

▲ The System Configuration Utility (Msconfig.exe) allows you to modify the system configuration temporarily to help with troubleshooting. It reduces the startup process to essentials.

▲ The Dr. Watson utility (Drwatson.exe) helps you troubleshoot applications by trapping errors in log files and taking a snapshot of the system.

▲ The System Configuration Editor (Sysedit.exe) is a text editor used to edit system files. When you run Sysedit, it automatically opens Protocol.ini, System.ini, Win.ini, Config.sys, and Autoexec.bat.

▲ Device Manager lists hardware devices installed on a system. For more information about a specific device in Device Manager, click the device and select **Properties**.

▲ When troubleshooting Windows 9x/Me boot problems, first check error messages, then boot in Safe Mode, then boot to the command prompt using the startup menu, and finally try booting from an emergency startup disk.

◢ To force the Windows 9x/Me startup menu to appear, hold down either the Ctrl key or the F8 key during the boot.

◢ You can reach Safe Mode either from the Windows startup menu or by pressing the F5 key while Windows is loading.

◢ Safe Mode starts Windows 9x/Me with a minimum default configuration to give you an opportunity to correct an error in the configuration.

◢ Choosing Command Prompt Only from the startup menu executes the contents of Autoexec.bat and Config.sys but does not start Windows. Instead it brings you to a DOS prompt. Use the WIN command to load Windows 9x/Me.

◢ Use the startup disk to recover from a failed boot when you cannot solve the problem using the startup menu or cannot boot from the hard drive. If you do not have a startup disk or the one you have has a virus, use a working computer to create a new disk.

>> KEY TERMS

For explanations of key terms, see the Glossary near the end of the book.

application programming interface (API) call	IFS (Installable File System)	System.ini
	initialization files	system tray
clean install	keys	upgrade install
comment line	memory paging	user component
Configuration Manager	pages	value data
disk thrashing	patches	virtual device driver (VxD)
Dosstart.bat	PIF (program information file)	virtual machine (VM)
Dr. Watson	Protocol.ini	VMM (Virtual Machine Manager)
DriveSpace	service pack	
dynamic VxDs	slack	WDM (Win32 Driver Model)
GDI (Graphics Device Interface)	static VxDs	Win.ini
General Protection Fault	Sysedit	Win386.swp

>> REVIEWING THE BASICS

1. What are the three core components of Windows 9x/Me?

2. Which are preferable to use: 32-bit drivers or 16-bit drivers?

3. What is the function of the Autorun.inf file included on the Windows 9x/Me installation CD? The Setup.exe file? The Readme.txt file?

4. List at least five things you need to do to prepare your hard drive for an upgrade installation of Windows 9x/Me.

5. What are the four types of installations that you can choose during setup of Windows 9x/Me?

6. What are the log files Setuplog.txt, Detlog.txt, and Detcrash.log used for?

7. What type of disk should you always create when prompted to do so during Windows 9x/Me setup? Why is this such an important step?

8. What is the Windows keyboard shortcut to display the startup menu while Windows is loading? To go through step-by-step confirmation of startup?

9. When installing hardware under Windows 9x/Me, how do you indicate that you want to use a Windows driver? A manufacturer-provided or downloaded driver?

10. Use the _____ applet in Control Panel when installing 32-bit software designed for Windows 9x/Me. Use the _____ option on the Start menu when installing older 16-bit software.

11. What is a comment line? How is a comment line noted within a file?

12. Explain the purpose of the System Configuration Utility. How would you use it in troubleshooting?

13. Name four configuration files that Windows 9x/Me includes for backward compatibility with legacy software and hardware.

14. The Windows 98/95 registry is contained in two files, _____ and _____. The Windows 95 backups of these files are called _____ and _____.

15. Which version of Windows includes the Registry Checker? How often does this utility back up the registry?

16. Explain the difference between the Regedit and Scanreg utilities.

17. Name the files that Sysedit automatically displays for editing. Give a short description of each.

18. List the five phases of the Windows 9x/Me boot process and give a short description of each.

19. Explain how the program Setver.exe is used in Windows 9x/Me.

20. What Msdos.sys entry can be used to backtrack from a Windows 9x/Me installation to the underlying version of DOS? What happens when this entry is set to =0? To =1?

21. What command do you enter in the Run dialog box to load Registry Checker under Windows?

22. List the options on the Windows 9x/Me startup menu and give a short description of each. Which option appears for Windows 95 but not for Windows 98, and why? Which option appears for Windows 95/98, but not for Windows Me?

23. Which startup menu options execute Autoexec.bat and Config.sys? Which do not?

24. What Windows utility allows you to control what drivers are loaded during Windows startup?

25. _____ is a Windows utility that can record detailed information about the system, errors that occur, and the programs that caused them in a log file.

26. What parts of the Windows load does Safe Mode not execute?

27. Name two ways to end an application that is hung without rebooting the PC.

28. After using the Windows 98 startup menu to boot the system to a command prompt, what command can you use to load the Windows desktop?

29. What is the name of the third file Windows Me added to store the registry that was not used with Windows 95/98?

30. What function key do you press during bootup to start Windows 98 in Safe Mode?

>> THINKING CRITICALLY

1. An application loads at startup. List the steps you would take to stop an application from loading at this time.

2. Place these tools in the order you would use them when troubleshooting the Windows 9x/Me boot process: emergency startup disk, Safe Mode, error messages, and the command prompt.

3. You attempt to install a new hardware device, but Windows 98 locks up during the boot. You remove the device and try to reboot, but Windows 98 still locks up. Which tools do you use to solve the problem and what do you do with them? (*Note*: You might use more than one of these tools.)

▲ Device Manager

▲ System Information utility

▲ Windows 98 startup disk

▲ Scanreg

▲ Registry Checker

>> HANDS-ON PROJECTS

PROJECT 7-1:   Installing a Windows Component

Using the Add/Remove Programs applet in Control Panel, look for Windows components that are not installed, and install one. You need access to the Windows 98 CD, or the files on the CD must be copied to the hard drive or a network drive.

PROJECT 7-2:   Using Shortcuts

Create a shortcut on your desktop to Notepad (Notepad.exe), a text editor. Using a second method for creating shortcuts, add a shortcut to the Windows command prompt (Command.com). First, locate the two program files on your hard drive by clicking **Start, Find,** and using the Find dialog box. Then create the shortcuts. List the steps you took to create each shortcut.

PROJECT 7-3:   Using the Windows 9x/Me Startup Menu

As soon as your computer displays the message "Starting Windows 95/98" during the boot process, press the **F8** function key. Select **Logged(\Bootlog.txt)**. After the boot is complete, open the file **Bootlog.txt** and print its contents. Shut down Windows, reboot the computer, and then press the **F8** key again. Select the **Safe Mode** option, and note the differences in the screen's appearance. Shut down Windows, reboot the computer, and then press the **F8** key again. This time, choose the **Step-by-step confirmation** option. Write down each command that executes.

PROJECT 7-4:   Using Windows Utilities and Files

1. Place a shortcut to Task Manager on your desktop. Print a screen shot of the Properties window of the shortcut. Test the shortcut.

2. Cause Sysedit to launch automatically at startup. Print the screen showing how you did this.

3. Edit Msdos.sys so that it automatically displays the startup menu when loading Windows. Print the contents of the file.

PROJECT 7-5:   Troubleshooting a Boot Problem

Edit the Config.sys file on your PC. If you are using an installation of Windows 9x/Me that does not use a Config.sys file, then create one. Enter a command line in the file that you know will cause an error. Boot the PC. Press the **F8** key during the boot, and walk through the boot process to demonstrate how this procedure can help you diagnose a problem with startup files.

Correct the command line in Config.sys, reboot, and walk through each command in the boot process.

PROJECT 7-6:   Tools for Troubleshooting a Device Driver

Using Automatic Skip Driver Agent (ASDA), disable one or more devices at startup. Print a screen shot of ASDA showing the disabled devices. Reboot and verify that the devices are not available. Using ASDA, enable the devices, reboot, and verify that the devices work.

Be sure you have the drivers for the devices available on the hard drive, floppy disk, or CD. Using Device Manager, uninstall a device. Print a screen shot of Device Manager showing that the device is not installed. Reinstall the device and verify that it is working.

PROJECT 7-7:   Preparing a Hard Drive for the Installation of Windows 9x/Me

Do the following to prepare a hard drive for a new installation of Windows 9x/Me:

1. Boot from a Windows 9x/Me startup disk, and then use Fdisk to create primary and extended partitions on the drive. The primary partition will contain drive C. If there is room on the drive, create two logical drives in the extended partition.

2. Format all three logical drives, placing system files on drive C.

3. Verify that you can boot to drive C, get a C prompt, and access all three drives.

4. Use the DIR command to print a directory of each drive to a local printer. Use these or similar commands: DIR C:> PRN, DIR D:> PRN, and DIR E:> PRN.

5. Using ScanDisk, scan each logical drive disk surface for errors.

> **Caution**
>
> This project requires that you completely erase everything on your hard drive. If you have important data on the drive, don't do this project!

>> REAL PROBLEMS, REAL SOLUTIONS

REAL PROBLEM 7-1:   Installing Windows 9x/Me

Follow the instructions in this chapter to install Windows 9x/Me using a Typical installation. Create the rescue disk when prompted to do so. Write down each decision you have to make as you perform the installation. If you get any error messages during the installation, write them down and list the steps you took to recover from the error. How long did the installation take?

Windows on a Network

In this chapter, we discuss how to use Windows to connect PCs in networks and how to access resources on a network. You'll learn about the technologies used to build networks and how Windows supports and manages a network connection, including how computers are identified and addressed on a network. You'll also learn to connect a computer to a network and share its resources with others on the network.

Wireless networking is becoming more and more popular, so you'll also learn how to connect a PC or notebook to a wireless network. You'll also learn how to set up and secure a wireless network. And you'll learn to troubleshoot a network connection. In the next chapter, you'll learn how to connect to the Internet and how to use the resources on it.

PHYSICAL NETWORK ARCHITECTURES

A+ ESS
5.1

A+
220-602
5.1

In this first part of the chapter, you'll learn about the various types of networking technologies and designs. We'll first look at the different sizes of networks, the different technologies used by networks, and some networking terms. Then, we'll turn our attention to the details of the types of networks you are most likely to encounter as a Windows support technician, which include Ethernet, wireless networks, and VoIP telephone networks.

SIZES OF NETWORKS

A computer network is created when two or more computers can communicate with each other. Networks can be categorized by several methods, including the technology used and the size of the network. When networks are categorized by size or physical area they cover, these are the categories used:

▲ *PAN*. A PAN (personal area network) consisting of personal devices at close range such as a cell phone, PDA, and notebook computer in communication. PANs can use wired connections (such as USB or FireWire) or wireless connections (such as Bluetooth or infrared).

▲ *LAN*. A LAN (local area network) covers a small local area such as a home, office, or other building or small group of buildings. LANs can use wired (most likely Ethernet) or wireless (most likely 802.11) technologies. A LAN is used for workstations, servers, printers, and other devices to communicate and share resources.

▲ *MAN*. A MAN (metropolitan area network) covers a large campus or city. (A small MAN is sometimes called a CAN or campus area network.) Newer technologies used are wireless and Ethernet with fiber-optic cabling. Older technologies used are ATM and FDDI.

▲ *WAN*. A WAN (wide area network) covers a large geographical area and is made up of many smaller networks. The best known WAN is the Internet.

ADDITIONAL TERMS USED IN NETWORKING

Before we get into the details of network architecture, you need to know a few terms and what they mean:

▲ A node, or host, is one device on the network. It can be a workstation, server, printer, or other device.

▲ A PC makes a direct connection to a network by way of a network adapter, which might be a network port embedded on the motherboard or a network interface card (NIC), using a PCI slot, such as the one shown in Figure 8-1. In addition, the adapter might also be an external device connecting to the PC using a USB port, SCSI external port, or serial port. The adapter might provide a port for a network cable or an antenna for a wireless connection. The adapter must match the type and speed of the physical network being used, and the network port must match the type of connectors used on the network. Laptops can make connections to a network through a PC Card NIC, a built-in network port, a wireless connection, or an external device that connects to the laptop by way of a USB port.

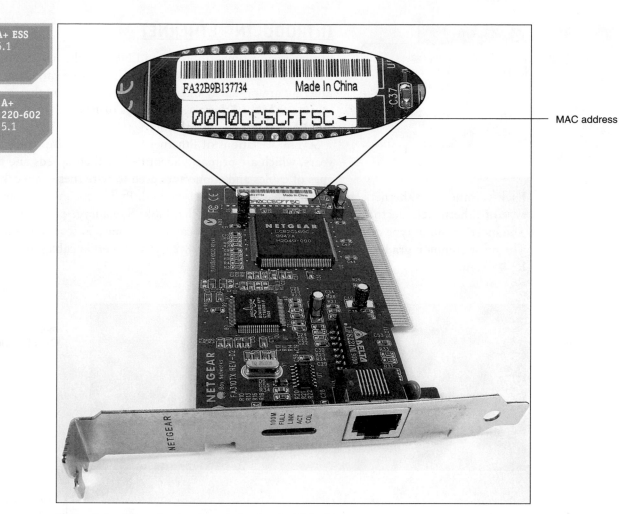

MAC address

Figure 8-1 Ethernet network card showing its MAC address

▲ Every network adapter (including a network card, onboard wireless, or wireless NIC) has a 48-bit (6-byte) number hard-coded on the card by its manufacturer that is unique for that adapter, and this number is used to identify the adapter on the network. The number is often written in hex and is called the **MAC (Media Access Control) address, hardware address, physical address, adapter address,** or Ethernet address. An example of a MAC address is 00-0C-6E-4E-AB-A5. Part of the MAC address refers to the manufacturer; therefore, no two adapters should have the same MAC address. Most likely the MAC address is written on the card, as shown in Figure 8-1.

▲ Communication on a network follows rules of communication called network protocols. Communication over a network happens in layers. The OS on one PC communicates with the OS on another PC using one set of protocols, and the network card communicates with other hardware devices on the network using another set of networking protocols. Examples of OS protocols are TCP/IP and NetBEUI, and examples of hardware protocols are Ethernet and Token Ring. You'll learn more about these protocols later in the chapter.

▲ Data is transmitted on a network in pieces called **packets, datagrams,** or **frames.** Information about the packet that identifies the type of data, where it came from, and where it's going is placed at the beginning and end of the data. Information at the beginning of the data is called a header, and information at the end of the data is called a trailer. If the data to be sent is large, it is first divided into several packets small enough to travel on the network.

A+ ESS
2.1
5.1

A+
220-602
2.1
5.1
5.3

A+ Tip

The A+ Essentials exam expects you to be familiar with many networking terms. This chapter is full of key terms you need to know for the exam.

INTRODUCING ETHERNET

Ethernet (sometimes abbreviated ENET) is the most popular network architecture used today. The three variations of Ethernet are primarily distinguished from one another by speed: 10-Mbps Ethernet, 100-Mbps or Fast Ethernet, and 1000-Mbps or Gigabit Ethernet.

Several variations of Ethernet have evolved over the years, which are primarily identified by their speeds and the types of cables and connectors used to wire these networks. Each variation of Ethernet can use more than one cabling method. By far, the most common type of Ethernet connector is called an RJ-45 connector that looks like a large phone jack. The most common type of Ethernet cable is twisted-pair cable that comes in several grades. The most common grades are CAT5 and CAT5E. Figure 8-2 shows Ethernet cables and a RJ-45 connector.

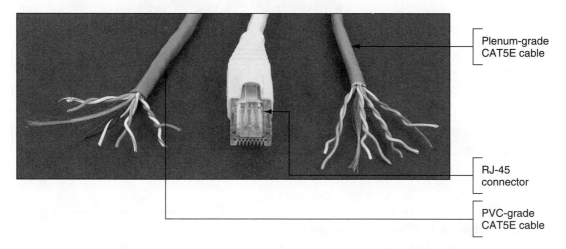

Plenum-grade
CAT5E cable

RJ-45
connector

PVC-grade
CAT5E cable

Figure 8-2 The most common networking cable for a local network is UTP cable using an RJ-45 connector

APPLYING|CONCEPTS   PATCH CABLES AND CROSSOVER CABLES

Two types of network cables can be used when building a network: a patch cable and a crossover cable. A **patch cable** (also called a straight-through cable) is used to connect a computer to a hub or switch. A **crossover cable** is used to connect two PCs (when a hub or switch is not used) to make the simplest network of all.

The difference in a patch cable and a crossover cable is the way the read and write lines are wired in the connectors at each end of the cables. A crossover cable has the read and write lines reversed so that one computer reads off the line to which the other computer writes. For older hubs, it was necessary to use a crossover cable to connect a hub to another hub. However, today you can connect a hub or switch to another hub or switch using the more common patch cables because these devices have a special port (called the uplink port) to use for the connection. Also, most switches use auto-uplinking, which means you can connect a switch to a switch using a patch cable on any port.

A+ ESS
2.1
5.1

A+
220-602
2.1
5.1
5.3

A patch cable and a crossover cable look identical and have identical connectors. One way to tell them apart is to look for the labeling imprinted on the cables, as shown in Figure 8-3.

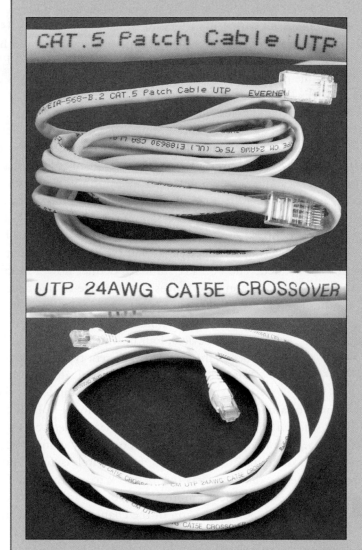

Figure 8-3   Patch cables and crossover cables look the same but are labeled differently

A+ ESS
2.1
5.1
6.1

A+
220-602
2.1
5.1
6.2
6.3

WI-FI WIRELESS NETWORKS

Wireless networks, as the name implies, use radio waves or infrared light instead of cables or wires to connect computers or other devices. A Wireless LAN (WLAN) covers a limited geographical area and is popular in places where networking cables are difficult to install, such as outdoors, in public places, and in homes that are not wired for networks. They are also useful in hotel rooms.

By far, the most popular technology for desktop and notebook computer wireless connections is IEEE 802.11, first published in 1990. Most new wireless LAN devices operate under the IEEE 802.11g standard, which is backward compatible with the earlier and slower IEEE 802.11b standard. These standards are also called **Wi-Fi (Wireless Fidelity)**.

802.11g and 802.11b use a frequency range of 2.4 GHz in the radio band and have a distance range of about 100 meters. 802.11b/g has the disadvantage that many cordless phones use the 2.4-GHz frequency range and cause network interference. 802.11g runs at

A+ ESS
2.1
5.1
6.1

A+
220-602
2.1
5.1
6.2
6.3

54 Mbps and 802.11b runs at 11Mbps. Apple Computer calls 802.11b **AirPort**, and it calls 802.11g AirPort Extreme.

Another IEEE standard is 802.11a, which works in the 5.0-GHz frequency range and is, therefore, not compatible with 802.11b/g. It has a shorter range from a wireless device to an access point (50 meters compared with 100 meters for 802.11b/g), supports 54 Mbps, and does not encounter interference from cordless phones, microwave ovens, and Bluetooth devices, as does 802.11b/g. Most wireless devices today support all three IEEE standards; look for **802.11a/b/g** on the packages. Another standard is 802.11d, which is designed to run in countries outside the United States where other 802.11 versions do not meet the legal requirements for radio band technologies.

As wireless networks become more and more popular and our wireless devices become more mobile, new IEEE standards are being developed to deal with the new demands on the technology. 802.11k and 802.11r are two standards designed to help manage connections between wireless devices and access points. Normally, if a wireless device senses more than one access point, by default, it connects to the access point with the strongest signal, which can cause an overload on some access points while other access points are idle. The 802.11k standard defines how wireless network traffic can better be distributed over multiple access points covering a wide area so that the access point with the strongest signal is not overloaded. The 802.11r standard defines how a mobile wireless device can easily and quickly transition as it moves out of range of one access point and into the range of another.

Wireless connections using 802.11b/g/a can be made with a variety of devices, four of which are shown in Figure 8-4. Notice in the figure the different types of antennae.

Wireless devices can communicate directly (such as a PC to a PC, which is called Ad Hoc mode), or they can connect to a LAN by way of a wireless **access point (AP)**, as shown in Figure 8-5. Multiple access points can be positioned so that nodes can access at least one access point from anywhere in the covered area. When devices use an access point, they communicate through the access point instead of communicating directly. Often a wireless access point is doing double duty as a router, a device that connects one network to another (see Figure 8-6).

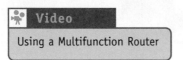

You'll learn more about routers in the next chapter. Also, in a later section of the chapter, you will learn how to configure a wireless device in a computer and connect it to a wireless network.

VoIP TELEPHONE NETWORKS

A+ ESS
2.1
5.1

A+
220-602
2.1
5.1

VoIP (Voice over Internet Protocol), also called Internet telephone, was once a novelty on the Internet, but not very useful because of all the problems with poor voice quality and dropped connections. However, VoIP has recently come of age and has become a viable residential and business alternative to regular phone service. Using VoIP, voice is converted to digital data for transmission over the Internet and to connect to POTS so that people can make and receive calls to VoIP subscribers as well as those using regular telephone service.

Just as with Ethernet, VoIP uses packets of data to communicate, and these voice packets can travel over the Internet using various paths rather than using a single closed circuit as does the PSTN network. Therefore, charges for VoIP are usually based on data sent rather than connect time.

A+ ESS
2.1
5.1
6.1

A+
220-602
2.1
5.1
6.2
6.3

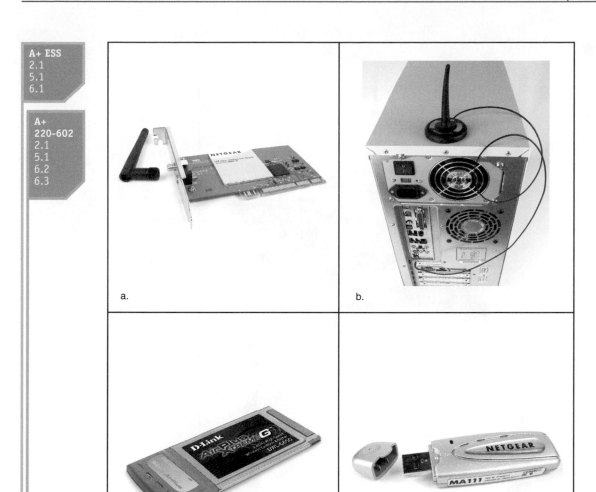

a.

b.

c.

d.

Figure 8-4 Four different types of wireless network adapters: (a) wireless NIC that fits in a PCI slot; (b) onboard wireless with an antenna that can be moved; (c) PC Card wireless NIC with embedded antenna; and (d) wireless NIC that uses a USB port on a desktop or notebook computer

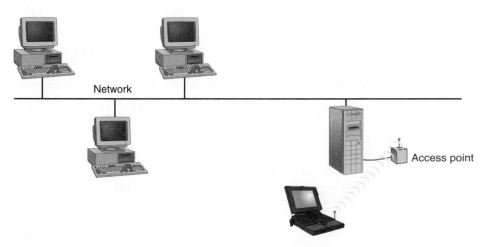

Network

Access point

Figure 8-5 Nodes on a wireless LAN connect to a cabled network by way of an access point

Front

Rear

Figure 8-6 This multifunction device is a router and also serves as a wireless access point to connect computers wirelessly to the local network

To use VoIP, you need a broadband Internet connection such as a cable modem or DSL and a subscription to a VoIP provider. Regular analog or digital telephones can be used, which connect to the Internet by way of a network cable just as your computer connects, as shown in Figure 8-7. The digital phone is this figure connects to a network port on a router or to a network wall jack using an RJ-45 connector labeled in the figure. The AC power adapter plugs into a power outlet and provides power to the phone by way of the one cord to the phone. This one cord is doing double duty as a power cord and a network cable. Also, WiFi telephones are beginning to appear on the market that can use a WiFi hot spot to send and receive VoIP wireless data. Because a WiFi phone is a node on a wireless network, it can have an always-up connection to the Internet. Some expect WiFi phones to ultimately replace cell phones. You'll learn more about VoIP in the next chapter.

A+ ESS
2.1
5.1

A+
220-602
2.1
5.1

AC power
adapter

RJ-45 network
connector

Figure 8-7 This VoIP digital telephone connects to a local network and on to the Internet by way
of a network cable

WINDOWS ON A NETWORK

A+ ESS
5.1

A+
220-602
5.1

As a system of interlinked computers, a network needs both software and hardware to work. Software includes an operating system installed on each computer on the network, and perhaps an **NOS (network operating system)** such as Windows Server 2003 or Unix to control the entire network and its resources. If the network is small (fewer than 10 computers), it can be a **peer-to-peer network,** in which each computer on the network has the same authority as the other computers.

Recall from Chapter 2 that a Windows peer-to-peer network is called a workgroup. Larger networks use the **client/server** model, in which access to a network is controlled by an NOS using a centralized database. A **client** computer provides a user ID and password to a **server** that validates the data against the security database. In a Windows network, this server is called the domain controller, and the network model is called a domain. Popular network operating systems are Windows 2003 Server, Novell NetWare, Open Enterprise Server, Unix, and Linux. Windows has client software built in for Windows and Novell NetWare servers. Alternately, for Novell NetWare, you can install Novell client software.

A network can have more than one workgroup or domain in operation, and some computers might not belong to any workgroup or domain. A computer joins a workgroup or domain in order to share resources with other computers and devices in the group or domain. Company policy controls how many workgroups or domains can exist within the company network. This number is based on user needs, security concerns, and administrative overhead required to manage the groups.

> **A+ Tip**
>
> The A+ Essentials exam expects you to understand the differences between a peer-to-peer network and a client/server network.

A+ ESS
5.1

A+
220-602
5.1

FOUR SUITES OF PROTOCOLS

At the physical network level, Windows supports Ethernet, ATM, Token Ring, and other networking protocols. At the operating system level, Windows supports the four suites of protocols shown in Figure 8-8 and described in the following list. The figure also shows the different ways a computer or other device on the network can be addressed.

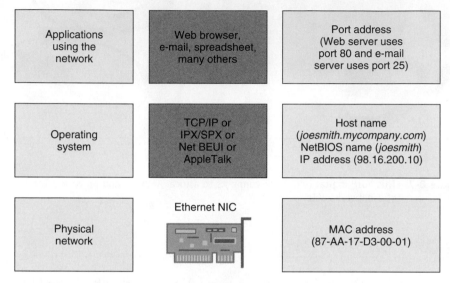

Figure 8-8 An operating system can use more than one method to address a computer on the network, but at the network level, a MAC address is always used to address a device on the network

Use figure 8-8 as a reference point throughout this section to understand the way the protocols and addresses relate on the network.

- ▲ **TCP/IP (Transmission Control Protocol/Internet Protocol)** is the protocol suite used on the Internet and so should be your choice if you want to connect your network to the Internet, with each workstation having Internet access. Novell NetWare, Linux, Unix, and Mac OS also support TCP/IP.
- ▲ **IPX/SPX (Internetwork Packet Exchange/Sequenced Packet Exchange)** is an NWLink protocol suite designed for use with the Novell NetWare operating system. IPX/SPX is similar to TCP/IP but is not supported on the Internet. **NWLink** is Microsoft's version of the IPX/SPX protocol suite used by Novell NetWare. When a Windows PC is a client on a Novell NetWare network, the Windows PC must be configured to use NWLink, which includes the IPX/SPX protocol.
- ▲ **NetBEUI (NetBIOS Extended User Interface**, pronounced *net-bouie*) is a proprietary Windows protocol suite used only by Windows computers. NetBEUI supports **NetBIOS (Network Basic Input/Output System)**, a protocol that applications use to communicate with each other. NetBEUI is faster than TCP/IP and easier to configure but does not support routing to other networks, and, therefore, is not supported on the Internet. It should be used only on an isolated network. Windows XP does not automatically install NetBEUI, because Microsoft considers NetBEUI and NetBIOS to both be legacy protocols.
- ▲ **AppleTalk** is a proprietary networking protocol suite for Macintosh computers by Apple Corporation.

To use one of these protocols on a network, the first step is to physically connect the computer to the network by installing the NIC in the computer and connecting the network cable to the switch, router, or other network device. (For wireless LANs, after installing the NIC, you put the computer within range of an access point.) After the drivers for the NIC are installed, the NIC is automatically associated with an OS networking protocol in a process called binding. **Binding** occurs when an operating system–level protocol such as TCP/IP associates itself with a lower-level hardware protocol such as Ethernet. When the two protocols are bound, communication continues between them until they are unbound, or released.

A+ Tip

The A+ Essentials exam expects you to be familiar with these networking protocols: TCP/IP, IPX/SPX, NWLink, and NetBIOS.

You can determine which protocols are installed in Windows by looking at the properties of a network connection. For example, in Windows XP you can right-click **My Network Places** and select **Properties** from the shortcut menu to open the Network Connections window, as shown on the left side of Figure 8-9. Then right-click the **Local Area Connection** icon and select **Properties** from the shortcut menu. The Local Area Connection Properties dialog box opens, as shown on the right side of the figure.

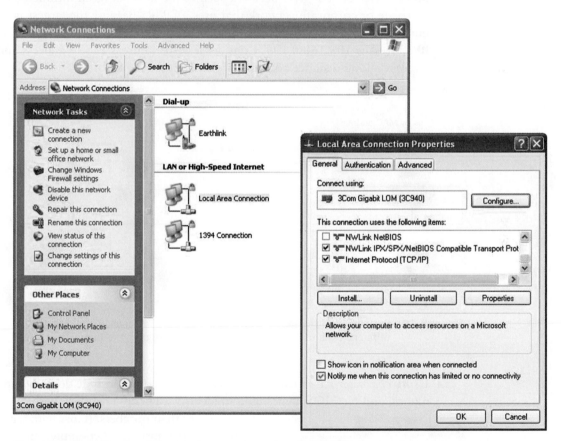

Figure 8-9 Three Windows XP network protocols are installed and two protocols are bound to this network card

You can see that two of the three available protocols are bound to the NIC because they are checked. In this situation, the PC is using a TCP/IP network, but one network printer uses IPX/SPX and does not support TCP/IP. Because the PC uses that printer, it must have IPX/SPX installed. (A **network printer** is a printer that any user on the network can access using one of those methods: (1) through its own network card and connection to the network, (2) through a connection to a standalone print server, or (3) through a connection to a computer as a local printer, which is shared on the network.)

A+ ESS
5.1

There is no problem with more than one operating system protocol operating on the network at the same time. Also, if you want to use a protocol and it is not listed, click **Install** in the Local Area Connection Properties window to select the protocol and install it.

A+
220-602
5.1

ADDRESSING ON A NETWORK

Every device on a network has a unique address. Part of learning about a network is learning how a device (such as a computer or a printer) or a program (such as a Web server) is identified on the network. On a network, four methods are used to identify devices and programs:

▲ *Using a MAC address.* As you learned earlier, a MAC address is a unique, 48-bit address permanently embedded in a NIC and identifying a device on a LAN. The MAC address is used only by devices inside the local network, and is not used outside the LAN.

▲ *Using an IP address.* An **IP address** is a 32-bit address consisting of a series of four 8-bit numbers separated by periods. An IP address identifies a computer, printer, or other device on a TCP/IP network such as the Internet or an intranet. (An **intranet** is a private or corporate network that uses TCP/IP.) Because the largest possible 8-bit number is 255, each of the four numbers can be no larger than 255. An example of an IP address is 109.168.0.104. Consider a MAC address a local address and an IP address a long-distance address, as shown in Figure 8-10.

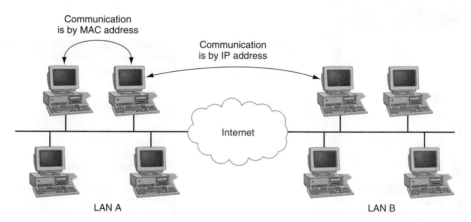

Figure 8-10   Computers on the same LAN use MAC addresses to communicate, but computers on different LANs use IP addresses to communicate over the Internet

▲ *Using character-based names.* Character-based names include domain names, **host names**, and NetBIOS names used to identify a PC on a network with easy-to-remember letters rather than numbers. (Host names and NetBIOS names are often just called **computer names**.)

> **A+ Tip**
>
> The A+ Essentials exam expects you to know each of the methods of identifying devices and programs on a network.

▲ *Using a port address.* A port address is a number that one application uses to address another application installed on a remote computer on the network. Port addresses are covered in the next chapter.

A+ ESS
5.1

A+
220-602
5.1

APPLYING|CONCEPTS EXAMINING YOUR NETWORK CONFIGURATION

If your PC is connected to the Internet or any other TCP/IP network, you can use some Windows utilities to report how the network connection is configured. For Windows 2000/XP, to display the IP address and the MAC addresses of all installed NICs, in a command prompt window, use the command **ipconfig /all**. The screen shown in Figure 8-11 appears.

Figure 8-11 Use the ipconfig /all command to display TCP/IP configuration data

For Windows 9x/Me, use the Winipcfg utility instead of Ipconfig. Enter **winipcfg** in the Run dialog box and press **Enter**. The IP Configuration window opens (see Figure 8-12). Select the NIC in the drop-down list of network devices.

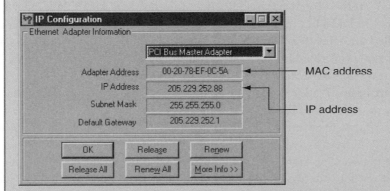

Figure 8-12 Use the Windows 9x/Me Winipcfg utility to display a PC's IP address and MAC address

A+ ESS
5.1

A+
220-602
5.1

When we use a browser to access a Web site on the Internet, it's interesting to know that we can use an IP address and port number in the place of a domain name. For example, you can access the Microsoft Web site by entering this domain name in your browser address box: *www.microsoft.com*. However, you can also use the IP address and port number instead of the domain name (see Figure 8-13). The IP address (207.46.20.30 in the browser address box) identifies the computer and the port number (80, which follows the IP address and is separated by a colon) identifies the application. The application, service, or program that is responding to requests made to port 80 on this computer is a Web server program that is serving up Web pages. An example of a Web server program is Internet Information Services (IIS) by Microsoft. Also note that if you enter only an IP address in a browser address box without a port number, port 80 is assumed.

Figure 8-13   A Web site can be accessed by its IP address and port number

Now let's turn our attention to the details of understanding how IP addresses and computer names are used on a network.

IP ADDRESSES

All protocols of the TCP/IP suite identify a device on the Internet or an intranet by its IP address. An IP address is 32 bits long, made up of 4 bytes separated by periods, as in this address: 190.180.40.120. The largest possible 8-bit number is 11111111, which is equal to 255 in decimal, so the largest possible IP address in decimal is 255.255.255.255, which in binary is 11111111.11111111.11111111.11111111. Each of the four numbers separated by periods is called an octet (for 8 bits) and can be any number from 0 to 255, making a total of 4.3 billion potential IP addresses (256 x 256 x 256 x 256). Because of the allocation scheme used to assign these addresses, not all of them are available for use.

The first part of an IP address identifies the network, and the last part identifies the host. It's important to understand how the bits of an IP address are used in order to understand how routing happens over interconnected networks such as the Internet, and how TCP/IP can locate an IP address anywhere on the globe. When data is routed over interconnected networks, the network portion of the IP address is used to locate the right network. After the data arrives at the local network, the host portion of the IP address is used to identify the one computer on the network that is to receive the data. Finally, the IP address of the host must be used to identify its MAC address so the data can travel on the host's LAN to that host. The next section explains this in detail.

A+ ESS
5.1

A+
220-602
5.1

CLASSES OF IP ADDRESSES

When a business, college, or some other organization applies for IP addresses, a range of addresses appropriate to the number of hosts on the organization's networks is assigned. IP addresses that can be used by companies and individuals are divided into three classes: Class A, Class B, and Class C, based on the number of possible IP addresses in each network within each class. IP addresses are assigned to these classes according to the scheme outlined in Table 8-1.

Class	Network Octets (Blanks in the IP Address Stand for Octets Used to Identify Hosts)	Total Number of Possible Networks or Licenses	Host Octets (Blanks in the IP Address Stand for Octets Used to Identify Networks)	Total Number of Possible IP Addresses in Each Network
A	0.__.__.__ to 126.__.__.__	127	__ .0.0.1 to __.255.255.254	16 million
B	128.0.__.__ to 191.255.__.__	16,000	__.__.0.1 to __.__.255.254	65,000
C	192.0.0.__ to 223.255.255.__	2 million	__.__.__.1 to __.__.__.254	254

Table 8-1 Classes of IP addresses

You can determine the class of an IP address and the size or type of company to which an address is licensed by looking at the address. More important, you also can determine what portion of an IP address is dedicated to identifying the network and what portion is used to identify the host on that network.

Figure 8-14 shows how each class of IP address is divided into the network and host portions. A Class A address uses the first (leftmost) octet for the network address and the remaining octets for host addresses. A Class A license assigns a single number that is used in the first octet of the address, which is the network address. The remaining three octets of the IP address can be used for host addresses that uniquely identify each host on this network. The first octet of a Class A license is a number between 0 and 126. For example, if a company is assigned 87 as its Class A network address, then 87 is used as the first octet for every host on this one network. Examples of IP addresses for hosts on this network are 87.0.0.1, 87.0.0.2, and 87.0.0.3. (The last octet does not use 0 or 255 as a value, so 87.0.0.0 is not valid.) In the example address 87.0.0.1, the 87 is the network portion of the IP address, and 0.0.1 is the host portion. Because three octets can be used for Class A host addresses, one Class A license can have approximately 256 x 256 x 254 host addresses, or about 16 million IP addresses. Only very large corporations with heavy communication needs can get Class A licenses.

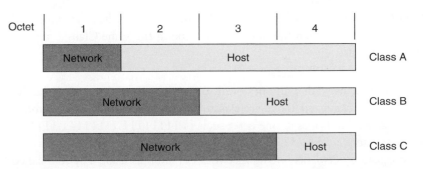

Figure 8-14 The network portion and host portion for each class of IP addresses

A Class B address uses the first two octets for the network portion and the last two for the host portion. A Class B license assigns a number for each of the two leftmost octets, leaving the third and fourth octets for host addresses. How many host addresses are there in one Class B license? The number of possible values for two octets is about 256 x 254, or about 65,000 host addresses in a single Class B license. (Some IP addresses are reserved, so these numbers are approximations.) The first octet of a Class B license is a number between 128 and 191, which gives about 63 different values for a Class B first octet. The second number can be between 0 and 255, so there are approximately 63 x 256, or about 16,000, Class B networks. For example, suppose a company is assigned 135.18 as the network address for its Class B license. The first two octets for all hosts on this network are 135.18, and the company uses the last two octets for host addresses. Examples of IP addresses on this company's Class B network are 135.18.0.1, 135.18.0.2, and 135.18.0.3. In the first example listed, 135.18 is the network portion of the IP address, and 0.1 is the host portion.

A Class C license assigns three octets as the network address. With only one octet used for the host addresses, there can be only 254 host addresses on a Class C network. The first number of a Class C license is between 192 and 223. For example, if a company is assigned a Class C license for its network with a network address of 200.80.15, some IP addresses on the network would be 200.80.15.1, 200.80.15.2, and 200.80.15.3.

Class D and Class E IP addresses are not available for general use. Class D addresses begin with octets 224 through 239 and are used for **multicasting**, in which one host sends messages to multiple hosts, such as when the host transmits a video conference over the Internet. Class E addresses begin with 240 through 254 and are reserved for research.

SUBNET MASK

A **subnet mask** is a group of four dotted decimal numbers that tells TCP/IP if a computer's IP address is on the same or a different network than another computer. For example, the following are three subnet masks:

▲ *11111111.11111111.11111111.00000000, which can be written as 255.255.255.0.*
Using this subnet mask, for computers to be in the same network, the first three octets of their IP addresses must match. For example, if the IP address of a computer is 192.40.18.10, then another IP address of 192.40.18.19 will be in the network, but 192.40.101.12 will not be in the network, because the first three octets don't match. When locating this last IP address, a router managing network traffic knows to expand the search for this IP address beyond the limits of the immediate Class C network.

▲ *11111111.11111111.00000000.00000000, which can be written as 255.255.0.0.*
IP addresses that match the first two octets will be in the same Class B network that uses this subnet mask.

▲ *11111111.00000000.00000000.00000000, which can be written as 255.0.0.0.*
IP addresses that match the first octet will be in the same Class A network that uses this subnet mask.

Subnet masks that use either all ones or all zeroes in an octet are called **classful subnet masks**. The three subnet masks listed above are classful subnet masks. A **classless subnet mask** can have a mix of zeroes and ones in one octet such as 11111111.11111111.11110000.00000000, which can be written as 255.255.240.0. These types of **classless subnet masks** are used to segment large corporate networks into subnetworks or subnets using a system called Classless Interdomain Routing (CIDR).

A+ ESS
5.1

A+
220-602
5.1

For example, suppose a computer in a subnet is assigned the subnet mask of 255.255.240.0 and an IP address of 15.50.212.59. When it wants to communicate with a computer assigned IP address 15.50.235.80, in order to know if these two computers are in the same subnet, a router will determine if the first two octets match and then compares the binary values of the third octet, like this:

```
212 = 11010100

235 = 11101011
```

To be in the same subnet, the first four bits must match, which they don't. Therefore, these two computers are not in the same subnet. However, an IP address that is in the same subnet as 15.50.212.59 is 15.50.220.100, because the first two octets match and the first four bits of the third octet match (comparing 11010100 to 11011100).

Sometimes using CIDR notation, an IP address and subnet mask are written using a shorthand notation like this: 15.50.212.59/20, where the /20 means that the subnet mask is written as 20 ones followed by enough zeroes to complete the full 32 bits.

> **A+ Tip**
>
> The A+ Essentials exam expects you to be familiar with a classful subnet mask.

DIFFERENT WAYS OF ASSIGNING IP ADDRESSES

When a small company is assigned a Class C license, it obtains 254 IP addresses for its use. If it has only a few hosts (for example, fewer than 25 on a network), many IP addresses go unused, which is one reason there is a shortage of IP addresses. But suppose that the company grew, now has 300 workstations on the network, and is running out of IP addresses. There are two approaches to solving this problem: Use private IP addresses or use dynamic IP addressing. Many companies combine both methods. An explanation of each of these solutions follows. Then we'll look at how Network Address Translation is used so that computers assigned private IP addresses can still use the Internet.

Public, Private, and Reserved IP Addresses

When a company applies for a Class A, B, or C license, it is assigned a group of IP addresses that are different from all other IP addresses and are available for use on the Internet. The IP addresses available to the Internet are called **public IP addresses**.

One thing to consider, however, is that not all of a company's workstations need to have Internet access, even though they might be on the network. So, although each workstation might need an IP address to be part of the TCP/IP network, those not connected to the Internet don't need addresses that are unique and available to the Internet; these workstations can use private IP addresses. **Private IP addresses** are IP addresses used on private intranets that are isolated from the Internet. Because the hosts are isolated from the Internet, no conflicts arise.

In fact, a small company most likely will not apply for a license of public IP addresses at all, but instead rely solely on private IP addresses for its internal network. A company using TCP/IP can make up its own private IP addresses to use on its intranet. IEEE recommends that the following IP addresses be used for private networks:

- 10.0.0.0 through 10.255.255.255
- 172.16.0.0 through 172.31.255.255
- 192.168.0.0 through 192.168.255.255

A+ ESS
5.1

A+
220-602
5.1

> **Notes**
>
> IEEE, a nonprofit organization, is responsible for many Internet standards. Standards are proposed to the networking community in the form of an RFC (Request for Comment). RFC 1918 outlines recommendations for private IP addresses. To view an RFC, visit the Web site *www.rfc-editor.org*.

When assigning isolated IP addresses, also keep in mind that a few IP addresses are reserved for special use by TCP/IP and should not be assigned to a device on a network. Table 8-2 lists these reserved IP addresses.

IP Address	How It Is Used
255.255.255.255	Broadcast messages
0.0.0.0	Currently unassigned IP address
127.0.0.1	Indicates your own workstation

Table 8-2   Reserved IP addresses

All IP addresses on a network must be unique for that network. (Figure 8-15 shows the Windows XP error that appears when two computers on the network have been assigned the same IP address.) A network administrator might assign an IP address to a standalone computer (for example, if someone is testing networking software on a PC that is not connected to the network). As long as the network is a private network, the administrator can assign any IP address, although a good administrator avoids using the reserved addresses.

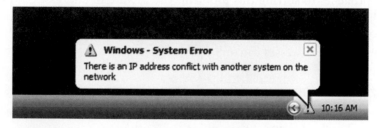

Figure 8-15   An error occurs when two networked computers use the same IP address

Dynamically Assigned IP Addresses

If an administrator must configure each host on a network manually, assigning it a unique IP address, the task of going from PC to PC to make these assignments and keeping up with which address is assigned to which PC can be an administrative nightmare. The solution is to have a server automatically assign an IP address to a workstation each time it comes onto the network. Instead of permanently assigning an IP address (called **static IP addresses**) to a workstation, an IP address (called a **dynamic IP address**) is assigned for the current session only. When the session terminates, the IP address is returned to the list of available addresses.

In most networks, not all workstations are online at all times. Thus, with dynamic IP addressing, fewer IP addresses than the total number of workstations can satisfy the needs of the network. Also, you can use private IP addresses for the range of IP addresses that can be assigned to workstations. When a workstation has an IP address assigned to it, it is said that the workstation is leasing the IP address. **Internet service providers (ISPs)**,

A+ ESS
5.1

A+
220-602
5.1

organizations through which individuals and businesses connect to the Internet, customarily use dynamic IP addressing for their individual subscribers and static IP addresses for their business subscribers.

The server that manages dynamically assigned IP addresses is called a **DHCP (Dynamic Host Configuration Protocol)** server. Workstations that work with DHCP servers are called DHCP clients. DHCP software resides on both the client and the server to manage the dynamic assignments of IP addresses. DHCP client software is built in to Windows 2000/XP and Windows 9x/Me.

> **A+ Tip**
>
> The A+ Essentials exam expects you to know what a DHCP server is and understand how to use static and dynamic IP addressing.

When you configure a DHCP server, you specify the range of IP addresses that can be assigned to clients on the network. Figure 8-16 shows the configuration window for a DHCP server embedded as firmware on a router. (Routers are used to connect networks and are discussed in the next chapter.) To access the configuration window using a Web browser on the network, enter the IP address of the router in the Web browser address box, and then press **Enter**. In the figure, you can see that the router's IP address is 192.168.1.1, and the starting IP address to be assigned to clients is 192.168.1.100. Because the administrator specified that the server can have up to 50 clients, the range of IP addresses is, therefore, 192.168.1.100 to 192.168.1.149. Also shown in the figure is a list of currently assigned IP addresses and the MAC address of the computer that currently leases that IP address.

When a PC first connects to the network, it attempts to lease an address from the DHCP server. If the attempt fails, it uses an **Automatic Private IP Address (APIPA)** in the address range 169.254.*x*.*x*. How to configure a Windows workstation to use dynamic or static IP addressing is covered later in the chapter.

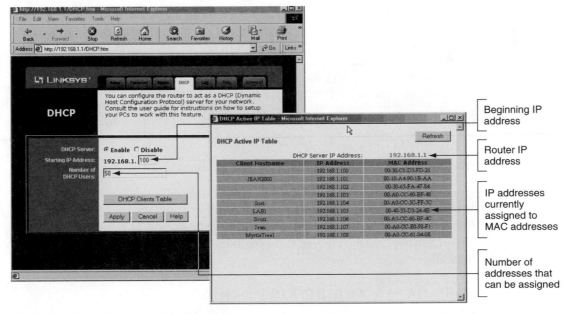

Figure 8-16   A DHCP server has a range of IP addresses it can assign to clients on the network

Network Address Translation

If hosts on a network using private IP addresses need to access the Internet, a problem arises because the private IP addresses are not allowed on the Internet. The solution is to use **NAT (Network Address Translation)**, which uses a single public IP address to access the Internet on behalf of all hosts on the network using other IP addresses. Using NAT, a networked computer trying to access the Internet must go through a server, router, or other device that substitutes its own IP address for that of the computer requesting the information. Because the device is standing in proxy for other hosts that want Internet access, it is called a **proxy server**. Figure 8-17 shows how a proxy server stands between the network and the Internet. This proxy server has two network cards installed. One card connects to the LAN, and the other connects to a cable modem and then to the ISP and the Internet.

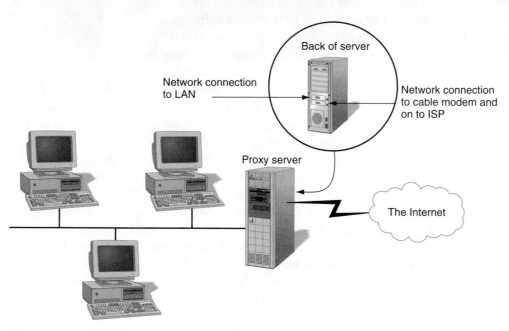

Back of server

Network connection to LAN

Network connection to cable modem and on to ISP

Proxy server

The Internet

Figure 8-17   A proxy server stands between a private network and the Internet

> **Notes**
>
> Windows 2000/XP, Windows Me, and Windows 98 SE offer a NAT service called Microsoft Internet Connection Sharing (ICS). With it, two or more PCs on a home network can share the same IP address when accessing the Internet. Under ICS, one PC acts as the proxy server for other PCs on the home network.

Because a proxy server stands between a LAN and the Internet, it often does double duty as a firewall. Recall that a firewall is software or hardware that protects a network from illegal entry. Because networks are so often attacked by worms and hackers from the Internet, even a small LAN often has a router or other device between the LAN and the Internet that serves as a proxy server, DHCP server, and firewall. As a firewall, it filters out any unsolicited traffic coming from the Internet. Chapter 10 gives more information about firewalls.

HOST NAMES AND NETBIOS NAMES

Each computer on a TCP/IP network is assigned an IP address, but these numbers are hard to remember. Host names and NetBIOS names use characters rather than numbers to identify computers on a network and are easier to remember and use than IP addresses. In addition, a company might have a domain name that can be used to identify the network. An example of a domain name is *amazon.com*. Domain names are covered in the next chapter.

Before TCP/IP became such a popular protocol, Windows assumed that the protocol of choice would be NetBEUI and that all computers on a network would be assigned a

NetBIOS name such as *joesmith* or *Workstation12*. These names usually are assigned when the operating system is installed. In contrast, TCP/IP identifies computers by IP addresses, but TCP/IP also allows a computer to be assigned a character-based host name such as *joesmith*. The host name can also have a domain name attached that identifies the network: *joesmith.mycompany.com*. On a TCP/IP network, the NetBIOS name or host name must be associated with an IP address before one computer can find another on the network. This process of associating a character-based name with an IP address is called **name resolution**.

Two name resolution services track relationships between character-based names and IP addresses: **DNS** (Domain Name System, also called **Domain Name Service**) and Microsoft **WINS** (Windows Internet Naming Service). DNS tracks host names and WINS tracks NetBIOS names. A **DNS server** and a **WINS server** are computers that can find an IP address for another computer when only the host name and domain name are known, using either the DNS or WINS system. Windows networks sometimes use a combination of DNS and WINS; DNS is the more popular method.

Windows 98 assumes that a computer name is a NetBIOS name, which can have only 15 characters, but Windows 2000 and Windows XP assume that the computer name is a host name that uses the TCP/IP convention for host names. If the name is 15 characters or fewer, it works as a NetBIOS name or a TCP/IP name. If a host name is used, it can be up to 63 characters, including letters, numbers, and hyphens, as long as the computer is not part of a workgroup. If the computer is part of a workgroup, the host name should not exceed 15 characters. Microsoft now considers the default naming convention to be TCP/IP host names rather than NetBIOS names.

> **⊙ A+ Tip**
>
> The A+ 220-602 exam expects you to be familiar with DNS and WINS services.

HOW COMPUTERS FIND EACH OTHER ON A LAN

You need to understand how one computer finds another computer on a local network so that you can solve problems when this process of name resolution fails. When an application wants to communicate with another computer on the same TCP/IP LAN, the requesting computer knows the name of the remote computer. Before TCP/IP communication can happen between the two computers, the first computer must discover the IP address of the remote PC. For Windows 98 using NetBIOS names, the computer runs through the following checklist in the order shown to discover the IP address. (A Windows 2000/XP computer using just TCP/IP and not NetBEUI uses DNS to resolve the name, not WINS, and begins at Step 5. If NetBEUI is running on this Windows 2000/XP computer, it tries DNS first, beginning at Step 5, and then turns to NetBEUI in Steps 1 through 4 to resolve the name.)

1. The computer checks the NetBIOS name cache. This cache is information retained in memory from name resolutions made since the last reboot.

2. If the computer has the IP address of a WINS server, it queries the server. A WINS server on the network, such as Windows Server 2003, maintains a database of NetBIOS names and IP addresses.

3. The computer sends a broadcast message to all computers on the LAN asking for the IP address of the computer with the broadcasted NetBIOS name.

4. The computer checks a file named **LMHosts**, which is stored on the local computer. This file, called a host table, contains the NetBIOS names and associated IP addresses of computers on the LAN if someone has taken the time to manually make the entries in the file.

5. If the IP address is still not discovered, the computer assumes that the network is using DNS instead of WINS, so it checks the file named Hosts stored on the local computer. The Hosts file is another host table that contains host names and associated IP addresses, and is similar to the information kept by DNS servers.

6. If the computer has the IP address of a DNS server, it queries the DNS server.

Both the LMHosts and Hosts host tables are stored in the \Windows\System32\drivers\etc folder of a Windows 2000/XP computer or in the \Windows folder of a Windows 9x/Me computer. LMHosts serves as a local table of information similar to that maintained by a WINS server for NetBIOS names, and Hosts serves as a local table of information similar to that kept by a DNS server.

If you look in the \Windows\System32\drivers\etc folder of a Windows 2000/XP computer or in the \Windows folder of a Windows 9x/Me computer, you will see a sample of each file named LMHosts.SAM and Hosts.SAM, where the SAM stands for sample. Open each file with Notepad to examine it. Entries in a host table file beginning with the # symbol are comments and are not read by the name resolution process. The sample files contain many commented lines. You can add your entries to the bottom of the file without the # symbol. Then save the file in the same folder as the sample file, naming it Hosts or LMHosts with no file extension. An example of a Hosts file is shown in Figure 8-18. It tells this computer the IP address of the domain name *apache.test.com*. Recall that a domain name is a name of a network. In the example, apache is the host name, and the domain name is test.com. The **fully qualified domain name (FQDN)** is *apache.test.com*, which is often loosely called the domain name.

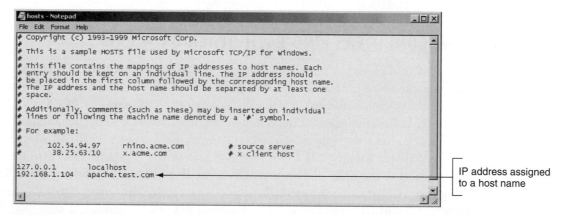

Figure 8-18   An entry in your client Hosts file will tell the client the IP address of an intranet Web site when no DNS service is running on the network

In this example, the computer named *apache.test.com* is used as a Web server for a private network. In order for people on the network to use this domain name, the Hosts file on each PC must have the entry shown in Figure 8-18, and the Web server must have the same IP address at all times. One way to accomplish this is to assign a static IP address to the server. Alternately, if your DHCP server supports this feature, you can configure it to assign the same IP address to your Web server each time if you tell the DHCP server your Web server's MAC address.

Now that you know about the operating system protocols used on a network and how various types of addresses identify computers and devices on the network, let's turn our attention to how to configure a newly-installed NIC and how to configure the OS to access and use resources on a network.

CONFIGURING A NETWORK CARD AND CONNECTING TO A NETWORK

To connect a PC to a network, you'll need a patch cable and a device for the PC to connect to, such as a switch or router. For most corporate environments, the switch is located in an electrical closet centrally located in the building, and patch cables connect the device to network wall jacks. In this situation, the patch cable connects from the PC to the wall jack.

Installing a network card and connecting the PC to a network involves three general steps: (1) Put the NIC in the PC, and install the NIC's drivers; (2) configure the NIC using Windows, so that it has the appropriate addresses on the network and the correct network protocols; and (3) test the NIC to verify that the PC can access resources on the network. This section discusses these steps to configure a wired NIC using Windows 2000/XP and Windows 9x/Me after it is already physically installed in the PC. (The steps to physically install a hardware device inside a computer case are not covered in this book.) It also discusses how to configure a wireless NIC in a notebook.

INSTALLING A NIC USING WINDOWS 2000/XP

To install a NIC using Windows 2000/XP, do the following:

> **Video**
>
> Setting up a Network with Crossover Cables

1. Read the instructions that come bundled with the NIC. Should you install the NIC first or the drivers first? In these steps, we are installing the NIC first, but always follow specific instructions of the manufacturer.

> **A+ Tip**
>
> The A+ Essentials exam expects you to know how to configure a Windows 2000/XP network connection.

2. Physically install the network card in the PC. (The details of this step are outside the scope of this book.)

3. Turn on the PC. The Found New Hardware Wizard launches to begin the process of loading the necessary drivers to use the new device. It is better to use the manufacturer's drivers, not the Windows drivers. If given the opportunity to choose between Windows drivers and the manufacturer drivers on CD, choose the manufacturer drivers. If Windows completes the installation using its own drivers without giving you the opportunity to install the manufacturer's drivers, after the NIC is installed, you can use Device Manager to update the drivers using the manufacturer's drivers.

4. After the Windows desktop loads, verify that the drivers installed successfully. Open **Device Manager**, right-click the card from the list of devices, and click **Properties**. The card's Properties dialog box opens (see Figure 8-19). Look for any conflicts or other errors reported by Device Manager on the General tab and the Resources tab of this dialog box.

5. If errors are reported or you want to replace Windows drivers with the manufacturer's drivers, click the **Driver** tab and then click **Update Driver**. Follow the instructions onscreen to use the network card manufacturer's drivers. You'll find other troubleshooting tips for installing NICs later in this chapter.

> **Video**
>
> Setting up a Network with Hub and Patch Cables

A+ ESS
5.2

A+
220-602
5.2
5.3

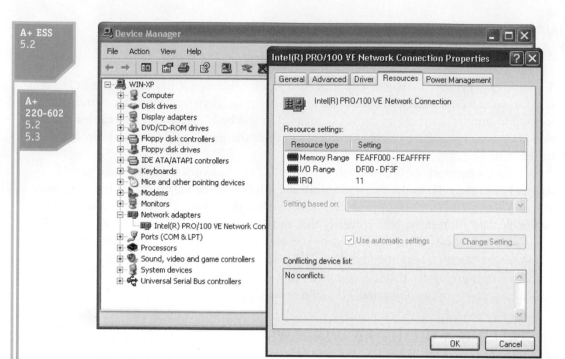

Figure 8-19 A network adapter's resources show in the Properties dialog box of the Device Manager window

6. Connect a network patch cable to the NIC port and to the network switch or a wall jack connected to a switch. You are now ready to configure the NIC to access the network.

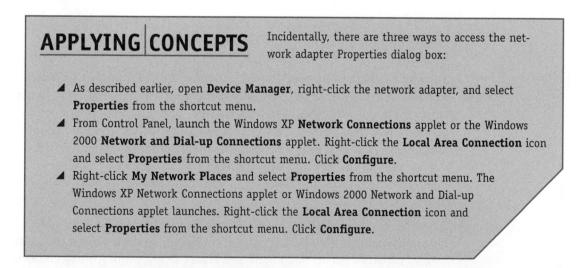

APPLYING CONCEPTS Incidentally, there are three ways to access the network adapter Properties dialog box:

◢ As described earlier, open **Device Manager**, right-click the network adapter, and select **Properties** from the shortcut menu.
◢ From Control Panel, launch the Windows XP **Network Connections** applet or the Windows 2000 **Network and Dial-up Connections** applet. Right-click the **Local Area Connection** icon and select **Properties** from the shortcut menu. Click **Configure**.
◢ Right-click **My Network Places** and select **Properties** from the shortcut menu. The Windows XP Network Connections applet or Windows 2000 Network and Dial-up Connections applet launches. Right-click the **Local Area Connection** icon and select **Properties** from the shortcut menu. Click **Configure**.

CONFIGURING WINDOWS 2000/XP TO USE A NETWORK

The first step to configure Windows 2000/XP to use a network is to give the computer a name. Remember that if you plan to use NetBEUI as a networking protocol instead of TCP/IP, limit the computer name to 15 characters. For Windows 2000/XP, the protocol is TCP/IP by default. Follow these directions to name a computer:

1. Right-click **My Computer** and select **Properties** from the shortcut menu. The System Properties dialog box opens.

8

2. For Windows XP, click the **Computer Name** tab, then click the **Change** button. The Computer Name Changes dialog box opens (see Figure 8-20). For Windows 2000, click the **Network Identification** tab, and then click the **Properties** button. The Identification Changes window opens.

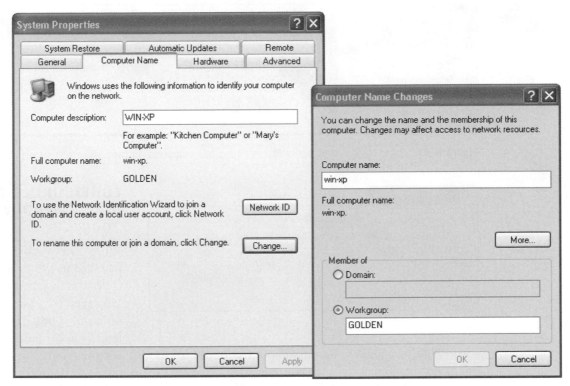

Figure 8-20 Windows XP uses the Computer Name Changes dialog box to assign a host name to a computer on a network

3. Enter the Computer name (**win-xp** in the example shown in Figure 8-20). Each computer name must be unique within a workgroup or domain.

4. If the computer is connecting to a workgroup, select **Workgroup** and enter the name of the workgroup (**GOLDEN** in this example). Recall that a workgroup is a group of computers on a network that shares files, folders, and printers. All users in the workgroup must have the same workgroup name entered in this window. If the PC is to join a domain (a network where logging on is controlled by a server), select **Domain**, enter the name of the domain here, such as *mycompany.com*. When configuring a PC on a network, always follow the specific directions of the network administrator responsible for the network.

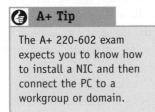

A+ Tip

The A+ 220-602 exam expects you to know how to install a NIC and then connect the PC to a workgroup or domain.

5. Click **OK** to exit the Windows XP Computer Name Changes dialog box or the Windows 2000 Identification Changes window, and click **OK** to exit the System Properties dialog box. You will be asked to reboot the computer for changes to take effect.

6. After rebooting a Windows XP system, click **Start, My Network Places**, and then click **View workgroup computers** to view this computer and others on the network. On the Windows 2000 desktop, open **My Network Places**, and double-click **Computers Near Me**. Figure 8-21 shows an example of My Network Places.

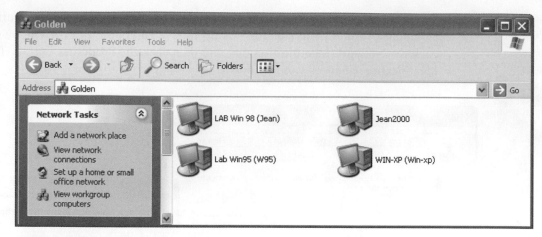

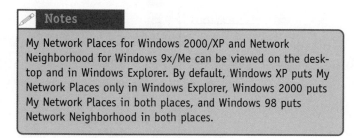

Figure 8-21   Windows XP My Network Places shows all computers on the LAN in a common workgroup

> **Notes**
>
> My Network Places for Windows 2000/XP and Network Neighborhood for Windows 9x/Me can be viewed on the desktop and in Windows Explorer. By default, Windows XP puts My Network Places only in Windows Explorer, Windows 2000 puts My Network Places in both places, and Windows 98 puts Network Neighborhood in both places.

CONFIGURING TCP/IP USING WINDOWS 2000/XP

When a network card is installed in Windows 2000/XP, TCP/IP is installed by default. However, if TCP/IP has been uninstalled or gives you problems, you can install it again. Also, Windows makes some assumptions about how TCP/IP is configured, and these settings might not be appropriate for your network. This section addresses all these concerns.

Before you configure TCP/IP, you might need to ask the network administrator the following questions:

1. Will the PC use dynamic or static IP addressing?

2. If static IP addressing is used, what are the IP address, subnet mask, and default gateway for this computer?

3. Do you use DNS? If so, what are the IP addresses of your DNS servers?

4. Is a proxy server used to connect to other networks (including the Internet)? If so, what is the IP address of the proxy server?

In dynamic addressing, the computer asks a DHCP server for its IP address each time it connects to the network. The server also gives the PC its subnet mask and default gateway, so that the computer knows how to communicate with other hosts that are not on its own network. A **gateway** is a computer or other device that allows a computer on one network to communicate with a computer on another network. A **default gateway** is the gateway a computer uses to access another network if it does not have a better option.

Most likely, you will be using dynamic IP addressing, and you will obtain the DNS server address automatically. The DHCP server might also act as the proxy server so that computers inside the network can make connections to computers outside the network using the proxy server's public IP address.

> **A+ Tip**
>
> The A+ 220-602 exam expects you to be familiar with a gateway, subnet mask, and static and dynamic (or automatic) address assignments.

A+ ESS
5.2

A+
220-602
5.2
5.3

To set the TCP/IP properties for a connection, follow these steps:

1. For Windows XP, open the **Network Connections** applet, and for Windows 2000, open the **Network and Dial-up Connections** applet. Right-click the **Local Area Connection** icon, and then select **Properties** from the shortcut menu. See Figure 8-22.

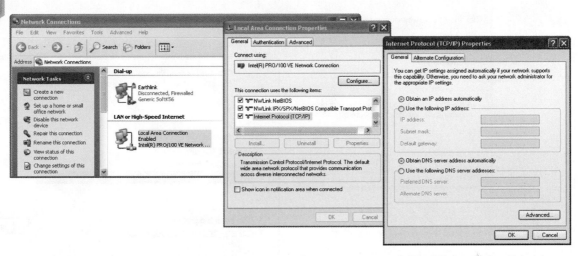

Figure 8-22 To configure TCP/IP under Windows XP, use the Internet Protocol (TCP/IP) Properties dialog box

2. Select **Internet Protocol (TCP/IP)** from the list of installed components, and then click the **Properties** button. The Internet Protocol (TCP/IP) Properties dialog box opens, which is also shown in Figure 8-22.

3. For dynamic IP addressing, select **Obtain an IP address automatically**. (This is the most likely choice.) For static IP addressing, select **Use the following IP address**, and enter the IP address, subnet mask, and default gateway.

4. To disable DNS until the DHCP server gives the computer the DNS server address, select **Obtain DNS server address automatically**. (This is the most likely choice.) If you have the IP addresses of the DNS servers, click **Use the following DNS server addresses**, and enter the IP addresses. Click **OK** twice to close both windows.

5. Open **My Network Places** and verify that your computer and other computers on the network are visible. If you don't see other computers on the network, reboot the PC.

CONFIGURING THE NWLINK AND NETBEUI PROTOCOLS

Instead of or in addition to TCP/IP, a computer might use the NWLink or NetBEUI protocol. These protocols can be used to communicate on a network, but not over the Internet, and a computer can use a combination of TCP/IP, NWLink, and NetBEUI.

A Novell network can use TCP/IP or IPX/SPX. If the network is using IPX/SPX, each Windows computer on the network must be configured to use the NWLink protocol. Do the following to install and use NWLink:

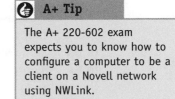

A+ Tip

The A+ 220-602 exam expects you to know how to configure a computer to be a client on a Novell network using NWLink.

1. NWLink is not normally installed. To install it, right-click the **Local Area Connection** icon in the Network Connections window and select **Properties**. The properties dialog

box opens, which lists the installed protocols (refer back to Figure 8-22). If NWLink is not listed, click **Install**. The Select Network Component Type dialog box opens, as shown in Figure 8-23. Select **Protocol** and click **Add**.

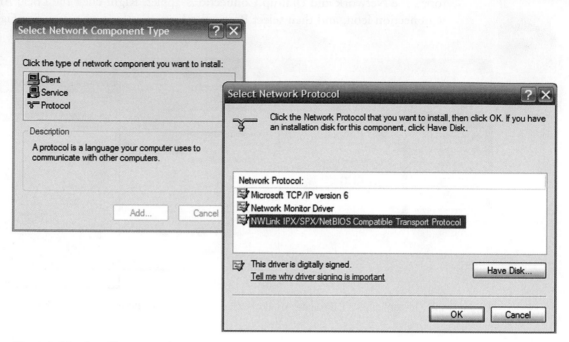

Figure 8-23 Installing network components

2. In the dialog box that opens, also shown in Figure 8-23, select **NWLink IPX/SPX/NetBIOS Compatible Transport Protocol** and click **OK**.

3. You should now see NWLink listed as an installed protocol in the Local Area Connection Properties dialog box (see the left side of Figure 8-24). Make sure that when the NIC used for your network connection is displayed near the top of the properties dialog box, the NWLink IPX/SPX/NetBIOS Compatible Transport Protocol is checked and, therefore, bound to the selected NIC.

4. Check for network connectivity by opening My Network Places and browsing the network. If you have problems with the connection, open the **Local Area Connection Properties** dialog box (see Figure 8-24), select the **NWLink** protocol, and click **Properties**. On the resulting dialog box, shown on the right side of Figure 8-24, verify that **Auto Detect** is selected so that NWLink is able to automatically detect the type of hardware network technology that is present (most likely Ethernet).

NetBEUI is used to support legacy applications that require a NetBIOS interface. To connect a Windows 2000 computer to a network using NetBEUI, use the Properties dialog box of the local area connection to install the NetBEUI Protocol, which automatically binds itself to the NIC providing this local network connection. Then assign a name to the computer. Remember to limit the name to 15 characters. Windows XP does not normally support NetBEUI. However, you can manually install it using the Windows XP Setup CD. For directions, see the Microsoft Knowledge Base Article 301041 at *support.microsoft.com*.

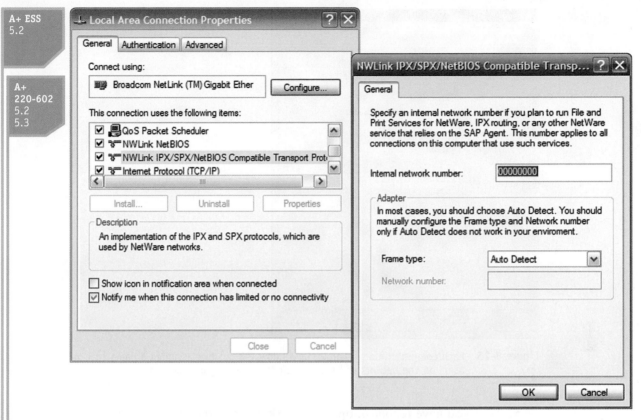

A+ ESS
5.2

A+
220-602
5.2
5.3

Figure 8-24 NWLink protocol is installed and bound to the NIC

INSTALLING A NIC USING WINDOWS 9X/ME

After a NIC is physically installed and the PC is turned on, Windows 9x/Me automatically detects the card and guides you through the process of installing drivers. After the installation, verify that the card is installed with no errors by using Device Manager. In Device Manager, the network card should be listed under Network adapters. Right-click the card and select **Properties** to view the card's properties. Last, connect a network patch cable to the NIC port and to the network hub or a wall jack connected to a hub. You are now ready to configure the NIC to access the network.

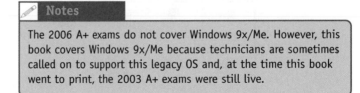

> **Notes**
>
> The 2006 A+ exams do not cover Windows 9x/Me. However, this book covers Windows 9x/Me because technicians are sometimes called on to support this legacy OS and, at the time this book went to print, the 2003 A+ exams were still live.

ASSIGNING A COMPUTER NAME

To assign a name to a Windows 9x/Me computer, follow these directions:

1. Access **Control Panel** and double-click the **Network** icon.

2. Click the **Identification** tab (see Figure 8-25).

3. Enter the computer name (**Patricia** in this example). Enter the name of the workgroup (**Golden** in this example). Each computer name must be unique within the workgroup.

4. Click **OK** to exit the window. You will be asked to reboot the system.

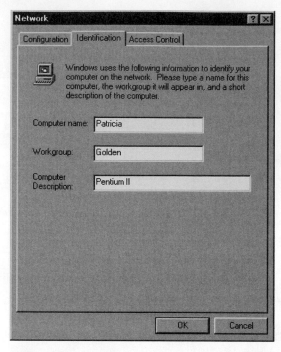

Figure 8-25 Each computer in a workgroup in Windows 98 must be assigned a name that other users on the network will see in their Network Neighborhood window

5. After you have rebooted, open **Network Neighborhood** on the Windows desktop. You should be able to see this computer and others on the network. Figure 8-26 shows an example of Network Neighborhood. If you cannot see other computers, you might have to install and configure TCP/IP, as described next.

Figure 8-26 Windows 98 Network Neighborhood shows all computers on the LAN in a common workgroup

INSTALLING AND CONFIGURING TCP/IP USING WINDOWS 98

If TCP/IP is not already installed, you must install it. For Windows 98, do the following:

1. Access **Control Panel** and double-click the **Network** icon. The Network window opens.

2. Click **Add** to display the Select Network Component Type window, as shown in Figure 8-27.

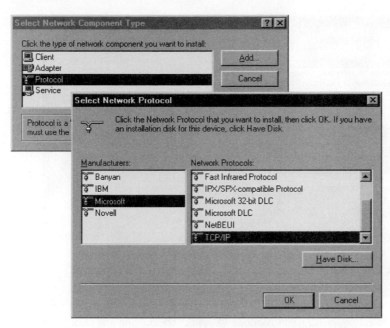

Figure 8-27 To install TCP/IP in Windows 98, use the Select Network Component Type window

3. Select **Protocol** and click **Add**. The Select Network Protocol window opens. Select **Microsoft** on the left and **TCP/IP** on the right (see Figure 8-27). Click **OK**. The system asks for the Microsoft Windows 98 CD and requests that you reboot the system.

4. When you return to the Network window, notice that TCP/IP is automatically bound to any network cards or modems that it finds installed.

The next step is to configure TCP/IP. Most likely, you will be using dynamic IP addressing, and the DNS service is initially disabled (later the DHCP server will tell the PC to enable it). In Windows 98, do the following to configure TCP/IP that has been bound to a NIC to communicate over a local network:

1. In the Network window, select the item where TCP/IP is bound to the NIC. (On the left side of Figure 8-28, that item is TCP/IP->NETGEAR FA311 Fast Ethernet PCI Adapter.) Then, click **Properties**. The TCP/IP Properties dialog box opens, as shown on the right side of the figure.

2. If static IP addressing is used, click **Specify an IP address,** and then enter the IP address and subnet mask supplied by your administrator. If dynamic IP addressing is used (as is usually the case), click **Obtain an IP address automatically**.

3. Click the **DNS Configuration** tab and choose to enable or disable DNS (see Figure 8-29). If you enable DNS, enter the IP addresses of your DNS servers. If your network administrator gave you other specific values for the TCP/IP configuration, you will find the tabs for these settings on this window. But in most cases, the above steps will work for you to configure TCP/IP.

4. When finished, click **OK** to exit the Properties dialog box, and then click **OK** to exit the Network window.

5. On the desktop, verify that you can see your computer and others on the network in Network Neighborhood. If you don't see others on the network, reboot the PC.

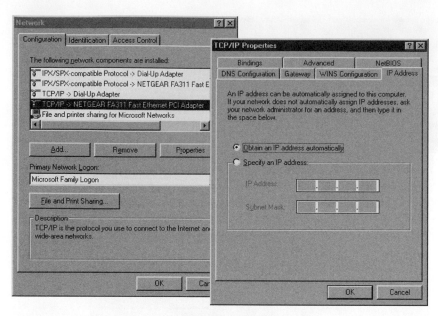

Figure 8-28   To configure TCP/IP in Windows 98, select the binding and click Properties to view the TCP/IP Properties dialog box

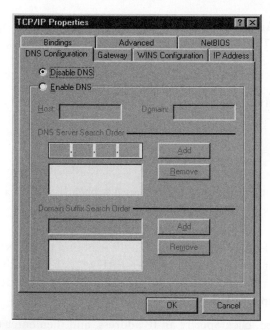

Figure 8-29   Configure DNS service under TCP/IP for Windows 98

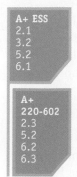

A+ ESS
2.1
3.2
5.2
6.1

A+
220-602
2.3
5.2
6.2
6.3

Notes

To use NetBEUI on a Windows 9x/Me network, first verify that NetBEUI is installed or install it as you do TCP/IP. It should automatically bind itself to any network adapters installed. NetBEUI needs no other configuration.

INSTALLING A WIRELESS ADAPTER IN A NOTEBOOK

For a notebook computer, a wireless adapter will use a USB port or a PC Card slot. Most new adapters use the USB port, such as the wireless adapter shown in Figure 8-30. The adapter will come with a setup CD and some documentation and maybe an accessory or two.

8

A+ ESS
2.1
3.2
5.2
6.1

A+
220-602
2.3
5.2
6.2
6.3

Cradle and
extension
cable

Drivers and
manual on
CD

Wireless
adapter

Figure 8-30 This 802.11g wireless adapter by Linksys uses a USB port to connect to a notebook or desktop computer

Do the following to install the adapter:

1. Read the installation directions that come with the wireless adapter to find out if you install the software first or the adapter first. For the Linksys wireless adapter used in this example, the instructions clearly say to first install the software (see Figure 8-31).

Figure 8-31 This label makes it clear you need to install the software before installing the wireless adapter

2. Insert the CD in the CD drive. The opening screen for this adapter is shown in Figure 8-32. Click **Click Here to Start** and follow the directions onscreen to install the device drivers and the utility to configure the wireless connection.

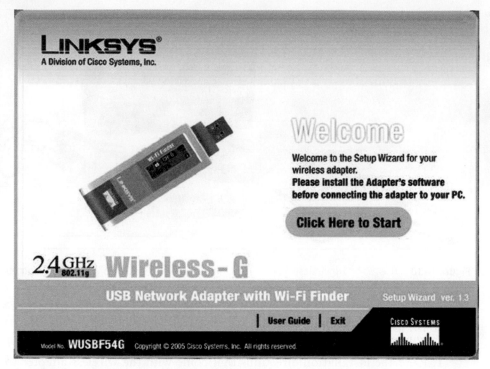

Figure 8-32 Install the wireless adapter software

3. Next, plug the wireless adapter into a USB port. See Figure 8-33. The Found New Hardware bubble appears. See Figure 8-34. Click the bubble to launch the Found New Hardware Wizard. Follow the wizard to install the device.

Figure 8-33 Plug the wireless USB adapter into the USB port

A+ ESS
2.1
3.2
5.2
6.1

A+
220-602
2.3
5.2
6.2
6.3

Figure 8-34   Windows XP recognizes the presence of a new USB device

When a new device is being installed, Windows might recognize that the drivers were not digitally signed by Microsoft. If this is the case, it displays a dialog box similar to that in Figure 8-35 (for a Netgear wireless adapter). Now you have a decision to make. You can stop the installation and go to the manufacturer's Web site to try to find approved drivers, or you can continue with the installation. For most devices, it is safe to continue the installation using unsigned drivers. To do that, click **Continue Anyway**.

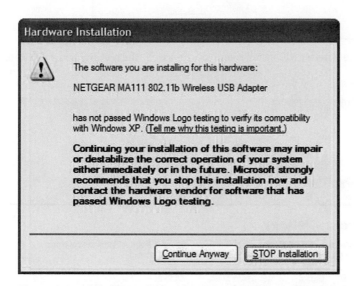

Figure 8-35   Windows asks you for a decision about using unsigned drivers

At another point in the installation, the wizard might ask if you want to disable the Windows XP Configuration Manager, which means you are choosing to use the manufacturer's utility to configure the wireless adapter (see Figure 8-36). Unless you have a good reason to do otherwise, click **Yes** to choose to use the manufacturer's utility. This utility will most likely be easier to use and allow you to better manage the wireless NIC than would the Windows XP Network Connections window. (Later, if you change your mind about which utility to use, you might have to uninstall and reinstall the device.)

After the wireless adapter is installed, the next step is to configure it. Read the adapter's documentation to find out how to use the software. Most likely during installation an icon was added to your system tray. Double-click the icon to open the configuration window. Figure 8-37 shows the configuration window for the Linksys wireless adapter. Click **Manual Setup** to configure the adapter.

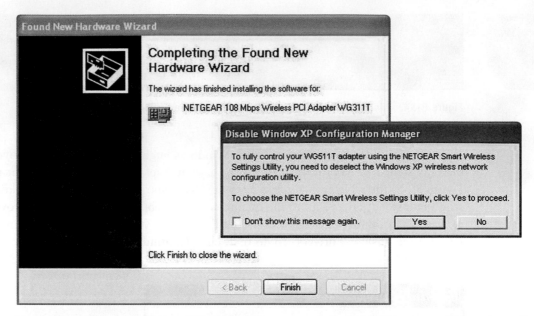

Figure 8-36 During the wireless NIC installation, you are asked which utility you want to use to configure the NIC

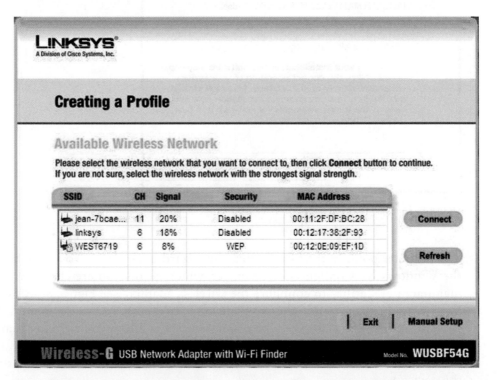

Figure 8-37 Opening screen to configure a Linksys wireless adapter

Each manufacturer has a different configuration utility, but all utilities should allow you to view information and manage the wireless device using these parameters. Information displayed about the current connection should include:

▲ *The MAC address of the access point device that the adapter is currently using.*
▲ *The current channel the connection is using.* 802.11b/g uses 14 different channels. The United States can use channels 1 through 11. The access point device is configured to use one of these 11 channels.

8

A+ ESS
2.1
3.2
5.2
6.1

A+
220-602
2.3
5.2
6.2
6.3

▲ *Current transmission rate*. For 802.11b networks, the transmission rate (Tx rate) is about 11 Mbps. For 802.11g, expect about 54 Mbps.

▲ *Throughput, link quality*, and *signal strength*. These values indicate throughput rate and how strong the signal is. For most wireless devices, there is nothing for you to configure to get a connection. If the signal strength is poor, look for a way to scan for a new access point. For the utility shown in Figure 8-37, click the **Refresh** button. If the wireless signal strength is still not good enough, try moving your notebook around a bit.

Configuration changes you can make for a wireless device include:

▲ *Mode or network type*. The mode indicates whether the computer is to communicate through an access point (Infrastructure mode) or directly with another wireless device (Ad Hoc mode).

▲ *SSID*. The SSID (service set identifier) is set to ANY by default, which means the NIC is free to connect to any access point it finds. You can enter the name of an access point to specify that this NIC should connect only to a specific access point. If you don't know the name assigned to a particular access point, ask the network administrator responsible for managing the wireless network. For public hot spots, if you don't know the SSID, try "Hotspot". For some public hot spots, the access point is hidden so you must pay to know its name. Figure 8-38 shows the configuration screen for the Linksys adapter where you can choose the mode and enter an SSID.

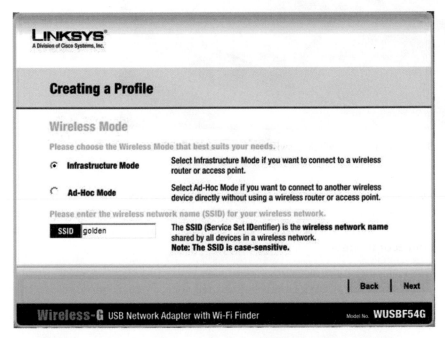

Figure 8-38 Configure the wireless mode and the SSID of the access point

▲ *Encryption settings*. Most wireless devices today support one or more standards for encrypted wireless transmission. When you try to connect to a secured network, if the connection is set for encryption, you'll be required to enter a secret passphrase or key to be used for the encryption. This passphrase is a word, such as "ourpassphrase," which generates a digital key used for encryption. Every computer user on the same wireless network must enter the same passphrase or key, which an administrator can change at any time.

A+ ESS
2.1
3.2
5.2
6.1

A+
220-602
2.3
5.2
6.2
6.3

▲ *Tx rate.* For some adapters, you can specify the transmission rate or leave it at fully automatic so that the adapter is free to use the best transmission rate possible.

▲ *TCP/IP configuration.* Some wireless configuration utilities provide a screen to configure the TCP/IP settings to static or dynamic IP addressing. If your utility does not do that, after you configure the adapter, you'll need to use the Network Connections window to verify the TCP/IP settings. Initially, they'll be set for dynamic IP configuration.

After you have made all configuration changes, you should immediately be able to use your browser. If you can't, then try rebooting the computer. Also, try moving the computer to a better hot spot and click the button to reconnect.

Here are the steps to connect to a public hot spot for a notebook computer that has embedded wireless ability and uses Windows XP network configuration:

1. Turn on your wireless device. For one notebook, that's done by a switch on the keyboard (see Figure 8-39).

Figure 8-39 Turn on the wireless switch on your notebook

2. Right-click **My Network Places** and select **Properties**. The Network Connections window opens. Right-click the **Wireless Network Connection** icon and select **View Available Wireless Networks** from the shortcut menu. The Wireless Network Connection window opens (see Figure 8-40).

3. Select an unsecured network from those listed and click **Connect**. (Incidentally, if you select a secured network that is protected with an encryption key, to continue, you must enter the key in a dialog box shown in Figure 8-41.)

A+ ESS
2.1
3.2
5.2
6.1

A+
220-602
2.3
5.2
6.2
6.3

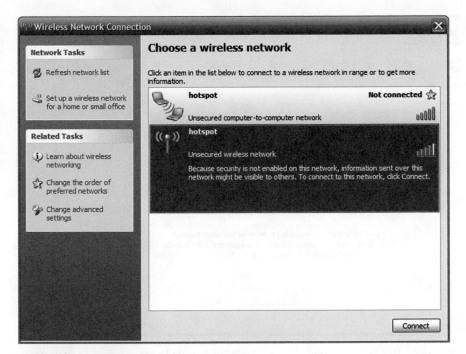

Figure 8-40 Available wireless hot spots

Figure 8-41 To use a secured wireless network, you must know the encryption key

4. Open your browser to test the connection. For some hot spots, a home page appears and you must enter a code or ticket number to proceed (see Figure 8-42).

5. You can see the status of the wireless connection by double-clicking the Wireless Network Connection icon in the Network Connections window or by double-clicking the wireless icon in the system tray. Either way, the status window shown in Figure 8-43 appears.

A+ ESS
2.1
3.2
5.2
6.1

A+
220-602
2.3
5.2
6.2
6.3

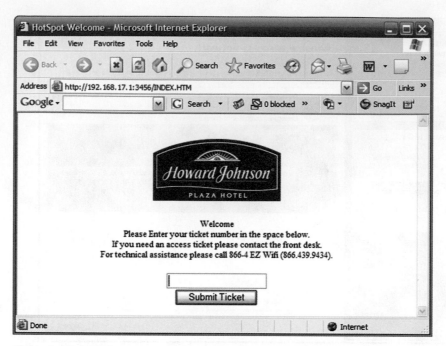

Figure 8-42   This hot spot requires a ticket number or code to use the wireless network

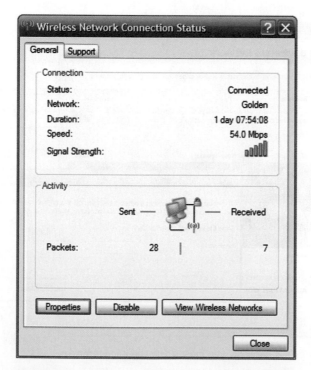

Figure 8-43   Status of the current wireless connection

If you have problems connecting, do the following:

1. If you know the SSID of the hot spot, on the Wireless Network Connection window, click **Change advanced settings**. The Wireless Network Connection Properties dialog box opens. Click the **Wireless Networks** tab (see Figure 8-44).

A+ ESS
2.1
3.2
5.2
6.1

A+
220-602
2.3
5.2
6.2
6.3

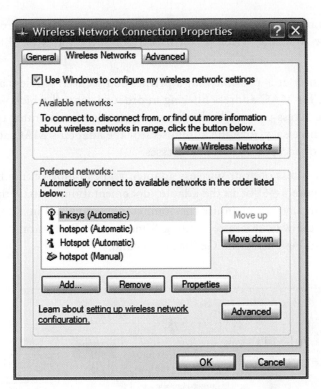

Figure 8-44 Manage wireless hot spots using the Wireless Network Connection Properties dialog box

2. Click **Add**. The Wireless network properties window opens (see Figure 8-45). Enter the SSID of the network and make sure that Network Authentication is set to **Open** and Data encryption is set to **Disabled**. Click **OK**. When a dialog box opens to warn you of the dangers of disabling encryption, click **Continue Anyway**. Click **OK** to close the Wireless Network Connection Properties dialog box.

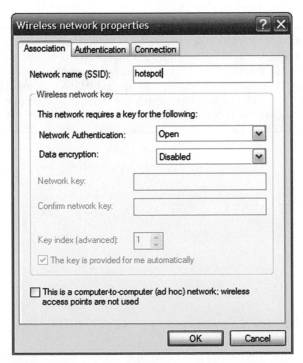

Figure 8-45 Enter the SSID of a hot spot to which you want to connect

A+ ESS
2.1
3.2
5.2
6.1

A+
220-602
2.3
5.2
6.2
6.3

3. In the Network Connections window, right-click the **Wireless Network Connection** icon and select **View Available Wireless Networks.** You should now be able to connect to the hot spot.

4. If you still can't connect, it is possible that a private and secured wireless access point has been configured for MAC address filtering in order to control which wireless adapters can use the access point. Check with the network administrator to determine if this is the case; if necessary, give the administrator the adapter's MAC address to be entered into a table of acceptable MAC addresses.

5. To know the MAC address of your wireless adapter, you can look on the back of the adapter itself (see Figure 8-46) or in the adapter documentation. Also, if the adapter is installed on your computer, you can use the command **ipconfig /all** in a command prompt window. By the way, if you're running Windows XP Professional, you can also display your MAC address using the Getmac command.

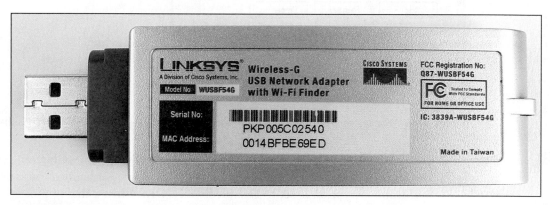

Figure 8-46   The MAC address is printed on the back of this USB wireless adapter

Notes

For a desktop computer, know that a wireless NIC uses an internal or external antenna. To install an NIC that uses an external antenna, remove the antenna from the NIC. Turn off the computer, unplug the power cord, open the case, and install the NIC. For an external antenna, screw the antenna on the NIC and raise it to an upright position (see Figure 8-47). Turn on the computer. The computer immediately detects the device and launches the Found New Hardware Wizard. The installation then proceeds the same way as for a wireless NIC installed in a notebook computer.

A+ ESS
2.1
3.2
5.2
6.1

A+
220-602
2.3
5.2
6.2
6.3

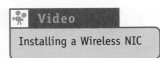
Video
Installing a Wireless NIC

Figure 8-47 Raise the antenna on a NIC to an upright position

USING RESOURCES ON THE NETWORK

A+ ESS
3.1
4.1

A+
220-602
5.2

So far in the chapter, you have learned how networks are structured, how to configure NICs, and how to set up Windows networking. Let's look next at how to use resources on a network after it's been set up. This section covers how to share folders, files, applications, and even entire hard drives. In Chapter 11, you will learn how to share printers on a network.

SHARING FILES, FOLDERS, AND APPLICATIONS

If users on a LAN working on a common project need to share applications, files, or printers, then all these users must be assigned to the same workgroup or domain on the LAN. Recall that Windows 2000/XP makes shared resources available by way of My Network Places, and Windows 9x/Me uses Network Neighborhood. Open either applet to see the names of all computers on the network. Figure 8-48 shows My Network Places for Windows XP. Drill down to see shared files, folders, and printers in your workgroup. Using Network Neighborhood or My Network Places, you can copy files from one computer to another, use shared applications installed on one computer from another computer, and share printers.

Workgroups can be effective when several people work on a common project. For example, if a group of people is building a Web site, sharing resources on the LAN is an effective method of passing Web pages around as they are built. Or one computer on the LAN can be designated as the file server. The user of this computer makes a portion of hard drive space available for the Web site files. All users have access to this one resource, and the Web site files are kept neatly in a single location. When using workgroups, each user is responsible for protecting shared resources by using password protection for read and write privileges to files and folders.

A+ ESS
3.1
4.1

A+
220-602
5.2

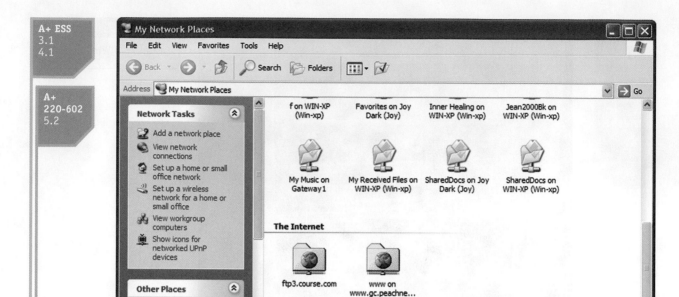

Figure 8-48   View and access shared resources on the network using My Network Places in Windows XP

HOW TO SHARE WINDOWS 2000/XP FILES, FOLDERS, AND APPLICATIONS

Using Windows 2000/XP, do the following to share files, folders, and applications with others on the network:

1. Two Windows components must be installed before you can share resources: Client for Microsoft Networks and File and Printer Sharing. Client for Microsoft Networks is the Windows component that allows you to use resources on the network made available by other computers, and File and Printer Sharing allows you to share resources on your computer with others. To verify these components are installed, open the **Network Connections** window, right-click the **Local Area Connection** icon, and select **Properties** from the shortcut menu. The Local Area Connection Properties dialog box opens. See Figure 8-49.

2. Verify **Client for Microsoft Networks** and **File and Printer Sharing for Microsoft Networks** are both checked. If you don't see these items in the list, click **Install** to install them. When you're done, close all windows.

8

A+ ESS
3.1
4.1

A+
220-602
5.2

Figure 8-49 Use the Network Connections applet to install a network client, service, or protocol using Windows XP

3. Using Windows Explorer, select the folder or file you want to share. In this example, we're using a folder named **C:\data**. Right-click the folder name. Select **Sharing and Security** (see Figure 8-50). The Data Properties dialog box opens, as shown in Figure 8-51.

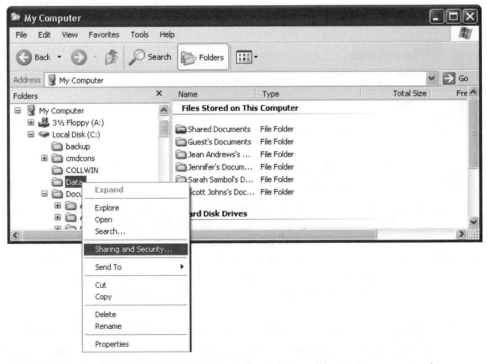

Figure 8-50 Use Windows Explorer to share a file or folder with others on a network

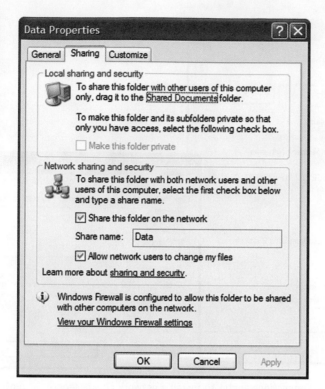

Figure 8-51   A user on a network can share a folder with others on the network

4. Check **Share this folder on the network**. If you want to allow others to change the contents of the folder, check **Allow network users to change my files**. Click **Apply**, and close the window. Other users on the network can now see the folder when they open My Network Places on their desktop. In Chapter 10, you'll learn how you can configure Windows so that you have more control over how other users are able to access shared resources.

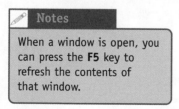

Notes

When a window is open, you can press the **F5** key to refresh the contents of that window.

Applications can also be shared with others in the workgroup. If you share a folder that has a program file in it, a user on another PC can double-click the program file in My Network Places and execute it remotely on his or her desktop. This is a handy way for several users to share an application that is installed on a single PC.

HOW TO SHARE WINDOWS 9X/ME FILES, FOLDERS, AND APPLICATIONS

To share Windows 9x/Me resources, you must first install Client for Microsoft Networks and File and Printer Sharing. Client for Microsoft Networks is the Windows component that allows you to use resources on the network made available by other computers, and File and Printer Sharing allows you to share resources on your computer with others in your workgroup. After these components are installed, the last thing to do is to share the folders, files, or printers that you want others to be able to access. All these steps are covered in this section.

Installing Windows 9x/Me Components Needed to Share Resources

To install Client for Microsoft Networks and File and Printer Sharing in Windows 98, open the **Network** applet in Control Panel and click **Add**. Select **Client** and then click **Add**.

The Select Network Client window opens. Select **Microsoft** on the left and **Client for Microsoft Networks** on the right. You might need the Windows 9x/Me CD. Using the same method, install File and Printer Sharing for Microsoft Networks.

After these two components are installed, you must choose to enable File and Print Sharing. In the Network window, click the **File and Print Sharing** button (see Figure 8-52). The File and Print Sharing window opens. Check both options to share both files and printers, and then click **OK**.

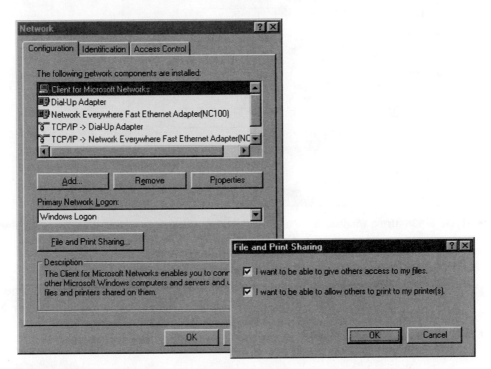

Figure 8-52 Turn on Windows 98 File and Print Sharing so others on the LAN can access resources on this PC

When they are installed, Client for Microsoft Networks and File and Printer Sharing should automatically bind themselves to the TCP/IP protocol. You can verify this by accessing the TCP/IP Properties dialog box and clicking the **Bindings** tab. On this tab, you can verify that Client for Microsoft Networks and File and Printer Sharing are checked.

Sharing Files and Folders with the Workgroup

After the computer is configured for File and Print Sharing, do the following to make a folder or file available to others on the LAN:

1. Using Windows Explorer, select the folder or file. In this example, we are using a folder named **C:\data**. Right-click the folder name and select **Sharing** from the shortcut menu. The data Properties dialog box opens, as shown in Figure 8-53.

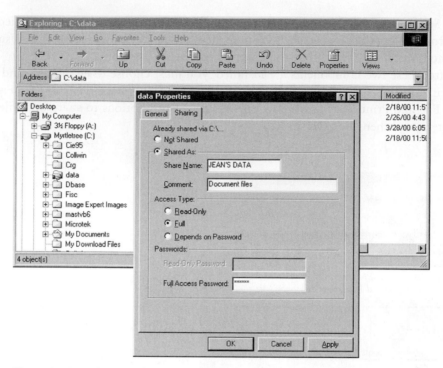

Figure 8-53 Using Windows 98, a user on a network can share a folder with others on the network

2. Click the **Shared As** option button. Enter a name for the shared folder. In the figure, the name is JEAN'S DATA. This action makes the folder available to others on the network. They can see the folder when they open My Network Places or Network Neighborhood on their desktop.

3. Click the **Depends on Password** option button in the Access Type section.

4. To allow others the right to make changes to the folder, enter a password under **Full Access Password**. For read-only access, enter a different password. Click **OK** to exit the window.

When using the Depends on Password option, be sure to enter a password in both the Read-Only Password and Full Access Password fields. If you leave a password field empty, then no password is required for a user to have the corresponding read-only or full access to the folder. Distribute the two passwords to people who need to access the folder. You control the access rights (permissions) by selecting which password(s) you give.

NETWORK DRIVE MAPS

A **network drive map** is one of the most powerful and versatile methods of communicating over a network. A network drive map makes one PC (the client) appear to have a new hard drive, such as drive E, that is really hard drive space on another host computer (the server). This client/server arrangement is managed by a Windows component called the Network File System (NFS), which makes it possible for files on the network to be accessed as easily as if they are stored on the local computer. NFS is a type of distributed file system (DFS), which is a system that shares files on a network. Even if the host computer uses a different OS, such as Unix, the drive map still functions.

8

Using a network drive map, files and folders on a host computer are available even to network-unaware DOS applications. The path to a file simply uses the remote drive letter instead of a local drive such as drive A or drive C. Also, network drive maps are more reliable than when using My Network Places or Network Neighborhood to access folders on the network.

> 📝 Notes
>
> A computer that does nothing but provide hard drive storage on a network for other computers is called a file server or a network attached storage (NAS) device. Other computers on the network can access this storage using a network drive map.

To set up a network drive under Windows 2000/XP or Windows 9x/Me, follow these steps:

1. On the host computer, using directions given earlier in the chapter, share the drive or folder on a drive to which you want others to have access.

2. On the remote computer that will use the network drive, connect to the network and access **Windows Explorer**. Click the **Tools** menu and select **Map Network Drive**.

3. The Map Network Drive dialog box opens, as shown in Figure 8-54. Select a drive letter from the drop-down list.

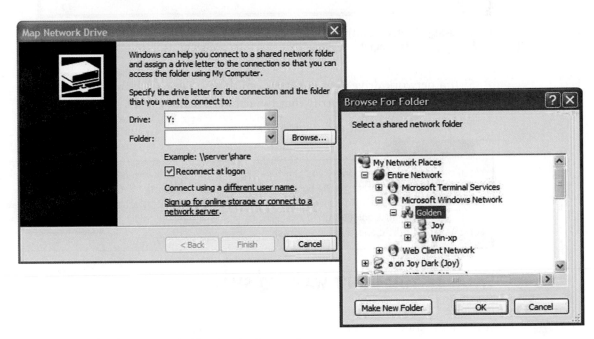

Figure 8-54   Mapping a network drive to a host computer

4. Click the **Browse** button and locate the shared folder or drive on the host computer. Click **OK** to close the Browse For Folder dialog box, and click **Finish** to map the drive. The folder on the host computer now appears as one more drive in Explorer on your computer (see Figure 8-55).

A+
220-602
3.1

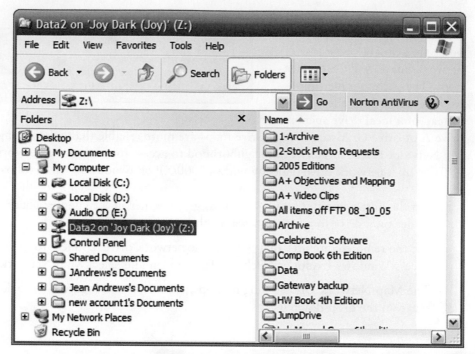

Figure 8-55   Contents on the right side of Windows Explorer belong to the host computer; this computer sees the contents as belonging to its drive Z

5. If a network drive does not work, go to My Network Places or Network Neighborhood, and verify that the network connection is good.

 Notes

When mapping a network drive, you can type the path to the host computer rather than clicking the Browse button to navigate to the host. To enter the path, in the Map Network Drive dialog box, use two backslashes, followed by the name of the host computer, followed by a backslash and the drive or folder to access on the host computer. For example, to access the Public folder on the computer named Scott, enter **\\Scott\Public** and then click **Finish**.

A+
220-602
5.2

WHAT IF YOU DON'T WANT TO SHARE?

If you're concerned about others on your network getting to information on your computer, you can do some things to make sure your PC is secure:

▲ *Disable File and Printer Sharing*. In the Network Connections window, under the Local Area Connection Properties dialog box, uncheck **File and printer sharing for Microsoft Networks**.

▲ *Hide your computer from others looking at My Network Places*. For Windows 2000/XP, in Control Panel, open the **Administrative Tools** applet and double-click **Service**. Right-click the **Computer Browser** service and select **Properties** from the shortcut menu. Under Startup type, select **Disabled** and click **Apply**. When you restart the PC, it will not be visible in My Network Places over the network.

▲ *Hide a shared folder*. If you want to share a folder, but don't want others to see the shared folder in their My Network Places or Network Neighborhood window, add a $ to the end of the folder name. Others on the network can access the folder only when they know its name. For example, if you name a shared folder MyPrivateFolder$, in order to

8

A+
220-602
5.2

access the folder, a user must enter \\Computername\MyPrivateFolder$ in the Run dialog box on the remote computer.

▲ *Make your personal folders private.* If you are using the NTFS file system, folders associated with your user account can be made private so that only you can access them. To make a personal folder and all its subfolders private, in Windows Explorer, drill down to a folder that is part of your user profile under the Documents and Settings folder. Right-click the folder and select **Sharing and Security** from the shortcut menu. The folder properties dialog box opens (see Figure 8-56). Check **Make this folder private** and click **Apply**. (It's interesting to see that in Figure 8-51, shown earlier in the chapter, the Make this folder private check box is grayed out because that folder is not part of a user profile in the Documents and Settings folder.) When you make a personal folder private, be sure you have a password associated with your user account. If you don't have a password, anyone can log on as you and gain access to your private folders.

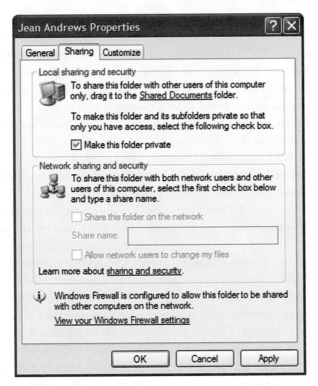

Figure 8-56 A folder that belongs to a user profile can be made private

HOW TO SET UP YOUR OWN WIRELESS NETWORK

A+ ESS
6.1

Setting up your own wireless network involves buying a wireless access point and configuring it and your wireless computers for communication. The key to successful wireless networking is good security. This section first looks at what you need to know about securing a wireless network, then shows how to choose the equipment you'll need and how to set up a wireless network.

A+
220-602
6.2
6.3

SECURITY ON A WIRELESS LAN

Wireless LANs are so convenient for us at work and at home, but the downside of having a wireless network is that if we don't have the proper security in place, anyone with a wireless computer within range of your access point can use the network—and, if they know how,

A+ ESS
6.1

A+
220-602
6.2
6.3

can intercept and read all the data sent across the network. They might even be able to hack into our computers by using our own wireless network against us. For all these reasons, it's terribly important to secure your wireless network.

Securing a wireless network is generally done in these ways:

▲ *Disable SSID broadcasting*. Normally, the name of the access point (called the SSID) is broadcast so that anyone with a wireless computer can see the name and use the network. If you hide the SSID, a computer can see the wireless network, but can't use it unless the SSID is entered in the wireless adapter configuration.

▲ *Filter MAC addresses*. A wireless access point can filter the MAC addresses of wireless NICs that are allowed to use the access point. This type of security prevents uninvited guests from using the wireless LAN, but does not prevent others from receiving data in the air.

▲ *Data encryption*. Data sent over a wireless connection can be encrypted. The three main methods of encryption for 802.11 wireless networks are **WEP (Wired Equivalent Privacy)**, **WPA (WiFi Protected Access)**, and **WPA2**. With either method, data is encrypted using a firmware program on the wireless device and is only encrypted while the data is wireless; the data is decrypted before placing it on the wired network. With WEP encryption, data is encrypted using either 64-bit or 128-bit encryption keys. (Because the user can configure only 40 bits of the 64 bits, 64-bit WEP encryption is sometimes called 40-bit WEP encryption.) Because the key used for encryption is static (doesn't change), a hacker who spends enough time examining data packets can eventually find enough patterns in the coding to decrypt the code and read WEP-encrypted data. WPA encryption, also called TKIP (Temporal Key Integrity Protocol) encryption, is stronger than WEP and was designed to replace it. With WPA encryption, encryption keys are changed at set intervals. The latest and best wireless encryption standard is WPA2, also called the 802.11i standard or the AES (Advanced Encryption Standard) protocol. As of March 2006, for a wireless device to be WiFi certified, it must support the WPA2 standard, which is included in Windows XP Service Pack 2. When buying wireless devices, be sure the encryption methods used are compatible!

▲ *Change firmware default settings*. Default settings are easy to guess. For example, a default password is often set to "password" and the default SSID is often set to the brand name of the device, such as Linksys or Netgear. For added security, be sure to change all default settings so they are not so easy to guess. Change the SSID to keep someone from guessing the SSID when it is not broadcasted. Also, change the default password and username for the configuration utility. You can also disable DHCP and use static IP addressing so others cannot obtain an IP address.

▲ *Update firmware*. For added security, keep the firmware on your wireless access point updated with downloads from the device manufacturer.

▲ *Use a firewall*. If the access point has firewall capability, be sure to turn it on. In addition, be sure to use a software firewall on every computer using the wireless network. How to manage firewalls is covered in Chapter 10.

▲ *Virtual private network (VPN)*. A VPN requires a password for entrance and encrypts data over both wired and wireless networks. The basic difference between WEP or WPA encryption and VPN encryption is that VPN encryption applies from the user's PC all the way to the host computer regardless of the type of network used. A VPN uses a technique called tunneling, in which a packet of data is encrypted, as shown in Figure 8-57. The encryption methods used by VPN are stronger than WEP or WPA and are the preferred method when transmitting sensitive data over a wireless connection. How to set up a VPN is beyond the scope of this chapter.

8

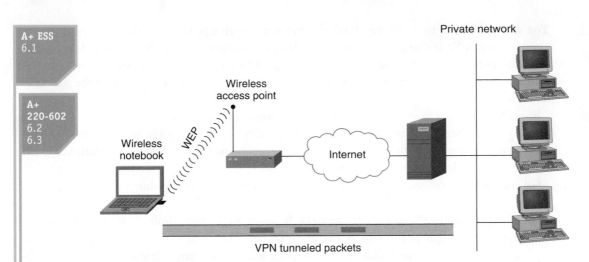

Figure 8-57 With tunneling, packets can travel over a wireless LAN and the Internet in a virtual private network (VPN), but WEP or WPA applies only to the wireless connection

CHOOSING A WIRELESS ACCESS POINT

When selecting a wireless access point, look for the ability to use all the security measures listed in the previous section. Also, be sure the access point supports 802.11 b/g. And, as always, before you buy, search the Internet to read hardware reviews about the device. Only buy a device that consistently gets good reviews. If you're also in need of a wireless adapter to use for the computers that will use your wireless networks, for best results, try to find adapters and an access point made by the same manufacturer.

A wireless access point can be a standalone device such as the one in Figure 8-58 by D-Link, which supports 802.11b/g. This particular access point advertises that it can support transfer rates up to 108 Mbps, but be aware that to get this high rate, you must use a compatible D-Link wireless adapter on your notebook or desktop computer. An access point can also serve more than one purpose, such as the Linksys router shown earlier in Figure 8-6.

Figure 8-58 This wireless access point by D-Link supports 802.11b/g

CONFIGURE AND TEST YOUR WIRELESS NETWORK

To install a standalone access point, position it centrally located to where you want your hot spot to be and plug it in. It will have a network or USB cable that you can connect to a computer so you can configure the access point. A wireless access point includes firmware.

A+ ESS
6.1

A+
220-602
6.2
6.3

(You might be able to update or flash the firmware with updates downloaded from the manufacturer's Web site.) The firmware includes a configuration utility. You access this utility by entering the IP address of the access point in a browser on a computer connected to the access point. Any changes you make to the configuration are stored on the access point device.

Run the setup CD that comes with the access point. If you don't have the setup CD, you can open your browser and enter the IP address of the device, which should launch a firmware utility you can use to configure it. All changes you make to the access point configuration will be saved on the device firmware memory.

Go through the following steps to configure the wireless access point:

1. It's very important to change the default password to the administrative utility to configure the access point. Unless you have disabled or secured the wireless access point, anyone outside your building can use your wireless network. If they guess the default password to the access point, they can change the password to hijack your wireless network. Also, your wireless network can be used for criminal activity. When you first install an access point, before you do anything else, change your password.

2. Look for a way to select the channel the access point will use, the ability to change the SSID of the access point, and the ability to disable SSID broadcasting. Figure 8-59 shows these three settings for one Linksys access point. Figure 8-60 shows how a wireless computer sees a wireless access point that is not broadcasting its SSID. This computer would not be able to use this access point until you entered the SSID in the configuration window shown in Figure 8-61.

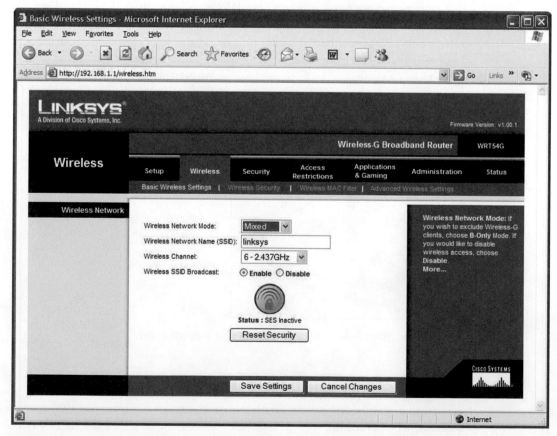

Figure 8-59 Look for the ability of the access point to disable SSID broadcasting

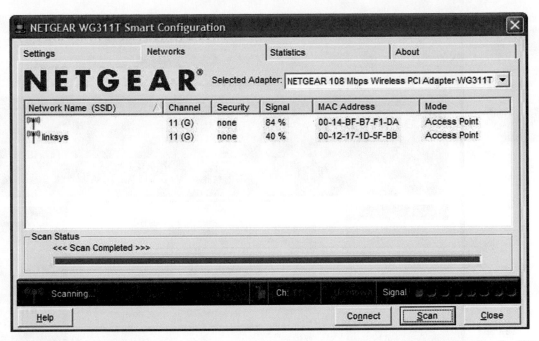

Figure 8-60 A wireless NIC shows it has located two access points, but one is not broadcasting its SSID

Figure 8-61 This wireless adapter configuration screen lets you enter the SSID of a hidden access point and also configure the wireless connection for WEP encryption

3. To configure data encryption on your access point, look for a wireless security screen similar to the one in Figure 8-62 where you can choose between several WPA, WEP, or RADIUS encryption methods. (RADIUS stands for Remote Authentication Dial-In User Service and uses an authentication server to control access.) WPA Personal is the one to choose unless one of your wireless adapters doesn't support it. For example, the wireless adapter configuration screen in Figure 8-61 shows it supports only WEP encryption, so your access point is forced to use that method. Enter the same passphrase for WEP encryption on the access point screen and all your wireless adapter configuration screens.

A+ ESS
6.1

A+
220-602
6.2
6.3

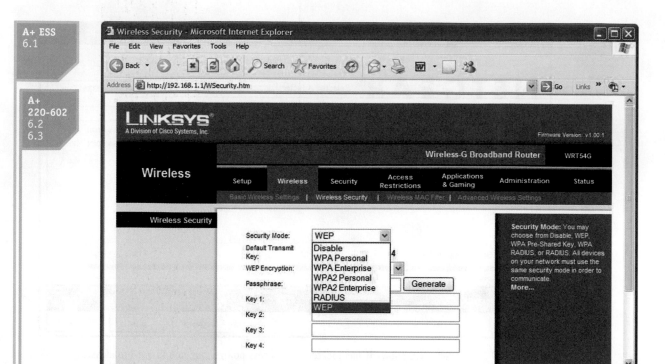

Figure 8-62 This wireless access point supports several encryption methods

4. Look for MAC filtering on your access point, similar to the screen in Figure 8-63. On this access point, you can enter a table of MAC addresses and decide if this list of MAC addresses is to be used to prevent or permit use of the access point.

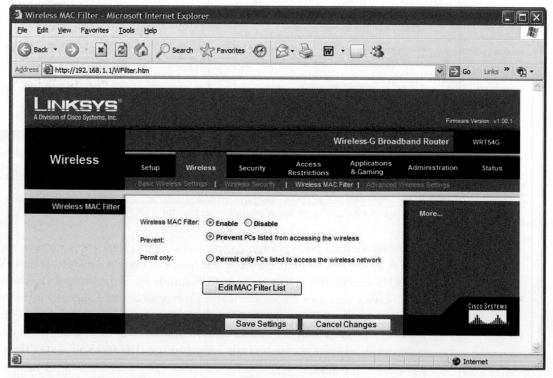

Figure 8-63 Configure how the access point will filter MAC addresses

A+ ESS
6.1

A+
220-602
6.2
6.3

5. Save all your settings for the access point and test the connection. To test it, on one of your wireless computers, open the configuration window for the wireless adapter and scan for access points. If the scan does not detect your access point, verify the wireless adapter is set to scan all channels or the selected channel of your access point. Try moving your access point or the computer. If you still can't get a connection, remove all security measures and try again. Then restore the security features one at a time until you discover the one causing the problem, or use encryption.

We've just configured your wireless access point to use several security features. Is it really necessary to use them all? Well, not really, but it can't hurt. Encryption is essential to keep others from hacking into your wireless data, and to keep others out of your network, you need to disable SSID broadcasting, filter MAC addresses, or use encryption.

TROUBLESHOOTING A NETWORK CONNECTION

A+ ESS
1.3
5.1
5.3

A+
220-602
1.2
3.1
5.3

APPLYING CONCEPTS

T.J. has just used a crossover cable to connect his two computers together. My Network Places on both computers refuses to display the other computer. What should T.J. check?

If you have problems connecting to the network, follow the guidelines in this section. First, here are some symptoms that might indicate the NIC is faulty:

▲ You cannot make a connection to the network.
▲ My Network Places or Network Neighborhood does not show any other computers on the network.
▲ You receive an error message while you are installing the NIC drivers.
▲ Device Manager shows a yellow exclamation point or a red X beside the name of the NIC. In the Network Connections window, you see a red X over the network icon.
▲ There are at least two lights on a NIC: One stays on steadily to let you know there is a physical connection (labeled LINK in Figure 8-64), and another blinks to let you know there is activity (labeled ACT in Figure 8-64). If you see no lights, you know there is no physical connection between the NIC and the network. This means there is a problem with the network cable, the card, or the switch, hub, or router to which the PC connects. Similar lights appear on the switch, hub, or router for each network port.
▲ The problem might not be caused by the NIC. Try replacing the network cable.

Figure 8-64 Lights on the back of a NIC can be used for troubleshooting

A+ ESS
1.3
5.1
5.3

A+
220-602
1.2
3.1
5.3

🎥 Video

Troubleshooting a Network

ⓘ **A+ Tip**

The A+ Essentials exam expects you to know how to troubleshoot network problems by using status indictors and activity lights on a NIC. You also need to know how and when to use the Ping and Ipconfig commands.

Sometimes you might have trouble with a network connection due to a TCP/IP problem. Windows TCP/IP includes several diagnostic tools that are useful in troubleshooting problems with TCP/IP. You will learn about several of these in the next chapter. The most useful is **Ping (Packet Internet Groper)**, which tests connectivity and is discussed here. Ping sends a signal to a remote computer. If the remote computer is online and hears the signal, it responds. Ipconfig under Windows 2000/XP and Winipcfg under Windows 9x/Me test the TCP/IP configuration.

Try these things to test TCP/IP configuration and connectivity:

1. For Windows 2000/XP, enter **Ipconfig /all** at the command prompt. For Windows 9x/Me, click **Start**, click **Run**, enter **Winipcfg** in the Run dialog box, and then click **OK**. If the TCP/IP configuration is correct and an IP address is assigned, the IP address, subnet mask, and default gateway appear along with the adapter address. For dynamic IP addressing, if the PC cannot reach the DHCP server, then it assigns itself an IP address. This is called IP autoconfiguration and the IP address is called an Automatic Private IP Address (APIPA). In this situation, the Winipcfg window and the results of the Ipconfig command both show the IP address as the IP Autoconfiguration Address, and the address begins with 169.254. In this case, suspect that the PC is not able to reach the network or the DHCP server is down.

2. Try to release the current IP address and lease a new address. To do this for Windows 9x/Me Winipcfg, select the network card, click the **Release** button, and then click the **Renew** button. For Windows 2000/XP, first use the **Ipconfig /release** command, and then use the **Ipconfig /renew** command. Or you can open the Network Connections window, right-click the network connection, and click **Repair** on the shortcut menu (see Figure 8-65).

3. Next, try the loopback address test. At a command prompt, enter the command **Ping 127.0.0.1** (with no period after the final 1). This IP address always refers to your local computer. It should respond with a reply message from your computer. If this works, TCP/IP is likely to be configured correctly. If you get any errors up to this point, then assume that the problem is on your PC. Check the installation and configuration of each component, such as the network card and the TCP/IP protocol suite. Remove and reinstall each component, and watch for error messages, writing them down so that you can recognize or research them later as necessary. Compare the configuration to that of a working PC on the same network.

4. Next, ping the IP address of your default gateway. If it does not respond, the problem might be with the gateway or with the network to the gateway.

5. Now try to ping the host computer you are trying to reach. If it does not respond, the problem might be with the host computer or with the network to the computer.

6. If you have Internet access and substitute a domain name for the IP address in the Ping command, and Ping works, you can conclude that DNS works. If an IP address works, but the domain name does not work, the problem lies with DNS. Try this command: **ping www.course.com**.

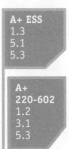

A+ ESS
1.3
5.1
5.3

A+
220-602
1.2
3.1
5.3

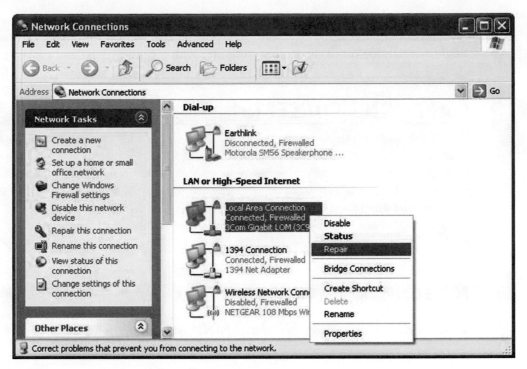

Figure 8-65 Use the Repair command to release and renew the IP address of a network connection

7. Determine whether other computers on the network are having trouble with their connections. If the entire network is down, the problem is not isolated to the PC and the NIC you are working on. Check the hub or switch controlling the network.

8. Make sure the NIC and its drivers are installed by checking for the NIC in Device Manager. Try uninstalling and reinstalling the NIC drivers.

9. If the drivers still install with errors, try downloading new drivers from the Web site of the network card manufacturer. Also, look on the installation CD that came bundled with the NIC for a setup program. If you find one, uninstall the NIC and run this setup program.

10. Some network cards have diagnostic programs on the installation CD. Try running the program from the CD. Look in the documentation that came with the card for instructions on how to install and run the program.

11. Check the network cable to make sure it is not damaged and that it does not exceed the recommended length for the type of network you are using. If the cable is frayed, twisted, or damaged, replace it. Be sure all network cables are securely attached to the wall or are up and out of harm's way so they will not be tripped over, stepped on, twisted, or otherwise damaged.

12. Connect the network cable to a different port on the hub. If that doesn't help, you might have a problem with the cable or the NIC itself. Uninstall the NIC drivers, replace the NIC, and then install new drivers. (Don't attempt to work inside the PC case unless you are aware of the dangers of static electricity.)

13. Check to see whether you have the most current version of your motherboard BIOS. The motherboard manufacturer should have information on its Web site about whether an upgrade is available.

A+ ESS
1.3
5.1
5.3

When a network drive map is not working, first check My Network Places or Network Neighborhood, and verify that you can access other resources on the remote computer. You might need to log on to the remote computer with a valid user ID and password.

A+
220-602
1.2
3.1
5.3

APPLYING CONCEPTS

Back to T.J.'s problem connecting his two computers. The problem might be the hardware or software. Begin with the hardware. Are the lights displayed correctly on the NICs? If so, T.J. can assume the hardware is functioning. Next, check the driver installation. Does Device Manager on both computers show no errors or conflicts with each network adapter? Next, check the configuration. In this situation, T.J. should have used static IP addressing. What is the IP address of each PC? Open a command window and try to ping the local computer, and then try to ping the remote computer. Does each computer have a computer name? Try rebooting each computer.

>> CHAPTER SUMMARY

◢ Networks are categorized in size as a PAN, LAN, MAN, or WAN.

◢ The most popular physical network architecture for LANs is Ethernet.

◢ An Ethernet hub broadcasts all data that flows through it to every node connected to it. It does not make decisions about where to send packets. Switches keep switching tables of nodes on the network and send packets only to the designated node.

◢ The most popular wireless technology for a LAN is 802.11b/g, also called Wi-Fi.

◢ VoIP telephone networks use the Internet for voice communication.

◢ A PC connects to a network using a NIC (network interface card) or network adapter, which communicates with NICs on other PCs using a set of hardware protocols (such as Ethernet). The OSs on the two computers use a different set of protocols (such as TCP/IP or NetBEUI) to communicate.

◢ The three protocols that Windows supports for network communications are TCP/IP (the protocol suite for the Internet), IPX/SPX (designed for use with Novell NetWare), and NetBEUI (a proprietary Windows protocol for use on networks isolated from the Internet). Only TCP/IP is supported on the Internet.

◢ The four types of addresses on a Windows network are MAC addresses, IP addresses, character-based names (such as NetBIOS names, host names, domain names), and port addresses.

◢ MAC addresses are used only for communication within a local network.

◢ IP addresses identify devices on the Internet and other TCP/IP networks. They consist of four numbers separated by periods. The first part of an IP address identifies the network, and the last identifies the host. The class of an IP address determines how much of the address is used as the network identifier and how much is used for the host identifier.

◢ IP addresses can either be public or private. For private IP addresses to be able to access the Internet, they must go through NAT (Network Address Translation) so that their requests all appear to be coming from a single public IP address for that network.

◢ Character-based names, such as fully qualified domain names, are used as an easy way to remember IP addresses.

◢ The IP address associated with a host name can change. DNS (Domain Name Service) and WINS (Windows Internet Naming Service) track the relationships between host names and IP addresses. DNS is more popular because it works on all platforms.

◢ Windows 2000 and Windows XP assume that a computer name is a host name, which follows the TCP/IP convention and can have up to 63 characters. Windows 98 assumes that a computer name is a NetBIOS name, which can have up to 15 characters.

◢ When installing a NIC, physically install the card, install the device drivers, install the OS networking protocol you intend to use (it might already be installed by default), configure the OS protocol, and give the computer a name.

◢ When configuring TCP/IP, you must know if IP addresses are statically or dynamically assigned.

◢ Before users on a network can view or access resources on a PC, Client for Microsoft Networks and File and Print Sharing must be installed and enabled, and the resources must be shared.

◢ Network drive mapping makes one PC appear to have a new hard drive when that hard drive space is actually on another host computer. Use Windows Explorer to map a network drive.

◢ When setting up a wireless network, configure the wireless access point to secure the network from unauthorized access. Use encryption to keep data from being stolen in transmission.

◢ When troubleshooting a NIC on a PC, check connections in the rest of the network, cabling and ports for the PC, the NIC itself (substituting one known to be working, if necessary), the BIOS, and the device drivers.

◢ Ping is a useful TCP/IP utility to check network connectivity.

◢ Two other useful troubleshooting tools are Ipconfig (Windows 2000 and Windows XP) and Winipcfg (Windows 9x/Me), which test TCP/IP configuration.

>> KEY TERMS

For explanations of key terms, see the Glossary near the end of the book.

802.11a/b/g
access point (AP)
adapter address
AirPort
Automatic Private IP Address (APIPA)
binding
classful subnet masks
classless subnet masks
client
client/server
computer name
crossover cable
datagram
default gateway
DHCP (Dynamic Host Configuration Protocol)
DNS (Domain Name System, or Domain Name Service)
DNS server
domain name
dynamic IP address

Ethernet
frame
fully qualified domain name (FQDN)
gateway
hardware address
host
host name
Hosts (file)
Internet service provider (ISP)
intranet
IP address
IPX/SPX (Internetwork Packet Exchange/Sequenced Packet Exchange)
LAN (local area network)
LMHosts
MAC (Media Access Control) address
MAN (metropolitan area network)
multicasting

name resolution
NAT (Network Address Translation)
NetBEUI (NetBIOS Extended User Interface)
NetBIOS (Network Basic Input/Output System)
network adapter
network drive map
network interface card (NIC)
network operating system (NOS)
network printer
node
NWLink
octet
packet
PAN (personal area network)
patch cable
peer-to-peer network
physical address
Ping (Packet Internet Groper)

private IP address
proxy server
public IP address
server
static IP address
subnet mask

TCP/IP (Transmission Control Protocol/Internet Protocol)
WAN (wide area network)
WEP (Wired Equivalent Privacy)
Wi-Fi (Wireless Fidelity)

WINS (Windows Internet Naming Service)
wireless LAN (WLAN)
WPA (WiFi Protected Access)
WPA2 (WiFi Protected Access 2)

>> REVIEWING THE BASICS

1. Name three types of Ethernet. What transmission speed does each support?

2. When using dynamic IP addressing, what type of server must be on the network?

3. Give an example of a classful subnet mask. Give an example of a classless subnet mask.

4. Which is more efficient for networking traffic, a switch or a hub? Why?

5. Is 172.16.50.100 intended to be a public or private IP address?

6. What are three ways a wireless network can be secured?

7. What connecting device do you use for a small LAN? For two or more connected networks?

8. Describe the structure of an IP address. How is it different from a MAC address?

9. How many potential IP addresses are there?

10. How many networks and addresses are available for Class A IP addresses? Class B? Class C?

11. Why are Class D and E addresses not available to individuals and companies?

12. Which octets are used for the network address and for host addresses in Class A? Class B? Class C?

13. In what class is the IP address 185.75.255.10?

14. In what class is the IP address 193.200.30.5?

15. Describe the difference between public and private IP addresses. If a network is using private IP addresses, how can the computers on that network access the Internet?

16. Why is it unlikely that you will find the IP address 192.168.250.10 on the Internet?

17. Which Windows operating system does not automatically include the NetBEUI protocol?

18. What are the two ways an IP address can be assigned to a PC? What is one advantage of each?

19. What are the Ping, Ipconfig, and Winipcfg utilities used for?

20. Of IPX/SPX, TCP/IP, and NetBEUI, which is routable and which is not?

21. When a PC reports it has used an automatic private IP address, what can you assume about the network configuration and current connectivity?

22. A network uses a subnet mask of 255.255.255.0 and has a computer on the network with the IP address of 120.12.12.3. Will the IP address 120.12.10.3 be on the network? Explain your answer.

23. What networking protocol was first used by Novell NetWare and is not supported on the Internet?

24. If you were going to connect two PCs together in a simple network using the network ports on each PC, what type of cable would you use?

25. Which name resolution service is used on the Internet, DNS or WINS? Why?

1. You have just installed a network adapter and have booted up the system, installing the drivers. You open My Network Places on a remote computer and don't see the computer on which you just installed the NIC. What is the first thing you check?

   a. Is File and Printer Sharing installed?

   b. Is the NetBEUI protocol installed?

   c. Are the lights on the adapter functioning correctly?

   d. Has the computer been assigned a computer name?

2. You work in the Accounting Department and have been using a network drive to post Excel spreadsheets to your workgroup as you complete them. When you attempt to save a spreadsheet to the drive, you see the error message, "You do not have access to the folder 'J:\'. See your administrator for access to this folder." What should you do first? Second?

   a. Ask your network administrator to give you permission to access the folder.

   b. Check My Network Places to verify that you can connect to the network.

   c. Save the spreadsheet to your hard drive.

   d. Using Windows Explorer, remap the network drive.

   e. Reboot your PC.

3. Your job is to support the desktop computers in a small company of 32 employees. A consulting firm is setting up a private Web server to be used internally by company employees. The static IP address of the server is 192.168.45.200. Employees will open their Web browser and enter *personnel.mycompany.com* in the URL address box to browse this Web site. What steps do you take so that each computer in the company can browse the site using this URL?

4. Linda has been assigned the job of connecting five computers to a network. The room holding the five computers has three network ports that connect to a switch in an electrical closet down the hallway. Linda decides to install a second switch in the room. The new switch has four network ports. She uses a crossover cable to connect one of the four ports on the switch to a wall jack. Now she has five ports available (two wall jacks and three switch ports). While installing and configuring the NICs in the five computers, she discovers that the PCs connected to the two wall jacks work fine, but the three connected to the switch refuse to communicate with the network. What could be wrong and what should she try next?

PROJECT 8-1: Investigating Your PC

If you are connected to the Internet or a network, answer these questions:

1. What is the hardware device used to make this connection (modem or network card)? List the device's name as Windows sees it.

2. If you are connected to a LAN, what is the MAC address of the NIC? Print the screen that shows the address.

3. What is the IP address of your PC?

4. What Windows utilities did you use to answer the first three questions?

5. Print the screen that shows which network protocols are installed on your PC.

PROJECT 8-2: Researching IP Address Classes

Use the Web site *www.flumps.org/ip/* by Paul Rogers to answer these questions:

1. List three companies that have a Class A IP address license.

2. List three companies that have a Class B IP address license.

3. Who owns IP address class license 9.x.x.x?

4. Find another Web site on the Internet that gives similar information. How does the information on the new site compare with the information on the *www.flumps.org/ip/* site?

PROJECT 8-3: Researching Switches

A PC support technician is often called on to research equipment to maintain or improve a PC or network and make recommendations for purchase. Find four Web pages advertising switches that meet these criteria:

1. Find two switches by different manufacturers that support Gigabit Ethernet and have at least five ports.

2. Find two switches by different manufacturers that support Fast Ethernet and have at least five ports.

3. Compare the features and prices of each switch. Which brand and type switch would you recommend for a small business network? What information might you want to know before you make your recommendation?

PROJECT 8-4: Sharing and Securing Folders

Using two computers, networked together, do the following to practice sharing and securing folders using Windows XP:

1. Create a user account on Computer 1 named User1. In the My Documents folder for that account, create a folder named Folder1.

2. On Computer 2, create a user account named User2. Try to access Folder1 on Computer 1. What is the result? What must you do so that the folder can be accessed?

3. Now make the folder private so that others cannot see or access it on the network. Describe how you did that.

PROJECT 8-5:   Researching a Wireless LAN

Suppose you want to connect two computers to your company LAN using a wireless connection. Use the Internet to research the equipment needed to create the wireless LAN, and answer the following:

1. Print a Web page showing an access point device that can connect to an Ethernet LAN.

2. How much does the device cost? How many wireless devices can the access point support at one time? How is the device powered?

3. Print three Web pages showing three different network adapters a computer can use to connect to the access point. Include one external device that uses a USB port and one internal device. How much does each device cost?

4. What is the total cost of implementing a wireless LAN with two computers using the wireless connection?

>> REAL PROBLEMS, REAL SOLUTIONS

REAL PROBLEM 8:1   Setting Up a Small Network

You've been using a Windows 98 desktop computer for several years, but finally the day has come! You purchase a wonderful and new Windows XP notebook computer complete with all the bells and whistles. Now you are faced with the task of transferring all your e-mail addresses, favorite Web site links, and files to your notebook.

Your old desktop doesn't have a CD burner, so burning a CD is out of the question. You considered the possibility of e-mailing everything from one computer to another or using floppy disks, but both solutions are not good options. Then the thought dawns on you to purchase a crossover cable and connect the two computers in the simplest possible network. Practice this solution by using a crossover cable to connect a Windows XP computer to a Windows 98 computer and share files between them.

CHAPTER
9

Windows on the Internet

In earlier chapters, you've learned much about how to support Windows, applications, and users, and how to connect a PC to a network. This chapter takes the next logical step in effectively using PCs by discussing connections to the Internet using Windows. You will learn how the TCP/IP suite of protocols is used, how to create and troubleshoot broadband and dial-up connections to the Internet, and how to install and use a router to enhance and secure an Internet connection. Then, you'll learn how to support many of the popular applications that use the Internet, such as Web browsers, e-mail clients, FTP software, Internet telephone, and Windows XP Remote Desktop.

THE TCP/IP SUITE OF PROTOCOLS

A+ ESS
5.1

A+
220-602
5.1

In Chapter 8, you learned how to configure the hardware and software necessary for networking, and how the operating system uses TCP/IP to make resources on a network available to the user. In this section of the chapter, you'll learn more about how TCP/IP works to support the major Internet applications.

Most applications that use the Internet are **client/server applications**, which means that two computers and two applications are involved. The client application on one computer makes a request for data from the server application on another computer. In this client/server environment, the application serving up data is called the server and the computer on which this server application is installed can also be referred to as the server. In other words, a server is any computer or application serving up data when that data is requested.

The World Wide Web itself is probably the most popular client/server application: The client is called a Web browser because it browses the Web, and the server is called a Web server or a Web host because it hosts a Web site. The requested data is called a Web page, which can have graphics, sound, and video embedded as part of the requested data (see Figure 9-1). Two examples of Web servers are Apache HTTP Server by The Apache Software Foundation (*www.apache.org*) and Internet Information Services (IIS), which is an integrated component of Windows Server 2003.

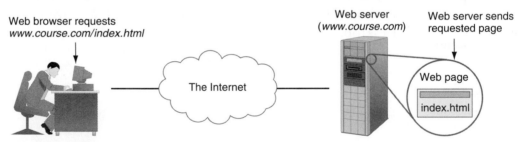

Figure 9-1   A Web browser (client software) requests a Web page from a Web server (server software); the Web server returns the requested file or files to the client

Client applications such as a Web browser or e-mail client software are installed on computers as any other application is installed. However, because a server application is waiting for a request from another program, it is installed on the computer as a service. Recall from earlier chapters that a service is managed under Windows 2000/XP using the Services console, or it can be managed using a utility program bundled with the server application.

To understand how TCP/IP is used to support client/server applications, let's first look at how a client application addresses a server application. Then, we'll look at the layers of protocols included in TCP/IP to support applications, the OS, and hardware. Finally, in this part of the chapter, we'll look at some utilities you can use when problems arise with TCP/IP communication.

USING IP AND PORT ADDRESSES TO IDENTIFY SERVICES

A computer on the Internet or an intranet might be running a Web server application, an e-mail server application, and an FTP server application, all at the same time. (You'll learn about FTP later in the chapter.) Recall that each of these server applications is running as a service on that computer.

A+ ESS
5.1

A+
220-602
5.1

Having multiple server applications running as individual services on one computer works fine as long as client applications requesting data know how to address a particular service. To understand how these services are addressed, let's start by using an example. Suppose that a computer is running a Web server and an e-mail server. The Web server is Apache HTTP Server and the e-mail server is Ntmail by Gordano LTD (*www.ntmail.co.uk*). The Apache and Ntmail programs are both running as background services on this one computer. How does a Web browser on a client PC say, "I want to speak with the Web server" and an e-mail program say, "I want to speak with the e-mail server," if both programs are running on the same computer using the same IP address? The answer is: they use an identifying number, called a **port, port address,** or **port number**, that has been assigned to each server application when it is started. (Don't confuse these port numbers or addresses with I/O addresses assigned to hardware devices, which were discussed in previous chapters.) Also, keep in mind that not every service running on a computer requires a port number; only those services that are server applications require port numbers.

Each server application "listens" at its assigned port. A network administrator can assign any port number to a server, but there are established port numbers for common servers and protocols. A Web server is normally assigned port 80, and an e-mail server receiving mail is normally assigned port 25, as shown in Figure 9-2. Port assignments are shown at the end of an IP address, following a colon. Using these default port assignments, the Web server would communicate at 138.60.30.5:80, and the e-mail server would communicate at 138.60.30.5:25.

Figure 9-2 Each server running on a computer is addressed by a unique port number

Unless the administrator has a good reason to do otherwise, he or she will usually use the common port assignments listed in Table 9-1. (One reason not to use the default port assignments is concern about security. You can make a Web site a secret site by using an uncommon port number.) If a Web server is assigned a port number different from the default port number, the Web server can be accessed by entering the server's IP address in the address box of the Web browser, followed by a colon and the port number of the Web server, like this: 138.60.30.5:8080.

Port	Protocol	Service	Description
20	FTP	FTP	File transfer data
21	FTP	FTP	File transfer control information
22	SSH	Secure Shell	Remote control to a networked computer
23	Telnet	Telnet	Telnet, an application used by Unix computers to control a computer remotely
25	SMTP	E-mail	Simple Mail Transfer Protocol; used by a client to send e-mail
80	HTTP	Web server	World Wide Web protocol
109	POP2	E-mail	Post Office Protocol, version 2; used by a client to receive e-mail
110	POP3	E-mail	Post Office Protocol, version 3; used by a client to receive e-mail
119	NNTP	News server	News servers that use the Network News Transfer Protocol (NNTP), the protocol used for newsgroups
143	IMAP	E-mail	Internet Message Access Protocol, a newer protocol used by clients to receive e-mail
443	HTTPS	Web server	HTTP with added security that includes authentication and encryption

Table 9-1   Common TCP/IP port assignments for well-known server applications

⊙ A+ Exam Tip

The A+ 220-602 exam expects you to know about these protocols used on the Internet: TCP/IP, SMTP, IMAP, HTTP, HTTPS, SSL, Telnet, FTP, DNS, and VoIP. All these protocols are covered in this chapter.

Notice in Table 9-1 that each service has one or more designated protocols. These protocols are the rules of communication between the client and server components of the applications, and they are each used for different types of communication between the client and server.

Recall from the last chapter that at the lowest networking level, the network or hardware protocol controls communication among physical networking devices such as Ethernet NICs and switches. The next layer up is the OS protocol used on the network, such as TCP/IP, AppleTalk, or NetBEUI. Now, on top of the hardware and OS protocols, we add a third level of protocols that control how applications such as those listed in Table 9-1 communicate using the network. That third level consists of the applications protocols.

Figure 9-3 shows how communication happens at the three levels. An application (1) uses an IP address and port number to send its request to the OS (2), which passes the request to the NIC (3), which puts the request on the physical network and on to the NIC on the server (4). On the receiving end, this NIC sends the request to the OS (5), which passes the request to the Web server application (6). The Web server responds by sending data to the OS (5), which passes it down to its NIC (4), which passes it onto the network, and, ultimately, the data is received by the browser. At these different levels, an application has a port address assigned to it, the OS has an IP address assigned, and the NIC has a MAC address.

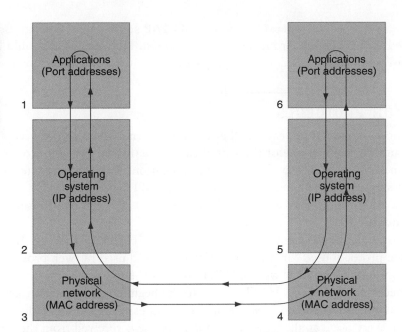

A+ ESS
5.1

A+
220-602
5.1

Figure 9-3 Applications, operating systems, and the physical network manage communication at all three levels

TCP/IP PROTOCOL LAYERS

Applications on the Internet all use protocols that are supported by TCP/IP. Figure 9-4 shows these different layers of protocols and how they relate to one another. As you read this section, this figure can serve as your road map to the different protocols.

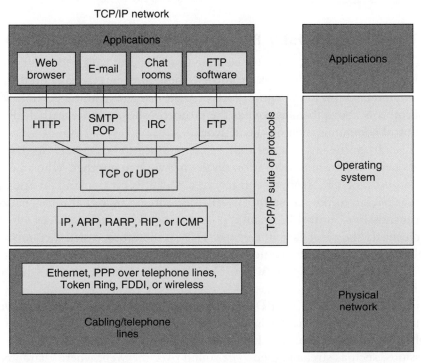

Figure 9-4 How software, protocols, and technology on a TCP/IP network relate to each other

Several types of protocols operate within the TCP/IP suite. The more significant ones are introduced in this section, from the top layer down. However, you should know that the TCP/IP protocol suite includes more protocols than just those mentioned in this chapter.

APPLICATION PROTOCOLS

Four of the most common applications that use the Internet are Web browsers, e-mail, chat rooms, and FTP. When one of these applications wants to send data to a counterpart application on another host, it makes an API (application programming interface) call to the operating system, which handles the request. (An API call is a common way for an application to ask an operating system to do something.) The API call causes the OS to generate a request.

For Web browsers, the OS generates an HTTP request. **HTTP (Hypertext Transfer Protocol)** is the protocol used for the World Wide Web and used by Web browsers and Web servers to communicate. In other words, HTTP formats the request, and encrypts and compresses it as necessary. It adds an HTTP header to the beginning of the data that includes the HTTP version being used and how the data is compressed and encrypted, if compression and encryption were done at all. Later, when the response is received from the server, the HTTP component of the OS decrypts and decompresses the data as necessary before passing it on to the browser.

After the response is passed to the browser, a session is established. **Sessions**, which are communication links created between two software programs, are managed by the browser and Web server using HTTP. However, TCP/IP at the OS level can also create a limited type of session.

Later in the chapter, you will learn more about Web and e-mail protocols and how they work.

Tip

Sessions are sometimes called **sockets** because they are established communication links.

TCP/IP PROTOCOLS USED BY THE OS FOR NETWORK COMMUNICATION

Looking back at Figure 9-4, you can see three layers of protocols between the application protocols and the physical network protocols. These three layers make up the heart of TCP/IP communication. In the figure, TCP or UDP manages communication with the applications protocols above them as well as the protocols shown underneath TCP and UDP, which control communication on the network.

Remember from the last chapter that all communication on a network happens by way of packets delivered from one location on the network to another. When a Web browser makes a request for data from a Web server, a packet is created and an attempt is made to deliver that packet to the server. In TCP/IP, the protocol that guarantees packet delivery is **TCP (Transmission Control Protocol)**. TCP makes a connection, checks whether the data is received, and resends it if it is not. TCP is, therefore, called a **connection-oriented protocol**. TCP is used by applications such as Web browsers and e-mail. Guaranteed delivery takes longer and is used when it is important to know that the data reached its destination.

On the other hand, **UDP (User Datagram Protocol)** does not guarantee delivery by first connecting and checking whether data is received; thus, UDP is called a **connectionless protocol** or a **best-effort protocol**. UDP is primarily used for broadcasting and other types of transmissions, such as streaming video or sound over the Web, where guaranteed delivery is not as important as fast transmission.

At the next layer, TCP and UDP pass requests to **IP (Internet Protocol)**, which is responsible for breaking up and reassembling data into packets and routing them to their destination.

A+ ESS
5.1

A+
220-602
5.1

When IP receives a request from one of these protocols (see Figure 9-5), the request has header information and data and is one long stream of bytes.

Figure 9-5 TCP turns to IP to prepare the data for networking

At this point, IP looks at the size of the data and breaks it into individual packets, which can be up to 4K in size. IP adds its own IP header, which includes the IP address of its host (source IP address) and that of the server (destination IP address), and then passes off the packet to the hardware.

If TCP is used to guarantee delivery, TCP uses IP to establish a session between client and server to verify that communication has taken place. When a TCP packet reaches its destination, an acknowledgment is sent back to the source (see Figure 9-6). If the source TCP does not receive the acknowledgment, it resends the data or passes an error message back to the higher-level application protocol. In Figure 9-6, the HTTP data is handled by the TCP protocol, which depends on the IP protocol for transmission. TCP on the receiving end is responsible for acknowledging the delivery.

Figure 9-6 TCP guarantees delivery by requesting an acknowledgment

Other protocols that operate in this part of the transmission process include the following:

▲ ARP (Address Resolution Protocol) is responsible for locating a host on a local network.
▲ RARP (Reverse Address Resolution Protocol) is responsible for discovering the Internet address of a host on a local network.
▲ ICMP (Internet Control Message Protocol) is responsible for communicating problems with transmission. For example, if a packet exceeds the number of routers it is permitted to pass through on its way to its destination, which is called a Time to Live (TTL) or hop count, a router kills the packet and returns an ICMP message to the source, saying that the packet has been killed (see Figure 9-7).

Figure 9-7 A router eliminates a packet that has exceeded its TTL

NETWORK PROTOCOLS USED BY HARDWARE

As you learned in the last chapter, the most popular hardware protocol for wired networks is Ethernet. Another hardware protocol that you will learn about later in the chapter is PPP, which is used for data communication over phone lines.

TCP/IP UTILITIES

When TCP/IP is installed as a Windows 2000/XP or Windows 9x/Me component, a group of utility tools is also installed that can be used to troubleshoot problems with TCP/IP. The most commonly used TCP/IP utilities are Ping, Winipcfg, and Ipconfig, which you learned about in the last chapter. Table 9-2 lists these and other TCP/IP utilities, and lists the purpose for each. The program files are found in the \Windows or \Winnt folder.

Utility	Description
ARP (Arp.exe)	Manages the IP-to-Ethernet address translation tables used to find the MAC address of a host on the network when the IP address is known
Getmac (Getmac.exe)	Displays the NIC's MAC address (Windows XP only)
Ipconfig (Ipconfig.exe)	Displays the IP address of the host and other configuration information (A command used by Unix similar to Ipconfig is config.)

Table 9-2 Utilities installed with TCP/IP on Windows

A+
220-602
3.1
5.3

Utility	Description
	Some parameters are: ▲ Ipconfig /all Displays all information about the connection ▲ Ipconfig /release Releases the current IP address ▲ Ipconfig /renew Requests a new IP address ▲ Ipconfig /? Displays information about Ipconfig
FTP (Ftp.exe)	Transfers files over a network
Nbtstat (Nbtstat.exe)	Displays current information about TCP/IP and NetBEUI when both are being used on the same network
Netstat (Netstat.exe)	Displays information about current TCP/IP connections
NSLookup (Nslookup.exe)	Displays information about domain names and their IP addresses
Ping (Ping.exe)	Verifies that there is a connection on a network between two hosts
Route (Route.exe)	Allows you to manually control network routing tables
Telnet (Telnet.exe)	Allows you to communicate with another computer on the network remotely, entering commands to control the remote computer
Tracert (Tracert.exe)	Traces and displays the route taken from the host to a remote destination; Tracert is one example of a trace-routing utility
Winipcfg (Winipcfg.exe)	A Windows 9x/Me utility to display IP address and other configuration information in a user-friendly window. In the Winipcfg window, use Release and Renew to release the current IP address and request a new one, which can sometimes solve TCP/IP connectivity problems when using a DHCP server.

Table 9-2   Utilities installed with TCP/IP on Windows (continued)

In addition to the utilities that are automatically installed with TCP/IP, another useful utility is the Microsoft SNMP Agent. This utility can be installed after you install TCP/IP; to do so, use the Add or Remove Programs applet in Control Panel. **SNMP (Simple Network Management Protocol)** provides system management tools for networks. A system administrator can monitor remote connections to computers running Windows clients with SNMP Agent. The administrator will most likely use the utility sparingly because it can be a security risk. For more information about SNMP, see RFC 1157 (*www.rfc-editor.org*).

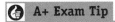

A+ Exam Tip

The A+ 220-602 exam expects you to know about the following TCP/IP utilities listed in Table 9-2: Ipconfig.exe, Ping.exe, Tracert.exe, and NSLookup. Know the filename of the utility's program file as well as how and when to use the utility.

APPLYING CONCEPTS

An interesting tool that lets you read information from the Internet name space is NSLookup, which requests information about domain name resolutions from the DNS server's zone data. Zone data is information about domain names and their corresponding IP addresses kept by a DNS server. The NSLookup utility program is included in Windows 2000/XP. For example, to use Windows XP to retrieve what the DNS server knows about the domain name *www.microsoft.com*, follow these directions:

1. Click **Start, Run**. Enter **Cmd** in the Run dialog box and press **Enter**. A command window opens.

A+
220-602
3.1
5.3

2. Enter the command **nslookup www.microsoft.com** and then press **Enter**. Figure 9-8 shows the results. Notice in the figure that the DNS server knows about eight IP addresses assigned to *www.microsoft.com*. It also reports that this information is nonauthoritative, meaning that it is not the authoritative, or final, name server for the *www.microsoft.com* computer name.

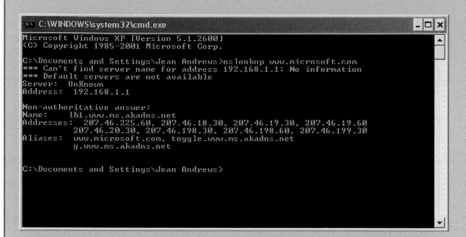

Figure 9-8 The Nslookup command reports information about the Internet name space

The Tracert (trace route) command can be useful when you're trying to resolve a problem reaching a destination host such as an FTP site or Web site. The command sends a series of requests to the destination computer and displays each hop to the destination. For example, to trace the route to the *www.course.com* site, enter this command in a command prompt window:

```
tracert www.course.com
```

The results of this command are shown in Figure 9-9. By default, the command makes 30 requests for up to 30 hops. The final 15 requests in the figure were not needed to show the complete path to the site, causing a "Request timed out" message to appear. Also, the Tracert command depends on ICMP information sent by routers when a packet's hop count has been exceeded. Some routers don't send this information. If a router doesn't respond, the "Request timed out" message appears.

A+
220-602
3.1
5.3

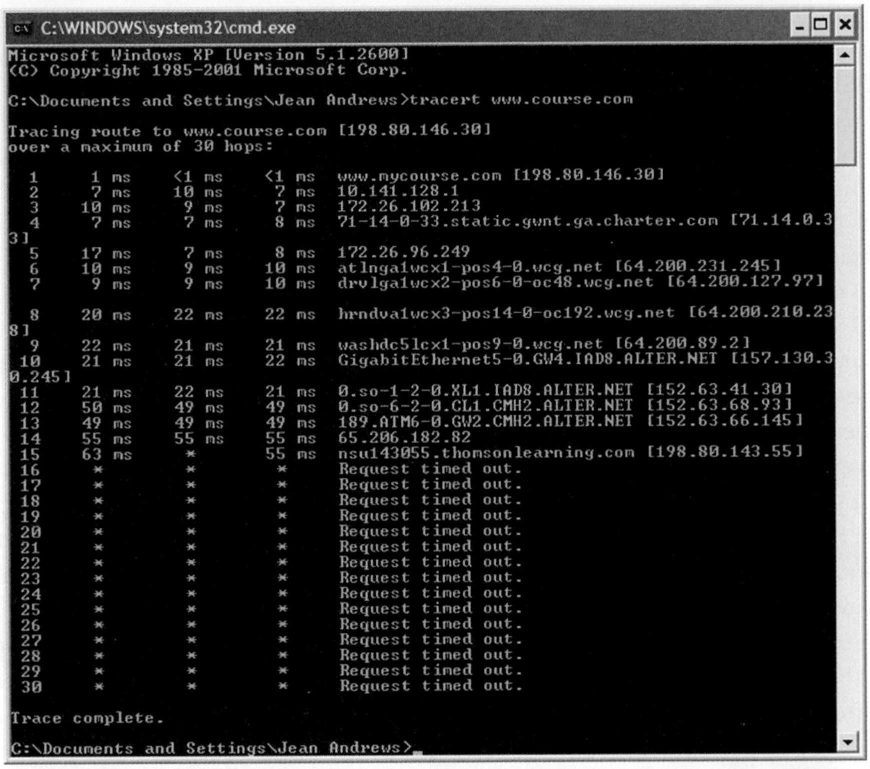

```
C:\WINDOWS\system32\cmd.exe                                    _ □ ×

Microsoft Windows XP [Version 5.1.2600]
<C> Copyright 1985-2001 Microsoft Corp.

C:\Documents and Settings\Jean Andrews>tracert www.course.com

Tracing route to www.course.com [198.80.146.30]
over a maximum of 30 hops:

  1     1 ms    <1 ms    <1 ms  www.mycourse.com [198.80.146.30]
  2     7 ms    10 ms     7 ms  10.141.128.1
  3    10 ms     9 ms     7 ms  172.26.102.213
  4     7 ms     7 ms     8 ms  71-14-0-33.static.gvnt.ga.charter.com [71.14.0.3
3]
  5    17 ms     7 ms     8 ms  172.26.96.249
  6    10 ms     9 ms    10 ms  atlnga1wcx1-pos4-0.wcg.net [64.200.231.245]
  7     9 ms     9 ms    10 ms  drvlga1wcx2-pos6-0-oc48.wcg.net [64.200.127.97]

  8    20 ms    22 ms    22 ms  hrndva1wcx3-pos14-0-oc192.wcg.net [64.200.210.23
8]
  9    22 ms    21 ms    21 ms  washdc5lcx1-pos9-0.wcg.net [64.200.89.2]
 10    21 ms    21 ms    22 ms  GigabitEthernet5-0.GW4.IAD8.ALTER.NET [157.130.3
0.245]
 11    21 ms    22 ms    21 ms  0.so-1-2-0.XL1.IAD8.ALTER.NET [152.63.41.30]
 12    50 ms    49 ms    49 ms  0.so-6-2-0.CL1.CMH2.ALTER.NET [152.63.68.93]
 13    49 ms    49 ms    49 ms  189.ATM6-0.GW2.CMH2.ALTER.NET [152.63.66.145]
 14    55 ms    55 ms    55 ms  65.206.182.82
 15    63 ms     *       55 ms  nsu143055.thomsonlearning.com [198.80.143.55]
 16     *        *        *      Request timed out.
 17     *        *        *      Request timed out.
 18     *        *        *      Request timed out.
 19     *        *        *      Request timed out.
 20     *        *        *      Request timed out.
 21     *        *        *      Request timed out.
 22     *        *        *      Request timed out.
 23     *        *        *      Request timed out.
 24     *        *        *      Request timed out.
 25     *        *        *      Request timed out.
 26     *        *        *      Request timed out.
 27     *        *        *      Request timed out.
 28     *        *        *      Request timed out.
 29     *        *        *      Request timed out.
 30     *        *        *      Request timed out.

Trace complete.

C:\Documents and Settings\Jean Andrews>_
```

Figure 9-9 The Tracert command traces a path to a destination computer

CONNECTING TO THE INTERNET

A+ ESS
5.1

In this part of the chapter, you'll learn how to connect a single PC to the Internet and then how to share that connection with other computers. Later in the chapter, you'll learn how to use a router to create a more sophisticated and secure Internet connection that can support multiple computers all accessing the Internet.

A+
220-602
5.1
5.3

A single computer or local network connects to the Internet by way of an Internet service provider (ISP) using one of the following bandwidth technologies:

▲ *Regular telephone lines.* Regular telephone lines, the most common and least expensive way to connect to an ISP, require an internal or external modem. A modem converts a PC's digital data (data made up of zeros and ones) to analog data (continuous variations of frequencies) that can be communicated over telephone lines.

▲ *Cable modem.* Cable modem communication uses cable lines that already exist in millions of households. Just as with cable TV, cable modems are always connected (always up). Cable modem is an example of broadband media. **Broadband** refers to any type of networking medium that carries more than one type of transmission. With a cable modem, the TV signal to your television and the data signals to your PC share the same cable. Just like a regular modem, a cable modem converts a PC's digital signals to analog when sending them and converts incoming analog data to digital.

▲ *DSL.* DSL (Digital Subscriber Line) is a group of broadband technologies that covers a wide range of speeds. DSL uses ordinary copper phone lines and a range of frequencies on the copper wire that are not used by voice, making it possible for you to use the same phone line for voice and DSL at the same time. The voice portion of the phone line requires a dial-up as normal, but the DSL part of the line is always connected or, in some regions, connects as needed. Asymmetric DSL (ADSL) uses one upload speed from the consumer to an ISP and a faster download speed. Symmetric DSL (SDSL) uses equal bandwidths in both directions.

▲ *ISDN.* ISDN (Integrated Services Digital Network) is a mostly outdated technology developed in the 1980s that also uses regular phone lines, and is accessed by a dial-up connection. For home use, an ISDN line is fully digital and consists of two channels, or phone circuits, on a single pair of wires called B channels, and a slower channel used for control signals, called a D channel. Each B channel can support speeds up to 64,000 bps. The two lines can be combined so that data effectively travels at 128,000 bps, about three to five times the speed of regular phone lines.

▲ *Satellite access.* People who live in remote areas and want high-speed Internet connections often are limited in their choices. DSL and cable modems might not work where they live, but satellite access is available from pretty much anywhere. Technology is even being developed to use satellites to offer Internet access on commercial airlines. Customers can use their own laptops to connect to the Internet through a connection at their seats to a satellite dish in the airplane. A satellite dish mounted on top of your house or office building communicates with a satellite used by an ISP offering the satellite service.

▲ *Wireless access.* Wireless refers to several technologies and systems that don't use cables for communication, including public radio, cellular phones, one-way paging, satellite, infrared, and private, proprietary radio. Because of its expense and the concern that increasing use of wireless might affect our health, as well as airplane control systems, pacemakers, and other sensitive electronic devices, wireless is not as popular as wired data transmission. Wireless is an important technology for mobile devices and for Internet access in remote locations where other methods are not an option.

> **✎ Notes**
>
> Another bandwidth technology used for Internet access is FiOS by Verizon. FiOS uses fiber-optic cabling from your ISP to your house. You'll learn more about FiOS in a project at the end of this chapter.

> **👍 Tip**
>
> The A+ Essentials and A+ 220-602 exams expect you to know how to connect to the Internet using a dial-up, cable modem, DSL, LAN, ISDN, satellite, and wireless connection. All these connections have many things in common. Skills learned in making one type of connection can be used when making another type.

In the following sections, you'll learn how to connect to the Internet using cable modem and DSL connections and a standard dial-up connection. You will learn how each type of connection is made as well as some advantages and disadvantages of each. Then, you'll learn how to share Internet connections using Windows. Finally, we'll look at how to use a software firewall to protect a computer from attacks.

CABLE MODEM AND DSL CONNECTIONS

Recall that DSL and cable modem are called broadband technologies because they support the transmission of more than one kind of data at once. These connections can carry voice, data, sound, and video simultaneously. The major differences and similarities between cable modem and DSL are as follows:

▲ Cable modem uses TV cable for transmission and you subscribe to cable modem bundled with your TV cable subscription. On the other hand, DSL uses phone lines for transmission and is bundled with your local phone service.

A+
220-602
5.1
5.3

▲ Cable modem and DSL both can be purchased on a sliding scale depending on the bandwidth you want to buy. Also, both subscriptions offer residential and the more-expensive business plans. Residential plans are likely to use dynamic IP addressing, and business plans are likely to have static IP addressing, increased bandwidth, and better support when problems arise.

▲ With cable modem, you share the TV cable infrastructure with your neighbors, which can result in service becoming degraded if many people in your neighborhood are using cable modem at the same time. I once used cable modem in a neighborhood where I found I needed to avoid Web surfing between 5:00 and 7:00 p.m. when folks were just coming in from work and using the Internet. With DSL, you're using a dedicated phone line, so your neighbors' surfing habits are not important.

▲ With DSL, static over phone lines in your house can be a problem. The DSL company provides filters to install at each phone jack, but still the problem might not be fully solved. Also, your phone line must qualify for DSL; some lines are too dirty (too much static) to support DSL.

▲ Setup of cable modem and DSL works about the same way, using either a cable modem box or a DSL box for the interface between the broadband jack (TV jack or phone jack) and the PC. Figure 9-10 shows the setup for a cable modem connection using a network cable between the cable modem and the PC.

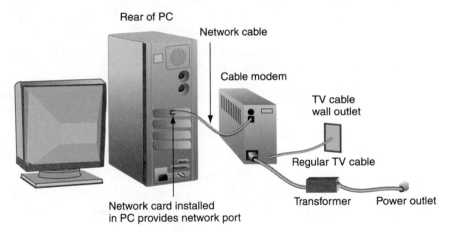

Figure 9-10 Cable modem connecting to a PC through a network card installed in the PC

▲ With either installation, in most cases, you can have the cable modem or DSL provider do the entire installation for you at an additional cost. A service technician comes to your home, installs all equipment, including a network card if necessary, and configures your PC to use the service.

▲ In most cases, cable modem and DSL use a network port or a USB port on the PC to connect to the cable modem or DSL box.

Generally, when setting up a cable modem or DSL connection to the Internet, the installation goes like this:

1. Connect the PC to the cable modem or DSL box. Connect the cable modem to the TV jack or the DSL box to the phone line. Plug up the power and turn on the broadband device.

2. Configure the TCP/IP settings for the connection to the ISP.

3. Test the connection by using a browser to surf the Web.

A+
220-602
5.1
5.3

Now let's look at the specific details of making a cable modem connection or DSL connection to the Internet.

INSTALLING A CABLE MODEM

To set up a cable modem installation to the Internet, you'll need the following:

- A computer with an available network or USB port
- A cable modem and a network or USB cable to connect to the PC
- The TCP/IP settings to use to configure TCP/IP provided by the cable modem company. For most installations, you can assume dynamic IP addressing is used. If static IP addressing is used, you'll need to know the IP address, the IP address of one or two DNS servers, the subnet mask, and the IP address of the default gateway (the IP address of a server at the ISP).

Then, follow these instructions to connect a computer to the Internet using cable modem:

1. Select the TV wall jack that will be used to connect your cable modem. You want to use the jack that connects directly to the point where the TV cable comes into your home with no splitters between this jack and the entrance point. Later, if your cable modem connection is constantly going down, you might consider that you've chosen the wrong jack for the connection because an inline splitter can degrade the connection. The cable company that installed the jacks should be able to tell you which jack is best to use for the cable modem (which is one good reason to have a technician come and hook you up for the first time).

2. Using coaxial cable, connect the cable modem to the TV wall jack. Plug in the power cord to the cable modem.

3. When using a network port on your PC, connect one end of the network cable to the network port on the PC and the other end to the network port on the cable modem.

4. You're now ready to configure Windows for the connection. Right-click **My Network Places** and select **Properties** from the shortcut menu. The Network Connections window opens. See Figure 9-11. Click **Create a new connection**.

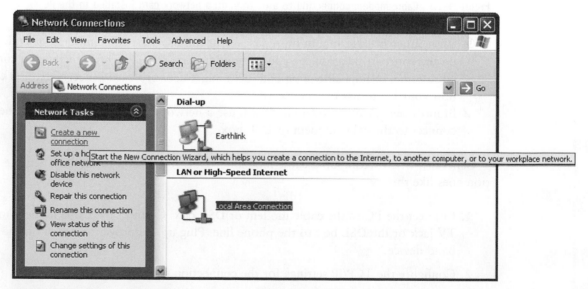

Figure 9-11   Using Windows XP, launch the New Connection Wizard

A+
220-602
5.1
5.3

5. The New Connection Wizard opens. Click **Next** to skip the welcome screen. On the next screen, select **Connect to the Internet** and click **Next**.

6. On the next screen, select **Set up my connection manually** and click **Next**. On the following screen (see Figure 9-12), select **Connect using a broadband connection that is always on** and then click **Next**. The wizard creates the connection. Click **Finish** to close the wizard.

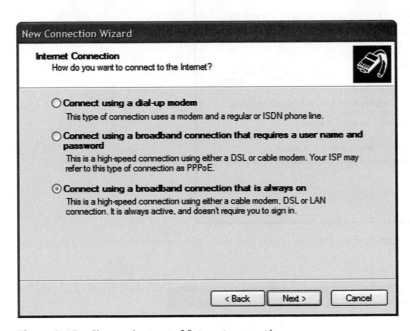

Figure 9-12   Choose the type of Internet connection

Windows XP makes assumptions about your connection. To view the configuration and make any necessary changes, do the following:

1. In the Network Connections window, right-click the connection icon and select **Properties** from the shortcut menu. The connection's Properties window opens. Click the **General** tab to select it, if necessary, as shown in Figure 9-13.

2. Select **Internet Protocol (TCP/IP)**, if necessary, and click **Properties**. The Internet Protocol (TCP/IP) Properties window opens, as shown in Figure 9-14.

3. Most likely, your ISP is using dynamic IP addressing for your connection, so you will need to select **Obtain an IP address automatically** and **Obtain DNS server address automatically**. If you are using static IP addressing (for example, if you have a business account with your ISP), select **Use the following IP address**, and enter the IP address given to you by the ISP, along with the IP address of the default gateway and the IP addresses of two or more DNS servers. Click **OK** to close the window.

4. On the connection properties window, click the **Advanced** tab and then, under Windows Firewall, click **Settings** and verify the firewall is up. Click **OK** to close the window, and then click **OK** again to close the connection's Properties window.

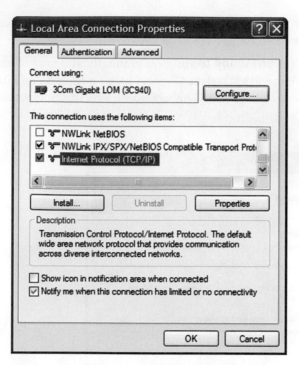

Figure 9-13 Configure an Internet connection using the Properties window of the connection icon

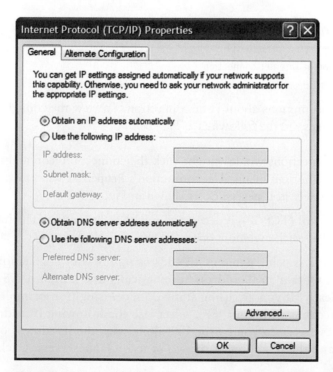

Figure 9-14 Configure TCP/IP for the connection

Follow these directions if you are using a USB cable to connect your cable modem to your computer:

1. When using a USB port on your PC, first read the directions that came with your cable modem to find out if you install the software before or after you connect the cable

modem and follow that order. For most installations, you begin with connecting the cable modem.

2. Connect a USB cable to your PC and to the cable modem. Turn on the cable modem and Windows XP will automatically detect it as a new USB device. When the Found New Hardware Wizard launches, insert the USB driver CD that came with your cable modem. The wizard searches for and installs these drivers, as shown in Figure 9-15. Click **Finish** to close the Found New Hardware Wizard. A new connection icon will be added to the Network Connections window. Check the properties of the connection to make sure TCP/IP is configured as you want it.

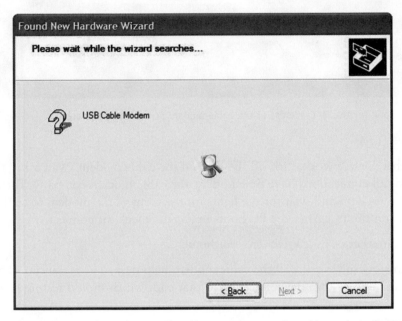

Figure 9-15 When using a USB cable to connect to the cable modem, the Found New Hardware Wizard will install the cable modem drivers

You are now ready to activate your service and test the connection. Do the following:

1. The cable company must know the MAC address of the cable modem you have installed. If you have received the cable modem from your cable company, they already have the MAC address listed as belonging to you and you can skip this step. If you purchased the cable modem from another source, look for the MAC address somewhere on the back or bottom of the cable modem. Figure 9-16 shows the information on one modem. Contact the cable company and tell them the new MAC address.

2. Test the Internet connection using your Web browser. If you are not connecting, try the following:

   ◢ Open the Network Connections window, right-click the connection and select **Repair** from the shortcut menu. For dynamic IP addressing, this releases and renews the IP address. (For Windows 2000, use **Ipconfig /release** and **Ipconfig /renew** to release and renew the IP address. For Windows 9x/Me, use **Winipcfg** to access the IP Configuration window. Select the network card and click **Release All**. Wait a moment, and then click **Renew**.) Now check for Internet connectivity again.

A+
220-602
5.1
5.3

Figure 9-16 Look for the MAC address of the cable modem printed on the modem

▲ If this doesn't work, turn off the PC and the cable modem. Wait a full five minutes until all connections have timed out at the cable modem company. Turn on the cable modem and wait for the lights on the front of the modem to settle in. Then turn on the PC. After the PC boots up, again check for connectivity.

▲ Try another cable TV jack in your home.

▲ If this doesn't work, call the cable modem help desk. The technician there can release and restore the connection at that end, which should restore service.

INSTALLING DSL

DSL service and the older technology, ISDN, are provided by the local telephone company. As with a cable modem, a technician from the phone company can install DSL for you, or they can send you a kit for you to install yourself. If you do the installation yourself, know that it works pretty much the same way as cable modem. Here are the steps that are different:

1. Install a telephone filter on every phone jack in your house that is being used by a telephone, fax machine, or dial-up modem. See Figure 9-17.

2. Connect the DSL modem, as shown in Figure 9-18. If necessary, you can use a Y-splitter on the wall jack (as shown on the left in Figure 9-17) so a telephone can use the same jack. Plug the DSL modem into the DSL port on a filter or directly into a wall jack. (Don't connect the DSL modem to a telephone port on the filter; this setup would prevent DSL from working.) Plug in the power to the DSL modem. Connect a network or USB cable between the DSL modem and the PC.

3. You're now ready to configure the network connection. If your DSL modem came with a setup CD, you can run that setup to step you through the configuration. You can also manually configure the network connection. To do that, using the Network Connections window, click **Create a new connection** and click **Next** to skip the welcome screen. Then click **Connect to the Internet** and click **Next**. Finally, click **Set up my connection manually**.

A+
220-602
5.1
5.3

Figure 9-17 Filters are needed on every phone jack when DSL is used in your house

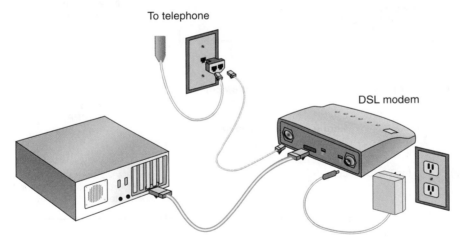

To telephone

DSL modem

Figure 9-18 Sample setup for DSL

4. On the next screen, shown in Figure 9-12, you have a choice to make, based on the type of DSL subscription you have. If you subscribed to always-up DSL, click **Connect using a broadband connection that is always on.** If you have a DSL subscription that is active only when you log on with a username and password, then click **Connect using a broadband connection that requires a user name and password.** This last type of connection is managed by a protocol called **PPPoE (Point-to-Point Protocol Over Ethernet)**, which is why the connection is sometimes called a PPPoE connection. Follow the wizard through to complete the setup.

 Notes

If your DSL subscription is not always up and requires you to enter your username and password each time you connect, using a router with autoconnecting ability can be a great help. It can automatically pass the username and password to your DSL provider without your involvement.

A+
220-602
5.1

DIAL-UP CONNECTIONS

Dial-up connections are painfully slow, but many times we still need them when traveling and they're good at home when our broadband connection is down or we just plain want to save money. Connecting to a network, such as the Internet, using a modem and regular phone line is called **dial-up networking**.

Dial-up networking works by using PPP (Point-to-Point Protocol) to send packets of data over phone lines, and is called a line protocol. (An earlier and outdated line protocol is Serial Line Internet Protocol (SLIP).) The network protocol, TCP/IP, packages the data, making it ready for network traffic, and then PPP adds its own header and trailer to these packets. Figure 9-19a shows how this works. The data is presented to the network protocol, which adds its header information. Then, the packet is presented to the line protocol, PPP, which adds its own header and trailer to the packet and presents it to the modem for delivery over phone lines to a modem on the receiving end.

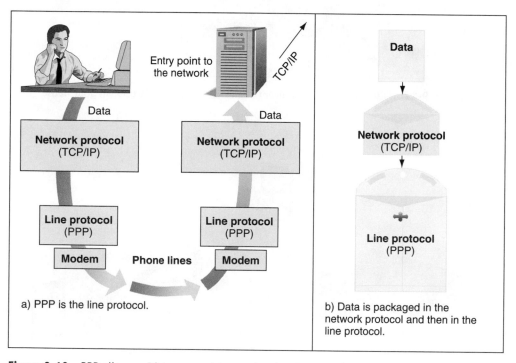

Figure 9-19   PPP allows a PC to connect to a network using a modem

The data packet is received by a computer at the ISP. The receiving computer strips off the PPP header and trailer information and sends the packet to the network still packaged in the TCP/IP protocols. In Figure 9-19b, these two protocols act like envelopes. Data is put in a TCP/IP envelope for travel over the network. This envelope is put in a PPP envelope for travel over phone lines. When the phone line segment of the trip is completed, the PPP envelope is discarded.

CREATING A DIAL-UP CONNECTION USING WINDOWS 2000/XP

To use dial-up networking to connect to the Internet, follow these directions:

1. Install an internal or external dial-up modem. After the modem is installed, you can check Device Manager to make sure Windows recognizes the modem with no errors (see Figure 9-20).

Video

Installing a Modem

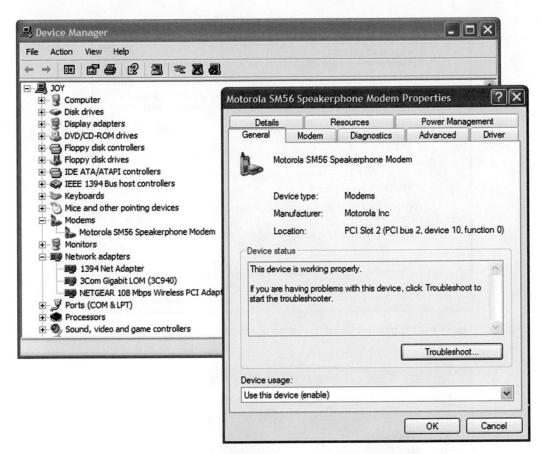

A+
220-602
5.1

Figure 9-20 Use Device Manager to verify the modem is recognized by Windows with no errors

2. To launch the New Connection Wizard in Windows XP, right-click **My Network Places** and select **Properties** from the shortcut menu. The Network Connections window opens. Click **Create a new connection**.

3. The New Connection Wizard opens. Click **Next** to skip the welcome screen. On the next screen, select **Connect to the Internet** and click **Next**.

4. On the next screen, select **Set up my connection manually** and click **Next**. On the following screen, select **Connect using a dial-up modem**. Click **Next**.

5. Enter a name to identify the connection, such as the name and city of your ISP. Click **Next**. On the following screen, enter the access phone number of your ISP. Click **Next**.

6. On the next screen (see Figure 9-21), enter your username and password at the ISP. This screen gives options to make the logon automatic and to make this the default connection to the Internet. Make your choices and click **Next**.

7. On the next screen, you can choose to add a shortcut to the connection on the desktop. Make your choice and click **Finish**. A connection icon is added to the Network Connections window; if you selected the option, a shortcut is added to the desktop.

8. To use the connection, double-click the connection icon. The Connect dialog box opens (see Figure 9-22). Click **Dial**. You will hear the modem dial up the ISP and make the connection.

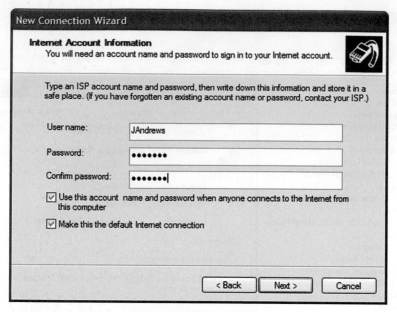

Figure 9-21 The New Connection Wizard asks how to configure the connection

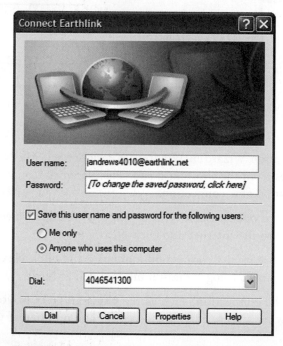

Figure 9-22 Make a dial-up connection to your ISP

To view or change the configuration for the dial-up connection, do the following:

1. In the Network Connections window, right-click the connection and select **Properties** from the shortcut menu. The connection Properties window opens, as shown in Figure 9-23.

A+
220-602
5.1

Figure 9-23 Configure an Internet connection using the Properties window of the connection icon

2. Use the tabs on this window to change Windows Firewall settings (Advanced tab), configure TCP/IP (Networking tab), control the way Windows attempts to dial the ISP when the first try fails (Options tab), and change other dialing features.

> **Video**
> Troubleshooting a Dial-Up Problem

If the dial-up connection won't work, here are some things you can try:

- Is the phone line working? Plug in a regular phone and check for a dial tone. Is the phone cord securely connected to the computer and the wall jack?
- Check the Dial-up Networking connection icon for errors. Is the phone number correct? Does the number need to include a 9 to get an outside line? Has a 1 been added in front of the number by mistake? If you need to add a 9, you can put a comma in the field like this "9,4045661200", which causes a slight pause after the 9 is dialed.
- Try dialing the number manually from a phone. Do you hear beeps on the other end?
- Try another phone number.
- When you try to connect, do you hear the number being dialed? If so, the problem is most likely with the phone number, the phone line, or the username and password.
- Does the modem work? Check Device Manager for reported errors about the modem. Does the modem work when making a call to another phone number (not your ISP)?
- Is TCP/IP configured correctly? Most likely, you need to set it to obtain an IP address automatically.
- Reboot your PC and try again.
- Using Device Manager, in the modem properties window, click the **Diagnostics** tab, as shown in Figure 9-24. Click **Query Modem** to have Windows attempt to communicate with the modem. If errors appear, assume the problem is related to the modem and not to the dial-up connection. You can also click **View log** to search for possible modem errors.

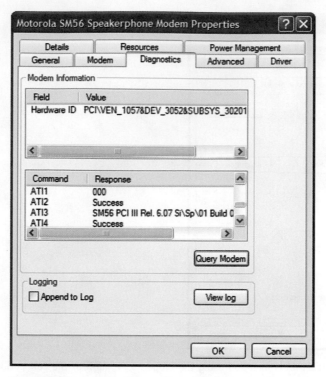

Figure 9-24 Use the Diagnostics tab on the modem's Properties window to search for modem problems

▲ Try removing and reinstalling the dial-up connection. If that doesn't work, try using
Device Manager to uninstall the modem and install it again. (Don't do this unless you
have with you the modem drivers on CD or on the hard
drive.)

> **Notes**
>
> If you want to disable call waiting while you're connected to the Internet, enter "*70" in front of the phone number (without the double quotes).

> **A+ Exam Tip**
>
> Even though Windows 9x/Me is not covered on the new 2006 A+ exams, this book is committed to covering both the new exams and the old 2003 exams that are still live at the time this book went to print.

CREATING A DIAL-UP CONNECTION IN WINDOWS 9X/ME

To use Windows 98 or Windows Me to communicate
with a network over phone lines, Dial-Up Networking
must be installed as an OS component on your PC using
the Add/Remove Programs applet in Control Panel.
(Network and Dial-Up Connections in Windows 2000
and Network Connections in Windows XP are installed
by default.)

When Windows 98 installs Dial-Up Networking, it also
"installs" a dial-up adapter. In terms of function, think of
this dial-up adapter as a virtual network card. Remember
that in the last chapter, you learned how TCP/IP is bound
to a network interface card. A dial-up adapter is a modem
playing the role of a network card for dial-up networking.
After Dial-Up Networking is installed, open the Device

Manager to see your "new" dial-up adapter listed under Network adapters, as shown in
Figure 9-25. You can also see it listed as an installed network component in the Network
window of Control Panel.

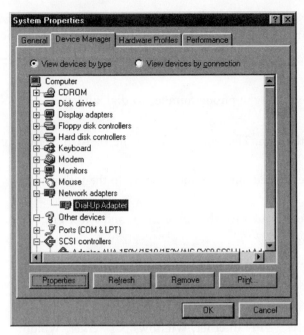

Figure 9-25 After Dial-Up Networking is installed, a new virtual network device,
a dial-up adapter, is listed as an installed hardware device

After you have verified the dial-up adapter is installed, you are now ready to create a
Dial-Up Networking connection. To create the connection in Windows 98:

1. After Dial-Up Networking is installed, click **Start**, point to **Programs, Accessories,**
and **Communications,** and then click **Dial-Up Networking**. The Dial-Up Networking
window opens, as shown on the left side of Figure 9-26.

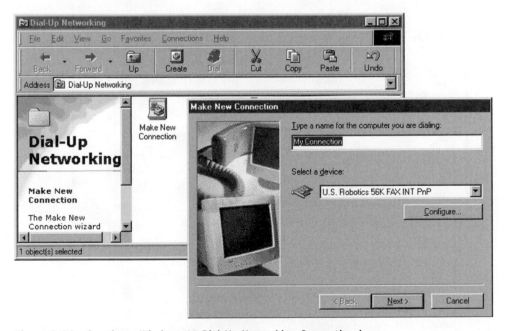

Figure 9-26 Creating a Windows 98 Dial-Up Networking Connection icon

2. Double-click **Make New Connection**. The Make New Connection Wizard appears, as shown on the right side of Figure 9-26. Click **Next** to move past the first screen.

3. Enter a name for the connection. If your modem is already installed, it appears in the modem list.

4. In the next dialog box, type the phone number to dial, and then click **Next** to continue.

5. Click **Finish** to build the icon. The icon appears in the Dial-Up Networking window.

Next, you will configure the connection. In Windows 98, do the following:

1. Right-click the icon you created for the connection, and select **Properties** from the shortcut menu.

2. Click the **General** tab. Verify that the correct phone number is entered for your ISP.

3. Click the **Server Types** tab. Figure 9-27 shows the resulting dialog box. Verify that these selections are made:

   ▲ Type of Dial-Up Server: **PPP: Internet, Windows NT Server, Windows 98**

   ▲ Advanced Options: Select **Enable software compression** (software compression is most likely enabled, but this option really depends on what the ISP is doing). Also, click **Log on to network**.

   ▲ Allowed Network Protocols: **TCP/IP**

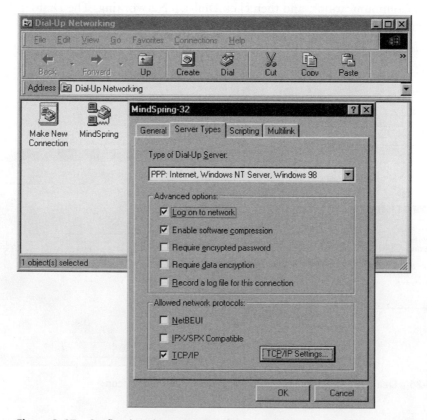

Figure 9-27 Configuring the server type for a connection to the Internet in Windows 9x/Me

4. Click **TCP/IP Settings** to open the TCP/IP Settings dialog box, as shown in Figure 9-28. Most likely, you will need to select:

◢ Server assigned IP address

◢ Server assigned name server addresses

◢ Use IP header compression

◢ Use default gateway on remote network

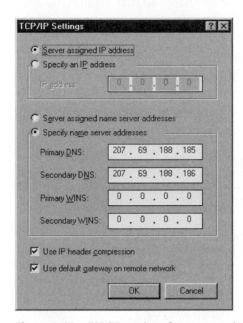

Figure 9-28   TCP/IP settings for a connection to the Internet in Windows 9x/Me

5. Click **OK** twice to complete the Dial-Up Networking connection.

6. To connect to your ISP, double-click the icon you created for it, which is now correctly configured. The first time you use the icon, enter the user ID and password to connect to your ISP. Check the option to remember the username and password if you don't want to have to enter them every time, but remember that this selection might not be wise if others who cannot be trusted have access to your PC.

7. Click **Connect**. You should hear the modem making the connection.

> ✎ **Notes**
>
> When troubleshooting problems with a modem using Windows 9x/Me, you can create a log file showing communication between Windows and the modem. To create the log file, open the **Network** applet in Control Panel, select **Dial-Up Adapter**, and then click **Properties**. In the Properties window, click the **Advanced** tab. In the Property box, select **Record A Log File**, and in the Value box, select **Yes**. Click **OK**. The file, Ppplog.txt, is created in the Windows folder. The file can get very large, so turn off logging when you don't need it. For tips on how to interpret the file, see the Microsoft Knowledge Base Article 156435, at *support.microsoft.com*.

A+
220-602
5.1

HIGH-SPEED DIAL-UP

Dial-up connections can be painfully slow when surfing the Web. If your ISP offers the option, you can speed up a dial-up connection to the Internet by using high-speed dial-up,

A+
220-602
5.1

which can almost double the average download times for much Web surfing. Two ISPs that support this feature are NetZero (*www.netzero.net*) and Earthlink (*www.earthlink.net*). Using high-speed dial-up, the phone line connection runs at the regular speed. However, downloading from the Internet is faster because the ISP provides these things to speed up downloading:

▲ *Abbreviated handshake.* When two modems first connect, they go through a handshaking routine to agree on protocols used for the connection. You hear the handshaking routine as a series of hisses and hums when the modems first connect. With high-speed dial-up, this handshaking process is abbreviated so that the initial connection to the ISP happens quickly.

▲ *Data compression.* The ISP uses an acceleration server, as shown in Figure 9-29, to compress data just before it is downloaded to you. Web pages, text, photos, and e-mails are compressed. The degree of compression depends on the type of data.

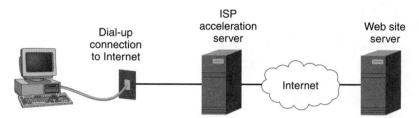

Figure 9-29 With high-speed dial-up, an acceleration server is used to improve download time

▲ *Filtering.* When your PC requests a Web page, many times that page is filled with unwanted pop-up ads. The acceleration server detects these ads and blocks them before downloading, thus reducing the amount of data to download and increasing the effective download speed.

▲ *Caching.* Recall from earlier chapters that caching is a technique that holds data until it's needed at a later time in order to speed up data access. Caching can happen on the server side (at the ISP) or on the client side (on your PC). These two types of caching are called **server-side caching** and **client-side caching**, as shown in Figure 9-30. When the acceleration server caches data, it holds Web pages that you have already requested in case you ask for them again, so that it doesn't have to go back a second time to the original Web site. With client-side caching, your browser holds in a cache Web pages that you've already seen in case you ask for the same page again. Also, caching software can be smart enough to request only part of the Web page—the part that might have changed—rather than requesting the entire page again. Internet Explorer normally uses caching, but with high-speed dial-up, the high-speed dial-up software you install on your PC when you subscribe to the service enhances IE caching so that it's smarter and works better.

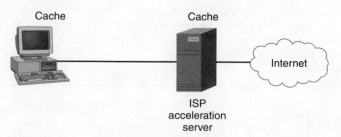

Figure 9-30 Server-side caching and client-side caching improve download times by reducing the number of requests for data

A+
220-602
5.2

SHARING A PERSONAL INTERNET CONNECTION

You have just seen how you can connect a single computer to the Internet using a cable modem, DSL, or dial-up connection. If the computer is networked with other computers, they, too, can access the Internet through this host computer, as illustrated in Figure 9-31. In Figure 9-31a, two computers are connected with a single crossover network cable, and in Figure 9-31b, a hub or switch is used to connect three or more computers in a small network. The host computer is the one that has the direct connection to the Internet.

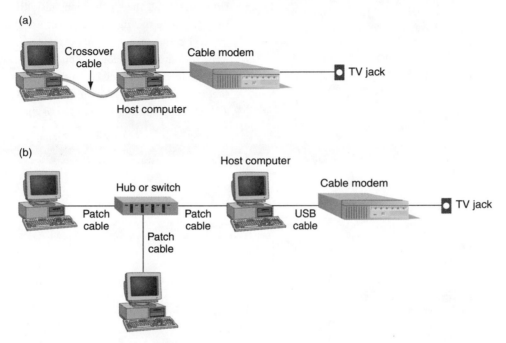

Figure 9-31 Two or more networked computers can share a single Internet connection

Windows XP and Windows 98 use **Internet Connection Sharing (ICS)** to manage these types of connections. Using ICS, the host computer uses NAT and acts as the proxy server for the LAN. Windows XP ICS also includes a firewall.

APPLYING | CONCEPTS To use Internet Connection Sharing in Windows XP or Windows 98, the computer that has a direct connection to the Internet by way of a phone line, cable modem, or DSL is the host computer. Follow these general directions to configure the LAN for Internet Connection Sharing using Windows XP:

1. Following directions earlier in the chapter, install and configure the hardware (modem, cable modem, or DSL) to connect the host computer to the Internet, and verify that the connection is working so that the host computer can browse the Web.

2. On the host computer, open the Network Connections window in the Windows XP Control Panel, and click the link to **Set up a home or small office network**. The Network Setup Wizard opens. Click **Next** in this window and the next.

3. Select the connection method for your host computer, which is **This computer connects directly to the Internet. The other computers on my network connect to the Internet through this computer.** Click **Next**.

A+
220-602
5.2

4. The wizard looks at your hardware connections (NIC or modem) and selects the one that it sees as a "live" connection. Verify that the wizard selected correctly and then follow the wizard to enter a description for your computer, your computer name, and your workgroup name.

Notes

To find out how to configure a Macintosh computer to connect to the Internet by way of a Windows computer providing an ICS connection, see the Microsoft Knowledge Base Article 230585 at *support.microsoft.com*.

5. The next screen of the wizard offers you the option of creating a Network Setup Disk (see Figure 9-32). If the other computers are not running Windows XP or Windows 98 and they have floppy disk drives, you'll need to create this disk so they can use the shared Internet connection. (If other computers on your network are running Windows 98 or Windows XP, there is no need to create the disk.) To create the disk, select the option to **Create a Network Setup Disk**, insert a blank floppy disk in the drive, and click **Next**.

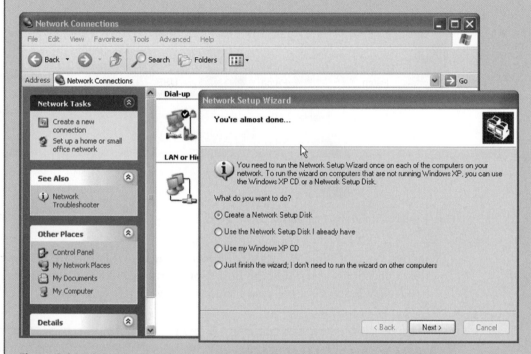

Figure 9-32 Create a Network Setup Disk to configure other computers on the LAN

6. The next screen gives you the option to format the disk. If it needs formatting, click **Format Disk**. Otherwise, click **Next**.

7. The wizard tells you that to use the disk, you must insert it into the next computer on the network, and run the program named Netsetup.exe from the disk. Click **Next** and then click **Finish**.

8. For the other computers in your network using Windows XP, open the **Network Connections** window and click the link to **Set up a home or small office network**. Follow the steps of the wizard to make the connection to the Internet. When given the opportunity, select **This computer connects to the Internet through a residential gateway or through another computer on my network**. Test that each computer can browse the Web. If you have problems, verify the TCP/IP configuration is correct. Try rebooting the PC.

A+
220-602
5.2

9. For all other computers, insert the Network Setup Disk in the floppy disk drive. At a command prompt, enter the command **A:Netsetup.exe** and then press **Enter**. After the program is finished, test that the computer can browse the Web. You might have to verify TCP/IP configuration and reboot the PC.

A+ ESS
6.1

A+
220-602
5.3
6.2
6.3

IMPLEMENTING A SOFTWARE FIREWALL

The Internet is a nasty and dangerous place infested with hackers, viruses, worms, and thieves. Knowing how to protect a single PC or a LAN is an essential skill of a PC support technician. The three most important things you can do to protect a single computer or network are to:

▲ Keep Windows updates current so that security patches are installed as soon as they are available.
▲ Use a software or hardware firewall.
▲ Run antivirus software and keep it current.

In earlier chapters, you learned how to keep Windows updates current. In the next chapter, you'll learn all about using antivirus software. In this section, you'll learn to use a software firewall. Software firewalls are appropriate when you're protecting a single personal computer or a host computer that is sharing an Internet connection with a few other computers. Then, in the later sections of this chapter, you'll learn how to use a hardware firewall.

A hardware or software firewall can function in several ways:

▲ Firewalls can filter data packets, examining the destination IP address or source IP address or the type of protocol used (for example, TCP or UDP).
▲ Firewalls can filter ports so that outside clients cannot communicate with inside services listening at these ports. Certain ports can be opened, for example, when your network has a Web server and you want Internet users to be able to access it.
▲ Firewalls can block certain activity that is initiated from inside the network—such as preventing users behind the firewall from using applications like FTP over the Internet. When evaluating firewall software, look for its ability to control traffic coming from both outside and inside the network.
▲ Some firewalls can filter information such as inappropriate Web content for children or employees, and can limit the use of the Internet to certain days or time of day.

Some examples of firewall software are ZoneAlarm (see Figure 9-33) by Zone Labs (*www.zonelabs.com*), Norton Personal Firewall by Symantec (*www.symantec.com*), Check Point Software by Check Point Software Technologies (*www.checkpoint.com*), McAfee Personal Firewall by McAfee (*www.mcafee.com*), Personal Firewall Pro by Sygate (*www.sygate.com*), and Windows XP Firewall.

> **Notes**
>
> Before Service Pack 2 for Windows XP was released, the firewall software for Windows XP was called Windows XP Internet Connection Firewall (ICF), and if this firewall was turned on, others on the LAN couldn't access resources on the PC. If you have Windows XP, be sure to install Service Pack 2 so that you have the benefit of the upgraded and much improved Windows Firewall.

A+ ESS
6.1

A+
220-602
5.3
6.2
6.3

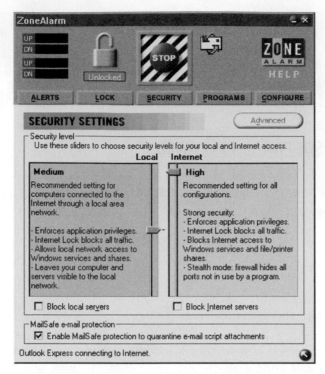

Figure 9-33   ZoneAlarm allows you to determine the amount of security the firewall provides

For Windows XP with Service Pack 2 applied, to manage Windows Firewall, open the **Network Connections** window. In the left pane, click **Change Windows Firewall settings**. The Windows Firewall window opens, as shown in Figure 9-34. Verify that **On (recommended)** is selected.

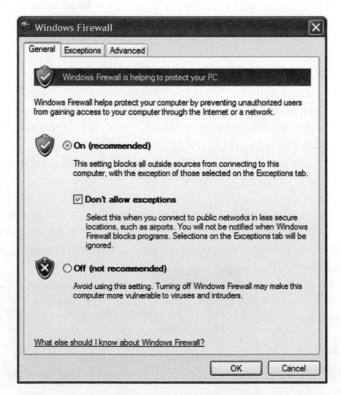

Figure 9-34   Windows Firewall is set for maximum protection

A+ ESS
6.1

A+
220-602
5.3
6.2
6.3

If you don't want to allow any communication to be initiated from remote computers, check **Don't allow exceptions**. This is the preferred setting when you're traveling or using public networks or Internet connections. If you are on a local network and need to allow others on the network to access your computer, uncheck **Don't allow exceptions**. Then click the **Exceptions** tab to select the exceptions to allow. For example, if you want to share files and folders on your local network, use the Exceptions tab shown in Figure 9-35, to allow File and Printer Sharing activity. Later in the chapter, you'll see another example of how to use this Exceptions tab to set up Windows XP Remote Desktop.

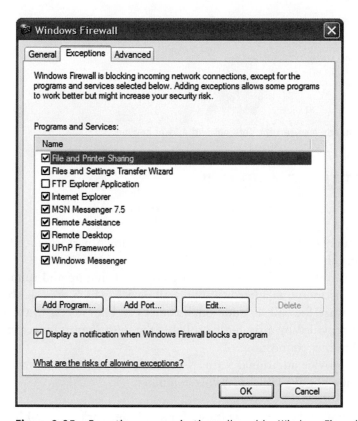

Figure 9-35 Exception communications allowed by Windows Firewall

USING A ROUTER ON YOUR NETWORK

A+
220-602
5.3

So far in the chapter, you've seen how one computer can connect to the Internet using a broadband or dial-up connection and also how this host computer can share that connection with others on a LAN. Two major disadvantages of this setup are that the host computer must always be turned on for others on the network to reach the Internet and the fact that security for your network is not as strong as it could be if you use a hardware firewall. Also, access to the Internet for other computers might be slow because of the bottleneck caused by the host computer. Installing a router solves all these problems.

Recall from the last chapter that a router is a device that manages traffic between two networks. In Figure 9-36, you can see how a router stands between the ISP network and the local network. The router takes the place of the host computer as the gateway to the Internet and also serves as a hardware firewall to protect your network.

A+
220-602
5.3

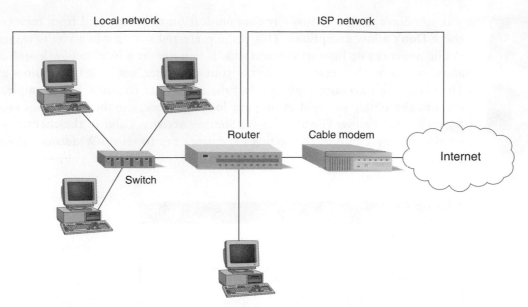

Figure 9-36   A router stands between the Internet and a local network

ADVANTAGES OF USING A ROUTER

The advantages of using a router rather than a host computer are:

◢ The host computer will not be a bottleneck to slow down performance for other computers using the Internet.
◢ Internet access is not dependent on the host computer being up and running.
◢ The router can also serve as a hardware firewall device, which provides better protection than a software firewall. In addition, a router can limit access to the Internet. This added security provided by a router is probably the most important reason to use a router for an Internet connection.
◢ The router can provide additional features—such as a DHCP server, switch, or wireless access point—not available on a host computer.

Three companies that make routers suitable for small networks are D-Link (*www.dlink.com*), Linksys (*www.linksys.com*), and NetGear (*www.netgear.com*). An example of a multifunction router is the Wireless-G Broadband Router by Linksys shown in Figure 9-37, which costs less than $60. It has one port for the broadband modem and four ports for computers on the network. The router is also an 802.11b/g wireless access point having two antennae to amplify the wireless signal and improve its range.

9

A+
220-602
5.3

Figure 9-37 This Linksys router allows computers on a LAN to share a broadband Internet connection and is an access point for computers with wireless adapters

The router shown in Figure 9-37 is typical of many brands and models of routers useful in a small office or small home network to manage the Internet connection. This router is several devices in one:

- ◢ As a router, it stands between the ISP network and the local network, routing traffic between the two networks.
- ◢ As a switch, it manages four network ports that can be connected to four computers or to a hub or switch that connects to more than one computer. In the small office setting pictured in Figure 9-38, this router connects to four network jacks that are wired in the walls to four other jacks in the building. Two of these remote jacks have switches connected that accommodate two or more computers.
- ◢ As a proxy server, all computers on the network route their Internet requests through this proxy server, which stands between the network and the Internet using NAT.

A+
220-602
5.3

Figure 9-38 A router and cable modem are used to provide Internet access for a small network

> **Notes**
>
> Recall that a proxy server adds protection to a network because it stands in proxy for other computers on the network when they want to communicate with computers on the Internet. The proxy server presents its own IP address to the Internet and does not allow outside computers to know the IP addresses of computers inside the network. This substitution of IP addresses is done using the NAT (Network Address Translation) protocol.

- ◢ As a DHCP server, all computers can receive their IP address from this server.
- ◢ As a wireless access point, a computer can connect to the network using a wireless device. This wireless connection can be secured using four different wireless security features.
- ◢ As a firewall, unwanted traffic initiated from the Internet can be blocked.
- ◢ As an Internet access restrictive device, the router can be set so that Internet access is limited.

INSTALLING AND CONFIGURING A ROUTER

To install a router that comes with a setup CD, run the setup program on one of your computers on the network (doesn't matter which one). Follow the instructions on the setup screen to disconnect the cable modem or DSL modem from your host computer and connect it to the router. Next, connect the computers on your network to your router. A computer can connect directly to a network port on the router, or you can connect a switch or hub to the router. Plug in the router and turn it on.

You'll be required to sign in to the utility using a default password. The first thing you want to do is reset this password so others cannot change your router setup.

9

A+
220-602
5.3

⚡ Caution

Changing the router password is especially important if the router is a wireless router. Unless you have disabled or secured the wireless access point, anyone outside your building can use your wireless network. If they guess the default password to the router, they can change the password to hijack your router. Also, your wireless network can be used for criminal activity. When you first install a router, before you do anything else, change your router password and disable the wireless network until you have time to set up and test the wireless security.

The setup program will then step you through the process of configuring the router. After you've configured the router, you might have to turn the cable modem or DSL modem off and back on so that it correctly syncs up with the router. If you don't get immediate connectivity to the Internet on all PCs, try rebooting each PC.

CONFIGURING THE ROUTER

Now let's look at how this Linksys router is configured, which is typical of what you might see for several brands and models of small office routers. Firmware on the router (which can be flashed for updates) contains a configuration program that you access using a Web browser from anywhere on the network. In your browser address box, enter the IP address of the router (for our router, it's 192.168.1.1) and press **Enter**. The main Setup window opens, as shown in Figure 9-39. For most situations, the default settings on this and other screens should work without any changes.

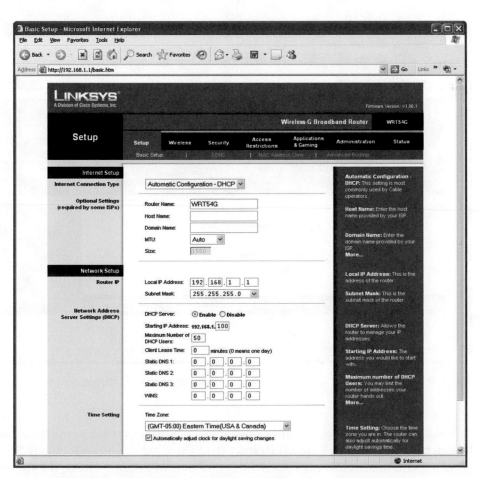

Figure 9-39 Basic Setup screen used to configure the router

A+
220-602
5.3

Using this Setup screen, under Internet Setup, you can change the host name and domain name if they are given to you by your ISP or leave them blank, which most often is the case. Under Network Setup, you can configure the DHCP server. Notice in the figure that the router can serve up to 50 leased IP addresses beginning with IP address 192.168.1.100. You can also disable the DHCP server if you want to use static IP addressing on your network or you already have another DHCP server on the network.

Video

Using a Hardware Firewall

After the router is configured as a DHCP server, you can configure each PC on your network to use dynamic IP addressing.

CONFIGURING A HARDWARE FIREWALL

In this section, you'll learn how to configure the Linksys router's firewall abilities to protect the network. You can use this information as a guide to configuring another router because, although the exact steps might vary, the basic principles will be the same.

Caution

Remember that you should always change the password to your router's setup utility. Default passwords for routers are easily obtained on the Web or in the product documentation. This is especially important for wireless routers.

To configure security on the firewall, click the **Security** link (as shown near the top of Figure 9-39). The window shown in Figure 9-40 appears. The most important item on this window is Block Anonymous Internet Requests. Enabling this feature prevents your network from being detected or accessed from others on the Internet without an invitation.

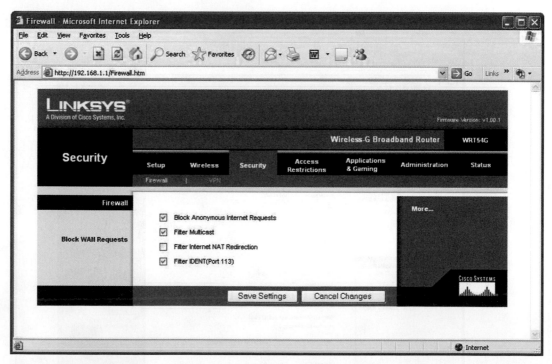

Figure 9-40 Configure the router's firewall to prevent others on the Internet from seeing or accessing your network

You can set policies to determine how and when users on your network can access the Internet. To do that, click **Access Restrictions**. The window shown in Figure 9-41 opens, allowing you to set policies about the day and time of Internet access, the services on the Internet that can be used, and the URLs and keywords that are not allowed.

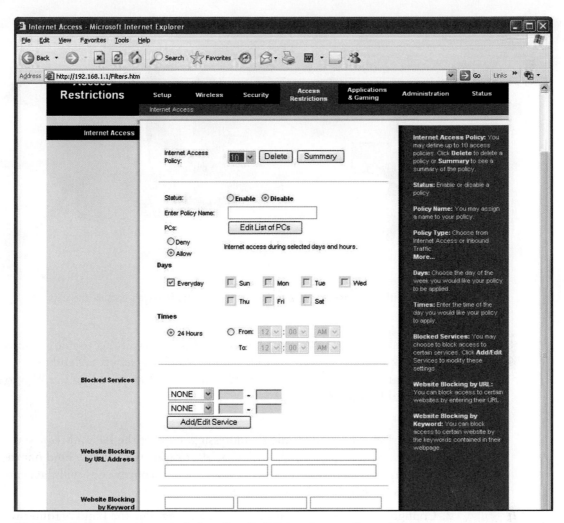

Figure 9-41 Configure the router's firewall to limit Internet access from within the network

PORT FILTERING AND PORT FORWARDING

Too much security is not always a good thing. There are legitimate times you want to be able to access computers on your network from somewhere on the Internet or allow others to do so, such as when you're hosting an Internet game or when you're traveling and want to use Remote Desktop to access your home computer. In this section, we'll look at how to drop your shields low enough so that the good guys can get in but the bad guys can't. However, know that when you drop your shields the least bit, you're compromising the security of your network, so be sure to use these methods sparingly. Here are the concepts that can be used; they are illustrated in Figure 9-42:

▲ Port filtering is used to open or close certain ports so they can or cannot be used. Remember that applications are assigned these ports. Therefore, in effect, you are filtering or controlling what applications can or cannot be used across the firewall.

▲ **Port forwarding** means that when the firewall receives a request for communication from the Internet, if the request is for a certain port, that request will be allowed and forwarded to a certain computer on the network. That computer is defined to the router by its IP address.

▲ For port forwarding to work, the local computer that is to receive this communication must have a static IP address.

Figure 9-42 With port forwarding, a router allows requests initiated outside the network

To demonstrate how to use port filtering and port forwarding to allow limited access to your network from the outside world, suppose you have set up a Web-hosting site on a computer that sits behind your firewalled router. To allow others on the Web to access your site, you would do the following:

1. If your ISP is using dynamic IP addressing, contact the ISP and request a static IP address. Most likely, the ISP will charge extra for this service. Find out the static IP address, which you can give to your friends. Your friends will then enter this IP address in their Web browsers to access your Web site.

2. Configure the router to use static IP addressing. For the Linksys router we're using as our example, the basic setup screen in Figure 9-43 shows how to configure the router for static IP addressing, using the gateway, and DNS server IP addresses and subnet mask provided by the ISP.

3. Next, configure your router to use port forwarding so that it will allow Web browser connections initiated from the Internet to pass through to your computer. Using your router's configuration utility, find the window that allows port forwarding, such as the one shown in Figure 9-44.

4. Enter the port that Web servers use, which, by default, is port 80, and the IP address of your desktop computer. In this example, the IP address chosen is 192.168.1.90. Check **Enable** to allow activity on this port to this computer. Save your changes.

5. Configure the computer that is running your Web server for static IP addressing and assign the IP address 192.168.1.90. Test the connection by using a computer that is somewhere on the Internet to access your Web site.

By the way, if you want your friends to be able to use a domain name rather than an IP address to access your Web site, you'll need to purchase the domain name and register it in the Internet name space to associate it with your static IP address assigned by your ISP. Several Web sites on the Internet let you do both; one site is by Network Solutions at *www.networksolutions.com*.

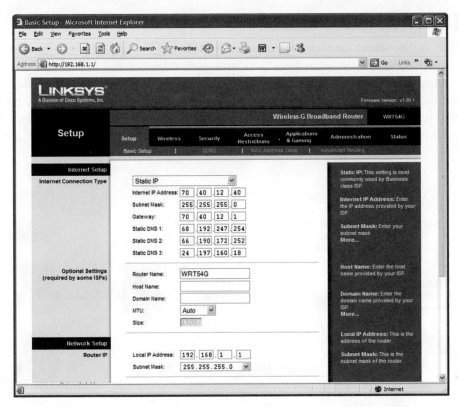

Figure 9-43 Configure the router for static IP addressing

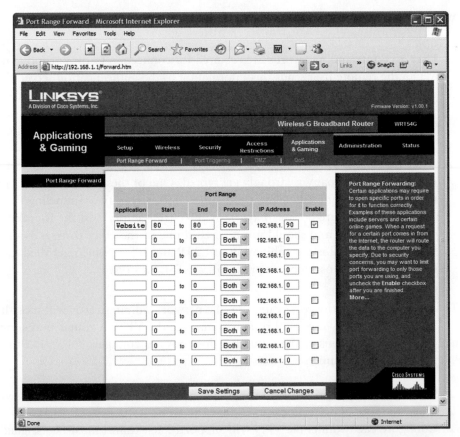

Figure 9-44 Using port forwarding, you can program your router to allow activity from the Internet
to initiate a session with a computer inside the network on a certain port

VIRTUAL PRIVATE NETWORK

Many people travel on their jobs or work from home, and the need is constantly growing for people to access private corporate data from somewhere on the Internet. Also growing are the dangers of private data being exposed in this way. The solution for securing private data traveling over a public network is a virtual private network (VPN) that you first learned about in the last chapter. Recall that a VPN works by using encrypted data packets between a private network and a computer somewhere on the Internet, as shown in Figure 9-45.

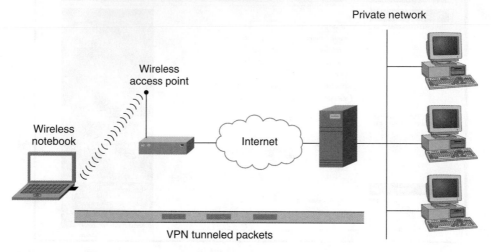

Figure 9-45 With a VPN, tunneling is used to send encrypted data over wired and wireless networks and the Internet

With a VPN, security is attained using both of these methods:

▲ User accounts and passwords are required for connection to the corporate network. When the remote user sends this information to the authentication server, the data is encrypted. The encryption protocols supported by Windows XP for the user account and password data are EAP (Extensible Authentication Protocol), SPAP (Shiva Password Authentication Protocol), CHAP (Challenge Handshake Authentication Protocol), and MS-CHAP (Microsoft CHAP).

▲ After the user is authenticated, a tunnel is created so that all data sent between the user and the company is strongly encrypted. One of these four tunneling protocols is used: Point-to-Point Tunneling Protocol (PPTP), Layer Two Tunneling Protocol (L2TP), SSL (Secure Sockets Layer), or IPsec (IP security). Of the four, PPTP is the weakest protocol and should not be used if one of the other three is available. The strongest protocol is a combination of L2TP and IPSec, which is called L2TP over IPSec. The two most popular protocols are SSL and IPsec.

To set up a VPN on the corporate side, the network administrator will most likely use a hardware device such as a VPN router to manage the VPN. A router that supports VPN is considerably more expensive than one that does not. To configure the router to support VPN, generally an administrator must:

▲ Select the encryption protocol used to encrypt the user account and password data.
▲ Select the tunneling protocol to use for the VPN.
▲ Configure each tunnel the VPN will support. Each tunnel must be assigned a user account and password, which is kept on the router.

A+ ESS
6.1
6.2
6.3

A+
220-602
6.2
6.3

Figure 9-46 shows a configuration window for a VPN router. The tunneling protocol has been selected to be IPSec. The next step in configuring this VPN is to add one tunnel for each remote user who will use the VPN. So far, no tunnels have been configured.

Figure 9-46 Configuring a VPN router

On the client end, to configure a VPN using Windows XP, a VPN network connection is created using the Windows XP Network Connections window. Follow these steps:

1. Open the **Network Connections** window and click **Create a new connection**. The New Connection Wizard launches. Click **Next**.

2. On the next screen, select **Connect to the network at my workplace**, and then click **Next**.

3. On the next screen (see Figure 9-47), select **Virtual Private Network connection**, and then click **Next**. Then enter the name of your company and click **Next**.

4. On the next screen, decide whether you want Windows to automatically dial up your ISP when you use the connection, and then click **Next**.

5. Enter the host name or IP address of the VPN (most likely, this is the static IP address that the ISP has assigned to your local network). Click **Next** and then click **Finish**. The VPN icon is added to your Network Connections window.

6. Windows XP automatically uses PPTP encryption. If you want to switch to L2TP over Ipsec (the other allowed protocol), right-click the network connection icon and select **Properties** from the shortcut menu. The properties window appears. Click the **Networking** tab and select **L2TP IPSec VPN** from the drop-down menu under Type of VPN (see Figure 9-48). To view and change the type of protocols allowed to encrypt the user account and password information, click the **Settings** button on the **Security** tab.

A+ ESS
6.1
6.2
6.3

A+
220-602
6.2
6.3

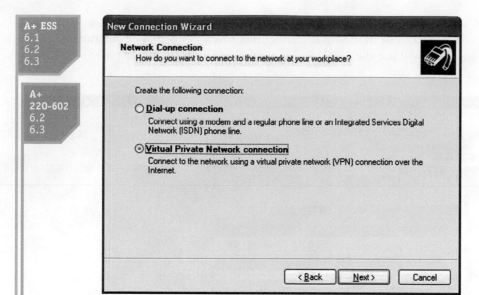

Figure 9-47   Use the New Connection Wizard to set up a connection to a VPN

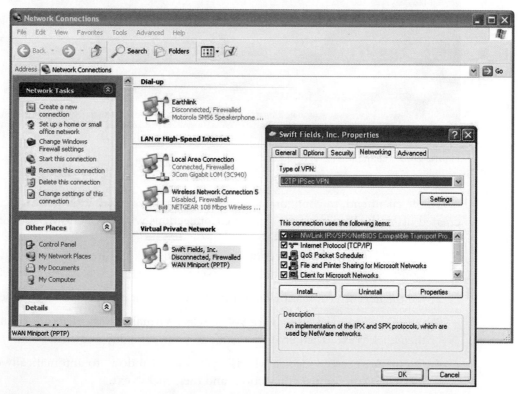

Figure 9-48   Properties window of a VPN connection

SUPPORTING INTERNET CLIENTS

A+
220-602
5.1

Now that you've learned how to connect to the Internet, let's look at some ways of using it. Earlier in the chapter in Table 9-1, you saw a list of application services that use the Internet. In this section, you will learn how to support some of the most common Internet clients: Web browsers, e-mail, FTP, VoIP, and Windows XP Remote Desktop.

A+
220-602
5.1
5.2

SUPPORTING WEB BROWSERS

A Web browser is a software application on a user's PC that is used to request Web pages from a Web server on the Internet or an intranet. A Web page is a text file with an .htm or .html file extension. It can include text coded in **HTML (Hypertext Markup Language)** that can be interpreted by a Web browser to display formatted text, graphics, and video, as well as play sounds. If the HTML code on the Web page points to other files used to build the page, such as a sound file or a photograph file, these files are also downloaded to the browser. In this section, you will learn about the addresses that Web browsers use to locate resources on a Web server, how to configure a browser, and how to solve problems with browsers. You'll also learn about using secure Web sites.

> **Notes**
>
> The HTTP protocol is used by browsers and Web servers for communication. The HTML language is used to build and interpret Web pages.

HOW A URL IS STRUCTURED

Earlier in the chapter you saw that a Web browser requests a Web page by sending an IP address followed by an optional port number. This works well on an intranet, but on the Internet, a more user-friendly address is preferred. That user-friendly address is a **URL (Uniform Resource Locator)**, which is an address for a Web page or other resource on the Internet. Figure 9-49 shows the structure of a URL.

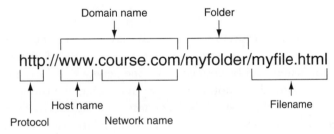

Figure 9-49   A URL contains the protocol used, the host name of the Web server, the network name, and the path and filename of the requested file

The first part of the URL shown in Figure 9-49 indicates the protocol, which in this case is HTTP. The protocol part of the URL specifies the rules, or protocol, the Web server should use when transmitting the page to the browser. A Web server is sometimes called an HTTP server.

Recall from Chapter 8 that a host name identifies a server or another computer within a network. In this last example, the host name is *www* (a Web server), and *course.com* is the name of the Course Technology network, sometimes called the domain name. A name that contains not only the network name (in this case, *course.com*) but also the host on that network is called a fully qualified domain name (FQDN), as you learned in Chapter 8. In this case, the FQDN is *www.course.com*. The Web page requested is located in the folder *myfolder* on the *www* server, and the file within that folder is named *myfile.html*. The FQDN must be resolved to an IP address before the request can happen.

The final segment, or suffix, of a domain name is called the **top-level domain** (*.com* in our example) and tells you something about the organization or individual who owns the name. Some domain names in the United States end in the suffixes listed in Table 9-3. There are other endings as well, including codes for countries, such as .uk for the United Kingdom. With the growth of the Internet, there has been a shortage of available domain names; because of this shortage, additional suffixes are being created.

A+
220-602
5.1
5.2

Domain Suffix	Description
.air	Aviation industry
.biz	Businesses
.com	Commercial institutions
.coop	Business cooperatives
.edu	Educational institutions
.gov	Government institutions
.info	General use
.int	Organizations established by international treaties between governments
.mil	U.S. military
.museum	Museums
.name	Individuals
.net	Internet providers or networks
.org	Nonprofit organizations
.pro	Professionals

Table 9-3 Suffixes used to identify top-level domain names

Domain names stand for IP addresses and provide an easy way to remember them, but domain names and IP addresses are not necessarily permanently related. A host computer can have a certain domain name, can be connected to one network and assigned a certain IP address, and then can be moved to another network and assigned a different IP address. The domain name can stay with the host while it connects to either network. It is up to a name resolution service, such as DNS or WINS, to track the relationship between a domain name and the current IP address of the host computer.

CONFIGURING A BROWSER

Many browsers are available for downloading from the Internet. The most popular browsers are Internet Explorer by Microsoft (*www.microsoft.com*), Firefox by Mozilla (*www.mozilla.com*), and Netscape Navigator by Netscape (*browser.netscape.com*). By far, the most popular browser is Internet Explorer because it comes installed as a part of Windows.

Depending on user needs, performance, and security requirements, some Internet Explorer settings you might need to change are listed next.

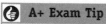 **A+ Exam Tip**

The A+ 220-602 exam expects you to know how to install and configure browsers, to enable and disable script support, and to configure proxy and other security settings. You will get practice installing a browser in a project at the end of this chapter.

Keep in mind that a few of these changes are for features that are available only if you have Internet Explorer version 6 or later.

▲ *Configure the pop-up blocker.* Internet Explorer version 6 and later has a pop-up blocker. To control Pop-up Blocker, open Internet Explorer, click **Tools**, and point to **Pop-up Blocker**, as shown in Figure 9-50. The first item in the menu in Figure 9-50 toggles between turning Pop-up Blocker on and off. To change settings, click **Pop-up**

9

A+
220-602
5.1
5.2

Blocker Settings. From the Pop-up Blocker Settings window that opens, you can create a list of Web sites that are allowed to present pop-ups and control how Pop-up Blocker informs you when it blocks a pop-up.

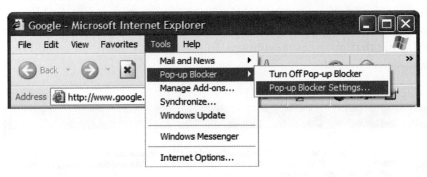

Figure 9-50   Internet Explorer Pop-up Blocker can be turned on or off and you can adjust its settings

---

✎ **Notes**

If Pop-up Blocker is turned on, you might have a problem when you try to download something from a Web site. Sometimes the download routine tries to open a Security Warning window to start the download, and your pop-up blocker suppresses this window and causes an error. To solve the problem, you can temporarily turn off Pop-up Blocker before you begin the download or you can allow the Security Warning window to appear by clicking the pop-up block message and selecting **Download File**, as shown in Figure 9-51. You can also hold down the Ctrl key while you click on a link to allow a pop-up even when Pop-up Blocker is turned on.

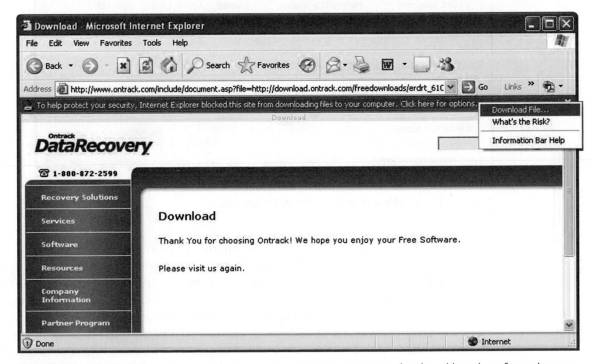

Figure 9-51   If your browser is set to block pop-ups, a message appears under the address bar of your browser

▲ *Manage IE add-ons.* Add-ons to Internet Explorer are small programs that are installed within IE to enhance the browser. Examples include an animated mouse pointer and various extra toolbars. An add-on can make your browser do what you

A+
220-602
5.1
5.2

don't want it to do, such as displaying a toolbar you don't need, and sometimes malicious software hides as an add-on. Add-on programs are controlled from the Tools menu. To see a list of add-ons already installed, click **Tools**, and then click **Manage Add-ons**. The Manage Add-ons window opens (see Figure 9-52). You can toggle between a list of currently loaded add-ons and previously used add-ons. And you can update, disable, and enable add-ons. Also notice in the figure that you can see the DLL file that provides the add-on. To permanently get rid of an add-on, search for and delete that file.

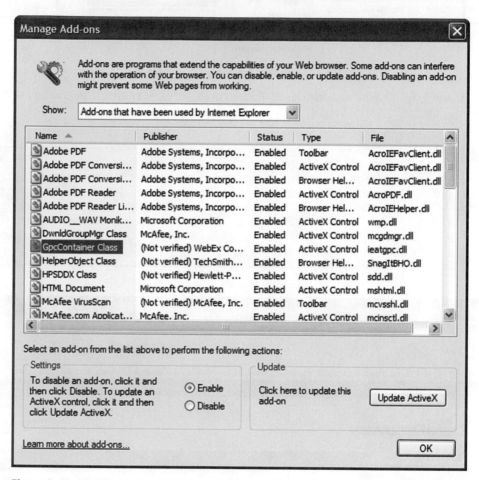

Figure 9-52   Disable and enable Internet Explorer add-ons

▲ *Set Internet Explorer security levels.* Internet Explorer offers several security options. To set them, click **Internet Options** on the Tools menu, and then click the **Security** tab (see Figure 9-53). Using the sliding bar on the left side of this window, you can choose the security level. (If the sliding bar is not visible, click the **Default Level** button to display the bar.) The Medium level is about right for most computers. If you click the Custom Level button, you can see exactly what is being monitored and controlled by this security level and change what you want. These settings apply to ActiveX plug-ins, downloads, Java plug-ins, scripts, and other miscellaneous settings and add-on programs. Adware or spyware can make changes to these security settings without your knowledge. These settings are not password protected, so they will not help if you are trying to secure the browser from what other users of this computer can do.

A+
220-602
5.1
5.2

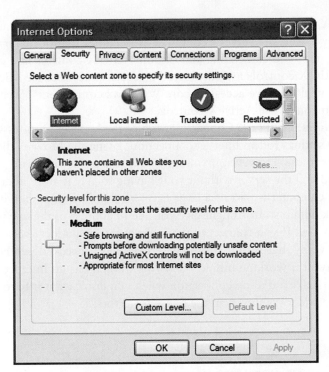

Figure 9-53 Set the security level of Internet Explorer using the Internet Options window

▲ *Control how and if scripts are executed.* Scripts are small programs embedded inside a Web page that control how the Web page functions. To enable and disable scripts or to cause a prompt to appear before a script is executed, click the **Security** tab (if necessary), and then click **Custom Level**. The Security Settings dialog box opens. Scroll down to the Scripting section (see Figure 9-54).

Figure 9-54 Enable and disable scripts on the Security tab of the Internet Options window

A+
220-602
5.1
5.2

◢ *Configure ActiveX controls.* An ActiveX control is a small add-on program that can be downloaded by a Web site to your computer (sometimes without your knowledge). Using the Security tab, you can enable and disable ActiveX controls and control how they are used. ActiveX controls are considered a security risk because Microsoft designed these controls to have access to core Windows components. Writers of malicious software sometimes use ActiveX controls.

◢ *Control proxy settings.* Under the **Connections** tab of the Internet Options window, you can control proxy settings for an Internet connection, giving the browser the IP address of the proxy server to use. However, if you only have one proxy server on your LAN, the browser should find the server without your having to give it an IP address. (On the other hand, if this computer is part of a large network that has more than one proxy server, the network administrator might give you the IP address of the one proxy server this computer is to use.) If you connect to the Internet through a local network, click **LAN Settings** and verify that **Automatically detect settings** is checked (see Figure 9-55). If your browser says it is working offline when you know it has an Internet connection or your PC tries to make a dial-up connection when you don't want it to, one thing you can do is check the windows shown in the figure for errors.

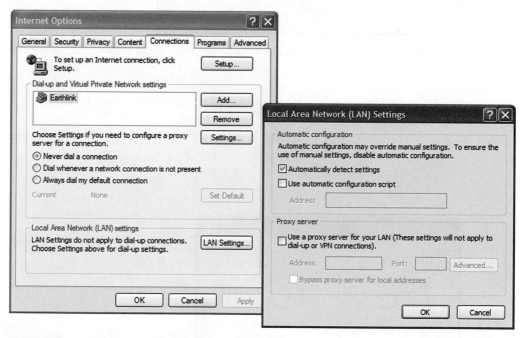

Figure 9-55   Connection settings for Internet Explorer

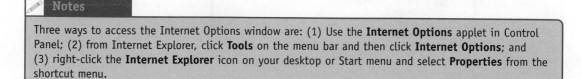

Notes

Three ways to access the Internet Options window are: (1) Use the **Internet Options** applet in Control Panel; (2) from Internet Explorer, click **Tools** on the menu bar and then click **Internet Options**; and (3) right-click the **Internet Explorer** icon on your desktop or Start menu and select **Properties** from the shortcut menu.

A+
220-602
3.2
5.2

SOLVING INTERNET EXPLORER PROBLEMS

If Internet Explorer gives errors or is slow, use the tools described in earlier chapters, such as Defrag, ScanDisk, and System Information, to make sure that you have enough free hard drive space, that the hard drive is clean, and that the virtual memory settings

A+
220-602
3.2
5.2

are optimized. Also, reduce the number of applications running and close any unneeded background tasks. After doing these things, if the browser is still slow or still gives errors, follow these steps:

1. *Clean out the cache that IE uses to hold temporary files.* Internet Explorer must search the entire cache each time it accesses a Web page. If the cache is too big, performance is affected. To clean out the cache, open the **Internet Options** window shown in Figure 9-56. Click **Delete Files** under the Temporary Internet files heading to clean out the IE cache. The Delete Files dialog box opens, asking you to confirm the deletion. Click **OK**. Click **Clear History** under the History heading to clean out the shortcuts cache. The Internet Options dialog box opens, asking you to confirm the deletions. Click **OK**. If this cache gets too big, performance slows down. Also, if you reduce the number of days that Internet Explorer keeps pages in the history folder, performance might improve because there will be less material for Internet Explorer to search. For example, change the number of days to keep pages in history from the default value of 20 to 7.

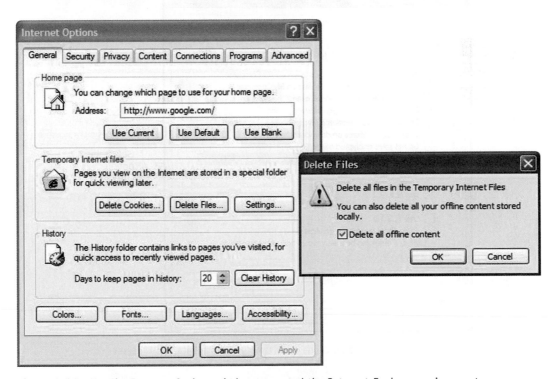

Figure 9-56 Use the Internet Options window to control the Internet Explorer environment

2. *Suppress downloading images.* Slow browser performance can be caused by a slow Internet connection. In this case, one thing you can do is to suppress the down-loading of images. Image files can be large and account for most of the downloaded data from Web sites. To suppress images, sound, animation, and video on the Internet Options window, click the **Advanced** tab. Scroll

> **Notes**
>
> Because other users might use the IE cache to trace your browsing habits, you might want to permanently eliminate the cache. To do that, in the Internet Properties window, click the **Advanced** tab (see Figure 9-57). Scroll down through the list of settings to the **Security** items. Check **Empty Temporary Internet Files folder when browser is closed** and click **Apply**.

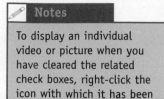

Notes

To display an individual video or picture when you have cleared the related check boxes, right-click the icon with which it has been replaced on the Web page.

down to the multimedia section of the check box list, and clear the check box or boxes for the feature or features that you do not want to display (**Show pictures, Play animations in web pages, Play videos in web pages,** or **Play sounds in web pages**).

3. *Repair a corrupted Internet Explorer cache.* If problems still persist, they might be caused by a corrupted IE cache. The easiest way to solve this problem is to delete the entire IE cache folder for the user account that has the problem. The next time the user logs on, the folder will be rebuilt. To delete the folder, first make sure you're logged on to the system using a different account that has administrative privileges. The folder you want to delete is C:\Documents and Settings*user name*\Local Settings\Temporary Internet Files. You will not be able to delete the folder if this user is logged on.

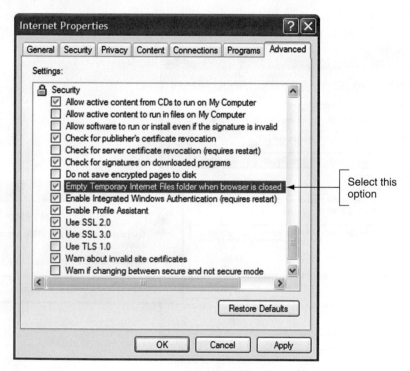

Figure 9-57 Empty the IE cache each time you close Internet Explorer

4. *Run antivirus software.* Unwanted pop-up ads or toolbars and other errors might be caused by malicious software, which can attack Internet Explorer as adware, spyware, browser hijackers, and viruses. Make sure your antivirus software is current and then scan your entire hard drive for viruses. You might also consider using anti-adware software such as Windows Defender by Microsoft (*www.microsoft.com*), Ad-Aware by Lavasoft (*www.lavasoftusa.com*), or SpyBot Search & Destroy by PepiMK Software (*www.safer-networking.org*). These products sometimes find malicious software attacking IE that antivirus software does not find. You'll learn more about ridding your system of malicious software in Chapter 10.

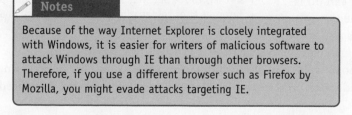

Notes

Because of the way Internet Explorer is closely integrated with Windows, it is easier for writers of malicious software to attack Windows through IE than through other browsers. Therefore, if you use a different browser such as Firefox by Mozilla, you might evade attacks targeting IE.

9

A+
220-602
3.2
5.2

5. *Update Internet Explorer.* Internet Explorer 6 is included in Windows XP Service Pack 2, and normal Windows updates include updates for IE as well as other system components. To get the latest Windows XP updates, including those for IE, connect to the Internet and then click **Start**, point to **All Programs**, and click **Windows Updates**. The Web site shown in Figure 9-58 appears. Click **Express** and follow the directions onscreen to get the updates. You might have to perform the update process more than once to get them all. If your problem is not solved, move on to the next step.

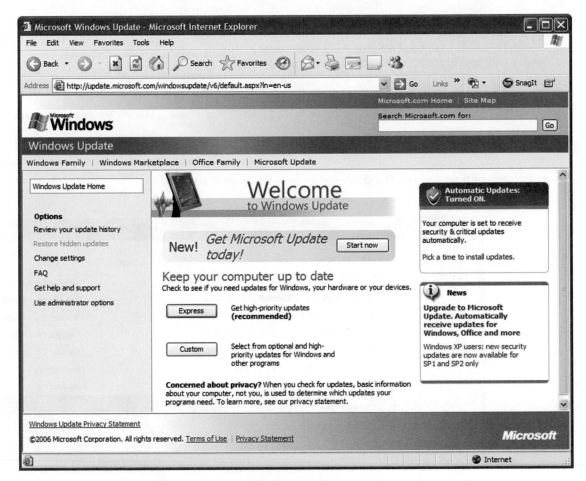

Figure 9-58 Updating Windows also updates Internet Explorer

6. *Use the Windows XP System File Checker (Sfc.exe) to verify Windows system files.* To use the utility to scan all Windows 2000/XP system files and verify them, first close all applications and then enter the command **sfc /scannow** in the Run dialog box. Click **OK**. The Windows File Protection window opens, as shown in Figure 9-59. Have your Windows setup CD handy in case it is needed during the scan, also shown in Figure 9-59. If you have problems running the utility, try the command **sfc /scanonce**, which scans files immediately after the next reboot. If your problem is still not solved after a reboot, move on to the next step.

7. *Remove and reinstall Internet Explorer 6.* For a Windows XP system, know that Internet Explorer 6 came with Windows XP Service Pack 2. Therefore, if you remove SP2, you also remove Internet Explorer 6. Beware, however, that you'll change other Windows components and settings other than IE when you do this. To remove Service Pack 2, open the Add or Remove Programs applet in Control

A+
220-602
3.2
5.2

Panel. Check the check box **Show updates,** as shown in Figure 9-60. Scroll down through the list of Windows updates and select **Windows XP Service Pack 2.** Click **Remove.** Follow the directions onscreen and reboot your computer when done. To reinstall SP2, first download the service pack at this Microsoft Web page: *www.microsoft.com/athome/security/protect/windowsxp/default.mspx.* If you have problems removing or installing the service pack, see the Microsoft Knowledge Base Article 875350 for additional help.

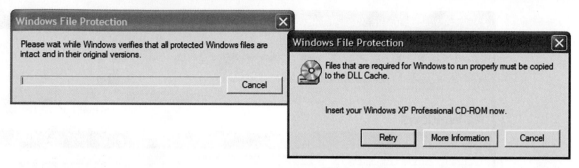

Figure 9-59 System File Checker might need the Windows setup CD

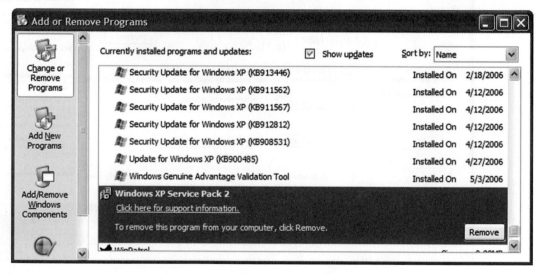

Figure 9-60 Use the Add or Remove Programs applet to uninstall Service Pack 2

At this point, if Internet Explorer is still not working, most likely you have a more serious problem than just IE and you need to refresh your entire Windows installation. Several methods and tools to do this are covered in Chapter 5 for Windows 2000/XP and in Chapter 7 for Windows 9x/Me.

Notes

If you cannot solve a problem with Internet Explorer without making considerable changes to your Windows installation, you might consider abandoning IE and installing another browser such as Firefox by Mozilla (*www.mozilla.com*). If you can't use your computer to access the Web site to download the installation file, go to another computer and download the file and burn it to a CD. Then use the CD to install the browser.

A+
220-602
5.1

USING SECURED WEB CONNECTIONS

When banking or doing some other private business on the Web, you might have noticed https in the address box of your browser, such as

A+
220-602
5.1

https://onlineservices.wachovia.com. **HTTPS (HTTP secure)** can mean HTTP over SSL or HTTP over TLS and tells you that the secure protocol being used is SSL or TLS. SSL and TLS can be used to secure several application protocols including HTTP, FTP, e-mail, and newsgroups. When SSL or TLS is used, all data communicated between the client and server is encrypted and the initial connection between the server and the client can be authenticated. However, know that only the communication over the Internet is secure. After the data reaches the server, SSL and TLS protocols don't apply. The purpose of these security protocols is to prevent others on the Internet from eavesdropping on data in transit or change that data. (This last type of intrusion is called a man-in-the-middle attack.) Here is some additional information about SSL and TLS:

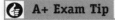

A+ Exam Tip

The A+ 220-602 exam expects you to know about HTTPS and SSL.

- ◢ **SSL (Secure Sockets Layer)** is the de facto standard developed by Netscape and used by all browsers; it uses an encryption system that uses a digital certificate. Public keys are secret codes used to encrypt and later decrypt the data, and are exchanged before data is sent (see Figure 9-61). A **digital certificate**, also called a **digital ID** or **digital signature,** is a code assigned to you by a certificate authority such as VeriSign (*www.verisign.com*) that uniquely identifies you on the Internet and includes a public key. Recall from Chapter 3 that Microsoft uses digital certificates to validate or digitally sign device drivers certified by Microsoft.

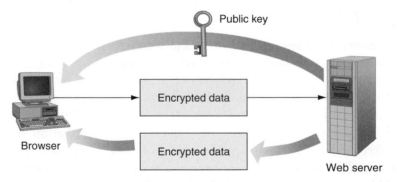

Figure 9-61 Using secure HTTP, a Web server and browser encrypt data using a public key before the data is transmitted

- ◢ **TLS (Transport Layer Security)** is an improved version of SSL. There are only slight differences between TLS and SSL, although the protocols are not interchangeable. Both client and server applications must support either SSL or TLS to create a secure connection, and all current browsers support both protocols.

To know if a connection to a Web site is secured, look for https in the browser address box and a lock icon at the bottom of the browser window, as shown in Figure 9-62.

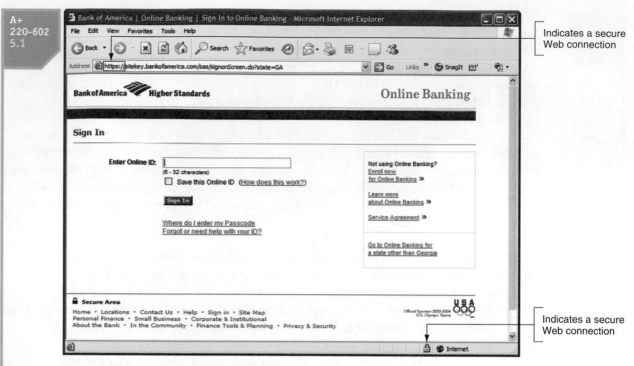

Indicates a secure Web connection

Indicates a secure Web connection

Figure 9-62   A secured connection from browser to Web server

SUPPORTING E-MAIL

E-mail is a client/server application used to send text messages to individuals and groups. When you send an e-mail message, it travels from your computer to your e-mail server. Your e-mail server sends the message to the recipient's e-mail server. The recipient's e-mail server sends it to the recipient's PC, but not until the recipient asks that it be sent by logging in and downloading e-mail. Different parts of the process are controlled by different protocols.

Figure 9-63 shows the journey made by an e-mail message as well as the protocols that control the different parts of the journey. The sender's PC and e-mail server both use **SMTP (Simple Mail Transfer Protocol)** to send an e-mail message to its destination. An improved version of SMTP is **SMTP AUTH (SMTP Authentication)**. This protocol is used to authenticate a user to an e-mail server when the e-mail client first tries to connect to the e-mail server to send e-mail. Using SMTP AUTH, an extra dialogue between the client and server happens before the client can fully connect that proves the client is authorized to use the service. After authentication, the client can then send e-mail to the e-mail server.

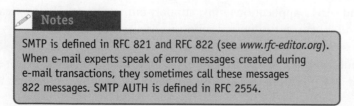

Notes

SMTP is defined in RFC 821 and RFC 822 (see *www.rfc-editor.org*). When e-mail experts speak of error messages created during e-mail transactions, they sometimes call these messages 822 messages. SMTP AUTH is defined in RFC 2554.

After the message arrives at the destination e-mail server, it remains there until the recipient requests delivery. The recipient's e-mail server uses one of two protocols to deliver the message: **POP (Post Office Protocol)** or **IMAP4 (Internet Message**

Access Protocol, version 4), which is a newer e-mail protocol. The current version of POP is version 3, often abbreviated as POP3. IMAP is slowly replacing POP for receiving e-mail.

9

A+
220-602
5.1

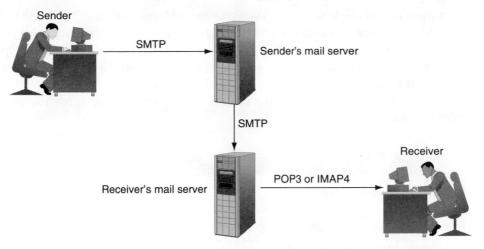

Figure 9-63 The SMTP protocol is used to send e-mail to a recipient's mail server, and the POP3 or IMAP4 protocol is used to download e-mail to the client

E-mail client software communicates with an e-mail server when it sends and receives e-mail. Two common e-mail clients are Eudora and Microsoft Outlook Express. Figure 9-63 shows a user with one e-mail server on his side of the transmission (there is a second e-mail server on the receiver's side of the transmission). However, it's possible to have two e-mail servers on the sender's side of the transmission; one would be for sending e-mail and the other for receiving e-mail. Figure 9-64 shows this arrangement.

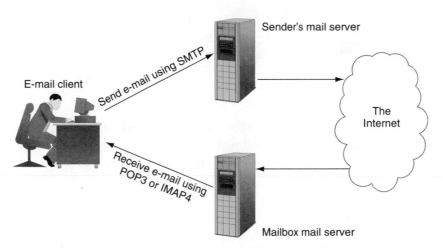

Figure 9-64 An e-mail client can use one server to send e-mail and another to receive e-mail

The e-mail server that takes care of sending e-mail messages (using the SMTP protocol) is often referred to as the SMTP server. The e-mail server from which you collect messages sent to you is often referred to as the POP server, because it uses the POP protocol.

When you configure your e-mail client software for the first time, you need to enter the addresses of your e-mail servers. If you are connecting to e-mail via an Internet service provider, the ISP can tell you these addresses. For example, if your ISP is *MyISP.net*, you might have an outgoing mail server address of *smtp.myISP.net*, *smtpauth.myISP.net*, or *mail.myISP.net* and an incoming mail server address of *pop3.myISP.net* or *pop.myISP.net*.

A+
220-602
5.1

In most e-mail client software, you enter the addresses of your POP or IMAP server and your SMTP server in a dialog box when setting up the program, along with your e-mail address you will use when sending e-mail. Look for menus or icons labeled Options, Preferences, Configuration, Setup, or similar names. Figure 9-65 shows a setup window in Microsoft Outlook where the outgoing mail server is named smtpauth.earthlink.net (using the SMTP AUTH protocol) and the incoming mail server is pop.earthlink.net (using the POP3 protocol).

Figure 9-65 Servers used for incoming and outgoing e-mail

After you enter the addresses, the software saves this and other configuration information in an initialization file, the Windows registry, or some other location. When you first connect to an e-mail server, the e-mail client can pass the account name and password to the server to access the account.

SUPPORTING FTP

A common task of communications software is file transfer, which is the passing of files from one computer to another. For file transfer to work, the software on both ends must use the same protocol. The most popular way to transfer files over the Internet is to use the File Transfer Protocol (FTP), which can transfer files between two computers using the same or different operating systems.

Many software vendors use FTP sites for downloading software to their customers. When you click a link on a Web site to download a file, if the protocol in your browser address box changes from http to ftp, then you are using FTP for the download. The FTP server application is most likely running on a Windows Server 2003 or Unix server. These servers are called FTP servers or FTP sites. A commercial FTP site might provide only the ability to download a file to your PC, but some FTP sites also give you the ability to copy, delete, and rename files; make and remove directories; and view details about files and directories, provided the user has the appropriate permissions on the FTP site.

A+
220-602
5.1

Most communications applications provide an FTP utility that has a unique look and feel, but the basics of file transfer are the same from one utility to another. If you don't have graphical FTP software installed on your PC, you can use FTP commands from a command prompt.

FTP FROM A COMMAND PROMPT

FTP can be initiated at a Windows 2000/XP, Windows 9x/Me, or DOS command prompt, if a connection to a network or the Internet is established. Table 9-4 shows a sample set of FTP commands entered at the command prompt.

Command Entered at the Command Prompt	Description
FTP	Execute the FTP program, ftp.exe.
OPEN 110.87.170.34	Open a session with a remote computer having the given IP address.
LOGIN: XXXXXX	The host computer provides a prompt to enter a user ID for the computer being accessed.
PASSWORD: XXXXXX	The host computer requests the password for that ID. Logon is then completed by the host computer.
CD /DATA	Change directory to the /DATA directory.
GET YOURFILE.DAT	Copy the file YOURFILE.DAT (or whatever file you want) from the remote computer to your computer.
PUT MYFILE.DAT	Copy the file MYFILE:DAT (or whatever file you want) from your computer to the remote computer.
BYE	Disconnect the FTP session.

Table 9-4   A sample FTP session from a command prompt

FILE TRANSFER USING FTP SOFTWARE

FTP client software can be downloaded from the Internet or directly from your ISP. In addition, any browser can be used as an FTP client. The following steps show you how to use FTP client software:

1. Start the FTP utility software. In this example, we are using CuteFTP by Globalscape (*www.globalscape.com*). The FTP utility screen that appears is similar to the one in Figure 9-66.

2. On the menu, click **File** and then click **Connect** to log on to an FTP site. A Site Properties dialog box opens, similar to the one in Figure 9-66.

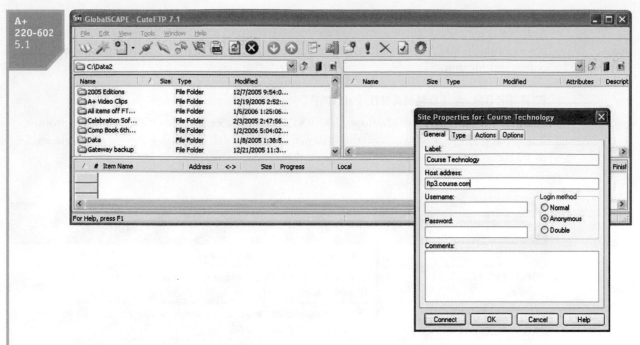

Figure 9-66   A typical FTP utility

3. Enter the Label (**Course Technology** in our example), Host address (**ftp3.course.com**), Username and Password, and then click **OK**.

4. The connection is made and your ID and password are passed to the host. After you have been authenticated by the host computer, a screen similar to that in Figure 9-67 appears.

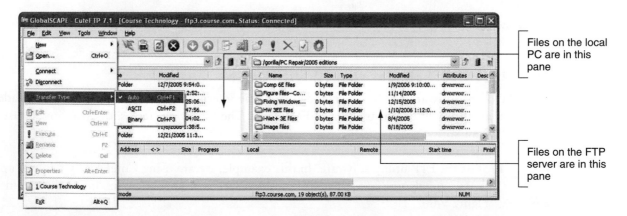

Files on the local PC are in this pane

Files on the FTP server are in this pane

Figure 9-67   An FTP utility screen showing local and remote files

5. The files on the left belong to you, and the files on the right belong to the remote host computer. You can drag and drop files either to or from the other computer. Notice in Figure 9-67 the choices you have when you click File, Transfer on the menu bar: Auto, ASCII, or Binary. These choices refer to the format to be used to transfer the files. Text files are written in ASCII code; therefore, use ASCII for text files, and use Binary for all others. If you are not sure which to use, choose **Auto**.

6. When the transfer of files is complete, click **File, Exit** to leave the utility.

9

A+
220-602
5.1

Many Web pages provide a link on the page offering you the ability to download a file. Click the link to download the file. This file is probably not being downloaded from the Web server, but from an FTP server. When you click the filename on the Web page, the program controlling the page executes FTP commands to the FTP server to download the file to you. If you receive an error, you can sometimes solve the problem by going directly to the company's FTP server and using an FTP utility (such as the one in the previous procedure) to download the file, or even see a list of other files that you might also like to download.

A Web browser such as Internet Explorer can also serve as an FTP client. To have it serve as an FTP client, enter the URL of the FTP server in the address box (for example, **ftp3.course.com**) and then press **Enter**. The browser changes menu options to become an FTP client. For example, the Login As command is added to the File menu. To log on to the FTP server in Internet Explorer, click **File** on the menu bar, and then click **Login As**. The Log On As dialog box opens for you to enter a user ID and password. Files and folders on the FTP server then display in the browser, as shown in Figure 9-68. You can drag files back and forth between the FTP server and your PC using this Internet Explorer FTP window and Windows Explorer opened on your desktop.

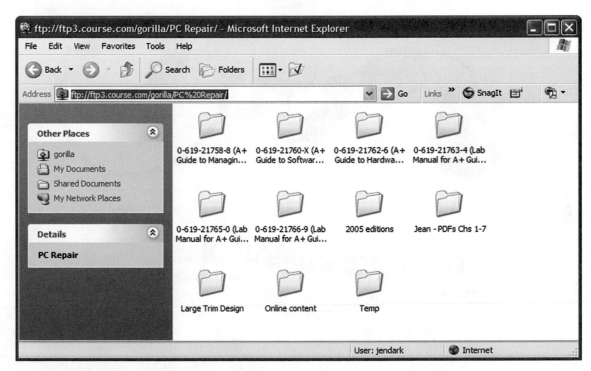

Figure 9-68 Using Internet Explorer as an FTP client

A+ ESS
5.1

SUPPORTING VoIP

A+
220-602
5.1
5.3

VoIP is a protocol that is used by Internet or intranet telephone networks to provide voice communication over a network. Using a VoIP service, you plug a digital telephone, such as the one shown in Figure 9-69, into a network port on a local network that is connected to the Internet and use that phone to make a phone call to anywhere on the planet. Notice in the figure the power cord and network cable share a common cable and connector to the phone. You can also use a regular analog phone as an Internet phone if you use an Analog Telephone Adapter (ATA), such as the one shown in Figure 9-70. Plug the phone into the ATA, which uses a network cable to connect to the network. Just as with mobile phones, the digital phone or ATA is programmed for a particular phone number.

A+ ESS
5.1

A+
220-602
5.1
5.3

AC adapter
supplies power
to the phone

RJ-45
connector

Figure 9-69   This digital telephone has a network port to connect to a network

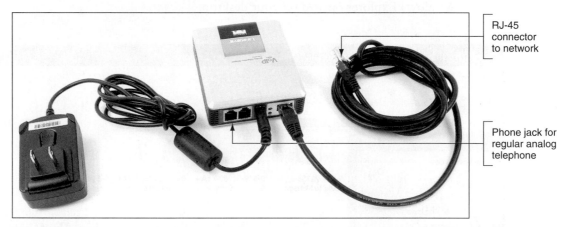

RJ-45
connector
to network

Phone jack for
regular analog
telephone

Figure 9-70   Use this ATA to turn an analog telephone into an Internet phone

APPLYING CONCEPTS

Quality of Service (QoS) refers to the success of communication over the Internet. Communication is degraded on the Internet when packets are dropped, delayed, delivered out of order, or corrupted. In order for VoIP to have the high quality it needs to compete with regular POTS voice communication, QoS on the Internet must be high. VoIP gave problems for many years with dropped lines, echos, delays, static, and jittered communication. ("Jitter" is the term used to describe a voice conversation that is mingled with varying degrees of delays.) However, more recently, many of these problems are for the most part solved to make VoIP a viable option for personal and business use. Recently, my daughter, Jill West, was responsible for selecting a telephone system for a small business. I asked her to describe the success and woes of having chosen a VoIP solution. Here is her story:

We planned our company so that we all can work from our home offices and live in several regions of the country, yet we compete in a market where we must present a unified front. More and more businesses are built this way these days, and, thankfully, technology is adapting.

When we first began investigating phone systems, we tried to patchwork together various telco (local telephone company) services, but with dismal results. Then we began researching several VoIP providers, from the industry flagship Vonage (www.vonage.com), to smaller and lesser-known companies. With a little searching, we found a company that provides the services important to us. Here are a few features:

▲ *We were able to buy the digital phones and ATA adapters from this company that configured and tested them for us before shipping and then taught us how to use them.*

A+ ESS
5.1

A+
220-602
5.1
5.3

▲ We were able to port our existing toll-free number to our new VoIP account.

▲ We are able to transfer live calls from one team member to another with three- or four-digit dialing and no long-distance charges for the transferred calls, even with our team spread over several states.

▲ We have an integrated voice-mail system using a Web portal. One window of our portal is shown in Figure 9-71.

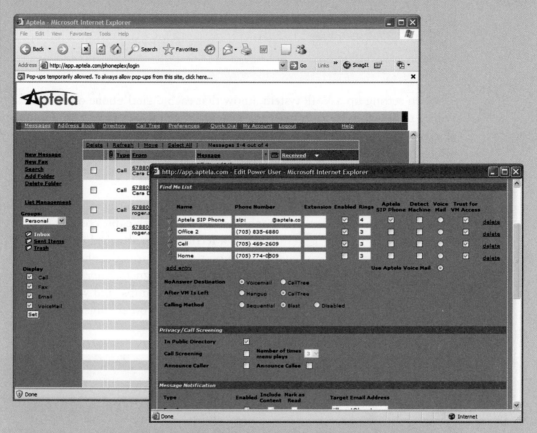

Figure 9-71 This Web portal is used to manage a VoIP service

▲ We can easily set up conference calls with the entire team.

▲ A single auto-attendant handles all incoming calls, or we can direct incoming calls to any number and still use the auto-attendant as a convenient backup.

▲ The company provided professional voice talent to record our auto-attendant message and other call-tree menu options.

▲ We have unlimited long distance, even for our high-volume salespeople.

▲ We can add or remove users as our company's payroll changes with no extensive implementation charges or technical difficulties.

▲ Each of our users can program various phone numbers into their account, such as cell phone, home phone, or home-office phone numbers. They can then tell the system at which phone to direct their individual incoming calls. Each call can be sent sequentially through the list of numbers, or "blast" all numbers simultaneously.

▲ Voice-mail messages and faxes can all be forwarded to our various e-mail accounts, and even the message itself is attached for immediate review.

▲ When we travel, we can take the service with us. I can pack my IP phone or ATA and plug it up wherever I am if I have high-speed Internet access. Even without the phone or adapter, I can still use a computer to access my Web portal and make calls from the portal Web site.

A+ ESS
5.1

A+
220-602
5.1
5.3

With all this, it seems there would be no drawbacks. But all is not well in paradise. We've had a few issues with dropped calls or annoying delays while talking. Sometimes we have to hang up and call the person back. Occasionally, the signal will phase out briefly, where one party can hear the other, but not vice versa. And, if your ISP drops your service for any reason, even just a temporary outage, you're pretty much without a phone. However, incoming calls are still directed through the auto-attendant, and messages are saved there until you again have access.

Overall, even with these drawbacks, VoIP was the right choice for our company. We're pleased with the features and are willing to tolerate the growing pains as technology catches up with our needs.

When setting up a VoIP system, know that each digital phone or ATA must be programmed with a phone number from the VoIP provider. Each device is also programmed to use dynamic IP addressing and must be assigned an IP address just like any other device on the network, which means your network must be using a DHCP server such as that provided by a multipurpose router. Plug up the devices to the network and then configure the VoIP service using the Web site of the VoIP provider.

✋ A+ Tip

The A+ 220-602 exam expects you to know how to eliminate electrical interference from a network.

Because electrical interference can be a problem with VoIP phones, each network cable connected to a VoIP phone needs a **ferrite clamp** attached (see Figure 9-72). Attach the clamp on the cable near the phone port. This clamp helps to eliminate electromagnetic interference. Some cables come with preinstalled clamps, and you can also buy ferrite clamps to attach to other cables.

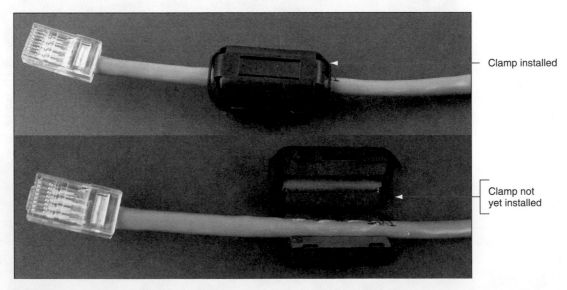

Clamp installed

Clamp not yet installed

Figure 9-72   Install a ferrite clamp on each network cable connected to a VoIP phone

A+
220-602
3.1
3.3

SUPPORTING REMOTE DESKTOP

Windows XP Professional Remote Desktop gives a user access to his or her Windows XP desktop from anywhere on the Internet. As a software developer, I find Remote Desktop extremely useful when I work from a remote location (my home office) and need to access a corporate network to support software on that network. Using the Internet, I can access a file server on

9

A+
220-602
3.1
3.3

these secured networks to make my software changes. It's easy to use and relatively safe for the corporate network. To use Remote Desktop, the computer you want to remotely access (the server) must be running Windows XP Professional, but the computer you're using to access it (the client) can be running Windows XP Home Edition or Windows XP Professional.

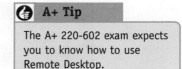

A+ Tip

The A+ 220-602 exam expects you to know how to use Remote Desktop.

In this section, you'll first see how Remote Desktop can be used, and then you'll see how to set it up for first use.

Notes

Many third-party applications besides Windows XP Remote Desktop exist that also allow you to remotely connect to another computer so that you can see and use the remote computer's desktop. One excellent product I've used for years is PC Anywhere by Symantec (*www.symantec.com*).

HOW TO USE REMOTE DESKTOP

To use Remote Desktop to connect to and use the desktop of your home or office computer, do the following from any Windows XP computer connected to the Internet:

1. Click **Start**, point to **All Programs**, point to **Accessories**, point to **Communications**, and then click **Remote Desktop Connection**. The Remote Desktop Connection window opens. Click **Options** and the window expands to full view, as shown in Figure 9-73.

Figure 9-73 Enter the IP address of the remote computer to which you want to connect

2. Enter the IP address of the Windows XP computer to which you want to connect and enter your user account name and password on the remote computer.

3. If you plan to transfer files from one computer to the other, click the **Local Resources** tab shown in Figure 9-74 and check **Disk drives**. If you want to print from the remote computer, also check **Printers**. Click **Connect** to make the connection.

A+
220-602
3.1
3.3

Figure 9-74 Allow files and printers to be shared using the Remote Desktop connection

4. The desktop of the remote computer appears, as shown in Figure 9-75. When you click the desktop, you can work with the remote computer just as if you were sitting in front of it, except response time is slower. To move files back and forth between computers, use Windows Explorer on the remote computer. Files on your local computer will appear under My Network Places in Windows Explorer on the remote computer. To close the connection to the remote computer, simply close the desktop window.

Local computer desktop

Remote computer desktop

Figure 9-75 The desktop of the remote computer is available on your local computer

A+
220-602
3.1
3.3

HOW TO PREPARE REMOTE DESKTOP FOR FIRST USE

To prepare a Windows XP Professional computer to be used as a Remote Desktop server so that you can access it from the Internet, you need to configure the computer for static IP addressing and also configure Remote Desktop for service. Here are the steps needed:

1. As described earlier in the chapter, you'll need a static IP address assigned to you by your ISP. If your computer is connected directly to your ISP, assign this IP address to your computer. If you are using a router on your network, configure the router for static IP addressing and assign it the IP address from the ISP. Then configure your computer for static IP addressing and assign it a private IP address (for example, 192.168.1.90).

2. If you are using a router on your network, configure the router for port forwarding and allow incoming traffic on port 3389. Forward that traffic to the IP address of your desktop computer. Figure 9-76 shows a setup screen for one router configured for these settings.

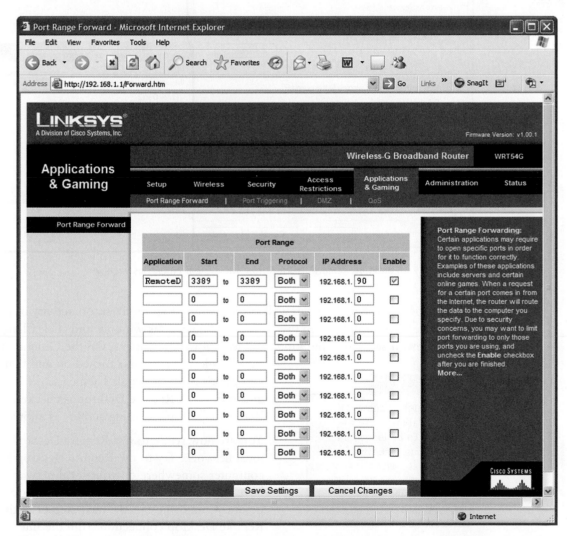

Figure 9-76   To set up a network for supporting a Remote Desktop server, configure your router for port forwarding on port 3389

3. Use your browser to verify you have Internet access before you continue to the next steps. If you have a problem, first try repairing your connection and then try rebooting your PC.

A+
220-602
3.1
3.3

You are now ready to configure Remote Desktop on your Windows XP Professional home or office computer. Do the following:

1. Right-click **My Computer** and click **Properties** to open the **System Properties** window, as shown in Figure 9-77. Click the **Remote** tab and check **Allow users to connect remotely to this computer**. Click **Select Remote Users**. In the dialog box that opens, also shown in Figure 9-77, add the users of this computer who will be using Remote Desktop. Users who have administrative privileges will be allowed to use Remote Desktop by default, but other users need to be added. Click **OK** twice to exit both windows.

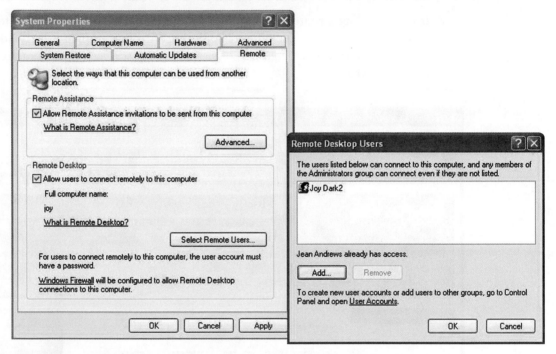

Figure 9-77   Configure Remote Desktop from the System Properties window

2. Verify that Windows Firewall is set to allow Remote Desktop activity to this computer. To do that, open the **Network Connections** window and click **Change Windows Firewall settings**. The Windows Firewall window opens. On the **General** tab, verify that Windows Firewall is turned on and that **Don't allow exceptions** is *not* selected. Then click the **Exceptions** tab and verify that **Remote Desktop** is checked so that Remote Desktop incoming activity is allowed.

3. You are now ready to test Remote Desktop using your local network. Try to use Remote Desktop from another computer somewhere on your local network. Verify you have Remote Desktop working on your local network before you move on to the next step of testing the Remote Desktop connection from the Internet.

Notes

Even though Windows XP normally allows more than one user to be logged on at the same time, this is not the case with Remote Desktop. When a Remote Desktop session is opened, all local users are logged off.

Is your desktop computer now as safe as it was before you programmed the router? Actually, no, so take this into account when you decide to use Remote Desktop. In a project at the end of this chapter, you'll learn how you can take further steps to protect the security of your computer when using Remote Desktop.

>> CHAPTER SUMMARY

▲ Ports are used to address particular software or services running on a computer. Common port assignments are port 80 for HTTP (Web browser requests), port 25 for SMTP (sending e-mail), port 110 for POP3 (receiving e-mail), and port 20 for FTP.

▲ Communication using TCP/IP involves communication at the application level, the OS level, and the hardware level.

▲ TCP guarantees that a packet reaches its destination and so is called a connection-oriented protocol. UDP does not guarantee delivery and so is called a connectionless or best-effort protocol.

▲ IP is responsible for breaking data into packets and passing them from TCP or UDP to the hardware.

▲ Some TCP/IP utilities useful in solving networking problems are Ipconfig, Winipcfg, Tracert, Nslookup, Ping, and Nbtstat.

▲ DSL and cable modem are broadband Internet connections that use a converter box, which can connect to a USB port or network port on a PC. In addition, a router is sometimes placed between the converter box and a single PC or local network.

▲ When a PC is connected directly to the Internet, the PC can share the Internet connection. Windows XP and Windows 98 use Internet Connection Sharing (ICS) to manage the connection on the host computer, or you can use a router that stands between the converter box and the network.

▲ Use a firewall on the host computer or router to protect the network from unsolicited activity from the Internet.

▲ A router can be configured to use port forwarding so that certain applications, such as a Web server, on a computer on the network can be accessed from the Internet.

▲ A virtual private network (VPN) can be used to authenticate a user and encrypt data when a user connects to a private network from somewhere on the Internet.

▲ A URL consists of a protocol, a host name, a network or domain name, and a top-level domain extension. Common top-level domains include .com for commercial institutions, .gov for divisions of government, and .org for nonprofit organizations.

▲ E-mail uses SMTP or SMTP AUTH to send messages and POP3 to receive messages. POP3 is being replaced by IMAP. Your ISP will provide you with information on the server types and addresses that it uses to send and receive e-mail.

▲ FTP is used to transfer files from one computer to another, regardless of whether the computers are using the same operating system. Both computers must have an FTP utility installed. It can be executed from user-friendly GUI software or from a command prompt.

▲ VoIP can be used to provide Internet phone service.

▲ Windows XP Remote Desktop is used to make a home or office computer's Windows XP Professional desktop available to the user anywhere on the Internet.

>> *KEY TERMS*

For explanations of key terms, see the Glossary near the end of the book.

ARP (Address Resolution
   Protocol)
best-effort protocol
broadband
cable modem
client/server application
client-side caching
connectionless protocol
connection-oriented protocol
dial-up networking
digital certificate
digital ID
digital signature
DSL (Digital Subscriber Line)
File Transfer Protocol (FTP)
hop count
HTML (Hypertext Markup
   Language)
HTTP (Hypertext Transfer
   Protocol)
HTTPS (HTTP secure)

ICMP (Internet Control Message
   Protocol)
IMAP4 (Internet Message Access
   Protocol, version 4)
Internet Connection Sharing (ICS)
IP (Internet Protocol)
ISDN (Integrated Services Digital
   Network)
Network News Transfer Protocol
   (NNTP)
POP (Post Office Protocol)
port
port address
port forwarding
port number
PPP (Point-to-Point Protocol)
PPPoE (Point-to-Point Protocol
   over Ethernet)
Quality of Service (QoS)
RARP (Reverse Address
   Resolution Protocol)

server-side caching
session
Serial Line Internet Protocol
   (SLIP)
SMTP (Simple Mail Transfer
   Protocol)
SMTP AUTH (SMTP
   Authentication)
SNMP (Simple Network
   Management Protocol)
socket
SSL (Secure Sockets Layer)
TCP (Transmission Control
   Protocol)
Time to Live (TTL)
TLS (Transport Layer Security)
top-level domain
UDP (User Datagram Protocol)
URL (Uniform Resource
   Locator)

>> *REVIEWING THE BASICS*

1. Explain how a single physical computer can be a Web server and an e-mail server at the same time.

2. What Windows XP component can be used to share an Internet connection with other computers on the LAN?

3. What protocol is commonly used to manage the connection between a broadband modem and a PC when the connection requires a username and password and is not always up?

4. Give the service and protocol for the following ports: port 21, port 25, port 80, and port 110.

5. Which protocol used by Web browsers and Web servers is responsible for guaranteeing delivery? For breaking data into packets? For decrypting and decompressing data as necessary?

6. Explain the difference between a connection-oriented protocol and a connectionless protocol, and give an example of each.

7. What TCP/IP utility would you use to display the route taken over the Internet by a communication between a Web browser and Web server?

8. What utility would you use to display information about the name space kept by a DNS server for a particular domain name?

9. Explain the functions of the following TCP/IP utilities: NSLookup, Winipcfg, Ipconfig, and Microsoft SNMP Agent.

10. What is the full command line to use Ipconfig to release the current IP address?

11. What utility new to Windows XP can be used to display a NIC's MAC address?

12. Place these stages of creating a dial-up networking connection in Windows 9x/Me in the correct order: creating a connection, verifying installation of the dial-up adapter, installing the Dial-up Networking feature, and entering configuration information for your ISP.

13. Explain at least four things you can try if you cannot make a connection to the Internet using a dial-up networking connection.

14. Label the component parts of this URL: http://www.companyabc.com/Reports/december2004.doc

15. Give the type of organization that would use the following top-level domains: .mil, .net, .air, .com, .org, .gov.

16. What are three things you can do to improve slow browser performance?

17. What protocol is used for sending e-mail? For receiving it?

18. Explain what FTP is used for.

19. What is the listening port for Windows XP Remote Desktop?

20. Explain the difference when a user sees http:// in a browser address box and when the user sees https:// in the address box.

21. Internet Explorer is the most popular browser. What is one security reason a user might choose to use a different browser such as Firefox by Mozilla?

22. When an ISP gives a user the two mail server addresses, smtp.myISP.net and pop.myISP.net, which address should be used for incoming mail and which should be used for outgoing mail?

23. When using a cable modem to connect to the Internet, the data transmission shares the cabling with what other technology?

24. What is the FTP command to close an FTP session?

25. Does it matter which TV jack in your house should be used by your cable modem? Why or why not?

26. What two methods can an ISP use to assign your computer or router an IP address?

27. When is it appropriate to delete the C:\Documents and Settings*user name*\Local Settings\Temporary Internet Files folder?

28. What device is required so that you can connect a regular telephone to a VoIP network?

29. Why is it necessary for your home or office computer to have a static IP address if it is to be set up for Remote Desktop?

30. Give two examples of broadband technology.

>> THINKING CRITICALLY

1. You are trying to connect to the Internet using a Windows XP dial-up connection. You installed a modem card and tested it, so you know it works. Next, you create a dial-up connection icon in the Network Connections window. Then, you double-click the icon and the Connect dialog box opens. You click Dial to make the connection. An error message appears saying, "There was no dial tone." What is the first thing you do?

   a. Check Device Manager for errors with the modem.

   b. Check with the ISP to verify that you have the correct phone number, username, and password.

   c. Check the phone line to see if it's connected.

   d. Check the properties of the dial-up connection icon for errors.

2. You connect to the Internet using a cable modem. When you open your browser and try to access a Web site, you get the error, "The Web page you requested is not available offline. To view this page, click Connect." What might be the problem(s) and what do you do?

   a. The browser has been set to work offline. On the File menu, verify that Work Offline is not checked.

   b. The cable modem service is down. In the Network Connections window, right-click the LAN connection and select Repair on the shortcut menu.

   c. Internet Connection Firewall is enabled on your PC. Disable it.

   d. The cable modem is down. Go to Device Manager and check for errors with the cable modem.

3. This question combines skills learned in this and previous chapters. You have set up a small LAN in your home with two Windows XP PCs connected to the Internet using a DSL connection. You have a DSL router box connected to the DSL and to a small hub. Your two PCs connect to the hub. You can browse the Internet from either PC. However, you discover that each PC cannot use the resources on the other PC. What is the problem and what do you do?

   a. The network hub is not working. Try replacing the hub.

   b. The NICs in each PC are not working. Try replacing one NIC and then the next.

   c. The LAN connections in the Network Connections window are not working. Delete the connections and re-create them.

   d. Files and folders are not shared on either PC. Use Windows Explorer to correct the problem.

>> HANDS-ON PROJECTS

PROJECT 9-1:   Practicing TCP/IP Networking Skills

While connected to the Internet or another TCP/IP network, answer these questions:

1. What is your current IP address?

2. Release and renew your IP address. Now what is your IP address?

3. Are you using dynamic or static IP addressing? How do you know?

4. What is your adapter address for this connection?

5. What is your default gateway IP address?

6. What response do you get when you ping the default gateway?

PROJECT 9-2:   Practicing Dial-Up Networking Skills with Windows 9x/Me

This project requires you to have a modem installed and working.

1. Open **My Computer** and open the **Dial-Up Networking** folder.

2. Double-click the **Make New Connection** option.

3. Enter the name **TEST** for the name of the computer that you are dialing. Click **Next**.

4. Enter your home phone number. Click **Next**.

5. Click the **Finish** button to create the Test dial-up.

6. Double-click the newly created **Test dial-up** icon, and confirm that it dials correctly. Describe what happens.

PROJECT 9-3: Investigating Verizon FiOS

Verizon (*www.verizon.com*) is currently offering an alternative to DSL and cable modem for broadband Internet access. FiOS is a fiber-optic Internet service that uses fiber-optic cable all the way to your house for both your residential telephone service and Internet access. Search the Web for answers to these questions about FiOS:

1. Give a brief description of FiOS and how it is used for Internet access.

2. What downstream and upstream speeds can FiOS support?

3. When using FiOS, does your telephone voice communication share the fiber-optic cable with Internet data?

4. What does Verizon say about FiOS cabling used for television?

5. Is FiOS available in your area?

PROJECT 9-4: Solving Browser Problems

Follow these instructions to solve problems with Microsoft Internet Explorer:

1. List the steps to access the Microsoft Web site and search for information about a problem. Search the site for information about Error 403.6, IP Restriction error. Print any information you find about the error.

2. Print the Microsoft Web site page that allows you to use the Update wizard to download the latest fixes for Internet Explorer. Download the update and apply it to your browser.

3. Perform the procedures discussed in the chapter to clean out the browser cache.

PROJECT 9-5: Using Pop-Up Blocker for Internet Explorer

Using Internet Explorer under Windows XP with Service Pack 2 applied, do the following:

1. Turn off pop-up blocker. Surf the Web until a pop-up window appears. What Web site produced the pop-up? Close your browser window.

2. Open the browser window again and turn on pop-up blocker. Surf the Web and open the same Web site from Step 1. Did the pop-up window appear?

3. If you trust this Web site and want to see its pop-up windows, how can you leave pop-up blocker turned on, but allow pop-ups from this one Web site?

PROJECT 9-6:   Practicing Using FTP

Practice using FTP by downloading the latest version of Firefox, a Web browser, using three different methods. Do the following:

1. Using your current browser, go to the Mozilla Web site at *www.mozilla.com* and download the latest version of Firefox. What is the version number? What is the name of the downloaded file? In what folder on your hard drive did you put the file?

2. Using your current browser as an FTP client, locate the same version of Firefox and the same file at the Netscape FTP site (*ftp-mozilla.netscape.com*) and download it to your PC. What is the path to the Firefox file on the FTP site? In what folder on your hard drive did you put the file?

3. Repeat the process to download Firefox, this time using FTP commands from a command prompt window. What FTP commands did you use?

>> REAL PROBLEMS, REAL SOLUTIONS

REAL PROBLEM 9-1:   Firewalling Your Home Network

At first, Santiago had only a single desktop computer, an ink-jet printer, and a dial-up phone line to connect to the Internet. Then, his wife, Maria, decided she wanted her own computer. And then they both decided it was time for a broadband connection to the Internet. After some research, they chose cable modem. So now, their home network looks like that shown earlier in the chapter in Figure 9-31a. Santiago chose to use a crossover cable to connect the two computers, and the cable modem connects to Santiago's computer using a USB cable.

Both computers are constantly plagued with pop-up ads and worms, so Santiago has come to you for some advice. He's heard he needs to use a firewall, but he doesn't know what a firewall is or how to buy one. You immediately show him how to turn on Windows XP Firewall on both PCs, but you know he really needs a better hardware solution. What equipment (including cables) do you recommend he buy to implement a hardware firewall? Also consider that his daughter, Sophia, has been begging for a notebook computer for her birthday, so plan for this expansion. By the way, Sophia has made it perfectly clear there's no way she'll settle for having to sit down in the same room with her parents to surf the Web, so you need to plan for a wireless connection to Sophia's bedroom.

REAL PROBLEM 9-2:   More Security for Remote Desktop

When Jacob travels on company business, he finds it's a great help to be able to access his office computer from anywhere on the road using Remote Desktop. However, he wants to make sure his office computer as well as the entire corporate network is as safe as possible. One way you can help Jacob add more security is to change the port that Remote Desktop uses. Knowledgeable hackers know that Remote Desktop uses port 3389, but if you change this port to a secret port, hackers are less likely to find the open port. Search the Microsoft Knowledge Base articles (*support.microsoft.com*) for a way to change the port that Remote Desktop uses. Practice implementing this change by doing the following:

1. Set up Remote Desktop on a computer to be the host computer. Use another computer (the client computer) to create a Remote Desktop session to the host computer. Verify the session works by transferring files in both directions.

2. Next, change the port that Remote Desktop uses on the host computer to a secret port. Print a screen shot showing how you made the change. Use the client computer to create a Remote Desktop session to the host computer using the secret port. Print a screen shot showing how you made the connection using the secret port. Verify the session works by transferring files in both directions.

3. What secret port did you use? What two Microsoft Knowledge Base Articles gave you the information you needed?

Securing Your PC and LAN

In today's computing environment, we all need to know how to keep our shields up. Security is an important concern for PC support technicians and many of the chapters of this book have addressed security concerns as appropriate within the content of each chapter. This chapter focuses on the tools and methods you need to know to protect a computer and a small network, and it summarizes several security tools and methods mentioned in other chapters. As you read this chapter, keep in mind that knowledge won't help much unless you use it. As a user or PC support technician, be sure to apply what you're about to learn!

Even with the best of security, occasionally a virus, worm, or some other type of malicious software gets into a computer. In these situations, it helps to understand how they work and how they hide. In this chapter, you'll learn about malicious software and then learn the step-by-step attack plan to get rid of it.

SECURING YOUR DESKTOP OR NOTEBOOK COMPUTER

A+ ESS
6.1
6.2

A+
220-602
6.1
6.2
6.3

Even though a desktop computer sits behind a firewall in a secured network, you still need to protect the system and its data from attacks within and from attacks that get into your network through security loopholes. In addition, when traveling with a notebook computer, security is especially important because your notebook is more exposed than when you're working in a more secured environment.

Here are the methods of securing a computer:

▲ Control access to a system by using strong authentication techniques.
▲ Limit use of the administrator accounts.
▲ Always use a personal firewall.
▲ Set AV software to run in the background and keep it current.
▲ Keep Windows updates current.
▲ Set Microsoft Internet Explorer for optimum security.
▲ Use alternate third-party client software.
▲ When supporting public Windows XP computers, use Microsoft Shared Computer Toolkit.
▲ Secure important files and folders.
▲ Physically protect your equipment.
▲ Beware of social engineering situations trying to lure you into compromising your security.
▲ Keep good backups of user data.
▲ Back up system files when you make major changes to your system.
▲ Make use of event logging and incident reporting.
▲ Destroy trash that might contain sensitive data.
▲ Perform monthly security maintenance chores.

All these techniques to secure a computer are covered in this part of the chapter. Later in the chapter, you'll learn about securing a wired or wireless network.

APPLYING|CONCEPTS

Three of the items listed earlier are so important to keep a secure system that Microsoft added the Windows Security Center to Windows XP Service Pack 2 to track these items. To open the Security Center, you can click its icon (looks like a shield) in the system tray or open the Security Center applet in Control Panel. Either way, the Windows Security Center window opens, as shown in Figure 10-1.

 Notes

If a Windows XP computer is configured to belong to a domain instead of a workgroup, all security is managed by the network administrator for the entire network. In this situation, the Windows Security Center does not alert you to problems with security or allow you, as the user, to adjust security settings.

A+ ESS
6.1
6.2

A+
220-602
6.1
6.2
6.3

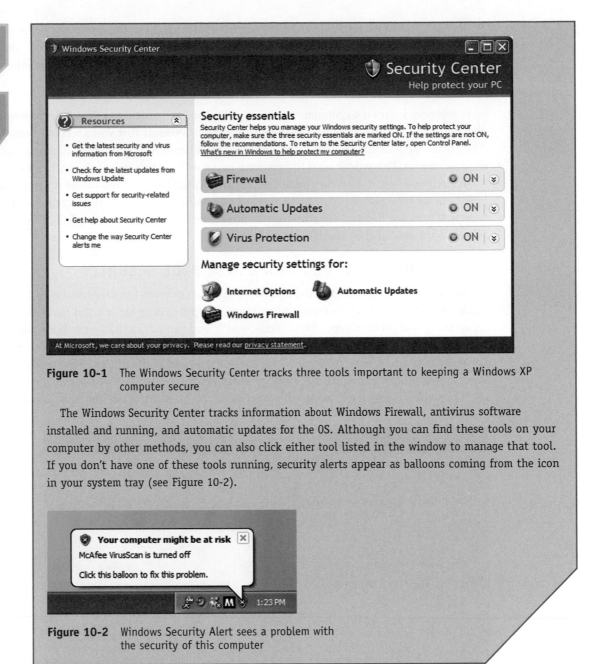

Figure 10-1 The Windows Security Center tracks three tools important to keeping a Windows XP computer secure

The Windows Security Center tracks information about Windows Firewall, antivirus software installed and running, and automatic updates for the OS. Although you can find these tools on your computer by other methods, you can also click either tool listed in the window to manage that tool. If you don't have one of these tools running, security alerts appear as balloons coming from the icon in your system tray (see Figure 10-2).

Figure 10-2 Windows Security Alert sees a problem with the security of this computer

Now let's turn our attention to all the different ways you can secure a computer.

ACCESS CONTROL

A+ ESS
1.1
6.1
6.2

Controlling access to a computer, file, folder, or network is done by using a combination of authentication and authorization techniques. First, let's look at a definition of these two key words:

◢ **Authentication** proves that an individual is who he says he is and is accomplished by a variety of techniques, including a username, password, personal identification number (PIN), smart card, or biometric data (for example, a fingerprint or iris scan). After an individual is authenticated, the individual is allowed access. (In practice, even though an individual is most often a person, sometimes an individual is a computer program or process.)

◢ **Authorization** determines what an individual can do in the system after he or she is authenticated. The privileges and rights the individual has are assigned to the identity of the individual. As you learned in Chapter 4, for Windows, these privileges and rights are assigned to a user account.

You can lock down a computer by using power-on passwords and Windows passwords. In addition, you need passwords to protect your online accounts that you access through Web sites. Also, many applications give you the option to set a password on the data files associated with the application. Passwords need to be strong passwords, which means they are not easy to guess.

To help you know how to control access to a computer and resources on that computer, let's look at how passwords can be used outside Windows and how to create strong passwords. Then, we'll turn our attention to how access control is accomplished inside Windows. Later in the chapter, you'll learn how to control access to networks.

POWER-ON PASSWORDS AND OTHER BIOS SECURITY

Power-on passwords are assigned in CMOS setup to prevent unauthorized access to the computer and/or to the CMOS setup utility. Power-on passwords are set and configured in CMOS setup using a security screen. Most likely, you'll find the screen under the boot menu options. For one BIOS, this security screen looks like that in Figure 10-3, where you can set a supervisor password and a user password. In addition, you can configure how the user password works. Also notice in Figure 10-3 that you can enable or disable boot sector virus protection so that a virus is less likely to be able to change the boot sectors of the hard drive.

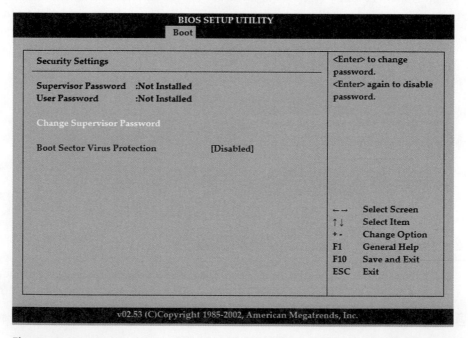

Figure 10-3 Set supervisor and user passwords in CMOS setup to lock down a computer

 A+ Tip

The A+ Essentials and A+ 220-602 exams expect you to know how to secure a workstation from unauthorized use.

After you enter a supervisor password, the security screen changes to that shown in Figure 10-4 where you can now set a user password and decide how that password will be used. The choices under User Access Level are **Full Access** (the user can access the CMOS setup utility and make any changes), **No Access** (the user cannot access the CMOS setup utility), **Limited** (the user can access

A+ ESS
1.1
6.1
6.2

A+
220-602
6.1
6.2
6.3

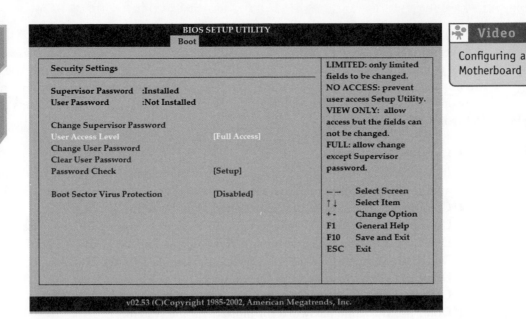

🎥 Video

Configuring a
Motherboard

Figure 10-4 Change the way a user password functions to protect the computer

CMOS setup and make a few changes such as date and time), and **View Only** (the user can access CMOS setup, but cannot make changes).

For added security, you can change the Password Check entry from Setup (the user must enter the password to enter CMOS setup) to Always (the user must enter the password to boot the system). If you use this last option, you can totally lock down the computer from unauthorized access.

> ✏️ **Notes**
>
> For added protection, configure the CMOS setup utility so that a user cannot boot from a removable device such as a CD, USB device, or floppy disk.

> ⚡ **Caution**
>
> Supervisor and user passwords that are required by startup BIOS when the computer is first turned on can be reset by setting a jumper on the motherboard. By setting this jumper, you can clear all CMOS setup customized settings and return CMOS setup to default settings. To keep someone from using this technique to access the computer, you can use a computer case with a lockable side panel and install a lock on the case (see Figure 10-5). If you are concerned that the computer case might be stolen, you can also install a lock and cable to securely tie the case to a table or other fixture.

> ✏️ **Notes**
>
> Never give out your passwords to anyone, not even to a supervisor or tech support person who calls and asks for it. These people should know how to access the system without your passwords.

Figure 10-5 This computer case allows you to use a lock and key to keep intruders from opening the case

A+ ESS
6.1
6.2

A+
220-602
6.1
6.2
6.3

HOW TO CREATE STRONG PASSWORDS AND PROTECT THEM

A fingerprint reader or other biometric device can be used in the place of a password to access your Windows user account and online accounts. However, these biometric solutions are not as secure as a strong password, which should be used to access corporate networks or protect sensitive data, such as financial information. A strong password meets all of the following criteria:

- ▲ Use eight or more characters (14 characters or longer is better).
- ▲ If your system allows it, a passphrase rather than a password is easier to remember and harder to guess. A **passphrase** is made of several words with spaces allowed.
- ▲ Combine uppercase and lowercase letters, numbers, and symbols.
- ▲ Use at least one symbol in the second through sixth position of your password.
- ▲ Don't use consecutive letters or numbers, such as "abcdefg" or "12345."
- ▲ Don't use adjacent keys on your keyboard, such as "qwerty."
- ▲ Don't use your logon name in the password.
- ▲ Don't use words in any language.
- ▲ Don't use the same password for more than one system.
- ▲ Don't store your passwords on a computer.

> **Notes**
>
> Microsoft offers a password checker at *www.microsoft.com/athome/security/privacy/password_checker.mspx*. Go to this link and enter your password on the window shown in Figure 10-6 for Microsoft to rate the strength of your password.

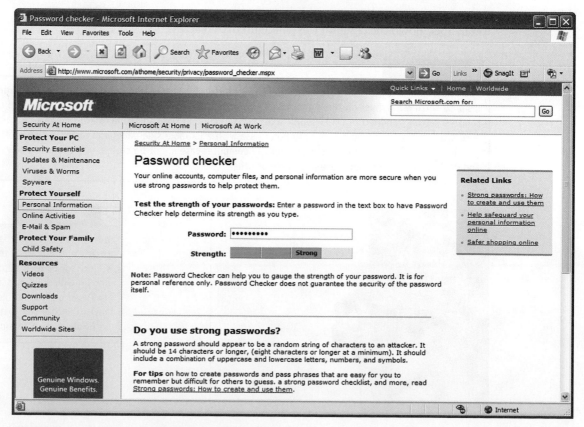

Figure 10-6 Microsoft password checker window

10

A+ ESS
6.1
6.2

A+
220-602
6.1
6.2
6.3

For Windows XP, in some situations, a blank password might be more secure than an easy-to-guess password such as "1234." That's because you cannot log on to a Windows XP computer from a remote computer unless the user account has a password. A criminal might be able to guess an easy password and log on remotely. For this reason, if your computer is always sitting in a protected room such as your home office, you might choose to use no password. However, for notebook computers that are not always protected in public places, always use a password. It's too easy for a criminal to log on to your Windows notebook if you use a blank password. You can use Group Policy to require that every account have a password.

If you write your password down, keep it in as safe a place as you would the data you are protecting. Don't send your passwords over e-mail or chat. Change your passwords regularly, and don't type your password on a public computer. For example, computers in hotel lobbies or Internet cafes should only be used for Web browsing—not for logging on to your e-mail account or online banking account. These computers might be running keystroke-logging software put there by criminals to record each keystroke. Several years ago, while on vacation, I entered credit card information on a computer in a hotel lobby in a foreign country. Months later, I was still protesting $2 or $3 charges to my credit card from that country. Trust me. Don't do it—I speak from experience.

ACCESS CONTROL USING WINDOWS

A+
220-602
5.2
6.1
6.2
6.3

Using Windows, controlling access to a computer or the resources on that computer is accomplished with user accounts and passwords. A password is used to authenticate a user, and the rights and permissions assigned a user account authorize what a user can or cannot do. For best security, recall from Chapter 4 that each user account that is set up on a Windows 2000/XP computer needs a password. As an administrator, when you first create an account, you can specify that the user is allowed to change the password at any time. And, as an administrator, you can reset a password if a user forgets it. Also, for added security, as you learned to do in Chapter 4, configure the Windows XP logon screen so that user accounts, including the powerful Administrator account, are not displayed on a Welcome screen. Using this method, a user must press Ctrl+Alt+Del to see the logon dialog box.

In Chapter 4, you also learned that you can share a file or folder with users in your workgroup. Remember that a limited or guest account cannot normally access files belonging to another account. Using the tools in Chapter 4, when you shared a file or folder, you had no control over which user or user group was allowed access to the shared file or folder. Using more advanced security techniques, you can control which user account or account group can access a shared file or folder. Follow these steps to configure which users are allowed access to certain files and folders:

1. Log on as an administrator to do all the following tasks.

2. To disable simple file sharing so that you have more control over file and folder access and can monitor that access, open the **Folder Options** applet in Control Panel and click the **View** tab of the Folder Options window (see Figure 10-7).

3. Scroll down to the bottom of the **Advanced settings** list, uncheck **Use simple file sharing (Recommended)** and click **Apply**. Close the window.

A+ ESS
6.1
6.2

A+
220-602
5.2
6.1
6.2
6.3

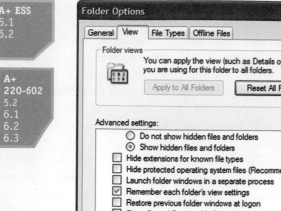

Figure 10-7 Turn off simple file sharing so that you have more control over access to files and folders

4. In Explorer, right-click a folder and select **Properties** from the shortcut menu. In our example, we're using the folder C:\Budget. Click the **Sharing** tab, shown in Figure 10-8. Notice the Sharing tab is now more complex than it was when simple sharing was enabled. (Also notice the new Security tab on the Properties window.)

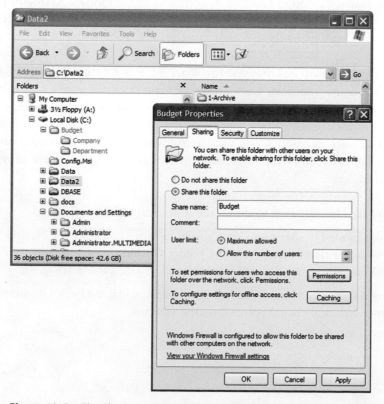

Figure 10-8 The Sharing tab for a folder when simple sharing is disabled

A+ ESS
6.1
6.2

A+
220-602
5.2
6.1
6.2
6.3

5. To share the folder, select **Share this folder**. To control who can access the folder, click **Permissions**. The Permissions dialog box opens, similar to the one shown in Figure 10-9.

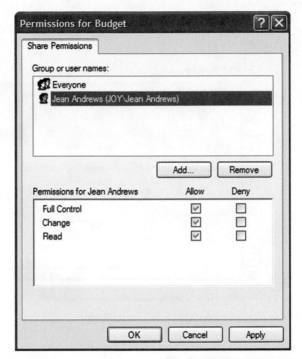

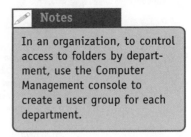

Figure 10-9 Control who can access a folder and the rights given that user or user group

6. By default, share permissions are assigned to everyone. To remove permissions from everyone, select **Everyone** and click **Remove**. To add permission to a particular user or user group, click **Add** and enter the name of the user or user group and click **OK**. To control the permissions for a user, select the user and then select the permissions in the bottom pane of the dialog box. In Figure 10-9, full control has been given to the selected user. Click **Apply** twice when you're done.

7. When a user logged on to this computer or a remote computer on the network tries to access this folder or file, Windows authenticates the user account and password. If the user account and password don't match, a dialog box appears asking for an authorized user account and password. (Figure 10-10 shows the dialog box to access the \Data2 folder on a remote computer.) If the user doesn't enter the expected information, an error occurs (see Figure 10-11).

In addition to the method just discussed, at a command prompt, you can use the Cacls command to control how user accounts can access files and folders. Suppose, for example, an administrator wants to give permission for a user account, JSmith, to have access to a file, Myfile.txt. Figure 10-12 shows the use of five Cacls commands that can be used. The first, third, and fifth commands display access information for the Myfile.txt file (Cacls Myfile.txt). The second command grants read-only access for the user JSmith. (In the command line, the /E parameter says to edit the list and the /G parameter says to grant permission to the following user. The :R parameter says the permission is read-only.) The fourth command revokes JSmith's access permission. To use the command, you do not have to turn off simple file sharing.

A+ ESS
6.1
6.2

A+
220-602
5.2
6.1
6.2
6.3

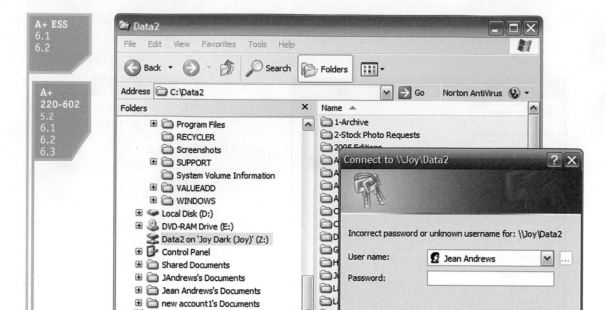

Figure 10-10 User account and password is authenticated to a remote folder

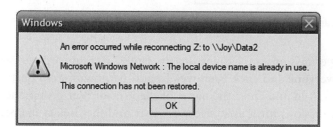

Figure 10-11 Access is denied to a remote folder

Figure 10-12 Use the Cacls command to change user permissions for files and folders

10

A+ ESS
6.1
6.2

A+
220-602
6.1
6.2
6.3

LIMIT USE OF THE ADMINISTRATOR ACCOUNT

Another thing you can do to secure your computer is to limit the use of the more powerful Administrator account. Recall that just after you complete a Windows XP installation or you buy a new computer with the OS already installed, you have two accounts, the Administrator account and the Guest account. You can't do much with the Guest account, so few people want to use it. Most of us find it convenient to log on each time as the Administrator, so we can install hardware and software and change any setting.

The problem is that a malware program might be at work while we're logged on and it will then most likely be running under our account with more privileges and the ability to do more damage than if we had been logged on under a less powerful account. For that reason, it's a good idea to create a Limited User account to use for your every-day normal computer activities. Then only use the Administrator account when you need to do maintenance or installation chores that require the power of the Administrator account.

To help you remember to limit the use of the Administrator account, change the desktop wallpaper and color scheme for this one account to something that stands out at a glance, such as that in Figure 10-13. Also, be sure to change the password of the Administrator account on a regular basis and use a strong password for this account.

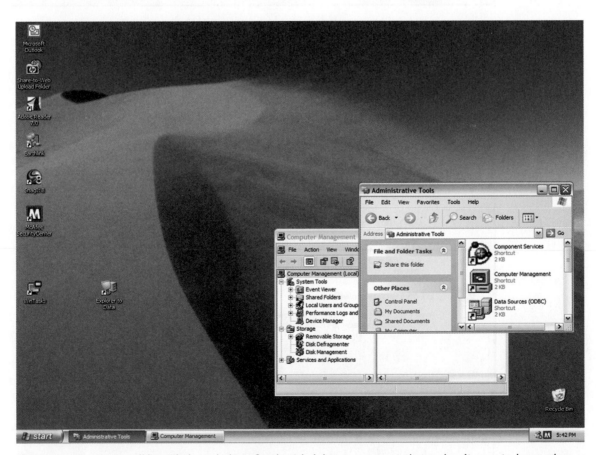

Figure 10-13 Use a striking Windows desktop for the Administrator account that makes it easy to know when you're logged on as the administrator

A+ ESS
6.1
6.2

A+
220-602
6.2
6.3

USE A PERSONAL FIREWALL

Never, ever connect your computer to an unprotected network without using a firewall. Recall that a firewall is software or hardware that prevents worms or hackers from getting into your system. In the last chapter, you saw how to configure a software firewall using Windows Firewall and a hardware firewall using a multipurpose router on a small network.

Here I go again telling you to not do what I did: Once while traveling, I used my Windows 2000 notebook to dial up my ISP before I remembered to turn on my McAfee firewall software. It was up no more than 10 minutes before I turned on the firewall, but in that time I received a nasty worm that infected my e-mail software. It sent out dozens of e-mail messages to Navy military addresses in that short time.

As you learned in the last chapter, for Windows XP with Service Pack 2 applied, you can use Windows Firewall as a personal firewall (see Figure 10-14). In that chapter, you learned to turn on Windows Firewall and configure it so that certain activity such as Remote Desktop and File and Printer Sharing can still be initiated from other computers on the network.

> **Notes**
>
> Even with Windows Firewall, Microsoft still recommends that you use a hardware firewall to protect your system from attack. Software firewalls are better than no firewall at all, but a hardware firewall offers greater protection.

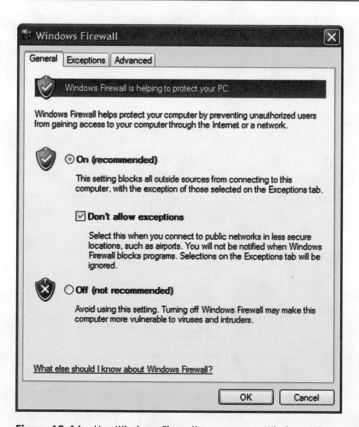

Figure 10-14   Use Windows Firewall to protect a Windows XP computer

10

A+ ESS
6.1
6.2

USE AV SOFTWARE

As a defensive and offensive measure to protect against malicious software, install and run antivirus (AV) software and keep it current. Configure the AV software so that it automatically downloads updates to the software and runs in the background. To be effective, AV software must be kept current and must be turned on. Set the AV software to automatically scan e-mail attachments.

AV software can only detect viruses identical or similar to those it has been programmed to search for and recognize. AV software detects a known virus by looking for distinguishing characteristics called **virus signatures**, which is why AV software cannot detect a virus it does not know. Therefore, it's important to have AV software regularly download updates to it. Figure 10-15 shows McAfee VirusScan software set to automatically stay current.

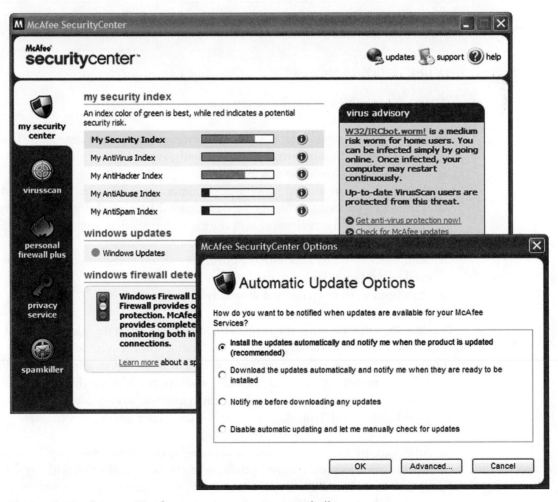

Figure 10-15 Set your AV software to stay current automatically

Table 10-1 lists popular antivirus software and Web sites that also provide information about viruses.

Antivirus Software	Web Site
AVG Anti-Virus by Grisoft	www.grisoft.com
Computer Associates	www.ca.com
F-Secure Antivirus by F-Secure Corp.	www.f-secure.com
eSafe by Aladdin Knowledge Systems, Ltd.	www.esafe.com
F-Prot by FRISK Software International	www.f-prot.com
McAfee VirusScan by McAfee Associates, Inc.	www.mcafee.com
NeaTSuite by Trend Micro (for networks)	www.trendmicro.com
Norman by Norman Data Defense Systems, Inc. (complicated to use, but highly effective)	www.norman.com
Norton AntiVirus by Symantec, Inc.	www.symantec.com
Panda Software	www.pandasoftware.com
PC-cillin by Trend Micro (for home use)	www.trendmicro.com

Table 10-1   Antivirus software and information

When selecting AV software, find out if it can:

▲ Automatically download new software upgrades and virus definitions from the Internet so that your software is continually aware of new viruses.
▲ Automatically execute at startup.
▲ Detect macros in a word-processing document as it is loaded by the word processor.
▲ Automatically monitor files being downloaded from the Internet, including e-mail attachments and attachments sent during a chat session, such as when using AOL Instant Messenger.
▲ Send virus alerts to your e-mail address to inform you of a dangerous virus and the need to update your antivirus software.
▲ Scan both automatically and manually for viruses.

Because AV software does not always stop adware or spyware, it's also a good idea to run anti-adware software in the background. The distinction between adware and spyware is slight and sometimes a malicious software program is displaying pop-up ads and also spying on you. There are tons of removal software products available on the Web, but I recommend the three in the following list. They all can catch adware, spyware, cookies, browser hijackers, dialers, keyloggers, and Trojans, which you'll learn about later in this chapter.

▲ Ad-Aware by Lavasoft (*www.lavasoft.com*) is one of the most popular and successful adware and spyware removal products. It can be downloaded without support for free.
▲ Spybot Search and Destroy by Patrick M. Kolla (*www.safer-networking.org*). This product does an excellent job of removing malicious software.
▲ Windows Defender by Microsoft (*www.microsoft.com*) is an up-and-coming product that, even in its current beta stage, does a great job removing malware.

KEEP WINDOWS UPDATES CURRENT

Although Unix, Linux, and the Apple Mac OS sometimes get viruses, Windows is plagued the most by far for two reasons. First, Windows is the most popular OS for desktop and notebook computers. Being the most popular also makes it the most targeted by authors of

10

A+ ESS
6.1
6.2

malware. Second, Windows is designed with highly integrated components and many user-level entry points into those components. After a program has penetrated a Windows user-mode process, it is possible to infect more than one component. Security holes are being found all the time, and Microsoft is constantly releasing patches to keep up. But you have to download and install those patches before they'll help you.

Recall from Chapter 2 that you can keep Windows updates current by using the Web site *windowsupdate.microsoft.com*. The easiest way to start the process is to click **Start, All Programs, Windows Update**. Recall that you can also set Windows XP to update in the background automatically without your involvement. To do that, right-click **My Computer**, select **Properties** on the shortcut menu, and then click the **Automatic Updates** tab. On this window, shown in Figure 10-16, select **Automatic (recommended)**. Figure 10-17 shows a balloon that is letting you know that it restarted during the night to install updates.

The only reason you might not want to keep this feature set to Automatic is if you don't use an always-up Internet connection and don't want to be bothered with the time spent downloading updates when you first connect to the Internet.

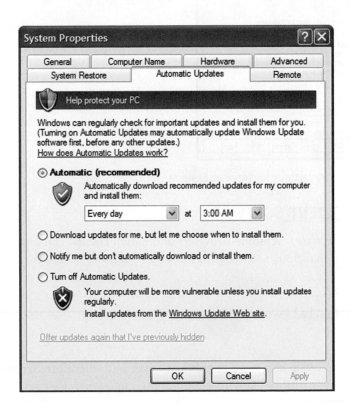

Figure 10-16 Turn on Automatic Updates

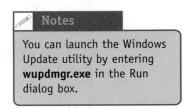

Notes

You can launch the Windows Update utility by entering **wupdmgr.exe** in the Run dialog box.

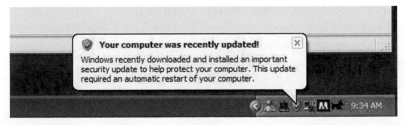

Figure 10-17 Automatic Updates might restart your computer to complete the process of installing Windows updates

SET INTERNET EXPLORER FOR OPTIMUM SECURITY

In the last chapter, you learned about the security features of Internet Explorer, which include the pop-up blocker, the ability to manage add-ons, the ability to block scripts and disable scripts embedded in Web pages, and the ability to set the general security level. Figure 10-18 shows the Internet Properties window where many of these options are configured. For most Web browsing, set the security level to Medium, as shown in the figure.

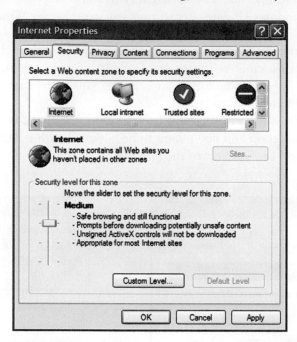

Figure 10-18   Control security settings for Internet Explorer

USE ALTERNATE CLIENT SOFTWARE

Using alternate client software, including browsers and e-mail clients, can give you an added layer of protection from malicious software that targets Microsoft products.

BROWSER SOFTWARE

Internet Explorer gets attacked by malware more than any other browser product for these reasons:

◢ Internet Explorer is by far the most popular browser, and, therefore, writers of malware know they are more likely to get more hits than when they write malware for less-popular browsers.

◢ Internet Explorer is written to more closely integrate with Windows components than other browsers. When malware penetrates Internet Explorer, it can then get to other Windows components that are inherently tied to IE.

◢ Internet Explorer is written to use ActiveX controls. An ActiveX control is a small program that can be downloaded by a Web site to your computer (sometimes without your knowledge). Microsoft invented ActiveX controls so that Web sites could use some nifty multimedia features. However, ActiveX controls allow Web pages to execute program code on your machine—and there's no way for you to know ahead of time whether that code is harmless or a malicious attack on your computer. For these reasons, you might consider using a different browser than Internet Explorer. One excellent browser is Firefox by Mozilla (*www.mozilla.com*). It's free and easy to use. See Figure 10-19.

A+ ESS
6.1
6.2

Figure 10-19 Firefox by Mozilla is not as vulnerable to malware as is Internet Explorer

If you do decide to stay with Internet Explorer, be sure to take advantage of its security features.

E-MAIL CLIENTS

Microsoft Outlook and Outlook Express are probably the most popular e-mail clients. That means they're also the most often attacked. They also support ActiveX controls and are closely integrated with Windows components, making your system more vulnerable to malware. To help stay out of the line of fire, you can use alternate e-mail clients. Personally, I use Eudora by Qualcomm (*www.eudora.com*). Mozilla offers Thunderbird, which others have told me is also a great product.

> **Notes**
>
> You might want to also consider using an alternate e-mail address. When you have to give an e-mail address to companies that you suspect might sell your address to spammers, use a second e-mail address that you don't use for normal e-mailing.

A+
220-602
6.1
6.2
6.3

CONSIDER USING MICROSOFT SHARED COMPUTER TOOLKIT FOR WINDOWS XP

If you are responsible for Windows XP computers used in a public place such as classrooms, labs, hotel lobbies, Internet cafes, and so forth, you might want to consider installing and running Microsoft Shared Computer Toolkit for Windows XP. Basically, this software locks down the drive on which Windows is installed so that a user cannot permanently change Windows configuration, installed software or hardware, user settings, or user data. A user can make

A+ ESS
6.1
6.2

A+
220-602
6.1
6.2
6.3

some changes to the drive, but when the system reboots, all these changes are undone and the system returns to its state when you enabled the toolkit. One feature of the tool is Windows Disk Protection, which prevents changes to the drive on which Windows is installed.

To learn more about the toolkit, go to the Microsoft Web site at *www.microsoft.com* and search for "Microsoft Shared Computer Toolkit for Windows XP." The toolkit can be downloaded for free to computers that are running a genuine Windows XP license (see Figure 10-20).

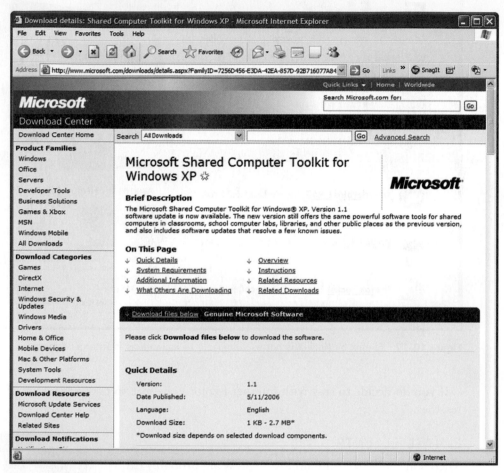

Figure 10-20   Microsoft Shared Computer Toolkit for Windows XP can secure a Windows installation on a computer used in public places

If you decide to use this tool, first get your drive in tip-top shape with everything just the way you want it. Then configure and enable the toolkit. You can configure it so that Windows updates can be installed when users are not working on the computer. Routinely, at least monthly, you need to check the computer to make sure any updates to applications are downloaded and installed.

HIDE AND ENCRYPT FILES AND FOLDERS

A+
220-602
3.1
6.2
6.3

In Chapter 8, you learned that you can do the following to protect files and folders from unauthorized access:

▲ Disable file and printer sharing so that others on the network cannot access resources on your computer.
▲ Hide your computer from others on the network.

A+ ESS
6.1
6.2

A+
220-602
3.1
6.2
6.3

▲ Hide a shared folder so that others must know the name of the folder to access it.

▲ Make your personal folders private.

Another way you can protect files and folders is to use the Windows 2000/XP **Encrypted File System (EFS)**, which works only when using the Windows 2000/XP NTFS file system. (Windows XP Home Edition does not provide encryption.)

Encryption puts data into code that must be translated before it can be accessed, and can be applied to either a folder or file. If a folder is marked for encryption, every file created in the folder or copied to the folder will be encrypted. At the file level, each file must be encrypted individually. Encrypting at the folder level is considered a best practice because it provides greater security: Any file placed in an encrypted folder is automatically encrypted so you don't have to remember to encrypt it. An encrypted file remains encrypted if you move it from an encrypted folder to an unencrypted folder on the same or another NTFS logical drive. A user does not have to go through a complex process of encryption to use EFS; from a user's perspective, it's just a matter of placing a file in a folder marked for encryption.

Now let's look at how to encrypt a file or folder, share an encrypted file, decrypt a file or folder, and use the Cipher command.

HOW TO ENCRYPT A FILE OR FOLDER

To encrypt a file or folder on an NTFS drive, do the following:

1. Right-click the folder or file you want to encrypt and select **Properties** from the shortcut menu. The Properties window for that file or folder opens, as shown on the left side of Figure 10-21.

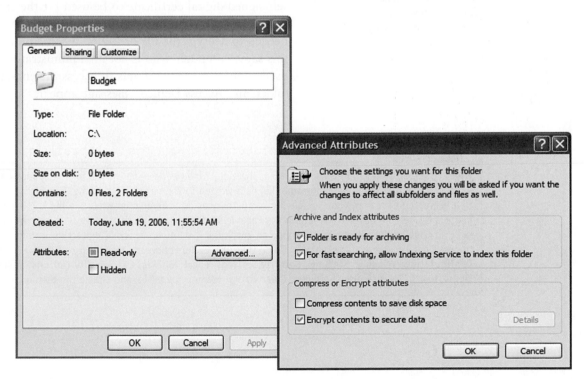

Figure 10-21 Encrypt a file or folder using the Properties window

A+ ESS
6.1
6.2

A+
220-602
3.1
6.2
6.3

2. Click the **Advanced** button. The Advanced Attributes dialog box opens, as shown on the right side of Figure 10-21.

3. To encrypt the folder or file, check **Encrypt contents to secure data** and click **OK**. On the Properties window, click **Apply**. The dialog box shown in Figure 10-22 opens, asking you if you want the encryption to apply to subfolders. Make your choice and click **OK**.

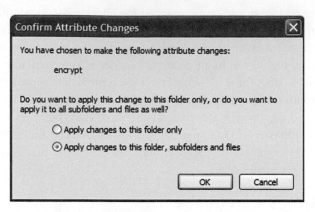

Figure 10-22   Encryption can apply to subfolders or just to the one folder

 A+ Tip

The A+ Essentials and A+ 220-602 exams expect you to know about encryption and encryption technologies.

Encrypted files or folders are displayed in Explorer in green. For a standalone computer that is not part of a Windows domain, the EFS encrypting process generates a self-signed digital certificate to be used for the encryption. This certificate contains both the private key and public key needed to decrypt the file or folder. If some other user on this same computer who is not an administrator or any user on the network attempts to access the encrypted file or folder, an "Access Denied" message appears.

 Notes

When you open an encrypted file with an application, Windows decrypts the file for the application to use. While the application is working on the file, data written to the virtual memory file, Pagefile.sys, might contain decrypted data from your file. If your computer goes into hibernation while the file is open, a criminal might later be able to read the data in the Pagefile.sys file by booting the system from another OS. For this reason, disable hibernation while working on encrypted files. Also, for added protection, configure Windows to clean out Pagefile.sys at shutdown. To do that, use Group Policy. In Group Policy, drill down to **Computer Configuration, Windows Settings, Security Settings, Local Policies**, and **Security Options**, as shown in Figure 10-23. Double-click **Shutdown: Clear virtual memory pagefile**, and enable the feature.

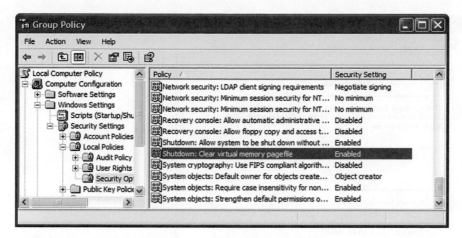

Figure 10-23 Use Group Policy to configure Windows to clear Pagefile.sys at shutdown

HOW TO SHARE AN ENCRYPTED FILE

You cannot share encrypted folders, but you can share encrypted files. In order to give another user on this same computer access to an encrypted file, you need to export your certificate and then the other user can import that certificate to be used to access the encrypted file. Here are the steps involved:

1. To export the certificate, on the file's properties window, click the **Advanced** button. The Advanced Attributes dialog box opens. Click **Details**. The Encryption Details dialog box opens, showing the users and recovery agents who can access the file, as shown on the left side of Figure 10-24. Click **Add**. The Select User dialog box opens, also shown in Figure 10-24.

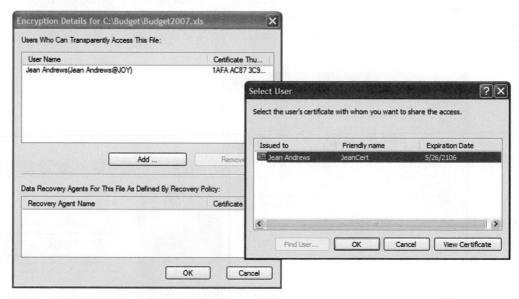

Figure 10-24 Encryption details for an encrypted file

2. Click **View Certificate**. The Certificate dialog box opens (see Figure 10-25). Notice on this dialog box that Windows does not recognize the certificate to be trusted. That's because the certificate was issued by EFS rather than obtained from a trusted certification authority (CA). A CA is an organization such as VeriSign (*www.verisign.com*) that issues digital certificates.

A+ ESS
6.1
6.2

A+
220-602
3.1
6.2
6.3

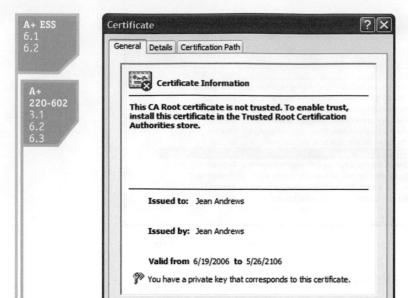

Figure 10-25   The Certificate dialog box shows information about the certificate used for encryption

3. Click the **Details** tab, as shown on the left side of Figure 10-26. Then click **Copy to File.** The Certificate Export Wizard launches, as shown on the right side of Figure 10-26. Follow the wizard to export the certificate. The wizard will give you the opportunity to name the file and decide in what folder it will be stored. Also, the wizard will ask you if you want to export the private key portion of the certificate, which you don't need to do. When the wizard completes, the file is created with a .pfx file extension.

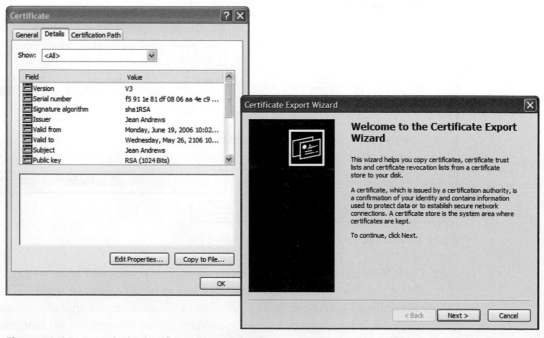

Figure 10-26   Launch the Certificate Export Wizard

A+ ESS
6.1
6.2

A+
220-602
3.1
6.2
6.3

4. Have the user who is to have access to the encrypted file log on to the system and import the certificate. To import the certificate, the user needs to locate the .pfx file in Explorer and double-click the file. The user can then access the encrypted file.

5. For added security, after all users who need access to the file have imported the certificate, delete the .pfx file.

The method just described to share an encrypted file might not work when you are part of a Windows domain. When you encrypt a file or folder on a Windows domain, the domain administrator might have set up the domain so that trusted certificates are used for the encryption. To know how to share an encrypted file on a Windows domain, check with your network administrator.

HOW TO DECRYPT A FILE OR FOLDER

To ensure that a file can be accessed if a user is not available or forgets the password to log on to the system, an administrator for the OS can decrypt a file. In this case, the administrator is called a data recovery agent (DRA).

Here are three ways to decrypt a file or folder:

◢ From the file's Properties dialog box, click the **Advanced** button. In the Advanced Attributes dialog box, uncheck **Encrypt contents to secure data**.

◢ Encryption is removed automatically when you move a file or folder to a FAT logical drive (volume) because the FAT file system does not support encryption. Figure 10-27 shows the message you see when an encrypted file is about to be moved to a jump drive.

◢ Use the Cipher command, which is discussed next.

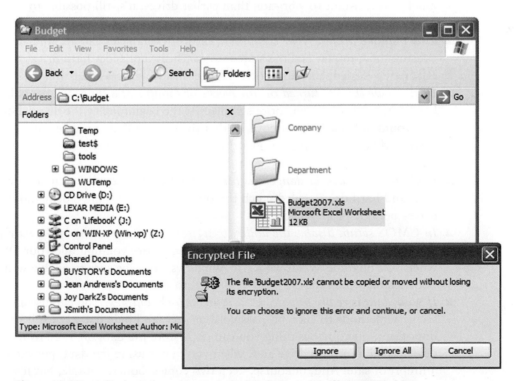

Figure 10-27 A file is no longer encrypted when it is moved off the NTFS drive

A+ ESS
6.1
6.2

A+
220-602
3.1
6.2
6.3

HOW TO USE THE CIPHER COMMAND

If you are encrypting a large number of files or folders from a command prompt or using a batch file, you can use the Cipher command:

CIPHER [/E, /D] [/S:*DIR*] [*PATHNAME*[. . .]]

Note the following about this command:

- ▲ /E encrypts the specified files or folders.
- ▲ /D decrypts the specified files or folders.
- ▲ /S:*DIR* applies the action to the specified folder (directory) and all its subfolders.
- ▲ *PATHNAME* is the path to and the name of the file or folder that is to be encrypted or decrypted.

For example, at the command prompt, to decrypt all files in the C:\Public folder, use this command:

```
CIPHER /D C:\Public\*.*
```

PHYSICALLY PROTECT YOUR EQUIPMENT

It's only common sense, but worth mentioning anyway. There are some things you can do to physically protect your computer equipment. Here is a list of do's and don'ts. You can probably add your own tips to the list:

- ▲ *Don't move or jar your computer when it's turned on.* Before you move the computer case even a foot or so, power it down. Don't put the computer case under your desk where it might get bumped or kicked. Although modern hard drives are sealed and much less resistant to vibration than earlier drives, it's still possible to crash a drive by banging into it while it's reading or writing data.
- ▲ *Don't smoke around your computer.* Tar from cigarettes can accumulate on fans, causing them to jam and the system to overheat. For older hard drives that are not adequately sealed, smoke particles can get inside and crash a drive.
- ▲ *Don't leave the PC turned off for weeks or months at a time.* My daughter once left her PC turned off for an entire summer. At the beginning of the new school term, the PC would not boot. We discovered that the boot record at the beginning of the hard drive had become corrupted. PCs, like old cars, can give problems after long spans of inactivity.
- ▲ *High humidity can be dangerous for hard drives.* I once worked in a basement with PCs, and hard drives failed much too often. After we installed dehumidifiers, the hard drives became more reliable.
- ▲ *In CMOS setup, disable the ability to write to the boot sector of the hard drive.* This alone can keep boot viruses at bay. However, before you upgrade your OS, such as when you upgrade Windows XP to Windows Vista, be sure to enable writing to the boot sector, which the OS setup will want to do.
- ▲ *If your data is really private, keep it under lock and key.* You can use all kinds of security methods to encrypt, password protect, and hide data, but if it really is that important, one obvious thing you can do is store the data on a removable storage device such as a flash drive and, when you're not using the data, put the flash drive in a fireproof safe. And, of course, keep two copies. Sounds simple, but it works.
- ▲ *Keep magnets away from your computer.* Don't work inside the computer case with magnetized screwdrivers or sit magnets on top of the computer case.

10

A+ ESS
6.1
6.2

▲ *Lock down the computer case.* As mentioned earlier in the chapter, some computer cases allow you to add a lock so that you can physically prevent others from opening the case. Besides this lock, you can also use a lock and chain to physically tie the case to a desk or other permanent fixture so someone can't walk away with it. As an added precaution, physically mark the case so it can be identified if it is later stolen. You embed an ID plate into the case or engrave your ID information into it. Record serial numbers and model numbers in a safe place separate from the equipment.

A+
220-602
6.4

BEWARE OF SOCIAL ENGINEERING

Generally speaking, the weakest link in setting up security in a computer environment is people. That's because people can often be tricked into giving out private information. Even with all the news and hype about identify theft and criminal Web sites, it's amazing how well these techniques still work. Many users naively download a funny screen saver, open an e-mail attachment, or enter credit card information into a Web site, without regard to security. In the computer arena, social engineering is the practice of tricking people into giving out private information or allowing unsafe programs into the network or computer. A good support technician is aware of the criminal practices used and is able to teach users how to recognize this mischief and avoid it. Most of the danger you need to be aware of comes over the Internet. Here are three common ways criminals might use the Internet to lure users into taking their bait:

▲ **Phishing** (sounds like "fishing") is a type of identity theft where the sender of an e-mail message scams you into responding with personal data about yourself. The scam artist baits you by asking you to verify personal data on your bank account, ISP account, credit card account, or something of that nature. Often you are tricked into clicking a link in the e-mail message, which takes you to an official-looking site complete with company or bank logos where you are asked to enter your user ID and password to enter the site.

▲ Scam artists use **scam e-mail** to lure you into their scheme. One scam e-mail I recently received was supposedly from the secretary of a Russian oil tycoon who was being held in jail with his millions of dollars of assets frozen. If I would respond to the e-mail and get involved, I was promised a 12 percent commission to help recover the funds.

▲ A **virus hoax** or e-mail hoax is e-mail that does damage by tempting you to forward it to everyone in your e-mail address book with the intent of clogging up e-mail systems or to delete a critical Windows system file by convincing you the file is malicious. Also, some e-mail scam artists promise to send you money if you'll circulate their e-mail message to thousands of people. I recently received one that was supposedly promising money from Microsoft for "testing" the strength of the Internet e-mail system. Beware! Always check Web sites that track virus hoaxes before pressing that Send button!

 A+ Tip

The A+ 220-602 exam expects you to be aware of social engineering situations that might compromise security.

Let's take a look at how to use the Internet responsibly, how to smoke out an e-mail hoax, and how to deal with suspicious scripts.

RESPONSIBLE INTERNET HABITS

In this section, we'll look at some best practices that, for the most part, simply equate to using good judgment when using the Internet to keep you out of harm's way.

Here is a list of what I'll call the Six Commandments for using the Internet:

1. *You shall not open e-mail attachments without scanning them for viruses first.* In fact, if you don't know the person who sent you the attachment, save yourself a lot of trouble and just delete it without opening it.

2. *You shall not click links inside e-mail messages.* These links might contain a malicious script. To keep the script from running, copy and paste the link to your browser address bar instead.

3. *You shall not forward an e-mail message without first checking to see if that warning is a hoax.* Save us all the time of having to delete the thing from our Inbox.

4. *You shall always check out a Web site before you download anything from it.* Freeware isn't so free if you end up with an infected computer. Only download from trusted sites.

5. *You shall never give your private information to just any ole Web site.* Use a search engine and search for information about a site before you trust it with your identity.

6. *You shall never trust an e-mail message asking you to verify your private data on a Web site with which you do business.* If you receive an e-mail that looks like it came from your bank, your PayPal account, or your utility company, don't click those links in that message. If you think it might be legitimate, open your browser, type in the link to the business's Web site, and check out the request.

HOW TO DEBUNK AN E-MAIL HOAX

An e-mail hoax is itself a pest because it overloads network traffic when naive users pass it on. Figure 10-28 shows an example of a virus hoax e-mail message I received.

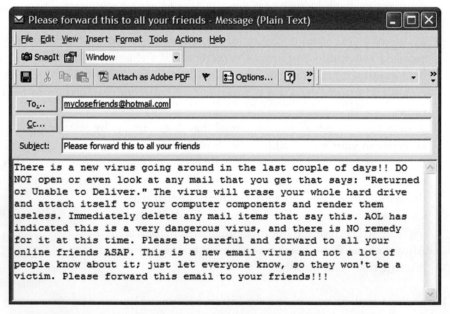

Figure 10-28 An example of a hoax e-mail message

Viruses grow more powerful every day, but this message is just absurd. It is unlikely that a virus can render computer components useless. No virus has been known to do actual physical damage to hardware, although viruses can make a PC useless by destroying programs or data, and a few viruses have been able to attack system BIOS code on the motherboard.

A+ ESS
6.1
6.2

A+
220-602
6.4

What's most important is not to be gullible and take the bait by forwarding the message to someone else. The potential damage a hoax like this can do is to overload an e-mail system with useless traffic, which is the real intent of the hoax. When I received this e-mail, over a hundred names were on the distribution list, sent by a friend who was innocently trying to help us all out.

Here are some Web sites that specialize in debunking virus hoaxes:

- ▲ *hoaxbusters.ciac.org* by Computer Incident Advisory Capability
- ▲ *www.hoaxinfo.com* by Jeff Richards
- ▲ *www.hoaxkill.com* by Oxcart Software
- ▲ *www.snopes.com* by Urban Legends
- ▲ *www.viruslist.com* by Kaspersky Lab
- ▲ *www.vmyths.com* by Rhode Island Soft Systems, Inc.

When you get a hoax, if you know the person who sent it to you, do us all a favor and send that person some of these links!

PROTECT AGAINST MALICIOUS E-MAIL SCRIPTS

One popular Trojan technique to spread a virus or worm is to put a malicious script in the body of an e-mail message or in an e-mail attachment. The e-mail is written with the intent of luring you to open the attachment or click a link in the e-mail text. For example, you receive spam in your e-mail, open it, and click the link "Remove me" to supposedly get removed from the spam list. However, by doing so, you spread a virus or worm, or install adware onto your PC.

To counteract this approach to spreading malicious software, let's take a look at how scripts work. Then we'll look at how you can protect yourself from malicious ones.

How Scripts Work

Scripts can be written in several scripting languages, such as VBScript or Jscript, and are executed in Windows using the Windows Scripting Host (WSH) utility, Wscript.exe. A script is stored in a file with a script file extension—the extension depends on the scripting language used to write the script. The scripting languages and file extensions that Windows recognizes by default are Jscript (.js file extension), Jscript Encoded (.jse), VBScript Encoded (.vbe), VBScript (.vbs), and Windows Script (.wsf). You can add other file extensions to this list.

The program that is used to handle a particular file type or file extension is determined by the Windows default settings. For instance, Windows does know how to handle a .txt file before any application is installed, because Notepad (the executable is Notepad.exe) is part of Windows, which is the program that is launched to open a .txt file.

On the other hand, file extensions that are not part of the Windows default settings can be added to the list of known file extensions when a new application is installed on a computer. For example, Windows will not know how to handle a .doc file until Microsoft Word has been installed. After Word is installed, when you double-click a .doc file, the Word executable, Winword.exe, is launched and then opens the document file.

How Scripts Are Spread

Now, let's use all this information to help protect a system against malicious scripts. Many times, a link that reads something like this one appears in an e-mail message from someone you don't know: "Click *www.symantec.com* to read about the latest virus attack." The link is not the URL to the Symantec Web site, but rather points to *www.symantec.com.vbs*, which is a script embedded in the e-mail message. When you click the link, the script with the .vbs file extension is executed by Wscript.exe and malicious software is spread to your computer.

Another malicious technique is to attach a file to an e-mail message. The filename is displayed, looking something like this: CoolPic.jpg. But because extensions of known file types are normally hidden, you are not aware that the real filename is CoolPic.jpg.vbs. When you click, thinking you're about to view a photo, you are executing a malicious script.

How to Help Protect Against Malicious Scripts

So, how do you protect yourself? Here is what you can do:

◢ Set Windows so that script file extensions display by default. If that e-mail attachment had appeared as CoolPic.jpg.vbs, you probably would not have opened it.
◢ Set Windows to not execute scripts, but rather to open them in a Notepad window. After you've examined a script, you can decide if you want to execute it.

Now let's see how to use both options. To display file extensions of scripts, do the following:

1. Using Windows Explorer or the Start menu, open **My Computer**. Click **Tools, Folder Options**. The Folder Options window opens. Click the **File Types** tab, as shown in Figure 10-29. Listed under *Registered file types* are all the file types that Windows knows how to handle.

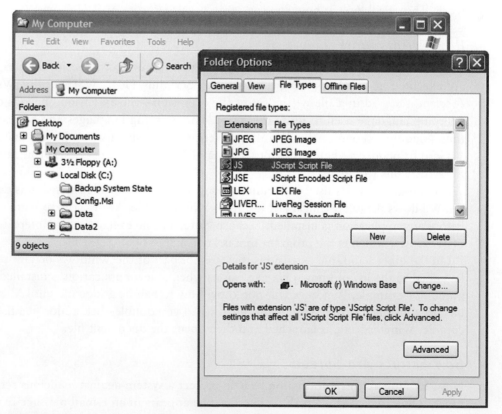

Figure 10-29   The File Types tab of the Folder Options window lists all the file types that Windows recognizes

A+ ESS
6.1
6.2

2. Select **JS** in the Extensions column and click **Advanced**. The Edit File Type window opens, as shown in Figure 10-30. Check the **Always show extension** check box. Click **OK**.

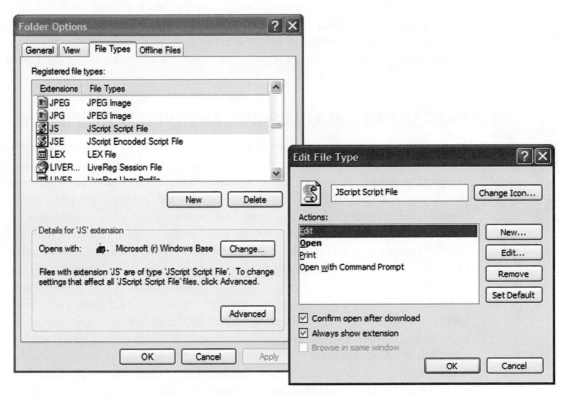

Figure 10-30 Use the Edit File Type window to change the way Windows displays and manages a file type

3. Do the same for the other script file types: JSE, VBE, VBS, and WSF. Click **Close** to close the Folder Options window.

A more drastic measure to protect yourself is to set Windows so that unknown scripts will not be executed. To do that, change the action that Windows takes each time you double-click a script file. Looking back at Figure 10-30, select **Edit** in the list of Actions (not the Edit button), click **Set Default**, and then click **OK**. The next time you double-click a script, it will be opened by Notepad for editing. Doing so will give you the opportunity to examine the script before it's executed. However, to actually execute the script, you have to manually use Wscript.exe to run it by entering this command at a command prompt (where Myscript.vbs is the name of the script):

```
Wscript.exe Myscript.vbs
```

KEEP GOOD BACKUPS OF USER DATA

One of the more important chores of securing a computer is to prepare in advance for disaster to strike. One of the most important things you can do to prepare for disaster is to make good backups of user data. You learned how to make backups in Chapter 4, so we won't repeat that information here.

A+ ESS
6.1
6.2

BACK UP SYSTEM FILES

Recall that in Chapter 3, you learned how to use Ntbackup.exe to back up the System State and registry before we edited the registry. You need to back up the System State after you have made major changes to the system, such as when you install a new hard drive or software application. If others in your organization have permission to install hardware or applications, you might need to explain to them the importance of backing up the System State. At the least, you can make it a routine part of your monthly maintenance tasks.

A+ ESS
3.3
6.1
6.2

A+
220-602
3.1
3.3
6.1
6.2

MAKE USE OF EVENT LOGGING AND INCIDENT REPORTING

As a part of managing the security of a computer or network, your organization might make you accountable to report incidents of unusual or atypical events. Incidents that you might be expected to report can include an attempt at breaking in to a secured computer or network, the security has been broken, an accident has occurred, property has been lost or damaged, a hazard has been reported, an alarm has been activated, unauthorized changes to a system or its data were made, or other such events. Reasons for incident reporting include the need for others to respond to an incident, the need to know about a weak security loophole that can be plugged, the need to be aware of trends in problems over the entire organization, and legal concerns.

For large networks, a computerized incident reporting tool is most likely already in place and your responsibility might be to learn how to use it, to know your user account and password to the system, and to make sure you report all incidents in a timely manner. On the other hand, old-fashioned paper reporting might be used. Either way, the incident-reporting forms will most likely include your name, job title, contact information, and full description of the incident. The description might include the system or systems affected, the people involved, the resulting damage, and if the problem is resolved or still active. Also included might be your recommendations or actions to resolve the problem.

You can use several monitoring tools to log events that can help you know if a computer or its security has been compromised. Several of these are discussed next.

MONITORING WINDOWS 2000/XP LOGON EVENTS

One event you might be expected to monitor is logging on to a local computer. Logging on to a domain is monitored at the domain level, but you can track logging on to a standalone computer or a computer in a workgroup by using Event Viewer. (Windows XP Home Edition does not support this feature.) You can track successful and/or failed attempts at logging on. For most situations, it is only required that you track failures. To set Event Viewer to track failures when people are attempting to log on to the system, do the following:

1. Log on to the system as an administrator. In Group Policy, drill down to **Computer Configuration, Windows Settings, Security Settings, Local Policies,** and **Audit Policy,** as shown in Figure 10-31.

2. Double-click **Audit account logon events.** The Audit logon events Properties dialog box opens, also shown in Figure 10-31. Check **Failure** and click **Apply.** Do the same for **Audit logon events** and then close the Group Policy window.

10

A+ ESS
3.3
6.1
6.2

A+
220-602
3.1
3.3
6.1
6.2

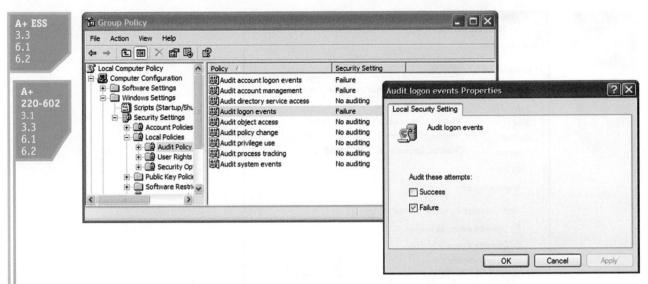

Figure 10-31 Set Windows XP to monitor logging on to the system

3. To see the events that are logged, open **Event Viewer** and select **Security** in the left pane (see Figure 10-32).

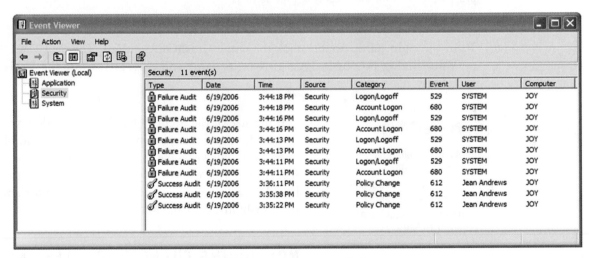

Figure 10-32 Event Viewer monitoring failures at logging on to Windows XP

4. Recall from earlier chapters that you can change the maximum allowed size of the log file. Besides changing the size of the Security log file, for added security, you can set the system to halt when the Security log file is full. To do that, right-click **Security** and select **Properties**. The Security Properties window opens (see Figure 10-33).

5. Select **Do not overwrite events (clear log manually)** and click **OK**. Close Event Viewer.

6. The next step is to edit the registry to tell the system to halt when the log file size is exceeded. First open the Registry Editor and navigate to this key:

```
HKLM\SYSTEM\CurrentControlSet\Control\Lsa.
```

7. To back up the key, right-click it and select **Export** from the shortcut menu; save the key to your desktop.

A+ ESS
3.3
6.1
6.2

A+
220-602
3.1
3.3
6.1
6.2

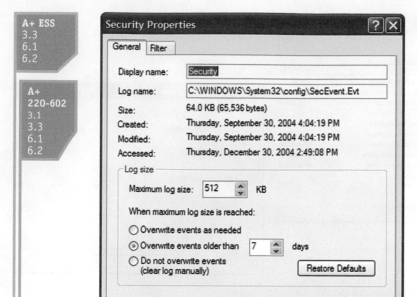

Figure 10-33   Control the Security log file settings

8. In the right pane, double-click the name **CrashOnAuditFail**. The Edit DWORD Value dialog box opens. Assign **1** to its value and click **OK**. Close the Registry Editor.

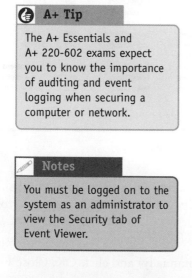

A+ Tip

The A+ Essentials and A+ 220-602 exams expect you to know the importance of auditing and event logging when securing a computer or network.

Notes

You must be logged on to the system as an administrator to view the Security tab of Event Viewer.

If the size of the Security log file is exceeded, you must restart the system, log on to the system as an administrator, open Event Viewer, save the log file, and then clear the log file. And, if you want the system to halt the next time the log file is full, you must use the Registry Editor and reset the CrashOnAuditFail value to 1.

MONITORING CHANGES TO FILES AND FOLDERS

Earlier in the chapter, you learned how to disable simple file sharing so that you can control which user accounts have access to a file or folder. After simple file sharing is disabled, you can also monitor access to a file or folder. Do the following:

1. To set the Group Policy to audit an object, open the **Group Policy** window. Then click **Computer Configuration, Windows Settings, Security Settings, Local Policies,** and **Audit Policy,** and then double-click **Audit object access** (see Figure 10-34). Check **Failure** and click **Apply.** Close the Group Policy windows.

2. Open the Properties window of the file or folder you want to monitor or audit and click the **Security** tab. Then click **Advanced.** The Advanced Security Settings window for the file or folder opens. Click the **Auditing** tab.

A+ ESS
3.3
6.1
6.2

A+
220-602
3.1
3.3
6.1
6.2

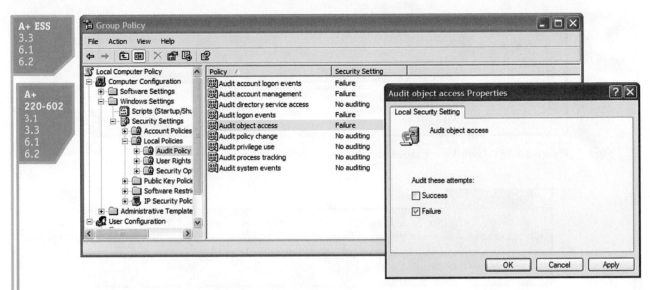

Figure 10-34 Set the Group Policy to audit an object

3. You can now add users that you want to monitor and decide what activity to monitor. To add a user, click **Add**. When you're done, click **Apply** to close the window and apply your changes. Figure 10-35 shows that all activity by the user BUYSTORY on the folder C:\Budget will be monitored. Close all windows when you're done.

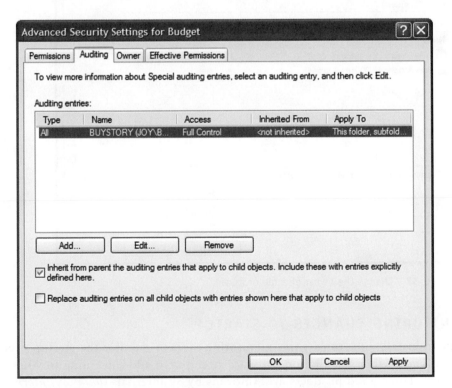

Figure 10-35 Specify the user and activity you want to monitor

4. To view the logged activity, open **Event Viewer** and double-click **Security**. Figure 10-36 shows the results when someone logged on using the Buystory account attempted to open the Budget folder for which they did not have permission to access.

A+ ESS
3.3
6.1
6.2

A+
220-602
3.1
3.3
6.1
6.2

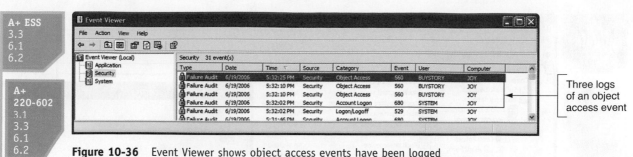

Three logs
of an object
access event

Figure 10-36   Event Viewer shows object access events have been logged

> ✎ **Notes**
>
> When simple file sharing is disabled, on the Properties window of a file or folder, you can use the Security tab to change the owner of the file or folder. If you are having a problem decrypting an encrypted file that belongs to another user, try changing the owner of the file. On the Security tab, click **Advanced**, and then click the **Owner** tab (see Figure 10-37).

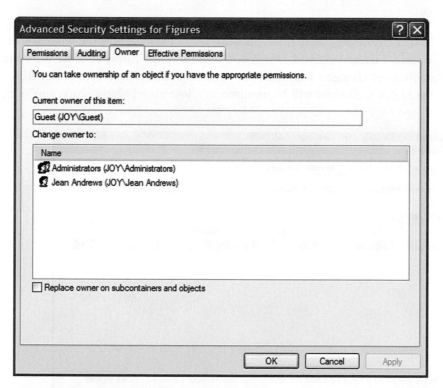

Figure 10-37   Change the owner of a file or folder

MONITORING CHANGES TO STARTUP

You can install some third-party monitoring tools to monitor the startup processes and let you know when installation software attempts to add something to your startup routines. Three good products are Autoruns by Sysinternals (*www.sysinternals.com*), WinPatrol by BillP Studios (*www.winpatrol.com*), and Startup Control Panel by Mike Lin (*www.mlin.net*). Figure 10-38 shows a window that displays when WinPatrol detected a startup process that was about to be added to a system.

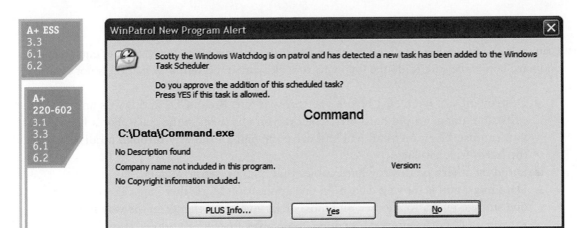

Figure 10-38 WinPatrol is asking permission to allow a startup process to be added

MONITORING NETWORK ACTIVITY

You can use Windows Firewall to monitor and log network activity. On the Windows Firewall window, click the **Advanced** tab, as shown on the left side of Figure 10-39. Under Security Logging, click **Settings**. The Log Settings window opens, as shown on the right side of Figure 10-39. Select what you want to log (dropped packets and/or successful connections) and click **OK**. Also notice the path and name of the log file: C:\Windows\pfirewall.log. A packet is a segment of data sent over a network connection and a dropped packet is a packet that could not be successfully delivered. Log dropped packets when you're trying to solve a connection problem and log successful connections when you want to monitor network activity.

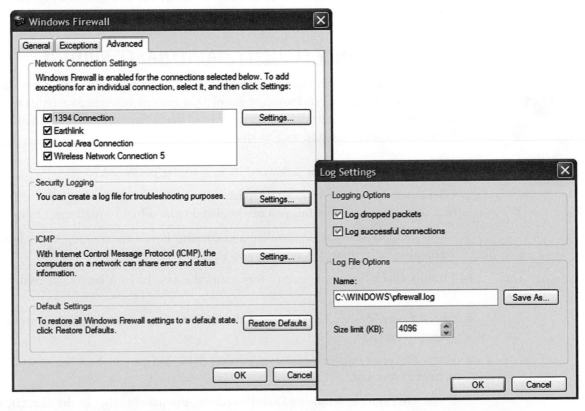

Figure 10-39 Using Windows Firewall, you can log dropped packets and successful connections

A+ ESS
6.1
6.2

DESTROY THE TRASH

Criminals can find out a lot about you by going through your trash. For computer equipment and hard copies, be sure to do the following to make sure important information is not exposed:

▲ Destroy all storage media before you throw it out. Break CDs and DVDs and physically do damage to old hard drives before you put them in the trash. For a hard drive, you can use a hammer and nail and drive the nail all the way through all disks inside the hard drive housing.

▲ Shred or otherwise destroy hard copies that contain sensitive data.

▲ **Data migration** is moving data from one application to another application or from one storage media to another, and most often involves a change in the way the data is formatted. For example, if accounts receivables for a small organization have been kept in Excel spreadsheets, and are now being moved into an Access database, that data must be migrated from Excel to Access. As the data is moved, keep in mind that sensitive data still needs to be encrypted and user access controlled. Then, after the migration is complete, be sure to destroy old data storage media that is no longer used.

▲ When retiring a computer system or when a user is no longer actively using a certain desktop or notebook computer, remnants of data and other sensitive information can accidentally be left on the system for criminals to find. The surest way to make certain that these data remnants are totally erased is to totally erase everything on the hard drive. The best way to totally erase everything on a hard drive is to use a **zero-fill utility** provided by a hard drive manufacturer. These utilities fill every sector on the drive with zeroes. For example, for Seagate (*www.seagate.com*) hard drives, download the DiscWizard Starter Edition diagnostic software, create a bootable floppy disk using the utility, and boot from the disk. Then select **Utilities Zero Fill Drive (Full)** from the startup menu, which fully erases all data on the drive. You can then repartition and reformat the drive to use it again.

A+ ESS
1.4
3.4
6.1
6.2

A+
220-602
3.4

PERFORM A MONTHLY SECURITY MAINTENANCE ROUTINE

Make it a habit to check every computer for which you are responsible each month. You can use the following checklist. However, know that routine maintenance tends to evolve over time based on an organization's past problems that might need special attention. Start with this list and then add to it as the need arises:

1. Change the administrator password. (Use a strong password.)

2. Check that Windows Automatic Updates is turned on and working. For applications that users routinely rely on, you might also download and install any critical updates.

3. Check that AV software is installed and current. If you are running anti-adware software, also verify that it is running and current.

4. Visually check the equipment to make sure the case has not been tampered with. Is the lock secure?

5. Check Event Viewer. Take a look at the Security list, looking for failed attempts to access the system.

6. Verify that user backups of data are being done and current backups of data and the System State exist.

7. If you are running Windows Disk Protection, discussed earlier in the chapter, you need to save any changes to disk that are required to update installed software.

SECURING YOUR WIRED OR WIRELESS NETWORK

Unsecured networks are like leaving your front door open when you go to work in the morning or signing every check in your checkbook and then leaving it lying around in a coffee shop. Don't even think about it! If you're responsible for a home or small office network, take security seriously. In this section, you'll see how to use a router to secure a small network, how to secure a wireless network, and about authentication techniques used for larger networks.

USE A ROUTER TO SECURE A SOHO NETWORK

For most networks for a small office or home office (SOHO), the device you'll want for security is a router that can be used to secure a wired network or provide a secured wireless network. Routers don't cost that much nowadays, and the investment is well worth it. In Chapters 8 and 9, you learned how to configure a hardware firewall built in to a multipurpose router and how to set up and secure a wireless network. To refresh your memory of that information, recall that a router can be used to limit communication from outside or inside the network in these ways:

▲ *Limit communication from outside the network*. Turn on the router's firewall so that anonymous communication initiated from outside the network is not allowed in.

▲ *Limit communication from within the network*. Access to the Internet can be limited to certain PCs on the network and certain times of day or days of the week. Also, certain services (such as gaming) can be blocked. Certain Web sites can be blocked (by entering the URL of the Web site in a list of blocked sites), and Web sites can be blocked by keywords contained in the Web pages. Figure 10-40 shows the setup screen for one router that allows you to limit Internet access.

▲ *Secure a wireless access point*. In Chapter 8, you learned that you can secure a wireless access point by renaming the SSID and disabling SSID broadcasting, filtering MAC addressing, encrypting data, using a firewall, and keeping the firmware updated.

▲ *Implement a virtual private network (VPN)*. Some high-end routers can create a virtual private network whereby users logged on to the network from a remote location on the Internet can have a private encrypted session with the corporate network using a technique called tunneling.

As part of your routine maintenance chores to secure a network, you can keep the router firmware up to date with the latest downloads to help make sure the router firewall is as secure as possible. Go to the Web site of the router manufacturer and download the firmware updates to a file on your hard drive. Then, using the router's setup utility, perform the upgrade. The Firmware Upgrade window for one router is shown in Figure 10-41.

A+ ESS
1.4
6.2

A+
220-602
6.2

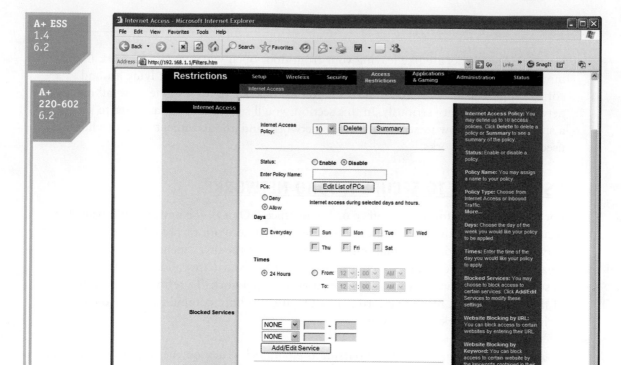

Figure 10-40 A router can be used to block Internet access

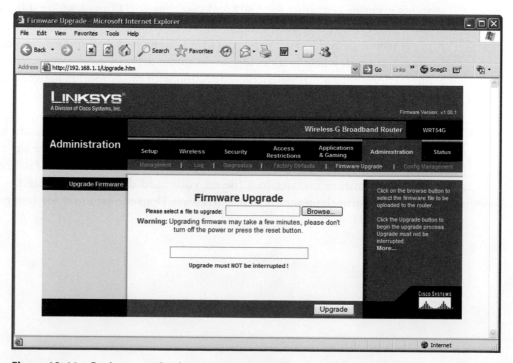

Figure 10-41 For best security, keep your hardware firewall firmware updated

A+ ESS
1.1
6.1
6.2

AUTHENTICATION TECHNOLOGIES FOR LARGER NETWORKS

Large corporate networks require more security than that provided by a multipurpose router or wireless access point. How to secure a large network is beyond the scope of this book. However, as a PC support technician, you might be called on to support the devices and techniques that are used to authenticate users when they first try to connect to a large network. In this part of the chapter, you'll learn how user accounts and passwords are encrypted as this information is sent over the network when authenticating the user. You'll also learn how smart cards and biometric data can be used to authenticate users.

ENCRYPTED USER ACCOUNTS AND PASSWORDS

When logging on to a network, such as that managed by Windows Server 2003, the user account and password must be passed over the network in order to be authenticated by the domain controller. If someone intercepts that information, the network security can be compromised. For this reason, user accounts and passwords are encrypted at the entry point to the network and decrypted just before they are validated. The protocols used to encrypt account names and passwords are called authentication protocols. The two most popular protocols are **CHAP (Challenge Handshake Authentication Protocol)** and **Kerberos**. Kerberos is the default protocol used by Windows 2000/XP.

SMART CARDS

Besides a user account and strong password, a network might require more security to control access. Generally, the best validation to prove you are who you say you are requires a two-factor authentication: You prove you have something in your possession and you prove you know something. For example, a user can enter a user ID and password and also prove he has a token in hand. This token can take on many forms. The most popular type of token is a **smart card**, which is any small device that contains authentication information that can be keyed into a logon window by a user or can be read by a **smart card reader** when the device is inserted in the reader. (You also need to know that some people don't consider a card to be a smart card unless it has an embedded microprocessor.)

> **A+ Tip**
>
> The A+ Essentials exam expects you to know about using smart cards and biometric devices for hardware and software security.

Here are some variations of smart cards:

- One type of smart card is a **key fob**, so called because it fits conveniently on a keychain. RSA Security (*www.rsasecurity.com*), a leader in authentication technologies, makes several types of smart cards, called SecurIDs. One SecurID key fob by RSA Security is shown in Figure 10-42. The number on the key fob changes every 60 seconds. When a user logs on to the network, she must enter the number on the key fob, which is synchronized with the network authentication service. Entering the number proves that the user has the smart card in hand.

Figure 10-42 A smart card such as this SecurID key fob is used to authenticate a user gaining access to a secured network

A+ ESS
1.1
6.1
6.2

▲ Other smart cards that look like a credit card also have an embedded microchip that displays a number every few seconds for a user to enter during the authentication process. The advantage of using smart cards that display a number to key in is that no special equipment needs to be installed on the computer. The disadvantage is that the smart card can only validate that the person has the token in hand but can provide no additional data about the user.

▲ Other smart cards have magnetic strips that can be read by a smart card reader that has a slot for the card (see Figure 10-43). Because these cards don't contain a microchip, they are sometimes called memory cards, and are sometimes used to gain entrance into a building. They can also be read by a smart card reader such as the one shown in Figure 10-44 that connects to a PC using a USB port. Used in this way, they are part of the authentication process into a network. The magnetic strip can contain information about the user to indicate their permissions on the system. Not only does the smart card validate the person has a token, but can also be used to control other functions on the network. The major disadvantage of this type of smart card is that each computer used for authentication must have one of these smart card reader machines installed. Also, in the industry, because a card with a magnetic strip does not contain a microchip, some in the industry don't consider it to fit into the category of a smart card, but rather simply call it a magnetic strip card.

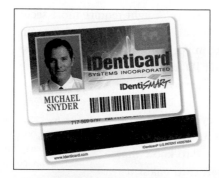 

Figure 10-43   A smart card with a magnetic strip can be used inside or outside a computer network

Figure 10-44   This smart card reader by Athena Smartcard Solutions (*www.athena-scs.com*) uses a USB connection

▲ Another type of smart card plugs directly into a USB port such as the one in Figure 10-45 by Aladdin (*www.aladdin.com*). The device is read by software installed

10

A+ ESS
1.1
6.1
6.2

on the computer and most likely contains one or more digital certificates that a user needs to authenticate into the private network and do business on the network. Digital certificates are transported over the Internet and verified using **PKI (Public-key Infrastructure)** standards. These smart cards are designed to encrypt any data sent over the Internet to the corporate network, such as that used by a VPN. In fact, many VPN solutions are based on a VPN router at the corporate office and a smart card token at the user end of the VPN tunnel. The advantage of this type of smart card is that it can contain sensitive data that can be read by a remote computer, but the computer does not need any special equipment to read the card. Remember that it's best to use two-factor authentication. Even though a user's password could be stored on this type of smart card, for added security, the user should still be expected to enter a password to gain access to the system.

Figure 10-45 This eToken by Aladdin can contain digital certificates so that a user can do business over a VPN

BIOMETRIC DATA

As part of the authentication process, rather than proving a person is in possession of a token, some systems are set to use biometric data to validate the person's physical body. Biometric data can include a fingerprint or an iris scan. These devices are not considered the stronger authentication techniques.

DEALING WITH MALICIOUS SOFTWARE

A+ ESS
3.3
6.1
6.2

A+
220-602
3.1

Even with the best of security, occasionally a virus, worm, or other type of malicious software penetrates a system. **Malicious software**, also called **malware** or a computer **infestation**, is any unwanted program that means you harm and is transmitted to your computer without your knowledge. The best-known malicious software is a virus, which is malicious software that can replicate itself by attaching itself to other programs. However, many types of malicious software have evolved over the past few years and there is considerable overlap in what they do, how they spread, and how to get rid of them.

A+ ESS
3.3
6.1
6.2

This part of the chapter covers all about dealing with malicious software. A PC support technician needs to know how to recognize that a system is infected, to understand how malicious software works, and to know how to clean up the mess.

A+
220-602
3.1

YOU'VE GOT MALWARE

Here are some warnings that suggest malicious software is at work:

▲ Pop-up ads plague you when surfing the Web.
▲ Generally, the system works much slower than it used to. Programs take longer than normal to load.
▲ The number and length of disk accesses seem excessive for simple tasks. The number of bad sectors on the hard drive continues to increase.
▲ The access lights on the hard drive and floppy drive turn on when there should be no activity on the devices. (However, sometimes Windows XP performs routine maintenance on the drive when the system has been inactive for a while.)
▲ Strange or bizarre error messages appear. Programs that once worked now give errors.
▲ Less memory than usual is available, or there is a noticeable reduction in disk space.
▲ Strange graphics appear on your computer monitor, or the computer makes strange noises.
▲ The system cannot recognize the CD-ROM drive, although it worked earlier.
▲ In Windows Explorer, filenames now have weird characters or their file sizes seem excessively large. Executable files have changed size or file extensions change without reason. Files mysteriously disappear or appear.
▲ Files constantly become corrupted.
▲ The OS begins to boot, but hangs before getting a Windows desktop.
▲ Your antivirus software displays one or more messages.
▲ You receive e-mail messages telling you that you have sent someone an infected message.
▲ Task Manager shows unfamiliar processes running.
▲ When you try to use your browser to access the Internet, strange things happen and you can't surf the Web. Your Internet Explorer home page has changed and you see new toolbars you didn't ask for.
▲ A message appears that a downloaded document contains macros, or an application asks whether it should run macros in a document. (It is best to disable macros if you cannot verify that they are from a trusted source and that they are free of viruses or worms.)

 Notes

Malicious software is designed to do varying degrees of damage to data and software, although it does not damage PC hardware. However, when boot sector information is destroyed on a hard drive, the hard drive can appear to be physically damaged.

A+ ESS
3.3
6.1
6.2

A+
220-602
3.1

HERE'S THE NASTY LIST

You need to know your enemy! Different categories of malicious software are listed next and are described in a bit more detail in this section:

▲ A **virus** is a program that replicates by attaching itself to other programs. The infected program must be executed for a virus to run. The program might be an application, a macro in a document, a Windows 2000/XP system file, or the boot sector programs. The damage a virus does ranges from minor, such as displaying bugs crawling around on a screen, to major, such as erasing everything written on a hard drive. Figure 10-46 shows the results of a harmless virus that simply displays garbage on the screen. The best way to protect against viruses is to always run antivirus (AV) software in the background.

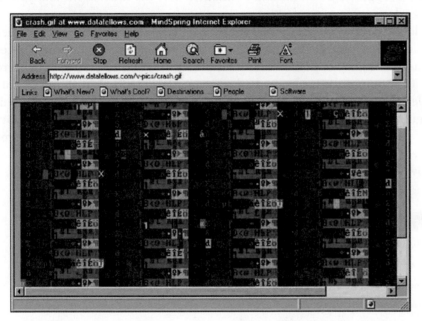

Figure 10-46 The crash virus appears to be destructive, making the screen show only garbage, but does no damage to hard drive data

▲ **Adware** produces all those unwanted pop-up ads. Adware is secretly installed on your computer when you download and install shareware or freeware, including screen savers, desktop wallpaper, music, cartoons, news, and weather alerts. Then, it displays pop-up ads based on your browsing habits. Sometimes when you try to uninstall adware, it deletes whatever it was you downloaded that you really wanted to keep. And sometimes adware is also spying on you and collecting private information.

▲ **Spam** is junk e-mail that you don't want, that you didn't ask for, and that gets in your way.

▲ **Spyware** is software that installs itself on your computer to spy on you, and collects personal information about you that it transmits over the Internet to Web-hosting sites that intend to use your personal data for harm. Spyware comes to you by way of e-mail attachments, downloaded freeware or shareware, instant messaging programs, or when you click a link on a malicious Web site.

▲ A **worm** is a program that copies itself throughout a network or the Internet without a host program. A worm creates problems by overloading the network as it replicates. Worms cause damage by their presence rather than by performing a specific damaging

A+ ESS
3.3
6.1
6.2

A+
220-602
3.1

act, as a virus does. A worm overloads memory or hard drive space by replicating repeatedly. When a worm (for example, Sasser or W32.Sobig.F@mm) is loose on the Internet, it can cause damage such as sending mass e-mailings. The best way to protect against worms is to use antivirus software and a firewall.

▲ A **browser hijacker**, also called a home page hijacker, does mischief by changing your home page and other browser settings. Brower hijackers can set unwanted bookmarks, redirect your browser to a porn site when you key in a wrong URL, produce pop-up ads, and direct your browser to Web sites that offer pay-per-view pornography.

▲ A **dialer** is software installed on your PC that disconnects your phone line from your ISP and dials up an expensive pay-per-minute phone number without your knowledge. The damage a dialer does is the expensive phone bill.

▲ A **keylogger** tracks all your keystrokes, including passwords, chat room sessions, e-mail messages, documents, online purchases, and anything else you type on your PC. All this text is logged to a text file and transmitted over the Internet without your knowledge. A keylogger is a type of spyware.

▲ A **logic bomb** is dormant code added to software and triggered at a predetermined time or by a predetermined event. For instance, an employee might put code in a program to destroy important files if his name is ever removed from the payroll file.

▲ A **Trojan horse** does not need a host program to work; rather, it substitutes itself for a legitimate program. In most cases, a user launches it thinking she is launching a legitimate program. Figure 10-47 shows a pop-up that appears when you're surfing the Web. Click OK and you've just introduced a Trojan into your system. A Trojan is likely to introduce one or more viruses into the system. These Trojans are called downloaders.

Figure 10-47   Clicking OK on a pop-up window might invite a Trojan into your system

Last year, I got fooled with a Trojan when I got an e-mail message near the actual date of my birthday from someone named Emilia, whom I thought I knew. Without thinking, I clicked the link in the e-mail message to "View my birthday card to you." Figure 10-48 shows what happened when I clicked.

10

A+ ESS
3.3
6.1
6.2

A+
220-602
3.1

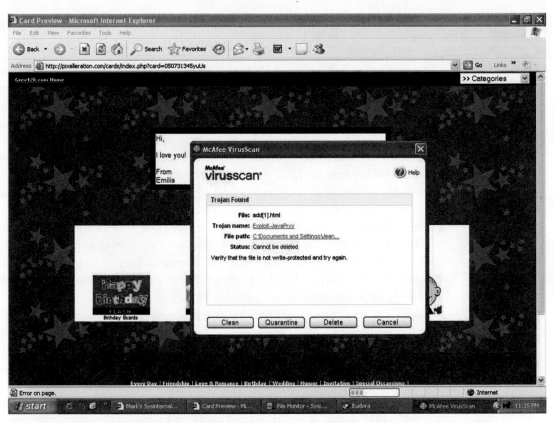

Figure 10-48 A Trojan can get in when you click a link in an e-mail message

HOW A VIRUS WORKS

A virus attacks your system and hides in several different ways. Consider the following:

- A **boot sector virus** hides in the boot sector program of a hard drive or floppy disk or in the master boot program in the Master Boot Record (MBR).
- A **file virus** hides in an executable (.exe, .com, or .sys) program or in a word-processing document that contains a macro.
- A **multipartite virus** is a combination of a boot sector virus and a file virus and can hide in either.
- A **macro** is a small program contained in a document that can be automatically executed either when the document is first loaded or later by pressing a key combination. For example, a word-processing macro might automatically read the system date and copy it into a document when you open the document.
- Viruses that hide in macros of document files are called macro viruses. **Macro viruses** are the most common viruses spread by e-mail, hiding in macros of attached document files.
- A **script virus** is a virus that hides in a script, which might execute when you click a link on a Web page or in an HTML e-mail message, or when you attempt to open an e-mail attachment.

HOW MALWARE REPLICATES AND HIDES

A virus or other malware can use various techniques to load itself in memory and replicate itself. Also, malware attempts to hide from antivirus (AV) software by changing its

A+ ESS
3.3
6.1
6.2

A+
220-602
3.1

distinguishing characteristics (its signature) and by attempting to mask its presence. Here are some techniques used by malware to start itself and prevent detection:

▲ A virus can search a hard drive for a file with an .exe extension and then create another file with the same filename but with a .com file extension. The virus then stores itself there. When the user launches the program, the OS first looks for the program name with the .com file extension. It then finds and executes the virus. The virus is loaded into memory and loads the program with the .exe extension. The user appears to have launched the desired program. The virus is then free to do damage or spread itself to other programs.

▲ Because AV software can detect a virus by noting the difference between a program's file size before the virus infects it and after the virus is present, the virus alters OS information to mask the size of the file in which it hides.

▲ The virus monitors when files are opened or closed. When it sees that the file in which it is hiding is about to be opened, it temporarily removes itself or substitutes a copy of the file that does not include the virus. The virus keeps a copy of this uninfected file on the hard drive just for this purpose. A virus that does this or changes the attributes of its host program is called a **stealth virus**.

▲ As a virus replicates, it changes its characteristics. This type of virus is called a **polymorphic virus**.

▲ Some viruses can continually transform themselves so they will not be detected by AV software that is looking for a particular characteristic. A virus that uses this technique is called an **encrypting virus**.

▲ The virus creates more than one process; each process is watching the other. If one process gets closed, it will be started up again by one of the other processes. (This method of preventing detection is also used by spyware.) Figure 10-49 shows a Task Manager window of an infected system. Look carefully at the two processes, both named pludpm.exe. On this system, when you try to stop one process, the other starts it back up.

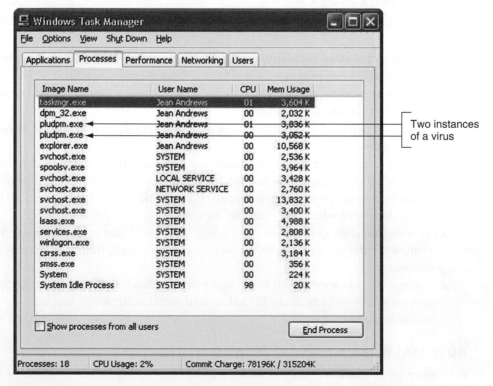

Figure 10-49 A virus running two instances of a process

A+ ESS
3.3
6.1
6.2

A+
220-602
3.1

A+
220-602
3.1
3.3

▲ Entries are often made in obscure places in the registry that allow the software to start when you start up Windows or launch Internet Explorer. (This method is used by several types of malware.)

▲ One type of malware, called a **rootkit**, loads itself before the OS boot is complete. Because it is already loaded when the AV software loads, it is sometimes overlooked by AV software. In addition, a rootkit hijacks internal Windows components so that it masks information Windows provides to user-mode utilities such as Task Manager, Explorer, the Registry Editor, and AV software—this helps it remain undetected.

STEP-BY-STEP ATTACK PLAN

This section is a step-by-step attack plan to clean up an infected system. We'll first use AV software and anti-adware software to do a general cleanup. But sometimes a system is so infected that normal measures of dealing with the problem are not going to help. So, to help you in these types of situations, we'll dig deeper to use some more complex tools and methods to smoke out any lurking processes that elude normal methods of de-infesting a system. When you're cleaning a system, as with solving any computer problem, be sure to keep good notes as you work. Document what you did and the outcome. These notes will be useful the next time you're faced with a similar problem.

RUN AV SOFTWARE

The first step to cleaning up an infected system is to run AV software. However, if you find yourself dealing with a highly infected system that does not have AV software already installed, you might not be able to download and install the software. Here are steps to use in this situation when AV software is not installed:

 Notes

It's handy to have AV software on CD, but recognize that this AV software won't have the latest updates and will need these updates downloaded from the Internet before it will catch new viruses.

1. Purchase the AV software on CD (see Figure 10-50).

2. Disconnect from the Internet so you won't open yourself up for more mischief.

Figure 10-50 AV software on CD means you don't need Internet access to install the software

A+ ESS
3.3
6.1
6.2

A+
220-602
3.1
3.3

> **Notes**
>
> If viruses are launched even after you boot in Safe Mode and you cannot get the AV software to work, try searching for suspicious entries in the subkeys under HKLM\System\ CurrentControlSet\Control\SafeBoot. Subkeys under this key control what is launched when you boot into Safe Mode. Also, if you are unable to boot into Safe Mode, system files might be infected. Chapter 5 covers how to deal with boot problems.

3. Boot into Safe Mode. To do that, press **F8** when Windows begins to load. The Windows XP Advanced Options menu appears. Choose **Safe Mode with Networking** and press **Enter**.

4. Insert the AV software CD. Most likely, the AV main menu will be displayed automatically, as shown in Figure 10-51. Choose to install the software.

Figure 10-51   Boot into Safe Mode and then install the AV software

5. When given the opportunity, enter the information to register the AV software so that you will be allowed to download updates. At this point, you won't be connected to the Internet to complete the registration, but at least the software is poised to register you later when the connection works (see Figure 10-52).

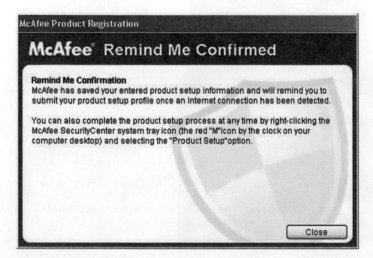

Figure 10-52   Choose to register your AV software so you can download updates

A+ ESS
3.3
6.1
6.2

A+
220-602
3.1
3.3

6. During the installation, when given the opportunity, choose to scan the system for viruses (see Figure 10-53). Set the software to scan all drives and all type files and to look for all types of malware.

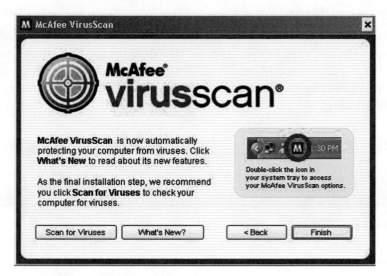

Figure 10-53 Choose to scan for viruses

7. Figure 10-54 shows the results of a McAfee scan that detected a bunch of adware, spyware, Trojans, and potentially unwanted programs (PUPs).

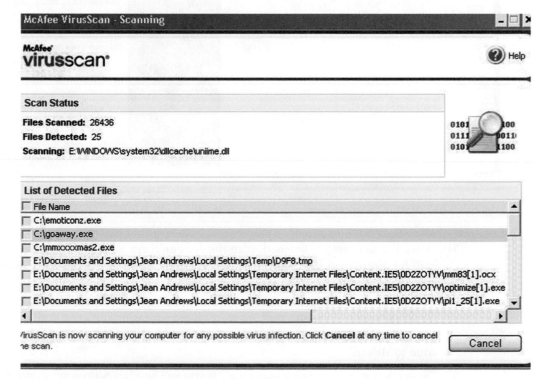

Figure 10-54 Virus scan detects unwanted programs

A+ ESS
3.3
6.1
6.2

A+
220-602
3.1
3.3

8. Sometimes, AV software detects a program that you know you have downloaded and want to keep, but the AV software recognizes it as potentially harmful. This type of software is sometimes called **grayware** or a PUP (potentially unwanted program). When the AV software displays the list of detected files, unless you recognize something you want to keep, I suggest you tell the AV software to delete them all.

9. Reboot into Safe Mode with Networking, connect to the Internet, and allow your AV software to get any current updates from the AV software Web site. Figure 10-55 shows that happening for McAfee VirusScan software. If the software requests you reboot the system for the installation to complete, be sure to reboot into Safe Mode with Networking.

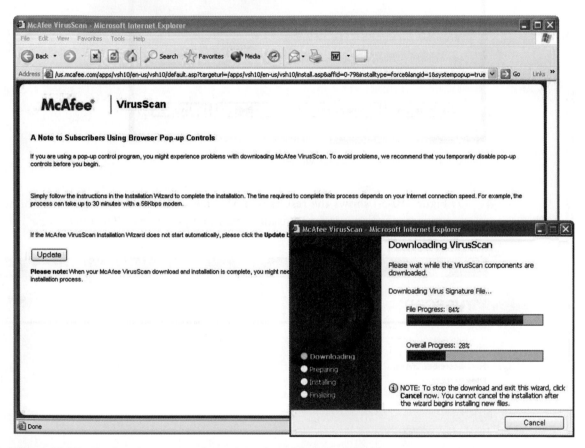

Figure 10-55 McAfee VirusScan getting updates from the McAfee Web site

10. After the updating is finished, scan the system again. Most likely, some new malware will be discovered for you to delete. For example, when I cleaned up an infected system using the McAfee CD version of the software, it found 34 viruses, Trojans, and adware. After all McAfee updates were applied, it found an additional 54 viruses, Trojans, adware, worms, and spyware. Keep repeating the scan until you get a clean scan. Reboot between scans and take notes of any program files the software is not able to delete.

11. Now it's time to see where you stand. If you use an always-up connection to the Internet, unplug your network cable. Reboot the system to the normal Windows 2000/XP desktop and check Task Manager. Do you see any weird processes, see pop-ups when you open your browser, or get strange messages like the one in Figure 10-56 asking permission to connect to the Internet? If so, you still have malware.

10

A+ ESS
3.3
6.1
6.2

A+
220-602
3.1
3.3

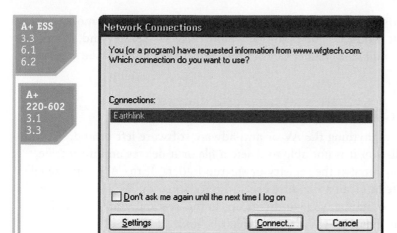

Figure 10-56 Evidence that malware is still infecting the system

It might be more fun to begin manually removing each program yourself, but it's probably quicker and more thorough to use anti-adware software next. I suggest you resist the temptation to poke around looking for the malware and move on to the next step.

RUN ADWARE OR SPYWARE REMOVAL SOFTWARE

Almost all AV software products today also search for adware and spyware. However, software specifically dedicated to removing this type of malware generally does a better job of it than does AV software. The next step in the removal process is to use anti-adware or anti-spyware software. Figure 10-57 shows what Windows Defender discovered on one computer.

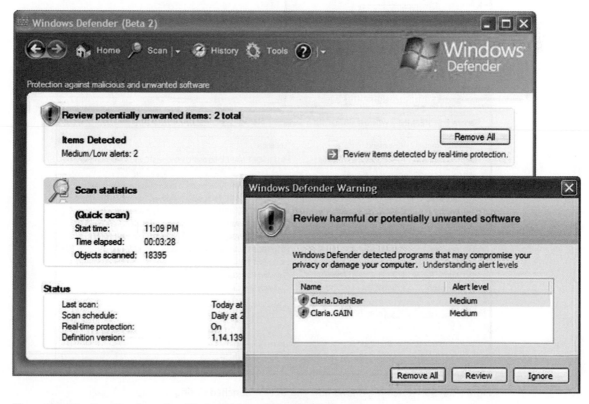

Figure 10-57 Results of running Windows Defender by Microsoft

To completely clean your system, you might have to run a removal product more than once or use several different products. For example, what Ad-Aware doesn't find, Windows Defender does, but what Windows Defender doesn't find, Ad-Aware finds. To be sure, run two products.

SEARCH OUT AND DESTROY WHAT'S LEFT

Next, you'll need to clean up anything the AV or anti-adware software left behind. Sometimes AV software tells you it is not able to delete a file or it deletes an infected file, but leaves behind an orphan entry in the registry or startup folders. If the AV software tells you it was not able to delete or clean a file, first check the AV software Web site for any instructions you might find to manually clean things up. In this section, you'll learn about general things you can do to clean up what might be left behind.

Respond to Any Startup Errors

On the first boot after AV software has found and removed malware, you might find some startup errors caused by incomplete removal of the malware. One example of such an error is shown in Figure 10-58. Somewhere in the system, the command to launch 0sis0ijw.dll is still working even though this DLL has been deleted. One way to find this orphan entry point is to use Msconfig. Figure 10-59 shows the Msconfig window showing us that the DLL is launched from a registry key.

Figure 10-58 Startup error indicates malware has not been completely removed

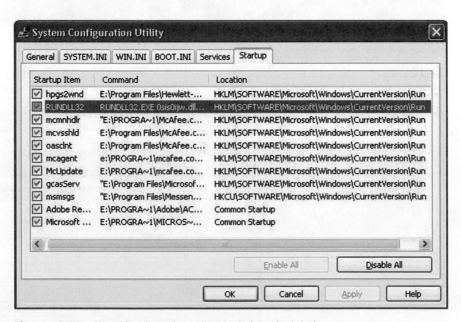

Figure 10-59 Msconfig shows how the DLL is launched during startup

A+ ESS
3.3
6.1
6.2

The next step is to back up the registry and then use Regedit to find and delete the key (see Figure 10-60).

A+
220-602
3.1
3.3

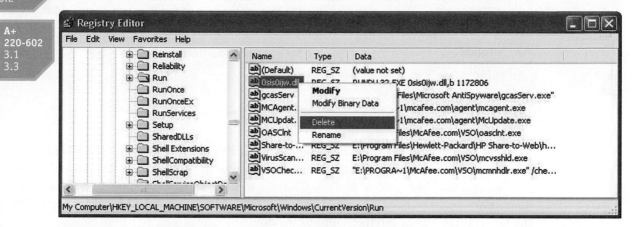

Figure 10-60 Delete orphan registry entry left there by malware

Delete Malicious Files

For each program file the AV software told you it could not delete, try to delete the program file yourself using Windows Explorer. For peace of mind, don't forget to empty the Recycle Bin when you're done. You might need to open a command prompt window and remove the hidden or system attributes on a file so that you can delete it. Figure 10-61 shows how this is done for the file C:\INT0094.exe. Table 10-2 explains each command used.

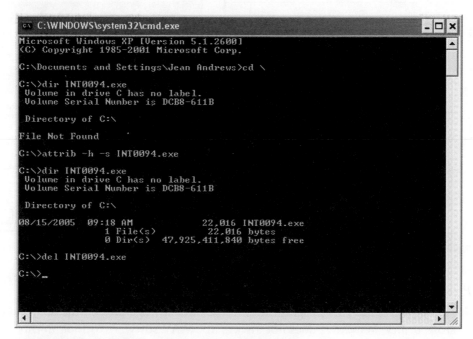

Figure 10-61 Commands to delete a hidden system file

A+ ESS
3.3
6.1
6.2

A+
220-602
3.1
3.3

Command	Explanation
cd \	Make the root directory of drive C the current directory
dir INT0094.exe	The file does not appear in the directory because it is hidden
attrib –h –s INT0094.exe	Remove the hidden and system attributes of the file
dir INT0094.exe	The Dir command now displays the file
del INT0094.exe	Delete the file

Table 10-2 Commands to delete a hidden system file

To get rid of other malware files, you might need to delete all Internet Explorer temporary Internet files. To do that, open the **Properties** window for drive C and click **Disk Cleanup** on the General tab. Then, from the Disk Cleanup window shown in Figure 10-62, make sure **Temporary Internet Files** is checked and click **OK**. (Alternately, you can click **Delete Files** on the General tab of the Internet Options window.)

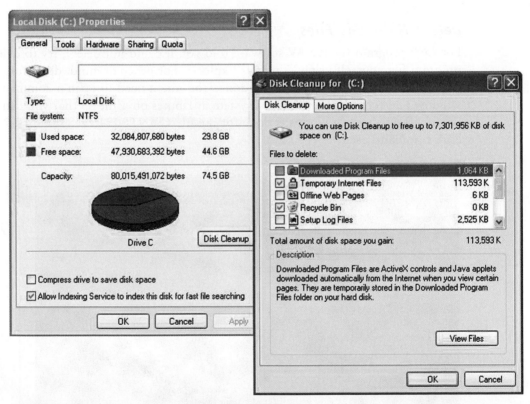

Figure 10-62 Delete all temporary Internet files

Purge Restore Points

Some malware hides its program files in the data storage area of the Windows XP System Restore utility. Windows does not always allow AV software to look in this storage area when it is scanning for malware. To get rid of that malware, you must turn off System Restore, reboot your system, and turn System Restore back on. How to do that was covered in earlier chapters. Turning off System Restore causes the data storage area to be purged. You'll get rid of any malware there, but you'll also lose all your restore points.

If your AV software is running in the background and reports it has found a virus in the C:\System Volume Information_Restore folder, it means malware is in a System Restore

A+ ESS
3.3
6.1
6.2

A+
220-602
3.1
3.3

point (see Figure 10-63). If you see a message similar to the one in Figure 10-63 or your AV software scan feature found lots of malware in other places on the drive, the best idea is to purge all restore points. Don't do this if, for some reason, you desperately need to keep a restore point you've previously made.

Figure 10-63 Malware found in a restore point

Clean the Registry

Sometimes AV software deletes a program file but does not delete the registry entries that launch the program at startup. In the last chapter, you learned how to search registry keys for startup processes. To get the job done more quickly, you can use Autoruns by Sysinternals to help you search for these registry entries. Figure 10-64 shows a screen shot where Autoruns is displaying a registry key used to launch the Pludpm.exe malware program. AV software had already found and deleted this program file, but it left the registry key untouched.

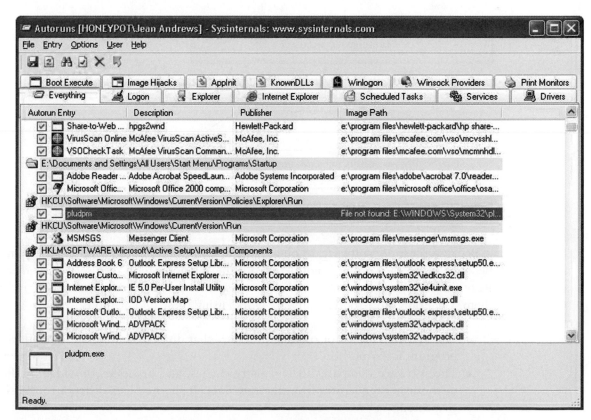

Figure 10-64 Autoruns finds orphan registry entries left there by AV software

Scan the Autoruns window looking for suspicious entries. Research any entries that you think might be used by malware. To get rid of these keys, back up the registry and then use Regedit to delete unwanted keys.

Root Out Rootkits

A rootkit is a program that uses unusually complex methods to hide itself on a system, and many spyware and adware programs are also rootkits. The term rootkit applies to a kit or set of tools used originally on Unix computers. In Unix, the lowest and most powerful level of Unix accounts is called the root account; therefore, this kit of tools was intended to keep a program working at this root level without interruption.

Rootkits can prevent Task Manager from displaying the running rootkit process, or might cause Task Manager to display a different name for this process. The program filename might not be displayed in Windows Explorer, the rootkit's registry keys might be hidden from the Registry Editor, or the Registry Editor might display incorrect information. All this hiding is accomplished in one of two ways, depending on whether the rootkit is running in user mode or kernel mode (see Figure 10-65). A rootkit running in user mode intercepts the API calls between the time when the API retrieves the data and when it is displayed in a window. A rootkit running in kernel mode actually interferes with the Windows kernel and substitutes its own information in place of the raw data read by the Windows kernel.

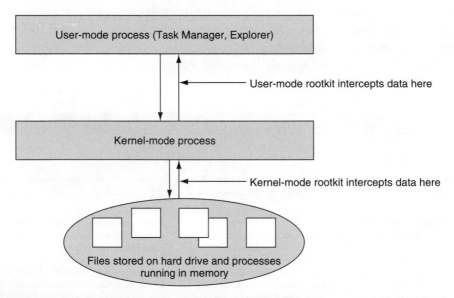

Figure 10-65   A rootkit can run in user mode or kernel mode

Because most AV software, to one degree or another, relies on Windows tools and components to work, the rootkit is not detected if the Windows tools themselves are infected. Rootkits are also programmed to hide from specific programs designed to find and remove them. Generally, anti-rootkit software works using these two methods:

- ◢ The software looks for running processes that don't match up with the underlying program filename.
- ◢ The software compares files, registry entries, and processes provided by the OS to the lists it generates from the raw data. If the two lists differ, a rootkit is suspected.

A+ ESS
3.3
6.1
6.2

A+
220-602
3.1
3.3

Two good anti-rootkit programs are:

◢ RootkitRevealer by Sysinternals (*www.sysinternals.com*)
◢ BackLight by F-Secure (*www.f-secure.com*)

After you have used other available methods to remove malware and you still believe you're not clean, you might want to download and run one of these products. Close all open applications and don't use the computer for any other task while the anti-rootkit software is running. If you change a file or the registry changes while the software is running, it might report a false positive because the list taken with the OS and without the OS might differ simply because you changed something between the times the two lists were taken. Figure 10-66 shows RootkitRevealer scanning for rootkits.

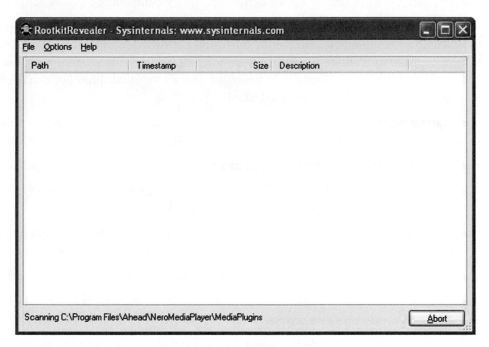

Figure 10-66   Rootkit Revealer scanning for rootkits

For best results when scanning for rootkits, run the anti-rootkit software from another computer so that the software is not dependent on the OS that might be infected. For example, you can share drive C on the network and then, from another computer on the network, run the anti-rootkit software and instruct it to scan drive C on the remote computer.

If the software detects a discrepancy that might indicate a rootkit is installed, you'll need to go to the Sysinternals or F-Secure Web site or do a general Web search to find information about the potential rootkit and instructions for removing it. Follow the instructions to manually remove the program and all its remnants. Sometimes the removal is so complicated, you might decide it makes more sense to just start over and reinstall Windows.

If you have tried all the techniques and products just described and still have malware, I'm sorry to say the next suggestion I have to offer is to restore the entire system from backups. If you don't have a current backup, as a last resort, you can back up your data, completely erase your hard drive, reinstall Windows and all your applications, and then restore your data.

>> CHAPTER SUMMARY

- ▲ Part of securing a Windows 2000/XP desktop or notebook computer includes securing the logon process, setting power-on passwords, using strong passwords, and limiting the use of the administrator account.

- ▲ All computers need to run a personal firewall such as Windows Firewall under Windows XP with SP2 applied.

- ▲ For AV software or anti-adware software to be effective, it must be kept current and it must always be running in the background.

- ▲ Keeping Windows updates current is necessary to plug up any security holes as they become known.

- ▲ Internet Explorer can be set for better security by controlling the way scripts are used.

- ▲ Because Internet Explorer and Outlook or Outlook Express are closely integrated with Windows components and are the most-popular browser and e-mail clients, they are more susceptible to malicious software than other client applications. Using less-popular clients such as Firefox by Mozilla (a browser) or Eudora by Qualcomm (an e-mail client) might mean you are less likely to be attacked.

- ▲ Practice and teach responsible Web surfing, such as never opening an e-mail attachment from unknown senders and never downloading from Web sites you have not carefully checked out.

- ▲ Microsoft Shared Computer Toolkit can be used to lock down a public personal computer.

- ▲ Files and folders can be hidden and made private and data within these files and folders can be encrypted using the Windows Encrypted File System (EFS).

- ▲ Physically protect the equipment for which you are responsible. You can buy locks and chains to tie the equipment down and keep others from opening the computer case.

- ▲ Social engineering techniques used by criminals include phishing, scamming, and virus hoaxes.

- ▲ To make it less likely you'll launch a malicious script on your computer, set Windows to display file extensions of scripts.

- ▲ You can configure Windows so that the file extensions of scripts are displayed within the e-mail program so that users are less likely to be tricked by a script masquerading as a picture or Web link.

- ▲ To secure a system, maintain good backups of user data and System State files.

- ▲ Monitor and log events concerning logon failures, access to files and folders, changes to startup, and network activity. When atypical events happen, record those events using the incident-reporting tools recommended by your organization.

- ▲ Don't throw away or recycle storage media without first destroying all data on the media.

- ▲ Maintain a monthly routine to check your security implementations to make sure all is working as it should and make any changes as appropriate.

- ▲ A small network can be secured using a router. For larger networks, a user can be authenticated on a network using encrypted user accounts and passwords, a token such as a smart card, and/or biometric data.

- ▲ Malicious software includes viruses, adware, spam, spyware, worms, browser hijackers, dialers, keyloggers, logic bombs, and Trojan horses.

◢ To clean a system of malicious software, run AV software and anti-adware software, respond to any startup errors, delete files, purge restore points, and remove orphan entries in the registry or other startup location.

>> KEY TERMS

For explanations of key terms, see the Glossary near the end of the book.

adware	infestation	scam e-mail
antivirus (AV) software	Kerberos	script virus
authentication	key fob	smart card
authorization	keylogger	smart card reader
boot sector virus	logic bomb	social engineering
browser hijacker	macro	spam
CHAP (Challenge Handshake	macro virus	spyware
Authentication Protocol)	malicious software	stealth virus
data migration	malware	Trojan horse
dialer	multipartite virus	virus
Encrypted File System (EFS)	passphrase	virus hoax
encrypting virus	phishing	virus signature
encryption	PKI (Public-key Infrastructure)	worm
file virus	polymorphic virus	zero-fill utility
grayware	rootkit	

>> REVIEWING THE BASICS

1. What encryption protocol does Windows XP use when sending an account name and password to a domain controller for validation?

2. Which policy in Group Policy must be enabled before you can monitor failed attempts at logging on to a Windows 2000/XP system?

3. Define and explain the differences between viruses, worms, logic bombs, and Trojan horses.

4. Where can viruses hide?

5. What is the best way to protect a computer or network against worms?

6. What is the best way to determine if an e-mail message warning about a virus is a hoax?

7. Are boot sector viruses limited to hard drives? Explain.

8. Which feature must you disable in the Folders Options applet of Control Panel before you can control which user group or user has access to a shared file or folder?

9. What is the most likely way that a virus will get access to your computer?

10. List three products to remove malicious software that can deal with adware and spyware.

11. Why is it best to run AV software in Safe Mode?

12. Which Windows tool do you use to view a recorded log of network activity?

13. What registry key keeps information about services that run when a computer is booted into Safe Mode?

14. What does AV software look for to determine that a program or a process is a virus?

15. What Windows tool can you use to solve a problem of an error message displayed at startup just after your AV software has removed malware?

16. What folder is used by Windows to hold System Restore restore points?

17. How can you delete all restore points and clean up the restore points' data storage area?

18. What two methods does anti-rootkit software use to detect a rootkit?

19. Name two anti-rootkit products.

20. What is the major disadvantage of using an AV software installation CD to install the AV software to rid a system of viruses?

21. Why does having Windows display known file extensions help prevent a system from being infected with malware?

22. How does a rootkit running in user mode normally hide?

23. What is the difference between spyware and adware?

24. What is the Windows Scripting Host utility used for, and what is the command line to execute it?

25. Why is using an ActiveX control considered a security risk?

26. What must you do before you can use the Windows Backup utility on a Windows XP Home Edition PC?

27. Name one browser other than Microsoft Internet Explorer.

28. Name two e-mail clients other than Microsoft Outlook or Outlook Express.

29. What are five file extensions that might be used for scripts?

30. Why might someone see better security when using a browser other than Internet Explorer?

>> THINKING CRITICALLY

1. A virus has attacked your hard drive and now when you start up Windows, instead of seeing a Windows desktop, the system freezes and you see a "blue screen of death" (an error message on a blue background). You have extremely important document files on the drive that you cannot afford to lose. What do you do first?

   a. Try a data recovery service even though it is very expensive.

   b. Remove the hard drive from the computer case and install it in another computer.

   c. Try GetDataBack by Runtime Software (*www.runtime.org*) to recover the data.

   d. Use Windows utilities to attempt to fix the Windows boot problem.

   e. Run antivirus software to remove the virus.

2. Just after you reboot after running AV software, an error message is displayed that contains a reference to a strange DLL file that is missing. What do you do first?

   a. Run the AV software again.

   b. Run Msconfig and look for startup entries that are launching the DLL.

    c. Run Regedit and look for keys that refer to the DLL.

    d. Search the Internet for information about the DLL.

3. Suppose a user has encrypted important data files and now is no longer working for your company. How do you decrypt these files so they can be read?

>> HANDS-ON PROJECTS

PROJECT 10-1: Learning to Use Autoruns

Download Autoruns by Sysinternals (*www.sysinternals.com*) and run it on your PC. How many registry keys does Autoruns list that contain startup items on your PC? Compare the list of startup items to that generated by Msconfig. Describe any differences between the two lists.

PROJECT 10-2: History of Rootkits

Rootkits became widely known when Sony included a rootkit with some of its audio CDs. The rootkit was intended to detect and prevent ripping or illegally copying the CDs. The rootkit was also written so it could not be detected or uninstalled by normal means. Use the Internet to research and answer these questions:

1. What are some of the audio CDs by Sony that contained the rootkit?

2. What are two software products that might be hidden on a Sony CD that contained the rootkit?

3. Describe Sony's response when consumers angrily protested the rootkit installation without their knowledge.

4. If you have used your computer to play a Sony audio CD that contained the rootkit, how can you best rid your computer of the rootkit?

PROJECT 10-3: Using the Internet to Learn About Viruses

One source of information about viruses on the Web is F-Secure Corporation. Go to the Web site *www.f-secure.com/v-descs/*, shown in Figure 10-67, for information about viruses; the viruses are listed alphabetically with complete descriptions, including any known sources of the viruses. Print a description of three viruses from this Web site, with these characteristics:

▴ One virus that destroys data on a hard drive

▴ One harmless virus that only displays garbage on the screen

▴ One virus that hides in a boot sector

The site also lists information about the most recent viruses. Search the Web site at *www.f-secure.com*, list five recent viruses, and describe their payloads.

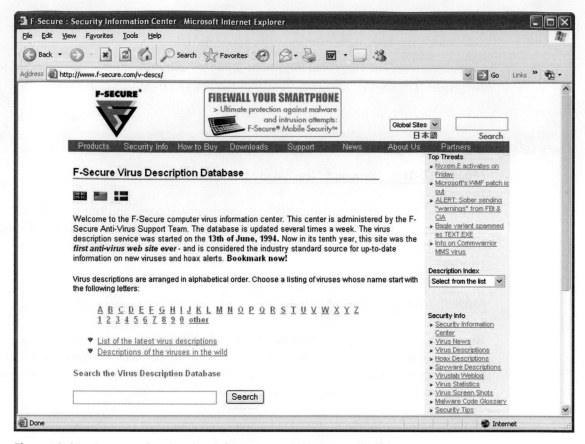

Figure 10-67 For comprehensive virus information, see the F-Secure Web site

PROJECT 10-4: Using Password Checker

Microsoft offers a password checker for users to know the strength of their passwords. To use the utility, go to the Microsoft Web site at *www.microsoft.com* and search for "Password Checker." Use this free Microsoft utility to verify that a password you have made up is a strong password. Based on the measure of the strength of several of your passwords, what do you think the password checker is looking for?

PROJECT 10-5: Downloading the Latest Update of AV Software

If you own antivirus software, download the latest antivirus (AV) definition list from the Internet. For example, for Norton AntiVirus, follow these directions:

1. Go to the Symantec Downloads page: *www.symantec.com/downloads*.

2. Click **Virus Definitions and Security Updates** and then click **Download Virus Definitions**. Select your Norton AntiVirus product and operating system.

3. Follow the directions to download the latest update and signature list for the particular version of your AV software.

4. While online, see if the site offers information on virus hoaxes and create a list of hoaxes if it does.

>> REAL PROBLEMS, REAL SOLUTIONS

REAL PROBLEM 10-1:   Cleaning Your System of Malware

Using the tools and techniques presented in this chapter, thoroughly clean your system of any malware. Take notes as you work and list any malware detected.

REAL PROBLEM 10-2:   E-Mail Hoax

Search your spam and junk mail for an e-mail you think might be a hoax. (Please don't click any links or open any attachments as you search.) Using the Web sites listed earlier in the chapter for debunking virus hoaxes, search for information about this potential hoax. You might need to enter the Subject line in the e-mail message into a search box on the Web site.

REAL PROBLEM 10-3:   Securing Your Computer

Using as many of the suggestions in the chapter as apply to your system, make your computer as secure as possible. Take notes as you work and record any problems you encounter. What other measures would you like to take to secure your computer that you don't know how to do or that cost too much?

CHAPTER 11

Supporting Printers and Scanners

This chapter discusses how to support printers and scanners. As you work through the chapter, you'll learn how to install a printer and scanner and how to share a printer with others on a network. Then, you'll learn about maintaining printers and scanners and troubleshooting printer and scanner problems. Local printers and scanners connect directly to a computer by way of a USB port, parallel port, serial port, wireless connection (Bluetooth, infrared, or WiFi), IEEE 1394 (FireWire) port, SCSI port, PC Card, or ExpressCard connection, or a computer can access a network printer by way of the network. Some printers support more than one method. Printers can also be combined with fax machines, copiers, and scanners in the same machine.

INSTALLING AND SHARING A PRINTER

A+ ESS
3.1
3.2
4.2

A+
220-602
4.2

Printers come in various sizes and use various technologies, such as the laser printer shown in Figure 11-1. Regardless of the size printer or the internal technology it uses, installing a printer under Windows works about the same. When a printer is connected to a port on a computer, the computer can share the printer with others on the network. There are also network printers with Ethernet ports that can connect the printer directly to the network.

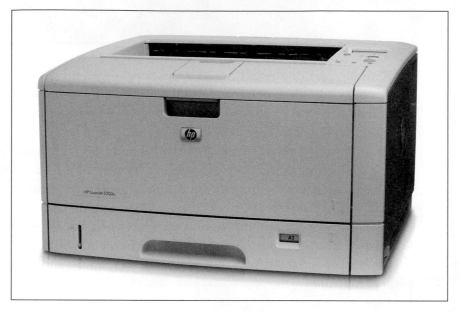

Figure 11-1 A desktop laser printer

Each computer on a network that uses the printer must have printer drivers installed so the OS on each computer can communicate with the printer and provide the interface between applications it supports and the printer. This section covers how to install a local printer and how to share that printer with others on the network.

 Notes

As you go through this part of the chapter, remember that a printer connected to a computer by way of a port on the computer is called a **local printer**, and a printer accessed by way of a network is called a **network printer**. A computer can have several printers installed. Of these, Windows designates one printer to be the **default printer**, which is the one Windows prints to unless another is selected.

INSTALLING A LOCAL PRINTER

Installing a local printer begins differently depending on the type of port you are using. For hot-pluggable ports such as a FireWire, USB, PC Card, ExpressCard, or wireless connection, you need to first install the software before connecting the printer. Remember that when using a hot-pluggable port, you don't need to power down a computer before plugging in or unplugging a hot-pluggable device. Follow these steps to install a local printer using a hot-pluggable port:

1. Log onto the system as an administrator. Begin the installation by running the setup program that came on the CD bundled with the printer before you install the printer.

11

A+ ESS
3.1
3.2
4.2

A+
220-602
4.2

If you don't have the CD, download the printer drivers from the printer manufacturer Web site and then execute that downloaded program. The setup program installs the drivers. For one HP printer, the setup program shows its progress in a window shown in Figure 11-2. Follow the directions onscreen to complete the printer installation.

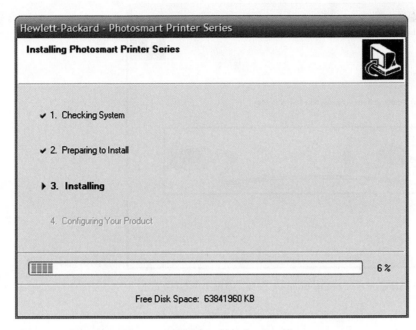

Figure 11-2   The printer setup program installs the drivers

2. At one point in the setup, you will be told to connect the printer (see Figure 11-3). Connect the printer to the port. For this printer, a USB port is used. For wireless printers, verify that the software for the wireless connection on your PC is installed and the wireless connection is enabled. For infrared wireless printers, place the printer in line of sight of the infrared port on the PC. (Most wireless printers have a status light that stays lit when a wireless connection is active.) Turn on the printer.

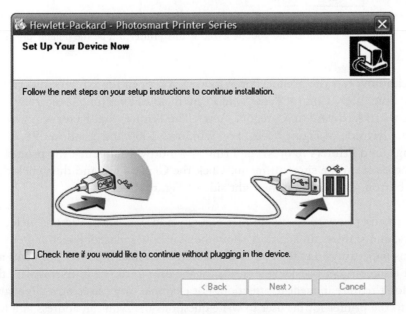

Figure 11-3   The printer setup program tells you when to connect the printer

3. The setup program detects the printer and tells you so, as shown in Figure 11-4. If Windows launches the Found New Hardware Wizard, it should close quickly. If not, cancel the wizard.

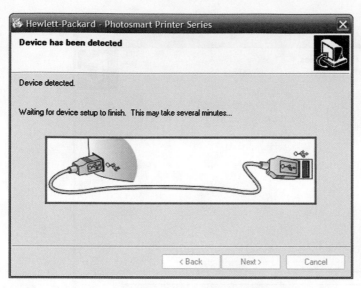

Figure 11-4 The printer setup program detects the printer

4. The setup program asks if you want this printer to be the default printer (see Figure 11-5). Click Yes or No to make your selection. The setup program finishes the installation.

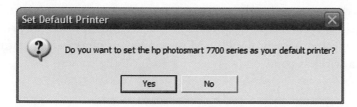

Figure 11-5 During the printer setup, you are asked if this printer will be the default printer

5. You can now test the printer. For Windows XP, open the Printers and Faxes window by clicking **Start, Control Panel**, and **Printers and Faxes** (in Classic view) or **Printers and Other Hardware** (in Category view). The Printers and Faxes window opens (see the left side of Figure 11-6). For Windows 2000 and Windows 98, click **Start, Settings**, and **Printers** to open the Printers window. Right-click the printer and select **Properties** from the shortcut menu. Click the **General** tab and then click the **Print Test Page** button, as shown on the right side of Figure 11-6.

6. Show the user how to use the printer and any add-ons. These add-ons include feeders, sorters, and staplers. In addition, show the user how to install paper and envelopes in the various paper trays. Let the user know whom to contact if printer problems arise. You might also consider providing a means for the user to record problems with the printer that don't require immediate attention. For example, you can hang a clipboard and paper close to the printer for the user to write questions that you can address at a later time.

A+ ESS
3.1
3.2
4.2

A+
220-602
4.2

Figure 11-6   To verify a printer installation, always print a test page as the last step in the installation

Here are the directions to install a local printer using an older port, such as a SCSI, serial, or parallel port, that is not hot-pluggable:

1. Plug in the printer to the port and turn on the printer. Now, you must decide how you want to install the drivers. You can use the setup program from the printer manufacturer or use the Windows installation process. First try using the setup program that came on the printer's setup CD or downloaded from the manufacturer's Web site. If you have problems with the installation, you can then try the Windows approach.

2. To use the manufacturer's installation program, launch the printer setup program from the printer setup CD or downloaded from the manufacturer's Web site and follow the directions onscreen to install the printer.

3. Alternately, you can use the Windows installation process to install the printer drivers. For Windows XP, open the Printers and Faxes window, or for Windows 2000 and Windows 98, open the Printers window. Click **Add a Printer**. The Add Printer Wizard launches, shown in Figure 11-7. Follow the directions onscreen to install the printer drivers.

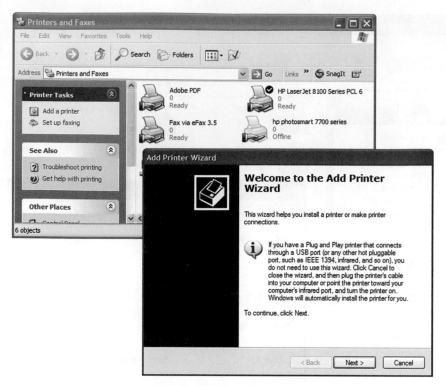

Figure 11-7 Use the Add Printer Wizard to install a printer

4. To test the printer after it is installed, in the Printers and Faxes window or the Printers window, right-click the printer and select **Properties** from the shortcut menu. Click **Print Test Page**.

✎ **Notes**

For Windows XP, by default, the Printers and Faxes window shows on the Start menu. If it is missing and you want to add it, right-click **Start** and select **Properties**. The Taskbar and Start Menu Properties dialog box opens. On the Start Menu tab, click **Customize** (see Figure 11-8). In the Customize Start Menu dialog box, click the **Advanced** tab. Check **Printers and Faxes**. Click **OK** to close the Customize Start Menu dialog box. Then click **Apply** and **OK** to apply your changes and close the Taskbar and Start Menu Properties dialog box.

SHARING A PRINTER WITH OTHERS IN A WORKGROUP

To share a local printer using Windows, File and Printer Sharing must be installed, and to use a shared printer on a remote PC, Client for Microsoft Networks must be installed. In most cases, it is easiest to simply install both components on all computers on the network. How to install the components under Windows 2000/XP and Windows 98 was covered in Chapter 17.

To share a local printer connected to a Windows 2000/XP workstation, do the following:

1. Open the Printers and Faxes window or Printers window. Right-click the printer you want to share, and select **Sharing** from the shortcut menu. The printer's Properties dialog box opens, as shown in Figure 11-9 for Windows XP; the dialog box in Windows 2000 is similar. Select **Share this printer** and enter a name for the printer.

2. If you want to make drivers for the printer available to remote users who are using an operating system other than the OS being used, click **Additional Drivers**.

A+ ESS
3.1
4.2

A+
220-602
4.2

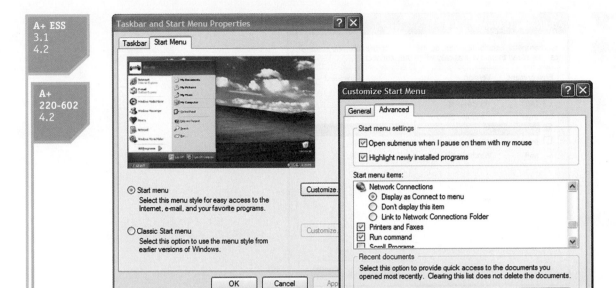

Figure 11-8 Add the Printers and Faxes item to the Start menu

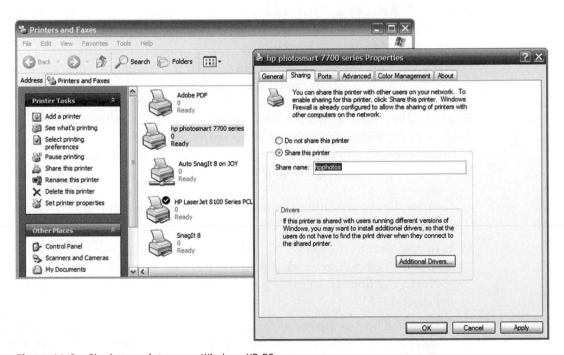

Figure 11-9 Sharing a printer on a Windows XP PC

3. The Additional Drivers window opens, as shown in Figure 11-10. Select the OS. In the figure, Windows 2000, XP, 95, 98, and Me are selected so that users of these OSs will have the printer drivers they need. Click **OK** twice to close both windows. You might be asked for the Windows installation CD or other access to the installation files. A shared printer shows a hand icon under it in the Printers and Faxes window, and the printer is listed in My Network Places or Network Neighborhood of other PCs on the network.

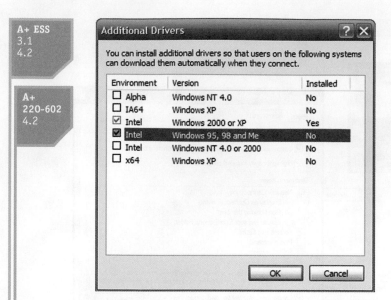

Figure 11-10   Make drivers for other operating systems available for the shared printer

You can share a printer on a Windows 9x/Me computer in the same way as for Windows 2000/XP, except the Additional Drivers option is not available.

USING A SHARED PRINTER

Recall that for a remote PC to use a shared network printer, the drivers for that printer must be installed on the remote PC. There are two approaches to installing shared network printer drivers on a remote PC. You can perform the installation using the drivers on CD (either the Windows CD or printer manufacturer's CD), or you can perform the installation using the printer drivers on the host PC. The installations work about the same way for Windows 2000/XP and Windows 98. The Windows XP installation is shown here, but differences for Windows 2000 and Windows 98 are noted.

To use a shared printer on the network by installing the manufacturer's printer drivers from CD, do the following using Windows XP:

1. Open the Printers and Faxes window and click **Add a printer**. The Add Printer Wizard opens. Click **Next**.

2. In response to the question, "Select the option that describes the printer you want to use:" select **A network printer, or a printer attached to another computer**. Click **Next**. The Specify a Printer page of the Add Printer Wizard opens, as shown in Figure 11-11.

3. Enter the host computer name and printer name. Begin with two backslashes and separate the computer name from the printer name with a backslash. Or, you can click **Browse**, search the list of shared printers on the network, and select the printer to install. (If your network is using static IP addressing and you know the IP address of the host PC, you can enter the IP address instead of the host name in this step.) Click **Next**.

4. Windows XP searches for Windows XP drivers on the host computer for this printer. If it finds them (meaning that the host computer is a Windows XP machine), the wizard skips to Step 6. If it doesn't find the drivers (the host computer is not a Windows XP machine), a message asks if you want to search for the proper driver. Click **OK**.

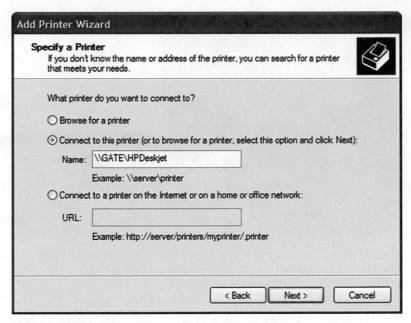

Figure 11-11 To use a network printer under Windows XP, enter the host computer name followed by the printer name, or have Windows XP browse the network for shared printers

5. Click **Have Disk** to use the manufacturer's drivers, or to use Windows drivers, select the printer manufacturer and then the printer model from the list of supported printers. Click **OK** when you finish.

6. In response to the question, "Do you want to use this printer as the default printer?" answer **Yes** if you want Windows to send documents to this printer until you select a different one. Click **Next**. Click **Finish** to complete the wizard.

7. The printer icon appears in the Printers and Faxes window. To test the printer installation, right-click the icon and select **Properties** from the shortcut menu. Click the **General** tab and then click **Print Test Page**.

Here are some additional things to know about installing a network printer using the Windows 98 Add Printer Wizard:

▲ When the wizard asks, "Do you print from MS-DOS-based programs?" answer Yes if you have any intention of ever doing so.

▲ The wizard gives you the opportunity to name the printer. You might include the location of the printer, such as 3rd Floor Laser or John's Laser.

▲ Sometimes, a DOS-based program has problems printing to a network printer. You can choose to associate the network printer with a printer port such as LPT1 to satisfy the DOS application. Click **Capture Printer Port**, and then select the port from the drop-down menu in the Capture Printer Port dialog box (see Figure 11-12).

▲ The Windows 98 Add Printer Wizard gives you the opportunity to print a test page on the last window of the wizard. It's always a good idea to print this test page to verify that the printer is accessible.

▲ Know that the Windows 98 Add Printer Wizard does not attempt to use the printer drivers on the host PC, but always installs local Windows 9x/Me drivers or uses the manufacturer's CD.

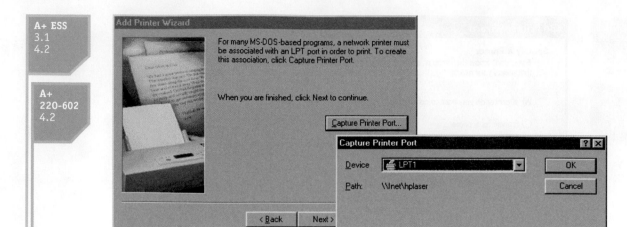

Figure 11-12   Associate a network printer with a printer port to help DOS applications in Windows 98

Another way to install a shared printer is to first use My Network Places or Network Neighborhood to locate the printer on the network. This method is faster because the remote PCs can use the printer drivers on the host PC. Do the following:

1. On a remote PC that uses Windows 2000/XP, open **My Network Places** and find the printer. Right-click the printer and select **Connect** from the shortcut menu. See Figure 11-13. (For Windows 9x/Me, open **Network Neighborhood** and find the printer. Right-click the printer and select **Install** from the shortcut menu.)

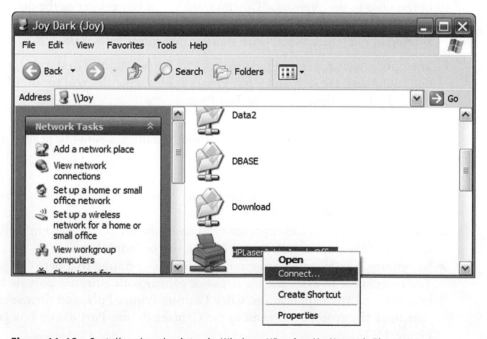

Figure 11-13   Install a shared printer in Windows XP using My Network Places

2. If the host computer is using the same OS as you are, or if you have a Windows 2000/XP host computer and the additional drivers for your OS have been installed, you can use those drivers for the installation. If Windows cannot find the right drivers, it sends you an error message and gives you the opportunity to install the drivers from your Windows CD or the printer manufacturer's CD.

11

A+ ESS
3.1
4.2

A+
220-602
4.2

> 🖉 **Notes**
>
> When installing a shared printer on a Windows 9x/Me PC where the host computer is also a Windows 9x/Me PC, you must first share the \Windows folder on the host PC so the remote PC can access the printer drivers. This is a security risk, so remove the share status on this important folder as soon as all remote PCs have the printer installed.

OTHER METHODS OF SHARING PRINTERS OVER A NETWORK

The three ways to make a printer available on a network are listed here:

- ◢ A regular printer can be attached to a PC using a port on the PC, and then that PC can share the printer with the network. (This method was described in the last section.)
- ◢ A network printer with embedded logic to manage network communication can be connected directly to a network with its own NIC.
- ◢ A dedicated device or computer called a print server can control several printers connected to a network. For example, HP has software called HP JetDirect, designed to support HP printers in this manner. For more information, see the HP Web site, *www.hp.com*.

If printers are available on the network using one of the last two methods, follow the printer manufacturer's directions to install the printer on each PC. If you don't have these directions, do the following:

1. Download the printer drivers from the printer manufacturer's Web site and decompress the downloaded file, if necessary.

2. Open the Printers and Faxes or Printers window and start the wizard to add a new printer. Select the option to install a local printer but do not ask Windows to automatically detect the printer.

3. On the next window shown in Figure 11-14, choose **Create a new port**. From the list of port types, select **Standard TCP/IP Port**. Click **Next** twice.

Figure 11-14 Configure a local printer to use a standard TCP/IP port

4. On the next window shown in Figure 11-15, you need to identify the printer on the network. If you know the IP address of the printer, enter it in the first box on this window and click **Next**. Some network printers have assigned printer names or the printer might have an assigned port name. To know how your network printer is configured, see the network printer's configuration window. How to access this window is discussed later in the chapter.

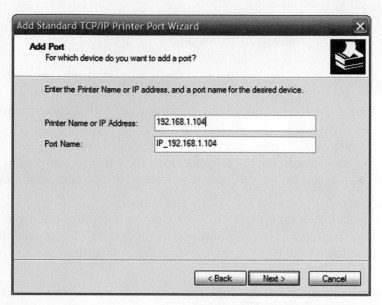

Figure 11-15   Enter the printer name or IP address to identify the printer on the network

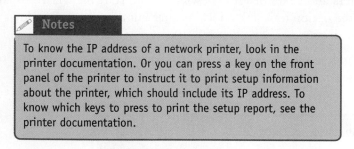

To know the IP address of a network printer, look in the printer documentation. Or you can press a key on the front panel of the printer to instruct it to print setup information about the printer, which should include its IP address. To know which keys to press to print the setup report, see the printer documentation.

5. On the next window (see Figure 11-16), click **Have Disk** so you can point to and use the downloaded driver files that will then be used to complete the printer installation.

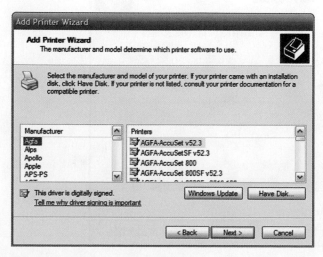

Figure 11-16   Select printer drivers

11

A+ ESS
3.1
4.2

6. When asked if you want this printer to be the default printer, make your selection. You'll also be given the opportunity to choose to share the printer. When asked if you want to print a test page, select **Yes**. Click **Finish** to close the wizard.

A+
220-602
4.2

> **✎ Notes**
>
> Because a network printer has no OS installed, the printer's NIC contains all the firmware needed to communicate over the network. For a PC, some of this software is part of Windows, including the network protocols TCP/IP and IPX/SPX. A network printer's NIC firmware usually supports TCP/IP and IPX/SPX. The network printer documentation will tell you which protocols are supported. One of these protocols must be installed on a PC using the printer.

One shortcut you might take to speed up the process of installing a printer connected directly to the network is to install the printer on one PC and then share it on the network. Then, you can install the printer on the other PCs by using My Network Places for Windows 2000/XP or Network Neighborhood for Windows 98, following the directions given earlier. Find the printer, right-click it, and then select **Connect** (for Windows 2000/XP) or **Install** (for Windows 9x/Me) from the shortcut menu. The disadvantage of using this method is that the computer sharing the printer must be turned on when other computers on the network want to use the printer.

MAINTAINING PRINTERS AND SCANNERS

A+ ESS
3.3
4.2

Printers and scanners generally last for years if they are properly used and maintained. To get the most out of a printer or scanner, it's important to follow the manufacturer's directions when using the device and to perform the necessary routine maintenance. For example, the life of a printer can be shortened if you allow the printer to overheat, don't use approved paper, or don't install consumable maintenance kits when they are required.

A+
220-602
3.3
4.2

When supporting printers using Windows, it is helpful to know about the protocols used by printers for communication between Windows and the printer, so we will begin our discussion of maintaining printers here. Then, we'll turn our attention to how you can use Windows to manage printers. Finally, you'll learn how to install and support a scanner.

PRINTER LANGUAGES

Years ago, all printers were dot matrix printers that could only print simple text using only a single font. Communication between the OS and the printer was simple. Today's printers can produce beautiful colored graphics and text using a variety of fonts and symbols, and communication between the OS and a printer can get pretty complicated.

The languages or methods the OS and printer use for communication and building a page before it prints are listed in the following. The method used depends on what the printer is designed to support and the printer drivers installed. If the printer has sophisticated firmware, it might be able to support more than one method. In this case, the installed printer drivers determine which methods can be used:

▲ *The printer uses PostScript commands to build the page.* For Windows 2000/XP or Windows 9x/Me using a PostScript printer, the commands and data needed to build a page to print are sent to the printer using the PostScript language. The printer firmware then interprets these commands and draws and formats the page in the printer memory before it is printed. PostScript is a language used to communicate how a page is to print and was developed by Adobe Systems. PostScript is popular with desktop publishing, the typesetting industry, and the Macintosh OS.

▲ *The printer uses PCL commands to build the page.* For Windows 2000/XP, a printer language that competes with PostScript is PCL (**Printer Control Language**). PCL was developed by Hewlett-Packard but is considered a de facto standard in the printing industry. Many printer manufacturers use PCL.

▲ *The Windows GDI builds the page and then sends it to the printer.* For Windows 2000/XP or Windows 9x/Me, a less-sophisticated method of communicating to a printer is to use the GDI (**Graphics Device Interface**) component of Windows. GDI draws and formats the page and then sends the almost-ready-to-print page to the printer in bitmap form. Because Windows, rather than the printer, does most of the work of building the page, a GDI printer needs less firmware and memory, and, therefore, generally costs less than a PCL or PostScript printer. The downside of using the GDI method is that Windows performance can suffer when printing a lot of complicated pages. Most low-end inkjet and laser printers are GDI printers. If the printer specifications don't say PCL or PostScript, you can assume it's a GDI printer. Many high-end printers support more than one protocol and can handle GDI, PCL, or PostScript printing.

▲ *Raw data is printed with little-to-no formatting.* Text data that contains no embedded control characters is sent to the printer as is, and the printer can print it without any processing. The data is called raw data. Dot matrix printers that can only print simple text receive and print raw data.

Normally, when Windows receives a print job from an application, it places the job in a queue and prints from the queue, so that the application is released from the printing process as soon as possible. Several print jobs can accumulate in the queue, which you can view in the Printers and Faxes or Printers window. This process is called **spooling**. (The word spool is an acronym for *s*imultaneous *p*eripheral *o*perations *o*n*l*ine.) Most printing from Windows uses spooling.

If the printer port, printer cable, and printer all support bidirectional communication, the printer can communicate with Windows. For example, Windows XP can ask the printer how much printer memory is available and what fonts are installed. The printer can send messages to the OS, such as an out-of-paper or paper-jam message.

USING WINDOWS TO MANAGE PRINTERS

From the Printers and Faxes window (for Windows XP) or the Printers window (for Windows 2000 and Windows 9x/Me), you can delete printers, change the Windows default printer, purge print jobs to troubleshoot failed printing, and perform other printer maintenance tasks. For example, to manage the print jobs for a printer, double-click the printer in the Printers and Faxes window. The printer window opens, and is similar to the one in Figure 11-17. From this window, you can see the status and order of the print jobs. If the printer reports a problem with printing, it will be displayed as the status for the first job in the print queue. To cancel a single print job, right-click the job and select **Cancel** from the shortcut menu, as shown in Figure 11-17. To cancel all print jobs, click **Printer** on the menu and select **Cancel All Documents**. (For Windows 9x/Me, click **Purge Print Documents**.)

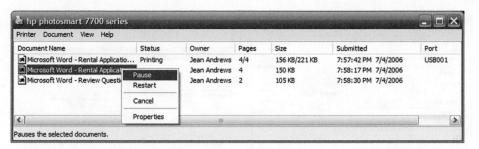

Figure 11-17 Manage print jobs using the printer window

> **Notes**
>
> When you use the Windows 2000/XP default settings, user accounts in the Everyone group are assigned the Print permission level, which means users can send documents to a printer. They cannot manage the print queue or change printer settings. Users in the Administrator and Power User groups are assigned the Manage Printers permission level, which means they have complete control over a printer, including printer settings and the print queue. A third permission level, Manage Documents, can be assigned to a user so that the user can manage the print queue while not being allowed to change printer settings.

The Printers and Faxes or Printers window can also be used to manage printer settings and options. For example, a printer that supports automatically printing on both sides of the paper (called duplex printing) needs to be configured in Windows to use this feature. On the printer's Properties window, click the **Configure** tab, shown in Figure 11-18. On this window, to enable duplexing, check **Duplexing Unit**. (Also notice the Mopier Enabled option on this window, which is the ability to print and collate multiple copies of a single print job.) To apply your changes, click **Apply** and then click **OK** to close the window. Now, when a user attempts to print from an application, the Print window gives the option to print on both sides of the paper. For example, when a user attempts to print a Word document, the Print window shown in Figure 11-19 appears. To print on both sides of the paper, the user can click **Properties** and then check **Print on Both Sides** in the window on the right side of Figure 11-19.

Figure 11-18 Configure printer options and settings using the printer's Properties window

A+ ESS
3.3
4.2

A+
220-602
3.3
4.2

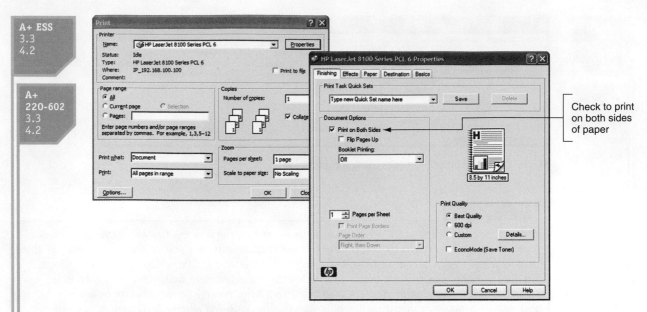

Figure 11-19 Printing on both sides of the paper

A printer might be able to accommodate different types of input trays and feeders for various envelopes, oversized paper, colored paper, transparencies, and other media. In addition, you can install on the printer staplers, sorters, stackers, binders, and output trays so that the printer can sort output by user (called mailboxes). After you have physically installed one of these devices, use the printer properties window to enable it. For example, suppose you have installed a 3,000-sheet stapler and stacker unit on the printer whose properties window is shown in Figure 11-18. To enable this equipment, in the drop-down list of Optional Paper Destinations, select **HP 3000-Sheet Stapler/Stacker** and click **Apply** (see Figure 11-20). Compare the picture of the printer in Figure 11-18 to the picture in Figure 11-20 where the equipment is enabled and drawn into the printer picture. After the equipment is enabled, when a user prints, the equipment is listed as an option in the Print window.

After this new equipment is installed or you have enabled a printer feature, users might see additional options available when they are printing. For example, when a user prints using Microsoft Word, the Print dialog box opens for the user to make selections for the print job. When the user clicks **Properties**, the printer properties dialog box opens. When the user clicks the **Paper** tab, she can then select the source tray for the print job, as shown in Figure 11-21.

Figure 11-20 Optional printer equipment has been installed by Windows

Figure 11-21 Select the source tray for print jobs

Some printers give you the option to install additional memory to hold fonts and print job buffers or a hard drive can be installed in some printers to give additional printer storage space. See the printer reference manual to find out how to install more memory or an internal hard drive. Most likely, you will use a screwdriver to remove a cover plate on the printer to expose a cavity where memory or a drive can be installed. After this equipment is installed, you must enable and configure it using the printer properties window. For example, for the HP 8100 printer properties window shown in Figure 11-18, when you click **More** under Other Options, the More Configuration Options dialog box opens, as shown in Figure 11-22. Using this dialog box, you can enable and configure the amount of additional printer memory or the size of a hard drive that you have just installed.

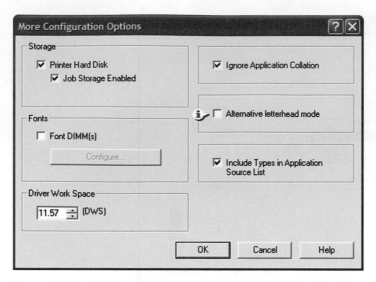

Figure 11-22 Enable and configure newly installed printer memory and hard drive

If a printer is giving you problems or you want to upgrade the printer drivers to add new functionality, search the printer manufacturer's Web site for the latest drivers for your printer and operating system. Download the drivers to a folder on the hard drive, such as C:\Downloads\Printer, and then double-click the driver file to extract files and launch the installation program to update the printer drivers.

INSTALLING A SCANNER

In this part of the chapter, you'll learn how to install a scanner. Scanners can use a variety of technologies, such as the flat-bed scanner shown in Figure 11-23. However, regardless of the type scanner, the Windows installation works about the same.

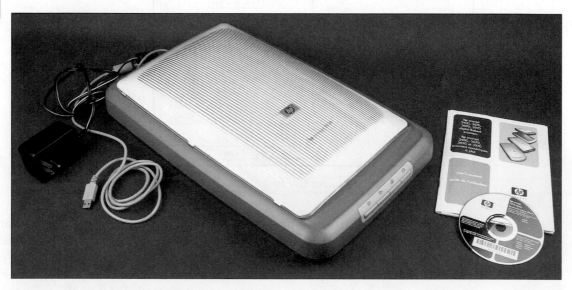

Figure 11-23 The HP Scanjet 3970 is a type of flat-bed scanner

A+ ESS
4.2

A+
220-602
4.3
4.4

The most common type of connector for a scanner intended to be used with a desktop system is a USB port, which means the scanner is hot-pluggable. Here are general directions for installing a scanner:

1. Read the manufacturer setup instructions and follow them in detail rather than using the general directions here. For USB scanners or other scanners that are hot-pluggable, most likely you'll be told to first run the setup CD before connecting the scanner.

2. Log on to the Windows 2000/XP system as an administrator.

3. Launch the setup program on the scanner setup CD and follow the onscreen instructions to install device drivers and other software. Figure 11-24 shows the main menu of one installation program for an HP scanner.

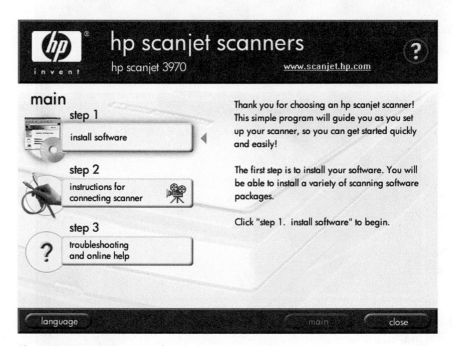

Figure 11-24 Main menu of a scanner setup program

4. Connect the scanner, plug it up, and turn it on.

5. Test the scanner by scanning a document or picture and saving it to a file. To scan an item, you can use the software that came bundled with the scanner or you can press a button on the front of the scanner. Generally, you have more control over scanning when you use the software rather than the buttons. For example, for one scanner, you launch the scanner software that displays a menu shown in Figure 11-25. To scan a picture, place the picture face down on the glass surface of the scanner and click **Scan Picture**.

6. The next window shows a preview of the scanned image (see Figure 11-26). Adjust the area of the page you want to scan and select your output type. Then click **Accept**. The scanner rescans and saves the image to a file. You can select the file format on the next window.

Figure 11-25   Scanner software main menu

Figure 11-26   Make adjustments before the final scan is made

Notes

Remember that you should not unplug or plug in a USB device into a USB port without first powering down or unplugging the device, turning off the device, or disconnecting it from its power source.

For older scanners that use a serial or parallel port, first power down your PC and connect the scanner. Then restart your PC. The Found New Hardware Wizard should launch and you can then install the software. For some products, the scanner installation instructions might tell you to first install the scanner drivers from the setup CD before connecting the scanner.

TROUBLESHOOTING PRINTERS AND SCANNERS

A+ ESS
1.3
3.3
4.3

A+
220-602
1.2
3.3
4.3
4.4

This section first discusses general printer troubleshooting and then explains how to troubleshoot problems with scanners. In these sections, you'll learn some general and specific troubleshooting tips. If you exhaust this list and still have a problem, turn to the manufacturer's Web site for additional information and support.

APPLYING | CONCEPTS Jill is the PC support technician responsible for supporting 10 users, their peer-to-peer network, printers, and computers. Everything was working fine when Jill left work one evening, but the next morning three users meet her at the door, complaining that they cannot print to the network printer and that important work must be printed by noon. What do you think are the first three things Jill should check?

As with all computer problems, begin troubleshooting by interviewing the user, finding out what works and doesn't work, and making an initial determination of the problem. When you think the problem is solved, ask the user to check things out to make sure he is satisfied with your work. And, after the problem is solved, be sure to document the symptoms of the problem and what you did to solve it.

PRINTER DOES NOT PRINT

When a printer does not print, the problem can be caused by the printer, the PC hardware or OS, the application using the printer, the printer cable, or the network. Follow the steps in Figure 11-27 to isolate the problem.

As you can see in the figure, the problem can be isolated to one of the following areas:

◢ The printer itself
◢ Connectivity between the PC and its local printer
◢ Connectivity between the PC and a network printer
◢ The OS and printer drivers
◢ The application attempting to use the printer

The following sections address printer problems caused by all of these categories, starting with hardware.

PROBLEMS WITH THE PRINTER ITSELF

To eliminate the printer as the problem, first check that the printer is on, and then print a self-test page. For directions to print a self-test page, see the printer's user guide. For example, you might need to hold down a button or buttons on the printer's front panel. If this test page prints correctly, then the printer works correctly.

A printer test page generally prints some text, some graphics, and some information about the printer, such as the printer resolution and how much memory is installed. Verify that the information on the test page is correct. For example, if you know that the printer should have 2 MB of on-board printer memory, but the test only reports 1 MB, then there is a problem with memory. If the information reported is not correct and the printer allows you to upgrade firmware on the printer, try doing that next.

A+ ESS
1.3
3.3
4.3

A+
220-602
1.2
3.3
4.3
4.4

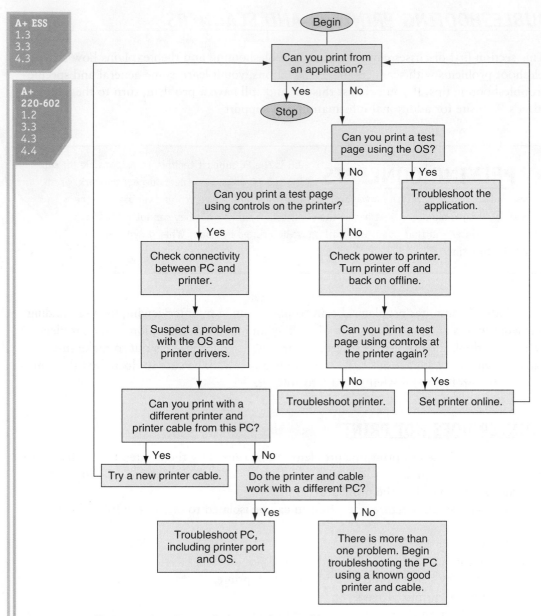

Figure 11-27   How to isolate a printer problem

If the self-test page does not print or prints incorrectly (for example, it has missing dots or smudged streaks through the page), then troubleshoot the printer until it prints correctly. Does the printer have paper? Is the paper installed correctly? Is there a paper jam? Is the paper damp or wrinkled, causing it to refuse to feed? Are the printer cover and rear access doors properly closed and locked? Try resetting the printer. For a laser printer, check that a toner cartridge is installed. For an inkjet printer, check that ink cartridges are installed. Has the protective tape been removed from the print cartridge? Check that power is getting to the printer. Try another power source. Check the user guide for the printer and the printer Web site for troubleshooting suggestions. For a laser printer, replace the toner cartridge. For inkjet printers, replace the ink cartridge. Check the service documentation and printer page count to find out if routine maintenance is due or if the printer has a history of similar problems. How to solve hardware problems with printers is not covered in this chapter.

A+ Exam Tip

The A+ Essentials exam expects you to know the importance of printing a test page when solving printer problems. You also need to know about using diagnostic tools available on the Web.

A+ ESS
1.3
3.3
4.3

A+
220-602
1.2
3.3
4.3
4.4

PROBLEMS WITH A LOCAL PRINTER CABLE OR PORT

If the printer self-test worked, but the OS printer test did not work, check for connectivity problems between the printer and the PC. For a local printer connected directly to a PC, the problem might be with the printer cable or the port the printer is using. Do the following:

◢ Check that the cable is firmly connected at both ends. For some parallel ports, you can use a screwdriver to securely anchor the cable to the parallel port with two screws on each side of the port.

◢ A business might use an older switch box (sometimes called a T-switch) to share one printer between two computers. A printer cable connects to the printer port of each computer. The two cables connect to the switch box. A third cable connects from the switch box to the printer. A switch on the front of the box controls which computer has access to the printer. Switch boxes were built with older dot matrix printers in mind. Some switch boxes are not recommended for inkjet or laser printers that use a bidirectional parallel cable, and can even damage a printer. For these printers, remove the switch box.

◢ Try a different cable. Use a shorter cable. (Parallel cables longer than 10 feet can sometimes cause problems.) Verify that a parallel cable is IEEE 1284-compliant.

◢ Try printing using the same printer and printer cable but a different PC.

◢ Enter Device Manager and verify the port the printer is using is enabled and working properly. Try another device on the same port to verify the problem is not with the port.

◢ Enter CMOS setup of the PC and check how the port is configured. Is it enabled? For a parallel port, is the port set to ECP or bidirectional? An ECP parallel port requires the use of a DMA channel, which might not be available. Try setting the port to bidirectional.

PROBLEMS WITH CONNECTIVITY FOR A NETWORK PRINTER

If the self-test page prints but the OS test page does not print and the printer is a network printer, the problem might be with connectivity between the PC on the network and the network printer. Try the following:

◢ Is the printer online?

◢ Turn the printer off and back on. Try rebooting the PC.

◢ If the printer is installed directly to one computer and shared with other computers on the network, check that you can print a test page from the computer that has the printer attached to it locally. Right-click the printer you want to test, and choose **Properties** from the shortcut menu. Click the **Print Test Page** button to send a test page to the printer.

◢ If you cannot print from the local printer, solve the problem there before attempting to print over the network.

◢ Verify that the correct default printer is selected.

◢ Return to the remote computer, and verify that you can access the computer to which the printer is attached. Go to Network Neighborhood or My Network Places, and attempt to open shared folders on the printer's computer. Perhaps you have not entered a correct user ID and password to access this computer; if so, you will be unable to use the computer's resources.

◢ Using the Printers and Faxes window, delete the printer, and then use Windows 2000/XP My Network Places or Windows 9x/Me Network Neighborhood to reconnect the printer.

◢ Is the correct network printer selected on the remote PC?

◢ Can you print to another network printer? If so, there might be a problem with the printer or its installation on the PC. Look at the printer's configuration.

◢ Is enough hard drive space available on the remote PC?

◢ For printers connected directly to the network, try pinging the printer. Try using another network port, and try using another network cable for the printer.

A+ ESS
1.3
3.3
4.3

A+
220-602
1.2
3.3
4.3
4.4

▲ Run diagnostic software provided by the printer manufacturer.

▲ If a PC cannot communicate with a network printer connected directly to the network, try installing a second network protocol that the network printer supports, such as IPX/SPX. If this works, then suspect that the firmware on the NIC is having a problem with TCP/IP. Try flashing the network printer's firmware.

PROBLEMS PRINTING FROM WINDOWS

If a self-test page works and you have already stepped through checking the printer connectivity, but you still cannot print a test page from Windows, try the following:

▲ The print spool might be stalled. Try deleting all print jobs in the printer's queue. Double-click the printer icon in the Printers and Faxes or Printers window. Select **Printer** on the menu bar, and then select **Cancel All Documents** (for Windows 2000/XP) or **Purge Print Documents** (for Windows 9x/Me). (It might take a moment for the print jobs to disappear.)

▲ Verify that the correct default printer is selected.

▲ Verify that the printer is online. See the printer documentation for information on how to determine the status from the control panel of the printer.

▲ If you still cannot print, reboot the PC. Verify that the printer cable or cable connections are solid.

▲ Try removing and reinstalling the printer driver. To uninstall the printer driver, right-click the printer icon in the Printers and Faxes or Printers window, and select **Delete**. Then reinstall the printer.

▲ Check the Web site of the printer manufacturer for an updated printer driver. Download and install the correct driver.

▲ Check Event Viewer for recorded events surrounding the printer or the port it is using. To access the log, in Control Panel, open the **Administrative Tools** applet and select **Event Viewer**. Then click **System**. For example, Figure 11-28 shows a recorded event about a print job.

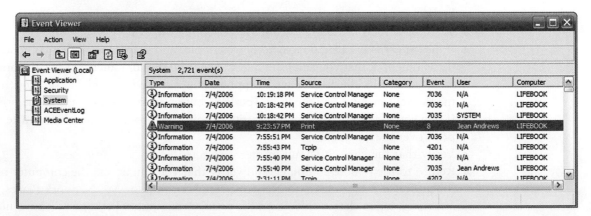

Figure 11-28 Check Event Viewer for recorded errors about the printer or its port

▲ In the printer's Properties dialog box, select the **Ports** tab (see Figure 11-29) and uncheck **Enable bidirectional support** for this printer. The PC and printer might have a problem with bidirectional communication.

▲ Verify printer properties. Try lowering the resolution.

▲ Try disabling printer spooling. On the printer's Properties dialog box, select the **Advanced** tab and then select **Print directly to the printer** (see Figure 11-30). Click **Apply**. Spooling holds print jobs in a queue for printing, so if spooling is disabled, printing from an application can be slower.

11

A+ ESS
1.3
3.3
4.3

A+
220-602
1.2
3.3
4.3
4.4

Figure 11-29 On this tab, you can enable and disable bidirectional support for a printer

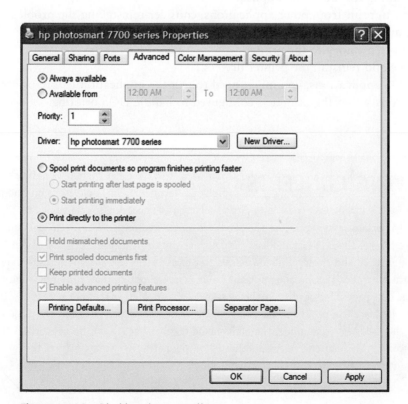

Figure 11-30 Disable printer spooling

A+ ESS
1.3
3.3
4.3

▲ If you have trouble printing from an application, you can also bypass spooling in the application by selecting the option to print to a file. Then drag that file to the icon representing your printer in the Printers and Faxes window.

▲ Verify that enough hard drive space is available for the OS to create temporary print files.

A+
220-602
1.2
3.3
4.3
4.4

▲ Use Chkdsk, Error-checking (Windows 2000/XP), or ScanDisk (Windows 9x/Me) to verify that the hard drive does not have errors. Use Defragmenter to optimize the hard drive.

▲ Boot Windows into Safe Mode and attempt to print. If this step works, there might be a conflict between the printer driver and another driver or application.

▲ Check the printer documentation for troubleshooting steps to solve printer problems. Look for diagnostic software that you can download from the printer manufacturer Web site or diagnostic routines you can run from the printer menu.

PROBLEMS PRINTING FROM APPLICATIONS

If you can print a Windows test page, but you cannot print from an application, try the following:

▲ Verify that the correct printer is selected in the Print Setup dialog box.

▲ Try printing a different application file.

▲ Delete any files in the print spool. From the Printers and Faxes or Printers window, double-click the printer icon. Click **Printer** on the menu bar of the window that opens, and then click **Cancel All Documents** or **Purge Print Documents**.

▲ Reboot the PC. Immediately enter Notepad or WordPad, type some text, and print.

▲ Reopen the application giving the print error and attempt to print again.

▲ Try creating data in a new file and printing it. Keep the data simple.

▲ Try printing from another application.

▲ If you can print from other applications, consider reinstalling the problem application.

▲ Close any applications that are not being used.

▲ Add more memory to the printer.

▲ Remove and reinstall the printer drivers.

▲ For DOS applications, you might need to exit the application before printing will work. Verify that the printer is configured to handle DOS printing.

A+ ESS
4.3

A+
220-602
1.2
4.3
4.4

APPLYING|CONCEPTS

Now back to Jill and her company's network printer problem. Generally, Jill should focus on finding out what works and what doesn't work, always remembering to check the simple things first. Jill should first go to the printer and check that the printer is online and has no error messages, such as a Paper Out message. Then, Jill should ask, "Can anyone print to this printer?" To find out, she should go to the closest PC and try to print a Windows test page. If the test page prints, she should next go to one of the three PCs that do not print and begin troubleshooting that PC's connection to the network. If the test page did not print at the closest PC, the problem is still not necessarily the printer. To eliminate the printer as the problem, the next step is to print a self-test page at the printer. If that self-test page prints, then Jill should check other PCs on the network. Is the entire network down? Can one PC see another PC on the network? Perhaps part of the network is down (maybe because of a switch or hub serving one part of the network).

TROUBLESHOOTING SCANNERS

Here are some troubleshooting tips if Windows cannot find an installed scanner or the scanner refuses to scan:

▲ Try turning off the scanner or unplugging it from its power source and then turning it back on.

▲ Try disconnecting the USB cable and then reconnecting it. If you are using a USB hub, remove the hub and connect the scanner directly to the PC.

▲ Try rebooting your computer.

▲ Is there enough free hard drive space? If necessary, clean up the hard drive.

▲ Many scanners have a repair utility and troubleshooting software that installs when the setup program runs. For example, looking back at Figure 11-24, to get help, click **troubleshooting and online help**. The resulting instructions give you suggestions of things to check. It also tells you that a repair utility is available from the Add or Remove Programs applet in Control Panel. In Control Panel, open the applet and select the scanner. Click **Change**. The installation wizard launches and gives you the opportunity to repair or remove the software (see Figure 11-31).

▲ Check the Web site of the scanner manufacturer for troubleshooting guidelines and other help. You might be able to post a question to a newsgroup on the site or start a chat session with technical support. Figure 11-32 shows help given at the HP site for one flat-bed scanner. Notice the two links to chat with an online technician and to e-mail technical support. Also notice the link to download drivers. Try downloading and installing new drivers for the scanner.

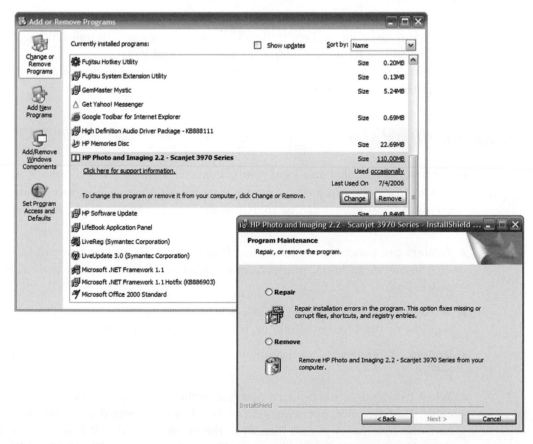

Figure 11-31 When a scanner gives problems, you can repair or remove the software

A+ ESS
4.3

A+
220-602
1.2
4.3
4.4

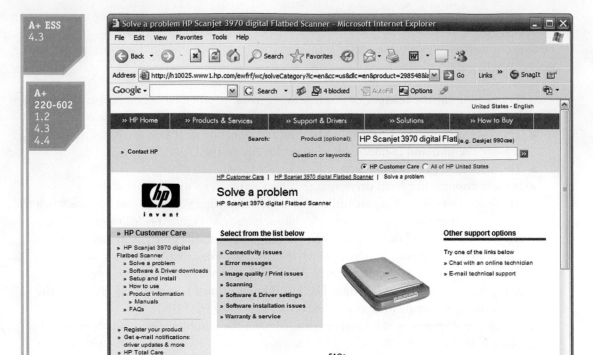

Figure 11-32   Online help for a scanner

▲ Try uninstalling and reinstalling the scanner software. To uninstall the software, use the Add or Remove Programs applet in Control Panel.

▲ Install the scanner on another computer to determine if the problem is with the computer or the scanner.

>> CHAPTER SUMMARY

▲ A printer is installed as a local printer connected directly to a computer, a network printer that works as a device on the network, or a network printer connected to a print server. A local printer can be shared so that others can use it as a resource on the network.

▲ Printers can process print jobs using PostScript, PCL (Printer Control Language), or GDI input. In addition, printers can receive raw data that can be printed with no processing.

▲ Windows manages and configures a printer using the Windows XP Printers and Faxes window or the Windows 2000 or Windows 9x/Me Printers window.

▲ Routine maintenance and cleaning help a printer or scanner to last longer and work better.

▲ When troubleshooting printers, first isolate the problem. Narrow the source to the printer, cable, PC hardware, operating system including the device driver, application software, or network. Test pages printed directly at the printer or within Windows can help narrow down the source of the problem.

>> KEY TERMS

For explanations of key terms, see the Glossary near the end of the book.

default printer	local printer	PostScript
GDI (Graphics Device Interface)	network printer	scanner
	PCL (Printer Control Language)	spooling

>> REVIEWING THE BASICS

1. What type of user account(s) must you use in Windows in order to manage the print queue?

2. What type of port will a desktop scanner most likely use?

3. What are two possible settings in CMOS for parallel port mode?

4. What two Windows components are used to share resources on a network and access those shared resources?

5. How do you share a local printer with others in the workgroup?

6. What are two ways to install a printer that is being shared by another computer on the network?

7. What company developed PostScript? PCL?

8. When you are isolating a printer problem, what are the four major possible sources of the problem?

9. How can you eliminate the printer as the source of a printing problem?

10. How can you be sure that a printer cable is not the source of a printer problem?

>> THINKING CRITICALLY

1. A Windows XP computer has a locally installed printer that you must make available to eight other Windows XP computers on the network. What is the best way to do this?

   a. Use the Add Printer icon in the Printers window for each of the eight PCs.

   b. Use My Network Places to install the printer on each of the eight PCs.

   c. Use the printer manufacturer's setup program from the printer's CD on each of the eight PCs.

   d. Install the printer on each of the eight PCs while sitting at the host PC. Use My Network Places on the host PC.

2. You are not able to print a Word document on a Windows XP computer to a network printer. The network printer is connected directly to the network, but when you look at the Printers and Faxes window, you see the name of the printer as \\SMITHWIN2K\HP LaserJet 8100. In the following list, select the possible sources of the problem.

   a. The SMITHWIN2K computer is not turned on.

   b. The HP LaserJet 8100 printer is not online.

  c. The SMITHWIN2K printer is not online.

  d. The Windows XP computer has a stalled printer spool.

  e. The HP LaserJet 8100 computer is not logged on to the workgroup.

3. You are not able to print a test page from your Windows 2000 PC to your local HP DeskJet printer. Which of the following are possible causes of the problem?

  a. The network is down.

  b. The printer cable is not connected properly.

  c. The Windows print spool is stalled.

  d. You have the wrong printer drivers installed.

  e. File and Printer Sharing is not enabled.

>> HANDS-ON PROJECTS

PROJECT 11-1: Sharing a Local Printer

Practice networking skills using Windows 2000/XP or Windows 9x/Me:

1. Share a local printer with others on the network.

2. Install a shared printer on a remote PC. Verify that you can print to the printer.

PROJECT 11-2: Researching Printer Web Sites

Your company plans to purchase a new printer, and you want to evaluate the printer manufacturers' Web sites to determine which site offers the best support. Research the Internet and answer these questions, supporting your answers with printed pages from the Web site:

1. Which Web site made it easiest for you to select a new printer based on your criteria for its use?

2. Which Web site made it easiest for you to find help for troubleshooting printer problems?

3. Which Web site gave you the best information about routine maintenance for its printers?

4. Which Web site gave you the best information about how to clean its printers?

PROJECT 11-3: Researching a Printer Maintenance Plan

You have been asked to recommend a maintenance plan for a laser printer. Search the manufacturer's Web site for information, and then write a maintenance plan. Include in the plan the tasks that need to be done, how often they need doing, and what tools and components are needed to perform the tasks. Use the Hewlett-Packard LaserJet 8100 DN printer unless your instructor tells you to use a different printer, perhaps one that is available in your lab.

>> REAL PROBLEMS, REAL SOLUTIONS

REAL PROBLEM 11-1:   Selecting a Color Printer for a Small Business

Jack owns a small real estate firm and has come to you asking for help with his printing needs. Currently, he has a color inkjet printer that he is using to print flyers, business cards, brochures, and other marketing materials. However, he is not satisfied with the print quality and wants to invest in a printer that produces more professional-looking hard copy. He expects to print no more than 8,000 sheets per month and needs the ability to print envelopes, letter-size and legal-size pages, and business cards. He wants to be able to automatically print on both sides of a legal-size page to produce a three-column brochure. Research printer solutions and do the following:

1. Print Web pages showing three printers to present to Jack that satisfy his needs. Include at least one laser printer and at least one other printer technology other than laser in your selections.

2. Print Web pages showing the routine maintenance requirements of these printers.

3. Print Web pages showing all the consumable products (other than paper) that Jack should expect to have to purchase in the first year of use.

4. Calculate the initial cost of the equipment and the total cost of consumables for one year (other than paper) for each printer solution.

5. Prepare a list of advantages and disadvantages for each solution.

6. Based on your research, which of the three solutions do you recommend? Why?

The Professional PC Technician

As a professional PC technician, you can manage your career by staying abreast of new technology, using every available resource to do your job well, and striving for top professional certifications. In addition, you should maintain excellent customer relationships and know how to communicate well and behave with professionalism. As you know, PC technicians provide service to customers over the phone or online, in person on-site, and sometimes in a shop where they have little customer contact. Although each setting poses specific challenges, almost all the recommendations in this chapter apply across the board.

> ✎ **Notes**
>
> If you meet someone who doesn't have a smile, give them yours.

JOB ROLES AND RESPONSIBILITIES

As a PC troubleshooter, you might have to solve a problem on your own PC or for someone else. As a PC technician, you might fulfill four different job functions:

- ▲ *PC support technician.* A PC support technician works on-site, closely interacting with users, and is responsible for ongoing PC maintenance. Of the four technician types listed here, a PC support technician is the only one responsible for the PC before trouble occurs, and, therefore, is able to prepare for a problem by keeping good records and maintaining backups (or teaching users how to do so). Some job titles that fall into this category include enterprise technician, IT administrator, PC technician, support technician, and PC support specialist.
- ▲ *PC service technician.* A PC service technician goes to a customer site in response to a service call and, if possible, repairs a PC on-site. PC service technicians are usually not responsible for ongoing PC maintenance but usually do interact with users. Other job titles might include field technician or field service technician.
- ▲ *Bench technician.* A bench technician works in a lab environment, might not interact with users of the PCs being repaired, and is not permanently responsible for them. Bench technicians probably don't work at the site where the PC is kept. They might be able to interview the user to get information about the problem, or they might simply receive a PC to repair without being able to talk to the user. A bench technician is sometimes called a depot technician.
- ▲ *Help-desk technician.* A help-desk technician provides telephone or online support. Help-desk technicians, who do not have physical access to the PC, are at the greatest disadvantage of the four types of technicians. They can interact with users only over the phone and must obviously use different tools and approaches than technicians at the PC. Other job titles in this category include remote support technician and call center technician.

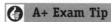 **A+ Exam Tip**

Presently, there are three A+ advanced exams: A+ 220-602 certifies a person to be a PC support technician or PC service technician, A+ 220-603 certifies a person to be a help-desk technician, and A+ 220-604 certifies a person to be a bench technician. For certification, you must also pass the A+ Essentials exam.

This chapter emphasizes the job of the on-site PC support technician. However, the special needs and perspectives of the service technician, bench technician, and help-desk technician are also addressed. Now let's look at the need to be certified, and then we'll look at the recordkeeping and information tools needed by a technician. Then, we'll turn our attention to what customers want and expect from PC support technicians beyond their technical know-how.

CERTIFICATIONS AND PROFESSIONAL ORGANIZATIONS

Many people work as PC technicians without any formal classroom training or certification. However, by having certification or an advanced technical degree, you prove to yourself, your customers, and your employers that you are prepared to do the work and are committed to being educated in your chosen profession. Certification and advanced degrees serve as recognized proof of competence and achievement, improve your job opportunities, create a higher level of customer confidence, and often qualify you for other training or degrees.

The most significant certifying organization for PC technicians is the Computing Technology Industry Association (CompTIA, pronounced "comp-TEE-a"). CompTIA sponsors the A+ Certification Program and manages the exams. The CompTIA home page for A+ Certification is *http://certification.comptia.org/a* and is shown in Figure 12-1. Follow the *Download exam objectives* link on this page to get the list of objectives for the exams. To become certified, all individuals must pass the A+ Essentials exam that covers content on hardware, operating systems, security, and soft skills (skills involving relationships with people). Passing the A+ Essentials exam validates entry-level skills in any PC repair job.

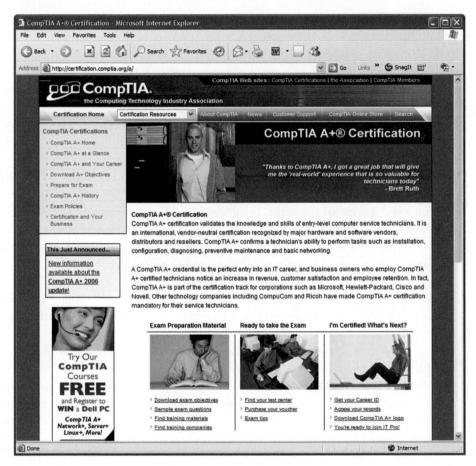

Figure 12-1 CompTIA A+ Certification Web page

In addition to passing the A+ Essentials exam, you must also pass one of the following advanced exams:

- A+ 220-602, which grants you the IT Technician designation
- A+ 220-603, which grants you the Remote Support Technician designation
- A+ 220-604, which grants you the Depot Technician designation

A+ Certification has industry recognition, so it should be your first choice for certification as a PC technician. CompTIA has more than 13,000 members from every major company that manufactures, distributes, or publishes computer-related products and services. For more information about CompTIA and A+ Certification, see the CompTIA Web site at *www.comptia.org*.

Other certifications are more vendor specific. For example, Microsoft, Novell, and Cisco offer certifications to use and support their products. These are excellent choices for additional certifications when your career plan is to focus on these products.

In addition to becoming certified and seeking advanced degrees, the professional PC technician should also stay abreast of new technology. Helpful resources include on-the-job training, books, magazines, the Internet, trade shows, interaction with colleagues, seminars, and workshops. One popular trade show is Interop by CMP Media (*www.interop.com*), where you can view the latest technology, hear industry leaders speak, and network with vast numbers of organizations and people.

RECORDKEEPING AND INFORMATION TOOLS

A+ ESS
1.3
3.3

If you work for a service organization, it will probably have most of the tools you need to do your job, including forms, online recordkeeping, procedures, and manuals. In some cases, help-desk support personnel might have software to help them do their jobs, such as programs that support the remote control of customers' PCs (such as Control-F1 by Blueloop and Windows XP Remote Assistance, which you learned about in Chapter 4), an online help utility, or a problem-solving tool developed specifically for their help desk.

Several types of resources, records, and information tools can help you support PCs, such as the following:

◢ The specific software or hardware you support must be available to you to test, observe, and study and to use to re-create a customer's problem whenever possible.

◢ You need a copy of the same documentation the user sees and should be familiar with that documentation.

◢ Hardware and software products generally have more **technical documentation** than just a user manual. A company should make this technical documentation available to you when you support its product.

◢ Online help targeted to field technicians and help-desk technicians is often available for a product. This online help will probably include a search engine that searches by topics, words, error messages, and the like.

◢ **Expert systems** software is designed and written to help solve problems. It uses databases of known facts and rules to simulate human experts' reasoning and decision making. Expert systems for PC technicians work by posing questions about a problem to be answered by the technician or the customer. The response to each question triggers another question from the software, until the expert system arrives at a possible solution or solutions. Many expert systems are "intelligent," meaning the system will record your input and use it in subsequent sessions to select more questions to ask and approaches to try.

◢ **Call tracking** can be done online or on paper. Most organizations have a call-tracking system that tracks: (1) the date, time, and length of help-desk or on-site calls; (2) causes of and solutions to problems already addressed; (3) who did what and when; and (4) how each call was officially resolved. Call-tracking software or documents can also help to escalate calls when necessary and track the escalation.

WHAT CUSTOMERS WANT: BEYOND TECHNICAL KNOW-HOW

A+ ESS
8.1
8.2

A+
220-602
8.1
8.2

Probably the most significant indication that a PC technician is doing a good job is that customers are consistently satisfied. You should provide excellent service and treat customers as you would want to be treated in a similar situation. One of the most important ways to achieve customer satisfaction is to do your best by being prepared, both technically and non-technically. Being prepared includes knowing what customers want, what they don't like, and what they expect from a PC technician.

Your customers can be "internal" (you both work for the same company, in which case you might consider the customer your colleague) or "external" (your customers come to you or your company for service). Customers can be highly technical or technically naive,

A+ ESS
8.1
8.2

A+
220-602
8.1
8.2

represent a large company or simply own a home PC, be prompt or slow at paying their bills, want only the best (and be willing to pay for it) or be searching for bargain service, be friendly and easy to work with or demanding and condescending. In each situation, the key to success is always the same: Don't allow circumstances or personalities to affect your commitment to excellence.

The following traits distinguish one competent technician from another in the eyes of the customer:

▲ *Have a positive and helpful attitude*. This helps establish good customer relationships. You communicate your attitude in your tone of voice, the words you choose, how you use eye contact, your facial expressions, how you dress, and in many other subjective and subtle ways. Generally, your attitudes toward your customers stem from how you see people, how you see yourself, and how you see your job.

▲ *Own the problem*. Taking ownership of the customer's problem builds trust and loyalty because the customer knows you can be counted on.

▲ *Be dependable*. Customers appreciate those who do as they say. If you promise to be back at 10:00 the next morning, be back at 10:00 the next morning. If you cannot keep your appointment, never ignore your promise. Call, apologize, let the customer know what happened, and reschedule your appointment.

▲ *Be customer-focused*. When you're working with or talking to a customer, focus on him or her. Make it your job to satisfy this person, not just your organization, your boss, your bank account, or the customer's boss. For example, when talking with a customer, be a good communicator and learn to listen carefully to what he or she is saying without interrupting.

▲ *Be credible*. Convey confidence to your customers. Being credible means being technically competent and knowing how to do your job well, but credible technicians also know when the job is beyond their expertise and when to ask for help.

▲ *Maintain integrity and honesty*. Don't try to hide your mistakes from your customer or your boss. Everyone makes mistakes, but don't compound them by a lack of integrity. Accept responsibility and do what you can to correct the error.

▲ *Know the law with respect to your work*. For instance, observe the laws concerning the use of software. Don't use or install pirated software.

▲ *Act professionally*. Customers want a technician to look and behave professionally. Dress appropriately for the environment. Consider yourself a guest at the customer's site. If a customer is angry, allow the customer to vent, keeping your own professional distance. (You do, however, have the right to expect a customer not to talk to you in an abusive way.)

▲ *Perform your work in a professional manner*. Troubleshoot the problem in a systematic way that portrays confidence and credibility. Get the job done and do it with excellence. Fill out the paperwork accurately and on time.

> **Notes**
>
> Your customers might never remember what you said or what you did, but they will always remember how you made them feel.

SUPPORT CALLS: PROVIDING GOOD SERVICE

Customers want good service. Even though each customer is different and might expect different results, the following characteristics constitute good service in the eyes of most customers:

▲ The technician responds and completes the work within a reasonable time.
▲ For on-site visits, the technician is prepared for the service call.
▲ The work is done right the first time.

A+ ESS
8.1
8.2

A+
220-602
8.1
8.2

▲ The price for the work is reasonable and competitive.

▲ The technician exhibits good interpersonal skills.

▲ If the work extends beyond a brief on-site visit or phone call, the technician keeps the customer informed about the progress of the work.

In the following sections of the chapter, you'll learn how to plan a good service call that is sure to satisfy your customers, how to make a good service call, and how to provide phone support. Because you won't be able to solve every problem you face, you'll also learn how to support customers when you can't fix their problems.

PLANNING FOR GOOD SERVICE

Whether you support customers and their computers on the phone or online, on-site, or in a shop, you need a plan to follow when you approach a service call. This section surveys the entire service situation, from the first contact with the customer to closing the call. Follow these general guidelines when supporting computers and their users:

▲ Almost every support project starts with a phone call or an Internet chat session. Follow company policies to obtain the specific information you should take when answering an initial call.

▲ Don't assume that an on-site visit is necessary until you have asked questions to identify the problem and asked the caller to check and try some simple things while on the phone with you. For example, the customer can check cable connections, power, and monitor settings and can look for POST error messages.

▲ Be familiar with your company's customer service policies. You might need to refer questions about warranties, licenses, documentation, or procedures to other support personnel or customer relations personnel. Your organization might not want you to answer some questions, such as questions about upcoming releases of software or new products or questions about your personal or company experience with supporting particular hardware or software.

▲ After reviewing your company's service policies, begin troubleshooting. Take notes, and then interview the customer about the problem so that you understand it thoroughly. Have the customer reproduce the problem, and carefully note each step taken and its results. This process gives you clues about the problem and about the customer's technical proficiency, which helps you know how to communicate with the customer.

▲ Search for answers. If the answers to specific questions or problems are not evident, become a researcher. Learn to use online documentation, expert systems, and other resources your company provides.

▲ Use your troubleshooting skills. Isolate the problem. Check for user errors. What works and what doesn't work? What has changed since the system last worked? Reduce the system to its essentials. Check the simple things first. Use the troubleshooting guidelines throughout this book to help you think of approaches to test and try.

▲ If you have given the problem your best, but still haven't solved it, ask for help. You learn when to ask for help from experience. After you have made a reasonable effort to help, and it seems clear you are unlikely to be successful, don't waste a customer's time.

▲ When you think you've solved the problem, allow the customer to decide when the service is finished to his or her satisfaction. Generally, the customer ends the call or chat session, not the technician.

▲ After a call, create a written record to build your own knowledge base. Record the initial symptoms of the problem, the source of the problem you actually discovered, how you made that discovery, and how the problem was finally solved. File your documentation according to symptoms or according to solutions.

A+ ESS
1.3
3.3
8.1
8.2

A+
220-602
8.1
8.2

MAKING AN ON-SITE SERVICE CALL

When a technician makes an on-site service call, customers expect him or her to have both technical and interpersonal skills. Prepare for a service call by reviewing information given you by whoever took the call. Know the problem you are going to address, the urgency of the situation, and what computer, software, and hardware need servicing. Arrive with a complete set of equipment appropriate to the visit, which might include a tool kit, flashlight, multimeter, grounding strap and mat, and bootable CDs.

INTERACTING WITH THE CUSTOMER

Set a realistic time for the appointment (one that you can expect to keep) and arrive on time. When you arrive at the customer's site, greet the customer in a friendly manner. Use Mr. or Ms. and last names rather than first names when addressing the customer, unless you are certain the customer expects you to use first names. The first thing you should do is listen; save the paperwork for later.

As you work, be as unobtrusive as possible. Don't make a big mess. Keep your tools and papers out of the customer's way. Don't use the phone or sit in the customer's desk chair without permission. If the customer needs to work while you are present, do whatever is necessary to accommodate that.

Ask the user questions to learn as much as you can about the problem. Refer to Chapter 4 for several sample questions, the most important being, "Can you show me how to reproduce the problem?" What procedure was taking place at the time? What had just happened? What recent changes did the user make? When did the computer last work? What has happened in the meantime? What error messages did the user see? Ask the user to listen while you repeat the problem to make sure you understand it correctly. Re-create the circumstances that existed when the computer stopped in as much detail as you can. Make no assumptions. All users make simple mistakes and then overlook them. And before you begin work, be sure to ask the very important question, "Does the system hold important data that is not backed up?"

Use diplomacy and good manners when you work with a user to solve a problem. For example, if you suspect that the user dropped the PC, don't ask, "Did you drop the PC?" Put the question in a less accusatory manner: "Could the PC have been dropped?" If the user is sitting in front of the PC, don't assume you can take over the keyboard or mouse without permission. Also, if the user is present, ask permission before you make a software or hardware change, even if the user has just given you permission to interact with the PC.

When working at a user's desk, consider yourself a guest and follow these general guidelines:

> ▲ Don't take over the mouse or keyboard from the user without permission.
> ▲ Ask permission again before you use the printer or other equipment.
> ▲ Don't use the phone without permission.
> ▲ Don't pile your belongings and tools on top of the user's papers, books, and so forth.
> ▲ Accept personal inconvenience to accommodate the user's urgent business needs. For example, if the user gets an important call while you are working, delay your work until the call is over.

> **A+ Tip**
>
> The A+ Essentials and A+ 220-602 exams expect you to know how to communicate with a user and how to respond when the user is angry.

A+ ESS
1.3
3.3
8.1
8.2

A+
220-602
8.1
8.2

Whether or not you are at the user's desk, you should follow these guidelines for good communication with the user:

▲ When you ask the user to describe the problem, be a good listener. Don't interrupt. If you don't understand exactly what the user is telling you, ask him or her to repeat it or ask good questions.

▲ When talking, use clear, concise, and direct statements.

▲ Don't talk down to or patronize the user. Don't make the user feel he or she is inferior.

▲ If the problem is simple to solve, don't make the user feel he or she has wasted your time. The user should always be made to feel that the problem is important to you.

▲ Don't use techie language or acronyms the user might not understand.

▲ Don't take drastic action, such as formatting the hard drive, before you ask the user about important data that might not be backed up.

▲ Provide users with alternatives where appropriate before making decisions for them.

▲ Protect the confidentiality of data on the PC, such as business financial information.

▲ Don't disparage the user's choice of computer hardware or software. Don't be judgmental or insulting.

▲ Don't be rude and answer your cell phone while the customer is speaking with you. Avoid unnecessary interruptions.

▲ If you make a mistake or must pass the problem on to someone with more expertise, be honest.

In some PC support situations, it is appropriate to consider yourself a support to the user as well as to the PC. Your goals can include educating the user as well as repairing the computer. If you want users to learn something from a problem they caused, explain how to fix the problem and walk them through the process if necessary. Don't fix the problem yourself unless they ask you to. It takes a little longer to train the user, but it is more productive in the end because the user learns more and is less likely to repeat the mistake.

WHEN THE CUSTOMER IS INVOLVED WITH SOLVING THE PROBLEM

If the problem is caused by hardware or software, keep the customer informed as you work. Explain the problem and what you must do to fix it, giving as many details as the customer wants. When a customer must make a choice, state the options in a way that does not unfairly favor the solution that makes the most money for you as the technician or for your company.

AFTER THE PROBLEM IS SOLVED

After you have solved the problem:

▲ Allow the customer enough time to be fully satisfied that all is working before you close the call. Does the printer work? Print a test page. Does the network connection work? Can the customer log on to the network and access data on it?

▲ If you backed up data before working on the problem and then restored the data from backups, ask the user to verify that the data is fully restored.

▲ If you changed anything on the PC after you booted it, reboot one more time to make sure you have not caused a problem with the boot.

▲ Review the service call with the customer. Summarize the instructions and explanations you have given during the call. This is an appropriate time to fill out your paperwork and explain to the customer what you have written.

A+ ESS
1.3
3.3
8.1
8.2

A+
220-602
8.1
8.2

A+ ESS
8.1
8.2

▲ Explain preventive maintenance to the customer (such as deleting temporary files from the hard drive or cleaning the mouse). Most customers don't have preventive maintenance contracts for their PCs and appreciate the time you take to show them how they can take better care of their computers.

PHONE SUPPORT

When someone calls asking for support, you must control the call, especially at the beginning. Follow these steps at the beginning of a service call:

▲ Identify yourself and your organization. (Follow the guidelines of your employer on what to say.)
▲ Ask for and write down the name and phone number of the caller. Ask for spelling if necessary. If your help desk supports businesses, get the name of the business the caller represents.
▲ Your company might require that you obtain a licensing or warranty number to determine whether the customer is entitled to receive your support free of charge or that you obtain a credit card number, if the customer is paying for the call. Get whatever information you need at this point to determine that you should be the one to provide service, before you start to address the problem.
▲ Open up the conversation for the caller to describe the problem.

Phone support requires more interaction with customers than any other type of PC support. To give clear instructions, you must be able to visualize what the customer sees at his or her PC. Patience is required if the customer must be told each key to press or command button to click. Help-desk support requires excellent communication skills, good phone manners, and lots of patience. As your help-desk skills improve, you will learn to think through the process as though you were sitting in front of the PC yourself. Drawing diagrams and taking notes as you talk can be very helpful.

If you spend many hours on the phone at a help desk, use a headset similar to the one shown in Figure 12-2 instead of a regular phone to reduce strain on your ears and neck. (Investing in a high-quality headset will be worth the money.)

Figure 12-2   Help-desk technicians can benefit from a hands-free headset

A+ ESS
8.1
8.2

A+
220-602
8.1
8.2

If your call is accidentally disconnected, call back immediately. Don't eat or drink while on the phone. If you must put callers on hold, tell them how long it will be before you get back to them. Don't complain about your job, your company, or other companies or products to your customers. A little small talk is okay and is sometimes beneficial in easing a tense situation, but keep it upbeat and positive. As with on-site service calls, let the user make sure all is working before you close the phone call. If you end the call too soon and the problem is not completely resolved, the customer can be frustrated, especially if it is difficult to contact you again.

WHEN THE CUSTOMER IS NOT KNOWLEDGEABLE

A help-desk call is the most difficult situation to handle when a customer is not knowledgeable about how to use a computer. When on-site, you can put a PC in good repair without depending on a customer to help you, but when you are trying to solve a problem over the phone, with a customer as your only eyes, ears, and hands, a computer-illiterate user can present a challenge. Here are some tips for handling this situation:

- Don't use computer jargon while talking. For example, instead of saying, "Open Windows Explorer," say, "Using your mouse, right-click the Start button and select Explore from the menu."
- Don't ask the customer to do something that might destroy settings or files without first having the customer back them up carefully. If you think the customer can't handle your request, ask for some on-site help.
- Frequently ask the customer what the screen displays to help you track the keystrokes and action.
- Follow along at your own PC. It's easier to direct the customer, keystroke by keystroke, if you are doing the same things.
- Give the customer plenty of opportunity to ask questions.
- Compliment the customer whenever you can to help the customer gain confidence.
- If you determine that the customer cannot help you solve the problem without a lot of coaching, you might need to tactfully request that the caller have someone with more experience call you.

> **Notes**
>
> When solving computer problems in an organization other than your own, check with technical support instead of working only with the PC user. The user might not be aware of policies that have been set on the PC to prevent changes to the OS, hardware, or applications.

WHEN THE CUSTOMER IS OVERLY CONFIDENT

Sometimes customers are proud of their computer knowledge. Such customers might want to give advice, take charge of a call, withhold information they think you don't need to know, or execute commands at the computer without letting you know, so you don't have enough information to follow along. A situation like this must be handled with tact and respect for the customer. Here are a few tips:

- When you can, compliment the customer's knowledge, experience, or insight.
- Show respect for the customer's knowledge. For example, you can ask the customer's advice. Say something like, "What do you think the problem is?" (However, don't ask this question of customers who are not confident because they most likely don't have the answer and might lose confidence in you.)
- Slow the conversation down. You can say, "Please slow down. You're moving too fast for me to follow. Help me understand."

A+ ESS
8.1
8.2

A+
220-602
8.1
8.2

- Don't back off from using problem-solving skills. You must still have the customer check the simple things, but direct the conversation with tact. For example, you can say, "I know you've probably already gone over these simple things, but could we just do them again together?"
- Be careful not to accuse the customer of making a mistake.
- Use technical language in a way that conveys you expect the customer to understand you.

WHEN THE CUSTOMER COMPLAINS

When you are on-site or on the phone, a customer might complain to you about your organization, products, or service or the service and product of another company. Consider the complaint to be helpful feedback that can lead to a better product or service and better customer relationships. Here are a few suggestions on how to handle complaints and customer anger:

- Be an active listener, and let customers know they are not being ignored. Look for the underlying problem. Don't take the complaint or the anger personally.
- Give the customer a little time to vent, and apologize when you can. Then start the conversation from the beginning, asking questions, taking notes, and solving problems. Unless you must have the information for problem solving, don't spend a lot of time finding out exactly whom the customer dealt with and what happened to upset the customer.
- Don't be defensive. It's better to leave the customer with the impression that you and your company are listening and willing to admit mistakes. No matter how much anger is expressed, resist the temptation to argue or become defensive.
- Know how your employer wants you to handle a situation where you are verbally abused. If this type of language is happening, you might say something like this in a very calm tone of voice: "I'm sorry, but my employer does not require me to accept this kind of talk."
- If the customer is complaining about a product or service that is not from your company, don't start off by saying, "That's not our problem." Instead, listen to the customer complain. Don't appear as though you don't care.
- If the complaint is against you or your product, identify the underlying problem if you can. Ask questions and take notes. Then pass these notes on to people in your organization who need to know.
- Sometimes simply making progress or reducing the problem to a manageable state reduces the customer's anxiety. As you are talking to a customer, summarize what you have both agreed on or observed so far in the conversation.
- Point out ways that you think communication could be improved. For example, you might say, "I'm sorry, but I'm having trouble understanding what you want. Could you please slow down, and let's take this one step at a time."

WHEN THE CUSTOMER DOESN'T WANT TO END A PHONE CALL

Some customers like to talk and don't want to end a phone call. In this situation, when you have finished the work and are ready to hang up, you can ease the caller into the end of the call. Ask if anything needs more explanation. Briefly summarize the main points of the call, and then say something like, "That about does it. Call if you need more help." Be silent about new issues. Answer only with yes or no. Don't take the bait by engaging in a new topic. Don't get frustrated. As a last resort, you can say, "I'm sorry, but I must go now."

A+ ESS
8.1
8.2

A+
220-602
8.1
8.2

WHEN YOU CAN'T SOLVE THE PROBLEM

You are not going to solve every computer problem you encounter. Knowing how to escalate a problem to those higher in the support chain is one of the first things you should learn on a new job. When escalation involves the customer, generally follow these guidelines:

▲ Before you escalate, first ask knowledgeable coworkers for suggestions for solving the problem, which might save you and your customer the time and effort it takes to escalate it.

▲ Know your company's policy for escalation. What documents do you fill out? Who gets them? Do you remain the responsible "support" party, or does the person now addressing the problem become the new contact? Are you expected to keep in touch with the customer and the problem, or are you totally out of the picture?

▲ Document the escalation. It's very important to include the detailed steps necessary to reproduce the problem, which can save the next support person lots of time.

▲ Pass the problem on according to the proper channels of your organization. This might mean a phone call, an online entry in a database, or an e-mail message.

▲ Tell the customer you are passing the problem on to someone who is more experienced and has access to more extensive resources. In most cases, the person who receives the escalation will immediately contact the customer and assume responsibility for the problem. However, you should follow through, at least to confirm that the new person and the customer have made contact.

▲ If you check back with the customer only to find out that the other support person has not called or followed through to the customer's satisfaction, don't lay blame or point fingers. Just do whatever you can to help within your company guidelines. Your call to the customer will go a long way toward helping the situation.

PROTECTING SOFTWARE COPYRIGHTS

As a computer support technician, you will be faced with the legal issues and practices surrounding the distribution of software. When someone purchases software from a software vendor, that person has only purchased a license for the software, which is the right to use it. The buyer does not legally *own* the software and, therefore, does not have the right to distribute it. The right to copy the work, called a copyright, belongs to the creator of the work or others to whom the creator transfers this right.

As a PC technician, you will be called upon to install, upgrade, and customize software. You need to know your responsibilities in upholding the law, especially as it applies to software copyrights. Copyrights are intended to legally protect the intellectual property rights of organizations or individuals to creative works, which include books, images, and software. While the originator of a creative work is the original owner of a copyright, the copyright can be transferred from one entity to another.

FEDERAL COPYRIGHT ACT OF 1976

The Federal Copyright Act of 1976 was designed in part to protect software copyrights by requiring that only legally obtained copies of software be used; the law also allows for one backup copy of software to be made. Making unauthorized copies of original software violates the Federal Copyright Act of 1976 and is called software piracy or, more officially, software copyright infringement. Making a copy of software and then selling it or giving it away is a violation of the law. Because it is so easy to do, and because so many people do it, many people don't realize that it's illegal. Normally, only the person who violated the copyright law is liable for infringement; however, in some cases, an employer or supervisor is also held responsible, even when the copies were made without the employer's knowledge. The Business Software Alliance (*www.bsa.org*) is a membership organization of software manufacturers and vendors, which has estimated that 26 percent of the business software in the United States is obtained illegally.

By purchasing a site license, a company can obtain the right to use multiple copies of software, which is a popular way for companies to provide software to employees. With this type of license, companies can distribute software to PCs from network servers or execute software directly off the server. Read the licensing agreement of any software to determine the terms of distribution.

INDUSTRY ASSOCIATIONS

One of two associations committed to the prevention of software piracy is the Software Information Industry Association, a nonprofit organization that educates the public and enforces copyright laws. Its Web address is *www.siia.net*, and its antipiracy hotline is 1-800-388-7478. The other organization, the Business Software Alliance, manages the BSA Anti-Piracy Hotline at 1-888-NOPIRACY. The BSA can also be reached at its e-mail address: *software@bsa.org*. Its Web site is *www.bsa.org*. These associations are made up of hundreds of software manufacturers and publishers in North and Latin America, Europe, and Asia. They promote software raids on large and small companies; in the United States, they receive the cooperation of the U.S. government to prosecute offenders.

Vendors might sometimes sell counterfeit software by installing unauthorized software on computers for sale. This practice is called hard-disk loading. Vendors have even been known to counterfeit disk labels and Certificates of Authenticity. Warning signs that software purchased from vendors is pirated include:

- ◢ No end-user license is included.
- ◢ There is no mail-in product registration card.
- ◢ Software is installed on a new PC, but documentation and original disks are not included in the package.
- ◢ Documentation is photocopied, or discs have handwritten labels.

WHAT ARE YOUR RESPONSIBILITIES UNDER THE LAW?

The Federal Copyright Act of 1976 protects the exclusive rights of copyright holders. It gives legal users of software the right to make one backup copy. Other rights are based on what the copyright holder allows. In 1990, the U.S. Congress passed the Software Rental Amendment Act, which prevents renting, leasing, lending, or sharing software without the express written permission of the copyright holder. In 1992, Congress instituted criminal penalties for software copyright infringement, which include imprisonment for up to five years and/or fines up to $250,000 for the unlawful reproduction or distribution of 10 or more copies of software.

Your first responsibility as an individual user is to use only software that has been purchased or licensed for your use. When you install software, one step in the installation is to agree to the end-user licensing agreement (EULA). Print and file this agreement as a record of the licensing requirements you have agreed to follow.

As an employee of a company that has a site license to use multiple copies of the software, your responsibility is to comply with the site license agreement. It is also your responsibility to purchase only legitimate software. Purchasers of counterfeit or copied software face the risk of corrupted files, virus-infected disks, inadequate documentation, and lack of technical support and upgrades as well as the legal penalties for using pirated software.

>> CHAPTER SUMMARY

▲ Four key job roles of a PC repair technician include PC support technician, PC service technician, bench technician, and help-desk technician.

▲ A+ Certification by CompTIA is the most significant and most recognized certification for PC repair technicians.

▲ Staying abreast of new technology can be done by attending trade shows, reading trade magazines, researching the Internet, and attending seminars and workshops.

▲ Customers want more than just technical know-how. They want a positive and helpful attitude, respect, good communication, ownership of their problem, dependability, credibility, and professionalism.

▲ The buyer of software does not legally own the software or have the right to distribute it. According to the Federal Copyright Act of 1976, you have the right to make one backup copy of software.

>> KEY TERMS

A+ Certification	escalate	license
call tracking	expert systems	site license
copyright	hard-disk loading	technical documentation

>> REVIEWING THE BASICS

1. Name four job roles that can be categorized as a PC technician.

2. Of the four jobs in Question 1, which one might never include interacting with the PC's primary user?

3. Assume you are a customer who wants to have a PC repaired. List five main characteristics you would want to see in your PC repair person.

4. What is one thing you should do when you receive a phone call requesting on-site support, before you make an appointment?

5. You make an appointment to do an on-site repair, but you are detained and find out that you will be late. What is the best thing to do?

6. When you arrive for an on-site service call, how important is your greeting? What would be a good greeting to start off a good business relationship?

7. When making an on-site service call, what should you do before making any changes to software or before taking the case cover off a computer?

8. What should you do after finishing your PC repair?

9. What is a good strategy to follow if a conflict arises between you and your customer?

10. If you are about to make an on-site service call to a large financial organization, is it appropriate to show up in shorts and a T-shirt? Why or why not?

11. You have exhausted your knowledge of a problem, and it still is not solved. Before you escalate it, what else can you do?

12. If you need to make a phone call while on a customer's site and your cell phone is not working, what do you do?

13. When someone calls your help desk, what is the first thing you should do?

14. List the items of information you would want to record at the beginning of a help-desk call.

15. What is one thing you can do to help a caller who needs phone support and is not a competent computer user?

16. Describe what you should do when a customer complains to you about a product or service your company provides.

17. What are some things you can do to make your work at a help desk easier?

18. Why is it important to be a certified technician?

19. Examine the EULA of some software installed on your PC. Is it legal for you to have it installed on your PC at work and also installed on your PC at home?

20. What organization offers A+ Certification?

>> THINKING CRITICALLY

1. You own a small PC repair company and a customer comes to you with a PC that will not boot. After investigating, you discover the hard drive has crashed. What should you do first?

   a. Install a hard drive the same size and speed as the original.

   b. Ask the customer's advice about the size drive to install, but select a drive the same speed as the original drive.

   c. Ask the customer's advice about the size and speed of the new drive to install.

   d. If the customer looks like he can afford it, install the largest and fastest drive the system can support.

2. You have repaired a broken LCD panel in a notebook computer. However, when you dis-assembled the notebook, you bent the hinge on the notebook lid so that it now does not latch solidly. When the customer receives the notebook, he notices the bent hinge and begins shouting at you. What do you do first? Second?

   a. Explain to the customer that you are sorry, but you did the best you could.

   b. Listen carefully to the customer and don't get defensive.

   c. Ask the customer what he would like you to do to resolve the problem.

   d. Tell the customer he is not allowed to speak to you like that.

>> HANDS-ON PROJECTS

PROJECT 12-1:   Interacting with the User

Rob, a PC service technician, has been called on-site to repair a PC. He has not spoken directly with the user, Lisa, but he knows the floor of the building where she works and can look for her name on her cubicle. The following is a description of his actions. Create a table with two columns. List in one column the mistakes he made and in the next column the correct action he should have taken.

Rob's company promised that a service technician would come some time during the next business day after the call was received. Rob was given the name and address of the user and the problem, which was stated as "PC will not boot." Rob arrived the following day at about 10 a.m. He found Lisa's cubicle, but she was not present. Because Lisa was not present, Rob decided not to disturb the papers all over her desk, so he laid his notebooks and tools on top of her work.

Rob tried to boot the PC, and it gave errors indicating a corrupted file system on the hard drive. He successfully booted from a CD and was able to access a C prompt. A DIR command returned a mostly unreadable list of files and subdirectories in the root directory. Next, Rob used Norton Utilities to try to recover the files and directories but was unable to do so. He began to suspect that a virus had caused the problem, so he ran a virus scan program that did not find the suspected virus.

He made a call to his technical support to ask for suggestions. Technical support suggested he try partitioning and formatting the hard drive to remove any possible viruses and recover the hard drive. Rob partitioned and formatted the hard drive and was on the phone with technical support, in the process of reloading Windows XP from the company's file server, when Lisa arrived.

Lisa took one look at her PC and gasped. She caught her breath and asked where her data was. Rob replied, "A virus destroyed your hard drive. I had to reformat."

Lisa tried to explain the importance of the destroyed data. Rob replied, "Guess you'll learn to make backups now." Lisa left to find her manager.

PROJECT 12-2:   Developing Help-Desk Skills

Work with a partner who will play the role of the user. Sit with your back to the user, who is in front of the PC. Troubleshoot the problem and talk the user through to a solution. Abide by these rules:

▲ A third person created an error so that the PC does not boot successfully. Neither you nor your partner knows what the third person did.
▲ The user pretends not to have technical insight but to be good at following directions and being willing to answer any nontechnical questions.
▲ Don't turn around to look at the screen.
▲ Practice professional mannerisms and speech.
▲ As you work, keep a log of the "phone call to the help desk," recording in the log the major steps toward diagnosing and correcting the problem.

When the problem is resolved, have the third person create a different problem that causes the PC not to boot correctly, and exchange roles with your partner.

PROJECT 12-3:   Researching PC Support

A PC support technician is expected to stay abreast of new technologies, and the Internet is an excellent source of information to do that. Access each of the Web sites listed in Table 12-1, and print one Web page from each site that shows information that might be useful for a support technician.

Organization	Web Site
CMP Media, LLC	*www.byte.com*
CNET, Inc.	*www.cnet.com*
F_Secure Corp	*www.f-secure.com*
How Stuff Works	*www.howstuffworks.com*
InfoHQ	*www.infohq.com*
Jupitermedia Corporation	*www.pcwebopedia.com*
Kingston Technology (information about memory)	*www.kingston.com*
Microsoft Technical Resources	*support.microsoft.com*
Michael Karbo	*www.karbosguide.com*
PC Today Online	*www.pctoday.com*
PC World	*www.pcworld.com*
Tom's Hardware Guide	*www.tomshardware.com*
ZDNet (publishes several technical magazines)	*www.zdnet.com*

Table 12-1 Web sites of technical information

>> REAL PROBLEMS, REAL SOLUTIONS

REAL PROBLEM 12-1: Looking for a PC Support Job

Suppose you've finished your PC repair curriculum and have achieved A+ Certification. Now it's time to find a job. Research the newspapers and online job sites for PC support jobs in your area. Look for jobs that require A+ Certification and also look for PC support-related jobs that don't require certification. Don't forget to check out retail jobs selling computers and computer parts. Find at least three job ads. If you can't find ads in your immediate area, branch out into nearby cites. Make printouts or copies of the three job ads and answer these questions:

1. What are the qualifications of each job?

2. What is the salary?

3. What additional experience or certification do you need to qualify for each job?

4. If you were actually looking for a PC support-related job, which of the three jobs would be your first choice? Why?

REAL PROBLEM 12-2: Researching the Latest Technology

Technology is constantly changing and you need to know how to research the latest technologies. Research and answer the following questions and print Web pages supporting your answers:

1. Make a list of the top three AMD processors, listing characteristics of each. What type of system uses each processor?

2. Describe the difference between a SATA and a SATA2 hard drive interface. What are the transfer rates for each?

3. Describe the intended uses of the latest USB standard, Wireless USB (WUSB). What is the transfer rate of WUSB devices set three meters apart? Print Web pages showing two WUSB devices.

APPENDIX A

How an OS Uses System Resources

Asystem resource is a tool used by either hardware or software to communicate with the other. When BIOS or a driver wants to send data to a device (such as when you save a file to the hard drive), or when a device needs attention (such as when you press a key on the keyboard), the device or software uses system resources to communicate. When you install a hardware device under DOS or Windows 9x/Me, it is sometimes necessary to configure which system resources a device will use. Therefore, for these operating systems, a technician needs a general understanding about system resources discussed in this appendix.

There are four types of system resources: interrupt request numbers (IRQs), memory addresses, I/O addresses, and direct memory access (DMA) channels. Table A-1 lists these system resources used by software and hardware, and defines each.

As you can see in Table A-1, all four resources are used for communication between hardware and software. Hardware devices signal the CPU for attention using an IRQ. Software addresses a device by one of its I/O addresses. Software looks at memory as a hardware device and addresses it with memory addresses, and DMA channels pass data back and forth between a hardware device and memory.

All four system resources depend on certain lines on a bus on the motherboard (see Figure A-1). A bus such as the system bus has three components: the data bus carries data, the address bus communicates addresses (both memory addresses and I/O addresses), and the control bus controls communication. (IRQs and DMA channels are controlled by this portion of the bus.)

System Resource	Definition
IRQ	A line of a motherboard bus that a hardware device can use to signal the CPU that the device needs attention. Some lines have a higher priority for attention than others. Each IRQ line is assigned a number (0 to 15) to identify it.
Memory addresses	Numbers assigned to physical memory located either in RAM or ROM chips. Software can access this memory by using these addresses. Memory addresses are communicated on the address bus.
I/O addresses	Numbers assigned to hardware devices that software uses to send a command to a device. Each device "listens" for these numbers and responds to the ones assigned to it. I/O addresses are communicated on the address bus.
DMA channel	A number designating a channel on which the device can pass data to memory without involving the CPU. Think of a DMA channel as a shortcut for data moving to and from the device and memory.

Table A-1 System resources used by software and hardware

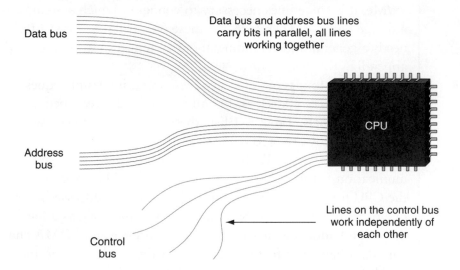

Figure A-1 A bus consists of a data bus, an address bus, and a control bus

Let's turn our attention to a more detailed description of the four resources and how they work.

INTERRUPT REQUEST NUMBER (IRQ)

When a hardware device needs the CPU to do something—for instance, when the keyboard needs the CPU to process a keystroke after a key has been pressed—the device needs a way to get the CPU's attention, and the CPU must know what to do once it turns its attention to the device. Getting the CPU's attention is known as a hardware interrupt, and the device creates a hardware interrupt by placing voltage on the designated interrupt request (IRQ) line assigned to the device. This voltage on the line serves as a signal to the CPU that the device has a request that needs processing. Often, a hardware device that needs attention from the CPU is referred to as "needing servicing." Interrupts initiate many processes that the CPU carries out, and these processes are said to be "interrupt-driven."

Table A-2 lists common uses for the sixteen available IRQs. The respective I/O addresses, which are listed in the second column of the table, are discussed in the third section of this appendix.

IRQ	I/O Address	Device
0	0040–005F	System timer
1	0060–006F	Keyboard controller
2	00A0–00AF	Access to IRQs above 7
3	02F8–02FF	COM2
3	02E8–02EF	COM4
4	03F8–03FF	COM1
4	03E8–03EF	COM3
5	0278–027F	Sound card or parallel port LPT2
6	03F0–03F7	Floppy drive controller
7	0378–037F	Printer parallel port LPT1
8	0070–007F	Real-time clock
9–10	N/A	Available
11	N/A	SCSI or available
12	0238–023F	Motherboard mouse
13	00F8–00FF	Math coprocessor
14	01F0–01F7	IDE hard drive
15	0170–017F	Secondary IDE hard drive or available

Table A-2   IRQs and I/O addresses for devices

In Table A-2, notice the COM and LPT assignments. A COM or LPT assignment is an agreed-on grouping of I/O addresses and an IRQ value. In the industry, it is agreed that when a device is configured to use COM1, it is using I/O addresses 03F8 through 03FF and IRQ 4. When all device and motherboard manufacturers agree to this and other COM and LPT assignments, it is less likely that devices will attempt to use conflicting resources, and it makes it easier to configure a device.

COM1 and COM2 are predetermined assignments that can be made to serial devices such as modems, and LPT1 and LPT2 are predetermined assignments that can be made to parallel devices such as printers. For example, a modem is built so that you can choose between using COM1 or COM2 for its resource assignments, rather than having to specify a particular IRQ or range of I/O addresses.

On motherboards, part of the chipset called the interrupt controller manages the IRQs for the CPU. The CPU actually doesn't know which IRQ is "up" because the interrupt controller manages that. If more than one IRQ is up at the same time, the interrupt controller selects the IRQ that has the lowest value to process first. For example, if a user presses a key on the keyboard at the same time that she moves the mouse configured to use COM1, the keystroke is processed before the mouse action, because the keyboard is using IRQ 1 and the mouse on COM1 is using IRQ 4. In other words, the interrupt controller is sort of the doorman to the CPU's apartment building. All devices wait outside the door while the interrupt controller decides who should be "let in" first, according to the IRQ value each holds in his hand.

The interrupt controller on early motherboards was designed to handle only eight different IRQs. To accommodate the need for more devices, a second group of IRQs was later added (IRQs 8 through 15), and a second interrupt controller was added to manage these new IRQs. This second controller did not have access to the CPU, so it had to communicate with the CPU through the first controller (see Figure A-2). To signal the first controller, the second controller used one of the first controller's IRQ values (IRQ 2). These last eight IRQs plug into the system using IRQ 2. Because of this, the IRQ priority level became: 0, 1, (8, 9, 10, 11, 12, 13, 14, 15), 3, 4, 5, 6, 7.

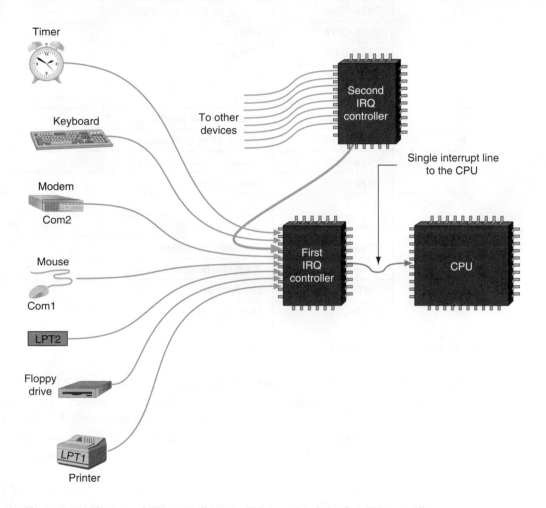

Figure A-2   The second IRQ controller uses IRQ 2 to signal the first IRQ controller

APPLYING | **CONCEPTS**   To see how the IRQs are assigned on your computer, you can use Device Manager for Windows 2000/XP and Windows 9x/Me. (For DOS, use a utility called MSD.) For Windows XP, click **Start**, right-click **My Computer**, and select **Properties** on the shortcut menu. For Windows 2000, right-click **My Computer** on the desktop and select **Properties** on the shortcut menu. The System Properties dialog box opens, as shown in Figure A-3. Click the **Hardware** tab and then click the **Device Manager** button. On the menu, click **View**, and then click **Resources by Type**, if necessary. Click the plus sign next to Interrupt request (IRQ) to open the list of assigned IRQs. Notice in the figure that IRQs 9 and 11 are each being shared by two devices.

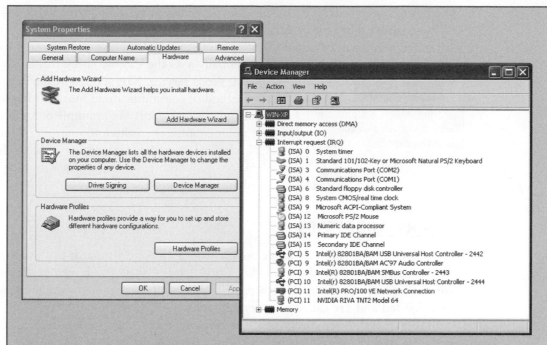

Figure A-3   Use Device Manager to see how your system is using IRQs and other system resources

To see current assignments in Windows 9x/Me, click **Start**, point to **Settings**, click **Control Panel**, and double-click **System.** Click the **Device Manager** tab, select **Computer,** and then click **Properties.** Figure A-4 shows the Computer Properties dialog box. Notice that IRQ 2 is assigned to the programmable interrupt controller because it is being used to manage IRQs 8 through 15.

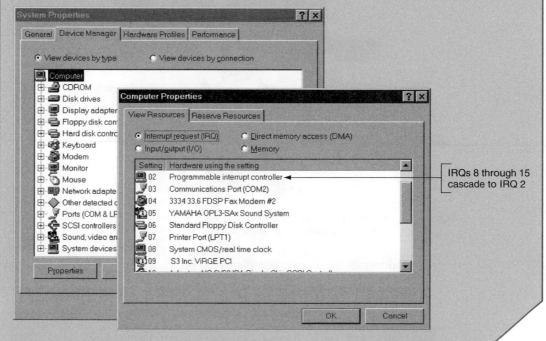

Figure A-4   Windows 9x/Me Device Manager shows current assignments for system resources

When using interrupts, the hardware device or the software does the work of getting the CPU's attention. However, the flow of "attention getting" can go the other way as well. This other way is called polling. With polling, software that was written for a specific hardware device constantly runs and occasionally asks the CPU to check this hardware device to see if it needs service. Not very many devices use polling as the method of communication; most hardware devices use interrupts. A joystick is one example of a device that does use polling. Software written to manage a joystick has the CPU check the joystick periodically to see if the device has data to communicate, which is why a joystick does not need an IRQ to work.

> **Notes**
>
> Sharing IRQs is not possible with ISA devices on the ISA bus. However, newer buses are designed to allow more than one device to share an IRQ.

MEMORY ADDRESSES

An operating system relates to memory as a long list of cells that it can use to hold data and instructions, somewhat like a one-dimensional spreadsheet. Each memory location or cell is assigned a number beginning with zero. These number assignments are made when the OS is first loaded and are called **memory addresses**.

Think of a memory address as a seat number in a theater (see Figure A-5). Each seat is assigned a number regardless of whether someone is sitting in it. The person sitting in a seat can be data or instructions, and the OS does not refer to the person by name, but only by the seat number. For example, the OS might say, "I want to print the data in memory addresses 500 through 650."

Figure A-5 Memory addresses are assigned to each location in memory, and these locations can store data or instructions

These addresses are most often displayed on the screen as hexadecimal (base 16 or hex) numbers in segment: offset form (for example, C800:5, which in hex is C8005 and in decimal is 819,205).

> **Notes**
>
> Windows offers a calculator that can quickly convert numbers in binary, digital, and hexadecimal. Enter a number in one number system, and then click another number system to make the conversion. To access the calculator in Windows 2000/XP or Windows 9x/Me, click **Start, Programs** (**All Programs** in Windows XP), **Accessories**, and then **Calculator**. To view the version of the calculator that can convert number systems, click **View, Scientific**.

I/O ADDRESSES

Another system resource made available to hardware devices is the input/output address, which is also known as an I/O address, a port address, or a port. I/O addresses are numbers the CPU can use to access hardware devices, in much the same way it uses memory addresses to access physical memory. Each device needs a range of I/O addresses so that the CPU can communicate more than one type of command to it.

The address bus on the motherboard sometimes carries memory addresses and sometimes carries I/O addresses. If the address bus has been set to carry I/O addresses, then each device "listens" to this bus (see Figure A-6). If a device (such as a hard drive, floppy drive, or keyboard) hears an address that belongs to it, then it responds; otherwise, it ignores the request for information. In short, the CPU "knows" a hardware device as a group of I/O addresses. If it wants to know the status of a printer or a CD drive, for example, it places a particular I/O address on the address bus on the motherboard.

Because IBM made many address assignments when it manufactured the first PC in the late 1970s, common devices such as a hard drive, a floppy drive, or a keyboard use a range of predetermined I/O addresses that never change. Their BIOS is simply programmed to use these standard addresses and standard IRQs. Legacy devices (devices that use older technologies) were designed to use more than one group of addresses and IRQs, depending on

how jumpers or DIP switches were set on the device. Newer devices, called Plug and Play devices, can use any I/O addresses or IRQ assigned to them during startup.

Notes

Refer back to Table A-2 for a listing of a few common assignments for I/O addresses. Because these addresses are usually written as hex numbers, you sometimes see them written with 0x first, such as 0x0040, or with the h last, like this: 0040h.

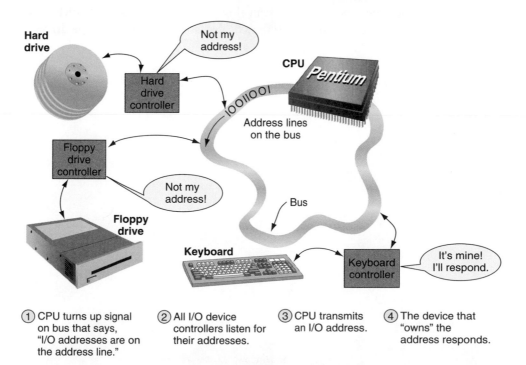

① CPU turns up signal on bus that says, "I/O addresses are on the address line."

② All I/O device controllers listen for their addresses.

③ CPU transmits an I/O address.

④ The device that "owns" the address responds.

Figure A-6 I/O address lines on a bus work much like people sitting in a waiting room waiting for their number to be called; all devices "hear" the addresses, but only one responds

DMA CHANNELS

Another system resource used by hardware and software is a direct memory access (DMA) channel, a shortcut method that lets an I/O device send data directly to memory. This bypasses the CPU and improves performance.

A chip on the motherboard contains the DMA logic and manages the process. Earlier computers had four DMA channels numbered 0, 1, 2, and 3. Later, channels 5, 6, and 7 were added. DMA channel 4 is used as IRQ 2 was used, as the entry point for the higher DMA channels to connect to the lower channels. This allows the higher channels a way to connect to the DMA controller on the motherboard and on to the CPU. In Figure A-7, you can see that DMA channel 4 is used to point to or cascade into the lower DMA channels.

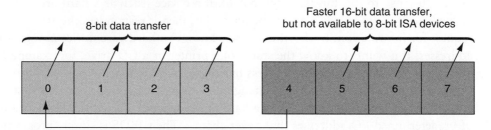

Figure A-7   DMA channel 4 is not available for I/O use because it is used to cascade into the lower-four DMA channels

Some devices, such as a printer, are designed to use DMA channels, and others, such as the mouse, are not. Those that use the channels might be able to use only a certain channel, say channel 3, and no other. Alternately, the BIOS might have the option of changing a DMA channel number to avoid conflicts with other devices. Conflicts occur when more than one device uses the same channel. DMA channels are not as popular as they once were, because their design makes them slower than newer methods such as a faster I/O bus. However, slower devices such as floppy drives, sound cards, and tape drives might still use DMA channels.

Introducing Linux

Unix is a popular OS used to control networks and to support applications used on the Internet. A variation of Unix is Linux (pronounced "Lih-nucks"), an OS created by Linus Torvalds when he was a student at the University of Helsinki in Finland. Basic versions of this OS are available for free, and all the underlying programming instructions (called source code) are also freely distributed.

Like Unix, Linux is distributed by several different companies, whose versions of Linux are sometimes called distributions. Popular distributions of Linux are shown in Table B-1. Linux can be used both as a server platform and a desktop platform, but its greatest popularity has come in the server market. Hardware requirements for Linux vary widely, depending on the distribution and version installed.

 Notes

For more information on Linux, see *www.linux.org* as well as the Web sites of the different Linux distributors.

Name	Comments	Web Site
Red Hat Linux	The most widely used distribution in the world, from Red Hat Software.	*www.redhat.com*
OpenLinux	Produced by The SCO Group (formerly Caldera International). Aimed at business users.	*www.sco.com*
UnitedLinux	A Linux distribution created by multiple Linux vendors as a common base product on which numerous Linux applications can be designed to run.	*www.unitedlinux.com*
TurboLinux	Focused on providing high-end, specialized server software to businesses.	*www.turbolinux.com*
Mandrake	Built on Red Hat Linux with many additional packages. Popular at retail outlets.	*www.mandrakelinux.com*
Stampede	A distribution optimized for speed.	*www.stampede.org*
Debian	A noncommercial Linux distribution targeted specifically to free software enthusiasts. Debian does not have a company behind it. It is created and maintained by developers of free software.	*www.debian.org*
SuSE	The leading German distribution. Increasingly popular in the United States.	*www.novell.com/linux/suse*
Yellow Dog Linux	A version of Linux for Macintosh computers, written for the PowerPC processor.	*www.yellowdoglinux.com*

Table B-1 Popular Linux distributions

Some of the advantages and disadvantages of Linux are:

- Linux rarely crashes.
- Basic versions can be downloaded and installed free of charge.
- Linux distributions that include technical support and software packages are available at a lower cost than other operating systems.
- Linux has strong features for handling network connections.
- Source code is available to users, enabling customization of the development environment.
- Linux on an inexpensive PC is an excellent training tool for learning Unix.
- Linux can be difficult to install, particularly for users who are not familiar with Unix commands.
- Most distributions of Linux run from a command line, which can be difficult for casual users to operate.
- Documentation can be spotty.
- Optimizing a Linux system can take a significant investment of time and research.
- Not as many desktop applications are available for Linux as for Windows, though a Windows-like office suite (Star Office) can be installed.

Network services such as a Web server or e-mail server often are provided by a computer running the Linux operating system. Linux is well suited to support various types of servers. Because Linux is very reliable and does not require a lot of computing power, it is sometimes used as a desktop OS, although it is not as popular for this purpose because it is not easy to use.

As a PC support technician, you should know a little about Linux, including a few basic commands, which are covered in this appendix. You will learn about root and user accounts, file structure, some common commands, and how to use the vi editor. Finally, we'll discuss window managers.

The material in this section is meant as a general introduction to the OS. The organization of files and folders, the desktop's appearance, and the way each command works might be slightly different with the distribution and version of Linux you are using.

ROOT ACCOUNT AND USER ACCOUNTS

Recall that an operating system is composed of a kernel, which interacts with the hardware and other software, and a shell, which interacts with the user and the kernel. Linux is a Unix-like operating system, and can use more than one shell, just as with other versions of Unix. The default shell for Linux is the Bash shell. The name stands for "Bourne Again Shell" and takes the best features from two previous shells, the Bourne and the Korn shells.

For a Linux or Unix server, the system administrator is the person who installs updates to the OS (called patches), manages backup processes, supports the installation of software and hardware, sets up user accounts, resets passwords, and generally supports users. The system administrator has root privileges, which means that he or she can access all the functions of the OS; the principal user account is called the root account. The administrator protects the password to the root account because this password gives full access to the system. When logged on, the administrator is logged on as the user root. You can use the *who* command to show a list of all users currently logged on to the system. In the following example, typing *who* shows that three users are currently logged on: the root user, James, and Susan.

```
who

root tty1 Oct 12 07:56

james tty1 Oct 12 08:35

susan tty1 Oct 12 10:05
```

> **Notes**
>
> The Linux command prompt for the root user is different from the command prompt for ordinary users. The root command prompt is #, and other users have the $ command prompt.

DIRECTORY AND FILE LAYOUT

The main directory in Unix and Linux is the root directory and is indicated with a forward slash. (In Unix and Linux, directories in a path are separated with forward slashes, in contrast to the backward slashes used by DOS and Windows.) Use the *ls* command, which is similar to the DOS Dir command, to list the contents of the root directory. The command (*ls -l /*) and its results are shown in Figure B-1.

Notice that the -*l* parameter is added to the command, which displays the results using the long format, and that there are spaces included before and after the parameters of the command. Also notice in the figure the format used to display the directory contents. The *d* at the beginning of each entry indicates that the entry is a directory, not a file. The other letters in this first column have to do with the read and write privileges assigned to the directory and the right to execute programs in the directory. The name of the directory is in the last column. The rights assigned the directory can apply to the owner of the directory, to other users, or to an entire group of users.

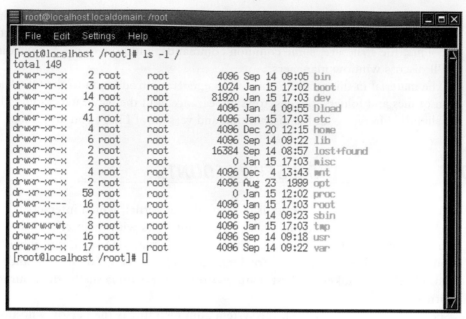

```
root@localhost.localdomain: /root                                    _ □ X
 File  Edit  Settings  Help
[root@localhost /root]# ls -l /
total 149
drwxr-xr-x    2 root     root         4096 Sep 14 09:05 bin
drwxr-xr-x    3 root     root         1024 Jan 15 17:02 boot
drwxr-xr-x   14 root     root        81920 Jan 15 17:03 dev
drwxr-xr-x    2 root     root         4096 Jan  4 09:55 Dload
drwxr-xr-x   41 root     root         4096 Jan 15 17:03 etc
drwxr-xr-x    4 root     root         4096 Dec 20 12:15 home
drwxr-xr-x    6 root     root         4096 Sep 14 09:22 lib
drwxr-xr-x    2 root     root        16384 Sep 14 08:57 lost+found
drwxr-xr-x    2 root     root            0 Jan 15 17:03 misc
drwxr-xr-x    4 root     root         4096 Dec  4 13:43 mnt
drwxr-xr-x    2 root     root         4096 Aug 23  1999 opt
dr-xr-xr-x   59 root     root            0 Jan 15 12:02 proc
drwxr-x---   16 root     root         4096 Jan 15 17:03 root
drwxr-xr-x    2 root     root         4096 Sep 14 09:23 sbin
drwxrwxrwt    8 root     root         4096 Jan 15 17:03 tmp
drwxr-xr-x   16 root     root         4096 Sep 14 09:18 usr
drwxr-xr-x   17 root     root         4096 Sep 14 09:22 var
[root@localhost /root]# []
```

Figure B-1   A directory listing using the ls command

Table B-2 lists directories that are created in the root directory during a typical Linux installation. The actual list of directories for a Linux computer that you work with might be a little different, because the directories created in the root directory depend on what programs have been installed.

Directory	Description
/bin	Contains programs and commands necessary to boot the system and perform other system tasks not reserved for the administrator, such as shutdown and reboot.
/boot	Consists of components needed for the boot process, such as boot loaders.
/dev	Holds device names, which consist of the type of device and a number identifying the device. Actual device drivers are located in the /lib/modules /[kernel version]/ directory.
/etc	Contains system configuration data, including configuration files and settings and their subdirectories. These files are used for tasks such as configuring a user account, changing system settings, and configuring a domain name resolution service.
/home	Contains user data. Every user on the system has a directory in the /home directory, such as /home/jean or /home/scott, and when a user logs on, that directory becomes the current working directory.
/lib	Stores common libraries used by applications so that more than one application can use the same library at one time. An example is the library of C programming code, without which only the kernel of the Linux system could run.
/lost+found	Stores data that is lost when files are truncated or when an attempt to fix system errors is unsuccessful.
/opt	Contains installations of third-party applications such as Web browsers that do not come with the Linux OS distribution.
/root	The home directory for the root user; contains only files specific to the root user. Do not confuse this directory with the root directory, which contains all the directories listed in this table.

Table B-2   Directories in a typical Linux root directory

Directory	Description
/sbin	Stores commands required for system administration.
/tmp	Stores temporary files, such as the ones that applications use during installation and operation.
/usr	Constitutes the major section of the Linux file system and contains read-only data.
/var	Holds variable data such as e-mail, news, print spools, and administrative files.

Table B-2   Directories in a typical Linux root directory (continued)

LINUX COMMANDS

This section describes some basic Linux and Unix commands, together with simple examples of how some are used. As you read along, be aware that all commands entered in Linux or Unix are case sensitive, meaning that uppercase and lowercase matter. Table B-3 shows some common commands for Linux and Unix. This is not meant to be a comprehensive list of commands, but simply a list you might find useful in working with files, directories, network connections, and system configuration. In the rest of the section, you will learn how to use a few common commands. For all of these procedures, assume that you are in your home directory (which would be /home/<*yourname*>/).

Command	Description
cat	Lets you view the contents of a file. Many Linux commands can use the redirection symbol > to redirect the output of the command. For example, use the redirection symbol with the cat command to copy a file: `cat /etc/shells > newfile` The contents of the shells file are written to newfile.
cd	Changes the directory. For example, `cd/etc` changes the directory to /etc.
chmod	This command changes the attributes assigned to a file and is similar to the DOS Attrib command. For example, to grant read permission to the file myfile: `chmod+r myfile`
clear	Clears the screen. This command is useful when the screen has become cluttered with commands and data that you no longer need to view.
cp	Used to copy a file: `cp <source> <destination>`
date	Entered alone, this command displays the current system date setting. Entered in the format date `<mmddhhmmyy>`, this command sets the system date. For example, to set the date to Dec 25, 2006 at 11:59 in the evening: `date 1225235906`
echo	Displays information on the screen. For example, to display which shell is currently being used, enter this command: `echo $SHELL`
fdisk	Creates or makes changes to a hard drive partition table: `fdisk <hard drive>`

Table B-3   Some common Linux and Unix commands

Command	Description
grep	Searches for a specific pattern in a file or in multiple files: `grep <pattern> <file>`
hostname	Displays a server's FQDN: `hostname`

ifconfig	Used to troubleshoot problems with network connections under TCP/IP. This command can disable and enable network cards and release and renew the IP addresses assigned to these cards. For example, to show all configuration information:
	
	`ifconfig -a`
	
	To release the given IP address for a TCP/IP connection named eth0 (the first Ethernet connection of the system):
	
	`ifconfig eth0 -168.92.1.1`

kill	Kills a process instead of waiting for the process to terminate: `kill <process ID>`
ls	The ls command is similar to the DOS Dir command, which displays a list of directories and files. For example, to list all files in the /etc directory, using the long parameter for a complete listing: `ls -l /etc`
man	Displays the online help manual, called man pages. For example, to get information about the echo command: `man echo` The manual program displays information about the command. To exit the manual program, type q.
mkdir	This command makes a new directory: `mkdir <directory>`
|more	Appended to a command to display the results of the command on the screen one page at a time. For example, to page the ls command: `ls |more`
mv	Moves a file or renames it, if the source and destination are the same directory: `mv <source> <destination>`
netstat	Shows statistics and status information for network connections and routing tables: `netstat`
nslookup	Queries domain name servers to look up domain names: `nslookup`
ping	Used to test network connections by sending a request packet to a host. If a connection is successful, the host will return a response packet: `ping <host>`
ps	Displays the process table so that you can identify process IDs for currently running processes (once you know the process ID, you can use the kill command to terminate a process): `ps`

Table B-3 Some common Linux and Unix commands (continued)

Command	Description
pwd	Shows the name of the present working directory: `pwd`
reboot	Reboots the system: `reboot`
rm	Removes the file or files that are specified: `rm <file>`
rmdir	This command removes a directory: `rmdir <directory>`
route	Entered alone, this command shows the current configuration of the IP routing table. Entered in the following format, it configures the IP routing table: `route[options]`
traceroute	Shows the route of IP packets; used for debugging connections on a network: `traceroute <host>`
useradd	Adds a user to a system: `useradd [option] <user>`
userdel	Removes a user from a system: `userdel <user>`
vi	Launches a full-screen editor that can be used to edit a file: `vi <file>`
whatis	Displays a brief overview of a command. For example, to get quick information about the echo command: `whatis echo`
who	Displays a list of users currently logged in: `who`

Table B-3   Some common Linux and Unix commands (continued)

EDITING COMMANDS

When you add options and file or directory names to a command, it can get quite long, and if you make a mistake while typing the command, you will want to edit it. Also, once the command has been entered, you can retrieve it, edit it, and press Enter to reissue the command. Some shells allow you to use the arrow, Backspace, Insert, and Delete keys to edit command lines, but other shells do not. Instead, you need to use the following keystrokes to edit a command line:

- Alt+D to delete a word
- Ctrl+K to delete from the current position to the end of the line
- Ctrl+A to move the cursor to the beginning of the command line
- Alt+B to move the cursor left one word
- Alt+F to move the cursor right one word

Follow these steps to edit a command line:

1. Type **who is this** but *do not* press Enter.

2. To move one word to the left, press **Alt+B** so that your cursor is positioned on the word "is."

3. To delete the word "is," press **Alt+D**.

4. To delete the portion of the command line that follows the current cursor position, press **Ctrl+K**.

5. To move the cursor to the beginning of the command line, press **Ctrl+A**.

VIEWING THE SHELLS FILE

The shells file in the /etc directory contains a list of available shells to use on a Linux system. Each shell incorporates slightly different support for programming and scripting languages. In addition, different Linux shells may use keystrokes other than the ones you just learned in supporting command-line editing; the keystrokes in the procedure in the last section work in Bash, the default Linux shell. To determine whether you are using the Bash shell, type **echo $shell** and press **Enter**. If you see the output /bin/bash, you are using the Bash shell. If you are not using the Bash shell, type **bash** and press **Enter** to change to the Bash shell.

To view a list of available shells:

1. Type **cat /etc/shells**, and then press **Enter**.

2. A list of available shells appears. This list might include the entries /bin/bash, /bin/bsh, /bin/csh, /bin/sh, /bin/tcsh, and /bin/zsh. Notice that all these shells are stored in the /bin directory. Type **clear,** and then press **Enter** to clear the screen.

3. Type **cat –n /etc/shells**, and then press **Enter**. Notice that this time, the same list of shells is displayed with a number before each line because you used the –n option. (See Figure B-2.) Notice in the figure that the current user is root.

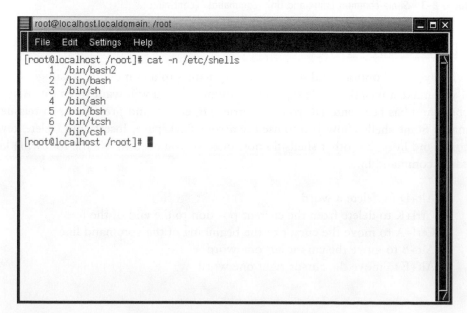

Figure B-2   Use the Cat command to display a list of shells

REDIRECTING OUTPUT

When you entered the command cat /etc/shells in the preceding procedure, the list of available shells, which is the output of that command, was sent to the screen. What if you wanted to save that list? You would use the **redirection symbol**, which is the greater-than (>) sign, to direct the output to a file, perhaps with the name available_shells. To do so, use these steps:

1. Go to the root directory by typing **cd /** and pressing **Enter**.

2. Type **cat /etc/shells > available_shells**, and then press **Enter**.

3. Notice that no command output appears on the screen, because the output has been saved to the new file available_shells (the file is created when the command is entered). To view the contents of the file, type **cat available_shells**, and then press **Enter**. The file is created in the current directory, which is the root directory.

CREATING A DIRECTORY

It is not a good idea to store data files in the root directory, so let's create a directory to which to move the new file available_shells:

1. Type **mkdir myfiles**, and then press **Enter**. This creates a directory named myfiles under the current directory, which is root.

2. Type **cd myfiles** to change from the current directory to the new directory.

3. Type **mv /available_shells .** and then press **Enter** (don't overlook the space and the period at the end of the command line; type them too). This moves the file from the root directory to the current directory, which is /myfiles. The source directory is the root and the destination directory is /myfiles. The period in a command line means the current directory.

4. Type **ls** to see the contents of the myfiles directory. The available_shells file is listed. (See Figure B-3.)

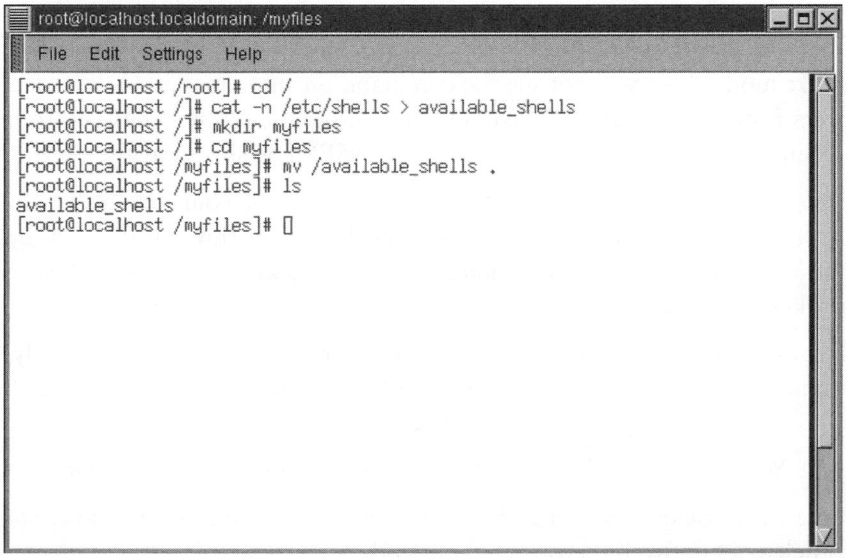

```
root@localhost.localdomain: /myfiles                    _ □ ×
 File   Edit   Settings   Help
[root@localhost /root]# cd /
[root@localhost /]# cat -n /etc/shells > available_shells
[root@localhost /]# mkdir myfiles
[root@localhost /]# cd myfiles
[root@localhost /myfiles]# mv /available_shells .
[root@localhost /myfiles]# ls
available_shells
[root@localhost /myfiles]# []
```

Figure B-3   Creating and moving files to a directory

USING THE VI EDITOR

You were introduced to the vi command in Table B-3 earlier in the appendix. This command launches the vi editor, which got its name because it is a visual editor; at one time, vi was the most popular Unix text editor. It is still used with shells that don't allow the use of the arrow, Delete, or Backspace keys. You can use the editor in insert mode, in which you can enter text, or command mode, which allows you to enter commands to perform editing tasks to move through the file. In this section, you will learn how to create and use commands on a text file in the vi editor. All of these commands are case sensitive.

Let's create and work with a file called mymemo.

1. To open the vi editor and create a file at the same time, type the command followed by the filename, as follows: **vi mymemo**, and then press **Enter**. The vi editor screen is shown in Figure B-4.

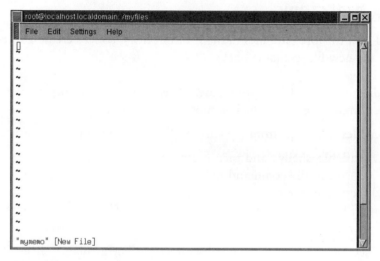

Figure B-4 The vi text editor

2. When you first open the vi editor, you are in command mode, which means that anything you type will be interpreted as a command by the vi editor. Type **i** to switch to insert mode. You will not see the command on the screen, and you do not need to press Enter to execute it. The command automatically switches you to insert mode. When you are in insert mode, the word INSERT is shown at the bottom of the screen.

3. Type the first two sentences of Step 2 as the text for your memo. If your shell supports it, practice using the arrow keys to move the cursor through the text, up, down, left, and right, one character at a time. If arrow keys are not supported, you can use keystrokes to move the cursor; these keystrokes are listed in Table B-4.

4. To switch back to command mode, press the **Esc** key. Now you are ready to enter commands to manipulate your text. Type **H** to move the cursor to the upper-left corner of the screen. You must use an uppercase H, because all these commands are case sensitive.

5. Type **W** repeatedly until you reach the beginning of the word "first."

6. Type **dw** to delete the word "first." To delete one character at a time, you would use x; to delete an entire line, you would use dd.

7. To save the file and exit the vi editor, type :x and press **Enter**. This will save the file and close the editor.

Table B-4 lists the vi editor commands to move the cursor. There are many more commands to manipulate text, set options, cancel, or temporarily leave a vi editor session. For a more complete list of vi editor commands, see a reference dedicated to Linux.

Command	Alternate	Description
Ctrl+B	Pg up	Back one screen
Ctrl+F	Pg down	Forward one screen
Ctrl+U	—	Up half a screen
Ctrl+D	—	Down half a screen
k	Up arrow	Up one line
j	Down arrow	Down one line
h	Left arrow	Left one character
l	Right arrow	Right one character
W	—	Forward one word
B	—	Back one word
0 (zero)	—	Beginning of the current line
$	—	End of current line
NG	—	Line specified by number *n*
H	—	Upper-left corner of screen
L	—	Last line on the screen

Table B-4 vi editor commands

WINDOW MANAGERS

Because many users prefer a Windows-style desktop, several applications have been written to provide a GUI for Unix and Linux. These GUIs are called window managers. One popular desktop environment application is GNU Network Object Model Environment (GNOME). GNOME (pronounced "guh-nome") provides a desktop that looks and feels like Windows 98, but is free software designed to use a Linux kernel. The major components of a GNOME window are shown in Figure B-5. For more information about GNOME, see the organization's Web site at *www.gnome.org*. Another popular Linux window manager is the KDE Desktop (*www.kde.org*).

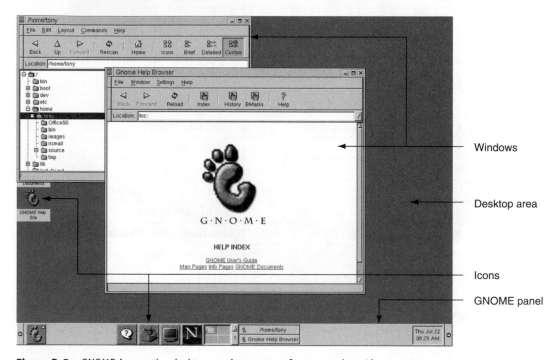

Figure B-5   GNOME is popular desktop environment software used on Linux systems

APPENDIX

C

Introducing the Mac OS

Mac OS X is the latest version of the proprietary OS for Apple Macintosh computers. This appendix covers the basic file and folder organization and startup process for the Mac OS. It is not intended to qualify you to support Macs, but rather to give you a passing familiarity with them, so that you will recognize some of the main features of the OS and know where to go for more information.

STARTING UP A MAC

When the Mac starts up, you see a graphical record of some of the events occurring in the startup process, such as the loading of the desktop and system applets, including the Finder window (which is used to explore the Mac system). Most of the startup process, however, is hidden from the user. Here are the main steps in the process:

1. Self-test, which is controlled from ROM, is conducted.
2. PRAM (parameter RAM) settings are retrieved.
3. System folder is located.
4. Mac OS ROM file is loaded.
5. Smiling Mac icon and welcome screen are displayed.
6. Enablers are loaded.
7. Disk First Aid runs if the Mac was not shut down properly.
8. Other System folder contents are located.
9. Mac desktop is displayed.
10. Finder and startup programs are loaded.

Each of these steps is described in more detail here, and major differences between Mac OS X and Mac OS 9 are noted.

▲ *Self-test is controlled from ROM.* When you press the power button on a Mac and power is sent to the motherboard, the ROM signals the Mac to perform a self-test. Components tested include the hard drive, the processor, ports, controllers, and expansion cards. The self-test ensures that they are operating correctly. Once this is confirmed, the Mac tests its RAM and halts the startup process if major damage or incorrect installations of RAM modules are detected. Minor damage to RAM might not be detected during the startup test of RAM but might show up in system malfunctions later.

▲ *PRAM settings are retrieved.* In the Mac, PRAM, or parameter RAM, stores configuration information for the Mac OS. After tests of components and RAM are completed, the Mac looks at the PRAM for settings that tell the system which drive is presently designated as the bootable drive (the startup disk). If it looks in that drive and does not find the Mac OS, it keeps looking in drives until it finds a bootable drive. If it cannot find one, the system displays a flashing question mark and pauses the startup process.

▲ *The System folder is located.* After the Mac locates a bootable disk, it looks for an active System folder, which is the folder that the system designates as the one from which the Mac OS is to be loaded. A System folder is required for a disk to be bootable. In Mac OS 9, the System folder is named System Folder, and in Mac OS X, the System folder is named System. See Figure C-1.

▲ *The Mac OS ROM file is loaded.* The first item that the Mac loads into memory from the System folder is the Mac OS ROM file, which contains commands required for interaction with hardware and the lower levels of the Mac OS. Before the iMac, these commands were stored in ROM on the motherboard in the Mac.

▲ *The smiling Mac icon and welcome screen are displayed.* When the smiling Mac icon is displayed, the system is loading the OS into RAM, beginning with the System file containing the libraries and commands that make up the core of the OS.

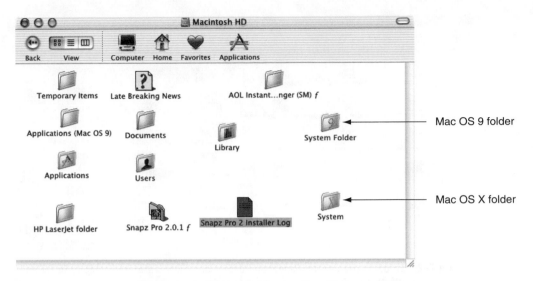

Figure C-1   Mac OS 9 is stored in the System Folder, but Mac OS X uses System

◢ *The system loads enablers for hardware components.* If Mac hardware is put on the market before the instructions to control it are included with the OS, an enabler file will be included with it that will enable it to function with the version of Mac OS being used on the computer. The enabler files are loaded after the System file. Generally, each revision of the Mac OS incorporates information included in enabler files that were necessary with the previous version.

◢ *Disk First Aid runs if the* system *was not shut down properly.* If the system is not shut down properly, the next time the computer starts up, the system will run Disk First Aid, a Mac disk utility, to search for and repair any problems that it finds with the hard drive. Disk First Aid runs after the System file and any enabler files are loaded.

◢ *Other contents of the System* folder *are located.* In Mac OS 9, in addition to the System file and enabler files, the System folder also contains the Control Panels and Extensions folders (see Figure C-2). The Control Panels folder controls system settings such as time and date, speaker volume, and the configuration of the Finder window and the desktop. The Extensions folder contains add-ons to provide new features to a Mac, as well as shared libraries and icons. These no longer exist in Mac OS X; their functions are incorporated into a single Library folder, which is shown in Figure C-3.

◢ *The Mac desktop is displayed.* The Mac desktop is displayed after the necessary contents of the System folder have been loaded. All the required components of the Mac OS have been loaded at this point.

◢ *The Finder window and startup* programs *are loaded.* After the Mac OS is completely loaded, the Finder window launches so that the user can access programs and files. The Finder itself is an application that is loaded automatically during the startup process, not a part of the OS. When the Finder window has been loaded, the system loads items in the Startup Items folder, which contains items that the user wants to open immediately upon startup. In Mac OS 9, it also opens the Launcher, which provides easy access to commonly used folders, programs, and files, if the Launcher control panel has been installed.

Figure C-2   In OS 9, the Control Panels and Extensions folders are used to contain OS and applications utilities

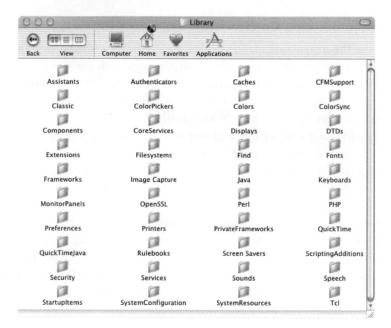

Figure C-3   In OS X, the Library folder replaces the Control Panels and Extensions folders of OS 9

USING THE MAC

Now that you've had an overview of the Mac OS startup process, let's look at some major features of the Mac interface and learn some important procedures and hints for using the Mac. In this section, you'll learn about the Finder window, the Apple menu, and procedures to help you work with files and applications in a Mac environment.

THE MAC DESKTOP

The Mac OS X desktop, with its major components labeled, is shown in Figure C-4. The Finder application is open and active. Because it is the currently active application, the menu bar for the Finder window is displayed at the top of the screen. The menu bar provides pull-down menus that contain options for working with applications, files, and the interface.

A new feature in the Mac OS X user interface is the **dock** that appears at the bottom of the desktop. It contains icons that provide access to frequently used applications. When you click the minus button to minimize a window, an icon representing that window appears in the dock. To open an application from its icon in the dock, just click it once. The icons in the dock that represent open applications have a small triangle underneath them. The Mac OS X desktop also includes shortcut icons that are usually located on the right side of the screen and provide quick access to files, folders, and programs.

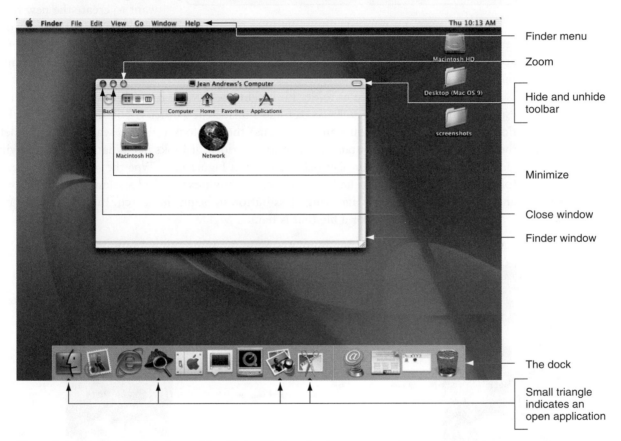

Figure C-4 The Mac OS X desktop with a Finder Window showing

The Mac OS X interface has been redesigned, and it does not use its own interface to run applications that were written for OS 9. Instead, it stores the Mac OS 9 applications in a separate folder and launches the OS 9 interface, which it calls the classic interface, whenever a user wants to use one of those applications. In this way, a user can still use older Mac applications with the newer Mac interface. In Figure C-4 you can see the icon on the right side of the screen to launch the Desktop (Mac OS 9) classic interface.

USING THE FINDER

The Mac's Finder window functions something like Explorer or My Computer in Windows, enabling the user to navigate and access the Mac's files and applications. The Finder window at the computer level, which is the top level of the Mac OS X's hierarchical file structure, shows an icon for the computer's hard drive as well as a Network icon to provide access to any other workstations to which the computer is connected. The Finder window and other windows contain a toolbar that appears at the top of the window and contains buttons that function much like the buttons in a Web browser, such as Back, Home, and Favorites. The Home button on the Mac OS X window toolbar takes the user back to the computer level.

> **Notes**
>
> If you use a folder frequently, such as the Documents folder, you can keep it open all the time without having it in your way. In Mac OS 9, drag it down to the bottom of the screen until it becomes a tab on the title bar. In Mac OS X, drag it down to the dock, and it will become an icon on the dock.

Besides allowing you to access programs, files, and folders, the Finder window provides you with a way to organize and manage them. For instance, to create a new folder, locate the folder in which you want to create the new folder using the Finder. When you've reached the desired folder, go to the File menu and click **New Folder.** The new folder will appear with its name highlighted. Type its new name and press the **Return** key to rename the folder.

It is easier to locate a file or folder in the Finder window if you know exactly where it is, especially if there are several levels of folders inside each other. If you don't know the location of the file or folder you want to find, use the Sherlock utility to search for it. By default, the dock in Mac OS X contains an icon for Sherlock; it looks like a hat and a magnifying glass. The search screen for Sherlock is shown in Figure C-5. Type the name of the file, folder, or text you want to find, click the check box next to the location you want to search, and then click the green magnifying glass button to begin the search. In the figure, you are searching the hard drive for a file that is named Myfile.

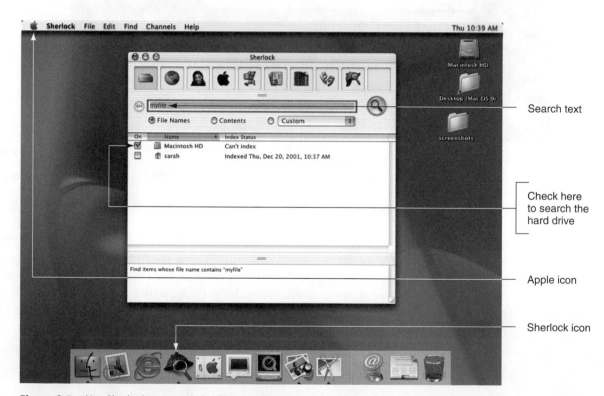

Figure C-5   Use Sherlock to search for files and folders

When you don't need a file or folder any more, just drag its icon to the Trash Can until the Trash Can is highlighted, and release the mouse button. Note that this is the only way you can delete icons from the Finder window. When an item is moved to the Trash Can, you can still recover it by double-clicking the Trash Can and locating the item. Items are not actually removed from the system until you chose File, Empty Trash from the menu.

USING THE APPLE MENU

The menu at the top of the Mac OS screen changes with each application that is active except for the Apple icon, which is always shown at the far left of the menu bar. The Apple menu, which opens when you click the Apple icon, and is similar to the Microsoft Windows Start menu, is present and is constantly accessible no matter what folder, window, or application you are using. It contains accessories to help you manage system tasks as well as programs such as media players, a calculator, search programs, and word-processing programs. The Mac OS X Apple menu is shown in Figure C-6.

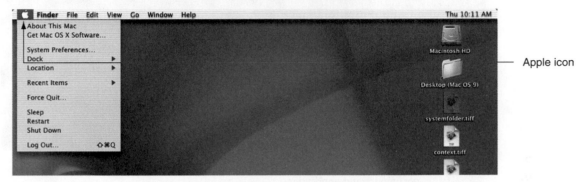

Figure C-6 The Apple menu is always available no matter what application is active

System Preferences on the Apple menu contains options for customizing the Mac interface. Click **Apple** and then click **System Preferences** to open the System Preferences window, shown in Figure C-7. Control Panels, which you learned about earlier in this appendix, are also accessible from the Apple menu in OS 9. In Mac OS 9, you can customize the Apple menu to contain anything you want by adding items to or removing items from the Apple folder, which is located in the System folder. You can create up to five levels of submenus under the Apple menu. In Mac OS X, the Apple menu is no longer customizable.

Figure C-7 The System Preferences window is used to customize the Mac interface

In Mac OS 9, there are three submenus on the Apple menu, called Recent Applications, Recent Documents, and Recent Servers. To customize these submenus, from the Apple menu, select **Control Panels, Apple Menu Options**. From this control panel, you can select whether to use recent menus and how many items to include on them. In Mac OS X, the Recent Items submenu on the Apple menu (shown in Figure C-8) gives you access to recently accessed documents and applications.

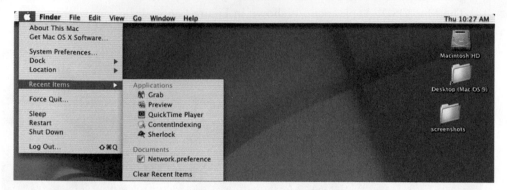

Figure C-8 Using Mac OS X, the Recent Items menu under the Apple menu lists recently accessed documents and applications

LAUNCHING AN APPLICATION

There are four ways to execute applications on the Mac:

- ◢ Double-click the icon for the application from the Finder window or another window or from the desktop.
- ◢ Choose the application from the Recent Applications submenu on the Apple menu.
- ◢ Double-click the icon of a file associated with that application, such as a text file saved from the Notepad application.
- ◢ Drag to the application's icon the icon of a document that you want to open with it.

The first two methods have already been discussed. The last option works well if you want to open a document with an application other than the one in which it was originally saved.

As you work with applications on the Mac, you may find that you want to have more than one application open at a time. In Mac OS 9, the Applications menu, which you can access from the upper-right corner of your screen, allows you to switch between open applications easily. The menu will show the icon and name of the currently active application. To access other open applications, click the menu and choose the name of the application you want to access. Recall that in Mac OS X, open applications are shown as icons in the dock with a small triangle under them.

SUPPORTING HARDWARE

In addition to working with files and applications, you will also need to know how to support hardware in a Mac system, such as monitors and hard drives, and including changing settings for video, understanding the file system used on the hard drive, and using system maintenance tools. Again, this section will not give you all you need to

C

know to work with Mac hardware; it is simply intended to show you some important tools for working with the system. For more information specific to working with Mac hardware, study books devoted specifically to the Mac, documentation and manuals that come with your system or with specific components, and the Apple Computer, Inc. Web site (*www.apple.com*).

ADJUSTING DISPLAY SETTINGS

To change display settings such as color depth and resolution, double-click the **Displays** icon under System Preferences. The Displays window appears, as seen in Figure C-9. You can change the following settings in the Displays window:

▲ *Resolution.* The resolution of a display affects how many pixels are shown on-screen. A resolution of 1024 x 768 means that there are 1,024 columns of pixels and 768 rows of pixels. When you change the resolution of your monitor, remember that the size of the items on the screen will change; the more pixels there are, the smaller items will be. This can be good if you want to see more items and space on your screen at one time, but it can be a drawback if you have vision problems. Two advantages to an 800 x 600 resolution are that it will produce a view close to what you will actually see in a printed document and that many Web pages are designed to be viewed at this resolution. A Web page optimized at 800 x 600 will look cramped at a lower resolution such as 640 x 480.

▲ *Contrast and brightness.* The sliders on the bottom of the Display tab of the Displays window enable you to control how much contrast there is between colors on your screen and how bright the overall display is. It is not a good idea to set a monitor to the highest brightness setting, because this can burn out the monitor prematurely.

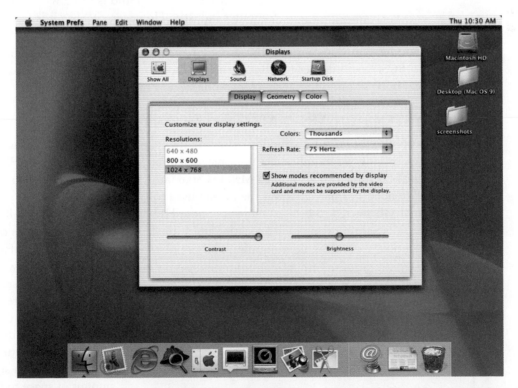

Figure C-9 The Displays window in the System Preferences window is used to adjust the display settings

◢ *Color depth*. Click the **Color** tab on the Displays window to view and change the settings for depth of color. The Color Depth box allows you to change how many colors can be shown on the screen: either 256, thousands, or millions. More colors mean a more realistic and more detailed picture. Sometimes a picture was created using a certain setting and will not be displayed correctly in a different setting. If a picture appears blurred or too gray, change the color depth until it appears correctly.

◢ *Display geometry*. Click the **Geometry** tab in the Displays window to reach options for changing the shape of the display on the screen. On most monitors, the display area is actually slightly smaller than the screen size, and you may see some black space around the display area. Use the Geometry settings to change the height, width, position, and shape of the display area.

SUPPORTING THE HARD DRIVE

As with other OSs, the Mac OS supports IDE and SCSI drive technologies and, for hard drives, there is a choice of file systems to use.

DRIVE TECHNOLOGIES: IDE AND SCSI

IDE is the most popular drive interface technology used for desktop computers. Two types of IDE drive interfaces are Parallel ATA (PATA) and Serial ATA (SATA). IDE drives follow an interface standard that allows for up to four PATA drives in a system or up to six PATA and SATA drives. SCSI drives are generally faster than IDE drives, and there can be up to 15 SCSI devices on a system. It is possible to mix IDE and SCSI devices on a system.

> **Notes**
>
> The terms *IDE* and *SCSI* refer not only to hard drives but also to other devices such as CD-ROM drives, Zip drives, and DVD drives.

In the mid-1990s, IDE became the main technology for connecting internal devices in a Mac, partially because it is less expensive than SCSI and is more widely used in the computer industry. However, because it is faster and can support more devices, SCSI can be a better choice for complex multimedia and graphics work. If you have a Mac that uses IDE technology and want to convert to SCSI, you can purchase a SCSI host adapter for that purpose. Choose a drive technology according to your needs, your budget, and what technology your system supports.

FILE SYSTEMS ON THE MAC

Recall that a file system is the overall structure that an OS uses to name, store, and organize files on a disk. The two main choices for a file system on a Mac hard drive are HFS (Hierarchical File System), also called Mac OS Standard Format, and HFS+, also called the Mac OS Extended Format. HFS was the format used for Mac disks before 1998, when drives larger than 1 GB started to become more common. HFS limited the number of allocation units on a disk to 65,536; how big each allocation unit was depended on the total size of the drive. These allocation units are called allocation blocks or simply blocks, and are similar to the Microsoft Windows file system's clusters; they are sets of hard drive sectors where the Mac's file system stores files. Files smaller than the size of a block still take up an entire block, which can cause a significant amount of space to be wasted; this wasted space is called slack.

> **Notes**
>
> In Mac OS 9, the File Exchange control panel is a component that can be installed to allow the Mac to use Microsoft Windows FAT16 and FAT32 partitions. Macs can read some NTFS or Linux/Unix file systems using utilities specially designed for that purpose. Mac OS X includes the ability to mount FAT drives but does not include a utility to format them as Mac OS 9 did.

In 1998, with the release of Mac OS 8.1, HFS was updated to HFS+, which allows for smaller blocks and can format drives up to 2048 GB. Any drive larger than 1 GB should be formatted with HFS+. Hard drives or removable media disks (such as floppy disks) smaller than 1 GB should be formatted with HFS, as should any hard drive that you plan to use with a Mac running Mac OS 8.1 or earlier.

The formatting of a hard drive with a file system creates blocks. It also creates a directory structure that allows the OS to access the drive. Some important elements of the directory structure are listed here.

- Boot blocks are the first two allocation blocks on the hard drive. They are initially empty, but once a System folder is installed on a computer, the boot blocks contain the location of the System folder so that the system can find and load the OS. You can correct damage to the boot blocks or replace erased boot blocks by installing a new System folder.
- Right after the boot blocks comes the volume information block, which holds information about the drive, including its format, name, number of files and folders, and allocation block size. This information must be present for a Mac to be able to access a drive. Because of the importance of the volume information block, a copy of it is stored in the next-to-last allocation block on the drive.
- A map of the allocation blocks on a hard drive is contained in the volume bit map, which uses a 1 to indicate that a block is storing files and a 0 to indicate that it is empty and is available for use. Damage to or corruption of the volume bit map does not prevent the Mac from being able to access the drive. However, when the Mac cannot determine from the volume bit map which allocation blocks are used, it might write new information to blocks that are full, overwriting the existing information. Regular disk maintenance (including use of the tools described in the next section) can help guard against this problem.
- The catalog tree is a database of the folders and files on a Mac hard drive, including information such as filenames and extensions, the application used to open a file, the creator of the file or folder, and the date the file or folder was created.
- The extents tree contains information about where the allocation blocks are located for files that take up more than one allocation block. When a file is larger than one allocation block, it is broken up into pieces called extents. One extent is stored in one allocation block. If a large proportion of the space on a hard drive is being used, the extents that make up a file might not be stored next to each other. The catalog tree and the extents tree work together and are both necessary for the Mac to be able to access data stored on the hard drive. They are the closest thing in the Mac to the FAT and the root directory in Windows.

DRIVE MAINTENANCE TOOLS

In Mac OS X, the Utilities folder (shown in Figure C-10) contains various system tools, including Disk Utility (shown in Figure C-11).

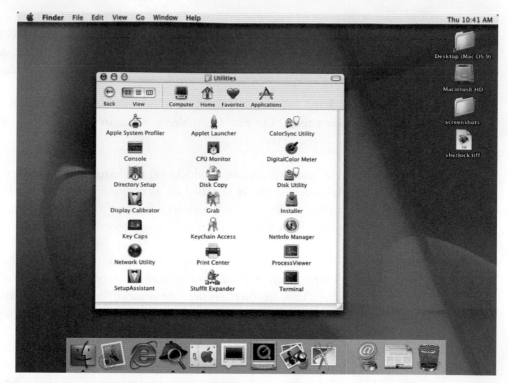

Figure C-10 The Max OS X Utilities folder contains several utilities, including those used to manage a hard drive

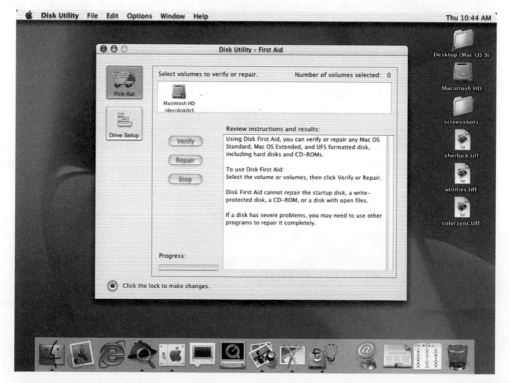

Figure C-11 The Mac OS X Disk Utility is in the Utilities folder and can be used to set up and repair a hard drive

DRIVE SETUP

The Drive Setup function can be used to format a hard drive when it is initially installed or to reformat a damaged hard drive. Remember that reformatting a drive erases all data and programs on it because the format process creates new allocation blocks and directory structures. When you format a drive, you can choose whether or not to create partitions on it. Partitioning a drive is not required, but can be done to divide the drive into one or more logical drives. Drive Setup can format most IDE and SCSI drives.

To use Drive Setup, on the Disk Utility window, click **Drive Setup,** select the disk you want to partition, and then click **Partition**. When you repartition a drive, all data on the current partitions is erased, and you cannot partition a drive that is currently used as the startup drive.

DISK FIRST AID

Disk First Aid is a disk repair tool that checks for errors on the hard drive and runs automatically on reboot when a Mac is not shut down properly. You can also run this tool manually as a preventive maintenance measure or as an attempt to address poor hard drive performance. Disk First Aid is part of the free Apple utility Disk Utility and is less powerful than third-party disk repair utilities such as Norton Disk Doctor, which is part of Norton Utilities, or Alsoft's Disk Warrior (*www.alsoft.com*). There are some problems that these utilities can repair that Disk First Aid can only detect.

Supporting Windows NT Workstation

Windows NT Workstation is a retired and pretty much dead operating system. However, at the time this book went to print, the CompTIA 2003 A+ exams were still alive, and the 2003 A+ Operating System Technologies exam does have coverage on Windows NT Workstation. The coverage of Windows NT is not extensive, but you should know about installing it and supporting the boot process. In this appendix, you'll learn the different ways to install Windows NT, and then we'll look at how to troubleshoot the Windows NT boot process.

INSTALLING WINDOWS NT AS THE ONLY OS

Windows NT comes with three disks that contain a simplified version of Windows NT, enough to boot a PC. If the hard drive does not contain an OS, the installation begins by booting from these three disks. After Windows NT is loaded from these three disks, it can access the CD-ROM drive, and installation continues from the CD. The program on the CD executed at that point is Winnt.exe, a 16-bit program. A faster version of Winnt.exe on the CD named Winnt32.exe, a 32-bit program, can be used instead of Winnt.exe in certain situations. Winnt32.exe can be run only after Windows NT has already been installed for the first time; it is used to upgrade from an older NT version to a newer version or to reinstall a corrupted version. It must be executed from within Windows NT.

The three startup disks can later be used to boot the PC if files on the hard drive become corrupted. You can also create a new set of bootable disks.

The Windows NT installation files are stored in the \i386 directory on the CD-ROM drive. If you have enough hard drive space, you can copy the contents of the \i386 directory and its subdirectories to the hard drive and install from there, which is faster because access to the hard drive is faster than access to the CD-ROM drive. If the computer is connected to a network, the contents of the \i386 directory can be copied to a network server, and the Winnt.exe program can be executed from the server to install Windows NT on the PC, if certain conditions exist. (Installations from servers are not covered in this appendix.) To perform an upgrade to Windows NT, boot the OS and execute the Winnt.exe program on the Windows NT CD.

TROUBLESHOOTING THE WINDOWS NT BOOT PROCESS

In this section, you will learn how to troubleshoot the Windows NT boot process and about some diagnostic tools that you can use for maintenance and troubleshooting. Many general troubleshooting tips you learned in earlier chapters apply to Windows NT as well. However, many troubleshooting tools, such as Safe Mode and Device Manager, which are available for Windows 2000/XP, don't exist under Windows NT.

 Notes

As Windows NT/2000/XP is booting, if it thinks there is a problem you should know about or the system is set for a dual boot, a boot loader menu appears and gives you options such as which OS you want to load or how you want to handle a problem.

APPLYING CONCEPTS   To recover from a failed Windows NT boot:

1. If the Windows NT boot loader menu appears, use the Last Known Good configuration to return to the last registry values that allowed for a successful boot. Any configuration changes since the last good boot will be lost.

2. If you cannot boot from the hard drive, boot using the three boot disks that came with the OS. If you don't have these three disks, you can create them on a working PC. Check for corrupted boot and system files that you can replace. (How to create the three boot disks is covered later in this section.)

D

3. Boot from the three disks, and select the option "To repair a damaged Windows NT version 4.0 installation."

4. Try reinstalling Windows NT in the same folder it currently uses. Tell the Setup program this is an upgrade.

5. As a last resort, if you are using the NTFS file system and you must recover data on the hard drive, move the hard drive to another system that runs Windows NT and install the drive as a secondary drive. You might then be able to recover the data.

LAST KNOWN GOOD CONFIGURATION

Just as with Windows 2000/XP, each time Windows NT boots and the first logon is made with no errors, the OS saves a copy of the hardware configuration from the registry, which is called the Last Known Good configuration. (All hardware configuration sets stored in the registry, including the Last Known Good, are called control sets.) If an error occurs the next time the PC boots, it can use the Last Known Good configuration.

If Windows NT detects the possibility of a problem, it adds the Last Known Good option to the Windows NT boot loader menu. You can select this Last Known Good option to revert to the control set used for the last good boot. For example, if you install a new device driver, restart Windows NT, and find that the system hangs, you can use the Last Known Good option to revert to the previous configuration.

> **Notes**
>
> The key in the registry that contains the Last Known Good configuration is HKEY_LOCAL_MACHINE\ HARDWARE.

Because the configuration information is not saved to the Last Known Good control set until after the logon, don't attempt to log on if you have trouble with the boot. Doing so causes the Last Known Good to be replaced by the current control set, which might have errors. For example, if you install a new video driver, restart Windows, and find the screen very difficult to read, don't log on. Instead, press the reset button to reboot the PC. When given the choice, select Last Known Good from the boot loader menu.

To prevent hard drive corruption, if you have problems booting Windows NT, wait for all disk activity to stop before pressing the reset button or turning off the PC, especially if you are using the FAT file system.

If you accidentally disable a critical device, Windows NT decides to revert to the Last Known Good for you. You are not provided with a menu choice.

Reverting to the Last Known Good causes the loss of any changes made to the hardware configuration since the Last Known Good was saved. Therefore, it is wise to make one hardware configuration change at a time and reboot after each change. That way, if problems during booting are encountered, only the most recent change is lost. When installing several hardware devices, install them one at a time, rebooting each time.

> **Caution**
>
> If you have problems booting in Windows NT, don't log on. If you do, you will overwrite your previous Last Known Good.

WINDOWS NT BOOT DISKS

Windows NT requires three disks to hold enough of Windows NT to boot the OS. If the original three disks to boot Windows NT become corrupted or are lost, you can make extra copies using Winnt32.exe if you are running Windows NT, or using Winnt.exe if you are running another OS, such as

DOS or Windows 9x. You do not have to be working on the PC where you intend to use the disks in order to make them, because the disks don't contain unique information for a specific PC.

CREATING WINDOWS NT BOOT DISKS

Do the following to create boot disks using Windows NT:

1. Click **Start,** click **Run,** and then enter one of the following commands in the Run dialog box. Substitute the letter of your CD drive for E in the command line, if necessary:

   ```
   E:\i386\winnt32.exe /ox

   E:\i386\winnt.exe /ox
   ```

   The /OX parameters cause the program to create only the set of three disks, without performing a complete installation. In Figure D-1, you can see the command line from within Windows NT used to create the disks when drive E contains the Windows NT installation CD.

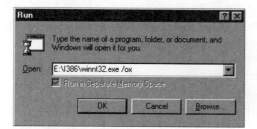

Figure D-1   Using Winnt32.exe to create a set of boot disks

2. The program asks for the location of the installation files. In this example, you would enter E:\i386. You are then prompted to insert three disks. The program creates the disks beginning with disk 3, then 2, then 1.

Windows NT does not have a Safe Mode, so if the PC later cannot boot Windows NT from the hard drive, these three disks can be used to load Windows NT, which loads using a generic VGA mode. After Windows NT is loaded, use a fourth disk—the Emergency Repair Disk (ERD)—to restore critical system files to their state at the time the last update was made to the ERD.

THE WINDOWS NT EMERGENCY REPAIR DISK

The Emergency Repair Disk (ERD) contains information unique to your OS and hard drive. You are given the opportunity to create the disk during installation. Always create this disk, because it is your record of critical information about your system that can be used to fix a problem with the OS.

D

The ERD enables restoration on your hard drive of the Windows registry, which contains all the configuration information for Windows. In addition, the disk includes information used to build a command window to run DOS-like commands. The files on the ERD are listed in Table D-1. Files stored on the ERD are also written to the hard drive during the installation. Using Explorer, you can see the files listed in the *\winnt_root*\repair folder.

In Microsoft documentation, *\winnt_root* is the folder in which Windows NT is installed, which most likely is C:\Winnt\.

File	Description
Setup.log	A read-only, hidden system file used to verify the files installed on a system
System._	A compressed file containing part of the registry
Sam._	A compressed file containing some of the security part of the registry
Security._	A compressed file containing some of the security part of the registry
Software._	A compressed file containing software information in the registry
Default._	A compressed file containing part of the registry
Config.nt	The Windows NT version of Config.sys used in creating a command window
Autoexec.nt	The Windows NT version of Autoexec.bat
Ntuser.da_	A compressed file containing information about authorized users of the system

Table D-1 Files on the Windows NT Emergency Repair Disk

After the installation, you can create a new ERD or update the current one by using the Rdisk.exe utility in the *\winnt_root*\system32 folder. You should update the disk any time you make any major changes to the system, for example, when you install hardware or software. To use the Rdisk.exe utility, click **Start**, then **Run**, and then either click **Browse** or enter the path to the utility. Add the /S option so that the utility also backs up the registry to the hard drive.

If Windows NT is stored on drive D, the command line is:

```
D:\Winnt\System32\rdisk.exe /s
```

First, files are updated in the D:\Winnt\Repair directory; then you are given the opportunity to create a new ERD.

USING THE BOOT DISKS AND THE ERD TO RECOVER FROM A FAILED BOOT

In the case of a hard drive failure, you can boot from the three boot disks that come with the Windows NT CD or that you made using either Winnt.exe or Winnt32.exe. The Windows NT programs on these disks might also request that you provide the ERD. Insert the first boot disk, and reboot. You will be

Windows NT does not have a Device Manager. When installing and troubleshooting hardware, look for individual icons in the Control Panel to manage hardware devices. For a detailed report of the system configuration, use the WinMSD command. At a command prompt enter **Winmsd /a /f**. The command creates the report in the current directory.

prompted to insert disk 2, followed by disk 3. The Setup menu in Figure D-2 then appears. Select the option to repair a damaged installation by pressing R, and follow directions on the screen.

```
Windows NT Workstation Setup

Welcome to Setup.
The Setup program for the Microsoft(R) Windows NT(TM) OS version 4.0
prepares Windows NT to run on your computer.

      *To learn more about Windows NT Setup before continuing, press F1
      *To set up Windows NT now, press ENTER
      *To repair a damaged Windows NT version 4.0 installation, press R
      *To quit Setup without installing Windows NT, press F3
```

Figure D-2 Windows NT Workstation Setup menu

APPENDIX E

CompTIA A+ Acronyms

CompTIA provides a list of acronyms which you need to know before you sit for the A+ exams. You can download the list from the CompTIA Web site at *www.comptia.org*. The list is included here for your convenience. However, CompTIA occasionally updates the list, so be sure to check the CompTIA Web site for the latest version.

Acronym	Spelled Out
AC	alternating current
ACPI	advanced configuration and power interface
ACT	activity
ADSL	asymmetrical digital subscriber line
AGP	accelerated graphics port
AMD	advanced micro devices
AMR	audio modem riser
APIPA	automatic private Internet protocol addressing
ARP	address resolution protocol
ASR	automated system recovery
AT	advanced technology
ATA	advanced technology attachment
ATAPI	advanced technology attachment packet interface
ATM	asynchronous transfer mode
ATX	advanced technology extended
BIOS	basic input/output system
BNC	Bayonet-Neill-Concelman or British navel connector
BRI	basic rate interface
BTX	balanced technology extended
CD	compact disc
CD-ROM	compact disc-read-only memory
CD-RW	compact disc-rewritable
CDFS	compact disc file system
CGA	color/graphics adapter
CMOS	complementary metal-oxide semiconductor
COM1	communication port 1
CPU	central processing unit
CRIMM	continuity-Rambus inline memory module
CRT	cathode-ray tube
DB-25	serial communications D-shell connector, 25 pins
DC	direct current
DDR	double data-rate
DDR RAM	double data-rate random access memory
DDR SDRAM	double data-rate symmetric dynamic random access memory
DFS	distributed file system
DHCP	dynamic host configuration protocol
DIMM	dual inline memory module
DIN	Deutsche Industrie Norm
DIP	dual inline package

Acronym	Spelled Out
DMA	direct memory access
DNS	domain name service or domain name server
DOS	disk operating system
DB-9	9-pin D shell connector
DRAM	dynamic random access memory
DSL	digital subscriber line
DVD	digital video disc
DVD-RAM	digital versatile disc-random access memory
DVD-ROM	digital video disc-read only memory
DVD-R	digital video disc-recordable
DVD-RW	digital video disc-rewritable
DVI	digital visual interface
ECC	error correction code
ECP	extended capabilities port
EDO SDRAM	extended data out symmetric dynamic random access memory
EEPROM	electrically erasable programmable read-only memory
EFS	encrypting file system
EGA	enhanced graphics adapter
EIDE	enhanced integrated drive electronics
EISA	extended industry standard architecture
EMI	electromagnetic interference
ENET	Ethernet
EPP	enhanced parallel port
ERD	emergency repair disk
ESD	electrostatic discharge
ESDI	enhanced small device interface
EVGA	extended video graphics adapter/array
EVDO	evolution data optimized or evolution data only
FAT	file allocation table
FAT12	12-bit file allocation table
FAT16	16-bit file allocation table
FAT32	32-bit file allocation table
FCC	Federal Communications Commission
FDD	floppy disk drive
FERPA	Family Educational Rights and Privacy Act
FPM	fast page-mode
FPM SDRAM	fast page-mode symmetric dynamic random access memory
FRU	field replaceable unit
FTP	file transfer protocol

Acronym	Spelled Out
GB	gigabyte
GDI	graphics device interface
GHz	gigahertz
GUI	graphical user interface
GRPS	general radio packet system
GSM	global system manager or graphics size modification or graphics screen manager
HCL	hardware compatibility list
HDD	hard disk drive
HDMi	high definition media interface
HPFS	high performance file system
HTML	hypertext markup language
HTTP	hypertext transfer protocol
HTTPS	hypertext transfer protocol over secure sockets layer
I/O	input/output
ICMP	Internet control message protocol
ICS	Internet connection sharing
IDE	integrated drive electronics
IEEE	Institute of Electrical and Electronics Engineers
IIS	Internet information server
IMAP	Internet mail access protocol
IP	Internet protocol
IPSEC	Internet protocol security
IPX	internetwork packet exchange
IPX/SPX	internetwork packet exchange/sequenced packet exchange
IR	infrared
IrDA	Infrared Data Association
IRQ	interrupt request
ISA	industry standard architecture
ISDN	integrated services digital network
ISO	Industry Standards Organization
ISP	Internet service provider
KB	kilobyte
LAN	local area network
LAT	local area transport
LCD	liquid crystal display
LED	light emitting diode
LPT	line printer terminal
LPT1	line printer terminal 1
LPX	low profile extended

Acronym	Spelled Out
LVD	low voltage differential
MAC	media access control
MAN	metropolitan area network
Mb	megabit
MB	megabyte
MBR	master boot record
MCA	micro channel architecture
MHz	megahertz
MicroDIMM	micro dual inline memory module
MIDI	musical instrument digital interface
MLI	multiple link interface
MMC	Microsoft management console
MMX	multimedia extensions
MP3	Moving Picture Experts Group Layer 3 Audio
MPEG	Moving Picture Experts Group
MSDS	material safety data sheet
MUI	multilingual user interface
NAS	network-attached storage
NAT	network address translation
NetBIOS	networked basic input/output system
NetBEUI	networked basic input/output system extended user interface
NFS	network file system
NIC	network interface card
NLI	not logged in or natural language interface
NLX	new low-profile extended
NNTP	network news transfer protocol
NTFS	new technology file system
NTLDR	new technology loader
OEM	original equipment manufacturer
OS	operating system
OSR	original equipment manufacturer service release
PAN	personal area network
PATA	parallel advanced technology attachment
PCI	peripheral component interconnect
PCIX	peripheral component interconnect extended
PCL	printer control language
PCMCIA	Personal Computer Memory Card International Association
PDA	personal digital assistant
PGA	pin grid array

Acronym	Spelled Out
PGA2	pin grid array 2
PIN	personal identification number
PnP	plug and play
POP	post office protocol
POP3	post office protocol 3
POST	power-on self test
PPP	point-to-point protocol
PPTP	point-to-point tunneling protocol
PRI	primary rate interface
PROM	programmable read-only memory
PS/2	personal system/2 connector
PSTN	public switched telephone network
PVC	permanent virtual circuit
QoS	quality of service
RAID	redundant array of independent disks
RAM	random access memory
RAMBUS	trademarked term
RAS	remote access service
RDRAM	Rambus dynamic random access memory
RF	radio frequency
RGB	red green blue
RIMM	Rambus inline memory module
RIP	routing information protocol
RIS	remote installation service
RISC	reduced instruction set computer
RJ	registered jack
RJ-11	registered jack function 11
RJ-45	registered jack-45
ROM	read only memory
RS-232	recommended standard 232
RTC	real-time clock
SAN	storage area network
SATA	serial advanced technology attachment
SCSI	small computer system interface
SCSI ID	small computer system interface identifier
SD card	secure digital card
SDRAM	symmetric dynamic random access memory
SEC	single edge connector
SFC	system file checker

Acronym	Spelled Out
SGRAM	synchronous graphics random access memory
SIMM	single inline memory module
SLI	scalable link interface or system level integration or scanline interleave mode
SMB	server message block
SMTP	simple mail transport protocol
SNMP	simple network management protocol
SoDIMM	small outline dual inline memory module
SOHO	small office/home office
SP	service pack
SP1	service pack 1
SP2	service pack 2
SPDIF	Sony-Philips digital interface format
SPGA	staggered pin grid array
SPX	sequenced package exchange
SRAM	static random access memory
SSH	secure shell
SSID	service set identifier
SSL	secure sockets layer
ST	straight tip
STP	shielded twisted pair
SVGA	super video graphics array
SXGA	super extended graphics array
TB	terabyte
TCP/IP	transmission control protocol/Internet protocol
TFTP	trivial file transfer protocol
UART	universal asynchronous receiver transmitter
UDF	user-defined functions or universal disk format or universal data format
UDMA	ultra direct memory access
UDP	user datagram protocol
UFS	universal file system
UPS	uninterruptible power supply
URL	uniform resource locator
USB	universal serial bus
UTP	unshielded twisted pair
UXGA	ultra extended graphics array
VESA	Video Electronics Standards Association
VFAT	virtual file allocation table
VGA	video graphics array
VoIP	voice over Internet protocol

Acronym	Spelled Out
VPN	virtual private network
VRAM	video random access memory
WAN	wide area network
WAP	wireless application protocol
WEP	wired equivalent privacy
WIFI	wireless fidelity
WINS	Windows Internet name service
WLAN	wireless local area network
WPA	wireless protected access
WUXGA	wide ultra extended graphics array
XGA	extended graphics array
XPR	is an AIX command-line utility
ZIF	zero-insertion-force
ZIP	zigzag inline package

GLOSSARY

This glossary defines the key terms listed at the end of each chapter and other terms related to managing and maintaining a personal computer.

32-bit flat memory mode   A protected processing mode used by Windows NT/2000/XP to process programs written in 32-bit code early in the boot process.

3-D RAM   Special video RAM designed to improve 3-D graphics simulation.

80 conductor IDE cable   An IDE cable that has 40 pins but uses 80 wires, 40 of which are ground wires designed to reduce crosstalk on the cable. The cable is used by ATA/66 and higher IDE drives.

802.11a/b/g   *See* IEEE 802.11a/b/g.

A+ Certification   A certification awarded by CompTIA (The Computer Technology Industry Association) that measures a PC technician's knowledge and skills.

access point (AP)   A device connected to a LAN that provides wireless communication so that computers, printers, and other wireless devices can communicate with devices on the LAN.

ACPI (Advanced Configuration and Power Interface)   Specification developed by Intel, Compaq, Phoenix, Microsoft, and Toshiba to control power on notebooks and other devices. Windows 98 and Windows 2000/XP support ACPI.

Active Directory   A Windows 2000 Server and Windows Server 2003 directory database and service that allows for a single point of administration for all shared resources on a network, including files, peripheral devices, databases, Web sites, users, and services.

active matrix   A type of video display that amplifies the signal at every intersection in the grid of electrodes, which enhances the pixel quality over that of a dual-scan passive matrix display.

active partition   The primary partition on the hard drive that boots the OS. Windows NT/2000/XP calls the active partition the system partition.

active terminator   A type of terminator for single-ended SCSI cables that includes voltage regulators in addition to the simple resistors used with passive termination.

adapter address   *See* MAC address.

adapter card   A small circuit board inserted in an expansion slot and used to communicate between the system bus and a peripheral device. Also called an interface card.

administrator account   In Windows NT/2000/XP, an account that grants to the administrator(s) rights and permissions to all hardware and software resources, such as the right to add, delete, and change accounts and to change hardware configurations.

Advanced Options menu   A Windows 2000/XP menu that appears when you press F8 when Windows starts. The menu can be used to troubleshoot problems when loading Windows 2000/XP.

adware   Software installed on a computer that produces pop-up ads using your browser; the ads are often based on your browsing habits.

AirPort   The term Apple computers use to describe the IEEE 802.11b standard.

ANSI (American National Standards Institute)   A nonprofit organization dedicated to creating trade and communications standards.

answer file   A text file that contains information that Windows NT/2000/XP requires in order to do an unattended installation.

antivirus (AV) software   Utility programs that prevent infection or scan a system to detect and remove viruses. McAfee Associates' VirusScan and Norton AntiVirus are two popular AV packages.

application program interface (API) call   A request from software to the OS to access hardware or other software using a previously defined procedure that both the software and the OS understand.

ARP (Address Resolution Protocol)   A protocol that TCP/IP uses to translate IP addresses into physical network addresses (MAC addresses).

ASCII (American Standard Code for Information Interchange)   A popular standard for writing letters and other characters in binary code. Originally, ASCII characters were seven bits, so there were 127 possible values. ASCII has been expanded to an 8-bit version, allowing 128 additional values.

AT command set   A set of commands that a PC uses to control a modem and that a user can enter to troubleshoot the modem.

ATAPI (Advanced Technology Attachment Packet Interface)   An interface standard, part of the IDE/ATA standards, that allows tape drives, CD-ROM drives, and other drives to be treated like an IDE hard drive by the system.

authentication   The process of proving an individual is who they say they are before they are allowed access to a computer, file, folder, or network. The process might use a password, PIN, smart card, or biometric data.

authorization   Controlling what an individual can or cannot do with resources on a computer network. Using Windows, authorization is granted by the rights and permissions assigned to user accounts.

autodetection   A feature of system BIOS and hard drives that automatically identifies and configures a new drive in CMOS setup.

Autoexec.bat   A startup text file once used by DOS and used by Windows to provide backward-compatibility. It executes commands automatically during the boot process and is used to create a16-bit environment.

Automated System Recovery (ASR)   The Windows XP process that allows you to restore an entire hard drive volume or logical drive to its state at the time the backup of the volume was made.

Automatic Private IP Address (APIPA)   An IP address in the address range 169.254.x.x, used by a computer when it cannot successfully lease an IP address from a DHCP server.

backup   An extra copy of a file, used in the event that the original becomes damaged or destroyed.

backup domain controller (BDC)   In Windows NT, a computer on a network that holds a read-only copy of the SAM (security accounts manager) database.

Backup Operator   A Windows 2000/XP user account that can back up and restore any files on the system regardless of its having access to these files.

bandwidth   In relation to analog communication, the range of frequencies that a communications channel or cable can carry. In general use, the term refers to the volume of data that can travel on a bus or over a cable stated in bits per second (bps), kilobits per second (Kbps), or megabits per second (Mbps). Also called data throughput or line speed.

baseline   The level of performance expected from a system, which can be compared to current measurements to determine what needs upgrading or tuning.

basic disk   A way to partition a hard drive, used by DOS and all versions of Windows, that stores information about the drive in a partition table at the beginning of the drive. Compare to dynamic disk.

batch file   A text file containing a series of OS commands. Autoexec.bat is a batch file.

baud rate   A measure of line speed between two devices such as a computer and a printer or a modem. This speed is measured in the number of times a signal changes in one second. *See also* bits per second (bps).

best-effort protocol   *See* connectionless protocol.

binary number system   The number system used by computers; it has only two numbers, 0 and 1, called binary digits, or bits.

binding   The process by which a protocol is associated with a network card or a modem card.

BIOS (basic input/output system)   Firmware that can control much of a computer's input/output functions, such as communication with the floppy drive and the monitor. Also called ROM BIOS.

bit (binary digit)   A 0 or 1 used by the binary number system.

bits per second (bps)   A measure of data transmission speed. For example, a common modem speed is 56,000 bps, or 56 Kbps.

block mode   A method of data transfer between hard drive and memory that allows multiple data transfers on a single software interrupt.

blue screen   A Windows NT/2000/XP error that displays against a blue screen and causes the system to halt. Also called a stop error.

Bluetooth   A standard for wireless communication and data synchronization between devices, developed by a group of electronics manufacturers and overseen by the Bluetooth Special Interest Group. Bluetooth uses the same frequency range as 802.11b, but does not have as wide a range.

boot loader menu   A startup menu that gives the user the choice of which operating system to load such as Windows 98 or Windows XP which are both installed on the same system, creating a dual boot.

boot partition   The hard drive partition where the Windows NT/2000/XP OS is stored. The system partition and the boot partition may be different partitions.

boot record   The first sector of a floppy disk or logical drive in a partition; it contains information about the disk or logical drive. On a hard drive, if the boot record is in the active partition, then it is used to boot the OS. Also called boot sector.

boot sector   *See* boot record.

boot sector virus   An infectious program that can replace the boot program with a modified, infected version, often causing boot and data retrieval problems.

Boot.ini   A Windows NT/2000/XP hidden text file that contains information needed to start the boot and build the boot loader menu.

bootable disk   For DOS and Windows, a floppy disk that can upload the OS files necessary for computer startup. For DOS or Windows 9x/Me, it must contain the files Io.sys, Msdos.sys, and Command.com.

bootstrap loader   A small program at the end of the boot record that can be used to boot an OS from the disk or logical drive.

bridging protocol   *See* line protocol.

Briefcase   A system folder in Windows 9x/Me that is used to synchronize files between two computers.

broadband   A transmission technique that carries more than one type of transmission on the same medium, such as cable modem or DSL.

broadcast   Process by which a message is sent from a single host to all hosts on the network, without regard to the kind of data being sent or the destination of the data.

browser hijacker   A malicious program that infects your Web browser and can change your home page or browser settings. It can also redirect your browser to unwanted sites, produce pop-up ads, and set unwanted bookmarks. Also called a home page hijacker.

buffer   A temporary memory area where data is kept before being written to a hard drive or sent to a printer, thus reducing the number of writes to the devices.

built-in user account   An administrator account and a guest account that are set up when Windows NT/2000/XP is first installed.

bus   The paths, or lines, on the motherboard on which data, instructions, and electrical power move from component to component.

bus mouse   A mouse that plugs into a bus adapter card and has a round, 9-pin mini-DIN connector.

bus speed   The speed, or frequency, at which the data on the motherboard is written and read.

byte   A collection of eight bits that can represent a single character.

cabinet file   A file with a .cab extension that contains one or more compressed files and is often used to distribute software on disk. The Extract command is used to extract files from the cabinet file.

cable modem   A technology that uses cable TV lines for data transmission requiring a modem at each end. From the modem, a network cable connects to an NIC in the user's PC, or a USB cable connects to a USB port.

call tracking   A system that tracks the dates, times, and transactions of help-desk or on-site PC support calls, including the problem presented, the issues addressed, who did what, and when and how each call was resolved.

CardBus   A PCMCIA specification that improved on the earlier PC Card standards. It improves I/O speed, increases the bus width to 32 bits, and supports lower-voltage PC Cards, while maintaining backward compatibility with earlier standards.

cards   Adapter boards or interface cards placed into expansion slots to expand the functions of a computer, allowing it to communicate with external devices such as monitors or speakers.

carrier   A signal used to activate a phone line to confirm a continuous frequency; used to indicate that two computers are ready to receive or transmit data via modems.

CCITT (Comité Consultatif International Télégraphique et Téléphonique)   An international organization that was responsible for developing standards for international communications. This organization has been incorporated into the ITU. *See also* ITU.

CD (change directory) command   A command given at the command prompt that changes the default directory, for example CD \Windows.

CDFS (Compact Disc File System)   The 32-bit file system for CD discs and some CD-R and CD-RW discs that replaced the older 16-bit mscdex file system used by DOS. *See also* Universal Disk Format (UDF).

CDMA (code-division multiple access)   A protocol standard used by cellular WANs and cell phones

CD-R (CD-recordable)   A CD drive that can record or write data to a CD. The drive may or may not be multisession, but the data cannot be erased once it is written.

CD-RW (CD-rewritable)   A CD drive that can record or write data to a CD. The data can be erased and overwritten. The drive may or may not be multisession.

central processing unit (CPU)   Also called a microprocessor or processor. The heart and brain of the computer, which receives data input, processes information, and executes instructions.

chain   A group of clusters used to hold a single file.

CHAP (Challenge Handshake Authentication Protocol)   A protocol used to encrypt account names and passwords that are sent to a network controller for validation.

checksum A method of checking transmitted data for errors, whereby the digits are added and their sum compared to an expected sum.

child directory *See* subdirectory.

child, parent, grandparent backup method A plan for backing up and reusing tapes or removable disks by rotating them each day (child), week (parent), and month (grandparent).

chipset A group of chips on the motherboard that controls the timing and flow of data and instructions to and from the CPU.

CHS (cylinder, head, sector) mode An outdated method by which BIOS reads from and writes to hard drives by addressing the correct cylinder, head, and sector. Also called normal mode.

circuit board A computer component, such as the main motherboard or an adapter board, that has electronic circuits and chips.

clean install Installing an OS on a new hard drive or on a hard drive that has a previous OS installed, but without carrying forward any settings kept by the old OS, including information about hardware, software, or user preferences. A fresh installation.

client/server A computer concept whereby one computer (the client) requests information from another computer (the server).

client/server application An application that has two components. The client software requests data from the server software on the same or another computer.

client-side caching A technique used by browsers (clients) to speed up download times by caching Web pages previously requested in case they are requested again.

clock speed The speed, or frequency, expressed in MHz, that controls activity on the motherboard and is generated by a crystal or oscillator located somewhere on the motherboard.

clone A computer that is a no-name Intel- and Microsoft-compatible PC.

cluster One or more sectors that constitute the smallest unit of space on a disk for storing data (also referred to as a file allocation unit). Files are written to a disk as groups of whole clusters.

CMOS (complementary metal-oxide semiconductor) The technology used to manufacture microchips. CMOS chips require less electricity, hold data longer after the electricity is turned off, are slower, and produce less heat than earlier technologies. The configuration, or setup, chip is a CMOS chip.

CMOS configuration chip A chip on the motherboard that contains a very small amount of memory, or RAM enough to hold configuration, or setup, information about the computer The chip is powered by a battery when the PC is turned off. Also called CMOS setup chip or CMOS RAM chip.

CMOS setup (1) The CMOS configuration chip. (2) The program in system BIOS that can change the values in CMOS RAM.

CMOS setup chip *See* CMOS configuration chip.

COAST (cache on a stick) Memory modules that hold memory used as a memory cache. *See* memory cache.

coaxial cable Networking cable used with10-Mbps Ethernet ThinNet or ThickNet.

cold boot *See* hard boot.

Command.com Along with Msdos.sys and Io.sys, one of the three files that are the core components of the real-mode portion of Windows 9x/Me. Command.com provides a command prompt and interprets commands.

comment A line or part of a line in a program that is intended as a remark or comment and is ignored when the program runs. A semicolon or an REM is often used to mark a line as a comment.

Compact.exe Windows 2000/XP command and program to compress or uncompress a volume, folder, or file.

Compatibility Mode utility A Windows XP utility that provides an application with the older Microsoft OS environment it was designed to operate in.

compressed drive A drive whose format has been reorganized in order to store more data. A Windows 9x compressed drive is really not a drive at all; it's actually a type of file, typically with a host drive called H.

compression To store data in a file, folder, or logical drive using a coding format that reduces the size of files in order to save space on a drive or shorten transport time when sending a file over the Internet or network.

computer name Character-based host name or NetBIOS name assigned to a computer.

Config.sys A text file used by DOS and supported by Windows 9x/Me that lists device drivers to be loaded at startup. It can also set system variables to be used by DOS and Windows.

Configuration Manager A component of Windows Plug and Play that controls the configuration process of all devices and communicates these configurations to the devices.

connectionless protocol   A protocol such as UDP that does not require a connection before sending a packet and does not guarantee delivery. An example of a UDP transmission is streaming video over the Web. Also called a best-effort protocol.

connection-oriented protocol   In networking, a protocol that confirms that a good connection has been made before transmitting data to the other end. An example of a connection-oriented protocol is TCP.

console   A window in which one or more Windows 2000/XP utility programs have been installed. The window is created using Microsoft Management Console, and installed utilities are called snap-ins.

conventional memory   DOS and Windows 9x/Me memory addresses between 0 and 640 K. Also called base memory.

copyright   An individual's right to copy his/her own work. No one else, other than the copyright owner, is legally allowed to do so without permission.

CRC (cyclical redundancy check)   A process in which calculations are performed on bytes of data before and after they are transmitted to check for corruption during transmission.

cross-linked clusters   Errors caused when more than one file points to a cluster, and the files appear to share the same disk space, according to the file allocation table.

crossover cable   A cable used to connect two PCs into the simplest network possible. Also used to connect two hubs.

CVF (compressed volume file)   The Windows 9x/Me file on the host drive of a compressed drive that holds all compressed data.

data bus   The lines on the system bus that the CPU uses to send and receive data.

data cartridge   A type of tape medium typically used for backups. Full-sized data cartridges are $4 \times 6 \times 2\frac{5}{8}$ inches in size. A minicartridge is only $3\frac{1}{4} \times 2\frac{1}{2} \times 2\frac{3}{5}$ inches in size.

data line protector   A surge protector designed to work with the telephone line to a modem.

data migration   Moving data from one application to another application or from one storage media to another, and most often involves a change in the way the data is formatted.

data path   The number of bits transported into and out of the processor.

data path size   The number of lines on a bus that can hold data, for example, 8, 16, 32, and 64 lines, which can accommodate 8, 16, 32, and 64 bits at a time.

data throughput   *See* bandwidth.

datagram   *See* packet.

default gateway   The gateway a computer on a network will use to access another network unless it knows to specifically use another gateway for quicker access to that network.

default printer   The printer Windows prints to unless another printer is selected.

Defrag.exe   Windows program and command to defragment a logical drive.

defragment   To "optimize" or rewrite a file to a disk in one contiguous chain of clusters, thus speeding up data retrieval.

desktop   The initial screen that is displayed when an OS has a GUI interface loaded.

device driver   A program stored on the hard drive that tells the computer how to communicate with an input/output device such as a printer or modem.

DHCP (Dynamic Host Configuration Protocol) server   A service that assigns dynamic IP addresses to computers on a network when they first access the network.

diagnostic cards   Adapter cards designed to discover and report computer errors and conflicts at POST time (before the computer boots up), often by displaying a number on the card.

diagnostic software   Utility programs that help troubleshoot computer systems. Some Windows diagnostic utilities are CHKDSK and SCANDISK. PC-Technician is an example of a third-party diagnostic program.

dialer   Malicious software installed on your PC that disconnects your phone line from your ISP and dials up an expensive pay-per-minute phone number without your knowledge.

dial-up networking   A Windows 9x/Me and Windows NT/2000/XP utility that uses a modem and telephone line to connect to a network.

differential backup   Backup method that backs up only files that have changed or have been created since the last full backup. When recovering data, only two backups are needed: the full backup and the last differential backup.

digital certificate   A code used to authenticate the source of a file or document or to identify and authenticate a person or organization sending data over the Internet. The code is assigned by a certificate authority such as VeriSign and includes a public key for encryption. Also called *digital ID* or *digital signature*.

digital ID   *See* digital certificate.

digital signature   *See* digital certificate.

DIMM (dual inline memory module)   A miniature circuit board installed on a motherboard to hold memory. DIMMs can hold up to 2 GB of RAM on a single module.

Direct Rambus DRAM   A memory technology by Rambus and Intel that uses a narrow network-type system bus. Memory is stored on a RIMM module. Also called RDRAM or Direct RDRAM.

Direct RDRAM   *See* Direct Rambus DRAM.

directory table   An OS table that contains file information such as the name, size, time and date of last modification, and cluster number of the file's beginning location.

discrete L2 cache   A type of L2 cache contained within the Pentium processor housing, but on a different die, with a cache bus between the processor and the cache.

disk cache   A method whereby recently retrieved data and adjacent data are read into memory in advance, anticipating the next CPU request.

disk cloning   *See* drive imaging.

disk compression   Compressing data on a hard drive to allow more data to be written to the drive.

disk imaging   *See* drive imaging.

Disk Management   A Windows 2000/XP utility used to display, create, and format partitions on basic disks and volumes on dynamic disks.

disk quota   A limit placed on the amount of disk space that is available to users. Requires a Windows 2000/XP NTFS volume.

disk thrashing   A condition that results when the hard drive is excessively used for virtual memory because RAM is full. It dramatically slows down processing and can cause premature hard drive failure.

Display Power Management Signaling (DPMS)   Energy Star standard specifications that allow for the video card and monitor to go into sleep mode simultaneously. *See also* Energy Star.

distribution server   A file server holding Windows setup files used to install Windows on computers networked to the server.

DMA (direct memory access) channel   A number identifying a channel whereby a device can pass data to memory without involving the CPU. Think of a DMA channel as a shortcut for data moving to/from the device and memory.

DMA transfer mode   A transfer mode used by devices, including the hard drive, to transfer data to memory without involving the CPU.

DNS (domain name service or domain name system)   A distributed pool of information (called the name space) that keeps track of assigned domain names and their corresponding IP addresses, and the system that allows a host to locate information in the pool. Compare to WINS.

DNS server   A computer that can find an IP address for another computer when only the domain name is known.

docking station   A device that receives a notebook computer and provides additional secondary storage and easy connection to peripheral devices.

domain   In Windows NT/2000/XP, a logical group of networked computers, such as those on a college campus, that share a centralized directory database of user account information and security for the entire domain.

domain controller   A Windows NT/2000 or Windows Server 2003 computer which holds and controls a database of (1) user accounts, (2) group accounts, and (3) computer accounts used to manage access to the network.

domain name   A unique, text-based name that identifies a network.

DOS box   A command window.

Dosstart.bat   A type of Autoexec.bat file that is executed by Windows 9x/Me in two situations: when you select Restart the computer in MS-DOS mode from the shutdown menu or you run a program in MS-DOS mode.

dot pitch   The distance between the dots that the electronic beam hits on a monitor screen.

Double Data Rate SDRAM (DDR SDRAM)   A type of memory technology used on DIMMs that runs at twice the speed of the system clock.

doze time   The time before an Energy Star or "Green" system will reduce 80 percent of its activity.

Dr. Watson   A Windows utility that can record detailed information about the system, errors that occur, and the programs that caused them in a log file. Windows 9x/Me names the log file \Windows\Drwatson\WatsonXX.wlg, where XX is an incrementing number. Windows 2000 names the file \Documents and Settings\user\Documents\DrWatson\Drwtsn32.log. Windows XP calls the file Drwatson.log.

drive imaging   Making an exact image of a hard-drive, including partition information, boot sectors, operating system installation, and application software to replicate the hard drive on another system or recover from a hard drive crash. Also called *disk cloning* and *disk imaging*.

DriveSpace   A Windows 9x/Me utility that compresses files so that they take up less space on a disk drive, creating a single large file on the disk to hold all the compressed files.

drop height   The height from which a manufacturer states that its device, such as a hard drive, can be dropped without making the device unusable.

DSL (Digital Subscriber Line)   A telephone line that carries digital data from end to end, and can be leased from the telephone company for individual use. Some DSL lines are rated at 5 Mbps, about 50 times faster than regular telephone lines.

dual boot   The ability to boot using either of two different OSs, such as Windows 98 and Windows XP.

dual channel   A motherboard feature that improves memory performance by providing two 64-bit channels between memory and the chipset. DDR and DDR2 memory can use dual channels.

dual-core processing   Two processors contained in the same processor housing that share the interface with the chipset and memory.

dual-scan passive matrix   A type of video display that is less expensive than an active-matrix display and does not provide as high-quality an image. With dual-scan display, two columns of electrodes are activated at the same time.

dump file   A file that contains information captured from memory at the time a stop error occurred.

DVD (digital video disc or digital versatile disk)   A faster, larger CD format that can read older CDs, store over 8 GB of data, and hold full-length motion picture videos.

dye-sublimation printer   A type of printer with photo-lab-quality results that uses transparent dyed film. The film is heated, which causes the dye to vaporize onto glossy paper.

dynamic disk   A way to partition one or more hard drives, introduced with Windows 2000, in which information about the drive is stored in a database at the end of the drive. Compare to basic disk.

dynamic IP address   An assigned IP address that is used for the current session only. When the session is terminated, the IP address is returned to the list of available addresses.

dynamic RAM (DRAM)   The most common type of system memory, it requires refreshing every few milliseconds.

dynamic volume   A volume type used with dynamic disks for which you can change the size of the volume after you have created it.

dynamic VxD   A VxD that is loaded and unloaded from memory as needed.

ECHS (extended CHS) mode   *See* large mode.

ECP (Extended Capabilities Port)   A bidirectional parallel port mode that uses a DMA channel to speed up data flow.

EDO (extended data out)   A type of outdated RAM that was faster than conventional RAM because it eliminated the delay before it issued the next memory address.

EEPROM (electrically erasable programmable ROM)   A type of chip in which higher voltage may be applied to one of the pins to erase its previous memory before a new instruction set is electronically written.

EIDE (Enhanced IDE)   A standard for managing the interface between secondary storage devices and a computer system. A system can support up to six serial ATA and parallel ATA IDE devices or up to four parallel ATA IDE devices such as hard drives, CD-ROM drives, and DVD drives.

electromagnetic interference (EMI)   A magnetic field produced as a side effect from the flow of electricity. EMI can cause corrupted data in data lines that are not properly shielded.

electrostatic discharge (ESD)   Another name for static electricity, which can damage chips and destroy motherboards, even though it might not be felt or seen with the naked eye.

Emergency Repair Disk (ERD)   A Windows NT record of critical information about your system that can be used to fix a problem with the OS. The ERD enables restoration of the Windows NT registry on your hard drive.

Emergency Repair Process   A Windows 2000 process that restores the OS to its state at the completion of a successful installation.

emergency startup disk (ESD)   *See* rescue disk.

Emm386.exe   A DOS and Windows 9x/Me utility that provides access to upper memory for 16-bit device drivers and other software.

Encrypted File System (EFS)   A way to use a key to encode a file or folder on an NTFS volume to protect sensitive data. Because it is an integrated system service, EFS is transparent to users and applications and is difficult to attack.

encrypting virus   A type of virus that transforms itself into a nonreplicating program in order to avoid detection. It transforms itself back into a replicating program in order to spread.

encryption   The process of putting readable data into an encoded form that can only be decoded (or decrypted) through use of a key.

Energy Star "Green" systems that satisfy the EPA requirements to decrease the overall consumption of electricity. *See also* Green Standards.

enhanced BIOS A system BIOS that has been written to accommodate large-capacity drives (over 504 MB, usually in the gigabyte range).

EPP (Enhanced Parallel Port) A parallel port that allows data to flow in both directions (bidirectional port) and is faster than original parallel ports on PCs that allowed communication only in one direction.

EPROM (erasable programmable ROM) A type of chip with a special window that allows the current memory contents to be erased with special ultraviolet light so that the chip can be reprogrammed.

error correction The ability of a modem to identify transmission errors and then automatically request another transmission.

escalate When a technician passes a customer's problem to higher organizational levels because he or she cannot solve the problem.

Ethernet The most popular LAN architecture that can run at 10 Mbps (ThinNet or ThickNet), 100 Mbps (Fast Ethernet), or 1 Gbps (Gigabit Ethernet).

Execution Trace Cache A type of Level 1 cache used by some CPUs to hold decoded operations waiting to be executed.

executive services In Windows NT/2000/XP, a group of components running in kernel mode that interfaces between the subsystems in user mode and the HAL.

expansion bus A bus that does not run in sync with the system clock.

expansion card A circuit board inserted into a slot on the motherboard to enhance the capability of the computer.

expansion slot A narrow slot on the motherboard where an expansion card can be inserted. Expansion slots connect to a bus on the motherboard.

expert systems Software that uses a database of known facts and rules to simulate a human expert's reasoning and decision-making processes.

ExpressCard The latest PCMCIA standard for notebook I/O cards that uses the PCI Express and USB 2.0 data transfer standards. Two types of Express-Cards are ExpressCard/34 (34 mm wide) and ExpressCard/54 (54 mm wide).

extended memory Memory above 1024 K used in a DOS or Windows 9x/Me system.

extended partition The only partition on a hard drive that can contain more than one logical drive.

external cache Static cache memory, stored on the motherboard or inside the CPU housing, that is not part of the CPU (also called L2 or L3 cache).

external command Commands that have their own program files.

faceplate A metal or plastic plate that comes with the computer case and fits over the empty drive bays or slots for expansion cards to create a well-fitted enclosure around them.

FAT (file allocation table) A table on a hard drive or floppy disk that tracks the clusters used to contain a file.

FAT12 The 12-bit wide, one-column file allocation table for a floppy disk, containing information about how each cluster or file allocation unit on the disk is currently used.

fault tolerance The degree to which a system can tolerate failures. Adding redundant components, such as disk mirroring or disk duplexing, is a way to build in fault tolerance.

Fiber Distributed Data Interface (FDDI) A ring-based network that does not require a centralized hub and can transfer data at a rate of 100 Mbps.

field replaceable unit (FRU) A component in a computer or device that can be replaced with a new component without sending the computer or device back to the manufacturer. Examples: power supply, DIMM, motherboard, floppy disk drive.

file allocation unit *See* cluster.

file extension A three-character portion of the name of a file that is used to identify the file type. In command lines, the file extension follows the filename and is separated from it by a period. For example, Msd.exe, where exe is the file extension.

file system The overall structure that an OS uses to name, store, and organize files on a disk. Examples of file systems are FAT32 and NTFS.

file virus A virus that inserts virus code into an executable program file and can spread whenever that program is executed.

filename The first part of the name assigned to a file. In DOS, the filename can be no more than eight characters long and is followed by the file extension. In Windows, a filename can be up to 255 characters.

firewall   Hardware or software that protects a computer or network from unauthorized access.

FireWire   *See* IEEE 1394.

firmware   Software that is permanently stored in a chip. The BIOS on a motherboard is an example of firmware.

flash ROM   ROM that can be reprogrammed or changed without replacing chips.

flat panel monitor   A desktop monitor that uses an LCD panel.

floppy disk drive (FDD)   A drive that can hold either a $5\frac{1}{4}$ inch or $3\frac{1}{2}$ floppy disk.

flow control   When using modems, a method of controlling the flow of data to adjust for problems with data transmission. Xon/Xoff is an example of a flow control protocol.

folder   *See* subdirectory.

folder redirection   A Windows XP feature that allows a user to point to a folder that can be on the local PC or somewhere on the network, and its location can be transparent to the user.

forgotten password floppy disk   A Windows XP disk created to be used in the event the user forgets the user account password to the system.

form factor   A set of specifications on the size, shape, and configuration of a computer hardware component such as a case, power supply, or motherboard.

formatting   Preparing a hard drive volume or floppy disk for use by placing tracks and sectors on its surface to store information (for example, FORMAT A:).

fragmentation   The distribution of data files on a hard drive or floppy disk such that they are stored in noncontiguous clusters.

fragmented file   A file that has been written to different portions of the disk so that it is not in contiguous clusters.

frame   The header and trailer information added to data to form a data packet to be sent over a network.

front-side bus (FSB)   *See* system bus.

FTP (File Transfer Protocol)   The protocol used to transfer files over a TCP/IP network such that the file does not need to be converted to ASCII format before transferring it.

full backup   A complete backup, whereby all of the files on the hard drive are backed up each time the backup procedure is performed. It is the safest backup method, but it takes the most time.

full-duplex   Communication that happens in two directions at the same time.

fully qualified domain name (FQDN)   A host name and a domain name such as *jsmith.amazon.com*. Sometimes loosely referred to as a domain name.

gateway   A computer or other device that connects networks.

GDI (Graphics Device Interface)   A core Windows component responsible for building graphics data to display or print. A GDI printer relies on Windows to construct a page to print and then receives the constructed page as bitmap data.

General Packet Radio Service (GPRS)   A protocol standard that can be used by GSM or TDMA on a cellular WAN to send voice, text, or video data in packets similar to VoIP.

General Protection Fault (GPF)   A Windows error that occurs when a program attempts to access a memory address that is not available or is no longer assigned to it.

Gigabit Ethernet   The next generation of Ethernet. Gigabit Ethernet supports rates of data transfer up to 1 gigabit per second but is not yet widely used.

gigahertz (GHz)   One thousand MHz, or one billion cycles per second.

global user account   Sometimes called a domain user account, the account is used at the domain level, created by an administrator, and stored in the SAM (security accounts manager) database on a Windows 2000 or Windows 2003 domain controller.

graphics accelerator   A type of video card that has an on-board processor that can substantially increase speed and boost graphical and video performance.

graphics DDR (G-DDR), graphics DDR2, graphics DDR3   Types of DDR, DDR2, and DDR3 memory specifically designed to be used in graphics cards.

grayware   A program that AV software recognizes to be potentially harmful or potentially unwanted.

Green Standards   A computer or device that conforms to these standards can go into sleep or doze mode when not in use, thus saving energy and helping the environment. Devices that carry the Green Star or Energy Star comply with these standards.

ground bracelet   A strap you wear around your wrist that is attached to the computer case, ground mat, or another ground so that ESD is discharged from your body before you touch sensitive components inside a computer. Also called static strap, ground strap, ESD bracelet.

group profile A group of user profiles. All profiles in the group can be changed by changing the group profile.

GSM (Global System for Mobile communication) An open standard for cellular WANs and cell phones that uses digital communication of data and is accepted and used worldwide.

guard tone A tone that an answering modem sends when it first answers the phone, to tell the calling modem that a modem is on the other end of the line.

Guest user A user who has limited permissions on a system and cannot make changes to it. Guest user accounts are intended for one-time or infrequent users of a workstation.

HAL (hardware abstraction layer) The low-level part of Windows NT/2000/XP, written specifically for each CPU technology, so that only the HAL must change when platform components change.

half life The time it takes for a medium storing data to weaken to half of its strength. Magnetic media, including traditional hard drives and floppy disks, have a half-life of five to seven years.

half-duplex Communication between two devices whereby transmission takes place in only one direction at a time.

handshaking When two modems begin to communicate, the initial agreement made as to how to send and receive data.

hard boot Restart the computer by turning off the power or by pressing the Reset button. Also called a cold boot.

hard copy Output from a printer to paper.

hard drive The main secondary storage device of a PC, a small case that contains magnetic coated platters that rotate at high speed.

hard drive controller The firmware that controls access to a hard drive contained on a circuit board mounted on or inside the hard drive housing. Older hard drives used firmware on a controller card that connected to the drive by way of two cables, one for data and one for control.

hard drive standby time The amount of time before a hard drive will shut down to conserve energy.

hard-disk loading The illegal practice of installing unauthorized software on computers for sale. Hard-disk loading can typically be identified by the absence of original software disks in the original system's shipment.

hardware The physical components that constitute the computer system, such as the monitor, the keyboard, the motherboard, and the printer.

hardware address *See* MAC address.

hardware cache A disk cache that is contained in RAM chips built right on the disk controller. Also called a buffer.

hardware interrupt An event caused by a hardware device signaling the CPU that it requires service.

hardware profile A set of hardware configuration information that Windows keeps in the registry. Windows can maintain more than one hardware profile for the same PC.

HCL (hardware compatibility list) The list of all computers and peripheral devices that have been tested and are officially supported by Windows NT/2000/XP (see *www.microsoft.com/whdc/hcl/default.mspx*).

head The top or bottom surface of one platter on a hard drive. Each platter has two heads.

hertz (Hz) Unit of measurement for frequency, calculated in terms of vibrations, or cycles per second. For example, for 16-bit stereo sound, a frequency of 44,000 Hz is used. *See also* megahertz.

hexadecimal notation (hex) A numbering system that uses 16 digits, the numerals 0–9, and the letters A–F. Hexadecimal notation is often used to display memory addresses.

hibernation A notebook OS feature that conserves power by using a small trickle of electricity. Before the notebook begins to hibernate, everything currently stored in memory is saved to the hard drive. When the notebook is brought out of hibernation, open applications and their data are returned to the state before hibernation.

hidden file A file that is not displayed in a directory list. Whether to hide or display a file is one of the file's attributes kept by the OS.

high memory area (HMA) In DOS or Windows 9x/Me, the first 64K of extended memory.

High Voltage Differential (HVD) A type of SCSI differential signaling requiring more expensive hardware to handle the higher voltage. HVD became obsolete with the introduction of SCSI-3.

high-level formatting Formatting performed by means of the DOS or Windows Format program (for example, FORMAT C:/S creates the boot record, FAT, and root directory on drive C and makes the drive bootable). Also called OS formatting.

Himem.sys The DOS and Windows 9x/Me memory manager extension that allowed access to memory addresses above 1 MB.

hive Physical segment of the Windows NT/ 2000/XP registry that is stored in a file.

hop count *See* time to live (TTL).

host Any computer or other device on a network that has been assigned an IP address. Also called node.

host adapter The circuit board that controls a SCSI bus supporting as many as seven or fifteen separate devices. The host adapter controls communication between the SCSI bus and the PC.

host bus *See* system bus.

host drive Using Windows 9x, typically drive H on a compressed drive. *See* compressed drive.

host name A name that identifies a computer, printer, or other device on a network.

hot-pluggable *See* hot-swappable.

hot-swappable A device that can be plugged into a computer while it is turned on and the computer will sense the device and configure it without rebooting, or the device can be removed without an OS error. Also called hot-pluggable.

HTML (HyperText Markup Language) A markup language used for hypertext documents on the World Wide Web. This language uses tags to format the document, create hyperlinks, and mark locations for graphics.

HTTP (HyperText Transfer Protocol) The communications protocol used by the World Wide Web.

HTTPS (HTTP secure) A version of the HTTP protocol that includes data encryption for security.

hub A network device or box that provides a central location to connect cables.

hypertext Text that contains links to remote points in the document or to other files, documents, or graphics. Hypertext is created using HTML and is commonly distributed from Web sites.

i.Link *See* IEEE 1394.

I/O addresses Numbers that are used by devices and the CPU to manage communication between them. Also called ports or port addresses.

I/O controller card An older card that can contain serial, parallel, and game ports and floppy drive and IDE connectors.

IBM Data Connector *See* IDC.

IBM-compatible PC A computer that uses an Intel (or compatible) processor and can run DOS and Windows.

ICMP (Internet Control Message Protocol) Part of the IP layer that is used to transmit error messages and other control messages to hosts and routers.

IDC (IBM Data Connector) A connector used with STP cable on a Token Ring network. Also called a *UDC (Universal Data Connector)*.

IDE (Integrated Drive Electronics or Integrated Device Electronics) A hard drive whose disk controller is integrated into the drive, eliminating the need for a controller cable and thus increasing speed, as well as reducing price. *See also* EIDE.

IEEE 1284 A standard for parallel ports and cables developed by the Institute for Electrical and Electronics Engineers and supported by many hardware manufacturers.

IEEE 1394 Standards for an expansion bus that can also be configured to work as a local bus. It is expected to replace the SCSI bus, providing an easy method to install and configure fast I/O devices. Also called FireWire and i.Link.

IEEE 1394.3 A standard, developed by the 1394 Trade Association, that is designed for peer-to-peer data transmission and allows imaging devices to send images and photos directly to printers without involving a computer.

IEEE 802.11a/b/g IEEE specifications for wireless communication and data synchronization. Also known as Wi-Fi. Apple Computer's versions of 802.11b/g are called AirPort and AirPort Extreme.

IFS (Installable File System) The Windows 9x/Me component that configures all devices and communicates these configurations to the device drivers.

IMAP4 (Internet Message Access Protocol version 4) Version 4 of the IMAP protocol, which is an e-mail protocol that has more functionality than its predecessor, POP. IMAP can archive messages in folders on the e-mail server and can allow the user to choose not to download attachments to messages.

incremental backup A time-saving backup method that only backs up files changed or newly created since the last full or incremental backup. Multiple incremental backups might be required when recovering lost data.

infestation Any unwanted program that is transmitted to a computer without the user's knowledge and that is designed to do varying degrees of damage to data and software. There are a number of different types of infestations, including viruses, Trojan horses, worms, and logic bombs. *See* malicious software.

information (.inf) file Text file with an .inf file extension, such as Msbatch.inf, that contains information about a hardware or software installation.

infrared transceiver A wireless transceiver that uses infrared technology to support some wireless devices such as keyboards, mice, and printers. A motherboard might have an embedded infrared transceiver, or the transceiver might plug into a USB or serial port. The technology is defined by the Infrared Data Association (IrDA). Also called an *IrDA transceiver* or *infrared port*.

initialization files Configuration information files for Windows. System.ini is one of the most important Windows 9x/Me initialization files.

inkjet printer A type of ink dispersion printer that uses cartridges of ink. The ink is heated to a boiling point and then ejected onto the paper through tiny nozzles.

Institute of Electrical and Electronics Engineers (IEEE) A nonprofit organization that develops standards for the computer and electronics industries.

instruction set The set of instructions, on the CPU chip, that the computer can perform directly (such as ADD and MOVE).

intelligent UPS A UPS connected to a computer by way of a USB or serial cable so that software on the computer can monitor and control the UPS. Also called *smart UPS*.

internal bus The bus inside the CPU that is used for communication between the CPU's internal components.

internal cache Memory cache that is faster than external cache, and is contained inside CPU chips (also referred to as primary, Level 1, or L1 cache).

internal command Commands that are embedded in the Command.com file.

Internet Connection Firewall (ICF) Windows XP software designed to protect a PC from unauthorized access from the Internet. Windows XP Service Pack 2 improved on ICF and renamed it Windows Firewall.

Internet Connection Sharing (ICS) A Windows 98 and Windows XP utility that uses NAT and acts as a proxy server to manage two or more computers connected to the Internet.

Internet service provider (ISP) A commercial group that provides Internet access for a monthly fee. AOL, Earthlink, and CompuServe are large ISPs.

intranet A private network that uses the TCP/IP protocols.

Io.sys Along with Msdos.sys and Command.com, one of the three files that are the core components of the real mode portion of Windows 9x/Me. It is the first program file of the OS.

IP (Internet Protocol) The rules of communication in the TCP/IP stack that control segmenting data into packets, routing those packets across networks, and then reassembling the packets once they reach their destination.

IP address A 32-bit address consisting of four numbers separated by periods, used to uniquely identify a device on a network that uses TCP/IP protocols. The first numbers identify the network; the last numbers identify a host. An example of an IP address is 206.96.103.114.

IPX/SPX (Internetwork Packet Exchange/Sequenced Packet Exchange) A networking protocol suite first used by Novell NetWare, and which corresponds to the TCP/IP protocols.

IrDA transceiver *See* infrared transceiver.

IRQ (interrupt request) line A line on a bus that is assigned to a device and is used to signal the CPU for servicing. These lines are assigned a reference number (for example, the normal IRQ for a printer is IRQ 7).

ISA (Industry Standard Architecture) slot An older slot on the motherboard used for slower I/O devices, which can support an 8-bit or a 16-bit data path. ISA slots are mostly replaced by PCI slots.

ISDN (Integrated Services Digital Network) A broadband telephone line that can carry data at about five times the speed of regular telephone lines. Two channels (telephone numbers) share a single pair of wires.

isochronous data transfer A method used by IEEE 1394 to transfer data continuously without breaks.

ITU (International Telecommunications Union) The international organization responsible for developing international standards of communication. Formerly CCITT.

JPEG (Joint Photographic Experts Group) A graphical compression scheme that allows the user to control the amount of data that is averaged and sacrificed as file size is reduced. It is a common Internet file format. Most JPEG files have a .jpg extension.

jumper Two wires that stick up side by side on the motherboard and are used to hold configuration information. The jumper is considered closed if a cover is over the wires, and open if the cover is missing.

Kerberos A protocol used to encrypt account names and passwords that are sent to a network controller for validation. Kerberos is the default protocol used by Windows 2000/XP.

kernel The portion of an OS that is responsible for interacting with the hardware.

kernel mode A Windows NT/2000/XP "privileged" processing mode that has access to hardware components.

key (1) In encryption, a secret number or code used to encode and decode data. (2) In Windows, a section name of the Windows registry.

key fob A device, such as a type of smart card, that can fit conveniently on a key chain.

keyboard A common input device through which data and instructions may be typed into computer memory.

keylogger A type of spyware that tracks your keystrokes, including passwords, chat room sessions, e-mail messages, documents, online purchases, and anything else you type on your PC. Text is logged to a text file and transmitted over the Internet without your knowledge.

LAN (local area network) A computer network that covers only a small area, usually within one building.

laptop computer *See* notebook.

large mode A mode of addressing information on hard drives that range from 504 MB to 8.4 GB, addressing information on a hard drive by translating cylinder, head, and sector information in order to break the 528-MB hard drive barrier. Also called ECHS mode.

large-capacity drive A hard drive larger than 504 MB.

laser printer A type of printer that uses a laser beam to control how toner is placed on the page and then uses heat to fuse the toner to the page.

Last Known Good configuration In Windows NT/2000/XP, registry settings and device drivers that were in effect when the computer last booted successfully. These settings can be restored during the startup process to recover from errors during the last boot.

LBA (logical block addressing) mode A mode of addressing information on hard drives in which the BIOS and operating system view the drive as one long linear list of LBAs or addressable sectors, permitting drives to be larger than 8.4 GB (LBA 0 is cylinder 0, head 0, and sector 1).

license Permission for an individual to use a product or service. A manufacturer's method of maintaining ownership, while granting permission for use to others.

Limited user Windows XP user accounts known as Users in Windows NT/2000, which have read-write access only on their own folders, read-only access to most system folders, and no access to other users' data.

line conditioner A device that regulates, or conditions, power, providing continuous voltage during brownouts and spikes.

line protocol A protocol used to send data packets destined for a network over telephone lines. PPP and SLIP are examples of line protocols.

line speed *See* bandwidth.

line-interactive UPS A variation of a standby UPS that shortens switching time by always keeping the inverter that converts AC to DC working, so that there is no charge-up time for the inverter.

LMHosts A text file located in the Windows folder that contains NetBIOS names and their associated IP addresses. This file is used for name resolution for a NetBEUI network.

local bus A bus that operates at a speed synchronized with the CPU frequency. The system bus is a local bus.

local I/O bus A local bus that provides I/O devices with fast access to the CPU. The PCI bus is a local I/O bus.

local printer A printer connected to a computer by way of a port on the computer. Compare to network printer.

local profile User profile that is stored on a local computer and cannot be accessed from another computer on the network.

local user account A user account that applies only to a local computer and cannot be used to access resources from other computers on the network.

logic bomb —A type of malicious software that is dormant code added to software and triggered at a predetermined time or by a predetermined event.

logical drive A portion or all of a hard drive partition that is treated by the operating system as though it were a physical drive. Each logical drive is assigned a drive letter, such as drive C, and contains a file system. Also called a volume.

logical geometry The number of heads, tracks, and sectors that the BIOS on the hard drive controller presents to the system BIOS and the OS. The logical geometry does not consist of the same values as the physical geometry, although calculations of drive capacity yield the same results. The use of communicating logical geometry is outdated.

Logical Unit Number (LUN) A number assigned to a logical device (such as a tray in a CD changer) that is part of a physical SCSI device, which is assigned a SCSI ID.

long mode A CPU processing mode that processes 64 bits at a time. The AMD Athlon 64 and the Intel Itanium CPUs use this mode.

lost allocation units *See* lost clusters.

lost clusters File fragments that, according to the file allocation table, contain data that does not belong to any file. The command CHKDSK/F can free these fragments. Also called lost allocation units.

low insertion force (LIF) socket   A socket that requires the installer to manually apply an even force over the microchip when inserting the chip into the socket.

low-level formatting   A process (usually performed at the factory) that electronically creates the hard drive tracks and sectors and tests for bad spots on the disk surface.

MAC (Media Access Control) address   A 48-bit hardware address unique to each NIC card and assigned by the manufacturer. The address is often printed on the adapter as hexadecimal numbers. An example is 00 00 0C 08 2F 35. Also called a physical address, an adapter address, or a hardware address.

macro   A small sequence of commands, contained within a document, that can be automatically executed when the document is loaded, or executed later by using a predetermined keystroke.

macro virus   A virus that can hide in the macros of a document file.

main board   *See* motherboard.

malicious software   Any unwanted program that is transmitted to a computer without the user's knowledge and that is designed to do varying degrees of damage to data and software. Types of infestations include viruses, Trojan horses, worms, adware, spyware, keyloggers, browser hijackers, dialers, and downloaders. Also called malware or an infestation.

malware   *See* malicious software.

mandatory user profile   A roaming user profile that applies to all users in a user group, and individual users cannot change that profile.

Master Boot Record (MBR)   The first sector on a hard drive, which contains the partition table and a program the BIOS uses to boot an OS from the drive.

master file table (MFT)   The database used by the NTFS file system to track the contents of a logical drive.

megahertz (MHz)   One million Hz, or one million cycles per second. *See* hertz (Hz).

memory   Physical microchips that can hold data and programming, located on the motherboard or expansion cards.

memory address   A number assigned to each byte in memory. The CPU can use memory addresses to track where information is stored in RAM.

Memory addresses are usually displayed as hexadecimal numbers in segment/offset form.

memory bus   *See* system bus.

memory cache   A small amount of faster RAM that stores recently retrieved data, in anticipation of what the CPU will request next, thus speeding up access. *See also* system bus.

memory dump   The contents of memory saved to a file at the time an event halted the system. Support technicians can analyze the dump file to help understand the source of the problem.

memory extender   For DOS and Windows 9x/Me, a device driver named Himem.sys that manages RAM, giving access to memory addresses above 1 MB.

memory paging   In Windows, swapping blocks of RAM memory to an area of the hard drive to serve as virtual memory when RAM is low.

memory-resident virus   A virus that can stay lurking in memory even after its host program is terminated.

microcode   A programming instruction that can be executed by a CPU without breaking the instruction down into simpler instructions. Typically, a single command line in a Visual Basic or C++ program must be broken down into numerous microcode commands.

MicroDIMM   A type of memory module used on subnotebooks that has 144 pins and uses a 64-bit data path.

microprocessor   *See* central processing unit (CPU).

Microsoft Management Console (MMC)   A utility to build customized consoles. These consoles can be saved to a file with an .msc file extension.

Mini PCI   The PCI industry standard for desktop computer expansion cards, applied to a much smaller form factor for notebook expansion cards.

minicartridge   A tape drive cartridge that is only $3\frac{1}{4}$ x $2\frac{1}{2}$ x $\frac{3}{5}$ inches. It is small enough to allow two drives to fit into a standard $5\frac{1}{2}$-inch drive bay of a PC case.

minifile system   In Windows NT/2000/XP, a simplified file system that is started so that Ntldr (NT Loader) can read files from any file system the OS supports.

mixed mode   A Windows 2000 mode for domain controllers used when there is at least one Windows NT domain controller on the network.

MMX (Multimedia Extensions)   Multimedia instructions built into Intel processors to add functionality such as better processing of multimedia, SIMD support, and increased cache.

modem   From MOdulate/DEModulate. A device that modulates digital data from a computer to an analog format that can be sent over telephone lines, then demodulates it back into digital form.

modem eliminator *See* null modem cable.

modem speed The speed at which a modem can transmit data along a phone line, measured in bits per second (bps). Also called line speed.

monitor The most commonly used output device for displaying text and graphics on a computer.

motherboard The main board in the computer, also called the system board. The CPU, ROM chips, SIMMs, DIMMs, RIMMs, and interface cards are plugged into the motherboard.

motherboard bus *See* system bus.

motherboard mouse *See* PS/2-compatible mouse.

mouse A pointing and input device that allows the user to move a cursor around a screen and select items with the click of a button.

MP3 A method to compress audio files that uses MPEG level 1. It can reduce sound files as low as a 1:24 ratio without losing much sound quality.

MPEG (Moving Pictures Experts Group) A processing-intensive standard for data compression for motion pictures that tracks movement from one frame to the next and only stores the data that has changed.

Msdos.sys In Windows 9x/Me, a text file that contains settings used by Io.sys during booting. In DOS, the Msdos.sys file was a program file that contained part of the DOS core.

MultiBank DRAM (MDRAM) A type of video memory that is faster than VRAM and WRAM, but can be more economical because it can be installed on a video card in smaller increments.

multicasting A process in which a message is sent by one host to multiple hosts, such as when a video conference is broadcast to several hosts on the Internet.

multimeter A device used to measure the various components of an electrical circuit. The most common measurements are voltage, current, and resistance.

multipartite virus A combination of a boot sector virus and a file virus. It can hide in either type of program.

multiplier The factor by which the bus speed or frequency is multiplied to get the CPU clock speed.

multi-processor platform A system that contains more than one processor. The motherboard has more than one processor socket and the processors must be rated to work in this multi-processor environment.

multisession A feature that allows data to be read from or written to a CD during more than one

session. This is important if the disk was only partially filled during the first write.

multitasking Doing more than one thing at a time. A true multitasking system requires two or more CPUs, each processing a different thread at the same time. Compare to cooperative multitasking and preemptive multitasking.

multithreading The ability to pass more than one function (thread) to the OS kernel at the same time, such as when one thread is performing a print job while another reads a file.

name resolution The process of associating a NetBIOS name or host name to an IP address.

NAT (Network Address Translation) A process that converts private IP addresses on a LAN to the proxy server's IP address before a data packet is sent over the Internet.

native mode A Windows 2000 mode used by domain controllers when there are no Windows NT domain controllers present on the network.

NetBEUI (NetBIOS Extended User Interface) A fast, proprietary Microsoft networking protocol used only by Windows-based systems, and limited to LANs because it does not support routing.

NetBIOS (Network Basic Input/Output System) An API protocol used by some applications to communicate over a NetBEUI network. NetBIOS has largely been replaced by Windows Sockets over a TCP/IP network.

network adapter *See* network interface card.

network drive map Mounting a drive to a computer, such as drive E, that is actually hard drive space on another host computer on the network.

network interface card (NIC) An expansion card that plugs into a computer's motherboard and provides a port on the back of the card to connect a PC to a network. Also called a network adapter.

network operating system (NOS) An operating system that resides on the controlling computer in the network. The NOS controls what software, data, and devices a user on the network can access. Examples of an NOS are Novell Netware and Windows Server 2003.

network printer A printer that any user on the network can access, through its own network card and connection to the network, through a connection to a standalone print server, or through a connection to a computer as a local printer, which is shared on the network.

NNTP (Network News Transfer Protocol) The protocol used by newsgroup server and client software.

node *See* host

noise An extraneous, unwanted signal, often over an analog phone line, that can cause communication interference or transmission errors. Possible sources are fluorescent lighting, radios, TVs, lightning, or bad wiring.

non-memory-resident virus A virus that is terminated when the host program is closed. Compare to memory-resident virus.

nonparity memory Eight-bit memory without error checking. A SIMM part number with a 32 in it (4 x 8 bits) is nonparity.

nonvolatile Refers to a kind of RAM that is stable and can hold data as long as electricity is powering the memory.

normal mode *See* CHS mode.

notebook A portable computer that is designed for travel and mobility. Notebooks use the same technology as desktop PCs, with modifications for conserving voltage, taking up less space, and operating while on the move. Also called a laptop computer.

NTFS (NT file system) The file system for the Windows NT/2000/XP operating systems. NTFS cannot be accessed by other operating systems such as DOS. It provides increased reliability and security in comparison to other methods of organizing and accessing files. There are several versions of NTFS that might or might not be compatible.

Ntldr (NT Loader) In Windows NT/2000/XP, the OS loader used on Intel systems.

NTVDM (NT virtual DOS machine) An emulated environment in which a 16-bit DOS application resides within Windows NT/2000/XP with its own memory space or WOW (Win16 on Win32).

null modem cable A cable that allows two data terminal equipment (DTE) devices to communicate in which the transmit and receive wires are cross-connected and no modems are necessary.

NWLink Microsoft's version of the IPX/SPX protocol suite used by Novell NetWare operating systems.

octet Term for each of the four 8-bit numbers that make up an IP address. For example, the IP address 206.96.103.114 has four octets.

on-board ports Ports that are directly on the motherboard, such as a built-in keyboard port or on-board serial port.

operating system (OS) Software that controls a computer. An OS controls how system resources are used and provides a user interface, a way of managing hardware and software, and ways to work with files.

operating system formatting *See* high-level formatting.

overclocking Running a processor at a higher frequency than is recommended by the manufacturer, which can result in an unstable system, but is a popular thing to do when a computer is used for gaming.

packet Segment of network data that also includes header, destination address, and trailer information that is sent as a unit. Also called data packet or datagram.

page fault An OS interrupt that occurs when the OS is forced to access the hard drive to satisfy the demands for virtual memory.

page file *See* swap file.

Pagefile.sys The Windows NT/2000/XP swap file.

page-in The process in which the memory manager goes to the hard drive to return the data from a swap file to RAM.

page-out The process in which, when RAM is full, the memory manager takes a page and moves it to the swap file.

pages 4K segments in which Windows NT/2000/XP allocates memory.

parallel ATA (PATA) An older IDE cabling method that uses a 40-pin flat data cable or an 80-conductor cable and a 40-pin IDE connector. *See also* serial ATA.

parallel port A female 25-pin port on a computer that can transmit data in parallel, 8 bits at a time, and is usually used with a printer. The names for parallel ports are LPT1 and LPT2.

parity An error-checking scheme in which a ninth, or "parity," bit is added. The value of the parity bit is set to either 0 or 1 to provide an even number of ones for even parity and an odd number of ones for odd parity.

parity error An error that occurs when the number of 1s in the byte is not in agreement with the expected number.

parity memory Nine-bit memory in which the ninth bit is used for error checking. A SIMM part number with a 36 in it (4 x 9 bits) is parity. Older PCs almost always use parity chips.

partition A division of a hard drive that can be used to hold logical drives.

partition table A table at the beginning of the hard drive that contains information about each partition on the drive. The partition table is contained in the Master Boot Record.

passphrase A type of password that can contain a phrase where spaces are allowed. A passphrase is stronger than a one-word password.

patch An update to software that corrects an error, adds a feature, or addresses security issues. Also called an update or service pack.

patch cable A network cable that is used to connect a PC to a hub, switch, or router.

path (1) A drive and list of directories pointing to a file such as C:\Windows\command. (2) The OS command to provide a list of paths to the system for finding program files to execute.

PC Card A credit-card-sized adapter card that can be slid into a slot in the side of many notebook computers and is used by modems, network cards, and other devices. Also called PCMCIA Card.

PC Card slot An expansion slot on a notebook computer, into which a PC Card is inserted. Also called a PCMCIA Card slot.

PCI (Peripheral Component Interconnect) bus A bus common on Pentium computers that runs at speeds of up to 33 MHz or 66 MHz, with a 32-bit-wide or 64-bit-wide data path. PCI-X, released in September 1999, enables PCI to run at 133 MHz. For some chipsets, it serves as the middle layer between the memory bus and expansion buses.

PCL (Printer Control Language) A printer language developed by Hewlett-Packard that communicates to a printer how to print a page.

PCMCIA (Personal Computer Memory Card International Association) Card *See* PC Card.

PCMCIA Card slot *See* PC Card slot.

PDA (Personal Digital Assistant) A small, handheld computer that has its own operating system and applications.

peer-to-peer network A network of computers that are all equals, or peers. Each computer has the same amount of authority, and each can act as a server to the other computers.

peripheral devices Devices that communicate with the CPU but are not located directly on the motherboard, such as the monitor, floppy drive, printer, and mouse.

phishing (1) A type of identity theft where a person is baited into giving personal data to a Web site that appears to be the Web site of a reputable company with which the person has an account. (2) Sending an e-mail message with the intent of getting the user to reveal private information that can be used for identify theft.

physical address *See* MAC address.

physical geometry The actual layout of heads, tracks, and sectors on a hard drive. Compare to logical geometry.

PIF (program information file) A file used by Windows to describe the environment for a DOS program to use.

pin grid array (PGA) A feature of a CPU socket whereby the pins are aligned in uniform rows around the socket.

Ping (Packet Internet Groper) A Windows and Unix command used to troubleshoot network connections. It verifies that the host can communicate with another host on the network.

pinout A description of how each pin on a bus, connection, plug, slot, or socket is used.

PIO (Programmed I/O) transfer mode A transfer mode that uses the CPU to transfer data from the hard drive to memory. PIO mode is slower than DMA mode.

pipelined burst SRAM A less expensive SRAM that uses more clock cycles per transfer than non-pipelined burst but does not significantly slow down the process.

pits Recessed areas on the surface of a CD or DVD, separating lands, or flat areas. Lands and pits are used to represent data on a disc.

pixel A small spot on a fine horizontal scan line. Pixels are illuminated to create an image on the monitor.

PKI (public key infrastructure) The standards used to encrypt, transport, and validate digital certificates over the Internet.

Plug and Play (PnP) A standard designed to make the installation of new hardware devices easier by automatically configuring devices to eliminate system resource conflicts (such as IRQ or I/O address conflicts). PnP is supported by Windows 9x/Me, Windows 2000, and Windows XP.

polling A process by which the CPU checks the status of connected devices to determine if they are ready to send or receive data.

polymorphic virus A type of virus that changes its distinguishing characteristics as it replicates itself. Mutating in this way makes it more difficult for AV software to recognize the presence of the virus.

POP (Post Office Protocol) The protocol that an e-mail server and client use when the client requests the downloading of e-mail messages. The most recent version is POP3. POP is being replaced by IMAP.

port (1) As applied to services running on a computer, a number assigned to a process on a computer so that the process can be found by TCP/IP.

Also called a port address or port number. (2) Another name for an I/O address. *See also* I/O address. (3) A physical connector, usually at the back of a computer, that allows a cable from a peripheral device, such as a printer, mouse, or modem, to be attached.

port address *See* I/O address.

port forwarding A technique that allows a computer on the Internet to reach a computer on a private network using a certain port when the private network is protected by a router using NAT as a proxy server. Port forwarding is also called tunneling.

port number *See* port.

port replicator A device designed to connect to a notebook computer in order to make it easy to connect the notebook to peripheral devices.

port settings The configuration parameters of communications devices such as COM1, COM2, or LPT1, including IRQ settings.

port speed The communication speed between a DTE (computer) and a DCE (modem). As a general rule, the port speed should be at least four times as fast as the modem speed.

POST (power-on self test) A self-diagnostic program used to perform a simple test of the CPU, RAM, and various I/O devices. The POST is performed by startup BIOS when the computer is first turned on, and is stored in ROM-BIOS.

PostScript A printer language developed by Adobe Systems which tells a printer how to print a page.

power conditioner A line conditioner that regulates, or conditions, power, providing continuous voltage during brownouts.

power scheme A feature of Windows XP support for notebooks that allows the user to create groups of power settings for specific sets of conditions.

power supply A box inside the computer case that supplies power to the motherboard and other installed devices. Power supplies provide 3.3, 5, and 12 volts DC.

power-on password A password that a computer uses to control access during the boot process.

PPP (Point-to-Point Protocol) A protocol that governs the methods for communicating via modems and dial-up telephone lines. The Windows Dial-up Networking utility uses PPP.

PPPoE (Point-to-Point Protocol over Ethernet) The protocol that describes how a PC is to interact with a broadband converter box, such as cable

modem, when the two are connected by an Ethernet cable, connected to a NIC in a PC.

preemptive multitasking A type of pseudo-multitasking whereby the CPU allows an application a specified period of time and then preempts the processing to give time to another application.

primary cache *See* internal cache.

primary domain controller (PDC) In a Windows NT network, the computer that controls the directory database of user accounts, group accounts, and computer accounts on a domain. *See also* backup domain controller.

primary partition A hard disk partition that can contain only one logical drive.

primary storage Temporary storage on the motherboard used by the CPU to process data and instructions. Memory is considered primary storage.

printer A peripheral output device that produces printed output to paper. Different types include dot matrix, ink-jet, and laser printers.

printer maintenance kit A kit purchased from a printer manufacturer that contains the parts, tools, and instructions needed to perform routine printer maintenance.

private IP address An IP address that is used on a private TCP/IP network that is isolated from the Internet.

process An executing instance of a program together with the program resources. There can be more than one process running for a program at the same time. One process for a program happens each time the program is loaded into memory or executed.

processor *See* central processing unit (CPU).

processor speed The speed, or frequency, at which the CPU operates. Usually expressed in GHz.

product activation The process that Microsoft uses to prevent software piracy. For example, once Windows XP is activated for a particular computer, it cannot be legally installed on another computer.

program A set of step-by-step instructions to a computer. Some are burned directly into chips, while others are stored as program files. Programs are written in languages such as BASIC and C++.

program file A file that contains instructions designed to be executed by the CPU.

protected mode An operating mode that supports preemptive multitasking, the OS manages memory and other hardware devices, and programs can use a 32-bit data path. Also called 32-bit mode.

protocol   A set of rules and standards that two entities use for communication.

Protocol.ini   A Windows initialization file that contains network configuration information.

proxy server   A server that acts as an intermediary between another computer and the Internet. The proxy server substitutes its own IP address for the IP address of the computer on the network making a request, so that all traffic over the Internet appears to be coming from only the IP address of the proxy server.

PS/2-compatible mouse   A mouse that plugs into a round mouse PS/2 port on the motherboard. Sometimes called a motherboard mouse.

public IP address   An IP address available to the Internet.

QIC (Quarter-Inch Committee or quarter-inch cartridge)   A name of a standardized method used to write data to tape. These backup files have a .qic extension.

Quality of Service (QoS)   A measure of the success of communication over the Internet. Communication is degraded on the Internet when packets are dropped, delayed, delivered out of order, or corrupted. VoIP requires a high QoS.

RAID (redundant array of inexpensive disks or redundant array of independent disks)   Several methods of configuring multiple hard drives to store data to increase logical volume size and improve performance, or to ensure that if one hard drive fails, the data is still available from another hard drive.

RAM (random access memory)   Memory modules on the motherboard containing microchips used to temporarily hold data and programs while the CPU processes both. Information in RAM is lost when the PC is turned off.

RAM drive   An area of memory that is treated as though it were a hard drive, but works much faster than a hard drive. The Windows 9x/Me startup disk uses a RAM drive. Compare to virtual memory.

RARP (Reverse Address Resolution Protocol)   A protocol used to translate the unique hardware NIC addresses (MAC addresses) into IP addresses (the reverse of ARP).

RDRAM   *See* Direct Rambus DRAM.

read/write head   A sealed, magnetic coil device that moves across the surface of a disk either reading data from or writing data to the disk.

real mode   A single-tasking operating mode whereby a program can use 1024 K of memory addresses, has direct access to RAM, and uses a16-bit data path. Using a memory extender (Himem.sys) a program in real mode can access memory above 1024 K. Also called 16-bit mode.

Recovery Console   A Windows 2000/XP command interface utility and OS that can be used to solve problems when Windows cannot load from the hard drive.

refresh   The process of periodically rewriting data, such as on dynamic RAM.

refresh rate   As applied to monitors, the number of times in one second an electronic beam can fill the screen with lines from top to bottom. Also called vertical scan rate.

registry   A database that Windows uses to store hardware and software configuration information, user preferences, and setup information.

Remote Assistance   A Windows XP feature that allows a support technician at a remote location to have full access to the Windows XP desktop.

rescue disk   A floppy disk that can be used to start up a computer when the hard drive fails to boot. Also called emergency startup disk (ESD) or startup disk.

resolution   The number of pixels on a monitor screen that are addressable by software (example: 1024 x 768 pixels).

restore point   A snapshot of the Windows Me/XP system state, usually made before installation of new hardware or applications.

REt (Resolution Enhancement technology)   The term used by Hewlett-Packard to describe the way a laser printer varies the size of the dots used to create an image. This technology partly accounts for the sharp, clear image created by a laser printer.

RIMM   A type of memory module developed by Rambus, Inc.

RJ-11   A phone line connection found on modems, telephones, and house phone outlets.

RJ-45 connector   A connector used with twisted-pair cable that connects the cable to the NIC.

roaming user profile   A user profile for a roaming user. Roaming user profiles are stored on a server so that the user can access the profile from anywhere on the network.

ROM (read-only memory)   Chips that contain programming code and cannot be erased.

ROM BIOS   *See* BIOS.

root directory   The main directory created when a hard drive or disk is first formatted. In Linux, it's indicated by a forward slash. In DOS and Windows, it's indicated by a backward slash.

rootkit   A type of malicious software that loads itself before the OS boot is complete and can hijack internal Windows components so that it masks information Windows provides to user-mode utilities such as Windows Explorer or Task Manager.

routable protocol   A protocol that can be routed to interconnected networks on the basis of a network address. TCP/IP is a routable protocol, but NetBEUI is not.

router   A device that connects networks and makes decisions as to the best routes to use when forwarding packets.

sampling rate   The rate of samples taken of an analog signal over a period of time, usually expressed as samples per second, or hertz.

scam e-mail   E-mail sent by a scam artist intended to lure you into a scheme.

scanner   A device that allows a computer to convert a picture, drawing, barcode, or other image into digital data that can be input into the computer.

script virus   A type of virus that hides in a script which might execute when you click a link on a Web page or in an HTML e-mail message, or when you attempt to open an e-mail attachment.

SCSI (Small Computer System Interface)   A fast interface between a host adapter and the CPU that can daisy chain as many as 7 or 15 devices on a single bus.

SDRAM II   *See* Double Data Rate SDRAM (DDR SDRAM).

secondary storage   Storage that is remote to the CPU and permanently holds data, even when the PC is turned off, such as a hard drive.

sector   On a disk surface one segment of a track, which almost always contains 512 bytes of data.

security accounts manager (SAM)   A portion of the Windows NT/2000/XP registry that manages the account database that contains accounts, policies, and other pertinent information about local accounts.

sequential access   A method of data access used by tape drives, whereby data is written or read sequentially from the beginning to the end of the tape or until the desired data is found.

serial ATA (SATA)   An ATAPI cabling method that uses a narrower and more reliable cable than the 80-conductor cable. *See also* parallel ATA.

serial ATA cable   An IDE cable that is narrower and has fewer pins than the parallel IDE 80-conductor cable.

serial mouse   A mouse that uses a serial port and has a female 9-pin DB-9 connector.

serial port   A male 9-pin or 25-pin port on a computer system used by slower I/O devices such as a mouse or modem. Data travels serially, one bit at a time, through the port. Serial ports are sometimes configured as COM1, COM2, COM3, or COM4.

server-side caching   A technique used by servers on the Internet to speed up download times by caching Web pages previously requested in case they are requested again.

service   A program that runs in the background to support or serve Windows or an application.

service pack   *See* patch.

session   An established communication link between two software programs. On the Internet, a session is created by TCP.

SFC (System File Checker)   A Windows tool that checks to make sure Windows is using the correct versions of system files.

SGRAM (synchronous graphics RAM)   Memory designed especially for video card processing that can synchronize itself with the CPU bus clock.

shadow RAM or shadowing ROM   ROM programming code copied into RAM to speed up the system operation, because of the faster access speed of RAM.

shared memory   When the video system does not have dedicated video memory, but is using regular RAM instead. A system with shared memory generally costs less than having dedicated video memory. Also called *video sharing*.

shell   The portion of an OS that relates to the user and to applications.

shielded twisted-pair (STP) cable   A cable that is made of one or more twisted pairs of wires and is surrounded by a metal shield.

shortcut   An icon on the desktop that points to a program that can be executed or to a file or folder.

Sigverif.exe   A Windows 2000/XP utility that allows you to search for digital signatures.

SIMD (single instruction, multiple data)   A process that allows the CPU to execute a single instruction simultaneously on multiple pieces of data, rather than by repetitive looping.

SIMM (single inline memory module)   A miniature circuit board used in older computers to hold RAM. SIMMs hold 8, 16, 32, or 64 MB on a single module.

simple volume   A type of dynamic volume used on a single hard drive that corresponds to a primary partition on a basic disk.

site license A license that allows a company to install multiple copies of software, or to allow multiple employees to execute the software from a file server.

slack Wasted space on a hard drive caused by not using all available space at the end of clusters.

sleep mode A mode used in many "Green" systems that allows them to be configured through CMOS to suspend the monitor or even the drive, if the keyboard and/or CPU have been inactive for a set number of minutes. *See also* Green Standards.

SLIP (Serial Line Internet Protocol) A line protocol used by regular telephone lines that has largely been replaced by PPP.

smart card Any small device that contains authentication information that can be keyed into a logon window or read by a reader to authenticate a user on a network.

smart card reader A device that can read a smart card used to authenticate a person onto a network.

SMARTDrive A hard drive cache program that came with Windows 3.x and DOS and can be executed as a TSR from the Autoexec.bat file (for example, Device = Smartdrv.sys 2048).

SMTP (Simple Mail Transfer Protocol) The protocol used by e-mail clients and servers to send e-mail messages over the Internet. *See* POP and IMAP4.

SMTP AUTH (SMTP Authentication) A protocol that is used to authenticate or prove that a client who attempts to use an email server to send email is authorized to use the server. The protocol is based on the Simple Authentication and Security Layer (SASL) protocol.

snap-ins A Windows utility that can be installed in a console window by Microsoft Management Console.

SNMP (Simple Network Management Protocol) A protocol used to monitor and manage network traffic on a workstation. SNMP works with TCP/IP and IPX/SPX networks.

social engineering The practice of tricking people into giving out private information or allowing unsafe programs into the network or computer.

socket *See* session.

SO-DIMM (small outline DIMM) A type of memory module used in notebook computers that uses DIMM technology and can have either 72 pins or 144 pins.

soft boot To restart a PC without turning off the power, for example, in Windows XP, by clicking Start, Turn Off Computer, and Restart. Also called warm boot.

soft power *See* soft switch.

soft switch A feature on an ATX or BTX system that allows an OS to power down the system and allows for activity such as a keystroke or network activity to power up the system. Also called soft power.

software Computer programs, or instructions to perform a specific task. Software may be BIOS, OSs, or applications software such as a word-processing or spreadsheet program.

software cache Cache controlled by software whereby the cache is stored in RAM.

solid ink printer A type of printer that uses sticks or blocks of solid ink. The ink is melted and then jetted onto the paper as the paper passes by on a drum.

solid state device (SSD) A storage device that uses memory chips to store data instead of spinning disks (such as those used by hard drives and CD drives). Examples of solid state devices are jump drives (also called key drives or thumb drives), flash memory cards, and solid state disks used as hard drives in notebook computers designed for the most rugged uses. Also called solid state disk (SSD).

solid state disk (SSD) *See* solid state device.

SO-RIMM (small outline RIMM) A 160-pin memory module used in notebooks that uses Rambus technology.

spam Junk e-mail you don't ask for, don't want, and that gets in your way.

spanned volume A type of dynamic volume used on two or more hard drives that fills up the space allotted on one physical disk before moving to the next.

spikes Temporary surges in voltage, which can damage electrical components. Also called swells.

spooling Placing print jobs in a print queue so that an application can be released from the printing process before printing is completed. Spooling is an acronym for simultaneous peripheral operations online.

spyware Malicious software that installs itself on your computer to spy on you. It collects personal information about you that it transmits over the Internet to Web-hosting sites that intend to use your personal data for harm.

SSE (Streaming SIMD Extension) A technology used by the Intel Pentium III and later CPUs and designed to improve performance of multimedia software.

SSL (secure socket layer) A secure protocol developed by Netscape that uses a digital certificate including a public key to encrypt and decrypt data.

standby time The time before a "Green" system will reduce 92 percent of its activity. *See also* Green Standards.

start bits Bits that are used to signal the approach of data.

startup BIOS Part of system BIOS that is responsible for controlling the PC when it is first turned on. Startup BIOS gives control over to the OS once it is loaded.

startup disk *See* rescue disk.

startup password *See* power-on password.

stateless Term for a device or process that manages data or some activity without regard to all the details of the data or activity.

static electricity *See* electrostatic discharge.

static IP address An IP address permanently assigned to a workstation.

static RAM (SRAM) RAM chips that retain information without the need for refreshing, as long as the computer's power is on. They are more expensive than traditional DRAM.

static VxD A VxD that is loaded into memory at startup and remains there for the entire OS session.

stealth virus A virus that actively conceals itself by temporarily removing itself from an infected file that is about to be examined, and then hiding a copy of itself elsewhere on the drive.

stop error An error severe enough to cause the operating system to stop all processes.

streaming audio Downloading audio data from the Internet in a continuous stream of data without first downloading an entire audio file.

striped volume A type of dynamic volume used for two or more hard drives that writes to the disks evenly rather than filling up allotted space on one and then moving on to the next. Compare to spanned volume.

subdirectory A directory or folder contained in another directory or folder. Also called a child directory or folder.

subnet mask A subnet mask is a group of four numbers (dotted decimal numbers) that tell TCP/IP if a remote computer is on the same or a different network.

subsystems The different modules into which the Windows NT/2000/XP user mode is divided.

surge suppressor or surge protector A device or power strip designed to protect electronic equipment from power surges and spikes.

Surround Sound A sound compression standard that supports six separate sound channels using six speakers known as Front Left and Right, Front Center, Rear Left and Right, and Subwoofer. Surround Sound 7.1 supports two additional rear or side speakers. Also known Dolby AC-3, Dolby Digital Surround, or Dolby Surround Sound.

suspend time The time before a "Green" system will reduce 99 percent of its activity. After this time, the system needs a warm-up time so that the CPU, monitor, and hard drive can reach full activity.

swap file A file on the hard drive that is used by the OS for virtual memory. Also called a page file.

swells *See* spikes.

switch A device used to segment a network. It can decide which network segment is to receive a packet, on the basis of the packet's destination MAC address.

synchronization The process by which files and programs are transferred between PDAs and PCs.

synchronous DRAM (SDRAM) A type of memory stored on DIMMs that runs in sync with the system clock, running at the same speed as the motherboard.

synchronous SRAM SRAM that is faster and more expensive than asynchronous SRAM. It requires a clock signal to validate its control signals, enabling the cache to run in step with the CPU.

SyncLink DRAM (SLDRAM) A type of DRAM developed by a consortium of 12 DRAM manufacturers. It improved on regular SDRAM but is now obsolete.

Sysedit The Windows 9x/Me System Configuration Editor, a text editor generally used to edit system files.

system BIOS BIOS located on the motherboard.

system board *See* motherboard.

system bus The bus between the CPU and memory on the motherboard. The bus frequency in documentation is called the system speed, such as 400 MHz. Also called the memory bus, front-side bus, local bus, or host bus.

system clock A line on a bus that is dedicated to timing the activities of components connected to it. The system clock provides a continuous pulse that other devices use to time themselves.

system disk Windows terminology for a bootable disk.

system partition The active partition of the hard drive containing the boot record and the specific files required to load Windows NT/2000/XP.

system resource A channel, line, or address on the motherboard that can be used by the CPU or a device for communication. The four system resources are IRQ, I/O address, DMA channel, and memory address.

System Restore A Windows Me/XP utility, similar to the ScanReg tool in earlier versions of Windows, that is used to restore the system to a restore point.

Unlike ScanReg, System Restore cannot be executed from a command prompt.

system state data In Windows 2000/XP, files that are necessary for a successful load of the operating system.

System Tray An area to the right of the taskbar that holds the icons for running services; these services include the volume control and network connectivity.

System.ini A text configuration file used by Windows 3.x and supported by Windows 9x/Me for backward-compatibility.

TAPI (Telephony Application Programming Interface) A standard developed by Intel and Microsoft that can be used by 32-bit Windows communications programs for communicating over phone lines.

taskbar A bar normally located at the bottom of the Windows desktop, displaying information about open programs and providing quick access to others.

TCP (Transmission Control Protocol) Part of the TCP/IP protocol suite. TCP guarantees delivery of data for application protocols and establishes a session before it begins transmitting data.

TCP/IP (Transmission Control Protocol/Internet Protocol) The suite of protocols that supports communication on the Internet. TCP is responsible for error checking, and IP is responsible for routing.

TDMA (time-division multiple access) A protocol standard used by cellular WANs and cell phones.

technical documentation The technical reference manuals, included with software packages and peripherals, that provide directions for installation, usage, and troubleshooting. The information extends beyond that given in user manuals.

telephony A term describing the technology of converting sound to signals that can travel over telephone lines.

thermal printer A type of line printer that uses wax-based ink, which is heated by heat pins that melt the ink onto paper.

thread Each process that the CPU is aware of; a single task that is part of a longer task or program.

TIFF (Tagged Image File Format) A bitmapped file format used to hold photographs, graphics, and screen captures. TIFF files can be rather large, and have a .tif file extension.

time to live (TTL) Number of routers a network packet can pass through on its way to its destination before it is dropped. Also called hop count.

TLS (Transport Layer Security) A protocol used to secure data sent over the Internet. It is an improved version of SSL.

token ring An older LAN technology developed by IBM that transmits data at 4 Mbps or 16 Mbps.

top-level domain The highest level of domain names, indicated by a suffix that tells something about the host. For example, .com is for commercial use and .edu is for educational institutions.

touch screen An input device that uses a monitor or LCD panel as a backdrop for user options. Touch screens can be embedded in a monitor or LCD panel or installed as an add-on device.

tower case The largest type of personal computer case. Tower cases stand vertically and can be as high as two feet tall. They have more drive bays and are a good choice for computer users who anticipate making significant upgrades.

trace A wire on a circuit board that connects two components or devices.

track One of many concentric circles on the surface of a hard drive or floppy disk.

training *See* handshaking.

transceiver The component on a NIC that is responsible for signal conversion. Combines the words transmitter and receiver.

translation A technique used by system BIOS and hard drive controller BIOS to break the 504-MB hard drive barrier, whereby a different set of drive parameters are communicated to the OS and other software than that used by the hard drive controller BIOS.

Travan standards A popular and improved group of standards for tape drives based on the QIC standards and developed by 3M.

triad Three dots of color that make up one composite dot on a CRT screen.

Trojan horse A type of infestation that hides or disguises itself as a useful program, yet is designed to cause damage when executed.

TSR (terminate-and-stay-resident) A program that is loaded into memory and remains dormant until called on, such as a screen saver or a memory-resident antivirus program.

UART (universal asynchronous receiver-transmitter) chip A chip that controls serial ports. It sets protocol and converts parallel data bits received from the system bus into serial bits.

UDP (User Datagram Protocol) A connectionless protocol that does not require a connection to send a packet and does not guarantee that the packet arrives at its destination. UDP is faster than TCP because TCP takes the time to make a connection and guarantee delivery.

unattended installation   A Windows NT/ 2000/XP installation that is done by storing the answers to installation questions in a text file or script that Windows NT/2000/XP calls an answer file so that the answers do not have to be typed in during the installation.

Universal Disk Format (UDF) file system   A file system for optical media used by all DVD discs and some CD-R and CD-RW discs.

unshielded twisted-pair (UTP) cable   A cable that is made of one or more twisted pairs of wires and is not surrounded by shielding.

upgrade install   The installation of an OS on a hard drive that already has an OS installed in such a way that settings kept by the old OS are carried forward into the upgrade, including information about hardware, software, and user preferences.

upper memory   In DOS and Windows 9x/Me, the memory addresses from 640 K up to 1024 K, originally reserved for BIOS, device drivers, and TSRs.

upper memory block (UMB)   In DOS and Windows 9x/Me, a group of consecutive memory addresses in RAM from 640 K to 1MB that can be used by 16-bit device drivers and TSRs.

UPS (uninterruptible power supply)   A device designed to provide a backup power supply during a power failure. Basically, a UPS is a battery backup system with an ultrafast sensing device.

URL (Uniform Resource Locator)   An address for a resource on the Internet. A URL can contain the protocol used by the resource, the name of the computer and its network, and the path and name of a file on the computer.

USB (universal serial bus) port   A type of port designed to make installation and configuration of I/O devices easy, providing room for as many as 127 devices daisy-chained together.

USB host controller   Manages the USB bus. If the motherboard contains on-board USB ports, the USB host controller is part of the chipset. The USB controller uses only a single set of resources for all devices on the bus.

user account   The information, stored in the SAM database, that defines a Windows NT/ 2000/XP user, including username, password, memberships, and rights.

user component   A Windows 9x/Me component that controls the mouse, keyboard, ports, and desktop.

user mode   In Windows NT/2000/XP, a mode that provides an interface between an application and the OS, and only has access to hardware resources through the code running in kernel mode.

user profile   A personal profile about a user that enables the user's desktop settings and other operating parameters to be retained from one session to another.

User State Migration Tool (USMT)   A Windows XP utility that helps you migrate user files and preferences from one computer to another in order to help a user make a smooth transition from one computer to another.

V.92   The latest standard for data transmission over phone lines that can attain a speed of 56 Kbps.

value data   In Windows, the name and value of a setting in the registry.

VCACHE   A built-in Windows 9x/Me 32-bit software cache that doesn't take up conventional memory space or upper memory space as SMARTDrive did.

VESA (Video Electronics Standards Association) VL bus   An outdated local bus used on 80486 computers for connecting 32-bit adapters directly to the local processor bus.

VFAT (virtual file allocation table)   A variation of the original DOS 16-bit FAT that allows for long filenames and 32-bit disk access.

video card   An interface card installed in the computer to control visual output on a monitor. Also called display adapter.

video sharing   *See* shared memory.

virtual device driver (VxD or VDD)   A Windows device driver that may or may not have direct access to a device. It might depend on a Windows component to communicate with the device itself.

virtual machine   One or more logical machines created within one physical machine by Windows, allowing applications to make serious errors within one logical machine without disturbing other programs and parts of the system.

virtual memory   A method whereby the OS uses the hard drive as though it were RAM. Compare to RAM drive.

virtual real mode   An operating mode that works similarly to real mode and is provided by a 32-bit OS for a 16-bit program to work.

virus   A program that often has an incubation period, is infectious, and is intended to cause damage. A virus program might destroy data and programs or damage a disk drive's boot sector.

virus hoax   E-mail that does damage by tempting you to forward it to everyone in your e-mail address book with the intent of clogging up e-mail systems or by persuading you to delete a critical Windows system file by convincing you the file is malicious.

virus signature   A set of distinguishing characteristics of a virus used by antivirus software to identify the virus.

VMM (Virtual Machine Manager)   A Windows 9x/Me program that controls virtual machines and the resources they use including memory. The VMM manages the page table used to access memory.

volatile   Refers to a kind of RAM that is temporary, cannot hold data very long, and must be frequently refreshed.

volt (V)   A measure of potential difference in an electrical circuit. A computer ATX power supply usually provides five separate voltages: +12 V, -12 V, +5 V, -5 V, and +3.3 V.

voltage   Electrical differential that causes current to flow, measured in volts. *See* volt.

voltage regulator module (VRM)   A device embedded or installed on the motherboard that regulates voltage to the processor.

voltmeter   A device for measuring electrical AC or DC voltage.

volume   *See* logical drive.

VRAM (video RAM)   RAM on video cards that holds the data that is being passed from the computer to the monitor and can be accessed by two devices simultaneously. Higher resolutions often require more video memory.

VxD   *See* virtual device driver.

wait state   A clock tick in which nothing happens, used to ensure that the microprocessor isn't getting ahead of slower components. A 0-wait state is preferable to a 1-wait state. Too many wait states can slow down a system.

WAN (wide area network)   A network or group of networks that span a large geographical area.

warm boot   *See* soft boot.

watt (W)   The unit used to measure power. A typical computer may use a power supply that provides 200 W.

wattage   Electrical power measured in watts.

WDM (Win32 Driver Model)   The only Windows 9x/Me Plug and Play component that is found in Windows 98 but not Windows 95. WDM is the component responsible for managing device drivers that work under a driver model new to Windows 98.

WEP (Wired Equivalent Privacy)   A data encryption method used on wireless networks that uses either 64-bit or 128-bit encryption keys that are static keys, meaning the key does not change while the wireless network is in use.

WFP (Windows File Protection)   A Windows 2000/XP tool that protects system files from modification.

Wi-Fi   *See* IEEE 802.11b.

wildcard   A * or ? character used in a command line that represents a character or group of characters in a filename or extension.

Win.ini   The Windows initialization file that contains program configuration information needed for running the Windows operating environment. Its functions were replaced by the registry beginning with Windows 9x/Me, which still supports it for backward compatibility with Windows 3.x.

Win16 on Win32 (WOW)   A group of programs provided by Windows NT/2000/XP to create a virtual DOS environment that emulates a 16-bit Windows environment, protecting the rest of the OS from 16-bit applications.

Win386.swp   The name of the Windows 9x/Me swap file. Its default location is C:\Windows.

WINS (Windows Internet Naming Service)   A Microsoft resolution service with a distributed database that tracks relationships between NetBIOS names and IP addresses. Compare to DNS.

WinSock (Windows Sockets)   A part of the TCP/IP utility software that manages API calls from applications to other computers on a TCP/IP network.

wireless LAN (WLAN)   A type of LAN that does not use wires or cables to create connections, but instead transmits data over radio or infrared waves.

word size   The number of bits that can be processed by a CPU at one time.

workgroup   In Windows, a logical group of computers and users in which administration, resources, and security are distributed throughout the network, without centralized management or security.

worm   An infestation designed to copy itself repeatedly to memory, on drive space or on a network, until little memory or disk space remains.

WPA (WiFi Protected Access)   A data encryption method for wireless networks that use the TKIP (Temporal Key Integrity Protocol) encryption method and the encryption keys are changed at set intervals while the wireless LAN is in use.

WPA2 (WiFi Protected Access 2)   A data encryption standard compliant with the IEEE802.11i standard that uses the AES (Advanced Encryption Standard) protocol. WPA2 is currently the strongest wireless encryption standard.

WRAM (window RAM)   Dual ported video RAM that is faster and less expensive than VRAM. It has its own internal bus on the chip, with a data path that is 256 bits wide.

zero-fill utility   A utility provided by a hard drive manufacturer that fills every sector on the drive with zeroes.

zone bit recording   A method of storing data on a hard drive whereby the drive can have more sectors per track near the outside of the platter.

INDEX

Connections applet, 424, 427
network client software built
in, 62–63
networks, 5
notebooks, 5
OSs (operating systems), 5–6
partition for installation, 81
PnP (Plug and Play), 5, 55
printing report of system
information, 44
product key, 99
Programs menu, 213
Recovery Console, 5
registry editors, 158
renaming computer, 40
requiring 650 MB, 76
searching hard drive for
partitions, 98–99
seriously corrupted, 268
Setup, 100
setup disks, 97
software, 5
Start, Settings, Control Panel
command, 18
steps to install, 97–100,
112–114
Task Manager, 161
Taskbar and Start Menu
Properties window, 31–32
testing cable modems, 483
testing printer, 610
transferring files and
preferences, 197–199
updates, 140
upgrade, 80, 100
versions, 5, 56–59
Welcome screen, 98
Welcome to Setup screen, 97
when to use, 74–75
Windows 2000 Advanced
Server, 59
Windows 2000 Datacenter
Server, 59
Windows 2000 Professional, 59
Windows 2000 Server, 59
Winnt32.exe installation
program, 97
Winnt.exe program, 97
your name and company
name, 99
Windows 2000 Advanced Server,
5, 59
Windows 2000 Datacenter Server,
5, 59

Windows 2000 Professional, 5, 59
Group Policy console
(Gpedit.msc), 209–212
recommended system
requirements, 5
*Windows 2000 Professional
Resource Kit*, 179, 262
Windows 2000 Repair Options
window, 267, 293
Windows 2000 Server, 59,
62–64, 186
Windows 2000 Setup, 100, 267
Windows 2000 setup CD, 267
Windows 2000/2003 domain
controllers, 63
Windows 2000/XP
16-bit device drivers, 22
32-bit device drivers, 24
active partition, 67
applications relating, 60
architecture, 60
automated installation, 83
automatically restarting,
262–263
available RAM, 76
boot disk verifying boot files,
288–290
boot partition, **67**
boot process, 246–252
Boot.ini file, 249–250
changing memory settings,
177–178
checklist to complete before
installing, 83–84
Chkdsk command, 221–223,
223
clean installation, 75, 79–81,
277, 294–295
Command Prompt window, 3
compression software, **224**
Computer Management,
130–131
configuring TCP/IP, 426–427
configuring to use network,
424–425
current CPU, 76
customizing startup, 250–252
Dependency Walker, 138–139
desktop, 28, 83
destroying current, 294–295
device drivers, 24
Device Manager, 41–42
DHCP client software, 419
dial-up connections,
486–490

Disk Cleanup (Cleanmgr.exe),
219
Disk Defragmenter, 206
Disk Management, 18, 76,
114, **116–119**
Diskpart command, 114–115
displaying IP address and
MAC addresses, 413
DNS, 421
DOS-like commands, 3
drivers, 78
dual boot, 75, 79–81
EFS (Encrypted File System),
561–566
Event Viewer, 134–138
Explore command, 34
extended partition, 67
failed boot, 330
FAT16 logical drives, 74
FAT32 file system, 69, 70
file creation, 37
files needed to start, 247–248
files used during load process
recorded in file, 261
FTP (File Transfer Protocol),
525
hard drive space available,
76–77
hardware working under, 78
hiding computer from
others, 450
ICS (Internet Connection
Sharing), 420
in-place upgrade, 277, 294
installation options, 75
installation process, 82–83
installing, 423–428
installing and supporting
applications, 124–130
installing hardware, 108–114
Ipconfig /all command, 458
kernel mode, 60–62
key folders used by, 249
Last Known Good
configuration, 262
loading normally, 261
logical drives, 114–116
logon, 64
managing hard drives, 65–74
managing memory, 175–179
monitoring logon events,
572–574
motherboard BIOS, 77–78
My Network Places, 426
naming computer, 424–425